INFORMATION TECHNOLOGY OUTSOURCING TRANSACTIONS

BECOME A SUBSCRIBER!
Did you purchase this product from a bookstore?

If you did, it's important for you to become a subscriber. John Wiley & Sons, Inc. may publish, on a periodic basis, supplements and new editions to reflect the latest changes in the subject matter that you *need to know* in order to stay competitive in this ever-changing industry. By contacting the Wiley office nearest you, you'll receive any current update at no additional charge. In addition, you'll receive future updates and revised or related volumes on a 30-day examination review.

If you purchased this product directly from John Wiley & Sons, Inc., we have already recorded your subscription for this update service.

To become a subscriber, please call **1-877-762-2974** or send your name, company name (if applicable), address, and the title of the product to:

mailing address: **Supplement Department**
John Wiley & Sons, Inc.
One Wiley Drive
Somerset, NJ 08875

e-mail: **subscriber@wiley.com**
fax: **1-732-302-2300**
online: **www.wiley.com**

For customers outside the United States, please contact the Wiley office nearest you:

Professional & Reference Division
John Wiley & Sons Canada, Ltd.
22 Worcester Road
Etobicoke, Ontario M9W 1L1
CANADA
Phone: 416-236-4433
Phone: 1-800-567-4797
Fax: 416-236-4447
Email: canada@wiley.com

John Wiley & Sons, Ltd.
The Atrium
Southern Gate, Chichester
West Sussex PO 19 8SQ
ENGLAND
Phone: 44-1243-779777
Fax: 44-1243-775878
Email: customer@wiley.co.uk

John Wiley & Sons Australia, Ltd.
33 Park Road
P.O. Box 1226
Milton, Queensland 4064
AUSTRALIA
Phone: 61-7-3859-9755
Fax: 61-7-3859-9715
Email: brisbane@johnwiley.com.au

John Wiley & Sons (Asia) Pte., Ltd.
2 Clementi Loop #02-01
SINGAPORE 129809
Phone: 65-64632400
Fax: 65-64634604/5/6
Customer Service: 65-64604280
Email: enquiry@wiley.com.sg

INFORMATION TECHNOLOGY OUTSOURCING TRANSACTIONS

PROCESS, STRATEGIES, AND CONTRACTS

2ND EDITION

JOHN K. HALVEY

BARBARA M. MELBY

JOHN WILEY & SONS, INC.

Copyright © 2005 by John Wiley & Sons, Inc. All rights reserved.

Published by John Wiley & Sons, Inc., Hoboken, New Jersey.
Published simultaneously in Canada.

Library of Congress Cataloging-in-Publication Data:

Halvey, John K.
　Information technology outsourcing transactions: process, strategies, and contracts / John K. Halvey, Barbara M. Melby.--2nd ed.
　　p. cm.
　Includes index.
　ISBN-13　978-0-471-45949-1 (cloth)
　ISBN-10　0-471-45949-6 (cloth)
　1. Information technology. 2. Contracting out. I. Melby, Barbara Murphy. II. Title.

T58.5.H35 2006
004'.068'4--dc22

　　　　　　　　　　　　　　　　　　　　　　　　　　　　　　　　2005045981

Printed in the United States of America

10　9　8　7　6　5　4　3　2　1

To Meghan... and for Harry W., who covered my retreat.

JKH

Thanks again to my parents, the 3 Gs and (of course) FF.

BMM

CONTENTS

Appendices

ABOUT THE AUTHORS

John K. Halvey is a partner in the New York office of the international law firm of Milbank, Tweed, Hadley & McCloy, LLP and the founder of the Technology & Strategic Sourcing Group. He practices in all areas of technology and sourcing law, with particular emphasis on information technology and business process outsourcing and private equity transactions involving technology or sourcing companies. Mr. Halvey has represented companies in many of the largest technology, telecommunications, and business process outsourcing transactions, including Deutsche Bank, BellSouth, Panasonic, DuPont, AT&T, Alcatel, Xerox, Boeing, Bombardier, General Atlantic, and the Commonwealth Bank of Australia.

His work in these areas has been the subject of articles in *Forbes, Information Week, ComputerWorld, CIO Magazine, The Daily Deal,* and *Venture Capital Journal.* Mr. Halvey has for many years been ranked by *Chambers and Partners* as one of the world's leading IT and outsourcing lawyers and in 2005 was the only lawyer in the United States to be ranked a "Star Performer" in the outsourcing industry.

In 1995, *Crain's* named Mr. Halvey on its list of the 40 most successful people under 40 in New York City. He is also listed in *The Best Lawyers in America.* He has published three other books: *Business Process Outsourcing Transactions: Process, Strategies and Contracts; Data Processing Contracts,* and *Computer Law and Related Transactions.* Mr. Halvey is a *magna cum laude* graduate of Tufts University, Emory University School of Business, and Emory University School of Law, where he was an executive editor of the *Law Review.*

Barbara M. Melby is a partner in the Global Outsourcing Group. Ms. Melby's practice focuses primarily on outsourcing transactions, including information technology and business process outsourcing, as well as other technology-related transactions, including development agreements, system implementation agreements, licensing and hosting agreements, technology services, joint ventures, and strategic alliances. Ms. Melby represents a large and diverse client base and has led or participated in nearly 100 major outsourcing transactions. Most recently she has completed a large offshore outsourcing transaction for a major insurance company, a global IT outsourcing (ITO) transaction for a leading international media company, a multi-tower outsourcing transaction for a major global pharmaceutical company, and a human resources outsourcing (HRO) transaction for large services provider. In addition to this book, Ms. Melby has co-authored *Business Process Outsourcing: Process, Strategies, and Contracts* (John Wiley& Sons, 2000). She also has written numerous articles in and has been widely quoted in a wide variety of publications to include *CIO Magazine, ITWorld, The Metropolitan Corporate Counsel,* and *The Pennsylvania Lawyer.* Ms. Melby is also a frequent speaker on outsourcing and technology transactions at various business, legal, and professional conferences. She is a graduate of Vassar College and received her law degree from Boston University, *magna cum laude.* While at Boston University, she served as an editor on the *Boston University Law Review* and was a Distinguished Scholar.

ABOUT THE WEB SITE

As a purchaser of this book, *Information Technology Outsourcing Transactions: Process, Strategies, and Contracts, 2nd Edition*, you have access to the supporting Web site:

www.wiley.com/go/information2e

The Web site contains files for the appendices that appear in this book (see Contents). These appendices are provided in Word format.

The password to enter this site is: outsourcing

PREFACE

Amid an unsteady economic recovery, outsourcing has become both a corporate buzzword and a galvanizing issue for many interest groups since the first publication of this book in 1994. Hardly a day goes by without national and international publications like *The Wall Street Journal, The New York Times, Business Week, Time*, and *The Economist* discussing the issue of outsourcing from a strategic, legal, and geopolitical point of view. While CNN's Lou Dobbs maintains a running list of American companies exporting jobs overseas,[1] no less than a dozen federal bills and resolutions meant to curb offshore outsourcing have been proposed,[2] and a majority of states have introduced antioutsourcing legislation of one type or another.[3] Yet, despite outsourcing's role as a lightning rod for campaign rhetoric, companies in a wide array of markets increasingly view outsourcing as a means to achieve cost or operational goals and as a tool for operational and cultural transformation.[4] As these companies embrace increasingly diverse outsourcing solutions, there has been an attendant need for increasingly sophisticated transaction structures, which, in turn, has brought outsourcing directly within the purview of corporate development groups.

The decision about what will or will not be outsourced has traditionally been one of determining what is strategically so important to the core competency of the business that it cannot be handed over to a third party. However, as the recent boom-bust economic cycle has demonstrated, business strategy is an evolving process, and the line of what is now deemed too critical to a company's operations to outsource has moved closer to the corporate offices of most organizations. Functions like HR, finance, marketing, project management, customer care, and customer acquisition—once viewed as too core to be handled by an

---

1. "Lou Dobbs Tonight" Web site, at http://www.cnn.com/CNN/Programs/lou.dobbs.tonight.
2. The list of proposed federal antioutsourcing legislation includes, among other measures, bans on offshoring federal contract work; reporting requirements for companies considering offshoring jobs; consumers' "right to know" measures for offshore call centers; restrictions on outsourcing-related work visas for foreign nationals; and ending the tax deferral for American companies' overseas profits. Global Sourcing Information: Table Tracking State and Federal Global Sourcing Legislation, National Foundation for American Policy Web site, at http://www.nfap.net/researchactivities/globalsourcing/appendix.aspx.
3. The list of proposed state antioutsourcing legislation includes, among dozens of other measures, bans on offshoring state contract work; restrictions on consumer information being sent offshore; consumers' "right to know" measures for offshore call centers; extending insurance benefits to workers who have been displaced through outsourcing; and advance notice to employees before their jobs can be sent offshore. Global Sourcing Information: Table Tracking State and Federal Global Sourcing Legislation, National Foundation for American Policy Web site, at http://www.nfap.net/researchactivities/globalsourcing/appendix.aspx.
4. Patrick Thibodeau, "Forrester adjusts outsourcing numbers upward," *ComputerWorld*, May 17, 2004, at http://www.computerworld.com/outsourcing/story/0,10801,93217,00.html.

outside party—are being outsourced with increasing frequency.[5] The confluence of this increased corporate outsourcing activity, the current political scrutiny, and the ever-developing sophistication of the outsourced solutions being offered has created a greater need for innovative corporate approaches in the outsourcing arena.

Although the outcome of any of the outsourcing regulatory proposals remains far from certain, outsourcing customers and their deal teams have nonetheless begun structuring (and restructuring) their outsourcing relationships in anticipation of a heightened regulatory environment. One such strategy involves how to control the outsourced solution. The threat of tighter regulations will prompt some companies to tighten the reins on the governance of the outsourced solution, ensuring that in the future the company can control its own compliance in a changing regulatory environment. For other companies, adapting to yet-unknown regulatory obstacles warrants becoming more hands off with the outsourced solution, easing the reins on the day-to-day mechanics of governance, and making the service provider responsible for compliance with changing laws. With either approach, the key to success is open dialogue between the company and service providers.

Current and pending data security and consumer protection laws have prompted some companies to seek firm assurances from their outsourcing vendors that the vendors' facilities, systems, and human resources policies have adequate security measures in place. In the wake of the Sarbanes-Oxley Act, and with new accounting rules being developed by the Securities and Exchange Commission (SEC) and Public Company Accounting Oversight Board (PCAOB), companies are seeking to bolster their rights to audit their outsourcing vendors' records, facilities, software, hardware, and security measures. With increased regulatory scrutiny of offshore service locations (not to mention the rise of global terrorism), the legal doctrine traditionally known as *force majeure* has taken on an added meaning, with companies demanding more robust business continuity and disaster recovery obligations on the part of the vendor. In addition, customers are paying greater attention to the corporate entities that are signatories to their outsourcing contracts so as to ensure that the customers are not simply contracting with local holding companies but, rather, with firms that have assets to stand behind the promises made in the contracts.

As these examples demonstrate, to successfully navigate an outsourcing transaction, and then manage the outsourcing relationship, in such dynamic times requires a combination of both corporate strategy and transaction process. Companies will continue to refine the focus on their core competencies (e.g., the sale of specialized goods or services) and seek to efficiently outsource the noncore elements of their business. As this decade unfolds, the competitive differentiation for most global organizations will be the ability to effectively manage multiple outsourced relationships and the myriad of business and legal issues those

---

5.   See, for example, Des Dearlove, "Hiring people to take care of your people," *The Financial Times,* June 8, 2004, at 29.

relationships entail. Managing an outsourced relationship involves having the right contract governance and management procedures in place, using effective communication, and dedicating the time, resources, energy, and commitment to leveraging the most from the outsourced relationship. Only through this process will companies realize the advantages of leveraging the outsourced model.

This new edition of *Information Technology Outsourcing Transactions* hopes to bring the reader up to date with changes and developments in outsourcing transactions and the process of doing outsourcing transactions in the past ten years. During this time, outsourcing has evolved from the last hope of broken IT departments to the solution of choice for the enhancement of an increasing number of business processes for an increasing number of Global 1000 companies. The practice of outsourcing has evolved in step with this movement from back office to front office and is now more complex, more challenging, and potentially more rewarding for all those involved. As with the previous edition, this book is not a substitute for legal, technical, financial, or accounting advice but, instead, serves as a guideline to effectively manage an outsourcing transaction.

CHAPTER 1

OVERVIEW OF THE IT OUTSOURCING INDUSTRY

1.1 BACKGROUND

Outsourcing—the assumption of management and operational responsibility for a noncore business function or functions by a third party—is at the forefront of strategic considerations by corporate and government information technology (IT) professionals. Virtually every Fortune 500 company in this country, and an increasing number of companies throughout the world, outsource some significant portion of their IT services. Meta Group, an analyst of the IT outsourcing industry, estimates that 70 percent of companies outsource and that all companies will embrace the model by 2006.[1] It is easy to understand, therefore, how IT outsourcing has become a $536 billion worldwide marketplace.[2]

Whereas, a decade ago, most companies engaged in a "build and maintain your own" strategy with respect to their IT infrastructure, corporate cost-cutting and the ever-increasing pace of technological innovation has spawned a generation of IT managers who accept—if not embrace—the underlying principles of outsourcing. The economies of scale that can be achieved by an outsourcing vendor, coupled with the ability to financially engineer the fees associated with outsourcing to achieve a desired goal with respect to payments, have given outsourcing an almost populist following.

Clearly, cost-cutting and financial engineering have been significant factors in fueling the outsourcing fire. In recent years, however, companies are also coming to view outsourcing as a means of transforming their IT operations without losing step with their competitors on a day-to-day basis. Transformational outsourcing is typically a two-step process—with the outsourcing vendor first taking responsibility for the outsourcing customer's existing (or legacy) systems

---

1. "We'll All Be Outsourcing by 2006," *Computing*, July 10, 2003.
2. Gartner Dataquest forecasts that the $536 billion worldwide IT services industry will grow through 2007 to reach $707 billion, with a compound annual growth rate of 5.7 percent. Worldwide IT Services Market Forecast, 2002–2007 (Executive Summary).

and processes and then taking responsibility for implementing new, state-of-the-art systems and processes (thereby "transforming" the customer's environment) in a shorter time frame than would be possible if the customer implemented the changes itself and with greater resources than those available within the customer's organization.

Given the financial and strategic magnitude of the decision to outsource even a portion of a company's IT operations, more and more IT professionals seek to understand the process and intricacies of outsourcing. This typically entails determining precisely what to outsource and the best way to manage the process of structuring and negotiating an outsourcing relationship. In this regard, this book is intended to be a guide to structuring, negotiating, and implementing IT outsourcing transactions. As such, it does not, and could not, address all issues that may be germane to any given transaction. The examples given in the book are strictly hypothetical, taken from the various experiences of the authors' work in this area over many years. In reviewing and using this text, it is important to note that each industry approaches outsourcing differently and that each company must determine for itself the optimal method of achieving the results it seeks from entering into what is typically a long-term relationship with an outsourcing vendor.

It is our hope that by discussing the fundamentals of outsourcing, the process can be demystified to some extent and that much of the emotion and hyperbole associated with outsourcing can be abated. Nothing in this text should be construed as a criticism of any outsourcing vendor or its customers. The skill and experience that most outsourcing vendors bring to their tasks will undoubtedly sustain the industry's growth. In order to address the many business and legal issues that are contained in the typical outsourcing transaction, it is necessary to generalize with respect to the positions taken by both vendors and customers, and their professional advisors. Like all generalizations, those contained in this book may well not apply to any particular transaction.

Finally, notwithstanding the admittedly parochial interests of the authors, anyone entering into an outsourcing transaction—whether a vendor or a customer—should consider consulting with someone who is familiar with the process in order to ensure that the industry developments and lessons learned are appropriately vetted. The laws relating to outsourcing, and the business case analysis underlying any decision to outsource, vary from transaction to transaction and are subject to change at almost the same rate as technology.

1.2   IT OUTSOURCING INDUSTRY

Analysts continue to predict increased growth for the IT outsourcing industry. As noted previously, Gartner Dataquest has forecasted that the $536 billion worldwide IT services industry will grow through 2007 to reach $707 billion, with a compound annual growth rate of 5.7 percent.[3] Similarly, IDC expects the

---

3.   Worldwide IT Services Market Forecast, 2002–2007 (Executive Summary).

worldwide IT outsourcing market to grow 7.7 percent a year over the next five years, to reach nearly $100 billion in sales in 2007.[4]

The growth is being fueled by several factors, including an increase in nascent markets spawned by the traditional IT outsourcing model, such as business process outsourcing, offshoring, and Internet-enabled outsourcing. Not only is the IT outsourcing market seeing an increase in the number of outsourcing contracts, but at least one analyst has found that the size and scope of the average outsourcing contract has also increased. IDC estimates that in 2003 the 100 largest worldwide outsourcing contracts ranged from $80 million to $5 billion, with 43 percent of IT outsourcing contracts valued between $100 and $249 million. According to IDC, this represents an increase from 2001, when contracts valued at less than $100 million represented the largest price offering.[5] The growing drive toward globalization is likely a major factor in the increased value of IT outsourcing contracts, because more companies are looking for a single service solution for their global operations.

IT outsourcing is an evolving market. Customers are continually looking for creative ways to structure deals through such mechanisms as strategic alliances, co-marketing agreements, and joint ventures, in order to reap the most benefit from the proposed ongoing alliance. Outsourcing vendors continue to strive to refine established methodologies and processes, while adapting services and infrastructure to leverage new technologies, responding to demands for innovative service models (such as utility-based services), racing to deploy Internet-based products and services, and building the expertise and systems to service user demands.

In one respect, IT outsourcing is a mature market, having over the past decade experienced deals that have run their full term and others that have been renegotiated and terminated, thereby benefiting from lessons learned and risks taken. In another respect, with the emergence of a new generation of outsourcing providers supporting new business processes and moving to offshore models and the continuous drive to improve existing methodologies and process, IT outsourcing remains in many ways an uncharted frontier.

Some of the major trends in the IT outsourcing industry are highlighted as follows, with many of them discussed in more detail later in this book:

- *Business process outsourcing.* The buzzword in the outsourcing industry continues to be business process outsourcing (BPO). Companies are looking at almost every noncore function to determine the feasibility of outsourcing the function to a third party. Leading business processes that have been targeted for outsourcing include human resources, procurement, finance and accounting, call centers, claims processing, facilities management, and logistics. Once trumpeted by the big accounting firms looking to grasp a larger piece of the outsourcing services market, all of the major top-tier vendors now offer a wide range of BPO services as well as several specialty outsourcers, which focus on a particular process. The BPO

4. CNET News.com, October 1, 2003, Report: "Big Blue Still Biggest in IT Outsourcing."
5. The WHIR's Web Host News, June 9, 2003, "IDC: Outsourcing Future Is Bright."

market continues to quietly expand its reach, adapting to the changing needs of companies and the changing ways companies do business. Yankee Group predicts that, while worldwide IT outsourcing (networking and computing functions) will grow 10 to 12 percent annually to reach $273.9 billion by 2006, BPO will grow at a faster rate—as fast as 12 to 20 percent annually to reach $500 billion by 2006.[6] A more in-depth discussion of BPO is provided in Chapter 12.

- *Offshoring.* In 2004, by far the hottest outsourcing topic—fueling political debates at the local, state, and federal levels and at times recognized as a major issue by the presidential candidates—has been offshore outsourcing or *offshoring.* Although offshoring has been around for several years, the seemingly recent predictions made by outsourcing analysts regarding the growth in the offshore outsourcing industry have been meet with astonishment and calls by the legislature to limit offshoring in an effort to keep jobs in the United States (particularly outsourcing efforts by federal and state government entities).[7] Examples of some of the predictions include the following:

  - By 2015, Forrester predicts that a total of 3.4 million previously U.S.-based positions will have been relocated overseas.[8]

  - By 2008, global investment in offshore IT services will grow from nearly $7 billion in 2003 to $17 billion in 2008.[9]

  - Offshore BPO services will represent 14 percent of the total BPO market 2007, with India's share of supply around 57 percent.[10] India is currently the leading destination for offshore outsourcing; however, countries such as Russia, China, Mexico, Ireland, Malaysia, the Philippines, and Singapore are becoming serious competitors in this market. A more in-depth discussion of offshoring is provided in Chapter 11.

- *Internet-enabled outsourcing.* The Internet has spawned a new generation of technology outsourcers with acronyms that are often difficult to keep up with, such as system integrators (SIs), managed service providers (MSPs), application service providers (ASPs), and application service provider aggregators (ASPAs). Internet-based outsourcers include service providers using the Internet as a means or a platform for providing outsourcing services as well as outsourcers of a company's Web-based business operations. Established outsourcers (such as EDS, IBM,

---

6. *Business Communications Review,* July 1, 2003, "Outsourcing."
7. Helpful Web sites that track the status of federal and state legislation relating to offshoring are listed in footnotes 2 and 3 on page xix in the Preface.
8. "US Outsourcing Is Accelerating," news.bbc.co.uk, May 17, 2004.
9. Jacques, Robert, "Offshore Outsourcing to Reach $17 Billion by 2008," *PCW Inter@ctive,* October 19, 2004.
10. Pastore, Michael, "Gartner Says Tech Jobs Will Continue to Move Overseas," cioupdate.com, July 29, 2003.

and CSC), established software companies (such as Oracle, Sun, and Microsoft), and a myriad of new players entered the race to provide Internet-based outsourcing services. One example of a natural offspring of traditional IT outsourcing in the Internet world is the ASP model. By definition of the ASP Industry Consortium, an ASP is a service that deploys, hosts, and manages access to a packaged application to multiple parties from a centrally managed facility.[11] Internet-based outsourcers are forging new ground using more traditional IT outsourcing models as precedent for innovative service offerings and deal structures. Although many of the contract issues that arise in traditional IT outsourcing deals arise in Internet-based outsourcing deals, these issues (such as privacy, use of data, and exposure to hacking and viruses) may take on greater importance in an Internet context. A more in-depth discussion of Internet-enabled outsourcing is provided in Chapter 13.

- *Going global.* IT outsourcing has seen a significant growth in the number of global deals—deals that cover a company's global operations (rather than deals that are piecemeal by country)—as well as the number of deals being entered into outside the United States. The United Kingdom and Europe have seen the most growth in IT outsourcing. One analyst indicated that IT outsourcing deals continue to boom in the United Kingdom and Europe, with the total value of contract awards in 2004 predicted to match that of the United States—up from 2002, when the outsourcing contract volume in Europe was one-third that of the Americas, and 2003, when it was 68 percent of the volume in the Americas.[12] A discussion of issues impacting global outsourcing transactions is provided in Chapter 11.

- *Strategic alliances.* Companies continue to seek innovative deal structures, introducing new paradigms into the marketplace. The most basic of these structures is the strategic alliance—a loosely fitted joint venture or teaming arrangement pursuant to which the vendor and the customer, at least theoretically, share a risk and reward framework. Several of the larger transactions include an alliance component. In some instances, the customer and the vendor have become partners through equity participation in the vendor's company. In other instances, the strategic alliance has taken the form of royalty arrangements or "go to market" strategies designed to create business opportunities for both the customer and the vendor in new marketplaces.

- *Utility-based models.* With computing services becoming more "commoditized," there has been a growing push from outsourcing customers and outsourcing vendors for "pay as you use" or utility-based models. Most industry experts still believe that these models are relatively immature, but many customers are embracing the models in a drive for more flexible pricing. Gartner estimated 15 percent of North American enterprises will adopt

---

11. "Technology," *The Asian Banker Journal,* February 6, 2001.
12. McCure, Andy, "European Outsourcing to Catch US Market in 2004," Silicon.com.

utility computing services by 2003, and that the market will grow from $8.6 billion in 2003 to more than $25 billion in 2006, with 30 percent of North American enterprises having utility computing arrangements.[13]

- *Renegotiating deals.* With many of the large deals signed in the 1990s expiring or close to expiring, the market is experiencing a relatively new trend—the extension or renegotiation of existing deals. The maturing IT outsourcing market has seen some deals being extended, but it has also seen some deals being terminated earlier than originally anticipated. The reasons for early termination have run the gambit from a change in corporate management to an unanticipated merger or sale to nonperformance or unsatisfactory service. A more in-depth discussion of issues that arise in connection with renegotiating and terminating outsourcing transactions is provided in Chapter 15.

1.3 IT OUTSOURCING DEALS

The first companies entering into outsourcing deals were predominantly U.S. banks and financial institutions, but today companies of almost every size and across every industry have outsourced all or part of their IT operations. Literally thousands of companies and government agencies have entered into outsourcing agreements for IT services. Exhibit 1.1 lists public IT outsourcing deals by industry. The data contained in this exhibit has been gathered from annual reports, press releases, and other public information. This list is not exhaustive by any means. It is intended to provide a sampling of the types of deals that customers have been entering into in the last couple of years.

	CUSTOMER	VENDOR	ESTIMATED CONTRACT VALUE (MILLIONS)	TERM (YEARS)	POINTS OF INTEREST
1.	3Com	EDS			Manage IT infrastructure
2.	7-Eleven, Inc.	EDS	$175	7	Full IT package of integration, intelligent storage and full-scale hosting services
3.	AAA	AT&T	$138	3	Networking services
4.	ABN AMRO	EDS			Full range of services, including application hosting, data processing, and back-office processing
5.	ABN AMRO Bank N.V.	EDS	$1,300	5	

EXHIBIT 1.1 IT OUTSOURCING DEALS

---

13. *Business Communications Review*, July 1, 2003, "Outsourcing."

	CUSTOMER	VENDOR	ESTIMATED CONTRACT VALUE (MILLIONS)	TERM (YEARS)	POINTS OF INTEREST
6.	ABB	IBM	$1,100	10	Information systems infrastructure in 14 countries in Europe and North America
7.	ACNielsen	EDS			Mainframe computers
8.	Advantica Restaurant Group, Inc.	ACS			Data center operations, network management services, support for desktops, and development and maintenance of applications
9.	Affiliated Health Services	ACS			Application software implementation, hardware management, help desk/ operations support, education, desktop and network support, and telecommunications
10.	Affiliated Health Services	ACS		3	Implementation services application software implementation and support, hardware management, education, data repository and an electronic medical record
11.	Agere Systems	Hewlett-Packard		3	Manage its data centers and improve its operational efficiencies
12.	Air Canada	IBM	$900	7	E-enablement of Air Canada infrastructure, enhancement of customer service procedures, and new IT-based developments
13.	Air China	Sabre Holdings Corporation		3 months	Extensive IT audit to determine its future IT and applications needs
14.	Air Force Center for Environmental Excellence	DynCorp Systems & Solutions LLC		5	Environmental and IT consulting services
15.	Air Force's Central Design Activity	DynCorp	$20	5	Design, testing, and implementation, business process reengineering, information protection and assurance, software QA, and systems engineering

EXHIBIT 1.1 (CONTINUED) IT OUTSOURCING DEALS

	CUSTOMER	VENDOR	ESTIMATED CONTRACT VALUE (MILLIONS)	TERM (YEARS)	POINTS OF INTEREST
16.	Air Force's Electronic Systems Center	Titan Systems Corporation	$29.9	4	Technical and acquisition management support and management and administrative support in the areas of business management, financial management, training, logistics configuration control, and data management
17.	Air Force's Electronic Systems Center	Titan Systems Corporation	$41.5	4	Information technology and program management support
18.	Air Force's Electronic Systems Center	Titan Systems Corporation	$88	5	Sustainment and modernization of a worldwide network of command and control centers, surveillance sensors, and strategic communications systems
19.	Air Force's Electronic Systems Center	Titan Systems Corporation	$103	4.5	Program technical and management support
20.	Air Force's Electronic Systems Center Materiel Systems Group	Titan Systems Corporation	$24	3	Technical assistance in planning, managing, coordinating and executing Department of Defense IT processes
21.	Air Force's Electronic Systems Center Standard Systems Group	Titan Systems Corporation	$21.5	4.5	Program management support, systems engineering, security engineering, and acquisition management
22.	Akamai Technologies, Inc.	IBM			Primary supplier of servers
23.	Alberta Human Resources and Employment Ministry	CGI Group, Inc.	CDN$12	4	Application maintenance services
24.	Alberta's Ministry of Health and Wellness	CGI Group, Inc.	CDN$25	5	Support legacy systems, client server applications, and Web-based applications
25.	Alcan Inc.	CGI Group, Inc.	CDN$200	10	
26.	Alcatel	EDS			
27.	Alenia Marconi Systems Limited	CSC		6	
28.	Allders Department Stores	CSC	$42	5	
29.	Allied Domecq Spirits and Wine	EDS		7	

EXHIBIT 1.1   (CONTINUED)   IT OUTSOURCING DEALS

	CUSTOMER	VENDOR	ESTIMATED CONTRACT VALUE (MILLIONS)	TERM (YEARS)	POINTS OF INTEREST
30.	Altis Semiconductor	IBM		10	Consulting, implementing, rolling out and maintaining of applications, connecting and managing networks, managing mainframe production, managing the network of 160 distributed applications servers based on OS/2, Aix, and Windows platforms
31.	Amadeus North America, LLC	NCR Corporation	$40		Supporting IT infrastructure
32.	Amalgamated Bank	ALLTEL Information Services		7	Integrated end-to-end banking application, report management, and data warehouse system
33.	American Express Co.	IBM Global Services	$4,000	7	Flexible pricing
34.	American General Life Companies	ACS		5	Mainframe processing and support services
35.	Amica Mutual Insurance Co.	IBM			
36.	Amore Pacific	IBM	$100	10	
37.	AMP Limited	CSC	$290	5	Mainframe and midrange services, voice and data networks, service help desks, desktops, servers, and high-volume printing
38.	Amtrak	IBM	$229	7	
39.	Anthem Blue Cross and Blue Shield	ACS		3	Technology outsourcing services
40.	Anthem Blue Cross and Blue Shield's Colorado and Nevada operations	ACS			Migrate the HP3000 UNIX processing of systems operations, and provide data center and professional services
41.	Arbella Mutual Insurance Company	ACS	$40	6	Mainframe data processing, UNIX-based data warehouse, and extensive telecommunications network
42.	AstraZeneca	IBM	$1,700	7	Provision of IT infrastructure services to 45 countries
43.	AT&T Wireless	Convergys Corporation	$100+	2	Integrated contact center services
44.	Auna Telecommunications	IBM	$495	10	IT integration and management

EXHIBIT 1.1 (CONTINUED) IT OUTSOURCING DEALS

	CUSTOMER	VENDOR	ESTIMATED CONTRACT VALUE (MILLIONS)	TERM (YEARS)	POINTS OF INTEREST
45.	Aventis	IBM	$1,500	10	Management of computer centers, server operations, and the provision of Internet, e-mail, and help-desk services
46.	AXA Group	IBM	$1,000	6	
47.	BAE Systems	CSC	$102	61 months	
48.	BAE Systems	CSC	$2,200	6	Manage the IT infrastructure in the United States and the United Kingdom
49.	BancFirst	ALLTEL Information Services		5	On-site outsourcing of IT services
50.	Banco Sabadell	Accenture			Migrate the bank's information systems from multiple units to a single platform and develop new applications
51.	Bank Leuni	EDS		5 to 7	Overhaul and modernize applications
52.	Bank of America	Compaq Computer Corporation		3	Single-source service and support as well as hardware
53.	Bank of America	EDS	$4,500	10	
54.	Bank of Ireland	Accenture			
55.	Bank of Queensland	EDS	$250	10	IT infrastructure and back-office processes
56.	Bank of Scotland	IBM	$1,000	10	IT operational services
57.	Bank One	AT&T	$465		Data and voice-networking infrastructure
58.	Bank One	IBM	$168		Data center operations, including help-desk support and management of the bank's mainframe computers and midrange servers
59.	Barclaycard Merchant Services	CSC	$17		
60.	Barclays	Accenture	$790	6	Application development and management; over 900 Barclays employees transferred in the United Kingdom
61.	Barclays	EDS	$375	7	
62.	BCE Mobile Communications, Inc.	CGI Group, Inc.	CDN$100 in 1st year	10	
63.	Belgian government	Accenture			Develop, operate, and maintain a governmental portal

EXHIBIT 1.1 (CONTINUED) IT OUTSOURCING DEALS

	CUSTOMER	VENDOR	ESTIMATED CONTRACT VALUE (MILLIONS)	TERM (YEARS)	POINTS OF INTEREST
64.	Bell Helicopter Textron	IBM	$70	6	End-to-end desktop solution
65.	BellSouth	EDS			Midrange systems management
66.	BellSouth Corporation	Accenture		6	Range of technology IT applications
67.	BellSouth Technology Group, Inc.	EDS			Consolidation of data center operations
68.	Blue Cross Blue Shield of Michigan	Compaq Computer Corporation		5	Customer enterprise help desk support, on-site desk-side software support, remedial maintenance, and asset management services
69.	BNP Paribas	IBM	$1,200		Joint venture to transform bank's IT into an on-demand infrastructure
70.	Boeing	IBM	$160	3	
71.	Borland Software Corporation	EDS Ltd		3	IT infrastructure
72.	BP	IBM	$200	5	Application management and host services
73.	BP	SAIC	$250	5	Support and maintain applications, maintain legacy systems, institute a mechanism for the updating and infusion of technology including e-commerce initiatives, and manage third-party contracts
74.	BP	SAIC	$360	4	Data management, Web development, applications support and administration, and selected consultancy services
75.	BP Amoco Exploration	SAIC Ltd.	£11		Applications support, applications infrastructure care and maintenance, software development, systems integration, and project management
76.	Bristol-Meyers Squibb	SAIC			Technology IT support to research and development activities

EXHIBIT 1.1   (CONTINUED)   IT OUTSOURCING DEALS

	CUSTOMER	VENDOR	ESTIMATED CONTRACT VALUE (MILLIONS)	TERM (YEARS)	POINTS OF INTEREST
77.	Bristol-Meyers Squibb	SAIC		3	Applications help desk, performing testing and deploying activities for new and enhanced applications, and conducting maintenance and enhancement work on existing applications
78.	Brother Industries, Ltd.	Deloitte Consulting	$91	5	Systems implementation, application management, and infrastructure management
79.	Bumiputra-Commerce Bank	EDS	$250		Build and manage technology infrastructure
80.	Burger King	Perot Systems			Data center management, help desk support, enterprise systems management, and global network management
81.	Burlington Northern and Santa Fe Railway Company	IBM		10	Management of a large portion of BNSF's computing infrastructure
82.	California Department of Forestry and Fire Protection	Northrop Grumman Corporation	$18.30	5	Full life cycle maintenance and upgrade support
83.	California Power Exchange Corporation	Perot Systems Corporation	$35		Business consulting and applications development services and IT infrastructure management
84.	California State Computer Store	GE Capital IT Solutions			Professional IT management, internetworking, midrange, storage, hardware and software licensing solutions
85.	Calpine Corporation	SAIC	$31	3	Help desk, server, desktop support, network, voice and video services
86.	Canadian-Pacific Railways	IBM	$154	7	Servers, storage, and emergency recovery
87.	CAN Life	Wipro Technologies			Business processing system
88.	CareSteps, Inc.	ACS		2	Technological support for a secured, Web-based health management platform
89.	Catholic Healthcare West	Perot Systems Corporation	$600	10	IT operations and applications services
90.	Cendant Corporation	IBM	$1,400	10	
91.	Centennial Communications Corp.	ALLTEL Information Services		3	Information services outsourcing

EXHIBIT 1.1   (CONTINUED)   IT OUTSOURCING DEALS

	CUSTOMER	VENDOR	ESTIMATED CONTRACT VALUE (MILLIONS)	TERM (YEARS)	POINTS OF INTEREST
92.	Centers for Medicare and Medicaid Services	Lockheed Martin IT	$401	7.5	Agency-wide IT and infra-structure support services
93.	Certain former sub-sidiaries of Swissair Group (including SR Technics)	EDS			
94.	CGU Group Canada Ltd.	CGI Group, Inc.		5	
95.	CHA Health	Perot Systems Corporation		5	BPO and applications hosting
96.	Charrette Corporation	Siemens Business Services, Inc.	$5.6	5	SAP application hosting
97.	Checkers Drive-In Restaurants, Inc.	CompuCom Sys-tems, Inc.			Providing installation and ongoing outsourcing ser-vices, along with desktop and printer equipment
98.	ChevronTexaco Corp.	EDS		5	Network and server support, mainframe and help desk
99.	Childrens Hospital Los Angeles	CSC	$100		Manage business and clini-cal information systems, including mainframe and midrange computers, desktop computers, help-desk operations, voice and data communica-tions, and applications maintenance and development
100.	CIBC	HP	$1,500	7	
101.	City of Espoo, Finland	Hewlett-Packard			Help desk, security services, on-site support, maintain and manage the network and servers
102.	City of Houston	Compaq Computer Corporation	$30	3	Evaluated existing technol-ogy, implemented a plan to upgrade, consolidate, and manage technology infrastructure
103.	City of Indianapolis	ACS	$25	2	
104.	City of Irvine, California	ACS		1	Application support, project management, data center management, local area network and data com-munications manage-ment, and desktop support services
105.	City of Orange, California	ACS	$4	3	Management and operation of the city's information services department

EXHIBIT 1.1   (CONTINUED)   IT OUTSOURCING DEALS

	CUSTOMER	VENDOR	ESTIMATED CONTRACT VALUE (MILLIONS)	TERM (YEARS)	POINTS OF INTEREST
106.	City of Palmdale, California	ACS	$5	5	Information services
107.	City of Riverside, California	ACS			Integration and implementation services for the use of imaging technology
108.	City of Santa Clara, California	ACS	$7.40	2	Support user, technical, procedures, documentation and administrative functions to facilitate the business and technical uses of the financial, utility and data warehouse systems
109.	Clarian Health Partners	Cap Gemini Ernst & Young US LLC	$100		Assume responsibility for existing applications and infrastructure and implement the best available information technology solutions
110.	Coca-Cola FEMSA	EDS			Support servers, WANs, desktop computing, handheld terminals and help-desk functions
111.	Commerciant	EDS	$18	5	Transaction processing services
112.	Commonwealth of Pennsylvania	EDS	$100		Administrative and operational processes that support Pennsylvania's Medicaid program
113.	Commonwealth of Pennsylvania	IBM	$550	7	Combine data centers into one centralized data center and provide ongoing management and operational support
114.	Commonwealth of Virginia	ACS			Desktop personal computers
115.	Computing Devices Canada	CSC	$68	10	Applications, desktops, help desk, network operations, and servers
116.	Con Edison Communications	Compaq Computer Corporation			Advanced network and services management solutions
117.	Continental Airlines	EDS	$1,000		Inter-airline electronic ticketing and check-in
118.	Continental Tire North America Inc.	Siemens Business Services, Inc.	$6		SAP application hosting and IT architecture upgrades
119.	Co-Operators General Insurance Company	CGI Group, Inc.	CDN$100	5	All support services for the data center and the wide-area network
120.	Coors Brewing Company	EDS			

EXHIBIT 1.1   (CONTINUED)   IT OUTSOURCING DEALS

	CUSTOMER	VENDOR	ESTIMATED CONTRACT VALUE (MILLIONS)	TERM (YEARS)	POINTS OF INTEREST
121.	County of San Diego	Pennant Alliance (a CSC-led consortium)	$644	7	Information and telecommunications services
122.	County of Solano, California	ACS		3	Application support, project management, data center management, LAN, and data communications support of the county's web portal
123.	Covisint	EDS			Global customer service support
124.	Cox Insurance	CGI	$246	10	Entire IT infrastructure, including desktops and application support, 200 Cox employees transferred
125.	CP Kelco	Cap Gemini Ernst & Young US LLP		5	Consolidate multiple SAP instances onto a single SAP platform as well as providing ongoing IT outsourcing services for applications management and infrastructure management
126.	Cullen/Frost Bankers Inc.	ALLTEL Information Services	$28		
127.	CVS Corporation	AT&T			Virtual private network
128.	Cygnifi	CSC		3	Application infrastructure support services
129.	D&B	CSC	$560	10	
130.	Dah Sing Bank Limited	IBM China/Hong Kong Limited	$30	7	Data center operations
131.	Daishi Bank Ltd.	IBM	$270	10	Manage development, maintenance, and operations of its information systems
132.	Daughters of Charity Health System	Perot Systems Corporation	$60	7	Infrastructure, applications, help desk, intranet Web development and project management services
133.	Defense Finance and Accounting Service	CSC	$150	5	Technical support services
134.	Defense Finance and Accounting Service—Kansas City	CSC	$75	5	Software and systems services
135.	Defense Information System Agency	Northrop Grumman Corporation	$300	7	

EXHIBIT 1.1 (CONTINUED)   IT OUTSOURCING DEALS

	CUSTOMER	VENDOR	ESTIMATED CONTRACT VALUE (MILLIONS)	TERM (YEARS)	POINTS OF INTEREST
136.	Defense Information Systems Agency	CSC	$225	7	
137.	Defense Information Systems Agency	CSC	$1,500	5	Full range of IT solutions and professional services
138.	Defense Technical Information Center	DynCorp Information Systems, LLC	$25		Web architecture, application development, Web site development, systems and database administrative support
139.	Defense's Worldwide TRICARE Information Center	Northrop Grumman Corporation			Operations support including administrative and management services, systems development, and call center support
140.	Del Monte Foods Company	EDS		10	Applications development, manage midrange servers and networks, and provide managed application workspace services
141.	Delaware Department of Health and Social Services	ACS			Enterprise Data Warehouse/Decision Support System
142.	Dell Computer Corporation	IBM	$6,000	7	Computer-related services
143.	Delphi Automotive Systems	EDS			Support IT systems, desktops, servers, and routers
144.	Department of Defense Military Health System	SAIC	$4.1	1	Design, develop, test, and deploy web portal
145.	Department of Education	SAIC	$70	1	
146.	Department of Justice	DynCorp and Verizon Enterprise Solutions	$300	6	Hardware maintenance, software technical support and help desk to asset/configuration management, UNIX operating system administration, and operations support
147.	Department of Transportation	Booz Allen Hamilton	$10,000	7	Information Technology Onmibus Procurement
148.	Department of Veterans Affairs	Northrop Grumman Corporation	$650	10	
149.	Detroit Medical Center	Compuware Corporation	$1,000	10	Responsibility for 100% of IS program
150.	Detroit Public Schools	Compuware Corporation	$15		IT services for critical business systems
151.	Deutsche Bank	EDS			

EXHIBIT 1.1   (CONTINUED)   IT OUTSOURCING DEALS

	CUSTOMER	VENDOR	ESTIMATED CONTRACT VALUE (MILLIONS)	TERM (YEARS)	POINTS OF INTEREST
152.	Deutsche Bank	IBM	$2,500	10	Computer centers in continental Europe
153.	Deutsche Leasing AG	CSC			Complete IT operations and provide network, midrange, hosting, and desktop services
154.	Diageo	IBM	400		
155.	Dominion of Canada General Insurance Company	CGI Group, Inc.		5	
156.	Domtar Inc.	CGI Group, Inc.	CDN$18.5	5	Mainframe and midrange environment, providing server management services as well as managing the hardware
157.	dotLogix	Comdisco			Host application, database and middleware servers and provide help desk support, managed firewall services, network monitoring, tape backup and T1 connectivity
158.	Dow Chemical	IBM			Web hosting
159.	Driveway Corp.	IBM			Primary storage services provider
160.	Educational Testing Service	CSC	$300	10	Technology consulting and applications and IT infrastructure outsourcing services
161.	El Pollo Loco	ACS	$1.8	3	Help desk support, applications support, and field maintenance
162.	Emergency Medicare Associates, PC	Per-Se Technologies, Inc.			Coding, accounts receivable management, and billing services
163.	Entergy	SAIC	$400	5	IT application development and maintenance, data center management and operations, midrange and desktop support services, infrastructure management, and most infrastructure services
164.	Environmental Protection Agency	CSC	$285	7	Enterprisewide portal
165.	Ericsson	HP			
166.	Essent	IBM		4	Management of office automation and data centers in the Netherlands

EXHIBIT 1.1   (CONTINUED)   IT OUTSOURCING DEALS

	CUSTOMER	VENDOR	ESTIMATED CONTRACT VALUE (MILLIONS)	TERM (YEARS)	POINTS OF INTEREST
167.	Evansville Board of Public Works and Vanderburgh County Board of Commissioners	ACS	$1.3	1	IT services, e-government solutions, software development and support, server hosting, and network management
168.	factor-e plc	Perot Systems Corporation		5	Technology support
169.	FDIC	Lockheed Martin IT	$45		Support entire IT infrastructure from network performance management to desktops and peripherals
170.	Federal Systems Integration and Management Center	DynCorp	$8.2 for 1st year	7	Help desk operations, data center support and operations, technology deployment support, and technology test lab support
171.	Federal Systems Integration and Management Center	SAIC	$271	10	Full range of IT solutions
172.	Federal Systems Integration and Management Center		$81	6	Analysis, engineering, maintenance, installation, integration, LAN/WAN support, and commercial-off-the-shelf software support
173.	FedEx Corporate Services, Inc.	Convergys Corporation		3	Technical support services
174.	Fiat	IBM	$5,725	10	
175.	Fireman's Fund Insurance Company	CGI Group, Inc.	$380	10	Data center, 24-hour support
176.	First Financial Bancorp	ALLTEL Information Services			Provide an integrated end-to-end banking application
177.	First Genetic Trust, Inc.	Hewlett-Packard		5	Technology partner for its high-performance, high-security IT infrastructure
178.	FirstMile Technologies	ALLTEL Information Services			Manage services including account management and service activation
179.	Foamex	EDS			
180.	Fonterra Co-Operative Group, Ltd.	EDS	$380		
181.	Fossil, Inc.	GE Capital IT Solutions	$0.6		Replace the existing data network infrastructure

EXHIBIT 1.1   (CONTINUED)   IT OUTSOURCING DEALS

	CUSTOMER	VENDOR	ESTIMATED CONTRACT VALUE (MILLIONS)	TERM (YEARS)	POINTS OF INTEREST
182.	Four of Sweden's nuclear power plants—Ringhals, Oskarshamn, Fors-mark, Barseback —and the nuclear safety company KSU	Cap Gemini Ernst & Young Sver-ige AB		5	Applications management services
183.	Franklin Resources, Inc.	IBM	$480	10	
184.	Fuddruckers Restaurants	Inflow, Inc.			
185.	GE Aircraft Engines	Compaq Com-puter Corpora-tion	$95 million/ 5 years (extension)	5	Services and IT infrastruc-ture outsourcing
186.	General Electric Company	CSC		10	Mainframe and midrange data processing opera-tions in Europe
187.	General Electric Company	CSC	$300	10	Data processing operations, help-desk and disaster recovery services in the United Kingdom and other European countries
188.	General Mills	Hewlett-Packard		3	IT hardware needs
189.	General Motors	EDS		3	Desktop management ser-vices
190.	General Motors Corporation	Compaq Computer Corporation			Notebook, desktop solu-tions, and related services
191.	General Services Administration	CSC	$63	10	Distributed computing ser-vices
192.	General Services Administration	DynCorp	$1,200		Full range of IT and engi-neering services
193.	General Services Administration	Logicon Inc.	$79	10	Complete IT security solutions
194.	General Services Administration	SAIC	$100	5	Call center support services
195.	General Services Administration's ANSWER program	DynCorp	$752	8	IT management structure, organization, and resources
196.	Genie	Cap Gemini Ernst & Young Group			Global data platform function
197.	Geodis	IBM	$143	10	Logistics
198.	Global One	ENTEX IT Ser-vice, Inc.			Global help desk and other IT life cycle solutions

EXHIBIT 1.1 (CONTINUED) IT OUTSOURCING DEALS

	CUSTOMER	VENDOR	ESTIMATED CONTRACT VALUE (MILLIONS)	TERM (YEARS)	POINTS OF INTEREST
199.	Golden State Vintners	Accenture and Avasta			IT staffing, hardware and software maintenance, and a call center to support Web site and business applications
200.	Goodyear Tire & Rubber Company	Lockheed Martin IT			Mainframe infrastructure systems and support
201.	Goro Nickel S.A.	Accenture			IT infrastructure and desktop services, application design and maintenance, and ongoing day-to-day IT operations
202.	Groupama	Accenture			IT transformation initiative
203.	Groupe DANONE	Accenture			Worldwide deployment of SAP software
204.	Gulfstream Aerospace Corporation	CSC	$510	10	Mainframe, midrange, and desktop computer operations and development and maintenance of applications software
205.	Hamot Medical Center	Siemens Medical Solutions		10	
206.	Harris Bank of Chicago	ALLTEL Information Services	$160		
207.	Harris Savings Bank of Harrisburg, Pennsylvania	ALLTEL Information Services			Integrated platform solutions
208.	Harvard Pilgrim Health Care	Perot Systems Corporation	$700	10	Strategic integrated business and technology services agreement
209.	Hawaii Medicaid Prescription Benefit Management Program	ACS	$6.1	5	Support the Hawaii Medicaid Prescription Benefit Management Program
210.	Heidelberger Druckmaschinen AG	AT&T	$12	3	Global wide-area network service
211.	Hertz Corporation	IBM	$154	6	Manage portions of data center and provide application development and management services
212.	Hibernia National Bank	ALLTEL Information Services	$91	8	
213.	Hillcrest HealthCare System	Perot Systems Corporation	$65	10	Implement Perot Systems' strategic technical integration plan
214.	HOCHTIEF	Cap Gemini Ernst & Young		10	Efficient implementation of innovative IT concepts

EXHIBIT 1.1   (CONTINUED)   IT OUTSOURCING DEALS

	CUSTOMER	VENDOR	ESTIMATED CONTRACT VALUE (MILLIONS)	TERM (YEARS)	POINTS OF INTEREST
215.	Hong Kong SAR Government	Hewlett-Packard			Systems integration, network infrastructure, office systems, Web development, and security management
216.	Hughes Electronics Corporation	CSC	$60	2	Networks, desktops, help desk, electronic mail, mainframe and midrange operations, and applications maintenance
217.	Hyatt Hotels Corporation	AT&T	$1.2	3	Managed firewall, managed intrusion detection, tape backup and restoration capabilities
218.	ICI Paints	CSC	$10	3	Application management and maintenance
219.	Illinois Hospital Association	ACS		5	IT and business process outsourcing
220.	Immigration and Naturalization Service	CSC	$47.9	28 months	
221.	Inacom	ENTEX IT Service, Inc.			Immediate desk-side, help desk, break/fix, and LAN support services
222.	Inergi LP	Cap Gemini Ernst & Young Canada, Inc.	CDN $1,000	10	Inergi LP managing and operating existing business processes and technology-enabled services for Hydro One
223.	Inex Partners Oy	Cap Gemini Ernst & Young Finland Oy		3	Responsibility of applications and infrastructure management
224.	Infineon	Accenture	$48	7	
225.	ING Group	IBM	$600		
226.	Ingersoll-Rand	ACS	$220	7	Business process outsourcing and IT services
227.	Interac Association	CGI Group, Inc.		10	New network and supporting infrastructure
228.	Internal Revenue Service	Accenture	$33.6	5	Redesign and provide support for the IRS's Web site
229.	Invensys plc	IBM			Management of computing systems
230.	ISS A/S	CSC	$450	10	
231.	J Sainsbury plc	Accenture		7	IT infrastructure
232.	J.P. Morgan Chase & Co.	IBM	5,000	7	Data processing technology infrastructure
233.	Japan Airlines	IBM	$664	10	Systems development, operations, and other services
234.	Johnson Controls, Inc.	Hewlett-Packard		5	Management of its desktop and notebook computing environment

EXHIBIT 1.1 (CONTINUED) IT OUTSOURCING DEALS

	CUSTOMER	VENDOR	ESTIMATED CONTRACT VALUE (MILLIONS)	TERM (YEARS)	POINTS OF INTEREST
235.	KB Home	Perot Systems Corporation		7	
236.	KBC Bank and Insurance Holding Company	EDS		3	Development and management of software applications
237.	Kellwood Company	EDS		7	
238.	Kimberly-Clark Corporation	Compaq Computer Corporation	$100	3	Global services and technology agreement
239.	KLM Airlines	IBM			Office automation and support
240.	Kobe Steel	IBM	$579	10	Information systems development, maintenance, and operations
241.	La Caixa	EDS		4	Data center management and contingency; projects and applications management for both legacy and Internet platforms; call center management; and human resources management and administration outsourcing
242.	La Quinta Inns, Inc.	Perot Systems Corporation		7	IT services for critical business systems
243.	Laurentian Bank of Canada	CGI Group, Inc.	$194		Development and management of its IT services
244.	Lexington Services	CSC	$60	10	Enhance and support hotel reservations system
245.	Loma Linda University Medical Center	ACS			Technology and professional services in support of mainframe-based application requirements
246.	Los Angeles Food Stamp Program	ACS		3	Manage the system and the network
247.	Lufthansa Cargo AG	Perot Systems Corporation			Continued application development and maintenance of the electronic booking system
248.	Main Street Direct	EDS		3	Back-office processing
249.	Malaysia Airlines	IBM		10	
250.	Malaysian Banking	CSC	$340	10	
251.	Manulife Financial	IBM	$563	10	IT infrastructure, including data centers, help desks, PC support, and voice and data networks
252.	Marconi Corp.	CSC	$735	10	
253.	Matson Navigation	ACS	$11	5	
254.	Maxtor Corporation	EDS			Customer support

EXHIBIT 1.1   (CONTINUED)   IT OUTSOURCING DEALS

	CUSTOMER	VENDOR	ESTIMATED CONTRACT VALUE (MILLIONS)	TERM (YEARS)	POINTS OF INTEREST
255.	MCAP Financial Corporation	CGI Group, Inc.	CDN$6.5	5	Manage and support IT infrastructure including AS400's and client server platform, wide-area network services, and help desk services
256.	MCI WorldCom	EDS	$6,000		Network operations outsourcing
257.	MedUnite	EDS			Hosting
258.	Meiji Life Insurance	IBM	$533	10	Administration and management of the host computer and backup centers
259.	Memorial Medical Center	Siemens Medical Solutions			Information technology business office functions
260.	MetLife	Siemens Business Services, Inc.		5	Technology refresh, full acquisition services, asset tracking, remote LAN monitoring and administration
261.	Metromedia Restaurant Group	ACS		5	Business process and IT outsourcing agreement
262.	mg technologies ag	IBM	$1,000	15	Global technology services
263.	Michelin	IBM	$1,210	8	IT operations in North America and Europe
264.	Microcell Telecommunications	GE-Capital IT Solutions	$1.6		Service and repair server hardware
265.	Microsoft	ENTEX Information Services, Inc.			Providing assistance to Microsoft's Information Technology Group in the deployment and support of Windows 2000 Professional
266.	Microsoft	Hewlett-Packard			Centralized end user technical support
267.	Mid Coast Hospital	CSC		5	IT management
268.	Millennium Steel Services	TRW Inc.		5	Design a complete e-commerce enterprise system
269.	Mitsui Marine and Fire Insurance Co.	IBM	$235	10	Host systems operation and management
270.	Mitsui Mutual Life Insurance Co. of Japan	IBM	$1,000	10	Manage and maintain IT operations
271.	Motion Picture & Television Fund	ACS	$23		
272.	Motorola Semiconductor Products Sector	ACS	$25	5	Application portfolio management
273.	Mouvement Desjardins	CGI Group, Inc.	CDN$1,200	10	Data processing operations

EXHIBIT 1.1 (CONTINUED)   IT OUTSOURCING DEALS

	CUSTOMER	VENDOR	ESTIMATED CONTRACT VALUE (MILLIONS)	TERM (YEARS)	POINTS OF INTEREST
274.	MTV	HP			Server platform for advertising sales system
275.	NASA	ACS' Intellisource	$120	3	Total life cycle support and management for desktop, networking and telecommunications assets including technology refresh, asset management, and customer support
276.	NASA	SAIC	$100	5	Internet support and IT services
277.	NASA's Center for Computational Sciences	CSC	$144	6.5	Acquire, install, and manage the latest supercomputer systems on a multiyear technology refresh basis
278.	Nasdaq Europe	Cap Gemini Ernst & Young UK plc		5	Support and manage its IT systems
279.	National Account Service Company LLC	IBM	$300	10	
280.	National Bank of Canada	IBM	more than $700	10	Operations of the IT infrastructure, including Web environment and call centers
281.	National Imagery and Mapping Agency	Lockheed Martin IT	$17	1	Computer network support
282.	National Institutes of Health	Logicon Inc.		10	IT services and support
283.	National Library of Medicine	CSC	$233	10	Computing, network services, and other technology support
284.	National Security Agency	Logicon Inc.	$2,000	10	Telephony and network support services, distribute computing services and enterprise management
285.	National Security Agency	Eagle Alliance, a CSC-led joint venture	$2,000	10	Secure and nonsecure telephony and network services, distributed computing services, and enterprise and security management
286.	National Security Agency	General Dynamics Corporation	$2,000	10	IT services in the areas of telephony and network services, distributed computing services, and enterprise management

EXHIBIT 1.1   (CONTINUED)   IT OUTSOURCING DEALS

	CUSTOMER	VENDOR	ESTIMATED CONTRACT VALUE (MILLIONS)	TERM (YEARS)	POINTS OF INTEREST
287.	Naval Service Warfare Center	DynCorp	$268	8	IT, technical, engineering, operational, and ancillary services
288.	Navigation Technologies	ACS			Mainframe and midrange computing environments
289.	Netmarket Group, Inc.	Compuware Corporation			Exclusive information technology partner
290.	New Jersey Department of Human Services	ACS			Design and implement a Medicaid Management Information System Shared Data Warehouse
291.	New Swiss intercontinental carrier	EDS			Reservation, departure control, flight operations, and general IT outsourcing support services
292.	New York Daily News	ACS			Web hosting
293.	Nextel Communications Inc.	EDS	$234	5	Manage corporate data center, database administration, help desk, desktop services, and other technical functions
294.	Nextel Communications Inc.	IBM and Teletech Holdings	$1,200	8	Customer service, data center, phone, and Web-based support services
295.	Nisource	IBM			Multi-tower BPO
296.	Nokia	Hewlett-Packard	$75	3	Run and manage business infrastructure operation centers, manage groupware, messaging and file print and sharing services, and support these services and servers
297.	Nokia	IBM	$251.4		IT help desk
298.	Noritake Co., Ltd.	IBM Japan	$41	10	Operation, administration, development, and maintenance of information systems and network of personal computers
299.	Nortel Networks	CSC	$339	7	

EXHIBIT 1.1   (CONTINUED)   IT OUTSOURCING DEALS

	CUSTOMER	VENDOR	ESTIMATED CONTRACT VALUE (MILLIONS)	TERM (YEARS)	POINTS OF INTEREST
300.	Nortel Networks	CSC			Global desktop and help line support, computer infrastructure manage-ment, legacy application development, and sup-port and data center management
301.	Nortel Networks Germany	CSC		8	
302.	Nortel Networks, Inc.	Perot Systems Corporation	$37	5	Technology services
303.	North Carolina Com-munity College System	ACS			Data warehouse system
304.	North Carolina Department of Health and Human Services	ACS	$5	2	Prior authorization and help desk services
305.	Northern Territory Government—Australia	CSC	$103	5	IT services to Northern Ter-ritory Government in Australia
306.	Northwest Memorial Hospital	ACS		3	Provide technology and pro-fessional services in sup-port of mainframe-based application requirements
307.	Northwestern Memo-rial Hospital	ACS		3	
308.	NTL Inc.	IBM	$2,000	11	
309.	OK Q8	EDS		5	IT operations, including sys-tem development
310.	Okanagan IT Alliance	CGI Group, Inc.	CDN$16	7	All support services for the data center and the wide-area network
311.	ON Semiconductor	ACS	$25	5	Full outsourcing applica-tion portfolio manage-ment of all legacy applications
312.	Option One Mort-gage Corporation	ENTEX IT Ser-vice, Inc.			Technology migration
313.	Optus	IBM Global Ser-vices Australia	$500	10	Application development, enhancement, and main-tenance of IT systems
314.	Owens & Minor, Inc.	Perot Systems Corporation	$229	7	IT hosting and services
315.	Oxford Health Plans, Inc.	CSC		5	Data center operations for midrange computing, enterprise-wide desktop support, 24x7 help desk support, and network management

EXHIBIT 1.1   (CONTINUED)   IT OUTSOURCING DEALS

	CUSTOMER	VENDOR	ESTIMATED CONTRACT VALUE (MILLIONS)	TERM (YEARS)	POINTS OF INTEREST
316.	Participate.com	Comdisco			Host site and provide ongoing monitoring and support
317.	Partnership of public safety and transportation agencies in VA, MD and DC	IBM			Build a public safety data communications network
318.	Pechiney Plastic Packaging, Inc.	CGI Group, Inc.	$16	5	Data center, help desk support, and maintaining desktops
319.	Pennsylvania State Police	EDS	$2.2	9 months	Infrastructure support, Web development, document management, hardware and software services
320.	Philips Semiconductors	EDS			Server, desktop, applications, and telecommunications support
321.	Physicians Plus Insurance Corporation	Perot Systems Corporation	$50	10	Back-office and technology management services
322.	Pilot Insurance Company	CGI Group, Inc.		5	
323.	Pitney Bowes Office Systems, Inc.	CGI Group, Inc.	$25	5	IT infrastructure management and support
324.	PracticeOne	Interliant, Inc.			Web-based hosting of data
325.	Procter & Gamble	HP	$3,000	10	IT infrastructure
326.	Procter & Gamble	IBM	$400	10	Management of employee services such as payroll, benefits, compensation, expatriate and relocation services, and HR data management of 98,000 employees in 80 countries
327.	Q4i	EDS	$15	5	Web hosting and managed storage services
328.	Quintiles Transnational Corp.	Perot Systems Corporation	$108	5	IT project management and application development
329.	Quintiles Transnational Corp.	Perot Systems Corporation		3	Global IT services
330.	RAG American Coal Holding, Inc.	Accenture and Mincom Alliance	$16	3	Provide IT and business services
331.	Railinc Corporation	ACS	$60	5	Full-service IT infrastructure services
332.	Raytheon Company	CSC	$65 per year		Mainframes and data centers, help desk support, and network operations
333.	Raytheon Company	CSC	$350	8	Desktop support

EXHIBIT 1.1   (CONTINUED)   IT OUTSOURCING DEALS

	CUSTOMER	VENDOR	ESTIMATED CONTRACT VALUE (MILLIONS)	TERM (YEARS)	POINTS OF INTEREST
334.	Raytheon Company	CSC	$128	8	IT infrastructure, including mainframe and midrange computers, desktop, help desk operations, engineering computing, electronic messaging, voice and video telecommunications, and network servers
335.	Rehabilitation Hospital of the Pacific	ACS		7	
336.	Richardson (Texas) Independent School District	Compaq Computer Corporation	$30-35	5	Life cycle solution and provide ongoing maintenance, technical support, and a dedicated project manager
337.	Rouge Steel Company	Perot Systems Corporation		6	IT requirements, including operational and business systems and software development and support
338.	Royal & SunAlliance UK	IBM		10	Mainframe, midrange, and desktop computing services
339.	Royal & SunAlliance USA	ACS		7	Data center operations and technical support for all mainframe platforms, data center operations for the midrange platforms and overall management of the wide-area network
340.	Ryanair.com	Comdisco		5	Managed Web hosting services
341.	Sabre Holdings Corporation	EDS	$2.2	10	Manage IT systems
342.	Saint Vincent Catholic Medical Centers of New York	CSC	$200	7	
343.	Sal. Oppenheim Jr. & Cie.	EDS		5	Operational and project services for IT infrastructure environment
344.	Saskatchewan Health	CGI Group, Inc.	CDN$3.8	27 months	Outsourcing and support services
345.	Schroders	CSC	$240	7	Manage infrastructure and application services, including desktop computing, help desk, midrange and voice services, and certain applications development and support
346.	Scoot	IBM	$50	5	Web hosting and full IT support

Exhibit 1.1   (Continued)   IT Outsourcing Deals

	CUSTOMER	VENDOR	ESTIMATED CONTRACT VALUE (MILLIONS)	TERM (YEARS)	POINTS OF INTEREST
347.	Scotiabank	IBM	$600	7	Manage computer operations, including data centers, branches, Automated Banking Machines, and desktop computer systems
348.	Scottish and Southern Energy	IBM	$50	5	Improve the provision of application development and support services within its IT operations
349.	Sempra Energy	CSC	$70	5	
350.	Shanghai Stock Exchange	Hewlett-Packard			Project definition consultancy services
351.	Sherwin-Williams	IBM			Store technology infrastructure
352.	Shiseido Co., Ltd.	IBM		10	
353.	Siemens Energy and Automation	Siemens Business Services, Inc.		5	Integrated Desktop, Server and Remote Network Monitoring and System administration and Service Desk Utility support
354.	Silicon Manufacturing Company	EDS			
355.	SN Brussels Airlines	EDS			Industry-customized IT
356.	Social Security Administration	Compaq Computer Corporation	$30		Provide computers, peripherals, and services
357.	Solutia, Inc	EDS			
358.	Sonera Corporation	Hewlett-Packard		5	Outsourcing of data centers
359.	Sonofon	WM-data		4	Operations and support for central IT system
360.	South Carolina Department of Social Services	ACS		1	Design, development, implementation, maintenance, and marketing of the system
361.	Sprint	EDS			
362.	SRC Devices Inc.	OneNeck IT Services Corp.			Application support, database administration, and financial support
363.	SSP Solutions	EDS			Host, deploy, and manage network
364.	St. Joseph Health System	Perot Systems Corporation	$270	10	IT services, operations, and support
365.	State of Arkansas	EDS			Services to bring Medicaid management information systems into compliance with HIPAA
366.	State of Hawaii, Med-QUEST Division	ACS	$41	5	Support the state's Medicaid program

Exhibit 1.1   (Continued)   IT Outsourcing Deals

	CUSTOMER	VENDOR	ESTIMATED CONTRACT VALUE (MILLIONS)	TERM (YEARS)	POINTS OF INTEREST
367.	State of Indiana	EDS	$33	1	Managed administrative and operational processes for the Indiana Office of Medicaid Planning and Policy
368.	State of Kansas	EDS	$160	6	Transform the administrative and operational processes that support the state's Medicaid program
369.	State of Texas Department of Information Resources	Lockheed Martin IT	$200	7	
370.	Stelco Inc.	EDS		10	IT support and development services
371.	STI Knowledge	EDS		3	Convert STI Knowledge's traditional classroom instruction for its call center professionals to a Web-based platform
372.	StorageTek	EDS	$300	10	IT infrastructure, application maintenance and support, basic call center functions
373.	Sun Life Assurance Company of Canada	IBM Canada	CDN $250	7	Manage a portion of the IT structure
374.	Sun Life Financial	CGI Group [Europe] Limited	CDN$119	7	Mainframe, midrange, UNIX and NT systems, and desktops
375.	Sun Life Financial	IBM	$164	7	Web hosting, mainframe and midrange server management, e-mail services, support for Lotus Notes applications and network security services
376.	Swedish Post	IBM			IT and telephony
377.	Swissair Group	EDS			
378.	Swissport	EDS			Network support, departure control and applications hosting and management services
379.	Tally Systems	Siemens Business Services, Inc.			Host inventory service as a part of IT management services
380.	Tarari Inc.	CenterBeam			Base IT infrastructure
381.	Tata Steel	Hewlett-Packard			IT infrastructure management
382.	TD Bank	IBM	720	7	Data network and technology services
383.	Telecom Italia	HP	$244	5	Desktop management

EXHIBIT 1.1 (CONTINUED) IT OUTSOURCING DEALS

	CUSTOMER	VENDOR	ESTIMATED CONTRACT VALUE (MILLIONS)	TERM (YEARS)	POINTS OF INTEREST
384.	Telecom New Zealand	EDS	$800	10	
385.	Telecom New Zealand	EDS			Supply and manage desktop PCS and laptops
386.	Telecom New Zealand	EDS	$133	3	
387.	TeleCorp PCS Inc.	Convergys Corporation		3	Customer care services
388.	Telefónica Argentina	IBM	$252	6	Data center operations and maintenance, help desk, business continuity services, and distributed systems management
389.	Telefónica CTC Chile	IBM Chile	$87.3	5	
390.	Telefonica del Sur	IBM			
391.	Telstra Corporation Limited	Deloitte Consulting	$155	5	Applications development and maintenance of Enterprise Resource Planning
392.	Tenet Healthcare Corporation	Perot Systems Corporation	$15	9.5	Desktop, network, and telecommunication support
393.	Tenet Healthcare Corporation	Perot Systems Corporation	$550	10	
394.	Texaco	IBM	$100	5	Primary global IT service provider
395.	Texas Comptroller of Public Accounts	ACS	$9.1	5	Application outsourcing
396.	Texas Comptroller of Public Accounts	ACS	$6.1	3	Application and support services
397.	Texas Department of Protective and Regulatory Services	Logicon Inc.	$80	6	Desktop refresh, transition support, network monitoring, help desk services, disaster recovery, and other IT-related services
398.	Texas Department of Transportation	Compaq Computer Corporation	$2	4	Provide all laptop PC systems
399.	Texas Department of Transportation	Compaq Computer Corporation	$20	4	Desktops, key services
400.	Texas Instruments Incorporated	Siemens Business Services, Inc.		3	Management, maintenance, and install/move/add/change services for deskside PC hardware and software
401.	The Dow Chemical Company	EDS	$1,400	7	Designing, constructing, enhancing, and maintaining network

EXHIBIT 1.1 (CONTINUED) IT OUTSOURCING DEALS

	CUSTOMER	VENDOR	ESTIMATED CONTRACT VALUE (MILLIONS)	TERM (YEARS)	POINTS OF INTEREST
402.	The Dow Chemical Company	IBM			End-to-end Web-hosting services
403.	The Guardian Life Insurance Company	Siemens Business Services, Inc.	$12.50	3	IT infrastructure reshaping project
404.	The Minute Maid Company	IBM	$70	5.5	Core IT functions, including application development, server operations, help desk and maintenance, and networking operations
405.	The New Power Company	IBM	$1,500	10	Build, staff, and run core components of back-office functions
406.	The Queen's Medical Center	ACS	$28	7	Entire scope of IT services
407.	The Robert Plan Corporation	Perot Systems Corporation	$185	12	Data center management, desktop support, network management, applications development, help desk support, disaster recovery, and change management
408.	The Warehouse Group Limited	Oracle New Zealand			Hosting and ongoing technical management of its Oracle Applications
409.	The Winterthur Group	IBM	$420	10	Operation of its IT center, excluding networks and infrastructure
410.	Tour de France	CSC		3	IT supplier
411.	Transora	CSC			Supplier of computer hardware, software, and related services and developing full e-procurement capability and support of the IT procurement service
412.	Triton Container International Limited	Perot Systems Corporation	$50	7	Manage all information technology operations and execute applications development services
413.	TXU	Cap Gemini	$3,000	7	Hardware, software, maintenance, and other services
414.	U.S. Air Force	EDS		5	Wide range of IT-related engineering services. Provider of middleware technology and smart-card readers for the service-wide implementation of a smart-card initiative

EXHIBIT 1.1   (CONTINUED)   IT OUTSOURCING DEALS

	CUSTOMER	VENDOR	ESTIMATED CONTRACT VALUE (MILLIONS)	TERM (YEARS)	POINTS OF INTEREST
415.	U.S. Air Force	Northrop Grumman Corporation		4	Technical support for a messaging system
416.	U.S. Air Force Information Technology Services	General Dynamics Corporation	$41	5	Continuous network operations and management support
417.	U.S. Air Force Weather Agency	Logicon Inc.	$13	5	Computer operations and software programming
418.	U.S. Army Communications— Electronics Command	CSC	$70	3	Deploy the Joint Computer-aided Acquisition and Logistic Support system to Department of Defense
419.	U.S. Army Wholesale Logistics Modernization Program	CSC	$680	10	IT services required to reengineer and modernize the Army's wholesale logistics business processes
420.	U.S. Army's Warfighter Information Network—Tactical	General Dynamics Corporation	$6,000		Define and document the optimal architecture and develop and deliver a demonstration suite of hardware and software for government testing
421.	U.S. Department of State	CSC	$160	5	IT and professional/technical services
422.	U.S. Department of State	CSC with IBM Team	$10	10	Computing infrastructure and integration services
423.	U.S. Department of State's Diplomatic Telecommunications Services Program	CSC		8	Engineering, training, financial management network management, help desk, and logistics support
424.	U.S. Department of Transportation– John A. Volpe National Transportation Center	CSC	$190.5	5	On-site technical support services
425.	U.S. General Services Administration	AT&T			Web hosting and security services
426.	U.S. Joint Forces Command	Northrop Grumman Corporation	$28.3	5	Full range of IT services
427.	U.S. Navy Personnel Research, Studies and Technology/ Navy Personnel Command	DynCorp Information & Enterprise Technology, Inc.	$7.6	5	Comprehensive life cycle services—from research and development to test and validation—of prototype computer-based information management systems for military staffing management

EXHIBIT 1.1 (CONTINUED) IT OUTSOURCING DEALS

	CUSTOMER	VENDOR	ESTIMATED CONTRACT VALUE (MILLIONS)	TERM (YEARS)	POINTS OF INTEREST
428.	U.S. Navy Space and Naval Warfare Systems Center	CSC	$38	5	Development, operation, and maintenance of the S&T Network infrastructure
429.	U.S. Postal Service	Compaq Computer Corporation	$1,000	5	Full spectrum of Windows and Intel-based products and services
430.	UCAR International Inc.	CGI Group, Inc.	$75	10	Data center services, networks, desktops, telecommunications, and legacy systems
431.	UK Department of Health	CSC	$60	7	
432.	UK government's Defence Aviation Repair Agency	Cap Gemini Ernst & Young UK plc	£19		IT infrastructure as well as applications management and a help desk
433.	UK Inland Revenue	Cap Gemini Ernst & Young UK plc	£5,200.00	10	
434.	UK National Health Service	Accenture		10	
435.	UK National Health Service	Accenture		10	
436.	UK National Health Service	BT Group			
437.	UK National Health Service	CSC			
438.	UK National Health Service	EDS			National Web-based e-mail
439.	United States Air Force Electronic Systems Center	ACS	$12.1	1	
440.	United States Air Force Reserve Command	ACS	$63.0	7	Network services
441.	United States Tennis Association	ACS			IT services including desktop, server operations, network support, database administration and management, and information services application support and development
442.	United Technologies Corp.	CSC	$2,100	10	Support desktop computers, help desk, engineering workstations, networks, servers, and mainframes
443.	University of Pennsylvania Health System	ACS and First Consulting Group, Inc.	$100		

EXHIBIT 1.1   (CONTINUED)   IT OUTSOURCING DEALS

	CUSTOMER	VENDOR	ESTIMATED CONTRACT VALUE (MILLIONS)	TERM (YEARS)	POINTS OF INTEREST
444.	University of Tennessee	SAIC		5	IT consulting services
445.	University of Tennessee Medical Center	McKesson Information Solutions Inc.	$15	10	Remote outsourcing
446.	US Department of the Navy	EDS			Navy Marine Corps Intranet Program
447.	US Oncology, Inc.	Perot Systems Corporation		5	Provide IT support services for selected enterprise applications
448.	USDA Farm Service Agency and Natural Resources Conservation	SAIC	$175	5	IT development, software maintenance, and operational support of systems
449.	V&S Group	CSC	$25	5	
450.	VALOR Telecommunications, LLC	ALLTEL Information Services	$30	1.5	Comprehensive remote outsourcing
451.	VHA Inc.	ACS		5	IT outsourcing and application outsourcing
452.	Virgin Mobile USA	EDS			Back-office infrastructure
453.	Visteon	IBM	$2,000	10	IT operations takeover
454.	Vitro, S.A. de C.V.	EDS		5	Database management, technology renovations, data recovery, desktop platform, support table, information security, and voice and data network administration
455.	Vought Aircraft Industries Inc.	Logicon Inc.	$107 for 2 years	3	Support of all hardware, from desktops to mainframes; network services, including WANs and LANs; systems engineering support; application support; programming; consulting; disaster recovery; and help desk services
456.	Ward Manufacturing Inc.	Perot Systems Corporation		5	Managing and supporting current and future information technology requirements
457.	Washington Mutual	ACS			Integration and conversion services
458.	Welch Allyn, Inc.	Cap Gemini Ernst & Young US LLC		5	Implement a new Enterprise System and provide applications development and support of related business initiatives

EXHIBIT 1.1 (CONTINUED)   IT OUTSOURCING DEALS

	CUSTOMER	VENDOR	ESTIMATED CONTRACT VALUE (MILLIONS)	TERM (YEARS)	POINTS OF INTEREST
459.	WellPoint Health Networks Inc.	Perot Systems Corporation		6.5	Application service provider
460.	Westpac Banking Corporation	IBM	$2,300	10	IT infrastructure and tele-communications services and strategic e-business initiative
461.	Whitbread PLC	CSC	$75	7	
462.	Williams Cos.	IBM	$320		
463.	Willis Group Holdings	Compaq Computer Corporation			Global workforce
464.	XM Satellite Radio	Convergys Corporation		3	Integrated contact center services
465.	Zurich Financial	IBM	"pay per use" system		Consolidation and management of personal technology for all 64,000 employees of ZFS in five European countries, the United States, and Canada

EXHIBIT 1.1   (CONTINUED)   IT OUTSOURCING DEALS

OUTSOURCING IN THE PHARMACEUTICAL INDUSTRY[14]

Most, if not all, major pharmaceutical companies have outsourced, or are evaluating outsourcing, one or more noncore business functions to a third-party service provider. Looking back over the last five years, the most likely business function that would have been outsourced by a pharmaceutical company was all or part of a company's back-office information technology (IT) infrastructure, such as the mainframe, midrange, desktop, or application maintenance functions. Recently, however, pharmaceutical companies are becoming more innovative in the types of business functions that they consider ripe for outsourcing. Examples of functions that are being considered include human resources (operations or payroll), financial transaction processing (particularly accounts payable), procurement, distribution and logistics, and clinical data management.

WHY OUTSOURCE?

Like most other companies, the leading factors motivating pharmaceutical companies to outsource include the following:

- Overall cost savings
- Flexible/variable pricing (not fixed/dedicated resources)
- Access to a broad pool of competent, trained resources
- Continued and early access to state-of-the-art technologies and processes
- Rapid standardization or globalization

OUTSOURCING OPTIONS AND THE "OFFSHORING" ISSUE

There are several different types of outsourcing options to be evaluated. The most common options at this time are *onshoring* (where the provision of services is from the same country where the recipient of services is provided); *offshoring* (where the provision of services is from a low-cost country other than the country where the recipient of services is located, such as India, the Philippines,

---

China, or some of the Eastern Bloc countries); *nearshoring* (where the provision of services is from a lower-cost country that is close to the recipient country's borders, such as Canada, Mexico, or the Caribbean); and, finally, likely the most common, a hybrid of all or some of these types (where a portion of the services will be provided onshore and a portion will be provided offshore).

As one may have gleaned from the recent electoral campaigns, offshoring is the most controversial of the various types of outsourcing, largely due to the perception that offshoring means the loss of jobs in the United States. Despite the negative press surrounding offshoring, leading analysts continue to state that most, if not all, major companies have considered offshore outsourcing or offshoring as a strategic sourcing option. With heightened focus on offshore outsourcing by internal management at all levels, it is important to understand key due diligence and legal considerations that are unique to an offshore outsourcing transaction, as well as the current state of the anti-offshoring legislation.

DUE DILIGENCE.   One of the concerns that companies have about outsourcing is the implicit loss of control over day-to-day operations of a business function. This concern is amplified in an offshore transaction because the personnel responsible for the daily operations are not only not down the hall, they are not even in the same country. Because of the perception that the loss of control is greater when offshoring, the due diligence process around offshoring is often more comprehensive (and longer) than that around an onshore transaction.

Key action items that should be reviewed as part of the due diligence of an offshore outsourcing company or a U.S.-based company with offshore operations include the following:

- What is the financial viability of the offshore enterprise? What is the relationship with the onshore enterprise (if any)? How will disputes be handled? How will notices be served? Will there be an onshore presence for service of process purposes?

- What business continuity options are offered by the outsourcing service provider? Where is the secondary site? Can volumes be moved between sites or back onshore?

- What experience does the offshore service provider have in the U.S. markets? Who are the U.S. references?

- Does the offshore service provider have procurement and financial responsibility for obtaining certain software and hardware as required for service delivery? Are any specific requirements necessary to enable compatibility between customer and service provider systems? Does the service provider have expertise in all of the customer's technologies and processes?

- What type of data, network, and physical security infrastructure does the service provider have in place?

- Does the offshore service provider have the ability to recruit a broad employee base to allow for growth?

- Will there be a good cultural fit? Are there any language or cultural issues?

- Can the service provider provide on-site resources if requested? What are the visa/immigration issues? Which company is responsible for the cost of travel, for attending meetings, for knowledge transfer?

- What communication lines will the service provider put in place?

- Does the service provider have the necessary language capabilities?

ANTI-OFFSHORING LEGISLATION. Slow economic recovery, coupled with increasing offshore transaction volume and an election year, has led to a flurry of legislative proposals intended to reduce or prohibit offshore outsourcing. At this time, at least 36 states have pending anti-offshore legislation (with a total of more than 150 pending laws). The major categories of anti-offshore legislation include the following (with an example of each):

- *"Buy american" initiatives.* No performance of state/federal contract work by offshore workers or non-U.S. citizens (e.g., Dodd Amendment; many pending State laws)

- *Offshore call center law.* Any call must be rerouted to the United States if the caller requests (e.g., proposed N.J. Law)

- *Privacy initiatives.* No transmission of personal medical, financial, or other data offshore without individual's prior consent unless offshore privacy protections certified as adequate by FTC (e.g., H. Clinton sponsored S. 2312)

- *Immigration law initiatives.* Proposed Limitations on H-1B and L-1 Visa Legislation

UNIQUE LEGAL ISSUES. In addition to the myriad of issues that arise in connection with outsourcing (some of which are highlighted as follows), several specific issues have heightened significance in an offshore deal. Examples include the following:

- Data privacy
- Import/export
- Immigration issues
- Proprietary rights
- Local law concerns
- Enforcement issues
- Ability to relocate/terminate

The actual impact of this legislation is not known at this time. In the near term, it appears to largely affect outsourcing by government entities, but this may extend to government contractors and companies with government funding as well.

REGULATORY COMPLIANCE: A KEY DIFFERENTIATING FACTOR

The regulatory regime of the pharmaceutical industry mandates that both the customer and the service provider understand the specific compliance requirements applicable to the specific outsourcing transaction at hand. A key part of the negotiations will involve determining which laws the customer and the service provider will be responsible for monitoring and complying with and how the costs will be allocated for changes required by new laws (including different interpretation of existing ones). Some questions to consider include the following:

- Which company will be responsible for interpreting regulations specifically promulgated for implementation by the pharmaceutical industry (such as FDA)?

- If the customer retains responsibility for interpreting such pharm-specific laws, how will the service provider implement them? Will the customer provide guidelines or protocols?

- Will the service provider have validation responsibilities? Will the service provider have to validate its own software and hardware? Will it have to validate customer software and hardware, or maintain already validated software and hardware? Will the service provider follow the customer's validation procedures? Who will determine when software or hardware has been actually validated?

- How will Sarbanes-Oxley compliance be handled? What are the service provider's responsibilities? A key issue that the customer's auditors will want assurance on is the ability of the service provider to provide SAS No. 70 reports (if and when required).

- For business processes, is the customer or the service provider best suited for monitoring and complying with laws specific to the service (e.g., in HR deals, will the customer have retained the legal compliance function or will the relevant employees have been terminated or transferred to the service provider)?

QUICK CHECKLIST OF OTHER MAJOR LEGAL ISSUES

In addition to the industry-specific and offshore-specific issues discussed previously, there are many other issues for the legal, business, and technical teams to consider in connection with the outsourcing transaction. A checklist of some of the key legal issues is set forth as follows:

- Scope of services
- Terms applicable to the transfer of employees and assets

- Structure and approval rights over project staff
- Responsibility for third-party consents (e.g., software access/use rights)
- Performance standards and benchmarking
- Regulatory compliance issues
- Approval rights over service locations (and right to force relocation)
- Ownership and use rights in existing and newly developed intellectual property
- Audit rights
- Applicable fee structure (including adjustment mechanism, inflation risk, tax responsibility, and invoicing)
- Rights to terminate
- Exit rights and termination assistance

CONCLUSION

The complex nature of outsourcing transactions requires that the customer's negotiating team be knowledgeable about not only the company's business and current and future service environments, but also terms applicable to such issues as asset transfer, employee transfer, data privacy, audit, insurance, regulatory compliance, tax, business continuity, and risk management. In order to achieve a good business and legal deal and construct a contract that has the flexibility to survive for the duration of the deal (which can be for as long as 10 years), the team must fully understand all of the many issues that can arise in an outsourcing transaction and be able to formulate reasonable positions and alternative approaches.

CHAPTER 2

CONSIDERING OUTSOURCING: THE REQUEST FOR PROPOSAL AND VENDOR SELECTION

2.1 THE DIRECTIVE

With IT costs accounting for a significant percentage of a customer's[1] total expenses and with the emphasis on technology as a critical vehicle for changing the strategic direction of many customers, senior management is paying more attention to how the IT department is being run—looking for new ways to cut costs and increase profitability and performance. Outsourcing is seen by senior management as a means for handling either short-term or long-term IT issues and, in many cases, broader organizational needs. For example, the outsourcing vendor may be willing to pay the customer a much-needed upfront lump-sum payment for IT assets, or outsourcing may provide the resources to implement

---

1. Note: References to "customer" in this chapter refer to the potential outsourcing customer considering and evaluating outsourcing, and may include companies or government entities.

new systems more rapidly than the customer would have been able to accomplish with its own in-house staff. It is no surprise then that, in many cases, the directive to consider outsourcing comes from senior management, particularly since IT personnel often view outsourcing as placing their jobs at risk.

The reasons for considering outsourcing vary from customer to customer and may depend on whether the directive comes from senior management or from within the IT department. Senior management typically decides to evaluate outsourcing as part of:

- An organization-wide directive to outsource noncore functions
- An effort to globalize/standardize functions throughout the organization
- An organization-wide directive to downsize or cut costs
- The reorganization of IT, often in response to a reengineering study
- The redirection of IT in an effort to remain competitive
- An effort to enhance public perception (and perhaps boost stock prices)

The IT department, whose reasons for considering outsourcing are often more focused, typically targets outsourcing as an option:

- As part of the reorganization of all or part of IT
- As a means to cut IT costs
- As a means to focus more resources on IT strategy
- In an effort to enhance performance
- As part of the rollout of new technology (e.g., client/server)
- In order to provide lacking expertise/experience

The reasons behind initiating the evaluation of outsourcing will affect the process, timetable, and scope of the transaction. If, for example, senior management has decided to outsource noncore capabilities as part of an organization-wide downsizing initiative or the customer wishes to sign the contract by the end of its fiscal year, the customer may spend less resources on assessing the benefits and risks of outsourcing and move more quickly to the request for proposal or vendor selection stage. In other instances, for example, where the go-ahead to consider outsourcing comes from IT management and the primary objective is to improve performance, the evaluation and negotiation process may be longer.

2.2   OBTAINING SUPPORT AND FORMING THE OUTSOURCING TEAM

Once the decision is made to consider outsourcing all or part of a customer's IT functions, it will be necessary to ensure that the outsourcing effort is supported by both the IT department and senior management and, in some cases, by the board of directors. Support from within the IT department and from senior management is critical to moving the process along, particularly because the customer will need to commit significant resources to carrying out the evaluation, proposal, and negotiation processes. These resources include financial resources for such expenses as travel, meeting rooms, overtime, and consultant/legal fees, as well as personnel resources (top IT managers who will likely work exclusively on this project for several months). Many customers overlook the need to obtain board support or, with respect to government entities, fiscal appropriation. Because the total amounts to be expended in many outsourcing contracts can be substantial, the customer should consider whether the decision to outsource is subject to board approval before going forward with the evaluation process or, more likely, before signing a contract. Even if board approval is not necessary until later, it is often useful to get the board "on board" at an early stage so that any negative reactions can be dealt with before too many resources are expended.

The next step is selecting the customer's project leader, typically the chief information officer (CIO) or a direct report. It is important that the project leader has (1) clear directions as to what the customer's objectives are and the time frame for achieving these objectives and (2) the empowerment to carry out these directions and make decisions. The project leader typically organizes a team from:

- Within the IT department
- One or all of the following departments: purchasing, finance, human resources, legal, audit, tax, risk management, and other affected areas (e.g., mergers and acquisitions may get involved if there is an asset transfer)
- Outside consultants and lawyers

It is important to get all project team members involved at an early stage because some pieces of the transaction may require a substantial lead time.

2.3 GUIDELINES AND INTERNAL EVALUATION

Once the outsourcing team is formed, it should consider preparing guidelines for the project, including procedures relating to confidentiality and internal and external communications. It is prudent to implement a system for marking documents (e.g., proprietary and confidential, authorized access only). Many customers also set up separate working rooms for the team, with dedicated fax and telephone lines.

An essential step—before performing preliminary due diligence—is for the team to establish its top five to ten objectives for outsourcing. It is a common outsourcing myth that the main reason that companies or government entities outsource their IT operations is to cut IT costs. Although the potential for immediate capital and overall cost savings exists, it is not always realized, nor is it necessarily the primary or sole objective in pursuing outsourcing. In addition to cost savings, other common objectives include the following:

- Concentrating on core capabilities
- Implementing a variable cost approach
- Obtaining an immediate cash infusion (typically associated with the transfer of assets to the vendor)
- Improving overall performance
- Keeping current with industry IT trends
- Providing access to new technologies
- Reducing risk
- Sharing risks
- Implementing tools for growth
- Standardizing diverse systems
- Revamping the IT structure management
- Facilitating migration to new systems
- Refreshing existing systems
- Managing legacy systems
- Managing legacy systems while the customer implements new technology
- Obtaining new or additional resources
- Providing flexibility to increase or decrease resources

Once the list of objectives is compiled by the outsourcing team, it is useful to submit the list to senior and IT management at an early stage for their approval. This process enables the outsourcing team to evaluate whether its initial objectives were achieved when the final deal is presented to management.

The next step is for the outsourcing candidate to begin an internal evaluation process to determine whether outsourcing is desirable from a business, financial, technological, operational, regulatory, and legal perspective. Issues to consider as part of this initial due diligence include identifying what will be outsourced and whether there are any obstacles to outsourcing (e.g., corporate initiatives, acquisition, restructuring or divesture plans, restrictive relationships with third parties, regulations). In addition, the customer will want to determine whether any precedent for outsourcing exists within its organization and learn how employee and asset issues were dealt with in previous transactions or are being dealt with in contemporaneous transactions. The customer should also investigate whether there are any existing IT outsourcing relationships, who the vendors are, and the status of the relationship.

The customer should also initiate at an early stage an investigation into whether any regulatory or local law approvals or authorizations may be required. In addition, the customer should determine what type of corporate approval is necessary (e.g., board approval, parent approval, legislative approval). Subject to the organizations' confidentiality obligations, due diligence that has proved very useful is for the outsourcing candidate to talk to other organizations that have outsourced similar IT functions to learn from their experience (and successes and mistakes).

Any customer deciding whether to outsource will need to outline the benefits and risks of outsourcing and assess whether the benefits outweigh the risks. An example of a common risk/benefit analysis follows:

- Benefits
  - Cost savings/benefits
  - Enhanced ability to concentrate on core business
  - Implementation of organization-wide initiatives
  - Sale of assets (i.e., moving assets off books, capital infusion)
  - Greater resources to move to new environment/systems in a faster time frame
  - More and varied skills and resources
  - Better access to new technology
  - Reduced training expense
  - Enhanced flexibility

- Risks
  - Loss of control
  - Cost management
  - Tax liability
  - Difficulties in reassuming responsibility (or "insourcing")
  - Reduced flexibility

2.4 PREPARING A TIMETABLE

The period of time from which a customer decides to pursue the possibility of outsourcing until the actual outsourcing contract is signed may vary from two months to three years depending on the customer's reasons for outsourcing, the customer's and the vendor's negotiating flexibility, and the complexity of the transaction. For example, the outsourcing team may have only a couple of months to select a vendor and negotiate and sign a contract if senior management decides that the contract must be signed by a specific date so that the announcement of the outsourcing transaction coincides with the announcement of a larger organizational restructuring (e.g., a public offering). However, there may be fewer time constraints in situations where the IT department introduces the idea of outsourcing all or part of the customer's IT and wishes to perform due diligence before escalating the idea to a senior management level for approval. In more complex transactions (e.g., involving several international sites), regulatory and legal requirements, rather than the customer, may dictate the time frame of the transaction for the following reasons: (1) financial institutions may need to obtain the consent of regulatory authorities; (2) transborder data flow restrictions may require the customer to obtain government/agency consent; or (3) local law may impose a notice period before transitioning employees. From the vendor's perspective, it is almost always desirable to close the deal as quickly as possible.

The length of time that a customer has to conclude an outsourcing transaction often dictates the process. A truncated timetable invariably means cutting corners with respect to due diligence, vendor selection, and negotiation. The customer should weigh the advantages of completing the transaction within a certain period against the loss of leverage and thoroughness that may result from the short period of time. However, while it is desirable to spend time defining requirements, performing due diligence, preparing a comprehensive request for proposal, and negotiating the transaction, there are advantages to moving the process along as expeditiously as possible, most notably that the process uses a significant amount of personnel and may involve incurring significant expenses (e.g., travel, consultants, lawyers). In addition, some customers have found that a drawn-out process may be particularly damaging to employee morale. Timing is often used to obtain concessions from the party under time constraints. The vendor, for example, may wish to complete the transaction by the end of its fiscal year, which the customer may use to its advantage if it does not have similar time constraints.

Once the customer has determined, at least generally, the time that it wishes to commit to the due diligence and negotiation process, it is useful for the customer to prepare a timetable of key dates relating to the outsourcing process. What are considered key dates will depend on the scope of the transaction, whether the customer is putting the transaction out to bid, and whether there are regulatory restrictions. Exhibit 2.1 contains a list of key dates to keep in mind when developing the outsourcing timetable. This list is by no means exhaustive and will vary depending on the requirements of each deal. For example, a financial institution will likely have different time-sensitive regulatory requirements than a steel manufacturer.

2.5   INTERNAL COMMUNICATIONS

An important issue to consider early in the planning process is how employee/internal communications will be handled. Customers usually follow one of three general philosophies:

1. Wait until the deal is ready to be signed before telling employees.
2. Tell the employees that outsourcing is being considered and that no other information is available until contract negotiations are well underway (on a need-to-know basis).
3. Be very upfront with employees from the start.

Issue	Responsibility	Time Frame
Senior Management Directive		
Select and Form Internal Outsourcing Team		
List Outsourcing Objectives		
Obtain Management Support		
Determine Internal Communication Strategy		
Customer's Preliminary Evaluation		
Internal Meetings		
Site Visits		
Request for Information (RFI)		
Develop RFI		
Issue RFI		
Vendor Responses Due		
Evaluate Responses		
Request for Proposal (RFP)		
Issue RFP		
Vendor Responses Due		
Evaluate Responses		
Vendor Presentations		
Clarifications		
Develop Negotiation Strategy		
Select Preferred Vendor(s)		
Customer Due Diligence		
Financial		
Legal		
Regulatory		
Data Issues		
Employee-Related		
Site/Local Issues		
Vendor Due Diligence		
Begins		
Ends		
Term Sheet		
Prepare Term Sheet		
Negotiate Term Sheet		
Contract		
Prepare Contract		
Negotiate Contract		
Employee-Related Issues		
Develop Transition Plan		
Make Offers to Employees		
Employee Acceptance Date		
Employee Start Date		
Approvals/Authorizations		
Corporate Approvals		
Regulatory Approvals		
Local Approvals (for international transactions)		
Sign Contract		
Press Release		
Asset Transfer		
Notify Third-Party Vendors		
Contract Commencement Date		

EXHIBIT 2.1   OUTSOURCING TIMETABLE

Pros and cons for each approach are as follows:

Wait Until There Is a Deal

PROS

Negotiating position is not compromised by employee reactions and demands

Negotiations are not strained by fear that employees will resign during negotiations (particularly if all employees are not being transferred and there will be no stay incentives)

Less risk of leakage to the press

Avoid false alarm if decision is made not to outsource

CONS

Breeds distrust among general employee population

Employees may claim that they were not treated fairly

Allows employees little opportunity to evaluate options

On a Need-to-Know Basis

PROS

Breeds trust with employees

Likelihood that employees will not leave until they know what the situation is

Mitigates claims from employees that they were not adequately informed

CONS

Risk that employees will resign

Employees may still claim that they were not fully informed

Incomplete disclosure may result in unfounded rumors

Be Upfront from the Start

PROS

Breeds trust/loyalty with employees

Reduces risk of claims that employees were not fully informed

Often helps in the negotiation process to learn what employee concerns are

CONS

Risk that employees will resign (particularly those who will not be transferred to the vendor)

Negotiation process may be driven by employee reactions and demands

Poor employee morale may result in pressure to close the deal

Once a customer has chosen its philosophy, a communication strategy will need to be prepared. The strategy may differ, and become more complicated, for multisite and international transactions. The customer will need to ensure that employees receive the same information at as close to the same time as possible. This typically involves close communication with all sites and "prepping" before employee communications. A more detailed discussion of employee-related issues is set forth in Chapter 7.

2.6 DEFINING THE SCOPE OF THE TRANSACTION

(a) DEFINING THE GENERAL SCOPE. What IT functions are being considered for outsourcing? Some customers wish to outsource all of their IT functions. This is particularly true in instances where the outsourcing customer has an own-ership interest in the outsourcer (e.g., the customer is a joint venture partner or there is a parent/subsidiary relationship). Other customers target certain areas of IT that they wish to outsource (e.g., data center, telecommunications) or certain areas of IT that they wish to retain. For example, some customers believe that because application development in many ways controls the strategic direction of the customer, this function should be retained. Other customers feel that they are outsourcing as a means to change the strategic direction of the customer (e.g., to move to client/server, standardize systems) and that in order to facilitate the change, the vendor will need to assume at least some application develop-ment responsibility.

For some customers, defining what IT functions should be outsourced is easy. Part of the outsourcing directive, for example, may be to outsource all IT func-tions except for strategic planning and process control, or to outsource data cen-ter but not desktop. Other customers are not sure which functions to outsource, mostly because they are not sure what the vendor can deliver and how much it will cost. If a customer is not sure what to outsource, it may be beneficial to be overinclusive of what is to be outsourced and include a requirement that the ven-dor must unbundle, or provide separate pricing for, certain functions. For exam-ple, if a customer wants to outsource its data center but is not sure whether to outsource telecommunications, the customer may choose to include telecommu-nications in its initial plan, thereby giving the customer the flexibility to put out a bid for telecommunications with the right to withdraw this function from the deal after evaluating the outsourcing benefits and risks.

The IT functions that customers typically consider outsourcing either by themselves or bundled with other services include the following:

- Data center
- Application development
- Application maintenance
- Help desk
- Voice network

- Data network
- Desktop
- Office/field support
- Telecommunications
- Asset acquisition
- Disaster recovery
- Print management
- Training

In addition to defining what IT functions are in scope, many customers have a difficult time determining which sites will be in scope. Is just one site or are all sites to be outsourced? Will the deal just include the United States or will it be global? Will particular countries be out of scope? Many customers, particularly larger ones with geographically dispersed locations, spend a great deal of time assessing which sites should be outsourced and which should either stay in-house or be part of a separate transaction. The decision as to whether certain sites should be included in scope is in some instances guided by local law requirements. For example, if a state or country has prohibitively high services taxes or laws relating to employee transfers, the customer may decide not to out-source services provided to or from that site or country. Another factor affecting the scope is the customer's management structure. If a customer has a decentral-ized structure, it is often difficult to achieve a consensus regarding what sites should be outsourced. The managers often have conflicting ideas about whether outsourcing is the right solution for all sites. An option for customers that are hesitant about outsourcing is to first enter into a "proof of concept" phase, where a few sites are outsourced with the understanding that other sites will follow if the trial period is successful. There have been mixed reviews regarding this approach.

Determining where the services will be provided will aid in assessing the complexity and often the cost (and tax consequences) of the transaction. Even if the deal is United States only, questions are raised regarding state tax and state employment law issues. If foreign locations are to be included, more lead time will be necessary to assess the requirements for local consents and authoriza-tions. It is often a time-consuming (and costly) task to coordinate with these for-eign locations. One thing to keep in mind is that international transactions will often require local counsel and in some instances local consultants. The out-sourcing team may need to be expanded to include representatives from the var-ious local sites.

Other issues to consider when starting to define the scope of the transaction include the following:

- Does the customer currently provide IT services to other entities? Will such services be in scope?

- Who are the end users (e.g., employees, customers, suppliers, independent consultants)?
- Are any existing outsourcing/subcontracting arrangements in effect that cover in-scope services? Are there any costs associated with terminating or transferring these relationships?
- Will assets be transferred to the vendor?
- Will employees be transferred to the vendor?
- Should any alternative structures be considered, such as forming a joint venture with the vendor or spinning the IT department off into a separate entity and then selling the entity to the vendor?

Just as important as defining what services are to be outsourced is defining what services the customer wishes to keep in house. The scope of retained responsibilities may vary from function to function with respect to financial, administrative, and operational responsibilities. For example, the vendor may assume responsibility for managing third-party application maintenance while the customer retains financial responsibility for third-party maintenance contracts. Areas that are often retained in whole or in part by the customer include the following:

- Process control
- Strategic planning
- Asset acquisition
- Hardware/software upgrades and replacements
- Application development
- Facilities
- Disaster recovery
- Office-related services
- Payment of third-party invoices
- Off-site storage
- Print
- Microfiche
- Report distribution
- Data entry
- Telephone charges

(b) UNDERSTANDING YOUR EXISTING IT RESOURCES. It is important for any customer wishing to outsource to have a strong understanding of the tasks its IT staff (those responsible for the functions to be outsourced) performs today. This is an important task to address early in the transaction for several reasons:

(1) it is difficult to define what services the customer wants the vendor to provide if the customer does not know what it is doing today; (2) it makes writing the request for proposal and service exhibits to the outsourcing agreement less overwhelming; and (3) if the customer does not have a clear and comprehensive understanding of its current tasks, it loses much at the negotiating table, particularly if the vendor has done its due diligence. It is not uncommon for the vendor to know more about the customer's IT services than the customer thereby giving the vendor the upper hand.

Following is an overview of several areas that should be explored before issuing the request for proposal:

- *The IT budget.* A useful starting point in determining what the IT department's existing responsibilities are is a review of the IT budget. The budget is often what the vendor will use to show how it can perform the same services more efficiently and at a lower cost. It is important then to understand the IT budget and to be able to clearly define what is and what is not included.

- *Shadow support.* One thing the budget does not often reveal is the incidental or shadow support the IT department receives from other departments. If shadow organizations provide IT services that are not within the IT organization, the outsourcing team should be aware of these people and consider whether the outsourcing vendor should be responsible for these services. It is also helpful to understand all of the seemingly minor things for which the IT department is responsible. For example, if the president of the customer's organization receives special weekly reports, this should either be included in the list of services to be provided (or covered at least generally) or provided by some other group. If the service is not included, the president may request his or her report and the customer will have to pay extra for it if it is not an in-scope service or provide it through internal resources if possible.

- *Organizational structure.* If the customer has not already prepared a list of in-scope IT personnel, it is useful to do this early in the process. This can be done by preparing an organization chart, specifying the names, duties, and locations of each of the IT employees and subcontractors. For example, the chart should specify how many people (managers, full-time employees, part-time employees, contractors) are responsible for each function.

- *Management structure.* An area to pay particular attention to is the internal management structure. Does it work? Does it work efficiently? Outsourcing is a good time to reorganize or realign the existing management structure.

- *Inventories.* One area that is typically lacking (particularly with customers with numerous field sites) is the customer's inventory of hardware and software assets that it owns and that it leases or licenses. If the customer does not have an inventory of its assets, it will be difficult for the customer to evaluate whether to transfer its assets or simply allow the outsourcing vendor to use the assets to provide the services. In addition, it is difficult to understand what the upgrade, replacement, and refresh responsibilities will be without an inventory of existing assets.

- *Service levels.* Another topic to consider early on is service levels. What service levels does the customer measure today? What service levels does the customer want to measure that it does not measure today? What is industry standard? Service levels are one of the most important aspects of the outsourcing agreement, yet often little attention is paid to these levels until late in the transaction. Vendors typically will commit to what the customer is doing today or better. But what is the customer doing today? If the customer does not know before entering into the outsourcing transaction, or does not have historical data to look to, the vendor will often take the position that it will measure the service levels over a period of time ranging from 30 to 180 days after the effective date of the agreement. The more information the customer has regarding its existing service levels, the better service levels it will likely be able to negotiate.

- *Critical services.* Another area that is often overlooked until too late is the definition of critical services. The customer is outsourcing its IT functions. Which services does it really care about? Which services, if they are not provided for an hour, a couple of hours, a day, a week, would cause serious damage to the customer (would cause you to lose your job)? Customers often do not have a defined list of critical functions. If the customer has an understanding of its critical functions early on, it can negotiate more stringent remedies if these critical functions are not met. Defining a customer's critical functions is not always easy. In fact, in some instances, it may not be possible. For example, for a front-office outsourcing deal, what is critical? Is any function more important than the others? The question is easier to answer in mainframe deals, but for many customers may be just as important in desktop and network-related transactions.

(c) DEVELOPING A LONG-RANGE PLAN. Many customers find it useful to develop a long-range plan. Where does the customer see itself in the next five years? Where does it see its IT requirements? For example, does the customer wish to standardize? Globalize? In your analysis, it is important to keep in mind that the maintenance of the existing environments, as new or modified systems are rolled out, is just as important as planning for future environments.

The long-range plan should include, to the extent possible, a list of the projects that the customer foresees doing in the next five years. What are the anticipated costs of these projects? Does the customer want these projects included in scope? Does the customer want to include a pool of resources to perform these projects?

Other aspects of the long-range plan should include anticipated software and hardware upgrades and replacements. What is the customer's anticipated refresh cycle for hardware and software? The customer will need to consider whether software, as well as hardware, refreshes are part of the deal. Similarly, the customer will need to evaluate what additional equipment it will require. Does the customer anticipate any major volume changes?

The customer should consider its current and future business needs. This includes new and divested sites and anticipated expansion. More often than not, the outsourcing team works in a vacuum, and partway into negotiations a businessperson will tell the team that some significant restructuring or organization-wide initiative will affect the transaction. The outsourcing team must be tapped into management—its own and often its parent company's—to understand the direction the customer is going in.

2.7 SELECTING A GROUP OF POTENTIAL VENDORS

(a) MAKING THE FIRST MOVE. The customer has obtained the commitment to move forward with exploring outsourcing as an option; now it must identify the potential vendor(s) that can provide the required services. In some cases, the customer will not have to look far. Unless the decision to evaluate outsourcing has been kept confidential, the vendors will hear about this decision through the grapevine, through an existing relationship with the customer, or through previous marketing efforts. The organization may already be targeted as a potential outsourcing customer. Even if the customer has an existing relationship with the vendor and thinks that in the long run this vendor is the right match for the customer, the customer should consider performing at least minimal due diligence to see who else is out there that can provide similar services. Such due diligence enables the outsourcing team to demonstrate that it has evaluated all of its alternatives. Government agencies, government contractors, and publicly held companies should keep in mind that government or security regulations may require them to look at more than one vendor.

Some customers have an idea whom they should talk to, whereas others are not as familiar with the possible vendors (this is particularly true for international outsourcing deals because U.S. IT departments typically do not have reason to be familiar with vendors in foreign markets). If you have an idea of whom to talk to, or if you know the vendors that you wish to target, it is useful to draw up a long list, and after doing due diligence on the vendors, shortening this list to three to five target vendors. If you do not know who all of the potential vendors are, you could obtain vendor information from industry reports and surveys or by talking to other outsourcing customers.

(b) VENDOR EXPERIENCE AND RESOURCES. The next step is to commence due diligence on the vendors that have been targeted. Due diligence may include the following:

- Talking to the vendors' customers
- Visiting sites of the vendors' customers
- Visiting vendor sites
- Checking customer's previous experience with each of the vendors
- Performing a newspaper search for recent articles regarding the vendors
- Checking litigation involving the vendors
- Obtaining annual reports
- Obtaining industry surveys and reports

During due diligence, the customer is able to begin to sense which vendors have the resources and experience to provide the desired services. Useful questions to ask each of the vendors during due diligence include the following:

- *Vendor reputation.* What is the vendor's reputation in your industry? What is the vendor's reputation in each of the countries where the customer wishes to outsource? Are there any conflicts or problems? Will the vendor's reputation and culture fit with the customer's reputation and culture?

- *Vendor history.* What is the vendor's history? How long has it been in business? Have there been any unusual peaks or valleys? Has the vendor been in any significant or relevant disputes or litigations?

- *Financial security.* Is the vendor financially secure? What is the vendor's market share? Has the vendor acquired or divested entities recently? Ask for a copy of the most recent financial statement or annual report. Are there any pending or threatened claims that could affect the vendor's financial standing?

- *Organization.* How is the vendor organized? By industry? By value of contract? Is there one international outsourcing entity or is there a web of local entities that work together?

- *Resource distribution.* Where are the vendor's data centers? Where are the vendor's employees located? Does the vendor have resources in the locations where your organization requires them? What is the extent of these resources? (For example, does the vendor really have an office in Singapore?)

- *Experience: Technology.* Does the vendor have experience with your current and future environment? Does the vendor have the capabilities to provide other services (e.g., reengineering)? Ask for examples and references.

- *Experience: Industry.* Does the vendor have experience dealing with organizations in your particular industry? Ask for examples and references.

- *Employee transition.* What is the vendor's experience with transitioning employees? How many transitions has the vendor done? In what states and countries? Has the vendor ever been sued in connection with a transition?

- *New system rollout.* What is the vendor's experience with implementing new systems?

- *Customer base and references.* Ask for references and contact names.

- *Subcontractors and partners.* Does the vendor typically partner with another entity to provide certain services? Who? What is the relationship with the partner?

If a customer does not have access to information regarding certain vendors in which it is interested, one way to approach vendors is to issue a request for information (RFI). RFIs have proven to be particularly useful to (1) customers looking to outsource overseas who do not know much about potential overseas vendors and (2) customers not necessarily looking to do business with one of the top outsourcers. However, customers that have targeted vendors or are dealing in an industry that they are very familiar with typically feel that issuing an RFI delays the selection process. Much of the information requested in the RFI could be requested in the customer's request for proposal. In addition, some customers feel that vendors will not answer the questions other than by providing promotional materials. An example of a generic RFI is set forth in Appendix 2.2. The RFI will need to be tailored to your organization's particular outsourcing requirements.

(c) NARROWING THE VENDOR GROUP.   Most customers choose to narrow the actual group of vendors to whom the request for proposal will be distributed to between three and five vendors. The screening process typically involves taking the long list of vendors and determining who among the top vendors meets the customer's requirements. As part of the screening process, it is useful to distribute the following material to the outsourcing team (and members of management if appropriate): a list of the vendors, a list of criteria on which to judge the vendors, and a system by which the vendors can be ranked for each of the criteria. The results of the team's evaluations can then be compiled and used to select the top three to five vendors.

2.8   REQUEST FOR PROPOSAL

(a) SINGLE BID VS. MULTIPLE BIDS.   In some cases, customers decide early in the process that they are going to issue the request for proposal (RFP) to only one vendor. This is generally not the recommended approach, but it may make sense in situations where:

- The customer has a history with one particular vendor who is familiar with the customer's systems and organization.

- The customer is under considerable and real pressures to get the deal done.

There are, however, significant disadvantages to requesting only one vendor to submit a bid. The most obvious is that the customer forfeits substantial negotiating leverage. Where else can the customer turn? Other disadvantages may include the following:

- Impact on pricing and service-level commitments because the bid is not competitive

- No comparative data or pricing

- The vendor may be less flexible

- Sending a negative message to other vendors (why bid on other projects if they do not have a chance?)

Single bidding is not an option for some outsourcing candidates, including:

- Government contractors

- Government entities (usually required to go out to competitive bid)

- In some cases with publicly held companies (this is particularly true where the aggregate contract value is substantial; it is also useful for corporate audit purposes to show that the contract is competitive)

For most customers, requesting multiple bids is the preferred approach because it:

- Adds to project legitimacy

- Demonstrates that due diligence was performed

- May lead to competitive pricing and service levels

- Enables the customer to use the possibility of other interested vendors as a negotiating tool

- Provides access to alternative solutions and technologies

(b) SINGLE VENDOR VS. MULTIPLE VENDORS. Before issuing an RFP, the outsourcing customer should determine whether it wishes to have one or multiple vendors provide the IT services to be outsourced. There are significant differences between unisourcing and multisourcing. The most compelling difference between the two approaches is that they require different internal management structures. Multisourcing will require a broader internal management equipped to manage several vendors at a time. In addition, there are liability issues. Unisourcing allows the customer to look to one party for performance, whereas multisourcing may allow a vendor to point to the other vendors in the event of a performance failure.

There are also cost benefits and risks associated with the two approaches. Bundling services together may allow the vendor to quote a better overall price for the services. However, if the vendor is not a telecommunications expert—and therefore has to build the necessary infrastructure or hire a subcontractor—it may be more cost effective for the customer to contract directly with the subcontracting organization.

(c) PREPARING THE REQUEST FOR PROPOSAL.   The content of the RFP varies greatly from customer to customer. A checklist of common RFP topics is set forth below. A sample RFP is provided in Appendix 2.3.

Introduction

1. *Cover letter.*
   - Include a general cover letter outlining your intentions.
   - Note which provisions are binding on the vendor (e.g., confidentiality, response requirements).
   - Attach an Intent to Bid form and request the vendor to fill in the form within a week or so. This will give you early warning signs as to how many vendors will be bidding and whether there are any wild cards.

2. *RFP format.* Identify on the cover sheet what the document is meant to cover. Include a general confidentiality provision. Number the RFPs being distributed and fill in to whom the RFP was distributed. Include a table of contents and a list of appendices.

3. *Objectives and overview.* Describe in general terms the functions that the customer wishes to outsource. Describe what the customer's goals and objectives are (e.g., cost savings, enhanced performance, new environment).

4. *Proposal submission date.* Note the date the proposal is due.

5. *How to respond.* Describe how the vendor should respond—number of copies, copy on a disk (note disk requirements). Who should responses be sent to? Does the customer require sealed envelopes, no faxes?

6. *Proposal format.* Describe the format the proposal should follow. For evaluation purposes, it is useful for all proposals to follow the same format.

7. *Customer contacts.* Note whom the vendor may contact for which areas.

8. *Communications.* Outline how communications with the customer should be handled (e.g., in writing only, by phone).

9. *Clarifications.* Describe how questions or clarifications should be handled.

10. *Vendor presentations.* Include a provision either requiring or giving you the option to require that the vendor make a presentation at the customer's site.

11. *Confidentiality.* This provision may prove to be very important. Include a detailed confidentiality provision. You may even wish to require the vendor to sign a confidentiality agreement before disseminating the RFPs.

12. *Ownership.* Note that the customer will retain ownership of all of its data and that the vendor must return all customer data upon request. The customer may wish to identify who owns the proposal, or at least that the customer has the right to use any materials in the proposal.

13. *Scope of proposal.* Note that the vendor's proposal should be as comprehensive as possible and reflect the vendor's best bid. If the vendor will not be bidding on some or all of the services, this should be noted upfront.

14. *Multivendor proposals.* If the vendor is partnering or plans to subcontract any portion of the services, this should be specified. The vendor should describe the services to be provided by the other party, the role of the other party in the outsourcing relationship, and the relationship between the responding vendor and the other party.

15. *Timetable.* Outline the key dates in the RFP/proposal process.

16. *Firm offer.* Note that all offers must be firm for a period of 60 to180 days.

17. *No obligation.* Note that the customer is under no obligation to enter into an agreement with any vendor.

18. *Right to negotiate with other parties.* Include a sentence reserving the right to negotiate with other parties.

19. *Costs and expenses.* The vendor is typically responsible for paying all of its own costs and expenses incurred before contract signing.

Vendor Background Information

20. *General information.* Ask for general background information (e.g., number of employees, locations).

21. *Industry information.* What is the vendor's experience in the customer's industry?

22. *Financial information.* Ask for information regarding the vendor's financial status, annual revenue, and position in the industry. Ask for copies of vendor annual or quarterly reports and financial statements.

23. *Organization.* How is the vendor organized? What is the management structure?

24. *Resources.* How are the vendor's resources dispersed? Where are they located?

25. *Customer base and references.* Ask for a summary of the vendor's customer base and at least three references.

26. *Partners/subcontractors.* Ask for the same information for any partners/subcontractors.

Customer Background Information

27. *General description of customer.* Provide general background information—type of business, size, locations.

28. *Description of existing services.* Describe existing services to be outsourced (e.g., types of systems, locations). Generally describe if any of the in-scope services are outsourced today.

29. *Description of short- and long-term goals.* Describe where the customer would like to be in the future (e.g., 3, 5, 10 years).

Services to Be Provided

30. *Services.* Provide a description of existing services and the services that the vendor will be required to provide.

31. *Locations.* List affected locations and entities.

32. *Transition.* Ask for a description of the plan pursuant to which the vendor will assume responsibility for the customer's IT functions.

33. *Migration.* Ask for a description of the plan pursuant to which the vendor will migrate functions to vendor locations (if applicable).

34. *New systems and environments.* Describe new systems and environments. Ask the vendor to describe a proposed solution and implementation strategy.

35. *Projects.* Describe any projects that the vendor will be required to undertake.

36. *Services not provided.* Ask the vendor to list any services that it expressly will not be providing. In addition, ask the vendor to list those services that it expects the customer to provide.

Performance

37. *Service levels.* Describe current service-level measurements (if available). Specify service levels that the vendor will be required to meet.

38. *Liquidated damages.* Require the vendor to indicate how liquidated damages will be applied in the event that the vendor does not achieve service-level commitments.

39. *Root cause analysis.* Require the vendor to perform a root cause analysis for any service failures.

40. *Reports.* Describe reporting requirements with respect to service level.

41. *Benchmarking.* Describe benchmarking procedures.

42. *Customer satisfaction surveys.* How will the vendor implement customer satisfaction surveys?

Management and Control

43. *Management procedures.* Ask the vendor to describe these procedures.

44. *Change control.* How will changes be implemented?

Employee Issues

45. *Transfer of employees.* Will all employees be made offers by the vendor?

46. *Offers.* What compensation and benefits will offers include? The customer should clearly specify any desired employment terms (see Chapter 7).

47. *Transition plan.* How will the vendor transition the employees?

48. *Employment agreement.* Ask for a copy of any employment agreement that transferred employees will be asked to sign.

Project Staff

49. *Project executive.* There should be a requirement that the vendor provide the name and qualifications of the initial project executive. The customer should be provided the opportunity to meet and interview the candidate. The customer should also reserve approval rights over all project executive appointments. The vendor should also be prohibited from "churning" project executives (e.g., specify minimum duration of appointment).

50. *Key employees.* The vendor should be required to provide the names and qualifications of any employees who are key other than the project executive. This usually includes the project executive's direct reports as well as employees key to certain projects. The customer should be provided the opportunity to meet and interview the candidates. The customer should reserve approval rights over all key employee appointments. The vendor should also be prohibited from "churning" key employees (e.g., specify minimum duration of appointment).

51. *Organization.* Ask the vendor to provide an organizational chart.

Pricing

52. *Pricing.* Include IT budget. (Note: Some customers take the position that they do not want to provide their pricing information until they have chosen a preferred vendor.)

53. *Base case.* Ask the vendor to provide its best base case figures. The vendor should clearly specify what is included and what is not.

54. *Unbundle.* Ask the vendor to provide separate pricing for functions and projects (if desirable).

55. *Volumes.* How will changes in volume affect the price?

56. *Growth.* Is any growth built into the price?

57. *Hardware and software.* What is included or excluded?

58. *Baseline adjustments.* How will adjustments be handled? What are the customer's requirements?

59. *Incremental fees.* Describe the mechanism pursuant to which the vendor will increase or decrease services. Rates should be provided on an hourly, weekly, and monthly basis.

60. *Additional services.* How will additional services be priced?

61. *Significant changes.* Note that significant changes in business requirements should trigger renegotiation or changes to pricing structure.

62. *COLA.* How will cost-of-living adjustments (COLA) be handled?

63. *Currency.* What currency will payments be made in? Who bears the currency risk?

64. *Technology indexing.* How will unanticipated decreases in technology cost be handled? The customer and the vendor should share in unanticipated savings.

65. *Taxes.* Who will be responsible for services taxes?

66. *New and divested entities.* How will new and divested entities be handled?

67. *Invoicing.* Describe the desired timing for invoice payment. In addition, describe invoice detail.

Termination

68. *Termination.* Specify circumstances that may trigger termination, for example:

- ○ For convenience
- ○ For cause
- ○ For failure to provide critical services
- ○ For change of control
- ○ For certain unforeseen events

69. *Termination assistance.* What assistance will the vendor provide upon termination?

Contract Terms

70. *Intellectual property.* Who will own what rights?

71. *Required consents.* Who will be responsible for paying for and obtaining third-party consents?

72. *Insurance.* What are the customer's insurance requirements?

Appendices

73. *Reference exhibits.* In many cases, the customer will already have prepared a large amount of the information to be attached to the RFP (e.g., inventories).

Terms and Conditions

74. *T&Cs.* Consider attaching terms and conditions (T&Cs) to the RFP. Model terms and conditions are set forth in Appendix 3.1.

2.9   EVALUATING THE PROPOSALS

Once final proposals are received from the vendors, the outsourcing team will need to take some time to review each of the proposals and evaluate which vendor or vendors are best suited to provide the desired services. The time period allotted for proposal review and evaluation typically ranges from two to eight weeks. The structure and scope of the vendor evaluation process will vary depending on the customer's approach, the number of vendors being evaluated, time constraints, and audit and report requirements. Common steps include the following:

- Selecting key evaluation criteria
- Identifying who will be asked to participate in the ranking of vendors
- Establishing a scoring system
- Weighting the key criteria
- Implementing final sign-off procedures

By the end of the evaluation period, the customer should have identified a preferred vendor or vendors (depending on whether the customer elects to negotiate with one or more vendors).

(a) EVALUATION CRITERIA.   In order to facilitate the evaluation process, it is helpful to prepare a list of key criteria on which to judge the vendors and their proposals. The items included on this list should reflect the customer's list of objectives for outsourcing. For example, if one of the customer's main objectives for outsourcing is to cut costs, then the vendors' financial proposals will likely be a key criteria. Similarly, if a key objective for outsourcing is to move the customer to a new environment, then the vendors' technical solutions will likely be considered key. The types of criteria that a customer considers key will vary depending on the scope, value, and complexity of the proposed outsourcing transaction. A customer wishing to outsource data center services in the United States will have different (and likely fewer) criteria than a customer wishing to outsource data center, help desk, application development, and network in 10 countries. Examples of key criteria include the following:

The Proposed Solution

- Technology (hardware/software/network)
- Configuration
- Committed resources
- Innovativeness
- Flexibility
- Fit with customer's environment
- Willingness to share risk

Ability to Deliver Services

- Experience/skill levels of staff
- Technology (hardware/software/network)
- Vendor reputation
- Vendor experience
- Proposed implementation schedules
- Physical security
- Data security
- Compliance
- Disaster recovery/business continuation

Ability to Implement New Systems

- Technical resources/ability
- Access to new technologies
- Flexibility
- Innovativeness
- Open systems versus proprietary systems
- Willingness to use third-party packages

- Implementation schedules
- Remedies for failing to meet schedules

Ability to Meet Performance Standards

- Methodology
- Proposed service levels
- Remedies for failing to meet service levels
- Benchmarking technology
- Benchmarking service levels
- Technology indexing

Value-Added Services

- Profit sharing
- Incentive mechanisms
- Access to new technologies
- Cross-marketing

Financial Proposal

- Base pricing
- Variable pricing
- Cost savings
- IT budget comparison
- Ability to increase or decrease services
- Cost-of-living adjustments
- Taxes
- Payment schedule
- Expenses

Vendor Reputation/Financial Standing

- Financial stability
- Quality of personnel
- Vendor culture
- Prior/existing customer relationships
- Vendor presence in customer locations

Vendor Experience

- Outsourcing experience
- Experience in industry
- Experience with compliance issues
- References
- Number of clients
- Experience in relevant locations

Vendor Flexibility

- Adjustment of services
- Adjustment of fees
- Adjustment of service levels
- Ability to add or take away entities
- Ability to terminate early
- Ability to terminate in part

Access to New Technologies

- Hardware
- Software
- Network
- Methodologies
- Processes
- Tools

Terms and Conditions

- Proprietary rights in software
- Third-party consents
- Indemnities
- Insurance
- Rights to terminate
- Rights upon termination
- Audit rights
- Damages

Human Resources

- Number of employees to be transitioned
- Salary

- Health benefits
- Deductibles/co-payment
- Bonuses
- Savings plans
- Retirement plans
- Severance
- Preemployment screening
- Employment agreement

(b) THE RESPONDENTS. Once the evaluation criteria are agreed on by the outsourcing team, the customer should rank the vendors based on their fulfillment of the criteria. This can be done on a formal or an informal basis. In order to benefit from the judgment of each member of the outsourcing team, many customers implement a voting system allowing each team member to submit his or her individual assessment of the proposals and vendors. In many cases, the group of people participating in the evaluation process extends beyond the outsourcing team and may include other key players, such as the CIO and members of senior management. Certain members of the outsourcing team may only be asked to submit evaluations on certain criteria; for example, human resources may be asked only to evaluate the human resources piece of the proposal, while other members of the outsourcing team may not be asked to participate in the evaluation process at all. It is useful for audit and reporting purposes for the customer to keep or ask the respondents to keep any documentation or data used to support the respondents' assessments.

(c) SCORING. Next, a scoring system should be established. Each of the criteria should be assigned a score ranging from poor to outstanding. A common (and easy to tally) scoring system is to rank the vendors in each category from 1 to 10 with: 1 = poor, 5 = acceptable, and 10 = outstanding.

(d) WEIGHTING THE CRITERIA. Not all evaluation criteria may be of equal importance. For example, the technical solution and human resources may each be considered key criteria, whereas greater importance may be placed on one rather than the other depending on the transaction. Customers engaging in more formal (or structured) evaluation processes should consider weighting each of the criteria to reflect the importance given to each. A common approach for weighting the criteria is to assign a weight or percentage to each general category, with the total of all of the weights equaling 100 percent (see Exhibit 2.2).

Some customers assign weights to subcategories of the general categories in order to allow for a more detailed analysis. Again, weights or percentages are assigned to each subcategory, with the total of all of the weights equaling 100 percent (see Exhibit 2.3).

CRITERIA	WEIGHT	RAW SCORE	WEIGHTED SCORE
Proposed Solutions	25%		
Ability to Deliver Services	25%		
Financial Proposal	25%		
Terms and Conditions	5%		
Human Resources	20%		
Total	100%		

EXHIBIT 2.2   WEIGHTING THE CRITERIA USING GENERAL CATEGORIES

The Total Weighted Score of the subcategories should then be inserted as the Raw Score for the general category (i.e., Financial Proposal) on Exhibit 2.2.

(e) TALLYING THE BALLOTS.   After the evaluation ballots have been filled out and returned to the outsourcing team leader or his or her designee, the results should be tallied. Although the customer typically chooses to keep the individual ballots confidential, the tally of all of the ballots is usually distributed to the outsourcing team and senior management.

(f) FINAL SELECTION PROCESS.   Once the ballots have been tallied, the outsourcing team should take a final look at the top vendor or vendors. This can be done in several ways:

- An informal sign-off from the outsourcing team
- An informal sign-off from senior management
- A formal approval vote by the outsourcing team and/or senior management
- A formal letter of approval from senior management

FINANCIAL PROPOSAL	WEIGHT	RAW SCORE	WEIGHTED SCORE
Base Pricing	25%		
Variable Pricing	15%		
Overall Cost Savings	10%		
Ability to Increase/Decrease Services	20%		
Cost of Living Adjustments	10%		
Taxes	10%		
Payment Schedule	5%		
Expenses	5%		
Total	100%		

EXHIBIT 2.3   WEIGHTING THE CRITERIA USING SUBCATEGORIES

Some customers go so far as to have respondents who disagree with the top vendor or vendors to note the reasons for such disagreement.

2.10 NOTIFYING THE PREFERRED VENDOR(S)

(a) MAKING THE ANNOUNCEMENT. The manner in which the preferred vendor(s) are to be notified should be discussed by the outsourcing team with senior management. Depending on the size of the proposed transaction, a member of the customer's senior management may wish to contact a member of the vendor's senior management and advise him or her of the decision. In other cases, the outsourcing team leader will notify the lead contact person for the vendor or vendors of the decision. Issues for the customer to keep in mind when making the announcement include the following:

- Reserve the right to negotiate with other vendors
- Refrain from making any promises or representations regarding entering into a definitive agreement
- Identify key issues that must be resolved (e.g., the price must come down a certain percentage)
- Emphasize that all negotiations and communications are confidential
- Note that the vendor should not make statements to customer employees or the press without the customer's consent
- Obtain a commitment that the vendor will provide a top negotiating team that is empowered to make decisions
- Discuss the proposed schedule

(b) COMMITMENT AND COSTS. The preferred vendor(s) typically will need to (or be asked to) increase the number of personnel working on the potential deal. Such personnel may include the following:

- A senior manager empowered to make decisions
- Marketing representatives
- Proposed project executive(s)
- Systems experts
- Tax expert(s)
- A dedicated human resources representative
- Legal counsel
- Industry experts (e.g., retail consultant)
- Local representatives and counsel (for international deals)
- Temporary staff (if customer staff is at critically low levels)
- Due diligence team
- Contract administrators

This commitment may also include increasing nonpersonnel resources (e.g., access to certain technologies, temporary loan of hardware, travel expenditures). The customer will likely also need to increase its commitment of personnel and resources in order to keep up with the team put together by the vendor(s).

With the increase in personnel and resources committed by the customer and the vendor(s), there should be at least an understanding between the customer and the vendor(s) as to how costs and expenses will be allocated. Typically, the customer and the vendor(s) each bear their own costs and expenses. In some cases, however, the customer may agree to pay for some or all of a vendor's expenses (e.g., the provision of temporary staff in the event that a definitive agreement is not entered into with the vendor or certain travel expenses).

(c) LETTERS OF INTENT. The preferred vendor may push for the customer to enter into a letter of intent with the vendor that, at a minimum, sets out the general objectives of the parties. Vendors typically want to include a provision in the letter of intent that provides that the customer will enter into exclusive negotiations with the vendor for a certain number of days. Other common provisions include allocating costs and expenses, indemnifications for representations made to customer employees, and restatement of the parties' confidentiality obligations.

Letters of intent are usually not appropriate if the customer is negotiating with two or more vendors simultaneously. Obviously, the customer could not commit to an exclusivity arrangement if it intended to negotiate with more than one vendor at a time. Most customers resist signing anything with the indicia that there is a commitment between the parties before the signing of the definitive agreement. In cases where the customers have agreed to sign a letter of intent, the customers have been confident that they would ultimately sign a definitive agreement with the vendor. Examples of letters of intent are set forth in Appendices 2.8 and 2.9.

(d) COMMUNICATION STRATEGY. Once the customer has selected the preferred vendor(s), the customer will need to decide whether to make an internal announcement to employees and/or a formal announcement to the press. A customer's decision to announce the selection of a preferred vendor will depend largely on whether it has chosen one or multiple vendors with whom to continue negotiations. If the customer has decided to engage in simultaneous negotiations with several vendors, it is unlikely that the customer (or the vendors) will wish to announce this strategy.

If one vendor is selected, the decision to announce the selection of a preferred vendor often depends on the customer's communication strategy with its employees. Announcing the selection to customer employees often leads to a leakage to the press. Many customers choosing to announce the selection of a preferred vendor to employees simultaneously issue a press release.

Customers that elect not to make an announcement to employees or to the press at the preferred vendor selection phase typically do so because they feel that they may forfeit negotiating power, lose the interest of other vendors, cause unwarranted public speculation or, possibly, impact public perception (including stock prices).

NONDISCLOSURE AGREEMENT (MUTUAL PROTECTION)

CONFIDENTIAL

[ADDRESSEE]

[ADDRESS]

Dear **[NAME]**:

In connection with the evaluation, discussion, and negotiation of a potential arrangement with Customer pursuant to which Vendor would provide Customer with certain information technology services (the "Transaction"), each of Customer and Vendor hereby agree as follows:

1. To keep secret and confidential all information, specifications, know-how, trade secrets, materials, data and other communications, oral or written ("Confidential Information"), of the other Party and not reveal such Confidential Information to any person except such responsible employees of the Party as may be necessary for the purposes of evaluating, discussing, and negotiating the Transaction.

2. To ensure that it treat the Confidential Information of the other Party in the same manner and with the same degree of care as it applies with respect to its own confidential information of a similar character.

3. Not to use the Confidential Information of the other Party in any way whatever anywhere in the world except for the purpose stated in paragraph 1 above. Not to copy any Confidential Information of the other Party [Alt 1: except on a limited basis as necessary to effectively allow employees to evaluate the Transaction] [Alt 2: except as may be expressly approved in writing].

4. To keep safe all documents and other tangible property comprised within the Confidential Information of the other Party and not to release them or it out of its possession.

5. To immediately notify the other Party upon learning of any unauthorized use or disclosure of any Confidential Information.

6. That Confidential Information being disclosed by the Parties pursuant to this Letter Agreement is with the express understanding that Parties shall not be obligated to enter into any further agreement. That should the Parties not enter into any agreement to return to the other Party all Confidential Information supplied by such Party on demand within 24 hours, and immediately cease all use whatever of the Confidential Information of the other Party.

7. Each Party agrees that the Confidential Information of the other Party and all copyright and other proprietary rights therein shall remain such Party's property at all times and that the receiving Party shall on demand return it to the disclosing Party within 24 hours of a written or oral demand.

8. The undertakings and agreements made by each of the Parties hereunder shall continue to be binding for a minimum period of [***] years whether or not the Confidential Information has been returned to the other Party until such time (if ever) as the Confidential Information falls into the public domain otherwise than as a result of or arising from any disclosure by the receiving Party.

9. Confidential Information being disclosed by each of Customer and Vendor pursuant to this Letter Agreement is with the express understanding that neither Vendor nor Customer shall be obligated to enter into any further agreement relating to the provision of information technology services.

10. Each of Customer and Vendor recognize that the disclosure of Confidential Information of the other party may give rise to irreparable injury and acknowledge that remedies other than injunctive relief may not be adequate. Accordingly, each of Customer and Vendor has the right to equitable and injunctive relief to prevent the unauthorized disclosure of its Confidential Information, as well as such damages or other relief as is occasioned by such unauthorized use or disclosure.

11. This Letter Agreement shall be governed by and construed in accordance with the laws of [***].

12. Each of Customer and Vendor represents that it has the full authority and right to enter into this Letter Agreement and to disclose to the other party Confidential Information and that such disclosure will not violate the rights of any third party.

13. This Letter Agreement sets forth the entire agreement between Customer and Vendor as to the subject matter of this Letter Agreement. The terms of this Letter Agreement shall not be amended or modified except in writing signed by each of Customer and Vendor.

Please evidence your agreement with this Letter Agreement by executing in the space provided and returning to Vendor one of the two original copies of this Letter Agreement sent to you.

Sincerely yours,

[VENDOR]

By: **[Name]**
Name: [***]
Title: [***]

Date: [***]

ACKNOWLEDGED AND AGREED:

[CUSTOMER]

By: **[Name]**
Name: [***]
Title: [***]

Date: [***]

REQUEST FOR INFORMATION

[NAME OF CUSTOMER OR, IF CUSTOMER WISHES TO RETAIN ANO-NYMITY, DESCRIBE TYPE OF COMPANY/ORGANIZATION, E.G., A MULTINATIONAL MANUFACTURING COMPANY] is considering out-sourcing its [DESCRIBE FUNCTIONS] in [SPECIFY GEOGRAPHIC LOCA-TIONS]. [CUSTOMER OR A CONSULTANT ON CUSTOMER'S BEHALF] is issuing this request for information (this "RFI") to gain information regarding potential outsourcing vendors.

All questions and comments relating to this RFI should be directed to **[NAME OF CONTACT] at [CONTACT PHONE NUMBER/ADDRESS]**. Responses are due by **[TIME]** on **[DATE]**. Responses should be sent to: **[CON-TACT NAME AND ADDRESS]**

Customer is interested in obtaining information about the vendor as set forth below. More specific questions and requests for information are set forth in the pages that follow. Please format your response so that it corresponds to the num-bers in this RFI. If there is additional information that you think would be help-ful, please attach the information to your response as appendices.

A. OVERVIEW

1. VENDOR HISTORY	[OBJECTIVE: What is the vendor's history? How long has it been in business? What has its market share been during the period that it has been in business? Have there been any unusual peaks/valleys? Has the vendor been in any significant/relevant disputes/litigations?]
2. FINANCIAL STANDING/ STABILITY	[OBJECTIVE: Is the vendor financially secure? What is the vendor's market share? Has the vendor acquired/ divested entities recently? Ask for a copy of the most recent financial statements, annual report. Are there any pending or threatened claims that could affect the vendor's financial standing.]
3. ORGANIZATION	[OBJECTIVE: How is the vendor organized? By industry? By value of contract? Is there one international out-sourcing entity or is there a network of local entities that work together?]

4. RESOURCE DISTRIBUTION	[OBJECTIVE: Where are the vendor's data centers? Where are the vendor's employees located? Does the vendor have resources in the locations that your organization requires them? What is the extent of these resources (e.g., does the vendor really have an office in Singapore?)]
5. EXPERIENCE: TECHNOLOGY	[OBJECTIVE: Does the vendor have experience with your current/future environment? Does the vendor have the capabilities to provide other services (e.g., reengineering)? Ask for examples and references.]
6. EXPERIENCE: INDUSTRY	[OBJECTIVE: Does the vendor have experience dealing with customers in your particular industry? Ask for examples and references.]
7. EMPLOYEE TRANSITION	[OBJECTIVE: What is the vendor's experience transitioning employees? How many transitions has the vendor done? In what states/countries? Has the vendor ever been sued in connection with a transition?]
8. NEW SYSTEM ROLLOUT	[OBJECTIVE: What is the vendor's experience with implementing new systems?]
9. CUSTOMER BASE/ REFERENCES	[OBJECTIVE: Obtaining references and contact names.]
10. SUBCONTRACTORS	[OBJECTIVE: Does the vendor typically partner with another entity to provide certain services? Who? What is the relationship with the partner?]

B. SPECIFIC INQUIRIES IN REQUEST OF GENERAL CATEGORIES SET FORTH IN (A) ABOVE

1. VENDOR HISTORY

    a. Please provide marketing and other information regarding the vendor's business.

    b. Please describe the vendor's background, including how long it has been in business.

2. FINANCIALS

    a. Please provide the 200[*] annual report and (if available) the latest quarterly audited financial statements for your company.

    b. If applicable, please provide the 200[*] annual report and (if available) the latest quarterly financial statement for your parent.

    c. Specify any recent acquisitions, divestitures, and downsizings.

    d. Specify whether any pending or threatened claims could affect the vendor's financial standing.

3. ORGANIZATION

    a. Please describe how the vendor is organized (e.g., by industry, by value of contract).

    b. Please identify the vendor's main offices and service locations.

    c.   **[FOR INTERNATIONAL DEALS]** Please describe the vendor's global organization.

4. RESOURCE DISTRIBUTION

    a.   Customer has sites in the following locations: **[SPECIFY]**. Please indicate the locations where the vendor has data centers. Please indicate the locations where the vendor has employees located and the number of employees in each location.

    b.   Please indicate the annual revenue of the vendor allocable to each location listed pursuant to (a) above.

    c.   Provide a list of customers for whom the vendor provides services in **[LIST LOCATION]**.

5. EXPERIENCE: TECHNOLOGY [DESCRIBE CURRENT AND FUTURE TECHNOLOGIES OF CUSTOMER]

    a.   Please identify the location of vendor's data centers, include capacity of each data center.

    b.   Please specify the number of vendor personnel trained to operate **[DESCRIBE TECHNOLOGY]**.

    c.   Please specify the vendor's experience in implementing **[DESCRIBE FUTURE ENVIRONMENTS]**.

    d.   Please specify the software and hardware tools and methodologies used by the vendor.

    e.   **[CUSTOMER]** may decide to expand the scope of its outsourcing efforts. Please describe other areas in which the vendor has particular expertise.

6. EXPERIENCE: INDUSTRY

    a.   Please describe the vendor's experience dealing with customers in **[DESCRIBE INDUSTRY]** in **[LIST LOCATIONS]**.

    b.   Please provide [***] examples and contact names/numbers.

7. EMPLOYEE TRANSITION

    a.   Please specify the types and numbers of employee transitions that the vendor has managed.

    b.   Please identify the states and countries in which the vendor has managed employee transitions.

    c.   Please indicate any litigation/disputes arising in connection with a transition that the vendor has been involved in.

8. SUBCONTRACTORS/PARTNERS

    a.   Please indicate whether the vendor typically subcontracts, or enters into a teaming arrangement to provide, part of the services.

    b.   Specify the functional areas and locations for which the subcontractor/partner is typically responsible.

REQUEST FOR PROPOSAL

[CUSTOMER]

INFORMATION TECHNOLOGY SERVICES
REQUEST FOR PROPOSAL

[DATE]

CUSTOMER PROPRIETARY AND CONFIDENTIAL

[NUMBER] Submitted to [NAME]

1.   INTRODUCTION AND VENDOR INSTRUCTIONS

1.1 OVERVIEW.   Customer currently is evaluating outsourcing in the following areas: **[LIST AREAS]**
   This Request for Proposal (this "RFP") is intended to serve as an overview of Customer's information technology environments and its outsourcing requirements.

1.2 OBJECTIVES.   Customer's overall business objective is to **[DESCRIBE]**.
   Customer's primary objectives in entering into an outsourcing arrangement are to: **[INSERT]**

1.3 EVALUATION CRITERIA.   Key evaluation criteria will include:
[FOR ILLUSTRATIVE PURPOSES ONLY]

- Resources and ability to support and manage Customer's current and long-term information technology needs
- Improved management of resources
- Total cost advantage to Customer
- Ability to provide continuous, measurable, and improving service
- Transition approach and plan (technical and employee transition)
- Cost-effective access to new technologies
- Vendor traits and characteristics

1.4 DISCLAIMER.   EACH VENDOR MUST PERFORM ITS OWN EVALUATION OF ALL INFORMATION, AND DATA PROVIDED BY CUSTOMER. CUSTOMER MAKES NO REPRESENTATION OR WARRANTY REGARDING ANY INFORMATION OR DATA PROVIDED BY CUSTOMER.

1.5 CONFIDENTIALITY.   The vendor should treat as confidential all information contained in this RFP and obtained in subsequent communications with

Customer. None of the information described in this Section 1.5 may be duplicated, used, or disclosed without Customer's prior written consent.

[Prior to the receipt of this RFP, the vendor has entered into a Confidentiality Agreement with Customer. The information described in this Section 1.5 will be deemed confidential information for the purposes of such Confidentiality Agreement.]

The vendor shall not, without Customer's written consent, refer to Customer or Customer's outsourcing efforts in any media release or public announcement.

1.6 PROPOSAL DUE DATE AND TIME TABLE. All Proposals must be received by **[TIME]** a.m. (Eastern Standard Time) on **[DATE]**. Customer may reject any proposal received after the due date (and time).

Other key dates include:

RFP Issued	[ ]
Proposals Due	[ ]
Proposal Presentations	[ ]
(if requested)	
Due Diligence	[ ]

1.7 DELIVERY OF PROPOSALS. In order to facilitate the preparation of your Proposal, a [***] CD-ROM containing this RFP has been included with the text files in [COMPUTER PROGRAM] format.

The vendor must submit [NUMBER] printed copies in loose-leaf binders and one electronic copy (on [DESCRIBE FORMAT]) of its Proposal to:
    [SPECIFY CONTACT NAME AND ADDRESS]

1.8 USE OF PROPOSALS. Customer shall have the right to use the Proposals, including any content contained therein, as it deems necessary or appropriate regardless as to whether the vendor or another vendor is ultimately awarded a contract.

1.9 CONSENTS. The vendor hereby agrees to grant any consents or approvals necessary under an existing or further contracts with Customer in connection with the provision of the services contemplated by this RFP regardless as to whether the vendor or another vendor is ultimately awarded the contract.

1.10 RIGHT TO TERMINATE OR EXTEND EXISTING SERVICES
[ADD IF RELEVANT].

1.11 BINDING OFFER. The vendor's Proposal will remain valid until **[TIME]** (Eastern Standard Time) on **[DATE]**.

1.12 VENDOR COSTS AND SELECTION. All costs incurred by the vendor in preparing the Proposal and providing any additional information to Customer, and in connection with performing due diligence, shall be borne by the vendor. The issuance of this RFP does not obligate Customer to accept any of the resulting proposals. Customer makes no commitments, implied or otherwise, that this RFP process will result in a business transaction with one or more of the vendors.

1.13 PRESENTATIONS.   The vendor will, upon Customer's request, make an oral presentation of its Proposal. If requested to provide an oral presentation, Customer will make up to **[NUMBER]** hours available at Customer's **[LOCATION]** facility at an agreed-upon date and time.

1.14 AMENDMENTS TO THIS RFP.   The vendor will consider, and incorporate into its Proposal, any additional information provided by Customer.

1.15 COMMUNICATIONS/CLARIFICATIONS.   The Proposal, and all related questions and responses, must be submitted in writing to be considered part of the final vendor Proposal.

THIS PROJECT MAY BE DISCUSSED WITH ONLY THE FOLLOWING CUSTOMER PERSONNEL AT THE CONTACT NUMBERS PROVIDED BELOW:

[SPECIFY NAMES, ADDRESSES, AND TELEPHONE NUMBERS]

1.16 DUE DILIGENCE AND NEGOTIATIONS.   As part of the vendor's initial due diligence, Customer intends to provide each of the vendors access to certain information and data, including third-party contracts, asset listings, and financial information, relating to Customer's information technology functions to be outsourced pursuant to this RFP. Such information and data will be made available in a data room at Customer's [LOCATION] facility at dates and times agreed upon by Customer and the vendor. Any information or data provided to vendor in connection with this due diligence shall be deemed Customer's confidential information and shall be treated as such in accordance with Section 1.5. The vendors may not duplicate any of the information or data provided in the data room. Upon Customer's request, the vendor will immediately destroy or cause to be destroyed all notes, memoranda, summaries, analyses, compilations, or other writings relating to this due diligence prepared by it or its agents. Such destruction shall be certified in writing by an authorized officer of the vendor supervising the destruction. The vendor will notify Customer of any inaccurate or incomplete information revealed during due diligence.

1.17 PROPOSAL FORMAT.   The proposals must be submitted in a uniform format. The proposal sections are listed below and, except for Sections 1, 2, and 13, correspond to the numbers in this RFP. Except with respect to Sections [***] of the vendor's response, the requirements of which are described below, the sections of the Proposal should contain the vendor's response to all items listed in the corresponding section of this RFP. Additional information relevant to a section may be included at the end of such section of the vendor's response.

Section 1. Cover Letter. Submit a cover letter on your letterhead signed by an authorized representative of your organization, certifying the accuracy of all information in your proposal and acknowledging your agreement to be bound by and comply with the terms set forth in Section 1 of this RFP.

Section 2. Executive Summary. Submit an executive summary of your proposal, covering the main features and benefits that distinguish it.

Section 3. Vendor-Specific Information.

Section 4. Services to Be Provided by the Vendor.

Section 5. Performance Specifications and Service Levels.

Section 6. Transition Plan.

Section 7. Disaster Recovery.

Section 8. Services to Be Provided by Customer.

Section 9. Project Staff.

Section 10. Human Resources.

Section 11. Financial Information.

Section 12. Terms and Conditions.

Section 13. Appendices. Appendices are optional. The vendor may wish to submit additional material that it believes will clarify or enhance its proposal.

2.   CUSTOMER: BACKGROUND INFORMATION AND STRATEGY

2.1 BACKGROUND INFORMATION.   [STATISTICAL INFORMATION RE: CUSTOMER, E.G., TYPE OF BUSINESS, SIZE, LOCATION]

2.2 CUSTOMER'S INFORMATION TECHNOLOGY STRATEGY.   [DESCRIBE STRATEGY]

3.   VENDOR-SPECIFIC INFORMATION

3.1 VENDOR BACKGROUND.   Provide an overview of your company, including a description of your company's organization, current or long-range plans, major contracts, any litigation and any other relevant information that may impact Customer's selection of your company.

3.2 VENDOR ORGANIZATION.   Provide an organizational chart of the vendor, an overview of how you will staff/service the account, and information regarding all key employees to be assigned to the Customer account.

3.3 RESOURCES.

3.3.1 Document your company's [U.S.] [global] presence and approach to management of Customer's contract.

3.3.2 Describe your experience with the hardware and software used by Customer.

3.4 FINANCIAL PERFORMANCE. Attach financial statements for the last [NUMBER] years. Certified financial statements of annual reports must be submitted for all identified vendors and subcontractors to be used by the vendor to provide services to Customer.

3.5 MULTIVENDOR PROPOSALS.

3.5.1 All other vendors or subcontractors that vendor anticipates using to provide information technology services to Customer must be identified in the vendor's Proposal.

3.5.2 Specify the scope and duration of any third-party arrangements for the provision of services to Customer.

3.5.3 The vendor must retain all responsibility for services provided to Customer by third parties.

3.6 REFERENCES.

3.6.1 Provide at least [***] references from current clients who have similar arrangements in size, scope, and geographic dispersement of services.

3.6.2 Provide the above information for at least [***] outsourcing clients who have terminated their contracts with vendor or whose contracts have expired.

4. SERVICES TO BE PROVIDED

4.1 MAINFRAME OPERATIONS.

4.1.1 [Customer Environment]

[DESCRIBE CUSTOMER'S ENVIRONMENT INCLUDING DATA CENTER LOCATION(S); NUMBER AND TYPES OF CENTRAL PROCESSORS; VOLUMES (I.E., NUMBER OF MIPS AND GIGABYTES OF DASD STORAGE CAPACITY)]

4.1.2 [Data Center Migration]

(The transition of data center and other information technology responsibilities to the vendor are covered in Section 6.) Specify whether vendor plans to migrate Customer's data center(s) to a vendor facility. If so, identify benefits (including cost savings) associated with such migration and the vendor's plans/procedures for implementing such migration. The migration plan should specify scheduled downtime and reimplementation of parallel environments. The vendor should also propose a liquidated damages schedule in the event of excessive unscheduled down time.

- Customer reserves the right to approve the provision of service from or to any location other than locations set forth in the final outsourcing agreement.

- The proposal should include the cost for disconnect, packing materials, shipping preparation, shipping, and installation of all equipment at the vendor site.

4.1.3 [Computer Operations]

Computer operations include:

- Console operations

- Printing and distribution

- Backups for all platforms

- Tape mounts

- Help desk and network operations

- Systems programming support

- Remote archive tape and documentation storage

Computer operations is available **[NUMBER]** hours a day, **[NUMBER]** days a week to support all production activities for all computing platforms.

4.1.4 [Production Control]

Production support includes job scheduling functions, job problem analysis, and resolution **[INCLUDE OTHER FUNCTIONS]**.

4.1.5 [Inventory Management]

Inventory Management includes the maintenance of a database of all Customer MIS assets.

The inventory will be used to access information on an as-needed basis to verify billing reports and plan upgrades of equipment and to maintain information on Customer's technical architecture. The system should be on-line with download capability.

4.1.6 [Change Management]

Change Management includes the management of new processes and ongoing change in the Customer's IT environments.

Change must be introduced with as little impact to Customer's business as possible.

Provide a detailed change management process.

4.1.7 [Problem Management]

Problem management includes the problem determination, escalation, and resolution activities, such as problem reporting, problem assignment, problem resolution, problem escalation, dispatching repair personnel, and other associated problem management activities.

Provide a detailed problem management process.

4.1.8 [Capacity Planning/Analysis]

Capacity planning/analysis includes the forecasting and planning for ongoing resource and equipment users on a [MONTHLY, QUARTERLY AND ANNUAL] basis. [DESCRIBE ANY FORECASTED GROWTH]

Please provide incremental pricing for:

	Growth		Decrease	
	CPU	DASD	CPU	DASD
10%				
20%				
30%				

Provide a detailed plan for capacity planning/analysis, including the types and timing of capacity reports.

4.1.9 [Distribution Services]

Distribution Services include **[DESCRIBE CUSTOMER DISTRIBUTION SERVICES INCLUDING TYPES, VOLUMES AND FACILITY LOCATIONS]**.

4.1.10 [Hardware]
[DESCRIBE HARDWARE REQUIREMENTS]
4.1.11 [Software]
[DESCRIBE SOFTWARE REQUIREMENTS]
4.1.12 [Data Security]

Provide a detailed description as to how the vendor plans to ensure data security. Specify vendor and any Customer responsibilities, including procedures to be followed in the event of a security breach. Before migrating or relocating any Services to a shared environment, vendor will provide, for Customer's approval, a proposal for such migration or relocation, including benefits or risks to Customer during the term of the outsourcing agreement.

Vendor will implement arrangements, satisfactory to Customer, to ensure that competitors of Customer will not have access to Customer's information.

4.2 AS/400 OPERATIONS AND MANAGEMENT.

4.2.1 [Customer Environment]
[DESCRIBE LOCATION(S); NUMBERS AND TYPES OF MACHINES]
4.2.2 [Migration/Consolidation]

(The transition of AS/400 and other information technology responsibilities to the vendor are covered in Section 6.)

Specify any plans to migrate/consolidate Customer's AS/400s to a vendor facility. If so, identify benefits (including cost savings) associated with such migration/consolidation and the Vendor's plans/procedures for implementing such migration/consolidation. The migration/consolidation plan should specify scheduled downtime and implementation of parallel environments. The vendor should also propose a liquidated damages schedule in the event of excessive unscheduled downtime.

Customer reserves the right to approve the provision service from or to any location other than the locations set forth in the final outsourcing agreement.

The proposal should include the cost for disconnect, packing materials, shipping preperation, shipping, and installation of all equipment at the vendor site.

4.2.3 [Production Control]

Production control includes job scheduling functions, job problem analysis, and resolution [INCLUDE OTHER FUNCTIONS].

4.2.4 [Change Management]

Change management includes the management of new processes and ongoing change to the Customer's I/T environments.

Change must be introduced with as little impact to Customer's business as possible.

Provide a detailed change management process for AS/400s.

4.2.5 [Problem Management]

Problem management includes problem determination, escalation, and resolution activities, such as problem reporting, problem assignment, problem resolution, problem escalation, dispatching repair personnel, and other associated problem management activities.

Provide a detailed problem management process.

4.2.6 [Capacity Planning/Analysis]

Capacity planning/analysis includes the forecasting and planning for ongoing resource and equipment needs on a [monthly, quarterly and annual] basis. [DESCRIBE ANY FORECASTED GROWTH]

4.2.7 [Distribution Services]

Distribution services include [DESCRIBE CUSTOMER DISTRIBUTION SERVICES INCLUDING TYPES, VOLUMES AND FACILITY LOCATIONS]

4.2.8 [Hardware]

[DESCRIBE HARDWARE REQUIREMENTS]

4.2.9 [Software]

[DESCRIBE SOFTWARE REQUIREMENTS]

4.3 DESKTOP SYSTEMS AND MANAGEMENT.

4.3.1 [Customer Environment]

[DESCRIBE CUSTOMER ENVIRONMENT]

4.3.2 [Requirements]

Customer currently supports and maintains the systems in Appendix [NUMBER]. [DESCRIBE CUSTOMER REQUIREMENTS]

4.3.3 [New Equipment/Refresh]

The selected vendor will be responsible for new terminal/workstation planning, configuration, and installation. Describe the scope of services vendor will provide and how vendor will provide them.

Customer anticipates that it will need to refresh approximately [NUMBER] percent of its workstations every year (resulting in [NUMBER] percent of the workstations being refreshed every [NUMBER] years). Please describe how vendor plans to manage and implement this refresh and provide a detailed listing of the costs associated with such refresh (including asset costs as well as delivery, installation, and testing costs). In addition, please provide incremental pricing in the event that Customer wishes to increase or decrease the number of workstations to be refreshed. (For inventory information, please refer to Appendix [NUMBER].)

4.4 DATA AND VOICE NETWORK.
4.4.1 [Data Network Environment]
[DESCRIBE DATA NETWORK ENVIRONMENT]
4.4.2 [Data Network Requirements]
[DESCRIBE DATA NETWORK REQUIREMENTS]
4.4.3 [Voice Network Environment]
[DESCRIBE VOICE NETWORK ENVIRONMENT]
4.4.4 [Voice Network Requirements]
[DESCRIBE VOICE NETWORK REQUIREMENTS]
4.4.5 [EDI Services]
[DESCRIBE EDI REQUIREMENTS]

4.5 HELP DESK.
4.5.1 [Customer Environment]
[DESCRIBE CUSTOMER ENVIRONMENT]
4.5.2 [Requirements]
[DESCRIBE CUSTOMER REQUIREMENTS]

4.6. LONG-RANGE INFORMATION TECHNOLOGY PLAN.   The vendor will assist Customer in developing and maintaining a long range information technology plan. The objectives of this plan are to:

- Develop an understanding and confirm the business requirements
- Identify new projects, accompanied by a high-level cost-benefit analysis and a preliminary schedule
- Review and, where appropriate, update Customer hardware, software, and network architectures

5.   PERFORMANCE SPECIFICATIONS AND SERVICE LEVELS

5.1 COMMITMENT AND APPROACH.   The vendor should describe its commitment and approach to each of the following:

- Initial service-level commitments
- Commitment to improving service levels
- Approach to defining missing service levels
- Commitment to provide measurement tools
- Service level reporting

5.2 SERVICE-LEVEL REQUIREMENTS.

5.2.1 [Data Center]
[SPECIFY SERVICE LEVELS]

5.2.2 [AS/400]
[SPECIFY SERVICE LEVELS]

5.2.3 [Desktop]
[SPECIFY SERVICE LEVELS]

5.2.4 [Network]
Data Network: [SPECIFY SERVICE LEVELS]
Voice Network: [SPECIFY SERVICE LEVELS]
EDI: [SPECIFY SERVICE LEVELS]

5.3 MANAGEMENT AND ADJUSTMENT.

5.3.1 Describe the practices and procedures that the vendor will use to manage and monitor service levels.

5.3.2 All service levels must be reviewed quarterly and adjusted as required annually.

5.4 PERFORMANCE CREDITS. The vendor is required to describe its approach to defining and calculating performance credits in the event of a failure to meet agreed-upon service levels and other performance measurement standards. Include your approach for calculating performance credits and how these amounts will be paid or credited to Customer.

5.5 ROOT CAUSE ANALYSIS. In the event the vendor fails to provide the services in accordance with the service levels, the vendor will, at no cost to Customer, (1) perform root cause analysis to identify the cause of such failure, (2) correct such failure, (3) provide Customer with a report detailing the cause of, and procedure for correcting, such failure, and (4) provide Customer with reasonable evidence that such failure will not recur.

5.6 CUSTOMER SATISFACTION SURVEY. Describe the vendor's proposed approach for administering and evaluating customer satisfaction surveys, including how the survey results will be used by the vendor to improve performance.

5.7 BENCHMARKING. Customer expects the vendor to engage at [vendor's cost] an independent party agreed upon by Customer to conduct benchmarking of Customer's technology and service levels. Describe the vendor's proposed use of benchmarking to measure Customer's technology and service levels.

6.   TRANSITION PLAN

The vendor will perform all functions and services necessary to accomplish a smooth transition of the outsourcing of the identified services.

The vendor will perform the transition such that during the process of the transition, Customer will not experience any additional costs or expenses or any degradation in services or performance.

During and following the transition, the vendor will not change the way any services or processes are performed in a manner that materially and adversely impacts the way Customer conducts its business operations, including procedures for inputting data or formats of reports, without Customer's consent.

During the transition, the vendor will meet or exceed the service levels provided before the commencement of the transition.

Provide a detailed transition plan with key dates and responsibilities, including:

- Overall approach
- Major activities and schedules
- Specific staffing plan during transition
- Testing processes

7. DISASTER RECOVERY

7.1 DATA CENTER. [DESCRIBE DISASTER RECOVERY REQUIRE-MENTS]

7.2 AS/400. [DESCRIBE DISASTER RECOVERY REQUIREMENTS]

7.3 DESKTOP. [DESCRIBE DISASTER RECOVERY REQUIREMENTS]

7.4 DATA AND VOICE NETWORK. [DESCRIBE DISASTER RECOVERY REQUIREMENTS]

8. SERVICES TO BE PROVIDED BY CUSTOMER

8.1 OVERVIEW. Customer will retain responsibility for the following areas: **[INSERT]**

8.2 FACILITIES. Describe Customer's responsibilities with respect to facilities, office equipment, and computer equipment. The vendor will be responsible for all office and data processing equipment upgrades, replacements, and additions in use by all vendor personnel, including the transitioned personnel.

8.3 OTHER AREAS. Please detail any other areas for which Customer will retain responsibility.

9. PROJECT STAFF AND MANAGEMENT

9.1 STRUCTURE.

9.1.1 Please describe the vendor's proposed account management structure.

9.1.2 Please describe the vendor's proposed staffing plans.

9.2 PROJECT MANAGER. The selected vendor will appoint a project executive to Customer's account. Customer must approve of such appointment. In addition, the vendor will not replace or reassign the project executive without Customer's consent.

9.3 KEY EMPLOYEES. Customer will designate certain members of the vendor's project staff as key employees. The vendor will not replace or reassign any of the key employees without Customer's consent.

9.4 SUBCONTRACTORS. The selected vendor will not subcontract any of the services to be provided without Customer's consent. In addition, specify any proposed subcontractors and the services they will provide.

9.5 PROCEDURES MANUALS AND PERIODIC MANAGEMENT REPORTS. Describe your approach to developing, providing, and maintaining a procedures manual and periodic management reports.

10. HUMAN RESOURCES

Note: This is applicable to U.S. employees only. Additional or replacement language will need to be added for non-U.S. employees.

Customer expects to transfer [all] [substantially all] of its information technology employees to the selected vendor (the "Affected Employees"). The Affected Employees are currently located in the United States. Customer anticipates that all vendors will offer employment compensation packages to the Affected Employees comparable to those being provided by Customer. The value of these packages should meet or exceed the current value of compensation and benefits currently enjoyed by each employee. In addition, it is intended that the transfer of the Affected Employees will not result in any severance or redundancy obligations on behalf of Customer.

10.1 EMPLOYMENT OFFERS.

10.1.1 [Affected Employees]

(a) The selected vendor will be required to offer employment to substantially all of the Affected Employees, including those Affected Employees on leave of absence or disability. Please describe your plans for offering employment to the Affected Employees.

(b) Specify whether any Affected Employees will be offered employment with a subcontractor or an affiliate of the vendor (rather than the vendor). In addition, identify the proposed subcontractors and affiliates, as well as the Affected Employees who will be offered employment by such subcontractors and affiliates.

10.1.2 [Compensation]

Each offer of employment to an Affected Employee will include an initial base salary of not less than the base salary that each Affected Employee received from Customer.

10.1.3 [Positions]

(a) The selected vendor will be required to offer employment to the Affected Employees for positions comparable to the positions in which such Affected Employees are currently employed.

(b) [The Affected Employee will be offered a position at the same location where the Affected Employee was employed by Customer before that time.]

10.1.4 [Health Benefits]

(a) Each Affected Employee will be eligible as of his or her start date for enrollment in the vendor's health care plans, including major medical, life insurance, hospitalization, dental, vision, long-term disability, pharmacy, and personal accident coverage. The vendor will provide each Affected Employee with health care coverage so that on the start date, he or she (and any family and dependents) is covered by such health care plans and all preexisting condition exceptions and exclusionary provisions and waiting periods are waived with respect to the Affected Employee (and any family and dependents). The vendor will be responsible for any medical or health expenses incurred by the Affected Employees incurred on or after the start date.

(b) The vendor will credit to or reimburse each Affected Employee the amount paid by such Affected Employee toward his or her medical deductible and copayments under Customer's medical benefit plans for the plan year in effect as of the start date for such Affected Employee.

10.1.5 [Vacation]

(a) The Affected Employees will be allowed to carry over up to [NUMBER] days accrued but unused vacation.

(b) The selected vendor will calculate time off for paid vacation and sick leave for each Affected Employee using each Affected Employee's length of service with Customer and the vendor.

10.1.6 [Savings Benefits]

Describe how you will handle the Affected Employee's existing savings benefits (including 401(k)). If the Affected Employees will have the option to roll over their savings benefits into a vendor plan, please describe this option and how it could be implemented.

10.1.7 [Retirement Benefits]

(a) Describe how you will handle the Affected Employee's existing retirement benefits.

(b) Describe your retirement benefit plans.

10.1.8 [Severance/Redundancy]

[FURTHER DISCUSSION NECESSARY]

10.1.9 [Other Benefits]

[The vendor will be responsible for providing (as part of the base fees) equal or substantially comparable benefits that the Affected Employees currently receive. This will be determined on a country-by-country basis and may include such benefits as car, housing, and meal allowances. It is the general intent of Customer that the transition to the vendor will not result in any severance or redundancy obligations on behalf of Customer. If any such obligations are triggered as a result of the transition, the vendor will be responsible for any severance/redundancy pay.]

10.1.10 [Work Hours]

The work days, including daily work hours and holidays, of the Affected Employees located at any Customer's location will be the same as the work hours in effect at that Customer's location.

10.1.11 [Service Credit]

The Affected Employees will be given credit for prior service with Customer for purposes of determining eligibility and accrual rates for vacation, sick leave, disability benefits, severance and health plans, and other plans and programs that are service-related. The Affected Employees will be given credit for prior service with Customer for purposes of determining retiree benefits eligibility.

10.1.12 [Hiring Requirements]

There will not be any conditions (e.g., preemployment screening) to the offers of employment to the Affected Employees.

10.2 TRANSITION TO VENDOR.

10.2.1 Specify the duration and timing of the employee transition period, the procedures that will be followed, and the date on which the Affected Employees accepting offers will start work with the vendor.

10.2.2 The selected vendor will be responsible for filling the positions of any Affected Employees not hired by vendor with replacements of comparable skill levels. The vendor will be responsible for the salary and benefits of such replacements.

10.2.3 The selected vendor will appoint a human resources representative who will be responsible for the transition of the Affected Employees from Customer to the vendor. The vendor will not replace or reassign the representative until after the Affected Employees' start date with the vendor.

10.2.4 Specify any planned reduction/relocation of any of the Affected Employees.

10.3 EMPLOYMENT AGREEMENT.   Attach a copy of any employment contract or procedures that would apply to the Affected Employees.

11.   FINANCIAL INFORMATION

11.1 BASE FEES.

11.1.1 Specify vendor's overall base fees, presented as fixed annual payments over the term.

11.1.2 At a minimum, the vendor's base charges should include information technology services that Customer provides for itself through its own personnel as of the date of the outsourcing agreement, as such services may evolve during the term.

11.1.3 [The base fees should include a compounded annual growth rate of [NUMBER] percent.]

11.1.4 [The vendor must reconcile its final pricing structure to Customer's [***] budget, which is attached as Appendix [NUMBER].]

11.1.5 All cost areas, including vendor responsible, pass-through, and Customer-retained cost areas, should be detailed by subarea (e.g., data center, AS/400s) over each of the years of the term.

11.1.6 Provide your base fees, broken down into separate pricing for each of the following subareas for each of the years of the term:

- Data center
- AS/400s
- Desktop systems
- Voice and data network
- Help desk
- Projects

11.2 INCREMENTAL USAGE.   Describe how increased/reduced usage will be handled. Provide unit rates that will be charged for any additional resources used and that will be credited for any resources not used by Customer (including hourly, daily, weekly, monthly rates). Rates will be the same for increased and reduced usage.

11.3 BASELINE ADJUSTMENTS.   Customer wishes to have the flexibility to adjust the resource baselines upon notice to the vendor, with an appropriate adjustment to the fees. Describe the mechanism pursuant to which baselines will be adjusted.

11.4 INFLATION.   There will not be any adjustments of the charges due to inflation or cost of living during the term.

11.5 NEW SERVICES.

11.5.1 Provide a detailed description of the approach, method, and treatment of the new services. These descriptions should be illustrated with examples whenever possible.

11.5.2 Customer reserves the right to solicit, negotiate, and award those capital and discretionary projects and services, which are outside the scope of this RFP, to a third-party vendor at its sole discretion.

11.6 SAVINGS.   Customer must achieve a **[NUMBER]** percent or more reduction in information technology expenses during the first year of the outsourcing agreement and **[NUMBER]** percent or more during each subsequent year during the term. Describe how the vendor will meet these requirements. In addition, identify how you will provide continuous cost savings to Customer.

11.7 TECHNOLOGY INDEXING.   Each calendar year during the term of the outsourcing agreement, the vendor will review (1) the actual information technology price/performance benchmarks during the calendar year as determined by a third party agreed upon by Customer and the vendor and (2) how the vendor's price/performance benchmarks during such calendar year compare with the actual improvements. If the actual improvements are greater than those improvements anticipated by the vendor, the vendor will issue to Customer a credit against fees for the following calendar year by multiplying the fees by the percentage difference between the actual and anticipated improvements. The vendor will be responsible for paying the fees and expenses of any third party in connection with providing the services described in (1) above.

11.8 TAXES.   [***] will be responsible for all worldwide taxes (other than for taxes based on Customer's net income) levied on payments made by Customer to the vendor or services provided by the vendor.

11.9 FOREIGN CURRENCY.   [All payments will be in currencies designated by Customer.]

11.10 INVOICING.
     11.10.1 [DESCRIBE REQUIRED INVOICE DETAIL]
     11.10.2 Customer will pay vendor fees within [NUMBER] days of the end of the month following the month during which services were provided.

11.11 MOST-FAVORED CUSTOMER.   The vendor will provide Customer with its most-favored-customer status and benefits to Customer.

11.12 SERVICES FOR NEWLY ACQUIRED CUSTOMER ENTERPRISE OR ADDITIONAL CUSTOMER WORK.   Customer reserves the right to add or remove business units to or from the scope of the outsourcing agreement.

11.13 TREATMENT OF DISPUTED AMOUNTS.   Describe the procedure used to settle disputed payments or credit amounts, including the period of time to settle disputes, the process of verifying these disputed items, and the process of resolving disputes that cannot be resolved during the normal procedures specified above. The parties will be required to continue to perform under the outsourcing agreement in the event of a good faith dispute.

11.14 EXPENSES.   All vendor expenses should be included in the base fee.

12.   TERMS AND CONDITIONS

For each of the terms set forth in the chart below, the vendor must indicate whether the term is accepted. Each term must have a response of:

Yes: The term is accepted as stated. If the vendor wishes to propose a modification or alternative which is more favorable to Customer, please describe it in the "comments" column.

Or

No: The term is not accepted as stated. Propose specific alternative language that would be acceptable in the "comments" column.

In addition to responding to the items in the chart below, please attach to the end of Section 12 of your Proposal a copy of your standard contract for Customer's review. Customer reserves the right to draft the outsourcing contract.

13.   APPENDICES

Mainframe Data Center Operations and Management: **[LIST APPENDICES]**
AS/400 Operations and Management: **[LIST APPENDICES]**
Desktop Systems and Management: **[LIST APPENDICES]**
Voice and Data Network: **[LIST APPENDICES]**
Help Desk: **[LIST APPENDICES]**
Project Staff: Customer MIS Organization Charts
Human Resources
Personal Information
Customer Benefits Materials
Miscellaneous: Customer Annual Report

CUSTOMER REFERENCE QUESTIONS: SAMPLE[2]

In addition to the obvious questions on vendor name, customer name, location, and contact, the following areas should be formally explored with each Vendor Customer Reference Account. The Customer may wish to format these questions into a formal questionnaire that is used by each caller so that it gets consistent information from each contact. Each contact should be formally documented with the answer to each question entered under the question. At a minimum, the following areas should be explored:

1. Why did the company decide to outsource?
2. What process did it go through to select a partner?
3. Who bid on the outsourcing program, who won, and why?
4. What is the scope of the effort?
   - Scope of what is done
   - Single site, multiple, global dimension
   - Number of devices outsourced
   - Is training included and to what extent?
   - What support model is being used (e.g., centralized off-site help desk)?
5. Contract-specific items:
   - Length
   - Incentive based and what was it tied to?
   - Assets transferred (HW/SW/People) and how much transitioned in what window of time?
   - Is there a guaranteed infrastructure upgrade provision (what was the state of the environment before they started)?
   - How did they deal with obsolescence/technology refresh?

---

2. This appendix has been reprinted with permission from Ron Gallagher, President of Oust Consulting, Inc.

- o Did they project forward pricing for technology, and was benchmarking used (if so, how, what services, and what benchmarking service)?
- o Productivity clause
- o Is this a per-seat agreement or something else (e.g., fixed fee with bonus)?

6. How long has the contract been in effect and what have the results been so far?

7. What was projected as the return to the business?
- o First-year savings percentage
- o Year-by-year savings
- o Response time/service improvement
- o Customer satisfaction improvements

8. How are they doing against the targets?

9. How was the asset and people transfer handled? What were the biggest problems encountered? What was the transition process?

10. What treatment was offered to the transitioned employees, and are they happy on the whole?

11. Did they use outside resources to help and, if so, who?

12. What service-level objectives and goals did they set, and are they being achieved? If not, what is preventing them from getting there?

13. What contract oversight/management organization did they put in place?
- o Number of people
- o Responsibilities

14. What other services/responsibilities did they retain?

15. Given the process and experience to date, what would they do differently? Would they still outsource?

16. Do they have a formal exit plan?
- o For cause
- o For convenience
- o Other

17. How did they deal with out-of-contract/scope work? How is the outsourcer responding to changing requirements and ongoing support for normal business programs?

18. What provisions do they have for continuous service (high availability/DRP)? What were they doing before, and what did they ask the outsourcer to do to improve the situation?

19. Others that are specific to the planned outsourcing effort.

VENDOR PROPOSALS RELATING TO THE PROVISION OF INFORMATION TECHNOLOGY SERVICES EVALUATION

A. OVERVIEW OF VENDORS BEING CONSIDERED

Vendor	Vendor Representative	Address	Status

B. EVALUATION CRITERIA
[To be modified by Customer Project Team]

Criteria	Explanation

Examples of criteria:

- **Vendor Resources** (Financial stability of Vendor, ability of Vendor to meet its commitments over the term of the contract)
- **Experience in Customer's Industry** (Specialized skills in Customer's industry to ensure quality)
- **Previous Experience with Customer** (Past experience Customer has with Vendor that may impact selection)
- **Financial Considerations** (Anticipated savings, improved cash flow, increased revenues)
- **Services to Be Provided** (Experience, resources, and ability of Vendor to provide in-scope services)

- ○ **Mainframe Support** (Experience, resources, and ability of Vendor in consolidating data center locations and providing mainframe services)
- ○ **AS/400 Support** (Experience, resources, and ability of Vendor in consolidating AS/400 locations and resources and providing AS/400 services)
- ○ **Desktop Support** (Experience, resources, and ability of Vendor in providing end-user support, including LAN, personal computer, and remote site support)
- ○ **Help Desk Support** (Experience, resources, and ability of Vendor in consolidating help desk resources and providing help desk services)
- ○ **Network Support** (Experience, resources, and ability of Vendor in providing network services)
- ○ **Disaster Recovery** (Experience, resources, and ability of Vendor in providing disaster recovery services)

- • **Human Resources** (Transition of Customer employees to Vendor; terms of offers)
- • **Terms and Conditions** (Responses to Customer's terms and conditions)

C. OVERALL WEIGHTED RANKING

[To be modified by Customer Project Team]

	Criteria	Weight	Justification
1.	Vendor Resources		
2.	Experience in Customer's Industry		
3.	Previous Experience with Customer		
4.	Financial Considerations		
5.	Services to be Provided		
6.	Human Resources		
7.	Terms and Conditions		
	Total	**100%**	

D. VENDOR RESOURCES

Vendor	Annual Revenue	Parent Company Revenue	Overall Rank

Key:

10 = Superior

8 = Very Good

6 = Good

4 = Adequate

2 = Fair

0 = Poor

E. EXPERIENCE IN CUSTOMER'S INDUSTRY

Vendor	Related Experience: United States	Related Experience: International	Overall Rank

F. PREVIOUS EXPERIENCE WITH CUSTOMER*

Vendor	Description of Work	Fees	Comments	Overall Rank

---

* This shall be a brief description of any services provided by the relevant Vendor to Customer prior to the date of the RFP and any services provided by Vendor to Customer.

G. FINANCIAL CONSIDERATIONS

Vendor	Cost Structure	Overall Savings	Value-Added Services	Comments	Overall Ranking

H. SERVICES TO BE PROVIDED

	Mainframe		AS/400		Desktop		Help Desk		Network		Disaster Recovery		Overall Ranking
Weight	%		%		%		%		%		%		100%
	Raw Score	Weighted Score	Raw Score	Weighted Score	Raw Score	Weighted Score	Raw Score	Weighted Score	Raw Score	Weighted Score	Raw Score	Weighted Score	Total of Weighted Scores

1. WEIGHTING FOR "SERVICES TO BE PROVIDED" CATEGORY.   [To be modified by Customer Project Team]

	Criteria	Weight	Justification
1.	Mainframe		
2.	AS/400		
3.	Desktop		
4.	Help Desk		
5.	Network		
6.	Disaster Recovery		
	Total	100%	

2. MAINFRAME.

Vendor	Experience	Resources	Ability	Overall Rank

3. AS/400S.

Vendor	Experience	Resources	Ability	Overall Rank

4. DESKTOP.

Vendor	Experience	Resources	Ability	Overall Rank

5. NETWORK.

Vendor	Experience	Resources	Ability	Overall Rank

6. DISASTER RECOVERY.

Vendor	Experience	Resources	Ability	Overall Rank

I. HUMAN RESOURCES

Vendor	Transition	Terms of Offer	Overall Rank

J. TERMS AND CONDITIONS

Vendor	Compliance with RFP Requirements	Overall Rank

K. OVERALL RANKING OF VENDOR

	Vendor Resources		Experience in Customer Industry		Financial Considerations		Services to Be Provided		Human Resources		Terms and Conditions		Overall Ranking
Weight	%		%		%		%		%		%		100%
	Raw Score	Weighted Score	Raw Score	Weighted Score	Raw Score	Weighted Score	Raw Score	Weighted Score	Raw Score	Weighted Score	Raw Score	Weighted Score	Total of Weighted Scores

---

* Represents final score for each vendor for this ballot. To tally scores of all of the ballots, add final scores together. For example,

	Vendor #1	Vendor #2
Ballot #1	8	6
Ballot #2	9	8
Ballot #3	7	7
Ballot #4	8	5
Ballot #5	9	6
Total Score:	41	32

ASSESSING LEGAL RESOURCES REQUIRED (CUSTOMER FORM): QUESTIONNAIRE

CONFIDENTIAL
FOR INTERNAL [CUSTOMER] USE ONLY

[CUSTOMER]

QUESTIONNAIRE FOR ASSESSING NECESSARY LEGAL RESOURCES TO BE ASSIGNED TO BPO TRANSACTION

The purpose of this questionnaire is to provide to the **[CUSTOMER]** Legal Department general background information regarding the proposed BPO transaction. The information gathered through this questionnaire is intended to assist the **[CUSTOMER]** Legal Department in assessing the types and amount of legal resources that should be assigned or made available to the particular transaction. Please take the time to review this questionnaire and provide as much information as possible, with the understanding that the transaction and the required legal resources may change over the course of the transaction.

1. **KEY OBJECTIVES**: (List key objectives for outsourcing, e.g., cost savings, move to new environment)

2. **CONTRACT STRUCTURE**: (Describe proposed contract structure, e.g., two-phase transaction, including business process reengineering and ongoing day-to-day operations and services; joint venture/strategic alliance)

3. **SCOPE OF SERVICES**: (Describe scope of services to be outsourced)

4. **GEOGRAPHIC SCOPE**: (List all states/countries from which services will be provided, as well as all states/countries to which services will be provided)

5. **AFFECTED SITES**: (Name all [CUSTOMER] sites that will be outsourced)

6. **TRANSFER OF EMPLOYEES**: (If employees will be transferred to the vendor or a vendor subcontractor or affiliate, specify approximate

number of employees to be transferred (by [CUSTOMER] location if possible) and describe any other personnel issues)

7. **SALE/LEASE**:

   a. ASSETS: (If any assets will be sold/leased to the vendor, specify types of assets and general terms of sale/lease if known)

   b. FACILITIES: (If any facilities will be sold/leased to the vendor, specify facilities and general terms of sale/lease if known)

8. **VALUE OF TRANSACTION**: (Specify proposed value of outsourcing contract)

9. **DEGREE OF "CRITICALNESS"**: (Indicate the importance of the outsourcing arrangement to [CUSTOMER], e.g., contract value may be small but vendor nonperformance would greatly damage [CUSTOMER])

10. **PROPOSED TERM**: (Specify proposed term of transaction)

11. **RELEVANT ISSUES**: (Specify any particular concerns in the following areas)

    a. REGULATORY COMPLIANCE

    b. PERMITS/LICENSES

    c. ENVIRONMENTAL

    d. AUDIT

    e. TAX

    f. DATA PRIVACY

    g. INSURANCE

    h. SPECIAL ISSUES

12. **CORPORATE ACTIONS:** (Specify any corporate actions that are required if known, e.g., board approval)

13. **COMMUNICATIONS/PR:** (Specify any particular communications/public relation actions that have been or will be taken, e.g., employee communication plan, press release)

14. **TRANSACTION STATUS:** (Describe status of transaction, e.g., RFP prepared; RFP issued)

15. **SELECTION OF VENDOR:** (Indicate whether a vendor(s) has (have) been selected (at least preliminarily))

16. **HISTORY WITH VENDOR:** (Describe any existing or previous relationships between **[CUSTOMER]** and preferred vendor(s))

17. **TIMELINE:** (Describe the proposed schedule for the outsourcing process)

18. **ROLE OF COUNSEL:** (Describe desired role that counsel should take in transaction, e.g., review documents, negotiate)

19. **DESIRED LEGAL RESOURCES/TIME COMMITMENT:** (Indicate any specific legal resources desired at this time)

20. **DRAFTING RESPONSIBILITY:** (Indicate whether **[CUSTOMER]** or the vendor will have drafting responsibility for the contract (if known))

21. **EXHIBIT REVIEW:** (Describe the resources to be used to review the exhibits to the contract, e.g., technical experts, business team members; define the anticipated role legal will have in the exhibit review)

22. **TEAM MEMBERS**:

    a. **[CUSTOMER]** TEAM (Specify all of the members of the **[CUSTOMER'S]** outsourcing team)

    b. VENDOR TEAM (Specify all of the members of the vendor's outsourcing team)

23. **LOCATION OF DUE DILIGENCE/NEGOTIATIONS:** (Specify the location where due diligence and negotiations will take place)

24. **OTHER CONCERNS/NOTES:** (List any additional concerns or comments)

DUE DILIGENCE AGREEMENT[3]

[TO BE IN LETTER FORMAT]

Dear [***]:

I am writing to confirm that [**Customer**] ("Customer") and [**Vendor**] ("Vendor") have agreed to proceed with negotiations for the provision by Vendor of certain information technology services to Customer. In connection with such negotiations and prior to the execution of a definitive outsourcing agreement (the "Definitive Agreement), Vendor will perform due diligence, as described in more detail in the due diligence plan prepared by Vendor set forth in Appendix 1 ("Due Diligence") to (a) verify the data and information provided by Customer in its Request for Proposal, dated [**DATE**], as amended by [***] (collectively, the "RFP"); (b) verify certain assumptions made by Vendor in its Proposal, dated [**DATE**], as amended by [***] (collectively, the "Proposal"); and (c) enable Vendor to offer services, pricing, and baselines that reflect Customer's existing and future information technology environments.

This letter agreement (this "Letter Agreement") shall set forth the terms and conditions governing Due Diligence. In this regard:

1. *Due Diligence Representative.* Vendor shall appoint an individual who shall (a) be in charge of performing Due Diligence, (b) serve as the primary contact for Customer in dealing with Vendor with respect to Due Diligence, and (c) be empowered to act and make decisions on behalf of Vendor in connection with Due Diligence.

2. *Due Diligence Objectives.* Due Diligence shall be performed in respect of the following Customer locations: [**LOCATION(S)**]. Due Diligence shall involve the evaluation of the following functions: [**FUNCTION(S)**]. Due Diligence shall include an evaluation of the following areas: (a) Customer's budget items, (b) operating expenses, (c) inventories of machines, peripheral equipment, and software to be transferred, (d) third-party leases, licenses, maintenance, and services agreements,

---

3.   Note: This sample agreement is intended to illustrate the types of legal issues that vendors typically wish to address in connection with information technology outsourcing transactions. The provisions included in this sample agreement, while comprehensive, may not cover all of the issues that may arise in a particular transaction. Legal issues will likely vary depending on the type of information technology process being outsourced and the scope of the outsourcing transaction. This sample agreement or any part thereof should only be used after consultation with your legal counsel. Legal counsel should be consulted prior to entering into or negotiating any outsourcing transaction.

(e) Customer's existing and proposed future environments, (f) charge-back procedures, and (g) [**ADD ADDITIONAL ITEMS**]. A more detailed description of the activities to be performed during due diligence is set forth in Appendix 1.

3. *Scheduling.* Customer and Vendor shall agree upon the times during which and locations where Due Diligence shall take place. Vendor shall not contact any Customer employee or agent or attempt access to any Customer data, information, or facilities without Customer's consent. Customer reserves the right, in its sole discretion, to deny access to any facility or data and withhold consent to any due diligence activity. Customer shall cooperate with Vendor to identify other means for achieving the objectives of such activity.

4. *Completion.* Vendor shall complete all Due Diligence by [**DATE**].

5. *Documentation.* By [**DATE**], Vendor shall submit to Customer a detailed report summarizing the due diligence performed and documenting the findings and results of such due diligence.

6. *Discrepancies/Additional Information.* Vendor shall be responsible for informing Customer of any discrepancies, inaccuracies, errors, or omissions learned or disclosed during Due Diligence. Customer shall not be responsible for any discrepancies, inaccuracies, errors, or omissions that it is not informed of prior to the execution of the Definitive Agreement.

7. **[OPTIONAL: In connection with the proposed transaction between Customer and Vendor, Customer intends to transition certain of its employees to Vendor (the "Transitioned Employees"). In the event Customer and Vendor execute the Definitive Agreement, Customer and Vendor wish to complete the transition of the Transitioned Employees to Vendor on [DATE]. In order to complete such a transition, it will be necessary for Vendor to commence preemployment screenings and similar employee-related tasks prior to the date of the Definitive Agreement between Customer and Vendor. In this regard, Customer and Vendor have agreed to certain terms and conditions relating to the transition of the Transitioned Employees, attached as Appendix 2. Substantially similar terms and conditions will be included in the Definitive Agreement between Customer and Vendor in the event the Definitive Agreement is executed. The agreement of Customer and Vendor on such terms and conditions does not in any way obligate Customer and Vendor to enter into the Definitive Agreement. Each party shall indemnify the other party against and hold the other party harmless from any claims by the Transitioned Employees arising out of such party's conduct or representations during the period through [DATE].]**

8. *Customer's Responsibilities.* Customer shall cooperate with Vendor as may be necessary to enable Vendor to perform Due Diligence. Vendor acknowledges and agrees that completion of Due Diligence is primarily

the responsibility of Vendor and that Customer shall not be required to expend any significant level of effort or resources toward Due Diligence.

9. *Binding Nature*. It is understood that while this Letter Agreement constitutes a statement of mutual intentions of Customer and Vendor with respect to the proposed provision of certain information technology and related services by Vendor to Customer, it does not constitute an obligation binding on either side, nor does it contain all matters upon which agreement must be reached and, except with respect to Paragraphs 7, 10, and 11, this Letter Agreement shall create no rights in favor of either party. A binding commitment with respect to the proposed project will result only from the execution of the Definitive Agreement.

10. *Expenses*. In the event Customer and Vendor do not execute the Definitive Agreement, each of the parties will bear its own costs and expenses incurred in negotiating the Definitive Agreement, including any costs and expenses relating to the preliminary work performed by Vendor in connection with Due Diligence for the proposed transition of the Transitioned Employees.

11. *Confidentiality*. During the pendency of formal corporate approvals from Customer [and its parent] and final preparation and execution of the Definitive Agreement, it is expected the parties will exchange confidential information, including business data, budgets, inventories, strategies, and customer information ("Confidential Information"). In addition, the parties agree that negotiations that are intended to result in the Definitive Agreement and the terms, conditions, or other facts with respect to such possible agreement, including the status thereof, shall be treated as Confidential Information. Each of the parties undertakes and agrees to (a) keep secret and confidential all Confidential Information and not reveal such Confidential Information to any person except such responsible employees as may be necessary for the purposes of performing Due Diligence; (b) ensure that it treats the Confidential Information in the same manner and with the same degree of care as it applies with respect to its own confidential information of a similar character;(c) keep safe all documents and other tangible property comprised within the Confidential Information and not to release them or it out of its possession; (d) immediately notify the other party upon learning of any unauthorized use or disclosure of such party's Confidential Information; and (e) return all Confidential Information on demand within 24 hours and immediately cease all use whatsoever of the Confidential Information.

12. *Term of Agreement*. Formalization of this relationship is subject to appropriate corporate approvals by Customer [**and its parent**] and final preparation and execution of the Definitive Agreement. If the Definitive Agreement has not been executed or has not received the appropriate corporate approvals of Customer [and its parent] on or before [**DATE**], this Letter Agreement shall be of no further force and effect, except as provided herein with respect to the terms of Paragraphs 7, 10, and 11.

13. *Miscellaneous.*

    a. *Publicity.* Each party shall not publish or use any advertising, written sales promotion, press releases, or other publicity matters relating to this Letter Agreement in which the other party's name or mark is mentioned or language from which the connection of said name or mark may be inferred or implied without the other party's consent.

    b. *Entire Agreement.* This Letter Agreement represents the entire agreement between the parties with respect to its subject matter, and there are no other representations, understandings, or agreements between the parties relative to such subject matter. No amendment to, or change, waiver, or discharge of, any provision of this Letter Agreement shall be valid unless in writing and signed by an authorized representative of the party against which such amendment, change, waiver, or discharge is sought to be enforced.

    c. *Counterparts.* This Letter Agreement may be executed in any number of counterparts, all of which taken together shall constitute one single agreement between the parties.

    d. *Exclusivity.* Neither this Letter Agreement nor any other arrangement between the parties grants Vendor any exclusive right to negotiate with Customer.

    e. *Assignment/Subcontracting.* Neither party may assign or subcontract its rights or obligations under this Letter Agreement in whole or in part without the consent of the other party. Any purported assignment in contravention of this Paragraph shall be null and void.

    f. *Governing Law.* **THIS LETTER AGREEMENT AND THE RIGHTS AND OBLIGATIONS OF THE PARTIES HEREUNDER SHALL BE CONSTRUED IN ACCORDANCE WITH AND BE GOVERNED BY THE LAWS OF THE STATE OF [STATE], WITHOUT GIVING EFFECT TO THE PRINCIPLES THEREOF RELATING TO THE CONFLICTS OF LAW.**

Please evidence your agreement and acceptance of the terms and conditions of this Letter Agreement by signing both of the two copies enclosed and returning one of the original, fully executed copies to me.

Sincerely yours,

[Name, Title]

AGREED TO AND ACCEPTED THIS
[DAY] DAY OF **[MONTH]**, **[YEAR]**

By: **[Name, Title]**

LETTER OF INTENT (CUSTOMER FORM)

[CUSTOMER LETTERHEAD]
[DATE]

CONFIDENTIAL

[NAME]
[TITLE]
[ADDRESS]
Dear _____:

1.   This letter is addressed to **[VENDOR]** (*"Vendor"*) to confirm the interest of Vendor and **[CUSTOMER]** (*"Customer"*) in entering into a **[SPECIFY TYPE OF BUSINESS PROCESS]** services agreement (the *"Services Agreement"*) for Vendor's provision of certain **[SPECIFY TYPE OF BUSINESS PROCESS]** and related services to Customer.

2.   Formalization of our relationship is subject to appropriate corporate approvals by Customer **[and its parent]** and final preparation and execution of the Services Agreement. If the Services Agreement has not been executed or has not received the appropriate corporate approvals of Customer **[and its parent]** on or before **[DATE]**, this letter shall be of no further force and effect, except as provided herein with respect to the terms of paragraphs 3, 5, and 6.

3.   During the pendency of formal corporate approvals from Customer **[and its parent]** and final preparation and execution of the Services Agreement, it is expected the parties will exchange confidential information. The parties agree to treat such confidential information in accordance with the confidentiality provisions attached as *Attachment 1*. Substantially similar provisions will be included in the Services Agreement. In addition, the parties agree that negotiations that are intended to result in a definitive agreement are taking place between Customer and Vendor, and the terms, conditions, or other facts with respect to such possible agreement, including the status thereof, shall be treated as "Confidential Information" in accordance with the same confidentiality provisions.

4.   **[In connection with the proposed transaction between Customer and Vendor, Customer intends to transition certain of its employees to Vendor (the "Transitioned Employees"). In the event Customer and**

113

Vendor execute the Services Agreement, Customer and Vendor wish to complete the transition of the Transitioned Employees to Vendor on [DATE]. In order to complete such a transition, it will be necessary for Vendor to commence preemployment screenings and similar employee-related tasks prior to the date of the Services Agreement between Customer and Vendor. In this regard, Customer and Vendor have agreed to certain terms and conditions relating to the transition of the Transitioned Employees, attached as *Attachment 2*. Substantially similar terms and conditions will be included in the Services Agreement between Customer and Vendor in the event the Services Agreement is executed. The agreement of Customer and Vendor on such terms and conditions does not in any way obligate Customer and Vendor to enter into the Services Agreement.]

5.   Each party shall indemnify the other party against and hold the other party harmless from any claims by the Transitioned Employees arising out of such party's conduct or representations during the period through [DATE].

6.   In the event Customer and Vendor do not execute the Services Agreement, each of the parties will bear its own costs and expenses incurred in negotiating the Services Agreement, including any costs and expenses relating to the preliminary work performed by Vendor in connection with the proposed transition of the Transitioned Employees.

7.   It is understood that while this letter constitutes a statement of mutual intentions of Customer and Vendor with respect to the proposed provision of certain [SPECIFY TYPE OF BUSINESS PROCESS] and related services by Vendor to Customer, it does not constitute an obligation binding on either side, nor does it contain all matters upon which agreement must be reached and, except with respect to paragraphs 3, 5, and 6, this letter shall create no rights in favor of either party. A binding commitment with respect to the proposed project will result only from the execution of the Services Agreement.

Very truly yours,

[CUSTOMER]
By:_____
[NAME]
[TITLE]

AGREED TO AND ACCEPTED THIS_____ DAY OF _____, _____

[VENDOR]

By:_____
[NAME]
[TITLE]

LETTER OF INTENT (VENDOR FORM)

[VENDOR LETTERHEAD]

[DATE]

CONFIDENTIAL

[NAME]
[TITLE]
[ADDRESS]

Dear _____:

This letter (this "*Letter Agreement*") is addressed to **[CUSTOMER]** ("*Customer*") to confirm the interest of Customer in entering into a services agreement with **[VENDOR]** ("*Vendor*") (the "*Services Agreement*") for Vendor's provision of **[DESCRIBE SERVICES]** (the "*Services*") to Customer.

[IF EXCLUSIVE NEGOTIATIONS: In consideration of the time and efforts of each of the parties in negotiating the Services Agreement, Customer agrees and acknowledges that it will negotiate exclusively with Vendor for the provision of the Services, and will not contact, respond to proposals from, or negotiate with any other vendor or third party for or in connection with the provision of the Services, as of the date of this Letter Agreement and continuing up to and including **[SPECIFY DATE]** (the "*Exclusivity Period*"). **[IF CERTAIN RATES/TERMS ARE FIRM DURING EXCLUSIVITY PERIOD:** The rates set forth in [SPECIFY DOCUMENT] are only applicable during the Exclusivity Period only, unless otherwise agreed upon by the parties.] If the Services Agreement has not been executed before the expiration of the Exclusivity Period, the parties shall agree to either: (a) agree upon an extension to the Exclusivity Period, (b) continue to negotiate the Services Agreement in accordance with the terms of this Letter Agreement on a nonexclusive basis, or (c) cease negotiations and terminate this Letter Agreement, subject to the terms of this Letter Agreement.]

[IF SERVICES WILL BE COMMENCED PRIOR TO EXECUTION OF SERVICES AGREEMENT: Customer desires Vendor to commence the provision of [**OPTION 1:** those Services described in **[SPECIFY DOCUMENT]** (the "*Interim Services*")] [**OPTION 2:** the resources described in **[SPECIFY DOCUMENT]** (the "*Interim Resources*")] as of **[SPECIFY DATE]** until the earlier of the execution of the Services Agreement and the termination of this Letter Agreement (the "*Interim Service Period*"). Customer agrees and acknowledges that time is critical and that Vendor agrees to provide the [**OPTION 1:** Interim Services] [**OPTION 2:** Interim Resources] to Customer solely as a convenience to Customer. Vendor shall therefore not be liable for any damages incurred in connection with the provision of the [**OPTION 1:** Interim Services] [**OPTION 2:** Interim Resources] and Customer agrees to indemnify Vendor in connection with any claims relating to the provision of the Services pursuant to paragraph ___ below. Customer shall pay the fees for the [**OPTION 1:** Interim Services] [**OPTION 2:** Interim Resources] during the Interim Service Period [**OPTIONS FOR PRICING:** [**OPT A:** set forth in [**SPECIFY DOCUMENT**] on the terms and according to the time frames set forth in [**SPECIFY DOCUMENT**]] [**OPT B:** as agreed upon by the parties or where not so agreed in advance fair and reasonable renumeration when directed to do so by Vendor] [**OPT C:** on a time and materials basis] [**OPT D:** at Vendor's then-current commercial rates]. [**Vendor may change the fees upon ___ days' notice to Customer.**]]

During the negotiation of the Services Agreement, it is expected the parties will exchange confidential information. The parties agree to treat such confidential information in accordance with the confidentiality provisions set forth in [**SPECIFY DOCUMENT**]. Substantially similar provisions will be included in the Services Agreement. In addition, the parties agree that negotiations that are intended to result in a definitive agreement are taking place between Customer and Vendor and the terms, conditions, or other facts with respect to such possible agreement, including the status thereof, shall be treated as "Confidential Information" in accordance with the same confidentiality provisions.

[**IF EMPLOYEE TRANSFERS WILL COMMENCE PRIOR TO EXECUTION OF SERVICES AGREEMENT:** In connection with the proposed transaction between Customer and Vendor, Customer intends to transition certain of its employees to Vendor (the *"Transitioned Employees"*). In the event Customer and Vendor execute the Services Agreement, Customer and Vendor wish to complete the transition of the Transitioned Employees to Vendor on [**SPECIFY DATE**]. In order to complete such a transition, it will be necessary for Vendor to commence preemployment screenings and similar employee-related tasks prior to the date of the Services Agreement between Customer and Vendor. In this regard, Customer and Vendor have agreed to certain terms and conditions relating to the transition of the Transitioned Employees, set forth in [**SPECIFY DOCUMENT**]. Substantially similar terms and conditions will be included in the Services Agreement between Customer and Vendor in the event the Services Agreement is executed. The agreement of Customer and Vendor on such terms and conditions does not in any way obligate Customer and Vendor to enter into the Services Agreement.]

[**IF INTERIM SERVICES OR EMPLOYEE TRANSFER PARAGRAPHS INCLUDED:** Customer shall indemnify Vendor against and hold Vendor harmless from any claims (a) relating to the provision of services described in paragraph ___ above and (b) by or relating to the Transitioned Employees.]

Upon the termination of this Letter Agreement, [**OPTION 1:** each of the parties will bear its own costs and expenses incurred in negotiating the Services Agreement.] [**OPTION 2:** Customer shall (a) reimburse Vendor for any costs and expenses relating to **[the negotiation and due diligence performed in connection with the Services Agreement [up to [SPECIFY DOLLAR AMOUNT] and]** [**IF EMPLOYEE TRANSFER PARAGRAPH APPLIES:** the preliminary work performed by Vendor in connection with the proposed transition of the Transitioned Employees] [**IF INTERIM SERVICES PARAGRAPH APPLIES:** and (b) pay to Vendor any amounts incurred in connection with the provision of the services described in paragraph ___].] This paragraph and paragraphs **[LIST CONFIDENTIALITY AND INDEMNITY]** shall survive the termination of this Letter Agreement.

[When the Services Agreement is executed, the terms and conditions of the Services Agreement shall apply retroactively to any work performed under this Letter Agreement.] This Letter Agreement shall be governed by, and construed in accordance with, the laws of [SPECIFY LAW].

Upon your understanding of and agreement to the foregoing, please sign the two original copies of this Letter Agreement provided to you and return one fully executed original to me.

Very truly yours,

[CUSTOMER]

By:_____
[NAME]
[TITLE]

AGREED TO AND ACCEPTED THIS_____ DAY OF _____, ____

[VENDOR]

By:_____
[NAME]
[TITLE]

CONSENT LETTER (MANAGEMENT OF THIRD-PARTY PRODUCTS/SERVICES)

[DATE]

Re: Outsourcing Agreement Between **[CUSTOMER]** and **[VENDOR]**

[THIRD PARTY VENDOR]
[ADDRESS]

To whom it may concern:

This is to inform you that Customer ("Customer") and Vendor ("Vendor") have entered into an agreement pursuant to which Vendor will provide certain information technology and related services to Customer. In connection with this transaction, **[Customer will provide Vendor and its affiliates and subcontractors access to and/or require the right to install on machines of vendor and its affiliates and subcontractors] [Vendor will have managerial, administrative, and financial responsibility for] [FILL IN PRODUCT/SERVICE]** (the "Third-Party Product/Service"). **[Note: Add worldwide if access/use will be outside the United States.]** Please confirm your consent to such access/assumption of responsibility by to Vendor by signing both copies of this letter and returning one signed original to me as soon as possible.

Vendor will be **[financially]** responsible for Customer's obligations to you for the Third-Party Product/Service. Vendor will also have managerial and administrative responsibility of the agreements relating to the Third-Party Product/Service. Therefore, all correspondence and invoices concerning such agreements as of this date should be mailed to the address currently used by Customer, c/o Vendor.

I would appreciate if the signed original was sent no later than **[***]** to the following: **[CUSTOMER]**

Sincerely yours,

[CUSTOMER]

ACCEPTED AND AGREED:

[THIRD-PARTY VENDOR]

By: **[NAME]**
[Title:]
[Date:]

CHAPTER 3

NEGOTIATIONS: STRATEGY AND PROCESS

3.1 INTRODUCTION

The methodology and strategy of negotiating an outsourcing agreement is determined by two basic factors: (1) the relative bargaining positions of the parties and (2) the type of contract being negotiated; that is, whether the underlying objective of the customer is to reduce costs, gain a competitive advantage in its industry, provide flexibility to its users, or (as is typically the case) some combination of those or other factors. Despite today's competitive marketplace, it is unlikely that a customer will be able to obtain the optimal contract because a negotiation is by definition a process of give and take. It is possible, however, for the parties to obtain a fair contract that will anticipate the likely occurrences over a five- to ten-year term and establish a mechanism for resolving disputes and adding work without resorting to a bureaucratic or adversarial process.

In order for both sides to accomplish this goal, each must first evaluate the basic risks and rewards with respect to the transaction. The customer must decide precisely why it is entering into an outsourcing arrangement. Most customers are able to develop a list of three to five key reasons, and these factors become the foundation from which negotiations begin. All too often, however, this is the only strategy the customer applies during negotiations. As a result, the customer often finds itself at a disadvantage during the negotiation process because the vendor is, at least presumably, experienced in negotiating outsourcing agreements and more familiar with the ebb and flow of the negotiations process.

The principal cause of this power imbalance is that the typical customer does not view negotiating the contract as part of the outsourcing process. Instead, he or she merely regards the contract as a necessary evil. The vendor, on the other hand, regards the contract as the final stage in the sales cycle, and its representatives are schooled on how best to close the deal while protecting the vendor to the greatest extent possible given the value of the transaction. An outsourcing transaction that is essentially a financing arrangement in which cost reduction is the customer's primary goal will likely be a different type of contract in substance and form than one in which the quality of the services, as opposed to their cost, is the customer's main concern. Similarly, if the outsourcing arrangement includes a significant amount of IT transformation, the contract must consider different elements than if it were a traditional IT structure outsourcing deal.

It is important to note at this point that senior management's primary interest in the negotiations is typically the financial benefits and technological advances to be derived from outsourcing, not the niceties of the contract. Thus, while all levels of the organization are likely to focus on vendor selection, forging the legal relationship between the parties is all too often regarded as an administrative task to be performed with as little involvement of senior management as possible. Although it is true that lawyers often plan the divorce before consummating the marriage, it is equally true that too many businesspeople take the wedding vows before reading the prenuptial agreement. The contract must be regarded as part of the outsourcing process—perhaps not the most important part, but a significant part. Accordingly, the customer's representatives must be well versed in the various subject matters that are dealt with in an outsourcing agreement or that subject matter experts be involved as necessary (e.g., HR).

This will allow the customer to manage the negotiation process as it would manage the selection process and, hopefully, to avoid unnecessary conflicts over issues with little or no practical effect on the project.

At this point, a brief examination of the contract's role is in order. A contract is a sword or shield to be used in the event of a dispute between the parties. This ultimate purpose should be kept in mind during the negotiation and the preparation of the agreement. It can be safely assumed that most businesspeople desire to live up to their obligations and that most of them substantially do so. The contract, then, must address the various matters that are to be accomplished and to focus responsibility on the party whose obligation it is to accomplish each. Most disputes arise when the parties have failed to consider some potential problem and have, therefore, neglected to specify in the contract who will be responsible.

Finally, this chapter is not intended as a text on negotiation, but instead will concentrate principally on the subject matter to be negotiated rather than on the strategy of negotiation. However, the general methodology of contract negotiation and the techniques that are most useful in defining a comprehensive contract are outlined in this chapter. This discussion is not an argument for tough contracts; it is a plea for well-thought-out, clearly articulated, and detailed contracts. If the duties, obligations, and expectations of each party are expressed, negotiated, agreed to (with an understanding of their implications), and clearly set forth in a written agreement, the chances that both parties will be satisfied with the contract are increased immensely.

3.2 NEGOTIATING PROCESS

While most IT professionals approach an outsourcing analysis differently than a hardware purchase or lease analysis, they tend to regard all contracts as having been created equally. There is often a false impression on the part of business people that the details of the contract are secondary to the project. In order to avoid the conflict that can result when the sales cycle has not included a robust discussion of the underlying legal relationship between the parties, the customer's representative all too often reviews the vendor's standard contract in light of business issues that arose during other projects, rather than as legal issues unique to the particular project. This, in turn, engenders the classic businessperson–lawyer conflict in which the lawyer points out that the supposed intent of many of the contract's provisions is not reflected in the actual language of the agreement. This approach ignores one of the fundamental truths of the outsourcing industry: the standard form is invariably inadequate from the customer's perspective.

This is not to suggest that customers steadfastly refuse to negotiate from the vendor's form (although as a general matter, the customer should draft the agreement whenever possible to better control the process). It does, however, suggest that customers should not rely on the oral representations of the vendor concerning the intent of the contract and that counsel should be involved as soon as possible. Ideally, this should take place before the vendor is selected. A vendor's willingness to be reasonable in its legal relationship with the customer should be a significant (although not determinative) factor in the selection process. Just as the IT professional will focus on the vendor's ability to perform when selecting the vendor, the customer should rely on its lawyer to assess the specific legal risks associated with each vendor, particularly as the regulatory implications of outsourcing continue to increase.

Fundamental to this approach is the need for the customer to be prepared for the negotiation. Taking the following steps before beginning the negotiation can help the customer achieve a more viable contract:

- *Define the transaction.* The subject matter of the contract is determined by the services being outsourced. As discussed earlier, however, the reasons for outsourcing the services determine the substance and form of the transaction. The definition of the transaction—the process by which a customer prioritizes its goals—is the most basic step in any negotiation. This list must be reviewed and updated throughout the negotiation, because issues may arise that will affect the priority and content given to key objectives. The customer must determine what role it intends to take during the negotiation. Will it control the process by drafting the agreements, setting the timetable for the negotiations, and dictating the content of the meetings, or will it allow the vendor to perform these tasks? In an ideal situation, a framework for the negotiations is established mutually, but as a practical matter, the customer must either lead or follow. Most vendors are accustomed to dominating the negotiation process and are reluctant to disturb the protective blanket of the standard form. The customer should make it apparent to the vendor, early in the selection process, that it will not accept the vendor's form contract and that the customer has certain contract terms that must be included in any agreement between the parties. If the customer allows the vendor to believe that this will be an ordinary negotiation process until the vendor delivers signed copies of its standard form, the resulting disturbance in the business relationship may not be worth any improvement in the legal relationship. The customer must be careful not to be confrontational in suggesting changes or demanding additional protection. Vendors are more inclined to accept modifications than to make concessions. Although clarifying the legal relationship between the parties is useful and sometimes essential, the customer should never lose sight of the fact that the parties must be willing to cooperate after the contract is signed. If the negotiation has dampened the vendor's enthusiasm for the business, the real objective of the contract (the successful outsourcing of service) will not be achieved regardless of how well crafted the contract is. In addition, certain rules of engagement must be established.

- *Define roles.* Many customers fail to realize that regardless of the type of transaction or the scope of the work, the contract's terms and its form are subject to negotiation. As noted previously, there are instances where the customer can and should insist on drafting the agreement. In addition, the customer must determine what roles each individual on the negotiation team will play. Will a businessperson take a lead role in raising and framing issues, or will attorneys take on that responsibility? The negotiation of any contract is an adversarial process because of the competing interests of the parties. This does not, however, mean that each contract negotiation should be adversarial. The customer should enter into the negotiations with the intent to advocate its interests through the reasonableness of its position. Despite the customer's best intentions, it is likely that the lead negotiator will at some point be regarded as confrontational by the vendor. This feeling, in turn, could carry over to the postcontract period and make the relationship between vendor and customer difficult. For this reason, many customers appoint counsel as the lead negotiator. Lawyers are familiar with the role of articulating positions and typically are less inclined to respond emotionally to the vendor's counterproposals. Similarly, having the lawyer serve as the lead negotiator establishes a distance between the positions advocated by the lawyer and those of the customer, and enables the customer to play the role of problem solver. Before placing this responsibility on the lawyer, the customer should make certain that the lawyer fully understands the customer's position on the issues and that the lawyer is willing to defer to the customer's judgment at the appropriate time.

- *Find a lawyer.* Although many businesspeople prefer not to involve lawyers in a project until it is absolutely necessary (and while it may seem to be in the authors' parochial interests to say so), it is advisable to choose a lawyer early in the selection process and to have that lawyer assess the legal risks associated with the legal relationship presented by each vendor. If the customer's organization has a corporate counsel's office, an effort should be made to identify a lawyer there who has experience with outsourcing contracts. If it is necessary to engage outside counsel, the customer should seek recommendations from other outsourcing customers and should ensure that the lawyer chosen has extensive experience in drafting and negotiating outsourcing agreements on behalf of customers. Once a lawyer is chosen, the customer's representative should clearly identify the lawyer's responsibilities and should decide the best method of involving the lawyer in the selection process.

- *Term sheet.* To the extent possible, the customer should seize the initiative in the negotiation process by preparing a term sheet for delivery to the vendor. The term sheet is a document that defines the customer's position on the salient terms of the contract. This document can be used to inform the vendor of the customer's positions or as a checklist for use in determining the adequacy of the vendor's form contract. Ideally, the term sheet should be issued together with the customer's RFP and should require the vendor to note any objection to its terms in the vendor's proposal. This allows the customer to seize the high ground in determining the legal relationship between the parties by establishing the terms from which this relationship will evolve. Each proposal can then be evaluated in terms of the vendor's willingness to accept the basic contract terms. If the vendor does not issue a formal proposal, the customer may wish to use the term sheet as an outline from which to inform the vendor of the customer's expectations.

  Regardless of whether the term sheet is issued to the vendor or employed by the customer as a point of reference, it is a vital document in the negotiation process, because it provides a framework within which the customer can build a viable contract. There are, however, several other reasons for developing a comprehensive term sheet. The first and perhaps most important reason is that developing such a document forces the customer to consider the operational and legal issues associated with the project. Through the analytical process of selecting and framing the applicable clauses, the key elements of the project are reinforced, and the customer becomes aware of the ramifications that a decision regarding one such element will have on another. This, in turn, gives the customer the advantage in the inevitable jousting over contract terms, because it will have considered most issues before they arise during the negotiation. In addition, if the term sheet has been issued to the vendor, it sets the framework of the transaction from the viewpoint of the customer and psychologically requires the vendor to tailor its needs within that framework.

The term sheet also provides an early insight into the vendor's position and a focus on weaknesses in the customer's positions that need to be corrected. The position of other vendors included in the selection process but not selected is also helpful in the negotiation and is obtained through the term sheet. Thus, if the customer knows that one vendor is willing to concede a specific issue, this information can be used in the actual negotiating sessions to induce another vendor to concede that point. The term sheet, when issued to all vendors involved in the process, will provide valuable input to the negotiator.

The vendors' responses to the document must be evaluated and the vendors ranked on their willingness to negotiate. This ranking should be added to the selection process criteria matrix in order to determine which vendor is most willing to negotiate.

- *Determine value attributed by vendor.* In negotiating with a vendor, it is important to understand clearly the vendor's position, as well as the positions of the individuals participating in the negotiation. Negotiations are performed by individuals whose viewpoints often differ from the corporate policy. Therefore, the negotiator should understand the positions not only of the organization the individuals represent but also of the individuals themselves. It is also important to understand what the value of the contract is to the vendor as a means of gauging how much the vendor will be willing to concede. This value may not only be economic. In addition to revenue (and, most notably, profits), the vendor must consider the public relations value of the contract, entry into a new industry, the breakthrough in establishing even a small relationship with the particular customer, or the prestige associated with the customer's name. Even though the economic value of a contract usually predominates, the customer should attempt to forecast what the total value of this contract might be to the vendor.

  In addition to the direct value of the contract, which is partly determined on the basis of the profits it can generate, other values to the vendor can be quantified. It is clear, for example, that a successful vendor will have a significant probability of selling additional services during the life of the contract. This means that the probability of future profits can and should be assessed. As a rule of thumb, therefore, it might be appropriate to assume that the vendor will derive a total profit equal to twice the profit in the initial outsourcing contract.

  There is also a psychological and financial impact associated with not getting the contract. The vendor has made an investment in the proposal (often worth millions of dollars on direct and indirect costs) in order to develop the proposal, entertain the customer, and incur unreasonable personnel costs. This investment is lost if the contract is not executed.

There is also a psychological loss, which is the converse of the public relations benefit of obtaining the contract. The absolute value of the loss can be important, and allowing another vendor to enter a new market or obtain a new client can be equally important. All of these factors, both economic and psychological, should be analyzed for negotiating purposes. It is clear that the negotiation will fail if the customer's negotiating team demands more than the value of the contract or more than the losses associated with not obtaining it. Thus, the negotiating team should carefully balance demands with value and recognize what is available to be negotiated.

3.3   EXPOSURE ANALYSIS

To further assess the impact of a contract, or the impact of not having coverage in areas where protection is desirable, a brief analysis of exposure can be made, in recognition of the risk, on an area-by-area basis.

The first step in this analysis is to divide the contract terms in the term sheet into categories of importance. These categories could be identified as follows:

- Key contract terms
- Significant contract terms
- Minor contract terms
- Terms with no quantifiable impact

An alternative approach is to classify terms by the amount of risk associated with each term. In a typical outsourcing contract, this might result in the following:

- A risk of $0–$50,000
- A risk of $50,000–$250,000
- A risk of $250,000–$1,000,000
- A risk of more than $1,000,000

Regardless of the method of classification, the contract clauses can be identified by category. It is then possible to assign weights to each category and to determine the total number of points associated with each weight. By evaluating the responses of each vendor to each clause, a particular score is obtained. This allows an assessment of the responsiveness of the vendor and its willingness to negotiate.

This is a mechanistic method of assessing the exposure of a contract, and it may not be specific enough or too specific in certain areas. It is only a tool used to assess the contract and to identify areas where it can be improved. It should never be used as a sole basis for negotiation, because common sense obviously will override the purely numerical conclusions this technique provides. However, the technique is useful in providing an insight into the vendor's responsiveness and willingness to negotiate, thereby providing the negotiator with added impetus for ensuring the best deal with any vendor.

3.4   PEOPLE NEGOTIATE, NOT COMPANIES

It is axiomatic that negotiations are performed by individuals whose values and opinions may be different from those adopted by the vendor. To the salesperson, for example, the contract being negotiated may be the most significant opportunity of the year (or, indeed, a career). It may mean a large bonus or a potential promotion. The salesperson as an individual has a great deal more to gain or lose from the contract than the vendor. Accordingly, the salesperson is likely to be most oriented toward negotiating a balanced contract. The salesperson is, in most cases, often least able to commit the vendor to any significant concessions. Yet, by knowing the vendor's internal organization, he or she can often facilitate compromise.

Next in line in terms of interest in finalizing the contract is typically the vendor's account manager (e.g., the individual who will administer the contract). In many cases, this individual receives some commission, and in all cases, account managers are held responsible for meeting the quota for their business unit. Thus, the vendor's account manager is equally interested in being awarded the contract. This level of management is responsible for a budget and must maintain its total concessions with customers within a specified fraction of the total sales of the business unit.

Finally, most removed from the interest of the customer, and typically the most difficult to deal with, is the vendor's legal representative. In most instances, the legal representative has been established as a protector of the vendor, with the responsibility of ensuring that the customer does not obtain a contract more favorable than the vendor's policy permits. Normally, the vendor organization has a very strong representative in its legal or contract negotiating representative. This person will create the greatest difficulty in the negotiating process and should be isolated as quickly as possible as part of the negotiation.

In attempting to understand the position of the other side in the negotiation, the personality of the individuals concerned should also be a consideration. In addition to a checklist of value items that the negotiator prepares, he or she should also prepare a short biographical synopsis of the individuals participating on the opposing side. Each synopsis should indicate the background of the individual, his or her current position, and personality traits. Traits such as quickness to become angry or willingness to compromise should be identified where possible to ensure that the negotiating team has a realistic understanding of the participants' personalities and can appeal to those characteristics most likely to result in negotiating advantages to the customer.

3.5 NEGOTIATING STRATEGY

As mentioned earlier, although this is not a text on negotiating strategy, some points will be mentioned to ensure that the negotiating process is carried out in a reasonable manner.

Although it may seem obvious, customers need to be constantly reminded that it is not desirable or productive to present the other side with an overwhelming series of requests at the beginning of the negotiations. If the vendor has already received the term sheet and has responded to it, the vendor is aware of the fact that the customer has requested a fairly significant change from the standard contract. The vendor, therefore, has already been placed on guard. Further demands might create a difficult situation in which the vendor might decide to walk out rather than deal with a massive problem in the contract. If the vendor has made it to the negotiating table despite having seen the term sheet, then the vendor is prepared to negotiate and compromise. Accordingly, it is not desirable to overwhelm the vendor at the initial negotiating session.

Clauses should be grouped into categories so that not all major ones are discussed at the beginning. For this reason, it is beneficial to discuss the sequence of clauses before the start of the negotiation. Many vendors will attempt to engage the customer in a line-by-line review and discussion of the agreement at the onset of negotiations. This is a decidedly unproductive approach because the participants' attention span undoubtedly declines as they conduct a seemingly endless march through the contract. A line-by-line analysis of the agreement is best postponed until the major issues have been resolved and, as a threshold matter, should be conducted by the lawyers off-line until the issues that arise from this discussion can be distilled to a manageable number.

A negotiating session will have a varying number of phases. Difficult periods of argument and acrimony should be alternated with periods of attention to clauses or agreements that are considered reasonable by both parties so there is the opportunity to establish a friendly relationship during the negotiation. The regular alternation of these periods ensures that neither party walks out of the negotiation without just cause.

Similarly, a negotiating session, of necessity, is a process of give and take. These trade-offs should be used carefully. When the negotiator is prepared to accede to a request from the vendor, or realizes that he or she has no choice but to accede because the vendor is intractable on a point, then the negotiator should use the trade-off capability. At that point, the negotiator might go back to a clause that had been suspended because no agreement was reached and indicate that he or she will accede to the point in question if the vendor will agree to accede to the previous point.

If it is impossible to reach an agreement on a particular issue, the customer should be prepared to drop that issue and suspend it until the next session. It is possible that in subsequent discussion the issue might become irrelevant, or a resolution or alternative may be found if time passes. In the next negotiating session, the negotiator should determine if either party is prepared to move from the position taken earlier. Resuscitation of these issues might take place as part of a trade-off or a give-up of another issue.

It is desirable to always have a fallback position for each issue under discussion and for the negotiation as a whole. A fallback position for a specific clause might simply be a softening of that clause or preparedness to accept an inferior position. This can be brought out when the vendor is unprepared to accept the clause as written. If the vendor offers an alternative, then the fallback position can be tried if it is better for the customer than the offered alternative, or if it can be made to appear as a reasonable compromise between the vendor's position and the customer's. If the vendor is totally intractable, then the fallback position can be brought out as a compromise between the customer's requirements and the vendor's unwillingness to provide any kind of response.

In addition to the fallback in each clause, there must be an overall fallback position. Remember that the vendors were selected on the basis of the commitments they were prepared to make either in the proposal or as a result of separate discussions. If the prime vendor becomes unwilling to make such commitments in a written contract, then perhaps the selection of this vendor was an error in the first place and the second-ranked vendor would be the better choice. If at any time the vendor declines its previous commitments, or if the negotiating position of the vendor is so intractable as to render a potential contract meaningless, it may be desirable to actually switch the negotiation to the second-ranked vendor. The authority and the knowledge that it is possible to shift to another vendor will make the negotiator more effective, even if this option is never exercised.

Finally, there may be occasions during the negotiation when it is better to stop all further discussion rather than generate further acrimony. If the negotiations have broken down, or if there is considerable disagreement and no apparent resolution is in sight, there should be some exit opportunities during which the situation can be reconsidered. At this point, the vendor and customer personnel should separate and perhaps discuss among themselves the approaches to be taken. For example, the vendor salesperson or sales manager might convince the vendor's negotiator to soften his or her position. Thus, opportunities to break and separate for dinner, for coffee, or just to regroup are desirable in any negotiating session.

MODEL TERM SHEET

SUMMARY OF KEY TERMS AND CONDITIONS

Agreement Structure. The parties will enter into a [services agreement] [master services agreement "MSA"] that will set out the [*if a MSA*: general] terms and condition applicable to Vendor's provision of services to Customer.

[If a MSA: Vendor and Customer will enter into specific service agreements [for each Customer site] [describing the responsibilities and obligations specific to the applicable services].]

The parties will simultaneously enter into [DESCRIBE ANY OTHER AGREEMENTS THAT WILL BE ENTERED INTO AS PART OF THE TRANSACTION, E.G., LEASES, PURCHASE AND SALE, CONSULTING SERVICES].

[*If the parties will be forming a joint venture or strategic alliance*: The parties will enter into an agreement to form [DESCRIBE JV/STRA-TEGIC ALLIANCE].]

Term. The term of the [services agreement] [MSA] will commence on [SPECIFY DATE] and continue until [SPECIFY DATE].

[*If a MSA*: The term of [IDENTIFY SPECIFIC SERVICE AGREE-MENTS] will commence on [SPECIFY DATE] and continue until [SPECIFY DATE].]

Scope of Services. Vendor [will provide] [will be the exclusive provider of] the following services to Customer (the "Services"): [PROVIDE GEN-ERAL DESCRIPTION OF SERVICES].

Vendor will have responsibility for: [DESCRIBE ANY KEY RESPONSIBILITIES THAT WILL IMPACT PRICE, E.G., UPGRADES, REFRESHES, NEW/ADDITIONAL EQUIPMENT, BUSINESS RECOVERY].

The following services are expressly excluded from scope: [LIST EXCLUDED SERVICES].

Customer Sites/Entities Receiving Services. Vendor will provide the Ser-vices to the following Customer sites: [LIST SITES].

The Customer entities receiving the Services under the [services agreement] [MSA] will be: [LIST ENTITIES].

Permits/Licenses/Consents. [Customer] [Vendor will have [administrative] [financial] responsibility for all governmental and third party operating, discharge, release and other permits, licenses and consents required [or desirable] in connection with the provision and receipt of the Services.

[MAY NEED TO DISTINGUISH BETWEEN GOVERNMENT CONSENTS/APPROVAL AND THIRD-PARTY CONSENTS APPROVALS.]

[ADD LANGUAGE RE: LIENS IF APPLICABLE]

Projects. Vendor will have the following project responsibilities: [DESCRIBE PROJECTS IF APPLICABLE].

The fees for the projects are [included] [not included] in the [base fees].

Contract Administration. Vendor will have [administrative] [financial] responsibility for the third-party contracts specified in Exhibit __.

Transition of Employees. [DETERMINE WHETHER CUSTOMER EMPLOYEES WILL BE TRANSFERRED TO VENDOR OR VENDOR SUBCONTRACTOR; IF SO, DETERMINE TERMS OF HIRING BY VENDOR; ALLOCATE SEVERANCE/REDUNDANCY RESPONSIBILITIES.]

Staffing. [SPECIFY ANY SPECIAL STAFFING REQUIREMENTS; ANY RESTRICTIONS ON SUBCONTRACTING.]

Purchase of Assets/Facility(ies). Vendor will purchase from Customer the following [assets] [facility(ies)]: [LIST ASSETS/FACILITY(IES)].

Vendor will pay to Customer the following amounts in consideration of such purchase on [SPECIFY DATE]: [SPECIFY PURCHASE PRICE].

Service Levels. Vendor will perform the Services in accordance with [SPECIFY SERVICE LEVELS].

If Vendor fails to meet the service levels specified above, [DESCRIBE CONSEQUENCES FOR PERFORMANCE FAILURE].

[Service levels credits shall not be an exclusive remedy.]

Customer Responsibilities. Customer will retain the following responsibilities: [DESCRIBE RETAINED RESPONSIBILITIES OF CUSTOMER, E.G., PROVISION OF SPACE, OFFICE EQUIPMENT, SUPPLIES].

Pricing. In consideration for providing the Services, Customer will pay to Vendor the following amounts: [DESCRIBE PRICING STRUCTURE].

Payment Terms. Vendor will deliver an invoice on or about the [first] day of each month for the Services [to be performed during such month] [performed during the preceding month] and each such invoice will be due within [FILL IN NUMBER OF DAYS] of receipt by Customer.

Taxes. Except for Vendor's obligation to pay employee-related taxes and taxes owed by Vendor measured by the net income of Vendor, all payments of compensation made by Customer hereunder will [be exclusive of] [include] any withholdings and of any federal, state or local sales or use tax, or any other tax or similar charge based on or measured by Vendor's gross receipts. [DISCUSS STATE LAW CONCERNS.]

Benchmarking. [DESCRIBE ANY BENCHMARKING OR CUSTOMER SATISFACTION PROVISIONS.]

Proprietary Rights. *Customer Intellectual Property*: Customer will grant to Vendor a nonexclusive right to use any intellectual property owned or licensed by Customer and used in connection with the provision of the Services.

Vendor Intellectual Property: Vendor will grant to Customer a nonexclusive right to use any intellectual property owned or licensed by Vendor and used in connection with the provision of the Services. [DETERMINE RIGHTS DURING TERM AND AFTER EXPIRATION/TERMINATION.]

Developments: All intellectual property developed by Vendor as part of the Services will become the property of [Customer] [Vendor].

[*Tools*: Vendor will retain all right, title, and interest in and to any and all ideas, concepts, know-how, development tools, methodologies, processes, procedures, technologies, or algorithms ("Tools"), which are based on trade secrets or proprietary information of Vendor.]

Audits. *Verification of Fees*: Upon reasonable notice from Customer, Vendor will provide Customer access to all relevant documentation and facilities for the purpose of confirming that fees billed are in accordance with the terms of the [services agreement] [MSA].

Access: Upon reasonable notice from Customer, Vendor will provide Customer access to all relevant facilities and equipment for the purpose of auditing the services and service levels.

Termination. *By Vendor*: Vendor will have the right to terminate the [services agreement] [MSA] if: (1) Customer fails to pay any amounts due or (2) Customer enters into bankruptcy.

By Customer: Customer will have the right to terminate the [services agreement] [MSA] if: (1) Vendor fails to perform any of its material obligations and does not cure such default within [SPECIFY NUMBER OF DAYS] or (2) Vendor enters into bankruptcy.

[SPECIFY ANY OTHER TERMINATION RIGHTS, E.G., TERMINATION FOR CONVENIENCE.]

Rights upon Termination. Vendor will provide transition services to be agreed to Vendor for up to [SPECIFY NUMBER OF DAYS] [before] [after] the effective date of termination for up to of the Service Agreement.

[SPECIFY ANY RIGHTS/OBLIGATIONS WITH RESPECT TO THE TRANSFER OF ASSETS OR AGREEMENTS AND THE RIGHT TO USE INTELLECTUAL PROPERTY.]

[SPECIFY ANY RESTRICTIONS ON THE SOLICITATION OF EMPLOYEES.]

Indemnification. The [services agreement] [MSA] will provide appropriate indemnification provisions for items such as intellectual property infringement, tangible and personal property damage, [environmental compliance] and other items to be agreed.

Dispute Resolution. [SPECIFY DISPUTE ESCALATION PROCEDURES.]

Force Majeure. [ADD APPLICABLE FORCE *MAJEURE* PROVISION.]

Insurance. [SPECIFY INSURANCE REQUIREMENTS.]

Standard Miscellaneous Provisions. The [services agreement] [MSA] will include standard provisions regarding, e.g., confidentiality, notice, assignment, governing law, compliance with laws.

OUTSOURCING CONTRACT

4.1   OVERVIEW

The most common form of IT contract involves the transfer of control and ownership of all or part of a customer's IT operations to an outsourcing vendor. In return, the customer agrees to compensate the vendor according to a negotiated fee schedule. The transfer of IT operations to the vendor[1] typically includes some or all of the following:

- The transfer to the vendor of customer assets used to manage and facilitate the IT operations being outsourced (e.g., facilities and office equipment used by the IT department) and other related tangible assets

---

1. In IT outsourcing transactions where the vendor is teaming with other service providers or subcontracting a major piece of the services, the transfers, assignments, licenses, and sublicenses described in the following list may be to the vendor's teaming partner or subcontractor.

- The assignment or license to the vendor of proprietary methodologies and/or technology used by the customer in connection with its IT operations

- The assignment or sublicense to the vendor of any third-party methodologies and/or technologies previously used by the customer in connection with its IT operations

- The transfer to the vendor of all or a significant portion of the customer employees previously involved in providing the outsourced services to the customer's organization

Thereafter, the vendor assumes responsibility for operating and managing the customer's IT operations and providing the IT services previously provided by the employees and consultants of the customer (except for certain responsibilities specifically retained by the customer, e.g., strategic control).

Given the wide variety of business issues and the many different legal disciplines involved in even the simplest form of outsourcing transaction, it should come as no surprise that one of the most difficult, if not the most difficult, stages of an outsourcing transaction is drafting and negotiating the contract. To an attorney familiar with general corporate practice, an outsourcing agreement may resemble a hybrid asset purchase and sale agreement and sale/leaseback agreement, in that there is typically a sale of assets or transfer of operations, a transfer of employees, and a lease back to the customer of the IT services that were divested. In an increasing number of IT outsourcing transactions, the basic structure of the deal resembles a project finance arrangement. Add to this the fact that an outsourcing contract is essentially a services agreement, and one can see how the IT outsourcing contract may be more than a hundred pages long.

Although it may seem daunting, drafting and negotiating an IT outsourcing contract can be distilled into five basic issues that must be considered and addressed by the parties:

1. What is it?
2. Who does it?
3. Who owns it?
4. How much is paid for it?
5. What happens if it is not done?

If, at the end of the contract negotiation process, the parties are confident that these five issues have been fairly and comprehensively addressed, it is likely that the relationship between the parties will survive the inevitable day-to-day disputes that arise in complex contractual relationships and, hopefully, flourish as methodologies and technology advance.

It is important to note at this point that a fair contract is not one that is necessarily ideal from either party's perspective. As discussed in Chapter 3, a negotiation with respect to an outsourcing arrangement is not one that either party should seek to win. A fair contract may well be one that requires both parties to perform in a way that will not result in optimal economic performance (as each party may define it). Similarly, there is no bright line for determining when a contract is sufficiently comprehensive, because comprehensiveness is in the eye of the beholder. A contract that might be deemed comprehensive for one organization could, in the eyes of another organization, be deemed insufficiently detailed to allow the customer to realize the anticipated benefits.

In any event, the threshold concern in addressing the five basic issues set forth earlier is to determine what the "it" is. From the vendor's perspective, the "it" is a sufficient level of detail so that the vendor is not required to perform services it did not anticipate in its cost models (or, perhaps more important, services it did anticipate at service levels it did not account for in its cost models) and for the customer to receive the services it anticipated receiving when it made the decision to enter into the agreement. With respect to the customer's employees who are being transitioned to the vendor, the "it" is to adequately address the terms under which such employees will be hired and fired (e.g., to define the benefits the employees will be receiving).

As with any contract, the contracting party must identify and evaluate the fundamental risks and anticipated benefits associated with the transaction before negotiations begin. As discussed in Chapter 3, the key risk and reward factors must serve as the basis for any negotiation strategy (regardless of which side of the transaction you represent) and should be reviewed and updated as the negotiations proceed.

4.2 USE OF ATTORNEYS

One virtually unavoidable consequence of entering into an outsourcing transaction is that the customer will need the services of an attorney, whether corporate or outside counsel. Most vendors make extensive use of corporate (and to some extent outside) counsel, as well as "contract professionals" who often function in the role that an attorney would typically fill. In addition, many companies have rules requiring the involvement of an attorney with respect to any contract for more than a specified amount of money. In many instances, it is simply the complexity of the vendor's standard form or the obvious attempts by the vendor to limit its liability and disclaim all forms of warranties that leads the customer to seek legal advice.

Regardless of whether the attorney involved is a conscript or a volunteer, he or she is all too often used in an inappropriate manner. Business professionals who would never consider entering into a new project without clear-cut objectives, a timetable for development, and contingency plans in the event the project fails will assume that the attorney involved will be able to accurately capture in detail that which is often reflected by only the barest of writings. Perhaps the best advice to give to a business professional with respect to the proper use of counsel in an outsourcing transaction is to view the attorney as one would view a project leader who has been asked to draft a project plan that will consider the various contingencies that may arise over the long term (perhaps as long as 10 years), accurately reflect the hundreds of obligations that the parties need to perform, and make specific provision for what happens in the event that none of the foregoing happens—and to do all of this as soon as possible. Just as the success of the project leader in this example would be largely contingent on the input he or she was given, even the most obstreperous and recalcitrant attorney can be effectively managed by his or her client—and provide value—if the client takes the time to consider what information the attorney will need to perform his or her tasks, periodically monitors these tasks to ensure that they are being handled in an efficient and effective manner, and perhaps most important, realizes that a deal that has taken several months to forge cannot usually be codified overnight.

In addition to drafting and assisting in the negotiating of the agreement, an attorney can be useful as a lightning rod around which difficult issues can be discussed. An outsourcing agreement is at its essence a service agreement, and it is important that the individuals who will be involved on an ongoing basis in providing and receiving the services develop a candid but professional relationship during the negotiations. As discussed in Chapter 3, conflict is inevitable during any negotiations, and, while this does not necessarily mean that the negotiations have to be adversarial, discussions often become heated. The focus of these conflicts should be primarily the parties' legal representatives, not the parties themselves. This will allow each side to articulate its perspective openly without personalizing the discussion. The resolution of most difficult issues is often left to businesspeople, but attorneys should be responsible for framing the issue and, ideally, for proposing alternative solutions.

4.3   KEY CONTRACT ISSUES

This section provides a general discussion of certain key clauses that are typically included in (or at least considered when drafting) the IT outsourcing contract. The content, and in some instances the applicability, of many of the clauses discussed in this section will vary depending on the type of services being outsourced, the scope and duration of the transaction, the overall contract value, and the critical nature of the services (i.e., critical versus noncritical services). This section is intended to provide some guidance for structuring and negotiating the IT outsourcing contract, but it is not intended to be an exhaustive discussion of all of the possible contract issues that may arise. Parties negotiating an IT outsourcing contract also should be mindful that the enforceability and applicability of certain contract provisions (e.g., liability, disclaimers, liquidated damages, noncompetition, transfer of employees, nonsolicitation) may depend on the law governing the contract. These may be state or county laws and may differ even among the transaction documents for deals that involve multiple agreements, such as offshore, international and possibly multisite deals. Accordingly, legal and other counsel as appropriate (e.g., local counsel, regulatory, audit) should be consulted before entering into any IT outsourcing contract.

Ideally, such counsel should be part of the team considering outsourcing and responsible for negotiating the transaction in order to assist the relevant party in fleshing out any particularly troublesome legal issues as early as possible.

In addition to the discussion of key contract issues set forth in the following list, the reader may find useful the checklists for the IT outsourcing agreement set forth in Appendices 4.1, 4.2, and 4.3.

(a) STRUCTURE OF THE IT OUTSOURCING AGREEMENT. One of the first issues confronting legal counsel in the outsourcing process is how to structure the IT outsourcing contract. For a single-country transaction covering the ongoing provision of existing IT services only, a single services agreement setting out each party's responsibilities, obligations, and possible liabilities may be appropriate. However, for more complex transactions, the parties may wish to consider different contract structures. For example, multiple agreements may be necessary to document transactions that include some type of strategic alliance, such as a joint venture, joint marketing, or gainsharing agreement. For multi-country or even multisite transactions, the parties may wish to enter into a master agreement that sets out the general terms and conditions governing the overall provision of services, together with separate country or site agreements setting out the country- or site-specific services as well as any legal or regulatory provisions unique to the country or site. For transactions that include the provision of ongoing services as well as other related services (e.g., business process reengineering, development, or change management), multiple agreements may be appropriate to effectively capture the various components of the business deal. In transactions that involve multiple agreements, the parties will need to determine the interrelationships of the various agreements, such as duration of term, cross-termination, and set off of payments.

Other issues that may drive how a particular outsourcing arrangement is structured include the relationship between the various entities receiving and delivering the services (i.e., is the contracting entity for each of the parties able to bind each of the entities that will receive or deliver the services, or must each of the recipient or delivering entities formally agree to be bound by the terms of the IT outsourcing contract?), cost allocation requirements internal to the customer (e.g., chargebacks), and tax, currency, or other pricing requirements that would necessitate separate country or site agreements (particularly relevant in international transactions). The factors determining the structure of a particular IT outsourcing transaction are shaped largely by the scope and geographic reach of the business deal.

(b) SCOPE OF SERVICES. One of the most important parts of every IT outsourcing contract is the description of the services that will be provided by the vendor. This is often the most difficult part of the agreement to draft because a list of the services currently being provided by the in-house staff typically does not exist and is time consuming to create. The services are typically described in an exhibit or schedule (or a series of exhibits or schedules) to the agreement, which can vary from a broad statement of the services to be provided to a detailed specification of each service to be provided. As part of the effort to codify the services to the greatest extent possible, customers often hire a consultant familiar with IT outsourcing transactions to develop a list of the services and the service levels historically provided by the in-house personnel. When creating this list of the services to be provided by the vendor, the customer should be sure to include any ancillary services (e.g., consulting, training, storage, reporting) it will also require.

(c) TERM.   The term of the IT outsourcing agreement may run from as few as one to as many as ten years, with renewal options. The duration of the contract term typically depends on the customer's objectives in outsourcing, the scope of services being outsourced, whether employees are being transitioned and/or assets are being transferred, the ramp-up costs incurred by the vendor, and the pricing structure offered to the customer. Many vendors favor evergreen contracts in which the agreement remains in effect until terminated by a party for cause or upon a specified period of notice, but key provisions such as price are periodically adjusted. Many customers, however, are seeking shorter terms of one to five years in order to retain greater flexibility with respect to their IT operations.

In addition, many IT outsourcing arrangements involve the provision of IT services as well as other project-related services, such as business reengineering, consulting, or change management services. The agreements documenting these types of arrangements, in some instances, have been divided into two phases—the project phase followed by the ongoing services phase—with the option to terminate or reevaluate the agreement after the end of the first phase. In other instances, however, there is an overlap in the time period during which project services are provided and the time period during which IT services are provided, which makes a multiphase approach less appropriate.

(d) TRANSITION.   The parties should have a clear understanding, typically set out in a detailed transition plan, as to how operations, assets, and employees will be transitioned to the vendor. Depending on the type of operations to be transitioned to the vendor, the parties may want to consider including testing requirements in the agreement, as well as the operation of parallel operating environments for a specified period. In order to reduce customer dissatisfaction in the early phases of the outsourcing relationship, it is useful for the parties to have an understanding about the levels of service to be delivered to the customer during transition.

(e) INTEGRATION.   A critical, although often overlooked, issue is how the provision of IT services (including the introduction of new methodologies and/or technology) will be integrated into the existing customer's organization. For example, if the IT department has established a standardized environment (often after much difficulty), the parties should evaluate whether the new methodologies and/or technology to be introduced by the outsourcing vendor are compatible. The parties will also need to discuss how IT-related failures are to be handled (e.g., through the customer or vendor's help desk).

To flesh out any integration issues, it is important that the customer, and perhaps the vendor if there is a due diligence period, contact representatives from other business departments within the customer organization that may be impacted by the outsourcing arrangement.

(f) MEASURING PERFORMANCE. A brief overview of some of the key issues involving performance follows. A more detailed discussion of how the parties may measure performance under the IT outsourcing contract is provided in Chapter 9.

> *Service levels.* As discussed in Chapter 9, customers and most vendors view service levels as useful measures of ongoing performance. Areas that are commonly measured to assess the level of service provided to the customer include response times, delivery requirements, reporting requirements, customer satisfaction, and guaranteed savings or cost reductions. The types of service levels measured and monitored under an IT outsourcing transaction typically depend on which services the customer considers important to its overall business operations. There are several different approaches for documenting and monitoring service levels. Although the preferable approach is to document the existing service levels achieved by the customer's IT operations group before sending out the RFP or at least before contract signing, an increasing number of customers seek to streamline the process by entering into agreements in which service levels will be established by the joint efforts of the parties after the contract has been signed. Accordingly, many IT outsourcing agreements establish or include a methodology for establishing the service levels to be met by the vendor. Although most vendors agree to establish service levels and report ongoing adherence to service levels, a topic that is a bit more contentious is the consequence if service levels are not achieved. Most customers wish to tie some type of liquidated damage (see the discussion of liquidated damages later in this chapter) or credit to the vendor's nonperformance. The amount and schedule for paying any liquidated damage or credit varies from deal to deal and is typically driven by the overall value of the transaction, the potential damage if there is nonperformance, and the negotiation leverage of the customer.

> *Benchmarking.* Depending on the scope and duration of the IT outsourcing arrangement, the parties may wish to consider including in the contract a mechanism for benchmarking the customer's services and pricing against others in the industry. As discussed further in Chapter 9, if the parties agree to benchmark services and/or pricing, they will need to negotiate the scope of the benchmark (e.g., overall versus individual

services), the pool of organizations that will be benchmarked, and the benchmarker.

Customer satisfaction. A key reason for the customer to enter into an IT outsourcing transaction is to improve user and/or management satisfaction. Increasingly, customers include a requirement that the vendor or a third party perform regular satisfaction surveys, often with an obligation to improve survey results periodically. In instances where the parties agree to include a mechanism for measuring customer satisfaction in the IT outsourcing contract, the parties typically negotiate the content of the satisfaction survey as well as the group of individuals to be surveyed.

Gainsharing. While gainsharing is not receiving as much attention as it once did, some customers still wish to consider gainsharing opportunities. Examples of gainsharing mechanisms include payment to the vendor of an incentive based on customer profits, providing options to the customer, and the payment to the vendor of an incentive based on actual savings generated by the vendor. A more detailed discussion of gainsharing is set forth in Chapter 9.

(g) CURRENCY COMPLIANCE.   The question that arises for customers and vendors is whether the methodologies and technology used by the customer in connection with its IT operations or used, developed, or acquired by the vendor in connection with the provision of IT services are or will be able to convert relevant financial and other data to account for use of the Euro and then read and process data using the Euro.

In negotiating the IT outsourcing contract, the parties should consider the impact, if any, of the Euro or other new currency. Obviously, the issue is more relevant for companies with European operations or those that do business in Europe (keeping in mind that electronic transactions and transactions over the Internet broaden the geographic activities of many companies).

Both the customer and the vendor should ensure that the IT outsourcing contract provides adequate protections regarding the use of the Euro and each party's responsibility and liability in the event the relevant methodologies and technology does not convert, read, and/or process data correctly using the Euro or there are systems or business failures or errors caused by the inability to convert, read, and/or process data using the Euro.

(h) LEGAL AND REGULATORY COMPLIANCE.   One of the more contentious issues that often arises when negotiating an IT outsourcing contract is responsibility for compliance with laws and regulations. The customer typically takes the position that the vendor should be responsible for keeping up to date with respect to all existing and new laws and regulations that may impact the delivery or receipt of the services, as well as being responsible (both operationally and financially) for implementing any changes necessary to be in compliance. This position may apply to all laws and regulations, regardless as to whether they are generally applicable or applicable only to the customer's specific industry. The vendor, however, often takes the position that it is not a compliance company and that the customer is in the best position to keep abreast of, interpret, and bear the financial risk for implementing changes necessitated by laws and regulations applicable to the customer and the customer's industry. The outcome of the negotiations may depend on the type of services outsourced, the leverage of the parties, and whether the customer is in a regulated industry.

(i) TRANSFER OF EMPLOYEES.   If the IT outsourcing arrangement between the customer and the vendor anticipates that the customer will terminate some or all of its IT employees in the hope or with the express requirement that the vendor will hire these employees to provide services to the customer, the IT outsourcing contract should expressly state the nature of the vendor's obligations with respect to these employees. Any transaction of this sort is replete with employment and labor law issues, most notably those involving pension plans, severance payments, termination notice requirements, union rights, and wrongful termination.

The manner in which the termination of the customer's IT employees and the subsequent hiring of such employees by the vendor is handled can determine the success of the customer's decision to outsource. Regardless of how this transfer of employees will be structured, the customer and the vendor must cooperate to ensure that the rights of the customer's employees are not violated by the contract or subsequent conduct of the parties. In light of the potential for such suits, however, the customer should have the IT outsourcing contract reviewed by an attorney familiar with labor and employment issues before entering into any outsourcing arrangement to ensure that the contract does not, on its face, violate any local, state, federal, or country laws.

It is in both parties' interests to be as detailed as possible in the contract with respect to their obligations to the customer's former employees. In this regard, the IT outsourcing contract typically provides for a transition period during which the customer will provide notice to and terminate employees who will no longer be required to provide the applicable IT services. As these employees are terminated, the vendor then offers employment to the individuals it intends to hire. Transition periods may run from three to six months. Another important aspect of the transfer of employees from the customer to the vendor is that the customer's relationship with the vendor may not continue indefinitely. For this reason, the customer may wish to retain certain key employees familiar with its IT operations and requirements to ensure that any migration to another vendor will be adequately supported. Similarly, the customer may wish to expressly retain the right to solicit certain vendor personnel, most notably those who previously worked for the customer, upon expiration or termination of the IT outsourcing contract. A more detailed discussion of employee transfer issues is set forth in Chapter 7.

(j) STAFFING.   Each party typically appoints one individual to manage the IT outsourcing contract and the overall provision and receipt of services. The vendor's representative will play an important role in the customer's organization and will interface with the customer's senior management, so the customer usually wishes to have the right to interview and approve such an individual before appointment. Other possible restrictions on the vendor's representative include requirements that a particular individual remain on the account for a period of time and that this person be dedicated to the customer's account on a full-time basis. Similar provisions often apply to other employees of the vendor whom the parties consider key to the IT outsourcing relationship.

(k) TRANSFER OF ASSETS.   Many IT outsourcing arrangements include the transfer of all or some of the assets and/or facilities used to provide the IT process services or facilitate IT operations. This transfer is often a critical part of the business deal because it may enable the customer to move assets or facilities off its books and, in some instances, receive a much-needed cash infusion or lump-sum payment. In cases where there is an asset or facility transfer, the parties will need to negotiate a purchase and sale agreement (which is typically attached to the IT outsourcing contract as an exhibit).

(l) MANAGEMENT AND CONTROL.   The parties will need to discuss how the procedures for managing and performing the services will be handled. In many cases, the IT outsourcing contract will require the vendor to develop a management procedure manual, as well as a manual detailing the vendor's day-to-day procedures. In addition, the parties will need to discuss how changes to the scope of services, manner of delivery of services, and service levels will be handled. Finally, as earlier discussed under "Integration," the parties should negotiate the vendor's obligation to comply with the customer's standards, methodologies, and architectures as they may be in effect from time to time during the term of the IT outsourcing contract.

(m) CUSTOMER RESPONSIBILITIES.   Just as important as developing a detailed description of services to be provided by the vendor (discussed earlier under section 4.3(b), "Scope of Services") is identifying the roles and responsibilities of the customer. The customer typically wishes to retain certain strategic responsibility, which should be clearly set out in the IT outsourcing contract. In addition, the customer may be obligated to provide or make available certain services or assets, such as desktops, supplies, space, parking, and telephone services, as part of the business deal.

(n) INTELLECTUAL PROPERTY.   Because the outsourcing of a customer's IT operations will undoubtedly involve the access to and use or development of valuable intellectual property, issues relating to intellectual property envelop the IT outsourcing transaction. A discussion of several of these issues follows:

Ownership rights. As a general matter, the IT outsourcing contract should include provisions with respect to the ownership of, and each party's right to use, any intellectual property assigned or licensed to the vendor or used by the vendor in providing services to the customer. Examples of the types of intellectual property that may be addressed in the IT outsourcing contract include the following:

- Methodologies
- Tools
- Software
- Firmware
- Patents
- Inventions
- Improvements that are used or developed in connection with the provision of the IT outsourcing services
- Related documentation
- Residual knowledge
- Trademarks

Different ownership and use rights may apply to items that are customer proprietary, leased or licensed by the customer from a third party, vendor proprietary, leased or licensed by the vendor from a third party, and newly developed or acquired. Ownership and use rights with respect to third-party intellectual property and vendor intellectual property are highlighted next.

Third-party IP. In a typical outsourcing agreement, the customer assigns or licenses to the vendor its proprietary intellectual property that is used in connection with the services and assigns or sublicenses to the vendor any third-party intellectual property that is used in connection with the services. Before effecting any such assignment, license, or sublicense of intellectual property, the customer should determine whether it actually owns all of the rights in the intellectual property to be assigned or licensed or whether its agreements with the third-party licensors permit an assignment of the customer's license or sublicense. In most cases, the customer's agreement with a third-party licensor will expressly prohibit any assignment of the license or grant of a sublicense or will require that the licensor consent to any such assignment or sublicense or may prohibit use of, or access to, the intellectual property by a third party or to provide services to a third party. If the customer effects the assignment, grants the sublicense, or provides access in violation of its agreement with the third-party licensor, the customer runs the risk that the third-party licensor will obtain an injunction preventing the vendor and the customer from using the intellectual property, which could prevent the vendor from providing the services. In addition, the customer (and, perhaps, the vendor) could be liable for damages to the third-party licensor.

It is prudent, therefore, for the customer and the vendor to expressly state in the agreement which party is responsible for obtaining any required consents in respect of third-party intellectual property (or other proprietary material that may be transferred or licensed pursuant to the agreement) and to specify which party will be responsible for paying any additional transfer, access, or license fees that may be imposed by the third party. In many cases, the additional transfer, access, or license fees are significant enough that the failure to allocate how such fees will be paid (e.g., split equally by the parties) can materially reduce the anticipated cost savings.

Many vendors advocate simply proceeding with the transaction as contemplated and providing notice of or soliciting a consent to the assignment or sublicense to the relevant third parties after the agreement is signed. The logic underlying this approach is that a third party will be more likely to impose an unreasonable transfer or license fee if it knows that the outsourcing transaction cannot be implemented until the transfer fee or license fee is paid. Although this strategy may be successful, it is not without risk. The customer should, at the very least, identify any third parties to whom notice should be sent and from whom consent is necessary, and include any anticipated transfer fees in its economic analysis of the transaction.

Vendor IP. The customer should also determine whether the vendor intends to convert the customer to intellectual property that is different from that used by the customer. If this is the case or if such a possibility exists, the customer may wish to retain the right to disapprove of the vendor's selection of intellectual property as a means of retaining control over the services the customer receives. Finally, if the customer is assigning (as opposed to licensing) any proprietary intellectual property to the vendor, it may wish to take back a perpetual license to use the intellectual property in the event the outsourcing agreement expires or is terminated. One of the more controversial aspects of an outsourcing arrangement relates to the use of any vendor's proprietary intellectual property or vendor-licensed third-party intellectual property by the customer after the expiration or termination of the agreement. In many instances, without the right to continue to use the vendor's intellectual property, the customer runs the risk that the agreement will terminate without the customer having the right to continue its operations the day after the termination. The customer, therefore, may wish to include in the IT outsourcing contract an express right for it or its agent (such as another outsourcing vendor) to operate the vendor's intellectual property in the event of the expiration or termination of the agreement. As a result, many IT outsourcing contracts contain the salient provisions of an intellectual property license agreement as well. Another common approach is to incorporate a separate license agreement by reference into the outsourcing agreement. In any event, the customer may wish to ensure that the license granted to it will survive the termination of the agreement for any reason.

The parties should carefully consider the terms of the license offered by the vendor before finalizing the IT outsourcing contract. For example, will the customer be obligated to pay for any transfer or access fees that may arise as a result of the expiration or termination of the underlying outsourcing agreement? A provision requiring a subsequent outsourcing vendor to sign the original vendor's standard form confidentiality agreement may well prevent the customer from entering into any subsequent outsourcing agreements because the terms of these confidentiality agreements are typically onerous. The scope of the license and any restriction placed on the third-party maintenance of the intellectual property must also be considered. In addition, the customer should consider whether any of the vendor intellectual property (e.g., source code) should be placed in escrow for the customer's benefit in the event of the vendor's bankruptcy (or the bankruptcy of any of the vendor's licensors) or cessation of the vendor's business.

(o) REPORTS AND DOCUMENTATION. The IT outsourcing agreement typically specifies the types of reports that will be provided by the vendor to the customer, as well as the delivery times for each report. The parties should also discuss whether the vendor will provide any other documentation to the customer (e.g., manuals, user documentation) and, if so, which party owns such documentation.

(p) OWNERSHIP AND RETURN OF DATA. From the customer's perspective, it is important that the IT outsourcing contract specify that the customer owns any data it submits to the vendor and has the right to recover, in a suitable form, a copy of all of its proprietary data upon termination or expiration of the agreement for any reason. Many standard form IT outsourcing contracts provide only that the customer's data will be returned upon expiration, as opposed to termination, of the agreement and do not specify the form in which the data must be returned or the method of returning the data. This can result in the customer being unable to promptly retrieve its data if the agreement terminates as a result of the vendor's default or retrieve its data in a suitable form upon any other termination or expiration of the agreement.

Similarly, the customer should be wary of a clause that states that the vendor will return the customer's data provided that the customer has fully performed its obligations under the agreement at that time. Most disputes that arise under outsourcing agreements relate to whether the services are being performed according to the specified service levels. In these circumstances, it is common for the customer to withhold payment of all or a portion of the specified fees as a means of gaining negotiating leverage over the vendor.

Withholding of payments is typically in violation of the IT outsourcing contract, and a court might well find that the customer has not performed all of its obligations under the contract if the vendor invokes that clause as a means of forcing the customer to pay all outstanding amounts before returning the customer's data. In effect, the customer becomes a hostage to the vendor's refusal to return its data until the vendor is paid in full. The customer should also seek to limit its expense of recovering its data from the vendor and should require the vendor to delete all of the customer's data from the vendor's records upon expiration or termination of the agreement. Finally, the IT outsourcing contract should protect the customer against the risk of the vendor withholding the customer's data in the event of a dispute between the parties by periodically requiring the vendor to provide a copy of such data to the customer or a third-party escrow agent.

(q) CONFIDENTIAL INFORMATION.   The customer should assume that in any outsourcing transaction, the vendor will have access to some or all of the following information and data:

- Customer proprietary know-how, methodologies, and technology
- Lists of customers and prospective customers
- Internal financial data and projections
- Strategic plans
- New product development data
- Market surveys and analyses
- Research pricing, marketing, and inventory data and projections

The potential injury to the customer or to others who may make claims against the customer, by reason of the theft, misuse, misappropriation, or disclosure of information in the customer's possession, cannot be overstated.

For example, the customer may also have assembled a variety of information to which fiduciary obligations attach, such as the following:

- Personal data concerning employees
- Reports received from franchises or licensees
- Confidential information concerning customers

Similarly, the customer will undoubtedly have access to certain vendor information and data that the vendor considers confidential. Such data and information may include the following:

- Vendor proprietary know-how, methodologies, and technology
- Strategic plans
- New product development data

- Operating procedures
- Pricing models

Accordingly, the confidentiality of each party's data and information should be protected by the IT outsourcing contract. The agreement must require each party and its agents to keep the other's proprietary data and information confidential and prohibit the use of such data and information for any purpose other than providing or receiving the services. The agreement should also give the parties the express right to obtain injunctive relief (see the discussion under section 4.3(ai), "Injunctive relief") to prevent the unauthorized disclosure of its confidential information.

The IT outsourcing contract may also include the following data-related provisions: a data security provision, a provision requiring the vendor to implement certain security measures in the event the vendor provides services to the customer's competitors at the same facility or using the same resources, and a provision outlining how attorney–client privileged documents should be handled.

(r) BUSINESS RECOVERY. The customer should consider which obligations the vendor will assume with respect to business recovery in the event of a disaster or force majeure event (i.e., an event outside the vendor's control). For example, will the vendor be required to maintain a "hotsite" from which services can be provided until services can be restored at the regular service location? Will the vendor be required to interface with certain other vendors in the event of a disaster or follow certain escalation procedures? In addition, the customer may wish to consider limiting the duration of any interruption of the services by providing that the customer can terminate the agreement without liability or obtain services from a third party if the services are interrupted for more than a specified period. Finally, the contract should specify what priority will be given to the customer's services in the event of a disaster that affects more than one of the vendor's customers and may require the vendor to restore the customer's critical services within a specified period.

(s) PRICING/FEES. A discussion of pricing/fee structures typically implemented in IT outsourcing arrangements is set forth in Chapter 6.

(t) PAYMENTS. The parties will have to negotiate when invoices will be paid (e.g., in arrears, in advance), in which manner (e.g., wire transfer), and in what currency. Most vendors propose that payments be made in advance of the services being provided. Because the customer will lose the "cost of money" if payments are made in advance, the customer typically wishes to pay net 15 to 45 days. The customer's position may depend on its current payment practices with other vendors.

With respect to disputed amounts, the parties may wish to consider including a provision that allows the customer to withhold disputed amounts with an obligation to pay amounts in dispute exceeding a certain threshold into escrow. It is very important to the customer to include language that requires the vendor to continue to perform services in the event of a fee dispute.

(u) TAXES.   The parties should research the extent of the tax liability that will be imposed in connection with the IT outsourcing contract and any supplemental agreements before entering into any IT outsourcing arrangement and determine how any such liability will be allocated between them. The allocation of tax is becoming an increasingly controversial subject in outsourcing agreements because many states and countries impose a tax on services.

(v) DEALING WITH BUSINESS VARIABILITY.   No customer's business remains static over the term of the IT outsourcing contract (particularly when the term is as long as 10 years). Therefore, it is important that the parties consider during contract negotiations possible changes in the customer's (and the vendor's) business over the term of the IT outsourcing contract and include provisions in the outsourcing agreement that allows for business variability. Examples of provisions that deal with business variability include the following:

> *Additional and reduced resource charges.* The IT outsourcing contract typically includes rates at which the customer may receive additional resources or services, as well as rates by which the baseline fee will be reduced if lesser resources or services are used. The rates may vary depending on the amount of resource needed and the amount of notice given.

> *Renegotiation trigger.* The IT outsourcing contract may include a renegotiation right if the customer's demand for services increases or decreases above or below a certain level. An example of such a provision is:

>> In the event that Customer's use of the Services increases or decreases more than [***] percent in the aggregate [per Service], Customer and Vendor shall negotiate and implement an appropriate adjustment to the Fees. In the event Customer and Vendor cannot agree on the adjustment to the Fees required by this Section, such disagreement shall be submitted to dispute resolution.

> *Termination right.* The IT outsourcing contract may include a partial or full termination right if the customer's demand for services decreases below a certain level. Such a termination right may be tied to a termination fee.

(w) AUDIT.   The following topics should be considered regarding audits:

> *Services.* The customer typically wishes to retain the right for its auditors and agents to audit the vendor's operations and records to ensure that the vendor is complying with its obligations under the IT outsourcing contract, as well as governmental rules and regulations. Such an audit may include the right to periodically inspect the vendor's premises. The parties will need to discuss each party's obligation in the event that an audit

reveals noncompliance with agreed-on procedures, government rules, and regulations.

Fees. The customer should also have the right to audit the fees charged by the vendor. This right typically extends back for a reasonable period, and the vendor is obligated to provide sufficiently detailed financial information to verify the charges under the IT outsourcing contract. Vendors are particularly sensitive, with good cause, about an audit provision that could potentially allow the customer to access the cost data with respect to the vendor's fees. It is unlikely that the customer has a legitimate need for this cost data, and many customers simply choose to require that sufficiently detailed information be provided solely to verify the fees they have paid. In any event, the customer typically wishes to be able to recover the amount of any overcharges, plus interest from the date payment was made. Similarly, in most cases, the vendor may wish to be able to recover the amount of any undercharges.

Security and SAS 70 audits. More customers are including in the outsourcing contract a requirement that the vendor perform annual security and/or SAS 70-type audits. The timing and costs of such audits are often the subject of significant negotiation.

(x) REPRESENTATIONS AND WARRANTIES. Many agreements include extensive representation and warranty clauses. Most customers insist on warranties from the vendor to the effect that it will provide the services as specified in the agreement; it will accommodate a specified increase in the amount of the customer's use of the services; and any intellectual property provided by the vendor will not infringe upon the proprietary rights of any third party. Examples of other possible representations and warranties of the vendor are representations with respect to the vendor's financial viability, the number of vendor personnel who will be staffed on the project, and the vendor obtaining all necessary licenses and permits.

In an effort to reduce risk (and therefore liability exposure), the vendor also typically insists on certain representations and warranties from the customer. These representations and warranties may include that the customer is authorized to enter into the contract, the customer will pay any amounts due, including taxes, and any intellectual property provided by the customer will not infringe on the proprietary rights of a third party.

(y) LIABILITY. In the IT outsourcing marketplace, imposing some type of cap or limitation on direct and consequential damages, with certain exceptions, has become the norm. Vendors generally attempt to limit their liability to direct damages only by excluding consequential and indirect damages and place a cap on any direct damages that may arise (e.g., a multiple of XXX months' fees). In order to avoid a claim that a limitation of liability provision is, on its face, overreaching, such limitations often provide for a variety of exceptions, including, for example, gross negligence and intentional misconduct of a party, any liability arising in connection with the indemnification clause, and breach of confidentiality or security.

(z) LIQUIDATED DAMAGES. Damages cannot be awarded without proof of an economic loss. It is often difficult, if not impossible, however, for an aggrieved party to prove the dollar amount involved. The parties may agree to liquidated damages, an agreed-on monetary remedy, in instances where it is difficult to ascertain actual damages (e.g., failure to meet project milestones or failure to meet certain service levels). In many outsourcing agreements, liquidated damages take the form of adjustments to the base fee under the agreement. For example, if the vendor fails to perform according to the service levels for a specified period, then the liquidated damages to the customer might take the form of a credit against the next month's base fee.

   Liquidated damage clauses are closely scrutinized because the law typically will refuse to enforce any provision it deems a penalty. A penalty, simply defined, is an agreed-on damage that bears no reasonable relation to the complained-of injury. As a result, liquidated damage provisions should attempt to establish a fair approximation of what actual damages would have been if the process of establishing actual damages had been carried out. Thus, if the provision fixes an unreasonably large liquidated damage, it may be void as a penalty. The unreasonableness of a liquidated damages provision is judged as of the time the contract was entered into, as opposed to the time at which the damage arose. Although vendors typically resist including a liquidated damages clause in the agreement, a persistent customer can get the vendor to accept such a clause if the damages are reasonable and a cap is placed on the amount of such damages. Finally, it is important for the customer to realize that an enforceable liquidated damages provision may preclude a claim for actual damages for the complaint of breach of the agreement.

(aa) TERMINATION. The agreement should provide for a means by which the customer may terminate the agreement upon the occurrence of certain events. It is critical that the customer have the express right to terminate the agreement in the event of a material breach of the agreement by the vendor. Agreements typically provide that, upon the failure of the vendor to perform any of its obligations under the agreement, the customer may give the vendor notice of such failure. The vendor is then given a certain number of days to cure the breach. If the vendor has not cured the breach within the specified period, the customer may terminate the agreement. The agreement may limit any such cure period to a certain number of days (e.g., 30, 60, 90). When establishing a cure period, the customer should consider how long it can realistically wait for the vendor to cure a failure to provide a critical service; in many cases, a 24-hour period during which services are not being provided will cripple the customer's business. As a result, it is often necessary to establish different cure periods for different defaults.

Customers, however, often try to limit the types of events that could trigger the vendor's right to terminate. At a minimum, the vendor should require a termination right for nonpayment.

In addition to termination for breach, the agreement may provide for termination upon the occurrence of other events (e.g., change in control of the customer's business, extraordinary or unforeseen events, a *force majeure* event exceeding a certain number of days, failure to respond within a certain time period). Agreements with initial and renewal terms may typically be terminated upon a certain number of days' notice before the expiration of a term. Evergreen agreements are typically terminable by either party upon six months' to a year's notice.

Finally, most customers wish to include a right to terminate at any time in whole or in part for convenience. Although such a right is typically granted to the customer, the vendor resists a broad termination for convenience provision. The parties need to negotiate the fees applicable in the event of an early termination.

(ab) EFFECT OF TERMINATION. Because of the critical nature of the services that the vendor is providing to the customer and the crucial nature of the data in the vendor's possession to the customer's business, IT outsourcing contracts frequently obligate the vendor to perform certain services after the termination or expiration of the contract. In this regard, the contract should require the vendor to provide post-termination services to support the customer's migration to another vendor or development of an internal organization for a specified period. This will also ensure that the vendor does not withhold performance as a means of gaining an advantage during a dispute about whether the termination of the agreement was appropriate. Another important post-termination obligation of the vendor should be to return to the customer all of its data and information, together with any customer-owned methodologies, technology, and assets. The customer may also wish to require the vendor to cease using (and, perhaps, destroy) any of the customer's forms or stationery. Finally, the customer should consider whether it will continue to need use of any vendor methodologies, technology, and assets during the post-termination transition period or after the termination or expiration of the IT outsourcing contract and, if so, include in the IT outsourcing contract a lease or license with respect to such methodologies, technology, and assets for the transition period or after contract termination or expiration.

Most outsourcing contracts include detailed exit rights, including rights with respect to software, equipment, third-party contracts, and vendor personnel. It is important to plan for the "divorce" at the onset of the relationship because, upon termination or expiration, there typically is not an even allocation of leverage.

(ac) TERMINATION ASSISTANCE. The IT outsourcing contract typically requires the vendor to provide termination assistance services upon expiration or termination so that the customer is assured of an orderly transition of the services. These services should include the express right of the customer to receive the base services for some reasonable period after the expiration or termination date, together with any other services that might be reasonably requested by a customer in connection with the transition of the services to another outsourcing vendor or back to the customer. Many contracts seek to limit the amount and types of charges the vendor can impose with respect to these termination assistance services under the theory that an unfettered right to charge will lead to excessive fees.

(ad) DISPUTE RESOLUTION.   Because operational disputes are an inevitable consequence of outsourcing arrangements, the IT outsourcing contract typically establishes an informal dispute resolution mechanism to deal with day-to-day operational disputes (e.g., processing priorities). Many IT outsourcing contracts provide for the formation of a management committee to administer such dispute resolution mechanisms. The management committee typically consists of both vendor and customer management personnel familiar with the arrangement between the parties and should be required to meet at specified times and in a specified location.

(ae) INDEMNITIES.   Most outsourcing contracts include well-negotiated indemnification clauses. Examples of some typical indemnities include indemnification for HR-related claims arising after (if the customer) or before (if the vendor) the commencement date of the IT outsourcing contract, certain property damage and personal injuries, certain security and confidentiality breaches, infringement claims based on the other party's intellectual property, and certain environmental claims.

(af) INTERNATIONAL ISSUES.   If the IT outsourcing transaction involves locations or services outside of the United States, additional legal issues may arise. Issues to consider include transborder data flow; data security; import/export controls; ownership of machines, software, methodologies, tools, and work product; audit requirements; methods of payment; currency and inflation risks; human resource issues; and taxes. A more detailed discussion of international issues is set forth in Chapter 11.

(ag) ASSIGNMENT.   An outsourcing agreement is analogous in many respects to a personal services agreement in that the customer has contracted for what it perceives are unique services from a particular source. Accordingly, the agreement typically provides that the vendor cannot assign the agreement to a third party without the customer's consent. At the least, this will prevent the vendor from assigning the agreement to a competitor of the customer. The vendor may request that the nonassignment obligations apply to the customer as well. The customer may, however, want to retain the right to assign the agreement under certain circumstances (e.g., merger or corporate reorganization) without the vendor's approval.

(ah) GOVERNING LAW AND VENUE. Virtually all standard form service contracts contain a provision setting forth the applicable law. In most instances, the vendor will assert that its corporate policy dictates the choice of governing law. Despite this assertion, the customer may insist on the governing law of its choice. For a contractual choice-of-law provision to be enforceable, the state's law chosen by the parties must bear a "reasonable relation" to the transaction involved. A court will not enforce a choice-of-law provision if the transaction has no relationship with a jurisdiction whose law is to apply.

Although a choice-of-law provision may seem innocuous, it can have a substantial effect on the parties' rights. For example, some states hold that an inconspicuous provision limiting or excluding express and implied warranties is nevertheless enforceable as long as it was read and understood; other states' courts disagree and require a conspicuous (i.e., large type size) display. Thus, the application of a particular state's law may substantially affect the outcome of any dispute under the agreement.

(ai) KEY MISCELLANEOUS PROVISIONS. The following miscellaneous provisions should also be considered:

Survival. Certain obligations of the parties, such as the indemnity and confidentiality obligations of each party, should survive any termination or expiration of the IT outsourcing contract.

Publicity. Each of the parties may wish to limit the other's right to use its name in connection with advertising or marketing efforts.

No solicitation. It is common for a party, most frequently the vendor, to prohibit the other party from soliciting or hiring its employees. Such clauses typically restrict a party's right to solicit or hire an employee of the other party during the term of the IT outsourcing contract for a certain period after termination or expiration. As discussed earlier, the customer may wish to expressly retain the right to solicit and hire its former employees upon termination or expiration of the contract.

No waiver. Most outsourcing agreements contain a clause providing that the waiver of any breach is not a waiver of any subsequent breaches. Without the inclusion of specific contract terms, and sometimes even in the face of such provisions, the law has recognized that a party's conduct may modify his or her prior agreement. Where the conduct of the parties after signing the agreement clearly indicates that certain provisions were not given effect by the parties, courts will frequently treat such provisions as inoperative. Waivers often arise in law by reason of the inaction of a party. For example, an agreement may require the vendor to deliver a particular report every 24 hours. If over a period of months or years the actual delivery practice has been 72 hours, judges can be led to the conclusion that the time requirement set forth in the agreement was not really important and, in any event, was waived by the practice of the parties.

As has been stated, many service agreements require continuing performance over an extended time period. Inaction, even if occasioned by mere lack of attention on the part of a party, can have disastrous effects on a clear and unequivocal agreement. Agreements generally provide that the only valid waiver is one reduced to writing and signed by the party to be charged with the waiver, that there will be no waiver implied by action or inaction, and that the waiver of a single breach shall not be deemed a waiver of any subsequent breach.

Injunctive relief. There is a slightly more liberal attitude on the part of courts toward stopping or preventing people from doing things that might injure others. Injunctions often involve contractual elements known as *restrictive covenants*. Restrictive covenants are agreements, or portions of agreements, in which a party has contracted not to engage in a particular activity. Before a party can get an injunction, he or she must prove that the injury that will be sustained if the act is carried out cannot be adequately compensated for by money; that the party will be irreparably banned if the action is not prohibited; and that the party has no other remedy. For example, a person who sells a business and agrees not to solicit or do business with the existing customers of the business being sold will be enjoined from violating that agreement. The release of genuine trade secrets, in the face of an agreement not to do so, will conventionally be enjoined. If a particular methodology is developed by a consultant as a proprietary product for the customer and if, in the face of a contractual prohibition, the consultant copies the relevant documentation and tries to sell that methodology to others, the courts will normally enjoin him or her from doing so. For restrictive covenants to be enforceable by injunction, they must be carefully drafted. Covenants that are overly broad, inadequately particularized, or unduly restrictive of free commerce will not be enforced by the judicial system. Restrictive covenants, when contracted for, are often of critical importance in a transaction and often involve matters in which monetary damages are inadequate. Accordingly, restrictive covenants should be drafted with great care.

4.4 RETAINING STRATEGIC CONTROL

One risk frequently identified when a customer is asked about the risks and benefits of outsourcing is loss of control over the strategic direction of the IT operations. The outsourcing customer, however, does not necessarily have to turn over all control of the IT operations to the outsourcing vendor. In fact, the retention of strategic control by the customer is often key to a successful outsourcing relationship because it ensures that the customer has control over its IT direction, which is core to the customer's business even if the actual implementation of it may not be. This section will touch on some of the ways a customer can retain a degree of control without micromanaging the vendor.

(a) TECHNICAL ARCHITECTURE AND PRODUCT STANDARDS. In an effort to retain control over the strategic direction of IT operations, many customers wish to include in the IT outsourcing contract a provision stating that the customer is responsible for dictating and/or approving all technical architecture and product standards and that the vendor is required to comply with all existing *and future* standards dictated by the customer (possibly with the vendor's consultation). The cost of compliance with existing standards is typically included in the base fees. The cost of compliance with future standards may either be borne by the vendor as part of the base fees or borne by the customer to the extent that any incremental costs are incurred by the vendor in connection with implementing any changes.

(b) IDENTIFYING CUSTOMER RESPONSIBILITIES.   It is important that the customer map out during the early stages of the IT outsourcing process which areas it considers strategic (e.g., the types of new methodologies or technology to be implemented) and what areas it considers operational (e.g., how the back office is run on a day-to-day basis). Examples of areas that customers may consider critical to their strategic direction include the following:

- Major changes in existing methodologies or technology (e.g., upgrades to existing hardware that will impact output or cost)
- Implementation of new methodologies or technology
- Changes to services
- Requirements for new projects
- Contract administration
- Internal liaison with corporate management

If an area is deemed strategic, and there are not overriding economic considerations, the customer should retain responsibility for that area either by maintaining that area in-house (e.g., some customers consider development of certain applications strategic and therefore wish to retain all or part of the development function in-house) or retaining control over that area (e.g., by having approval rights over how the function is carried out).

(c) IN-HOUSE CAPABILITIES.   In many cases, the IT outsourcing contract includes provisions to allow the customer to retain strategic control of its IT operations, but the customer does not retain an adequate number of qualified personnel to manage the outsourcing relationship and exercise the terms of the IT outsourcing contract. The customer will need to weigh its need to manage the vendor and administer the contract against its desire to transfer as much responsibility to the vendor as possible. In a full-scale IT outsourcing transaction (i.e., where all functions of the particular IT function are outsourced), the retained employees are typically managers and key technical personnel, such as the following:

- Project executive
- Project executive's direct reports
- Contract administrator
- Key operational and technical personnel (who understand and are able to manage and review day-to-day operations)

(d) RIGHTS OF APPROVAL.   The customer may wish to ensure that the IT outsourcing contract grants it adequate approval rights over strategic areas and functions. Examples of two key provisions are as follows:

1. Except as may be necessary on an emergency basis to maintain the continuity of the Services, Vendor shall not, without Customer's consent, modify (1) the composition or the nature of the Services or (2) the manner in which the Services are provided or delivered if such modification or modifications would have an adverse effect on the business of Customer.

2. Except as may be approved by Customer, Vendor shall not make any changes or modifications, to the Customer Intellectual Property, the Developed Intellectual Property or the Vendor Intellectual Property (the "Intellectual Property") that would adversely alter the functionality of the Intellectual Property, degrade the performance of the Intellectual Property or materially affect the day-to-day operations of Customer's business.

(e) VENDOR CONCERNS.   Following are some possible vendor concerns:

Micromanagement. The vendor will likely object to any constraints on its ability to perform the services on the grounds that the customer should be concerned about output, not operations. The vendor may argue that to be able to provide the services at lower cost, it must have the freedom to control how operations are run. Why, for example, does the customer care about the methodologies or technology being used, if the output is not impacted? The answer, from the customer's prospective, is that the methodologies and technology being used may impact other costs and efficiency and cause integration and compatibility issues with other areas of the customer's organizations. Although most customers agree that they should not micromanage the vendor, most also want to retain some control over the methodologies or technology being used.

Dedicated vs. shared environments. The vendor may take a different position on the amount of control retained by the customer for dedicated and shared environments. The customer has an easier argument for retaining approval rights in a dedicated environment because other customers are not exercising similar approval rights.

Cost considerations. The vendor may argue that if the customer wants methodologies or technology that the vendor would not otherwise implement, then it will only implement these methodologies or technology at the customer's cost. Similarly, the vendor may argue that if the customer will not approve a change, the vendor is not liable for any problems caused by the failure to implement the change.

4.5 ASSEMBLING THE TEAM

Because of the complex nature of the IT outsourcing transaction, it is useful for each party to assemble its team of experts as early in the transaction as possible. The team may include representatives from business, technical, finance, legal, audit, environmental, and human resources. If the transaction is international in scope, the team may need to be expanded to include local representatives from each of these categories.

KEY ISSUES IN OUTSOURCING AGREEMENTS[2]

KEY ISSUES IN OUTSOURCING AGREEMENTS

1. Structure of the Outsourcing Agreement
   - How will the outsourcing agreement be structured?
     - A single services agreement
     - A master agreement with site-specific, country-specific, or entity-specific service agreements
     - Separate agreements for reengineering, development, and ongoing management
     - Separate agreements documenting the terms applicable to a joint venture/strategic alliance relationship and the terms applicable to ongoing services
   - What is the inter-relationship between these agreements if separate (e.g., cross-termination, payment)?
   - Factors that may affect the agreement structure include:
     - *Scope of services.* Will Vendor be providing any reengineering or development services?
     - *Geographic scope.* Single country vs. international agreement
     - *Scope of services at specific sites.* Will all Customer sites receive the same services or will each Customer site receive different services?
     - *Types of entities receiving/delivering the services.* Is the contracting entity for each of the parties able to bind the entities that will receive/deliver the services or must each of the recipient/delivering entities agree to be bound by the master agreement?

---

2. Note: This checklist is intended to illustrate the types of legal issues that customers may wish to consider in connection with contracting for application services. The items included in this checklist may not cover all of the issues that may arise in a particular transaction. Legal issues will likely vary depending on the type of service being provided and the scope of the services. This checklist or any part thereof should only be used after consultation with your legal counsel. Legal counsel should be consulted prior to entering into or negotiating any transaction covering the provision of application services.

- *Cost allocation.* Are there any cost allocation requirements internal to customer that would drive separate site/entity agreements?
- *Taxes.* Are there any tax requirements that would drive separate service agreements?

2. Contracting Party
   - Who will sign the agreement on behalf of Customer? On behalf of Vendor?
   - If there is a master agreement with separate service agreements, will the same party that signs the master agreement sign the service agreements?

3. Entities Receiving Services from Vendor
   - Determine who will receive services from Vendor
   - Entities may include:
     - Customer affiliates
     - Joint ventures/alliances
     - Contractors
     - Suppliers
     - Clients of Customer
   - Will Customer have the option of adding/deleting entities over the term?
   - How will mergers/acquisitions/divestitures be handled? What will Customer's and Vendor's ongoing obligations be?
   - Which entity(ies) will have payment obligations? Are recipients of services third-party beneficiaries?

4. Entities Providing Services to Customer
   - Determine which entity (or entities) will provide the services to Customer.
   - Will there be any subcontracting/teaming relationships?
   - For international deals, how will Vendor provide resources/services in each country? Will Vendor use affiliated entities or subcontractors?
   - What are Customer's rights to approve/remove subcontractors?
   - Which entity(ies) will have performance/indemnification obligations?

5. Term
   - What is the commencement date of services? Will there be one commencement date for all sites? Will there be one commencement date for all services (e.g., reengineering, development, and ongoing management)?
   - How long is the term of the agreement? If the transaction includes multiple agreements, are all of the agreements co-terminus? If there is a master agreement with separate site/service agreements, are all of the agreements co-terminus?

      o   Will there be a pilot period?

      o   What are each party's renewal rights? What type of notice is required for renewal?

6.   Scope of Services

      o   Determine the general scope of services to be provided by Vendor.

      o   Determine those services that will be provided in-house by Customer or to Customer by a third party.

      o   Describe in detail the services (typically by service category) to be provided by Vendor.

      o   Define Customer's responsibilities with respect to the services to be provided by Vendor (i.e., definition of requirements, strategic direction, approvals).

      o   Define existing and future requirements (e.g., capacity requirements, volume changes, business changes). Allocate managerial and financial responsibility.

7.   Transition Plan

      o   How will the transition of services to Vendor be handled?

      o   Will there be any redundant/parallel environments?

      o   Determine the performance standards during transition.

      o   How long will the transition period be?

8.   Methodologies

      o   Assess methodologies to be used by Vendor. Are the methodologies proprietary to Vendor or licensed from a third party? If licensed from a third party, are there any use restrictions? What are Customer's rights to use during the term and after expiration/termination?

      o   Will any of Customer's methodologies continue to be used during the term of the transaction? What are Vendor's use rights (e.g., use in connection with services to Customer only; use in connection with other customers)?

      o   How will Vendor transition Customer to Vendor's methodologies (if applicable)?

      o   How will the methodologies introduced by Vendor be integrated with Customer's existing and future methodologies (with respect to the applicable business function as well as other business areas, e.g., information systems)?

      o   Will Vendor be developing/providing any new methodologies? If so, how will ownership/use rights be allocated? How will new methodologies be rolled out (e.g., define time period, consequences for failure to meet deadlines, each party's responsibilities)?

9.   Technology

o   Assess technology to be used by Vendor. Is the technology proprietary to Vendor or licensed from a third party? If licensed from a third party, are there any use restrictions? What are Customer's rights to use during the term and after expiration/termination?

o   Will any of Customer's technology continue to be used during the term of the transaction? What are Vendor's use rights (e.g., use in connection with services to Customer only; use in connection with other customers)?

o   Will the environment be dedicated/shared?

o   How will Vendor transition Customer to Vendor's technology (if applicable)?

o   How will the technology introduced by Vendor be integrated with Customer's existing or future technology (e.g., is Vendor technology compatible with technology used by Customer's information system group)?

o   Will Vendor be developing/providing any new technology? If so, how will ownership/use rights be allocated? How will new technology be rolled out (e.g., define time period, consequences for failure to meet deadlines, each party's responsibilities)?

10.   Assets

o   Will Vendor be purchasing any of Customer's assets (e.g., equipment, real estate)? If so, when will purchase be made (e.g., on date of signing)?

o   How will assets be valued (e.g., book value, fair market value)?

o   Is the transfer of assets necessary in conjunction with the transfer of employees in order to constitute an "automatic transfer" under the particular country's employment/redundancy laws?

11.   Projects

o   Identify any projects that Vendor will be responsible for implementing/managing as part of the transaction.

o   Will Vendor be responsible for any reengineering in connection with its provision of services? If so, what are each party's responsibilities? What are the consequences if the reengineering is not successful or performed by deadlines specified?

o   What is the inter-relationship of Vendor's reengineering responsibilities and Vendor's other services responsibilities (e.g., are they cross-terminable)?

o   Will Vendor be responsible for any new implementations? If so, what are each party's responsibilities? What are the consequences if the reengineering is not successful or performed by deadlines specified?

  ○ Which party will be responsible for purchase/license of third-party methodologies/technologies (if applicable)?

12.   Integration

  ○ How will the methodologies/technologies introduced by Vendor be integrated with other methodologies/technologies used by Customer?

  ○ Have other Customer business areas been contacted for input (e.g., information systems, human resources)?

13.   Transfer of Employees

  ○ Determine whether any or all of Customer employees will be offered employment by, or transitioned to, Vendor or a Vendor subcontractor.

  ○ Identify group of retained employees.

  ○ Review Customer's severance/redundancy policy, if any, to determine whether a transition to Vendor may invoke severance obligations. (If so, factor into Customer's cost analysis.)

  ○ Are there any claims with respect to any of the transitioned employees?

  ○ Compare Customer and Vendor benefits. Are any adjustments necessary?

  ○ Does Vendor require any special screening of employees (e.g., drug testing)?

  ○ Will Vendor require transitioned employees to sign an employment agreement?

  ○ Develop an employee communication plan.

  ○ Determine whether any stay bonuses/incentives are necessary.

14.   Project Staff

  ○ Identify management structure of Vendor as well as Customer in connection with the provision/receipt of services.

  ○ Are there any limitations/restrictions with respect to reassignment/replacement of key Vendor personnel?

  ○ Are there any limitations/restrictions with respect to "churning" of employees?

  ○ How will Customer complaints regarding Vendor personnel be handled?

  ○ Are any special clearances of Vendor personnel necessary?

  ○ Are there any limitations/restrictions with respect to subcontractors?

15. Retained Assets

   ○ Identify which assets Vendor will manage and, of those assets, which assets Vendor will have financial responsibility for.

   ○ Identify which assets Customer will continue to manage and, of those assets, whether Vendor will have any financial responsibility.

   ○ How will the parties act in the event it is not clear where a problem originates from (e.g., root cause analysis)?

16. Agreements to be Reviewed

   ○ Identify any third-party agreements/relationships that may be impacted by the outsourcing, including:
      • Maintenance agreements
      • Subcontracting relationships
      • Other service agreements
      • Methodology/technology licenses
      • Equipment/asset leases
      • Real estate leases/subleases

   ○ Are there any restrictions with respect to third-party management/access or assignment to a third party?

   ○ What are the terms relating to termination/renewal?

   ○ What are the pricing terms, and will they be impacted by the transaction?

   ○ Develop a strategy for notifying third parties, if applicable.

17. Third-Party Consents

   ○ Are any third-party consents necessary in connection with the commencement of the transaction? If so, which party is responsible for obtaining such consents and how will financial responsibility be allocated?

   ○ How will third-party consents be obtained upon the expiration/termination of the transaction (in order to transition agreements/assets back to Customer or Customer's designee)? How will financial responsibility be allocated?

18. Performance Standards

   ○ Identify those services that will have performance standards.

   ○ How will Vendor's performance be measured? Will existing performance standards be used or will performance standards be established on a going-forward basis?

   ○ Identify any permitted downtime and testing.

- ○ How will failures to meet performance standards be handled (e.g., liquidated damages or termination)?
- ○ Will there be any procedures for assessing/determining causes of failures to meet performance standards (e.g., root cause analysis)?
- ○ What performance standards will apply during transition/implementation?

19.   Customer Satisfaction

- ○ Will Vendor be responsible for any type of customer satisfaction reporting?
- ○ Determine pool of employees surveyed (e.g., management, end users).
- ○ How will the results of such surveys be used (e.g., as basis for performance standard)?

20.   Benchmarking

- ○ Determine whether the agreement will include any benchmarking procedures (e.g., benchmarking of services or prices).
- ○ Develop benchmarking procedures (e.g., scope of benchmark, group against which services/prices will be benchmarked).
- ○ Identify benchmarker (e.g., third party, Vendor group).
- ○ How will benchmarking results be reviewed and how will changes, if applicable, be implemented?

21.   Sarbanes-Oxley Considerations

- ○ Determine documentation and training requirements.
- ○ Are any special reports required (such as SAS 70)?

22.   Compliance Issues

- ○ Identify any regulatory/governmental requirements (e.g., timing, notice, consent). (Note: These requirements are typically driven by the type of transaction, e.g., rules governing accounting services, and the type of organization receiving services, e.g., rules governing financial institutions. In addition, compliance issues may vary from country to country or if the transaction involves more than one country.)
- ○ Are the software, equipment, systems, or other materials owned, used, or provided by Vendor in providing the services capable of correctly processing and/or operating without errors or omissions relating to the occurrence in or use by such software, equipment, systems, or other materials of dates or date-dependent data, including from different centuries or more than one century?

- o Are the software, equipment, systems, or other materials owned, used, or provided by Vendor in providing the services compliant with guidelines set forth by industry-specific regulatory bodies?

- o Determine which party is responsible for ensuring compliance. Allocate costs of compliance resulting from changes in laws, rules, or regulations after commencement.

- o Identify any license/permits required to be obtained by Customer and/or Vendor.

- o Consult with legal, regulatory, tax, and audit departments.

23. Transaction-Specific Issues

- o Identify any transaction-specific requirements (e.g., for warehouse distribution transactions, provisions regarding liens; for real estate management transactions, insurance, and environmental obligations; for accounting services transactions, provisions regarding accounting standards and filing deadlines).

- o Consult with legal, regulatory, tax, and audit departments.

24. Customer Responsibilities

- o Identify Customer's responsibilities (e.g., provision of supplies, computers, parking).

- o Will Customer be providing any space/facilities to house Vendor's employees? What are the terms of Vendor's use (e.g., sublease)?

- o Is Customer retaining staff necessary to perform the retained responsibilities (e.g., management, definition of requirements, approvals)?

25. Service Locations

- o Where will Vendor be providing the services from? If such locations are not Customer locations, are there any restrictions on where Vendor may provide services from?

- o Will the service locations be dedicated to Customer or shared facilities?

- o Describe physical security requirements. Are uniforms or other identification required? Does Customer or Vendor have specific codes of conduct?

- o How will breaches of security be handled?

- o Are there any environmental concerns?

26. Management Procedures

- o Will the parties develop management procedures to be used in connection with the provision of the services?

- o How will change control be handled?

27. Reports
   - Identify the performance and other reports that Customer currently generates or receives with respect to the services being outsourced.
   - Identify those reports that Customer wishes to receive from Vendor.
   - Establish deadlines for each report.
   - Will Customer be required to review the reports within a specific time period?
   - How will errors in reports be handled?

28. Data
   - Discuss procedures for handling Customer data. What are Vendor's use rights?
   - How will errors in Customer data be handled?
   - Describe data security requirements at service locations. Are passwords required?
   - How will breaches of security be handled?

29. Proprietary Rights
   - Establish Vendor's right to use Customer proprietary methodologies and technology during the term and after expiration/termination of the agreement.
   - Establish Vendor's right to use during the term and after expiration/termination of the agreement methodologies and technology licensed by Customer from third parties and used in connection with the provision of the services.
   - Establish Customer's right to use Vendor's proprietary methodologies and technology during the term and after expiration/termination of the agreement.
   - Establish Customer's right to use during the term and after expiration/termination of the agreement methodologies and technology licensed by Vendor from third parties and used in connection with the provision of the services.
   - Establish each party's ownership/use rights with respect to methodologies and technology developed or acquired as part of or in connection with the provision of the services.
   - Establish any restrictions governing the use of confidential information.
   - Establish any restrictions governing the use of mentally retained information.
   - Discuss whether noncompetition provisions are appropriate.

30. Audit

- o What are Customer's rights to audit the services and the service locations? How often may Customer exercise any such audit rights?
- o How will the results of any such audit be dealt with?
- o What are Customer's rights to audit the fees?
- o How will overpayments/underpayments be handled?
- o Will interest be charged?

31. Fees

- o Determine the applicable fee structure.
- o Customer should assess actual cost savings, if any. Such analysis should include any new taxes, employee transfer costs, training, and other expenses resulting from the outsourcing.
- o Vendor should assess actual profit margin.
- o Other Fee Provisions:
  - If a base fee structure is used, determine structure for increasing and decreasing fees/resources.
  - Determine the rights of the parties to set off monies owed.
  - To what extent, if any, will Customer be responsible for Vendor expenses (e.g., travel)? Will Vendor use Customer or Vendor expense guidelines?
  - Will there be any cost-of-living adjustments?
  - For international deals, is there any currency risk?
  - Consider a most-favored-customer provision.
  - How will fees be paid (e.g., in what currency, in what manner, and according to what schedule)?
  - How, when, and to what Customer entity(ies) will invoices be issued?
  - Determine the degree of detail to be included on invoices.
  - How will disputed fees/credits be handled (e.g., escrow)? What are the parties' obligations to perform in the event of a dispute?
  - How will changes in business volumes be handled?

32. Taxes

- o Determine liability for sales, use, and other taxes.
- o Determine liability for additional taxes resulting from Vendor's relocation of service locations or rerouting of services.

33.   Additional Services

- ○ How will the provision of additional services be handled? Will Vendor be required to submit a bid? Will any rights of first refusal be granted to Vendor?
- ○ What type of detail must be included in a Vendor proposal?
- ○ To what extent does Customer wish to reserve the right to contract with third parties?

34. Insurance

- ○ Specify Vendor's insurance requirements, for example:
  - Errors and omissions
  - Liability
  - Workers' compensation
  - Automobile
  - Environmental
- ○ Specify any specific bonding requirements.
- ○ Determine whether any parental or other type of guarantee is appropriate.

35. Termination

- ○ Consider early termination rights, for example:
  - Termination for convenience in whole
  - Partial termination for convenience
  - Termination upon change of control of Vendor
  - Termination upon change of control of Customer
  - Termination for breach
  - Termination for nonpayment
  - Termination for failure to provide critical services
  - Termination for failure to meet the performance standards
  - Termination for substantial changes in business
  - Termination for change in financial condition
  - Termination upon the occurrence of a regulatory event
  - Cross-termination with other agreements
- ○ Determine whether and in what instances termination fees are applicable. If so, establish formula for determining applicable termination fees.

36. Exit Rights

- ○ Determine each party's ongoing rights after expiration/termination with respect to proprietary and third-party methodologies, technology, equipment, facilities, subcontracting arrangements, and third-party service agreements.

  o Determine which party will be responsible for transfer/assignment fees imposed by third parties.

  o If Customer has right to purchase certain Vendor assets used to provide the services, how will the purchase price be determined?

37. Termination Assistance

  o Determine the types of assistance Vendor and/or its subcontractors will provide Customer upon expiration/termination.

  o Determine duration of Vendor's termination assistance obligations.

  o How will termination assistance be paid for (e.g., fee schedule, time schedule for payment)?

38. Liability Provisions

  o Assess liability exposure.

  o Determine any liquidated damages to be imposed upon Vendor (e.g., for failure to meet performance standards, for failure to meet implementation schedules).

  o What are each party's indemnification obligations (e.g., for claims of infringement, employee claims).

  o Determine the representations and warranties to be made by each party.

39. Dispute Resolution

  o How will disputes be handled? Will the agreement include an escalation procedure?

  o Will unresolved disputes be handled through arbitration or litigation?

40. Business Continuity

  o Does Vendor have redundant infrastructure?

  o What are Vendor's disaster recovery plans?

  o Where is the Vendor's secondary site?

  o What is Customer's existing business recovery plan? Will Customer's plans be terminated?

  o Specify response times for delivery of business recovery services. Describe escalation procedures.

41. Assignment

  o Specify each party's right to assign its rights/obligations under the agreement in whole or in part.

- ○ Will there be any special assignment rights in the event of a merger/acquisition/divestiture?

- ○ May either party assign to an affiliate/related entity?

42. Solicitation of Employees

- ○ Will there be any limitations/restrictions on Customer's or Vendor's right to solicit and/or hire the other party's employees?

- ○ When will such limitations/restrictions apply (e.g., during the term, after expiration/termination)?

- ○ Will there be any exceptions for blind solicitations (e.g., newspaper advertisements)?

43. Miscellaneous Provisions

- ○ *Notices*. How will notices be given (e.g., by hand, by facsimile)? To whom (e.g., to business manager and/or counsel)?

- ○ *Publicity*. Will there be limitations/restrictions on each party's ability to make public statements regarding the other party and/or the transaction?

- ○ *Governing law*. Determine which state/country law will govern the transaction (or if international transaction with multiple documents, determine which law will govern each part of the transaction).

- ○ *Venue*. Will there be a requirement that any action be brought in a particular venue?

- ○ *Import/export*. Provide any limitations/restrictions on the export/import of data and/or technology.

- ○ *Interpretation of documents*. How will the transaction documents be interpreted in the event of a dispute (e.g., the main agreement will take precedence over the exhibits/schedules, change orders will take precedence over earlier dated documents)?

- ○ *Counterparts*. Specify whether the various transaction documents may be executed in counterparts.

- ○ *Relationship of the parties*. Specify that Vendor is an independent contractor to Customer and that the provision of services does not constitute any type of partnership or joint venture (unless that is expressly the intent).

- ○ *Severability*. Specify that if any provision is held to be invalid that the remaining provisions shall remain in full force and effect.

- ○ *Waivers*. Specify that any delay or omission does not constitute a waiver of rights and that any waiver should not be construed to be a waiver of a subsequent breach/covenant.

- ○ *Entire agreement.* Specify that the transaction documents constitute the entire agreement between the parties.

- ○ *Amendments.* Specify how the transaction documents may be amended (e.g., by writing signed by both parties).

- ○ *Survival.* Specify which provisions of the agreement will survive termination and/or expiration of the agreement.

- ○ *Third-party beneficiaries.* Expressly state that there will not be any third-party beneficiaries under the transaction documents or, if there will be third-party beneficiaries, identify such beneficiaries.

- ○ *Covenant of further assurances.* Expressly state that each party will execute any documents or perform any actions necessary to effectuate the purposes of the agreement.

KEY ISSUES IN OFFSHORE OUTSOURCING AGREEMENTS[3]

1. **Initial Due Diligence**
   - Initial down selection diligence may include:
     - Financial viability
     - Business continuity plans and procedures
     - Experience in U.S. markets
     - Security infrastructure
     - Understanding and compliance with laws
     - Work quality and technical solutions
     - Employee base
     - Cultural fit: Does Vendor understand your corporate environment? Does Vendor have a good understanding of U.S. law and business practices?

2. **Structure of the Outsourcing Agreement**
   - How will the outsourcing agreement be structured?
     - A single services agreement
     - A master agreement with site-specific, country-specific, or entity-specific service agreements
     - Separate agreements for reengineering, development, and ongoing management
     - Separate agreements documenting the terms applicable to a joint venture/strategic alliance relationship and the terms applicable to ongoing services
   - What is the inter-relationship between these agreements if separate (e.g., cross-termination, payment)?

---

3. Note: This checklist is intended to illustrate the types of legal issues that customers may wish to consider in connection with contracting for application services. The items included in this checklist may not cover all of the issues that may arise in a particular transaction. Legal issues will likely vary depending on the type of service being provided and the scope of the services. This checklist or any part thereof should only be used after consultation with your legal counsel. Legal counsel should be consulted prior to entering into or negotiating any transaction covering the provision of application services.

   ○   Factors that may affect the agreement structure include:
   - *Scope of services.* Will Vendor be providing any reengineering or development services?
   - *Geographic scope.* Single country vs. international agreement
   - *Scope of services at specific sites.* Will all Customer sites receive the same services or will each Customer site receive different services?
   - *Types of entities receiving/delivering the services.* Is the contracting entity for each of the parties able to bind the entities that will receive/deliver the services or must each of the recipient/delivering entities agree to be bound by the master agreement?
   - *Cost allocation.* Are there any cost allocation requirements internal to customer that would drive separate site/entity agreements?
   - *Taxes.* Are there any tax requirements that would drive separate service agreements?

3.   Contracting Party

   ○   Who will sign the agreement on behalf of Customer? On behalf of Vendor?

   ○   If there is a master agreement with separate service agreements, will the same party that signs the master agreement sign the service agreements?

4.   Entities Receiving Services from Vendor

   ○   Determine who will receive services from Vendor

   ○   Entities may include:
   - Customer affiliates
   - Joint ventures/alliances
   - Contractors
   - Suppliers
   - Clients of Customer

   ○   Will Customer have the option of adding/deleting entities over the term?

   ○   How will mergers/acquisitions/divestitures be handled? What will Customer's and Vendor's ongoing obligations be?

   ○   Which entity(ies) will have payment obligations? Are recipients of services third-party beneficiaries?

5.   Entities Providing Services to Customer

   ○   Determine which entity (or entities) will provide the services to Customer.

   ○   Will there be any subcontracting/teaming relationships?

   ○   For international deals, how will Vendor provide resources/services in each country? Will Vendor use affiliated entities or subcontractors?

    o   What are Customer's rights to approve/remove subcontractors?

    o   Which entity(ies) will have performance/indemnification obligations?

6.   Term

    o   What is the commencement date of services? Will there be one commencement date for all sites? Will there be one commencement date for all services (e.g., reengineering, development, and ongoing management)?

    o   How long is the term of the agreement? If the transaction includes multiple agreements, are all of the agreements co-terminus? If there is a master agreement with separate site/service agreements, are all of the agreements co-terminus?

    o   Will there be a pilot period?

    o   What are each party's renewal rights? What type of notice is required for renewal?

7.   Scope of Services

    o   Determine the general scope of services to be provided by Vendor.

    o   Determine those services which will be provided in-house by Customer or to Customer by a third party.

    o   Describe in detail the services (typically by service category) to be provided by Vendor.

    o   Define Customer's responsibilities with respect to the services to be provided by Vendor (i.e., definition of requirements, strategic direction, approvals).

    o   Define existing and future requirements (e.g., capacity requirements, volume changes, business changes). Allocate managerial and financial responsibility.

8.   Transition Plan

    o   How will the transition of services to Vendor be handled?

    o   Will there be any redundant/parallel environments?

    o   Determine the performance standards during transition.

    o   How long will the transition period be?

9.   Methodologies

    o   Assess methodologies to be used by Vendor. Are the methodologies proprietary to Vendor or licensed from a third party? If licensed from a third party, are there any use restrictions? What are Customer's rights to use during the term and after expiration/termination?

    o   Will any of Customer's methodologies continue to be used during the term of the transaction? What are Vendor's use rights (e.g., use in connection with services to Customer only; use in connection with other customers)?

- How will Vendor transition Customer to Vendor's methodologies (if applicable)?

- How will the methodologies introduced by Vendor be integrated with Customer's existing and future methodologies (with respect to the applicable business function as well as other business areas, e.g., information systems)?

- Will Vendor be developing/providing any new methodologies? If so, how will ownership/use rights be allocated? How will new methodologies be rolled out (e.g., define time period, consequences for failure to meet deadlines, each party's responsibilities)?

10.   Technology

- Assess technology to be used by Vendor. Is the technology proprietary to Vendor or licensed from a third party? If licensed from a third party, are there any use restrictions? What are Customer's rights to use during the term and after expiration/termination?

- Will any of Customer's technology continue to be used during the term of the transaction? What are Vendor's use rights (e.g., use in connection with services to Customer only; use in connection with other customers)?

- Will the environment be dedicated/shared?

- How will Vendor transition Customer to Vendor's technology (if applicable)?

- How will the technology introduced by Vendor be integrated with Customer's existing or future technology (e.g., is Vendor technology compatible with technology used by Customer's information system group)?

- Will Vendor be developing/providing any new technology? If so, how will ownership/use rights be allocated? How will new technology be rolled out (e.g., define time period, consequences for failure to meet deadlines, each party's responsibilities)?

11.   Assets

- Will Vendor be purchasing any of Customer's assets (e.g., equipment, real estate)? If so, when will purchase be made (e.g., on date of signing)?

- How will assets be valued (e.g., book value, fair market value)?

- Is the transfer of assets necessary in conjunction with the transfer of employees in order to constitute an "automatic transfer" under the particular country's employment/redundancy laws?

12. Projects

- Identify any projects that Vendor will be responsible for implementing/managing as part of the transaction.
- Will Vendor be responsible for any reengineering in connection with its provision of services? If so, what are each party's responsibilities? What are the consequences if the reengineering is not successful or performed by deadlines specified?
- What is the inter-relationship of Vendor's reengineering responsibilities and Vendor's other services responsibilities (e.g., are they cross-terminable)?
- Will Vendor be responsible for any new implementations? If so, what are each party's responsibilities? What are the consequences if the reengineering is not successful or performed by deadlines specified?
- Which party will be responsible for purchase/license of third-party methodologies/technologies (if applicable)?

13. Integration

- How will the methodologies/technologies introduced by Vendor be integrated with other methodologies/technologies used by Customer?
- Have other Customer business areas been contacted for input (e.g., information systems, human resources)?

14. Transfer of Employees

- Determine whether any or all of Customer employees will be offered employment by, or transitioned to, Vendor or a Vendor subcontractor.
- Identify group of retained employees.
- Review Customer's severance/redundancy policy, if any, to determine whether a transition to Vendor may invoke severance obligations. (If so, factor into Customer's cost analysis.)
- Are there any claims with respect to any of the transitioned employees?
- Compare Customer and Vendor benefits. Are any adjustments necessary?
- Does Vendor require any special screening of employees (e.g., drug testing)?
- Will Vendor require transitioned employees to sign an employment agreement?
- Develop an employee communication plan.
- Determine whether any stay bonuses/incentives are necessary.

15.   Project Staff

- o   Identify management structure of Vendor as well as Customer in connection with the provision/receipt of services.
- o   Are there any limitations/restrictions with respect to reassignment/ replacement of key Vendor personnel?
- o   Are there any on-site/off-site requirements?
- o   Are there any limitations/restrictions with respect to "churning" of employees?
- o   How will Customer complaints regarding Vendor personnel be handled?
- o   Are there any special clearances of Vendor personnel necessary?
- o   Are there any limitations/restrictions with respect to subcontractors?
- o   Are there any visa requirements?
- o   What are Vendor's employment practices? Do they comply with local law? Do they comply with U.S. law?

16.   Retained Assets

- o   Identify which assets Vendor will manage and, of those assets, which assets Vendor will have financial responsibility for.
- o   Identify which assets Customer will continue to manage and, of those assets, whether Vendor will have any financial responsibility.
- o   How will the parties act in the event it is not clear where a problem originates from (e.g., root cause analysis)?

17.   Agreements to be Reviewed

- o   Identify any third-party agreements/relationships that may be impacted by the outsourcing, including:
  - • Maintenance agreements
  - • Subcontracting relationships
  - • Other service agreements
  - • Methodology/technology licenses
  - • Equipment/asset leases
  - • Real estate leases/subleases
- o   Are there any restrictions with respect to third-party management/ access or assignment to a third party?
- o   What are the terms relating to termination/renewal?
- o   What are the pricing terms, and will they be impacted by the transaction?
- o   Develop a strategy for notifying third parties, if applicable.

18. Third-Party Consents

- Are any third-party consents necessary in connection with the commencement of the transaction? If so, which party is responsible for obtaining such consents and how will financial responsibility be allocated?

- How will third-party consents be obtained upon the expiration/termination of the transaction (in order to transition agreements/assets back to Customer or Customer's designee)? How will financial responsibility be allocated?

19. Performance Standards

- Identify those services that will have performance standards.

- How will Vendor's performance be measured? Will existing performance standards be used or will performance standards be established on a going-forward basis?

- Identify any permitted downtime and testing.

- How will failures to meet performance standards be handled (e.g., liquidated damages or termination)?

- Will there be any procedures for assessing/determining causes of failures to meet performance standards (e.g., root cause analysis)?

- What performance standards will apply during transition/implementation?

20. Customer Satisfaction

- Will Vendor be responsible for any type of customer satisfaction reporting?

- Determine pool of employees surveyed (e.g., management, end users).

- How will the results of such surveys be used (e.g., as basis for performance standard)?

21. Benchmarking

- Determine whether the agreement will include any benchmarking procedures (e.g., benchmarking of services or prices).

- Develop benchmarking procedures (e.g., scope of benchmark, group against which services/prices will be benchmarked).

- Identify benchmarker (e.g., third party, Vendor group).

- How will benchmarking results be reviewed and how will changes, if applicable, be implemented?

22. Sarbanes-Oxley Considerations

- Determine documentation and training requirements.

- Are any special reports required (such as SAS 70)?

23. Compliance Issues
- Identify any regulatory/governmental requirements (e.g., timing, notice, consent). (Note: These requirements are typically driven by the type of transaction, e.g., rules governing accounting services, and the type of organization receiving services, e.g., rules governing financial institutions. In addition, compliance issues may vary from country to country or if the transaction involves more than one country.)
- Are the software, equipment, systems, or other materials owned, used, or provided by Vendor in providing the services capable of correctly processing and/or operating without errors or omissions relating to the occurrence in or use by such software, equipment, systems, or other materials of dates or date-dependent data, including from different centuries or more than one century?
- Are the software, equipment, systems, or other materials owned, used, or provided by Vendor in providing the services compliant with guidelines set forth by industry-specific regulatory bodies?
- Determine which party is responsible for ensuring compliance. Allocate costs of compliance due to changes in laws, rules, or regulations after commencement.
- Identify any license/permits required to be obtained by Customer and/or Vendor.
- Consult with legal, regulatory, tax, and audit departments.

24. Transaction-Specific Issues
- Identify any transaction-specific requirements (e.g., for warehouse distribution transactions, provisions regarding liens; for real estate management transactions, insurance, and environmental obligations; for accounting services transactions, provisions regarding accounting standards and filing deadlines).
- Consult with legal, regulatory, tax, and audit departments.

25. Customer Responsibilities
- Identify Customer's responsibilities (e.g., provision of supplies, computers, parking).
- Will Customer be providing any space/facilities to house Vendor's employees? What are the terms of Vendor's use (e.g., sublease)?
- Is Customer retaining staff necessary to perform the retained responsibilities (e.g., management, definition of requirements, approvals)?

26. Service Locations
- Where will Vendor be providing the services from? If such locations are not Customer locations, are there any restrictions on where Vendor may provide services from?

- Will the service locations be dedicated to Customer or shared facilities?
- Describe physical security requirements. Are uniforms or other identification required? Does Customer or Vendor have specific codes of conduct?
- How will breaches of security be handled?
- Are there any environmental concerns?

27. Management Procedures

- Will the parties develop management procedures to be used in connection with the provision of the services?
- How will change control be handled?

28. Reports

- Identify the performance and other reports that Customer currently generates or receives with respect to the services being outsourced.
- Identify those reports that Customer wishes to receive from Vendor.
- Establish deadlines for each report.
- Will Customer be required to review the reports within a specific time period?
- How will errors in reports be handled?

29. Data

- Discuss procedures for handling Customer data. What are Vendor's use rights?
- How will errors in Customer data be handled?
- Describe data security requirements at service locations. Are passwords required?
- How will breaches of security be handled?

30. Proprietary Rights

- Establish Vendor's right to use Customer proprietary methodologies and technology during the term and after expiration/termination of the agreement.
- Establish Vendor's right to use during the term and after expiration/termination of the agreement methodologies and technology licensed by Customer from third parties and used in connection with the provision of the services.
- Establish Customer's right to use Vendor's proprietary methodologies and technology during the term and after expiration/termination of the agreement.

- Establish Customer's right to use during the term and after expiration/termination of the agreement methodologies and technology licensed by Vendor from third parties and used in connection with the provision of the services.

- Establish each party's ownership/use rights with respect to methodologies and technology developed or acquired as part of or in connection with the provision of the services.

- Establish any restrictions governing the use of confidential information.

- Establish any restrictions governing the use of mentally retained information.

- Discuss whether noncompetition provisions are appropriate.

31. Audit

- What are Customer's rights to audit the services and the service locations? How often may Customer exercise any such audit rights?

- How will the results of any such audit be dealt with?

- What are Customer's rights to audit the fees?

- How will overpayments/underpayments be handled?

- Will interest be charged?

32. Fees

- Determine the applicable fee structure. Will payment be made in U.S. dollars?

- Customer should assess actual cost savings, if any. Such analysis should include any new taxes, employee transfer costs, training, and other expenses resulting from the outsourcing.

- Vendor should assess actual profit margin.

- Other Fee Provisions:
    - If a base fee structure is used, determine structure for increasing and decreasing fees/resources.
    - Determine the rights of the parties to set off monies owed.
    - To what extent, if any, will Customer be responsible for Vendor expenses (e.g., travel)? Will Vendor use Customer or Vendor expense guidelines?
    - Will there be any cost-of-living adjustments?
    - For international deals, is there any currency risk?
    - Consider a most-favored-customer provision.
    - How will fees be paid (e.g., in what currency, in what manner, and according to what schedule)?

- How, when, and to what Customer entity(ies) will invoices be issued?
- Determine the degree of detail to be included on invoices.
- How will disputed fees/credits be handled (e.g., escrow)? What are the parties' obligations to perform in the event of a dispute?
- How will changes in business volumes be handled?

33.   Taxes

- Determine liability for sales, use, and other taxes.
- Determine liability for additional taxes resulting from Vendor's relocation of service locations or rerouting of services.

34.   Additional Services

- How will the provision of additional services be handled? Will Vendor be required to submit a bid? Will any rights of first refusal be granted to Vendor?
- What type of detail must be included in a Vendor proposal?
- To what extent does Customer wish to reserve the right to contract with third parties?

35.   Insurance

- Specify Vendor's insurance requirements, for example:
  - Errors and omissions
  - Liability
  - Workers' compensation
  - Automobile
  - Environmental
- Specify any specific bonding requirements.
- Determine whether any parental or other type of guarantee is appropriate.

36.   Termination

- Consider early termination rights, for example:
  - Termination for convenience in whole
  - Partial termination for convenience
  - Termination upon change of control of Vendor
  - Termination upon change of control of Customer
  - Termination for breach
  - Termination for nonpayment
  - Termination for failure to provide critical services
  - Termination for failure to meet the performance standards
  - Termination for substantial changes in business

- Termination for change in financial condition
- Termination upon the occurrence of a regulatory event
- Cross-termination with other agreements

○ Determine whether and in what instances termination fees are applicable. If so, establish formula for determining applicable termination fees.

37. Exit Rights

○ Determine each party's ongoing rights after expiration/termination with respect to proprietary and third-party methodologies, technology, equipment, facilities, subcontracting arrangements, and third-party service agreements.

○ Determine which party will be responsible for transfer/assignment fees imposed by third parties.

○ If Customer has right to purchase certain Vendor assets used to provide the services, how will the purchase price be determined?

38. Termination Assistance

○ Determine the types of assistance Vendor and/or its subcontractors will provide Customer upon expiration/termination.

○ Determine duration of Vendor's termination assistance obligations.

○ How will termination assistance be paid for (e.g., fee schedule, time schedule for payment)?

39. Liability Provisions

○ Assess liability exposure.

○ Determine any liquidated damages to be imposed upon Vendor (e.g., for failure to meet performance standards, for failure to meet implementation schedules).

○ What are each party's indemnification obligations (e.g., for claims of infringement, employee claims).

○ Determine the representations and warranties to be made by each party.

40. Dispute Resolution

○ How will disputes be handled? Will the agreement include an escalation procedure?

○ Will unresolved disputes be handled through arbitration or litigation?

41. Business Continuity

○ Does Vendor have redundant infrastructure?

○ What are Vendor's disaster recovery plans?

- ○ Where is the Vendor's secondary site?

- ○ What is Customer's existing business recovery plan? Will Customer's plans be terminated?

- ○ Specify response times for delivery of business recovery services. Describe escalation procedures.

42.   Assignment

- ○ Specify each party's right to assign its rights/obligations under the agreement in whole or in part.

- ○ Will there be any special assignment rights in the event of a merger/acquisition/divestiture?

- ○ May either party assign to an affiliate/related entity?

43.   Solicitation of Employees

- ○ Will there be any limitations/restrictions on Customer's or Vendor's right to solicit and/or hire the other party's employees?

- ○ When will such limitations/restrictions apply (e.g., during the term, after expiration/termination)?

- ○ Will there be any exceptions for blind solicitations (e.g., newspaper advertisements)?

44.   Miscellaneous Provisions

- ○ *Notices.* How will notices be given (e.g., by hand, by facsimile)? To whom (e.g., to business manager and/or counsel)?

- ○ *Publicity.* Are there any limitations/restrictions on each party's ability to make public statements regarding the other party and/or the transaction?

- ○ *Governing law.* Determine which state/country law will govern the transaction (or if international transaction with multiple documents, determine which law will govern each part of the transaction).

- ○ *Venue.* Will there be a requirement that any action be brought in a particular venue?

- ○ *Import/export.* Provide any limitations/restrictions on the export/import of data and/or technology.

- ○ *Interpretation of documents.* How will the transaction documents be interpreted in the event of a dispute (e.g., the main agreement will take precedence over the exhibits/schedules, change orders will take precedence over earlier dated documents)?

- ○ *Counterparts.* Specify whether the various transaction documents may be executed in counterparts.

- ○ *Relationship of the Parties.* Specify that Vendor is an independent contractor to Customer and that the provision of services does not constitute any type of partnership or joint venture (unless that is expressly the intent).

o *Severability.* Specify that if any provision is held to be invalid that the remaining provisions shall remain in full force and effect.

o *Waivers.* Specify that any delay or omission does not constitute a waiver of rights and that any waiver should not be construed to be a waiver of a subsequent breach/covenant.

o *Entire agreement.* Specify that the transaction documents constitute the entire agreement between the parties.

o *Amendments.* Specify how the transaction documents may be amended (e.g., by writing signed by both parties).

o *Survival.* Specify which provisions of the agreement will survive termination and/or expiration of the agreement.

o *Third-party beneficiaries.* Expressly state that there will not be any third-party beneficiaries under the transaction documents or, if there will be third-party beneficiaries, identify such beneficiaries.

o *Covenant of further assurances.* Expressly state that each party will execute any documents or perform any actions necessary to effectuate the purposes of the agreement.

KEY ISSUES IN A DATA CENTER OUTSOURCING TRANSACTION[4]

1. Current vs. New Environment
    o   Is the vendor continuing to operate the current environment or will the vendor move to a new environment? Should there be separate scope exhibits for the current vs. the new?
    o   If new, what are the customer requirements for the new environment?

2. Migration from an Incumbent Provider or In-house Service
    o   Are there existing procedures manuals that the customer can share?
    o   If an incumbent provider, what are the termination assistance requirements?
    o   Will the existing personnel be available for knowledge transfer?
    o   What is the migration plan (e.g., timing, critical milestones, when does pricing commence)?

3. Employee Issues
    o   Determine whether any or all of the customer employees/temps/ contractors will be offered employment by, or transitioned to, the vendor or a vendor subcontractor.
    o   If not, are there any automatic transfer requirements?
    o   Identify group of retained employees.
    o   Review the customer's severance/redundancy policy, if any, to determine whether a transition to the vendor may invoke severance obligations. (If so, factor into the customer's cost analysis.)
    o   Are there any claims with respect to any of the transitioned employees?
    o   Compare the customer and the vendor benefits. Are any adjustments necessary?

---

4. Note: This checklist is intended to illustrate the types of legal issues that customers may wish to consider in connection with contracting for application services. The items included in this checklist may not cover all of the issues that may arise in a particular transaction. Legal issues will likely vary depending on the type of service being provided and the scope of the services. This checklist or any part thereof should only be used after consultation with your legal counsel. Legal counsel should be consulted prior to entering into or negotiating any transaction covering the provision of application services.

- Does the vendor require any special screening of employees (e.g., drug testing)?
- Will the vendor require transitioned employees to sign an employment agreement?
- Develop an employee communication plan.
- Determine whether any stay bonuses/incentives are necessary.

4. Asset Issues
   - Does the customer require any asset purchase or assumption of leases/licenses?
   - Consider facility, hardware, and software.

5. Hardware Due Diligence
   - What is the current hardware being used?
   - Will the vendor be required to purchase/lease/use the existing hardware?
   - Does the customer own or lease the hardware? What are the lease terms (e.g., length, right to access/relocate)?
   - What are the maintenance requirements?
   - What are the refresh requirements?
   - Is the hardware dedicated/shared?
   - Will the hardware be able to run future versions of the software? Whose responsibility is compatibility?
   - What are the current capacity requirements of the customer? What are the future capacity requirements? At what capacity is the hardware currently run? Who is responsible for additional hardware requirements?
   - Will the vendor's tools be able to run on the hardware? What impact will the tools have on capacity/performance?
   - What are the vendor's responsibility to purchase additional/new hardware?

6. Software Due Diligence (System and Applications)
   - What is the current software being used?
   - Will the vendor be required to purchase/license/use the existing software?
   - Does the customer own or license the software? What are the license terms (e.g., length, right to access/relocate)?
   - What are the maintenance requirements?
   - What are the refresh requirements?
   - Is the software dedicated/shared?

- Will the systems software be able to run future versions of the applications software? Whose responsibility is compatibility?
- Will the vendor's tools be able to run with the customer's software?
- Will the vendor be responsible for the rollout of new software? What if the existing software is no longer maintained by the third-party licensor?

7. Tool Requirements
- What are the customer's tool requirements?
- Will the vendor use the customer's tools?
- What tools will the vendor provide (during the term and at termination)?
- Does the vendor have all the necessary tools to monitor/report on the service levels?

8. Scope of Services
- Data center only (e.g., database administration, telecommunications, LAN network, data transmission, desktop, help desk)?
- Is this a requirements contract?
- Hours of operation
- Language requirements
- System operation (remote vs. onsite)
- Tape management
- Data entry
- File services
- Print and microfiche
- Print distribution
- Test environments
- Documentation of operation procedures
- Production control
  - Operate/monitor systems console
  - Manage schedules
  - Implement automated scheduling
  - Batch management
  - Report balancing
  - Special forms inventory
- Hardware planning and implementation
  - Upgrades
  - Replacements
  - Additional equipment

- ○ Systems management
  - Capacity management
  - Performance management
  - Change management
  - Problem management
  - Recovery management
  - Configuration management
  - Inventory management
- ○ Systems software
  - Requirements
  - Procurement
  - Acceptance testing
  - Maintenance
  - Upgrades
  - New releases
  - Enhancements
  - Replacements
  - Additional software
  - System monitoring
  - Performance tuning
  - Problem resolution
  - Backup
  - Vendor/subcontractor performance
  - Reporting
- ○ Application software
- ○ Facilities
- ○ Quality assurance
- ○ Customer satisfaction
- ○ Physical security
- ○ Data security
- ○ Data procedures
- ○ Help desk requirements
- ○ Third-party contract administration
- ○ Travel requirements
- ○ Existing/new projects
- ○ Customer-retained responsibilities

9.   Third-Party Agreements to Be Reviewed

- o   Identify any third-party agreements/relationships that may be impacted by the outsourcing, including:

  - Maintenance agreements

  - Subcontracting relationships

  - Other service agreements

  - Methodology/technology licenses

  - Equipment/asset leases

  - Real estate leases/subleases

- o   Are there any restrictions with respect to third-party management/access or assignment to a third party?

- o   What are the terms relating to termination/renewal?

- o   What are the pricing terms, and will they be impacted by the transaction?

- o   Develop a strategy for notifying third parties, if applicable.

10.   Third-Party Consents

- o   Are any third-party consents necessary in connection with the commencement of the transaction? If so, which party is responsible for obtaining such consents and how will financial responsibility be allocated?

- o   How will third-party consents be obtained upon the expiration/termination of the transaction (in order to transition agreements/assets back to the customer or the customer's designee)? How will financial responsibility be allocated?

11.   Performance Standards

- o   Identify those services that will have performance standards.

- o   How will the vendor's performance be measured? Will existing performance standards be used or will performance standards be established on a going-forward basis?

- o   Identify any permitted downtime and testing.

- o   How will failures to meet performance standards be handled (e.g., liquidated damages or termination)?

- o   Will there be any procedures for assessing/determining causes of failures to meet performance standards (e.g., root cause analysis)?

- o   What performance standards will apply during transition/implementation?

12. Reporting

  ○ Identify the performance and other reports that the customer currently generates or receives with respect to the services being outsourced.

  ○ Identify those reports that the customer wishes to receive from the vendor.

  ○ Establish deadlines for each report.

  ○ Will the customer be required to review the reports within a specific time period?

  ○ How will errors in reports be handled?

13. Vendor Personnel Requirements

  ○ Identify management structure of the vendor as well as the customer in connection with the provision/receipt of services.

  ○ Are there any limitations/restrictions with respect to reassignment/replacement of key the vendor personnel?

  ○ Are there any limitations/restrictions with respect to "churning" of employees?

  ○ How will the customer complaints regarding the vendor personnel be handled?

  ○ Are any special clearances of the vendor personnel necessary?

  ○ Are there any limitations/restrictions with respect to subcontractors?

14. Compliance Issues

  ○ Identify any regulatory/governmental requirements (e.g., timing, notice, consent). (Note: These requirements are typically driven by the type of transaction, e.g., rules governing accounting services, and the type of organization receiving services, e.g., rules governing financial institutions. In addition, compliance issues may vary from country to country or if the transaction involves more than one country.)

  ○ Check HIPAA, GLB, and privacy regulations.

  ○ Are there any Euro compliance issues?

  ○ Determine which party is responsible for ensuring compliance. Allocate costs of compliance due to changes in laws, rules, or regulations after commencement.

  ○ Identify any license/permits required to be obtained by the customer and/or the vendor.

  ○ Consult with legal, regulatory, tax, and audit departments.

15. Transaction-Specific Issues

- Identify any transaction-specific requirements.
- Consult with legal, regulatory, tax, and audit departments.

16. Service Locations

- Where will the vendor be providing the services from? If such locations are not the customer locations, are there any restrictions on where the vendor may provide services from?
- Will the service locations be dedicated to the customer or shared facilities?
- Describe physical security requirements. Are uniforms or other identification required? Does the customer or the vendor have specific codes of conduct?
- How will breaches of security be handled?
- Are there any environmental concerns?

17. Fee Structure

- Fixed fees and variable fees
- Utility pricing
- Fees by location
- Bundled fees vs. fees by service tower/category
- Prices for increases/decreases in volume
- Minimum fees
- Fees for new services
- Expenses
- COLA
- Currency of payment
- Currency risks
- Time of payment
- Late payment mechanism
- Amounts that can be withheld if there is a dispute

18. Taxes

- Determine liability for sales, use, and other taxes.
- Determine liability for additional taxes resulting from the vendor's relocation of service locations or rerouting of services.

19. Disaster Recovery

- Will the vendor have any business recovery responsibilities?

- ○ What are the customer's existing business recovery plan? Will the customer's plans be terminated?
- ○ Specify response times for delivery of business recovery services. Describe escalation procedures.

20. Termination
- ○ Consider early termination rights, for example:
  - • Termination for convenience in whole
  - • Partial termination for convenience
  - • Termination upon change of control of the vendor
  - • Termination upon change of control of the customer
  - • Termination for breach
  - • Termination for nonpayment
  - • Termination for failure to provide critical services
  - • Termination for failure to meet the performance standards
  - • Termination for substantial changes in business
  - • Termination upon the occurrence of a regulatory event
  - • Cross-termination with other agreements
- ○ Determine whether and in what instances termination fees are applicable. If so, establish formula for determining applicable termination fees.

21. Exit Rights
- ○ Determine each party's ongoing rights after expiration/termination with respect to proprietary and third-party methodologies, technology, equipment, facilities, subcontracting arrangements, and third-party service agreements.
- ○ Determine which party will be responsible for transfer/assignment fees imposed by third parties.
- ○ If the customer has right to purchase certain the vendor assets used to provide the services, how will the purchase price be determined?

22. Agreement Issues
- ○ Structure
- ○ Contracting parties
- ○ Entities receiving services from the vendor
- ○ Parental guarantee from the customer/vendor
- ○ Entities providing services to the customer (will the vendor be sub-contracting services?)
- ○ Term
- ○ Proprietary rights

- Audit
- Assignment rights
- Rights to solicit employees
- Governing law/jurisdiction
- Confidentiality/publicity

23. Damages
    - Direct damages
    - Damage exclusions
    - Data loss
    - Indemnities
    - No consequentials

24. Insurance Requirements
    - Specify the vendor's insurance requirements, for example:
      - Errors and omissions
      - Liability
      - Workers' compensation
      - Automobile
      - Environmental
    - Specify any specific bonding requirements.

INFORMATION TECHNOLOGY OUTSOURCING AGREEMENT (CUSTOMER FORM)[5]

---

5.   Note: This sample agreement is intended to illustrate the types of legal issues that vendors typically wish to address in connection with information technology outsourcing transactions. The provisions included in this sample agreement, while comprehensive, may not cover all of the issues that may arise in a particular transaction. Legal issues will likely vary depending on the type of information technology process being outsourced and the scope of the outsourcing transaction. This sample agreement or any part thereof should only be used after consultation with your legal counsel. Legal counsel should be consulted prior to entering into or negotiating any outsourcing transaction.

TABLE OF EXHIBITS

Exhibit 1: Statement of Work
[Exhibit 2: Assets]
Exhibit 3: Customer Third-Party Contracts
Exhibit 4: Critical Services
[Exhibit 5: Customer IP]
Exhibit 6: Service Locations
Exhibit 7: Affected Employees
[Exhibit 8: Customer Budget]
Exhibit 9: Designated Fees
Exhibit 10: Service Levels and Performance Credits
Exhibit 11: Variable and Resource Baselines
[Exhibit 12: Supporting Documentation]
Exhibit 13: Key Personnel
Exhibit 14: Transition Plan
[Exhibit 15: Technical Architecture and Product Standards Procedures]
[Exhibit 16: Form of General Assignment and Bill of Sale]
Exhibit 17: Reports
[Exhibit 18: Form of Initial Customer Satisfaction Survey and Related Procedures]
Exhibit 19: Safety and Security Procedures
Exhibit 20: Human Resources Provisions
Exhibit 21: Critical Milestones
Exhibit 22: Termination Fees

INFORMATION TECHNOLOGY SERVICES
AGREEMENT

by and between

[CUSTOMER]
and
[VENDOR]

Dated as of [SPECIFY DATE]

This INFORMATION TECHNOLOGY SERVICES AGREEMENT, dated as
of **[SPECIFY DATE]**, is by and between CUSTOMER and VENDOR.
W I T N E S S E T H:
WHEREAS, in response to the RFP, Vendor submitted the Proposal;
WHEREAS, based on the Proposal, Customer and Vendor have engaged in
extensive negotiations and discussions that have culminated in the formation of
the relationship described in this Agreement; and
WHEREAS, Vendor desires to provide to Customer, and Customer desires to
obtain from Vendor, the information technology and related services described
in this Agreement on the terms and conditions set forth in this Agreement.
NOW, THEREFORE, for and in consideration of the agreements set forth
below, Customer and Vendor agree as follows:

ARTICLE 1. DEFINITIONS AND CONSTRUCTION.

1.01 DEFINITIONS.   The following defined terms used in this Agreement shall
have the meanings specified below:

"*Additional Resource Charges*" shall mean the resource charges specified in
   Exhibit 11 for the use of Services above the resource baselines set forth
   in *Exhibit 11.*

"*Affected Employees*" shall mean those Customer Employees set forth in
   Exhibit 7.

["*Affected Project Staff Member*" shall have the meaning set forth in *Section 28.03.*]

["*Affected Resources*" shall have the meaning set forth in *Section 28.04.*]

"*Affiliate*" shall mean, as to any entity, any other entity that, directly or indirectly, Controls, is Controlled by, or is under common Control with such
   entity.

"Agreement" shall mean this Information Technology Services Agreement by
   and between Customer and Vendor.

["*Assets*" shall mean the [facilities] equipment, technology and related assets set forth in *Exhibit 2*.]

"*Assigned Agreements*" shall mean the third-party agreements that are assigned, in whole or in part, to Vendor and that are set forth in *Exhibit 3*.

"*Benchmarker*" shall mean the third party designated by Customer from time to time [upon [SPECIFY TIME PERIOD] days' notice to Vendor] to conduct the Benchmarking Process.

"*Benchmarking Process*" shall mean the objective measurement and comparison process (utilizing baselines and industry standards agreed upon by Customer and Vendor) established by Customer and Vendor.

"*Benchmark Results*" shall mean the final results of the Benchmarking Process delivered by the Benchmarker in a written report to each of Customer and Vendor, including any supporting documentation requested by Customer or Vendor to analyze the results of the Benchmarking Process.

"*Benchmark Review Period*" shall mean the [SPECIFY TIME PERIOD] period following receipt by Customer and Vendor of the Benchmark Results.

"*Change(s)*" shall mean any change to the Services [or the Systems] that would materially alter the functionality, performance standards [or technical environment of the Systems], the manner in which the Services are provided, the composition of the Services, or the cost to Customer of the Services.

"*Change Control Procedures*" shall mean the written description of the change control procedures applicable to any Changes under this Agreement.

"*Change in Control*" shall mean the (1) consolidation or merger of a Party with or into any entity (other than the consolidation or merger of a Party with an Affiliate of such Party in which such Party is the surviving entity); (2) sale, transfer, or other disposition of all or substantially all of the assets of a Party; or (3) acquisition by any entity, or group of entities acting in concert, of beneficial ownership of [SPECIFY PERCENT] or more (or such lesser percentage that constitutes Control) of the outstanding voting securities or other ownership interests of a Party.

"*Confidential Information*" of Customer or Vendor shall mean all information and documentation of Customer and Vendor, respectively, whether disclosed to or accessed by Customer or Vendor in connection with this Agreement, including (1) with respect to Customer, all Customer Data and all information of Customer or its customers, suppliers, contractors and other third parties doing business with Customer; (2) with respect to Customer and Vendor, the terms of this Agreement; and (3) any information developed by reference to or use of Customer's or Vendor's information, provided, however, that except to the extent otherwise provided by Law, the term "Confidential Information" shall not include information that (1) is independently developed by the recipient, as demonstrated by the recipient's written records, without violating the disclosing Party's proprietary rights, (2) is or becomes publicly known (other than through unauthorized disclosure), (3) is disclosed by the owner of such information to a third party free of any obligation of confidentiality, (4) is already known by the recipient at the time of disclosure, as demonstrated by the recipient's written records, and the recipient has no obligation of confidentiality other than pursuant to this Agreement or any confidentiality agreements between Customer and Vendor entered into before the Effective Date, or (5) is rightfully received by a Party free of any obligation of confidentiality, provided that (a) such recipient has no knowledge that such information is subject to a confidentiality agreement and (b) such information is not of a type or character that a reasonable person would have regarded it as confidential.

"Consents" shall mean all licenses, consents, authorizations, and approvals that are necessary to allow (1) Vendor and Vendor Agents to use (a) Customer's owned and leased assets, (b) the services provided for the benefit of Customer under Customer's third-party services contracts, (c) the Customer IP, (d) the Vendor IP, and (e) any assets owned or leased by Vendor; (2) Customer to assign the Assigned Agreements to Vendor pursuant to Section 7.03 and Vendor to manage and administer the Customer Third-Party Contracts pursuant to Article 7; (3) Vendor and Vendor Agents to (a) use any third-party services retained by Vendor to provide the Services during the Term and the Termination Assistance Period and (b) assign to Customer the New IP; **[and (4) after the expiration, termination or partial termination of this Agreement or the insourcing or resourcing of any portion of the Services, (a) Customer and its designee(s) to use the Vendor IP or, with respect to any Vendor IP that Vendor has licensed, leased, or otherwise obtained from third parties pursuant to *Section 28.02(3)*, Vendor to transfer, assign, or sublicense such Vendor IP, (b) Vendor and Vendor Agents assign the agreements and Vendor Machines to Customer and its designee(s) pursuant to *Section 28.02(5)* and *Section 28.02(6)*].**

"Contract Year" shall mean each 12-month period commencing, in the case of the first Contract Year, on the Effective Date and thereafter upon the completion of the immediately preceding Contract Year.

"Control" shall mean, with respect to any entity, the possession, directly or indirectly, of the power to direct or cause the direction of the management and policies of such entity, whether through the ownership of voting securities (or other ownership interest), by contract, or otherwise.

"*Critical Services*" shall mean those services described as Critical Services in *Exhibit 4*.

"*Customer*" shall mean **[CUSTOMER NAME]**, a **[SPECIFY TYPE, E.G., DELAWARE] [corporation] [partnership] [other]**.

"*Customer Agents*" shall mean the agents, subcontractors, and representatives of Customer, other than Vendor and Vendor Agents.

["*Customer Budget*" shall mean the [SPECIFY YEAR] budget for the information technology and related **services set forth in *Exhibit 8*.]**

"*Customer Contract Manager*" shall have the meaning set forth in *Section 6.01*.

"*Customer Data*" shall mean all data and information (1) submitted to Vendor or Vendor Agents by or on behalf of Customer, (2) obtained, developed, or produced by Vendor or Vendor Agents in connection with this Agreement, or (3) to which Vendor or Vendor Agents have access in connection with the provision of the Services.

"*Customer IP*" shall mean the IP **[including the IP set forth in *Exhibit 5*]** used in connection with the provision of the Services that is (1) owned, acquired, or developed by Customer or (2) licensed or leased by Customer from a third party.

"*Customer's Regulatory Requirements*" shall mean the Laws to which Customer is required to submit or voluntarily submits from time to time.

"*Customer Service Location(s)*" shall mean any Customer service location set forth in Exhibit 6 and any other service location owned or leased by Customer for which Vendor has received Customer's approval in accordance with *Section 10.01(3)*.

"*Customer Third-Party Contracts*" shall mean the Managed Agreements and the Assigned Agreements, collectively.

"*Data Safeguards*" shall have the meaning set forth in *Section 10.03*.

"*Default Cure Period*" shall have the meaning set forth in *Section 26.04(1)*.

"*Default Notice*" shall have the meaning set forth in *Section 26.04(1)*.

"*Designated Fees*" shall mean the fees for the Designated Services set forth in *Exhibit 9*.

"*Designated Service Levels*" shall mean the service levels and standards for the performance of the Designated Services as described in *Exhibit 10*.

"*Designated Services*" shall have the meaning set forth in *Section 3.01*.

["*Developed Software*" shall mean any Software, modifications, or enhancements to Software and Related Documentation developed pursuant to this Agreement by or on behalf of (1) Vendor, (2) Vendor Agents, (3) Vendor and Customer or Customer Agents jointly,

(4) Vendor Agents and Customer or Customer Agents jointly, or (5) Vendor, Vendor Agents, Customer, and Customer Agents jointly.]

"*DRP*" shall mean the disaster recovery plan.

"*Effective Date*" shall mean **[SPECIFY DATE]**.

["*EMU Compliant*" shall mean, with respect to Software, Tools, and Machines, that such Software, Tools, and Machines shall be capable of processing calculations relating to conversions of any currency to a European Monetary Unit.]

"*End Date*" shall have the meaning set forth in *Section 28.02*.

"*End Users*" shall mean users of the Services, as specified by Customer.

"*Extension Period*" shall have the meaning set forth in *Section 2.02*.

"*Fees*" shall mean the Designated Fees, the Additional Resource Charges, and any other amounts payable by Customer to Vendor pursuant to this Agreement.

["Force Majeure *Event*" shall have the meaning set forth in *Section 17.02*.]

"*Governmental Approval*" shall mean any license, consent, permit, approval, or authorization of any person or entity, or any notice to any person or entity, the granting of which is required by Law, including Customer's Regulatory Requirements, for the consummation of the transactions contemplated by this Agreement.

"*Governmental Authority*" shall mean any federal, state, municipal, local, territorial, or other governmental department, regulatory authority, judicial, or administrative body, domestic, international, or foreign.

"*Improvements*" shall mean any developments, including new developments in IP and Machines, that could reasonably be expected to have an impact on Customer's business, to the extent known and made available within or by Vendor.

"*Indemnified Party*" shall have the meaning set forth in *Section 29.03*.

"*Indemnifying Party*" shall have the meaning set forth in *Section 29.03*.

"*Initial Agreement Expiration Date*" shall mean **[SPECIFY DATE]**.

"*Initial Customer Satisfaction Survey*" shall have the meaning set forth in *Section 9.01*.

"*Initial Term*" shall have the meaning set forth in *Section 2.01*.

"*Interest*" shall mean interest at a rate of **[SPECIFY PERCENT]** per annum more than the prime rate established by Customer, but in no event to exceed the highest lawful rate of interest.

"*IP*" shall mean any (1) processes, methodologies, procedures, and trade secrets, (2) Software, Tools, and machine-readable texts and files, and

(3) literary work or other work of authorship, including documentation, reports, drawings, charts, graphics, and other written documentation.

"Key Personnel" shall mean the Vendor Contract Manager and such other individuals specified in *Exhibit 13*, collectively.

"Law" shall mean any declaration, decree, directive, legislative enactment, order, ordinance, regulation, rule, or other binding restriction of or by any Governmental Authority.

"Losses" shall mean any and all damages, fines, penalties, deficiencies, losses, liabilities, (including settlements and judgments) and expenses (including interest, court costs, reasonable fees and expenses of attorneys, accountants, and other experts or other reasonable fees and expenses of litigation or other proceedings or of any claim, default, or assessment).

"Machines" shall mean equipment used to provide the Services, including computers and related equipment, such as central processing units and other processors, controllers, modems, communications and telecommunications equipment (voice, data and video), cables, storage devices, printers, terminals, other peripherals and input and output devices, and other tangible mechanical and electronic equipment intended for the processing, input, output, storage, manipulation, communication, transmission, and retrieval of information and data.

"Managed Agreement Invoice(s)" shall mean any invoice submitted by third parties in connection with the Managed Agreements.

"Managed Agreements" shall mean the third-party agreements for which Customer retains financial responsibility and that are set forth in *Exhibit 3*.

"Management Committee" shall have the meaning set forth in *Section 13.01*.

"New IP" shall mean the IP developed or acquired by Vendor or Vendor Agents under this Agreement or in connection with the provision or delivery of the Services.

"New Service(s)" shall mean any service that is outside the scope of the Designated Services.

"New Service Level(s)" shall mean any service level established by Vendor and Customer in connection with a New Service.

"Parties" shall mean Customer and Vendor, collectively.

"Party" shall mean either Customer or Vendor, as the case may be.

"Performance Credits" shall mean the performance credits set forth in *Exhibit 10*.

"Privileged Work Product" shall have the meaning set forth in *Section 22.02*.

"Procedures Manual" shall have the meaning set forth in *Section 13.02*.

"*Project Staff*" shall mean the personnel of Vendor and Vendor Agents who provide the Services.

["*Proposal*" shall mean the Proposal, dated [SPECIFY DATE] and set forth in *Exhibit 12*, submitted by Vendor in response to the RFP.]

"*Reduced Resource Credits*" shall mean the credits in the amounts equal to the Additional Resource Charges specified in *Exhibit 11* for the use of Services below the resource baselines set forth in *Exhibit 11*.

"*Related Documentation*" shall mean, with respect to Software and Tools, all materials, documentation, specifications, technical manuals, user manuals, flow diagrams, file descriptions, and other written information that describes the function and use of such Software or Tools, as applicable.

["*RFP*" shall mean the Request for Proposal distributed by Customer that is set forth in *Exhibit 12*.]

"*Service Levels*" shall mean the Designated Service Levels and the New Service Levels, collectively.

"*Service Location(s)*" shall mean any Customer Service Location or Vendor Service Location, as applicable.

"*Services*" shall mean, collectively, the Designated Services, the New Services being provided by Vendor pursuant to this Agreement, and, during the Termination Assistance Period, the Termination Assistance Services.

["*Software*" shall mean the source code and object code versions of any applications programs, operating system software, computer software languages, utilities, other computer programs and Related Documentation, in whatever form or media, including the tangible media upon which such applications programs, operating system software, computer software languages, utilities, other computer programs, and Related Documentation are recorded or printed, together with all corrections, improvements, updates, and releases thereof.]

["*Systems*" shall mean the IP and the Machines, collectively, used to provide the Services.]

"*Term*" shall mean the Initial Term and any renewal or extension of the Initial Term pursuant to *Section 2.02*.

"*Termination Assistance Period*" shall mean a reasonable period of time designated by Customer during which Vendor shall provide the Termination Assistance Services in accordance with *Article 28*.

"*Termination Assistance Services*" shall mean (1) the terminated, insourced, or resourced Services (and any replacements thereof or substitutions therefore), to the extent Customer requests such Services during the Termination Assistance Period, (2) Vendor's cooperation with Customer or another service provider designated by Customer in the transfer of the terminated, insourced, or resourced Services to Customer or such other service provider in order to facilitate the transfer of the terminated, insourced, or resourced Services to Customer or such other service provider, and (3) any New Services requested by Customer in order to facilitate the transfer of the terminated, insourced, or resourced Services to Customer or another service provider designated by Customer.

[*"Tools"* **shall mean any Software development and performance testing tools, know-how, methodologies, processes, technologies, or algorithms and Related Documentation used by Vendor in providing the Services and based on trade secrets or proprietary information of Vendor or otherwise owned or licensed by Vendor.**]

"Transition Plan" shall mean the high-level transition plan set forth in *Exhibit 14.*

"Transition Schedule" shall mean the schedule for the transition of services and functions to Vendor from Customer, as set forth in the Transition Plan.

"Transition Services" shall have the meaning set forth in *Section 4.01.*

"Use" shall mean the right to load, execute, store, transmit, display, copy, maintain, modify, enhance, create derivative works, make, and have made.

"Variable Fee Report" shall mean the detailed invoice provided to Customer by Vendor on a monthly basis describing the Variable incurred by Customer and Vendor during the preceding month.

"Variable Fees" shall mean the Additional Resource Charges and the Reduced Resource Credits, collectively.

"Vendor" shall mean **[VENDOR NAME]**, a **[SPECIFY TYPE] [corporation] [partnership] [other]**.

"Vendor Agents" shall mean the agents, subcontractors, and representatives of Vendor.

"Vendor Contract Manager" shall have the meaning set forth in *Section 12.01.*

"Vendor IP" shall mean the IP used in connection with the Services or with Customer IP, which is (1) owned, acquired, or developed by or on behalf of Vendor or (2) licensed, leased, or otherwise obtained by Vendor from a third party, excluding in each case Customer IP and New IP.

"Vendor Machines" shall mean those Machines leased or owned by Vendor and Vendor Agents that are used by Vendor and Vendor Agents to provide the Services.

"Vendor Service Location(s)" shall mean any Vendor service location set forth in *Exhibit 6* and any other service location approved by Customer pursuant to *Section 10.01(3).*

1.02 REFERENCES.   In this Agreement and the Exhibits to this Agreement:

1. the Exhibits to this Agreement shall be incorporated into and deemed part of this Agreement and all references to this Agreement shall include the Exhibits to this Agreement;

2. references to an Exhibit, Section, or Article shall be to such Exhibit to, Section, or Article of this Agreement, unless otherwise provided;

3. references to any Law shall mean references to such Law in changed or supplemented form or to a newly adopted Law replacing a previous Law; and

4. references to and mentions of the word "including" or the phrase "e.g." shall mean "including, without limitation."

1.03 HEADINGS.   The Article and Section headings, Table of Contents, and Table of Exhibits are for reference and convenience only and shall not be considered in the interpretation of this Agreement.

1.04 INTERPRETATION OF DOCUMENTS.   Except as otherwise expressly set forth in the body of this Agreement or in any of the Exhibits, in the event of a conflict between the provisions in the body of the this Agreement and the Exhibits, the provisions in the body of this Agreement shall prevail.

ARTICLE 2. TERM

2.01 INITIAL TERM.   The initial term of this Agreement shall commence on the Effective Date and continue until 23:59 (**[SPECIFY TIME STANDARD]**) on the Initial Agreement Expiration Date, or such earlier date upon which this Agreement may be terminated pursuant to *Article 26* (the "*Initial Term*").

2.02 RENEWAL AND EXTENSION.   Unless this Agreement is terminated earlier pursuant to Article 26, Customer shall notify Vendor at least **[SPECIFY TIME PERIOD]** prior to the Initial Agreement Expiration Date as to whether Customer desires to renew this Agreement. If Customer provides Vendor with notice that it does not desire to renew this Agreement, this Agreement shall expire on the Initial Agreement Expiration Date. If Customer provides Vendor with notice that it desires to renew this Agreement and the Parties have not agreed on the terms and conditions applicable to the renewal of this Agreement **[SPECIFY TIME PERIOD]** prior to the Initial Agreement Expiration Date, then the term of this Agreement shall extend for a period as determined by Customer (the "*Extension Period*") of up to **[SPECIFY TIME PERIOD]** from the Initial Agreement Expiration Date, at the charges, terms, and conditions in effect as of the Initial Agreement Expiration Date. If during the Extension Period the Parties are unable to reach agreement on the terms and conditions applicable to the renewal of this Agreement, this Agreement shall expire at the end of the Extension Period.

ARTICLE 3. DESIGNATED SERVICES

3.01 GENERALLY. Commencing on the Effective Date and continuing throughout the Term, Vendor shall be responsible for providing to Customer:

1. the services described in this Agreement (including the services, functions, responsibilities, and projects described in the Statement of Work set forth as *Exhibit 1*);

2. the services, functions, and responsibilities being performed prior to the Effective Date by the Affected Employees or such other Customer employees whose services, functions, or responsibilities were eliminated as a result of this Agreement, even if the service, function, or responsibility is not specifically described in this Agreement; **[NOTE: MAY NEED TO ADDRESS CONTRACTORS]**

3. **[the services, functions, and responsibilities reflected in and contemplated by the Customer Budget;]** and

4. any services, functions, or responsibilities not specifically described in this Agreement, but which are required for the proper performance and delivery of the Services (clauses (1) through (4) of this Section, collectively, the "Designated Services").

Subject to *Section 18.02*, Vendor shall increase or decrease the amount of the Services according to Customer's request for the Services.

3.02 PROVISION OF METHODOLOGIES/TECHNOLOGY. In providing methodologies, technology, and the Services to Customer, Vendor shall (1) jointly with Customer, identify the least cost/highest benefit methods to implement proven methodologies and technology changes and, upon Customer's approval, implement proven methodologies and technology changes; (2) maintain a level of methodologies and technology that allows Customer to take advantage of advances in order to remain competitive in the markets which Customer serves; (3) provide to Customer the Improvements for Customer's evaluation in connection with the Services; and (4) meet with Customer at least once during every **[SPECIFY TIME PERIOD]** during the Term in accordance with the procedures agreed on by the Customer Contract Manager and the Vendor Contract Manager to inform Customer of any new methodologies and technology Vendor is developing or trends and directions of which Vendor is otherwise aware that could reasonably be expected to have an impact on Customer's business.

3.03 VENDOR LICENSES AND PERMITS. Vendor shall obtain and maintain all Governmental Approvals. Upon Vendor's request, Customer shall cooperate with and assist Vendor in obtaining any such Governmental Approvals, to the extent reasonably possible.
   [ADD LANGUAGE RE: NO LIENS IF APPLICABLE]

3.04 CHANGES IN LAW AND REGULATIONS.

1. Vendor shall promptly identify and notify Customer of any changes in Law, including Customer's Regulatory Requirements, that may relate to Customer's use of the Services or Vendor's delivery of the Services. Vendor and Customer shall work together to identify the impact of such changes on how Customer uses, and Vendor delivers, the Services. Vendor shall be responsible for any fines and penalties arising from any noncompliance with any Law relating to the delivery or use of the Services, except as set forth in the following sentence. Customer shall be responsible for any fines and penalties arising from any noncompliance by Customer with any Law relating to Customer's use of the Services, to the extent (a) Vendor notifies Customer in a timely manner of changes in such Law in accordance with this subsection and (b) such noncompliance was not caused by Vendor.

2. Vendor shall perform the Services regardless of changes in Law, including Customer's Regulatory Requirements. If such changes prevent Vendor from performing its obligations under this Agreement, Vendor shall develop and, upon Customer's approval, implement a suitable workaround until such time as Vendor can perform its obligations under this Agreement without such workaround; provided, however, that if such workaround results in an increase in the charges to Customer under this Agreement, then Customer shall have the right to terminate the affected portion of Customer's obligations without regard to *Section 26.04(1)* [and *Section 26.05*]. Upon the implementation of such workaround, the Parties shall negotiate and implement an equitable adjustment to the applicable Fees.

3.05 [TECHNICAL ARCHITECTURE AND PRODUCT STANDARDS. Vendor shall comply with Customer's information management technical architecture and product standards set forth in *Exhibit 15*, as the same may be modified by Customer from time to time during the Term and the Termination Assistance Period.]

3.06 KNOWLEDGE SHARING. At least once every Contract Year, or on request after at least **[SPECIFY TIME PERIOD]** notice from Customer, Vendor shall meet with representatives of Customer in order to **[(1) explain how the Systems work and should be operated,]** (2) explain how the Services are provided, and (3) provide such training and documentation as Customer may require for Customer to **[understand and operate the Systems and]** understand and provide the Services after the expiration or termination of this Agreement.

3.07 INSOURCING. Upon at least **[SPECIFY TIME PERIOD]** notice to Vendor, Customer may insource or obtain from a third party all, or any portion, of the Services.

3.08 [ASSET TRANSFER. **On the Effective Date, Vendor shall purchase the Assets for the purchase price specified in** *Exhibit 16*. **Vendor shall be responsible for and shall pay all sales, use, and other similar taxes arising out of or in connection with the transfer of the Assets by Customer to Vendor on the Effective Date. On the Effective Date, Customer shall assign and transfer to Vendor good and valid title in and to the Assets free and clear of all liens, except permitted liens, by delivery of one or more general assignments and bills of sale in the form of** *Exhibit 16*, **duly executed by Customer and Vendor.]**

3.09 REPORTS. Vendor shall provide to Customer, in a form acceptable to Customer, the **[on-line]** reports set forth in *Exhibit 17*, and such other reports as Customer may request from time to time.

ARTICLE 4. TRANSITION

4.01 TRANSITION SERVICES. Vendor shall perform all functions and services necessary to accomplish the transition of Customer's business process operations and capabilities to Vendor on or before **[SPECIFY DATE]** (the "*Transition Services*"). The Transition Services shall be performed in accordance with the Transition Plan and without causing a material disruption to Customer's business. Vendor shall designate an individual for each of Customer's facilities and functions being transitioned in accordance with this Agreement who shall be responsible for managing and implementing the Transition Services with respect to such functions or services. Until the completion of the applicable Transition Services, each individual shall review with the Customer Contract Manager the status of the Transition Services for which that individual is responsible as often as may be reasonably requested by the Customer Contract Manager.

4.02 EXTENSIONS TO THE TRANSITION SCHEDULE. Upon notice from Customer that Customer desires Vendor to extend the Transition Schedule by more than **[SPECIFY TIME PERIOD]** days, or if the Transition Schedule is extended for more than **[SPECIFY TIME PERIOD]** days as a result of delays caused by Customer or Customer Agents or as a result of Customer's Regulatory Requirements, (1) Vendor shall extend the Transition Schedule for the applicable period of time, and (2) Customer shall pay to Vendor an amount equal to Vendor's direct and actual costs associated with extending the Transition Schedule pursuant to this subsection, including any of Vendor's direct and actual costs that would otherwise have been reduced or eliminated if the transition had occurred as scheduled.

1. In the event the Transition Schedule is extended for more than **[SPECIFY TIME PERIOD]** as a result of delays caused by Vendor or Vendor Agents, (a) Customer shall continue to pay the Designated Fees, subject to Customer's deferral rights in accordance with *Section 18.06*, and (b)

Vendor shall pay to Customer an amount equal to Customer's direct and actual costs associated with extending the Transition Schedule in accordance with this subsection, including payment of occupancy expenses at the applicable Customer facilities and such other direct and actual costs retained by Customer that would have otherwise been reduced or eliminated if the transition had occurred as scheduled.

2. In the event Customer and Vendor agree to extend the Transition Schedule, Customer and Vendor shall negotiate an appropriate adjustment to the Fees.

3. In the event Customer or Vendor incurs costs in connection with the extension of the Transition Schedule for which the other Party will be responsible pursuant to this Section, the Party incurring the costs shall be obligated to use all commercially reasonable efforts to minimize such costs.

ARTICLE 5. NEW SERVICES

5.01 NEW SERVICES. Customer may from time to time during the Term request that Vendor perform a New Service. Upon receipt of such a request from Customer, Vendor shall provide Customer with a written proposal for such New Service which shall include:

1. a description of the services, function, and responsibilities Vendor anticipates performing in connection with such New Service;

2. a schedule for commencing and completing such New Service;

3. Vendor's prospective charges for such New Service, including a detailed breakdown of such charges;

4. when appropriate, a description of any new IP or Machines to be provided by Vendor in connection with such New Service;

5. a description of the human resources necessary to provide the New Service;

6. when appropriate, a list of any existing IP or Machines included in or to be used in connection with such New Service;

7. when appropriate, acceptance test criteria and procedures for [any new Software] or any products, packages, or services; and

8. such other information requested by Customer.

Vendor shall not begin performing any New Service until Customer has provided Vendor with authorization to perform the New Service from the Customer Contract Manager.
[CONSIDER WHETHER VENDOR SHOULD BE OBLIGATED TO PROVIDE CERTAIN SERVICES IF REQUESTED BY CUSTOMER.]

5.02 THIRD-PARTY SERVICES.   Notwithstanding any request made to Vendor by Customer pursuant to *Section 5.01* or any other provision in this Agreement, Customer shall have the right to contract with a third party to perform any New Service, including services to augment or supplement the Services. Upon Customer's request, Vendor shall assist Customer in identifying qualified third-party suppliers to provide New Services. In the event Customer contracts with a third party to perform any New Service, Vendor shall cooperate in good faith with Customer and any such third party, to the extent reasonably required by Customer, including by providing:

1. in writing, applicable requirements, standards, and policies for the Services, to the extent available;

2. assistance and support services to such third party; and

3. **[access to the Systems, to the extent that such access is required for the New Service and does not materially and adversely affect Vendor's ability to perform its obligations pursuant to this Agreement.]**

5.03 ADDITIONAL BUSINESS UNITS.   Customer reserves the right to add business units to this Agreement. Customer shall share such information with Vendor as may be necessary for Vendor to determine which resources will be required to meet Customer's needs. Customer shall not be obligated to obtain the Services from Vendor with respect to any additional entity or business unit or pursuant to an acquisition.

ARTICLE 6.   CUSTOMER RESPONSIBILITIES

6.01 CUSTOMER CONTRACT MANAGER.   Customer shall appoint an individual (the "*Customer Contract Manager*"), who from the date of this Agreement shall serve as the primary Customer representative under this Agreement. The Customer Contract Manager shall (1) have overall responsibility for managing and coordinating the performance of Customer's obligations under this Agreement, and (2) be authorized to act for and on behalf of Customer with respect to all matters relating to this Agreement. Notwithstanding the foregoing, the Customer Contract Manager may, upon notice to Vendor, delegate such of his or her responsibilities to other Customer employees, as the Customer Contract Manager deems appropriate.

6.02 [CUSTOMER RESOURCES.   Commencing on the Effective Date and continuing for so long as Vendor requires the same for the performance of the Services, Customer shall provide to Vendor, at no charge to Vendor and subject to *Section 6.03*, the following:

1. **the use of the space in Customer's premises that was utilized by the Affected Employees as of the Effective Date and any additional space in Customer's premises that Vendor may from time to time**

reasonably require in connection with the performance of the Services (in accordance with Customer's corporate policy), together with office furnishings, telephone equipment and services, janitorial services, utilities and office-related equipment, supplies, and duplicating services reasonably required in connection with the performance of the Services;

2. for use by personnel employed or managed by Vendor on Customer's premises, those personal computers, workstations, terminals, printers, and other equipment utilized by the Affected Employees as of the Effective Date, other than the Assets. Vendor shall maintain and replace such equipment, at its own expense, as may be necessary to perform the Services in accordance with the Service Levels. All equipment provided by Customer shall remain the property of Customer or its lessor; provided, however, that, to the extent that Vendor upgrades such equipment or replaces parts included in such equipment, Customer shall own the upgrades and replacement parts and Vendor shall own the replaced or removed equipment.]

6.03 [USE OF CUSTOMER FACILITIES.   Except as expressly provided in this Agreement, Vendor shall use the Customer Service Locations for the sole and exclusive purpose of providing the Services. Use of such facilities by Vendor does not constitute a leasehold interest in favor of Vendor or any of Vendor's customers.

1. Vendor shall use the Customer Service Locations in a reasonably efficient manner. To the extent that Vendor operates the space in a manner that unnecessarily increases facility costs incurred by Customer, Customer reserves the right to set off the excess utility costs of such practices.

2. Vendor and Vendor Agents shall keep the Customer Service Locations in good order, not commit or permit waste or damage to such facilities, not use such facilities for any unlawful purpose or act, and comply with all of Customer's standard policies and procedures as in effect from time to time, including procedures for the physical security of the Customer Service Locations.

3. Vendor shall permit Customer and Customer Agents to enter into those portions of the Customer Service Locations occupied by Vendor's staff at any time to perform facilities-related services.

4. Vendor shall not make any improvements or changes involving structural, mechanical, or electrical alterations to the Customer Service Locations without Customer's approval. [OWNERSHIP OF IMPROVEMENTS/CHANGES TO FACILITIES]

5. **When the Customer Service Locations are no longer required for performance of the Services, Vendor shall return such locations to Customer in substantially the same condition as when Vendor began using such locations.]**

[ADD OBLIGATIONS RE: HAZARDOUS MATERIALS/ENVIRON-MENTAL COMPLIANCE]

ARTICLE 7. CONTRACT ADMINISTRATION
[IF APPLICABLE]

7.01 MANAGED AGREEMENTS.   Vendor shall manage, administer, and maintain the Managed Agreements. Vendor shall provide Customer with reasonable notice of any renewal, termination, or cancellation dates and fees with respect to the Managed Agreements. Vendor shall not renew, modify, terminate, or cancel, or request or grant any consents or waivers under, any Managed Agreements without the consent of the appropriate entity or unit of Customer. Any fees or charges or other liability or obligation imposed on Customer in connection with any such renewal, modification, termination, or cancellation of, or consent or waiver under, the Managed Agreements, obtained or given without Customer's consent, shall be paid or discharged, as applicable, by Vendor.

7.02 MANAGED AGREEMENT INVOICES.   Vendor shall (1) receive all Managed Agreement Invoices, (2) review and correct any errors in any such Managed Agreement Invoices in a timely manner, and (3) submit such Managed Agreement Invoices to Customer within a reasonable period of time prior to the due date or, if a discount for payment is offered, the date on which Customer may pay such Managed Agreement Invoice with a discount. Customer shall pay the Managed Agreement Invoices received and approved by Vendor. Customer shall only be responsible for payment of the Managed Agreement Invoices and shall not be responsible to Vendor for any management, administration, or maintenance fees of Vendor in connection with the Managed Agreement Invoices. Customer shall be responsible for any late fees in respect of the Managed Agreement Invoices, provided that Vendor submitted the applicable Managed Agreement Invoices to Customer for payment within a reasonable period of time prior to the date any such Managed Agreement Invoice is due, but in no event later than **[SPECIFY TIME PERIOD]** prior to the due date of such Managed Agreement Invoice. If Vendor fails to submit a Managed Agreement Invoice to Customer for payment in accordance with the preceding sentence, Vendor shall be responsible for any discount not received or any late fees in respect of such Managed Agreement Invoice.

7.03 ASSIGNED AGREEMENTS.   As of the Effective Date, Vendor shall assume all responsibility for the Assigned Agreements. Vendor may, to the extent permitted by the Assigned Agreements, renew, modify, terminate, or cancel, or request or grant any consents or waivers under, any such Assigned Agreements. Any modification, termination, or cancellation fees or charges imposed upon Customer in connection with any modification, termination, or cancellation of, or consent or waiver under, the Assigned Agreements shall be paid by Vendor.

7.04 ASSIGNED AGREEMENT INVOICES. Vendor shall pay the invoices submitted by third parties in connection with the Assigned Agreements and shall be responsible for any late fees in respect of such third-party invoices.

7.05 PERFORMANCE UNDER AGREEMENTS. Vendor shall promptly notify Customer of any breach of, or misuse or fraud in connection with, any Managed Agreements of which Vendor becomes aware and shall cooperate with Customer to prevent or stay any such breach, misuse, or fraud. Vendor shall pay all amounts due for any penalties or charges (including amounts due to a third party as a result of Vendor's failure to promptly notify Customer pursuant to the preceding sentence), associated taxes, legal expenses, and other incidental expenses incurred by Customer as a result of Vendor's nonperformance of its obligations under this Agreement with respect to the Customer Third-Party Contracts.

ARTICLE 8. SERVICE LEVELS

8.01 DESIGNATED SERVICE LEVELS. Vendor shall perform the Designated Services in accordance with the Designated Service Levels and in accordance with *Exhibit 10.*

8.02 NEW SERVICE LEVELS. Vendor shall provide the New Services in accordance with the New Service Levels applicable to such New Services.

8.03 ADJUSTMENT OF SERVICE LEVELS. The Management Committee (1) shall review the Service Levels for the preceding 12 months during the last calendar quarter of every Contract Year, (2) with respect to any Service Levels that require periodic adjustment pursuant to this Agreement or are no longer appropriate because of an increase, decrease, or change to the Services, shall adjust the Service Levels for the subsequent Contract Year, and (3) with respect to all other Service Levels, may adjust the Service Levels for the subsequent Contract Year. In addition, either Party may, at any time upon notice to the other Party, initiate negotiations to review and, upon agreement by the Management Committee, adjust any Service Level that such Party in good faith believes is inappropriate at the time.

8.04 ROOT CAUSE ANALYSIS. Upon receipt of a notice from Customer with respect to Vendor's failure to provide the Services in accordance with the applicable Service Levels, Vendor shall, as soon as reasonably practicable, (1) perform a root cause analysis to identify the cause of such failure, (2) provide Customer with a report detailing the cause of, and procedure for correcting, such failure, (3) implement such procedure, and (4) provide Customer with assurance satisfactory to Customer that such failure will not recur following the completion of the implementation of the procedure.

8.05 MEASUREMENT AND MONITORING TOOLS.   As of the Effective Date, Vendor shall implement the measurement and monitoring Tools and procedures required to measure and report Vendor's performance of the Services against the applicable Service Levels. Such measurement and monitoring and procedures shall (1) permit reporting at a level of detail sufficient to verify compliance with the Service Levels and (2) be subject to audit by Customer or its designee. Vendor shall provide Customer and its designees with information concerning access to such measurement and monitoring Tools and procedures upon request, for inspection and verification purposes.

8.06 CONTINUOUS IMPROVEMENT AND BEST PRACTICES.   Vendor   shall, on a continuous basis (1) as part of its total quality management process, identify ways to improve the Service Levels, and (2) identify and apply proven techniques and Tools from other installations within its operations that would benefit Customer either operationally or financially. Vendor shall, from time to time, include updates with respect to such improvements, techniques, and Tools in the reports provided to Customer pursuant to *Section 3.09.*

8.07 PERFORMANCE CREDITS.   In the event of a failure to provide the Services in accordance with the applicable Service Levels, Vendor shall incur the Performance Credits identified in and according to the schedule set forth in *Exhibit 10.* The Performance Credits shall not limit Customer's right to recover, in accordance with this Agreement, other damages incurred by Customer as a result of such failure. If the Performance Credits incurred exceed **$[SPECIFY DOLLAR AMOUNT]** in any **[SPECIFY TIME PERIOD]** period during the Term, Customer may, upon notice to Vendor, terminate this Agreement, in whole or in part, without regard to *Section 26.04(1).* Nothing in this Section shall be deemed to limit or obviate Customer's right to terminate this Agreement pursuant to *Section 26.04(1).*

ARTICLE 9.   CUSTOMER SATISFACTION AND BENCHMARKING

9.01 INITIAL CUSTOMER SATISFACTION SURVEY.   During   the   *[SPECIFY TIME PERIOD]* period after the Effective Date, Vendor shall submit to Customer, for Customer's approval, the identity of the unaffiliated third party that shall conduct a initial customer satisfaction survey. Upon Customer's approval of such third party, Vendor shall engage such third party to conduct a initial customer satisfaction survey as approved by Customer for affected End Users approved by Customer (the *"Initial Customer Satisfaction Survey"*). The Initial Customer Satisfaction Survey shall be (1) of the content and scope set forth in *Exhibit 18*, (2) administered in accordance with the procedures set forth in

Exhibit 18, and (3) subject to Customer's approval. The results of the Initial Customer Satisfaction Survey shall be the baseline for measurement of the performance improvements described in *Section 9.02.*

9.02 CUSTOMER SATISFACTION SURVEY.

1. At least once every Contract Year during the Term, Vendor shall, upon Customer's request, engage an unaffiliated third party approved by Customer to conduct a customer satisfaction survey in respect of those aspects of the Services designated by Customer. The survey shall, at a minimum, cover a representative sampling of End Users and senior management of Customer, in each case as specified by Customer. The timing, content, scope, and method of the survey shall be consistent with the Initial Customer Satisfaction Survey and subject to Customer's approval. Vendor agrees that **[(a)]** increased measured customer satisfaction shall be a key performance incentive for the compensation of the Key Personnel **[and (b) customer satisfaction shall be measured as a service level pursuant to *Section 9.01*]**.

2. **[In the event that Customer disputes the results of the customer satisfaction survey, Customer may engage a third party, reasonably acceptable to Vendor, to conduct the customer satisfaction survey pursuant to this Section. The results of such survey shall be binding on the Parties.]**

9.03 BENCHMARKING OVERVIEW. The Benchmarking Process shall be conducted by the Benchmarker. In the event (1) a Benchmarker is no longer providing the services required to conduct the Benchmarking Process, (2) Customer and Vendor agree that the Benchmarker should be replaced, or (3) Customer and Vendor determine that another Benchmarker would be needed to take advantage of another system or methodology utilized by such Benchmarker to conduct the Benchmarking Process, Customer shall promptly designate a replacement Benchmarker. The fees and expenses charged by the Benchmarker shall be paid by xxx.

9.04 BENCHMARKING PROCESS. The Benchmarker shall conduct the Benchmarking Process annually in respect of each Contract Year. Within **[SPECIFY TIME PERIOD]** after the beginning of each Contract Year, or such later date agreed upon by the Parties, Customer and Vendor shall (1) agree upon the period during which the Benchmarking Process shall be conducted in such Contract Year and (2) review the Benchmarking Process used during the preceding Contract Year and adjust the Benchmarking Process as may be agreed upon by the Parties for the current Contract Year.

9.05 BENCHMARK RESULTS REVIEW PERIOD AND ADJUSTMENTS. Customer and Vendor shall review the Benchmark Results during the Benchmark Review

Period. **[ADD CONSEQUENCE IF BENCHMARK RESULTS REVEAL THAT VENDOR'S FEES/SERVICES ARE NOT COMPETITIVE.]**

ARTICLE 10.   SERVICE LOCATIONS.

10.01 SERVICE LOCATIONS.   The Services shall be provided **[(1) to the Customer Service Locations,]** (2) from the Vendor Service Locations, and (3) from any other location for which Vendor has received Customer's approval. Any incremental expenses incurred by Customer as a result of a relocation to, or use of, any location other than the locations set forth on *Exhibit 6* shall, at Customer's sole discretion, be paid by Vendor or reimbursed to Customer by Vendor. **[Except with respect to a Customer Service Location that Vendor is (a) the sole lessee of or (b) a sub-lessee and has management control of,]** Vendor and Vendor Agents may not provide or market services to a third-party from a Customer Service Location without Customer's consent.

10.02 SAFETY AND SECURITY PROCEDURES.   Vendor shall maintain and enforce at the Service Locations safety and security procedures that are at least equal to the most stringent of the following: (1) industry standards for locations similar to the Vendor Service Locations; (2) the procedures in effect at locations of other Vendor customers; (3) those procedures applicable to the Customer Service Locations as may be reasonably amended by Customer from time to time during the Term; and (4) any higher standard otherwise agreed upon by the Parties. Vendor shall comply with the safety and security procedures that are applicable to the Customer Service Locations, including the safety and security procedures set forth in *Exhibit 19*.

10.03 DATA SECURITY.   Vendor shall establish and maintain safeguards against the destruction, loss, or alteration of the Customer Data in the possession of Vendor (the *"Data Safeguards"*), which shall be no less rigorous than those data security policies in effect as of the Effective Date at each applicable Customer Service Location in respect of such Customer Service Location and Vendor Service Location. Vendor shall revise and maintain the Data Safeguards at Customer's request. In the event Vendor intends to implement a change to the Data Safeguards (including pursuant to Customer's request), Vendor shall notify Customer and, upon Customer's approval, implement such change. In the event Vendor or Vendor Agents discovers or is notified of a breach or potential breach of security relating to the Customer Data, Vendor shall immediately (1) notify the Customer Contract Manager of such breach or potential breach and (2) if the applicable Customer Data was in the possession of Vendor or Vendor Agents at the time of such breach or potential breach, Vendor shall (a) investigate and remediate the effects of the breach or potential breach and (b) provide Customer with assurance satisfactory to Customer that such breach or potential breach will not recur.

10.04 SECURITY RELATING TO COMPETITORS.   If (1) Vendor provides the Services to Customer from a Service Location that is shared with a third party or third parties or (2) any part of the business of Vendor or any such third party is now or is in the future competitive with Customer's business, then Vendor shall develop a process, subject to Customer's approval, to restrict access in any such shared environment to Customer's Confidential Information so that Vendor's employees or Vendor Agents providing services to such competitive business do not have access to Customer's Confidential Information.

ARTICLE 11. HUMAN RESOURCES

Transitioning of employees of Customer to Vendor shall be effected in accordance with the terms and conditions set forth in *Exhibit 20*.

ARTICLE 12. VENDOR STAFF

12.01 VENDOR CONTRACT MANAGER.   Vendor shall appoint an individual (the "*Vendor Contract Manager*"), who from the date of this Agreement shall serve, on a full-time basis, as the primary Vendor representative under this Agreement. Vendor's appointment of any Vendor Contract Manager shall be subject to Customer's prior approval. The Vendor Contract Manager shall (1) have overall responsibility for managing and coordinating the performance of Vendor's obligations under this Agreement and (2) be authorized to act for and on behalf of Vendor with respect to all matters relating to this Agreement.

12.02 KEY PERSONNEL.   With respect to the Key Personnel set forth in *Exhibit 13*, the Parties agree as follows:

1. Each Key Personnel shall be dedicated to the Customer account on a full-time basis.

2. Before assigning an individual to a Key Personnel position, whether as an initial assignment or as a replacement, Vendor shall (a) notify Customer of the proposed assignment, (b) introduce the individual to appropriate representatives of Customer, (c) provide Customer with a résumé and any other information regarding the individual that may be reasonably requested by Customer, and (d) obtain Customer's approval for such assignment. Vendor shall only assign an individual to a Key Personnel position who is approved by Customer.

3. Vendor shall not replace or reassign (a) the Vendor Contract Manager for **[SPECIFY TIME PERIOD]** from the Effective Date or (b) the other Key Personnel for **[SPECIFY TIME PERIOD]** from the Effective Date, unless Customer consents to such reassignment or replacement or such Key Personnel (i) voluntarily resigns from Vendor, (ii) is dismissed by Vendor for misconduct (e.g., fraud, drug abuse, theft),

(iii) fails to perform his or her duties and responsibilities pursuant to this Agreement, or (iv) dies or is unable to work due to his or her disability.

4.   If Customer decides that any Key Personnel should not continue in that position, then Customer may in its sole discretion and upon notice to Vendor require removal of such Key Personnel. Vendor shall, as soon as reasonably practicable, replace such Key Personnel.

5.   Vendor shall maintain backup procedures and conduct the replacement procedures for the Key Personnel in such a manner so as to assure an orderly succession for any Key Personnel who is replaced. Upon request, after a determination that a Key Personnel will be replaced, Vendor shall make such procedures available to Customer.

12.03 PROJECT STAFF.   Vendor shall appoint individuals with suitable training and skills to perform the Services to the Project Staff. Vendor shall provide Customer with a list of all Vendor personnel dedicated full-time to the Project Staff at the end of every **[SPECIFY TIME PERIOD]** period after the Effective Date. Except as otherwise approved by Customer (in its sole discretion), those Vendor personnel located on Customer's premises may only provide services on such premises which support Customer's operations. Vendor shall notify Customer as soon as possible after dismissing or reassigning any member of the Project Staff whose normal work location is at a Customer Service Location.

12.04 SUBCONTRACTORS.

1.   Prior to subcontracting any of the Services, Vendor shall notify Customer of the proposed subcontract and shall obtain Customer's approval of such subcontract. Prior to amending, modifying, or otherwise supplementing any subcontract relating to the Services, Vendor shall notify Customer of the proposed amendment, modification, or supplement and shall obtain Customer's approval thereof.

2.   No subcontracting shall release Vendor from its responsibility for its obligations under this Agreement. Vendor shall be responsible for the work and activities of each of the Vendor Agents, including compliance with the terms of this Agreement. Vendor shall be responsible for all payments to its subcontractors.

3.   Vendor shall promptly pay for all services, materials, equipment, and labor used by Vendor in providing the Services and Vendor shall keep Customer's premises free of all liens.

12.05 CONDUCT OF VENDOR PERSONNEL.   While at the Customer Service Locations, Vendor and Vendor Agents shall (1) comply with the requests, standard rules and regulations of Customer regarding safety and health, personal and professional conduct (including the wearing of a particular uniform, identification badge or personal protective equipment, and adhering to plant regulations and general safety practices or procedures) generally applicable to such Customer Service Locations and (2) otherwise conduct themselves in a businesslike manner. Vendor shall cause the Project Staff to maintain and enforce the confidentiality provisions of this Agreement. In the event that Customer determines that a particular member of the Project Staff is not conducting himself or herself in accordance with this Section, Customer may notify Vendor of such conduct. Upon receipt of such notice, Vendor shall promptly (1) investigate the matter and take appropriate action, which may include (a) removing the applicable person from the Project Staff and providing Customer with prompt notice of such removal and (b) replacing the applicable person with a similarly qualified individual or (2) take other appropriate disciplinary action to prevent a recurrence. In the event there are repeat violations of this Section by a particular member of the Project Staff, Vendor shall promptly remove the individual from the Project Staff as set forth above.

12.06 NONCOMPETITION. Vendor shall not assign a Key Personnel or member of the Project Staff to the account of any competitor of Customer without Customer's prior consent (1) while such Key Personnel or member of the Project Staff, as the case may be, is assigned to the Customer account and (2) for a period of **[SPECIFY TIME PERIOD]** years following the date that such Key Personnel or member of the Project Staff, as the case may be, is removed from, or ceases to provide services in connection with, the Customer account.

ARTICLE 13. MANAGEMENT AND CONTROL

13.01 MANAGEMENT COMMITTEE. Within **[SPECIFY TIME PERIOD]** of the Effective Date, the Customer Contract Manager and the Vendor Contract Manager shall appoint **[an equal number of]** representatives to serve on a management committee (the "Management Committee"). Customer shall designate one of its representatives on the Management Committee to act as the chairperson of the Management Committee. The Management Committee shall be authorized and responsible for (1) advising with respect to Customer's strategic and tactical decisions regarding the establishment, budgeting and implementation of Customer's priorities and plans for the Services and (2) monitoring and resolving disagreements regarding the provision of the Services and the Service Levels. A Party may change any of its representatives on the Management Committee upon notice to the other Party.

13.02 PROCEDURES MANUAL. Within **[SPECIFY TIME PERIOD]** after the Effective Date, Vendor shall deliver to Customer **[for Customer's approval]**, in the form and scope agreed upon by Customer and Vendor, a management procedures manual (the "*Procedures Manual*"). Vendor shall periodically prepare and provide to Customer updates to such Procedures Manual to reflect any changes in the procedures described therein within a reasonable time after such changes are made.

13.03 CHANGE CONTROL PROCEDURES.   Prior to the Effective Date, Vendor shall deliver to Customer, for its review and approval, the Change Control Procedures. The Change Control Procedures shall provide, at a minimum, that:

1.   No Change shall be implemented without Customer's approval, except as may be necessary on a temporary basis to maintain the continuity of the Services.

2.   With respect to all Changes, Vendor shall (a) other than those Changes made on a temporary basis to maintain the continuity of the Services, schedule Changes so as not to unreasonably interrupt Customer's business operations, (b) prepare and deliver to Customer each month a rolling schedule for ongoing and planned Changes for the next **[SPECIFY TIME PERIOD]** period, and (c) monitor the status of Changes against the applicable schedule.

3.   With respect to any Change made on a temporary basis to maintain the continuity of the Services, Vendor shall document and provide to Customer notification (which may be given orally provided that any oral notice must be confirmed in writing to Customer within five business days) of the Change no later than the next business day after the Change is made.

4.   Vendor shall update the Change Control Procedures as necessary and shall provide such updated Change Control Procedures to Customer for its approval.

ARTICLE 14. PROPRIETARY RIGHTS

14.01 CUSTOMER IP.   Customer hereby grants to Vendor solely to provide the Services a nonexclusive, nontransferable, limited right to have access to and Use, to the extent permissible under the applicable third-party agreements, the Customer IP. Vendor may sublicense, to the extent permissible under the applicable third-party agreements, to Vendor Agents the right to have access to and Use the Customer IP solely to provide those Services that such Vendor Agents are responsible for providing and as may otherwise be agreed to by the Parties.

14.02 VENDOR IP.   Vendor shall provide Customer with access to the Vendor IP during the Term and during the Termination Assistance Period in accordance with *Article 28*. Customer shall have the right to approve any Vendor IP prior to Vendor's use of such Vendor IP to provide the Services. Vendor hereby grants to Customer a global, perpetual, irrevocable, fully paid-up, nonexclusive license to Use and sublicense, and to permit a third party to Use, solely in connection with providing goods or services to or purchasing goods or services from Customer, the Vendor IP being used to provide the Services as of the date of expiration or termination of this Agreement. Upon Customer's request, Vendor shall provide Customer with a list of all Vendor IP being used to provide the Services as of the date of such request.

14.03 NEW IP.   New IP shall be owned by xxx. xxx shall have all right, title, and interest, including worldwide ownership of copyright and patent, in and to the New IP and all copies made from it. xxx hereby irrevocably assigns, transfers, and conveys, and shall cause xxx agents to assign, transfer, and convey, to xxx without further consideration all of its and their right, title, and interest in and to such New IP, including all rights of patent, copyright, trade secret, or other proprietary rights in such materials. xxx acknowledges, and shall cause xxx agents to acknowledge, that xxx and the successors and permitted assigns of xxx shall have the right to obtain and hold in their own name any intellectual property rights in and to such New IP. xxx agrees to execute, and shall cause xxx agents to execute, any documents or take any other actions as may reasonably be necessary, or as xxx may reasonably request, to perfect Customer's ownership of any such New IP. [Note: Ownership of new IP is subject of negotiation.]

ARTICLE 15. DATA

15.01 OWNERSHIP OF CUSTOMER DATA.   All Customer Data is, or will be, and shall remain the property of Customer and shall be deemed Confidential Information of Customer. Without Customer's approval (in its sole discretion), the Customer Data shall not be (1) used by Vendor or Vendor Agents other than in connection with providing the Services, (2) disclosed, sold, assigned, leased, or otherwise provided to third parties by Vendor or Vendor Agents, or (3) commercially exploited by or on behalf of Vendor or Vendor Agents. Vendor hereby irrevocably assigns, transfers, and conveys, and shall cause Vendor Agents to assign, transfer, and convey, to Customer without further consideration all of its and their right, title, and interest in and to the Customer Data. Upon request by Customer, Vendor shall execute and deliver, and shall cause Vendor Agents to execute and deliver, any financing statements or other documents that may be necessary or desirable under any Law to preserve, or enable Customer to enforce, its rights hereunder with respect to the Customer Data.

15.02 CORRECTION OF ERRORS.   Vendor shall promptly correct any errors or inaccuracies in the Customer Data and the reports delivered to Customer under this Agreement, to the extent caused by Vendor or Vendor Agents. At Customer's request and expense, Vendor shall promptly correct any other errors or inaccuracies in the Customer Data or such reports.

15.03 RETURN OF DATA.   Upon request by Customer at any time during the Term and upon expiration or termination of this Agreement, Vendor shall (1) promptly return to Customer, in the format and on the media requested by Customer, all or any part of the Customer Data and (2) erase or destroy all or any part of the Customer Data in Vendor's possession, in each case to the extent so requested by Customer. Any archival tapes containing Customer Data shall be used by Vendor and Vendor Agents solely for backup purposes.

ARTICLE 16. CONSENTS

Vendor, at its own cost, shall obtain, maintain, and comply with all of the Consents.

ARTICLE 17. CONTINUED PROVISION OF SERVICES

17.01 DISASTER RECOVERY PLAN.   Vendor shall (1) develop, submit to Customer for Customer's review, and implement a DRP acceptable to Customer within **[SPECIFY TIME PERIOD]** of the Effective Date, (2) periodically update and test the operability of the DRP during every **[SPECIFY TIME PERIOD]** period that the DRP is fully operational, (3) certify to Customer at least **[SPECIFY TIME PERIOD]** during every **[SPECIFY TIME PERIOD]** period that the DRP is fully operational, and (4) implement the DRP upon the occurrence of a disaster (as such term is defined in the DRP). Vendor shall reinstate the Critical Services within **[SPECIFY TIME PERIOD]** of the occurrence of a disaster. In the event the Critical Services are not reinstated within **[SPECIFY TIME PERIOD]**, Customer may terminate this Agreement, in whole or in part, without regard to *Section 26.04(1)*. In the event of a disaster, Vendor shall not increase its charges under this Agreement or charge Customer usage fees in addition to the Designated Fees or the Variable Fees.

17.02 *FORCE MAJEURE.*   [ADD APPLICABLE *FORCE MAJEURE* PROVISION]

ARTICLE 18. PAYMENTS TO VENDOR

18.01 DESIGNATED FEES.   In consideration of Vendor providing the Designated Services, Customer shall pay to Vendor the Designated Fees. Except as expressly set forth in this Agreement, there shall be no charge or fees payable by Customer in respect of Vendor's performance of its obligations pursuant to this Agreement.

18.02 VARIABLE FEES AND ADJUSTMENT OF BASELINES.   At the end of every month, Vendor shall review the amount of the Designated Services used by Customer during the preceding month. In the event Customer's use of such services (1) increases above the resource baselines set forth in *Exhibit 11*, Customer shall pay to Vendor, in addition to the Designated Fees, an amount equal to the Additional Resource Charges in connection with the services set forth in *Exhibit 11* or (2) decreases below the resource baselines set forth in *Exhibit 11*, Vendor shall credit Customer an amount equal to Reduced Resource Credits in connection with the services set forth in *Exhibit 11*. Upon notice to Vendor, and no more than once each Contract Year, Customer may adjust the resource baselines set forth in *Exhibit 11* and Customer and Vendor shall implement an appropriate adjustment to the Fees to reflect the adjustment of the resource baselines.

18.03 SUBSTANTIAL CHANGE IN BASELINES.   In the event that Customer's use of the Designated Services decreases or increases more than **[SPECIFY PERCENT]** in the aggregate from the baselines set forth in *Exhibit 11* for any consecutive **[SPECIFY TIME PERIOD]** period during the Term, Customer and Vendor shall negotiate and implement an appropriate reduction or increase to the Designated Fees. Customer shall not be obligated to obtain the Services from Vendor with respect to any newly acquired or formed entity or business unit.

18.04 [ADJUSTMENTS TO FEES.   There shall be no periodic adjustments to the Fees.]

18.05 EXPENSES.   Except as expressly set forth in this Agreement, all costs and expenses relating to the Services (including all costs and expenses related to the acquisition, maintenance, and enhancement of the IP and Machines) are included in the Fees and shall not be charged to or reimbursed by Customer.

18.06 CRITICAL MILESTONES.   In connection with the development of the Transition Plan, Customer and Vendor shall develop a list of milestones relating to Vendor's obligations pursuant to *Article 4,* which are critical to Customer, and, for each milestone (1) a description of the applicable triggering event from which achievement of that milestone shall be measured, (2) the duration of time from the triggering event for the completion of that milestone, and (3) an amount of the Designated Fees that Customer may defer with respect to that milestone in accordance with this Section. *Exhibit 21* contains lists of events and related information that Customer and Vendor agree shall be included in the final list. After development of the final list, Customer may defer, upon Customer's election, the specified amount of the Designated Fees if, as a result of Vendor's failure to perform its obligations pursuant to this Agreement, Vendor fails by more than **[SPECIFY TIME PERIOD]** days to achieve any specified milestone by the specified completion date. If and when Vendor achieves the specified milestone, all deferred fees shall be promptly paid to Vendor. Customer's deferral rights described in this Section shall not limit Customer's right to recover other damages incurred by Customer as a result of such failure or to terminate this Agreement pursuant to *Section 26.04(1).*

18.07 RIGHTS OF SET-OFF.   With respect to any amount that (1) should be reimbursed to Customer or (2) is otherwise payable to Customer pursuant to this Agreement, Customer may upon notice to Vendor deduct the entire amount owed to Customer against the charges otherwise payable or expenses owed to Vendor under this Agreement.

18.08 PRORATION.   All periodic Fees or charges under this Agreement are to be computed on a calendar month basis and shall be prorated on a per diem basis for any partial month.

18.09 REFUNDABLE ITEMS; PREPAID EXPENSES.   In the event Vendor receives any refund, credit, or other rebate (including deposits) in connection with a Customer Third-Party Contract or the Assets that is attributable to periods prior to the Effective Date or for which Customer retained financial responsibility after the Effective Date, then Vendor shall promptly (1) notify Customer of such refund, credit, or rebate and (2) pay to Customer the full amount of such refund, credit, or rebate. Vendor shall reimburse Customer for all prepaid amounts related to the Services.

18.10 UNUSED CREDITS.   Any unused credits against future payments owed to either Party by the other pursuant to this Agreement shall be paid to the applicable Party within 30 days of the earlier of the expiration or termination of this Agreement.

18.11 MOST-FAVORED CUSTOMER.   Vendor's charges to Customer for the Services shall be at least as low as Vendor's lowest charges for similar services to Vendor's best customer. Upon Customer's request, Vendor shall notify Customer that this Section has not been contradicted by any transaction entered into by Vendor since the later of (1) the Effective Date or (2) the date of the most recent notice provided by Vendor pursuant to this Section. If Vendor is unable to provide such notice because of a transaction entered into by Vendor contradicting this Section, Vendor shall offer to Customer an adjustment to the terms of this Agreement, including, if appropriate, the lowest charges included in any such transaction.

ARTICLE 19. PAYMENT SCHEDULE AND INVOICES

19.01 DESIGNATED FEES.   Within **[SPECIFY TIME PERIOD]** of the last day of each month of the Term, Vendor shall invoice Customer for the Designated Services performed in accordance with this Agreement during that month. **[Vendor shall invoice the Designated Fees in the currency specified by Customer.]** The Designated Fees for the first month of the Term shall be due and payable to Vendor within **[SPECIFY TIME PERIOD]** after the Effective Date. The Designated Fees for each subsequent month during the Term shall be due and payable to Vendor within **[SPECIFY TIME PERIOD]** of the later of (1) the end of the month in which Vendor provided the Services and (2) the date that Customer receives Vendor's invoice.

19.02 VARIABLE FEES.   During the first week of each calendar month of the Term after the first such month, Vendor shall provide Customer with the Variable Fee Report and an invoice for payment of the Additional Resource Charges. Customer shall pay such invoice within **[SPECIFY TIME PERIOD]** of Customer's receipt of such invoice or, in the event the Reduced Resource Credits are in excess of the Additional Resource Charges, Vendor shall provide Customer with a credit as set forth in the invoice for the Designated Fees for the following month. In the event Customer disapproves of any of the Variable Fees set forth in the Variable Fee Report, Customer shall provide Vendor with a list of any Variable Fees of which Customer disapproves and Vendor shall adjust the Variable Fee Report to reflect the changes indicated by Customer and agreed to by Vendor.

19.03 TIME OF PAYMENT.   Any sum due Vendor pursuant to this Agreement for which payment is not otherwise specified shall be due and payable **[SPECIFY TIME PERIOD]** after receipt by Customer of an invoice from Vendor.

19.04 DETAILED INVOICES.   Vendor shall provide invoices with varying degrees of detail (e.g., per end user, department, project, site), as requested by Customer.

19.05 FEE DISPUTE.   In the event of a dispute, Customer shall pay any undisputed amounts to Vendor and Vendor shall continue to perform its obligations under this Agreement.

ARTICLE 20. TAXES

1. The Fees paid to Vendor are inclusive of any applicable sales, use, gross receipts, excise, value-added, withholding, personal property, or other taxes attributable to periods on or after the Effective Date based on or measured by Vendor's cost in acquiring or providing equipment, materials, supplies, or services furnished or used by Vendor in performing or furnishing the Services, including all personal property and sales or use taxes, if any, due on the Vendor Machines. In the event that a sales, use, excise, gross receipts, or services tax is assessed on the provision of the Services by Vendor to Customer or on Vendor's charges to Customer under this Agreement, however levied or assessed, Vendor shall bear and be responsible for and pay the amount of any such tax. To the extent that any sales, use, gross receipts, excise, value-added, or services tax is required by Law to be separately identified in Vendor's billings to Customer, Vendor shall separately identify the tax and assume any and all responsibility for noncompliance, including tax, interest, and penalty assessments.

2. Any taxes assessed, as determined by Customer, including a gross-up thereon, on the provision of the Services for a particular site resulting from Vendor's relocating or rerouting the delivery of Services for Vendor's convenience to, from, or through a location other than the Service Location used to provide the Services as of the Effective Date shall be paid by Customer and Customer shall receive a credit with respect to the Fees invoiced under this Agreement equal to such payments made pursuant to this subsection.

3. Customer and Vendor shall each bear sole responsibility for all taxes, assessments, and other real property-related levies on its owned or leased real property.

4. Customer and Vendor shall cooperate to segregate the Fees into the following separate payment streams: (a) those for taxable Services; (b) those for nontaxable Services; (c) those for which a sales, use, or other similar tax has already been paid; and (d) those for which Vendor functions merely as a paying agent for Customer in receiving goods, supplies, or services (including leasing and licensing arrangements) that otherwise are nontaxable or have previously been subject to tax. In addition, each of Customer and Vendor shall reasonably cooperate with the other to more accurately determine a Party's tax liability and to minimize such liability, to the extent legally permissible. Each of Customer and Vendor shall provide and make available to the other any resale certificates, information regarding out-of-state sales or use of equipment, materials, or services, and any other exemption certificates or information requested by a Party.

ARTICLE 21. AUDITS

21.01 SERVICES. Upon notice from Customer, Vendor and Vendor Agents shall provide Customer, Customer Agents, and any of Customer's regulators with access to and any assistance (including reports) that they may require with respect to the Service Locations and the Systems for the purpose of performing audits or inspections of the Services and the business of Customer relating to the Services. If any audit by an auditor designated by Customer, a Customer Agent, or a regulatory authority results in Vendor being notified that Vendor or Vendor Agents are not in compliance with any Law or audit requirement, Vendor shall, and shall cause Vendor Agents to, promptly take actions to comply with such audit. Vendor shall bear the expense of any such response that is (1) required by a Law or audit requirement relating to Vendor's business or (2) necessary due to Vendor's noncompliance with any Law or audit requirement imposed on Vendor. To the extent the expense is not payable by Vendor pursuant to the preceding sentence, Customer shall bear the expense of any such compliance that is (a) required by any Law or audit requirement relating to Customer's business or (b) necessary due to Customer's noncompliance with any Law or audit requirement imposed on Customer.

21.02 FEES.

1. Upon notice from Customer, Vendor shall provide Customer and Customer Agents with access to such financial records and supporting documentation as may be requested by Customer, and Customer and Customer Agents may audit the Fees charged to Customer to determine if such Fees are accurate and in accordance with this Agreement (including *Section 18.11*).

2. If, as a result of such audit, Customer determines that Vendor has over-charged Customer, Customer shall notify Vendor of the amount of such overcharge and Vendor shall promptly pay to Customer the amount of the overcharge, plus Interest calculated from the date of receipt by Vendor of the overcharged amount until the date of payment to Customer.

3. In addition to Customer's rights set forth in *Section 21.02(2)*, in the event any such audit reveals an overcharge to Customer of 5 percent or more of a particular fee category, Vendor shall, at Customer's option, issue to Customer a credit against the Designated Fees or reimburse Customer for the cost of such audit.

21.03 RECORD RETENTION.   Vendor shall retain records and supporting documentation sufficient to document the Services and the Fees paid or payable by Customer under this Agreement in accordance with Customer's then-current record retention procedures, as in effect from time to time.

[ADD SECURITY AND SAS 70 REQUIREMENTS.]

21.04 FACILITIES.   Vendor shall provide to Customer[,]Customer Agents, **[and Customer's regulators]**, on Vendor's premises (or, if the audit is being performed of a Vendor Agent, the Vendor Agent's premises if necessary), space, office furnishings (including lockable cabinets), telephone and facsimile services, utilities, and office-related equipment and duplicating services as Customer or such Customer Agents may reasonably require to perform the audits described in this Article.

ARTICLE 22. CONFIDENTIALITY

22.01 GENERAL OBLIGATIONS.   All Confidential Information relating to or obtained from Customer or Vendor shall be held in confidence by the recipient to the same extent and in at least the same manner as the recipient protects its own confidential information. Neither Customer nor Vendor shall disclose, publish, release, transfer, or otherwise make available Confidential Information of, or obtained from, the other in any form to, or for the use or benefit of, any person or entity without the disclosing Party's consent. Each of Customer and Vendor shall, however, be permitted to disclose relevant aspects of the other's Confidential Information to its officers, directors, agents, professional advisors, contractors (including the Benchmarker), subcontractors, and employees and to the officers, directors, agents, professional advisors, contractors, subcontractors, and employees of its affiliates, to the extent that such disclosure is not restricted under this Agreement, any Assigned Agreements, any Managed Agreements, any Consents, or any Governmental Approvals and only to the extent that such disclosure is reasonably necessary for the performance of its duties and obligations, or exercise of its rights, under this Agreement; provided, however, that the recipient shall take all reasonable measures to ensure that Confidential Information of the disclosing Party is not disclosed or duplicated in contravention of the provisions of this Agreement by such officers, directors, agents, professional advisors, contractors, subcontractors, and employees. The obligations in this Section shall not restrict any disclosure pursuant to any Law (provided that the recipient shall give prompt notice to the disclosing Party of such order).

22.02 ATTORNEY–CLIENT PRIVILEGE.   Vendor recognizes that it may obtain access to client documents, data, and databases created by and for Customer and associated communications related thereto (collectively, *"Privileged Work Product"*), which are confidential attorney work products or subject to the attorney-client privilege. Vendor shall not intentionally reveal Privileged Work Product to third parties, and Vendor shall institute adequate safeguards to prevent the unintentional disclosure of Privileged Work Product to third parties. The only Project Staff who may have access to Privileged Work Product shall be those for whom such access is necessary to provide services to Customer as provided in this Agreement. All Project Staff who will need access to Privileged Work Product shall first sign and deliver to Customer a confidentiality agreement satisfactory to Customer. Vendor recognizes that Privileged Work Product has been prepared in anticipation of litigation and that Vendor is performing the Services in respect of Privileged Work Product as an agent of Customer, and that all matter related thereto is protected from disclosure by Rule 26 of the United States Federal Rules of Civil Procedure (or any similar Law in other local jurisdictions). Should Vendor ever be notified of any judicial or other proceeding seeking to obtain access to Privileged Work Product, Vendor shall (1) immediately notify Customer and (2) take such reasonable actions as may be specified by Customer to resist providing such access. Customer shall have the right and duty to represent Vendor in such resistance or to select and compensate counsel to so represent Vendor or to reimburse Vendor for reasonable attorneys' fees and expenses incurred in resisting such access.

22.03 UNAUTHORIZED ACTS.   Without limiting either Party's rights in respect of a breach of this Article, each Party shall:

1. promptly notify the other Party of any unauthorized possession, use, or knowledge, or attempt thereof, of the other Party's Confidential Information by any person or entity that may become known to such Party;

2. promptly furnish to the other Party full details of the unauthorized possession, use, or knowledge, or attempt thereof, and assist the other Party in investigating or preventing the recurrence of any unauthorized possession, use, or knowledge, or attempt thereof, of Confidential Information;

3. cooperate with the other Party in any litigation and investigation against third parties deemed necessary by the other Party to protect its proprietary rights; and

4. promptly use its best efforts to prevent a recurrence of any such unauthorized possession, use, or knowledge, or attempt thereof, of Confidential Information.

Each Party shall bear the cost it incurs as a result of compliance with this Section.

ARTICLE 23.   REPRESENTATIONS AND WARRANTIES

23.01 BY CUSTOMER.   Customer represents and warrants that:

1. Customer is a [corporation duly incorporated] [partnership duly organized,] [other,] validly existing and in good standing under the Laws of [SPECIFY LAWS];

2. Customer has all requisite [corporate] [partnership] [other] power and authority to execute, deliver, and perform its obligations under this Agreement;

3. the execution, delivery, and performance of this Agreement by Customer (a) has been duly authorized by Customer and (b) will not conflict with, result in a breach of, or constitute a default under any other agreement to which Customer is a party or by which Customer is bound;

4. Customer is duly licensed, authorized, or qualified to do business and is in good standing in every jurisdiction in which a license, authorization, or qualification is required for the ownership or leasing of its assets or the transaction of business of the character transacted by it, except where the failure to be so licensed, authorized, or qualified would not have a material adverse effect on Customer's ability to fulfill its obligations under this Agreement;

5. Customer is in compliance with all Laws applicable to Customer and has obtained all applicable permits and licenses required of Customer in connection with its obligations under this Agreement;

6. Customer has not disclosed any Confidential Information of Vendor **[; and**

7. **the Customer IP set forth in *Exhibit 5* does not infringe upon the proprietary rights of any third party]**.

[ADD ENVIRONMENTAL COMPLIANCE REP IF APPLICABLE]
[ADD ERISA COMPLIANCE REP IF APPLICABLE]

23.02 BY VENDOR.   Vendor represents and warrants that:

1. Vendor is a **[corporation duly incorporated,] [partnership duly organized,] [other,]** validly existing and in good standing under the Laws of **[SPECIFY LAWS]**;

2. Vendor has all requisite **[corporate][partnership][other]** power and authority to execute, deliver, and perform its obligations under this Agreement;

3. the execution, delivery, and performance of this Agreement by Vendor (a) has been duly authorized by Vendor and (b) will not conflict with, result in a breach of, or constitute a default under any other agreement to which Vendor is a party or by which Vendor is bound;

4. Vendor is duly licensed, authorized, or qualified to do business and is in good standing in every jurisdiction in which a license, authorization, or qualification is required for the ownership or leasing of its assets or the transaction of business of the character transacted by it, except where the failure to be so licensed, authorized, or qualified would not have a material adverse effect on Vendor's ability to fulfill its obligations under this Agreement;

5. Vendor is in compliance with all Laws applicable to Vendor and has obtained all applicable permits and licenses required of Vendor in connection with its obligations under this Agreement;

6. Vendor has not disclosed any Confidential Information of Customer;

7. there is no outstanding litigation, arbitrated matter, or other dispute to which Vendor is a party which, if decided unfavorably to Vendor, would reasonably be expected to have a material adverse effect on Customer's or Vendor's ability to fulfill its respective obligations under this Agreement; and

8. the Vendor IP does not infringe upon the proprietary rights of any third party.

23.03 DISCLAIMER. EXCEPT AS SPECIFIED IN *SECTION 23.01* AND *SECTION 23.02*, NEITHER CUSTOMER NOR VENDOR MAKES ANY OTHER WARRANTIES WITH RESPECT TO THE SERVICES OR THE SYSTEMS AND EACH EXPLICITLY DISCLAIMS ALL OTHER WARRANTIES, EXPRESS OR IMPLIED, INCLUDING THE IMPLIED WARRANTIES OF MERCHANTABILITY AND FITNESS FOR A SPECIFIC PURPOSE.

ARTICLE 24. ADDITIONAL COVENANTS

24.01 BY CUSTOMER. Customer covenants and agrees with Vendor that during the Term and the Termination Assistance Period:

1. Customer shall comply with all Laws applicable to Customer and, except as otherwise provided in this Agreement, shall obtain all applicable permits and licenses required of Customer in connection with its obligations under this Agreement[; **and**

2. the Customer IP set forth in *Exhibit 5* shall not infringe upon the proprietary rights of any third party (except as may have been caused by a modification by Vendor or Vendor Agents)].

24.02 BY VENDOR.   Vendor covenants and agrees with Customer that during the Term and the Termination Assistance Period:

1.   Vendor shall comply with all Laws applicable to Vendor and shall obtain all applicable permits and licenses required of Vendor in connection with its obligations under this Agreement;

2.   none of the Services, the New IP, the Vendor IP, the Vendor Machines, any enhancements or modifications to the Customer IP performed by Vendor or Vendor Agents, or any other resources or items provided to Customer by Vendor or Vendor Agents shall infringe upon the proprietary rights of any third party (except as may have been caused by a modification by Customer or Customer Agents).

3.   **[Vendor shall ensure that no viruses or similar items are coded or introduced into the Systems. Vendor agrees that, in the event a virus or similar item is found to have been introduced into the Systems, Vendor shall assist Customer in reducing the effects of the virus or similar item and, if the virus or similar item causes a loss of operational efficiency or loss of data, to assist Customer to the same extent to mitigate and restore such losses;]**

4.   **[without the consent of Customer, Vendor shall not insert into the Software used to provide the Services any code that would have the effect of disabling or otherwise shutting down all or any portion of the Services. Vendor further represents and warrants that, with respect to any disabling code that may be part of the Software used to provide the Services, Vendor shall not invoke such disabling code at any time, including upon expiration or termination of this Agreement, without Customer's consent;]**

5.   **[If a European Monetary Unit is required under any Law, or is permitted under any Law and any country adopts such European Monetary Unit, then (a) to the extent required to provide the Services, the Systems shall be EMU Compliant and (b) upon Customer's request Vendor shall provide Customer with test scripts to validate that such Systems are EMU Compliant.]**

[ADD ENVIRONMENTAL COMPLIANCE COVENANT IF APPLICABLE]
[ADD ERISA COMPLIANCE COVENANT IF APPLICABLE]

ARTICLE 25.   DISPUTE RESOLUTION

25.01 CONTRACT MANAGERS.   Any dispute arising under this Agreement shall be considered in person or by telephone by the Customer Contract Manager and the Vendor Contract Manager within **[SPECIFY TIME PERIOD]** of receipt of a notice from either Party specifying the nature of the dispute; provided, however, that a dispute relating to *Section 15.03* or *Article 22* shall not be subject to this Section. Unless the Customer Contract Manager and the Vendor Contract Manager otherwise agree in writing, either Party may pursue its rights and remedies under this Agreement after the occurrence of such meeting or telephone conversation.

25.02 CONTINUITY OF SERVICES.   Vendor acknowledges that the timely and complete performance of its obligations pursuant to this Agreement is critical to the business and operations of Customer. Accordingly, in the event of a dispute between Customer and Vendor, Vendor shall continue to so perform its obligations under this Agreement in good faith during the resolution of such dispute unless and until this Agreement is terminated in accordance with the provisions hereof.

25.03 EXPEDITED DISPUTE RESOLUTION.   Notwithstanding anything to the contrary contained in this Agreement, in the event of a dispute relating to or arising out of a Default Notice, the dispute resolution process described in this Article must be commenced and completed within the applicable Default Cure Period.

ARTICLE 26. TERMINATION

26.01 TERMINATION FOR CONVENIENCE.   Customer   may   terminate   this Agreement, in whole or in part, for convenience effective as of any time after the Effective Date by giving Vendor notice of the termination at least **[SPECIFY TIME PERIOD]** prior to the termination date specified in the notice.

26.02 TERMINATION FOR CHANGE IN CONTROL OF CUSTOMER.   In the event of a Change in Control of Customer, Customer may terminate this Agreement by giving Vendor notice of the termination at least **[SPECIFY TIME PERIOD]** prior to the termination date specified in the notice.

26.03 TERMINATION FOR CHANGE IN CONTROL OF VENDOR.   In the event of a Change in Control of Vendor, Customer may terminate this Agreement by giving Vendor notice of the termination at least **[SPECIFY TIME PERIOD]** prior to the termination date specified in the notice.

26.04 TERMINATION FOR CAUSE.

   1.   If Vendor defaults in the performance of any of its material obligations (or repeatedly defaults in the performance of any of its other obligations) under this Agreement (except as provided in *Section 26.05*), and does not cure such default within 30 days of receipt (the *"Default Cure Period"*) of a notice of default (the *"Default Notice"*), then Customer may, by giving notice to Vendor, terminate this Agreement as of the termination date specified in the notice.

2. If Customer fails to make undisputed payments due to Vendor under this Agreement and does not cure such default within 30 days of receipt of a Notice of Default from Vendor, then Vendor may, by giving notice to Customer, terminate this Agreement as of the Termination Date specified in the notice.

26.05 TERMINATION FOR FAILURE TO PROVIDE CRITICAL SERVICES.   If Vendor fails to provide (1) any Critical Service and does not, within **[SPECIFY TIME PERIOD]** after receipt of a notice from Customer with respect to such failure, cure such failure or, if such failure cannot be cured within **[SPECIFY TIME PERIOD]**, provide Customer with a workaround that allows Customer to receive such Critical Service or (2) any Critical Service more than **[SPECIFY TIME PERIOD]** times in any consecutive **[SPECIFY TIME PERIOD]** period during the Term, then Customer may, upon notice to Vendor, terminate this Agreement, in whole or in part, as of the termination date specified in the notice.

[ADD ADDITIONAL TERMINATION RIGHTS IF APPLICABLE]

26.06 OTHER TERMINATIONS.   In addition to the provisions of this Article, this Agreement may be terminated as provided in *Section 3.04(2), Section 8.07*, and *Section 17.01*.

ARTICLE 27. [TERMINATION FEES]

27.01 [CALCULATION OF TERMINATION FEES.]   **[Set forth in *Exhibit 22* are the only termination fees that would be payable to Vendor if this Agreement is terminated pursuant to *Section 26.01*, effective as of the end of any month during the remaining Contract Years during the Term. Any termination fees payable in accordance with this Article shall be due and payable on the End Date.]**

27.02 [FEE ADJUSTMENT UPON PARTIAL TERMINATION.]   **[If Customer terminates a portion of the Services pursuant to *Section 26.01* or any other provision of this Agreement, then the Designated Fees shall be adjusted in accordance with *Exhibit 22*.]**

27.03 [TERMINATION FEES.]   **[Except as otherwise specifically set forth in this Article, no termination fee shall be payable by Customer in connection with the termination of this Agreement.]**

ARTICLE 28. TERMINATION ASSISTANCE

28.01 TERMINATION ASSISTANCE SERVICES.   Vendor shall, upon Customer's request during the Termination Assistance Period, provide the Termination Assistance Services at Vendor's rates then in effect for such services immediately prior to the expiration, termination, or partial termination of this

Agreement, or the insourcing or resourcing of a portion of the Services, except to the extent that resources included in the Designated Fees being paid by Customer to Vendor after such expiration, termination, partial termination, insourcing, or resourcing can be used to provide the Termination Assistance Services. The quality and level of performance during the Termination Assistance Period shall not be degraded. After the expiration of the Termination Assistance Period, Vendor shall (1) answer questions from Customer regarding the terminated, insourced, or resourced Services on an "as-needed" basis at Vendor's then standard billing rates and (2) deliver to Customer any remaining Customer-owned reports and documentation relating to the terminated, insourced, or resourced Services still in Vendor's possession.

28.02 EXIT RIGHTS.   Upon the later of (1) the expiration, termination, or partial termination of this Agreement or the insourcing or resourcing of a portion of the Services, and (2) the last day of the Termination Assistance Period (the *"End Date"*):

1. The rights granted to Vendor and Vendor Agents in *Section 14.01* shall immediately terminate and Vendor shall, and shall cause Vendor Agents to, (a) deliver to Customer, at no cost to Customer, a current copy of the Customer IP in the form in use as of the End Date and (b) destroy or erase all other copies of the Customer IP in Vendor's or Vendor Agents' possession. Vendor shall, upon Customer's request, certify to Customer that all such copies have been destroyed or erased.

2. Vendor shall deliver to Customer a copy of the Vendor IP in the form in use as of the End Date, and Customer shall have the rights described in *Section 14.02*.

3. Upon Customer's request, with respect to any Vendor IP that Vendor has licensed, leased, or otherwise obtained from third parties, and is using to provide the Services as of the End Date, Vendor shall transfer, assign, or sublicense such Vendor IP to Customer and its designee(s) at no additional cost.

4. Vendor shall (a) deliver to Customer a copy of all of the New IP (if owned or licensed by customer), in the form in use as of the End Date and (b) destroy or erase all other copies of such New IP in Vendor's possession.

5. Upon Customer's request, with respect to (a) any agreements for maintenance, disaster recovery services, or other third-party services, and any Vendor Machines not owned by the Vendor, being used by Vendor or Vendor Agents to provide the Services as of the End Date and (b) the Assigned Agreements (not otherwise covered in *Section 28.02(5)(a)*), Vendor shall, and shall cause Vendor Agents to, transfer or assign such agreements and Vendor Machines to Customer and its designee(s), on terms and conditions acceptable to all applicable parties.

6.   Upon Customer's request, Vendor shall sell to Customer or its designee(s) (a) the Vendor Machines being used by Vendor or Vendor Agents to perform the Services as of the End Date and (b) any assets transferred by Customer to Vendor or Vendor Agents (not otherwise covered in *Section 28.02(6)(a)*), free and clear of all liens, security interests, or other encumbrances at the lesser of the fair market value, as shall be determined by an agreed-upon appraisal, and the book value.

28.03 HIRING OF PROJECT STAFF.   Upon the occurrence of the delivery to Vendor by Customer of a notice of intent to (1) terminate this Agreement, or (2) insource or resource a portion of the Services pursuant to *Section 3.07*, with respect to each then-current member of the Project Staff performing the portion of the Services that are being terminated, insourced, or resourced (each an *"Affected Project Staff Member"*), Vendor shall (a) not terminate, reassign, or otherwise remove from the Project Staff any Affected Project Staff Member and (b) to the extent not prohibited by applicable laws or governmental rules or regulations, (i) provide Customer with the name of each Affected Project Staff Member's position and a description of job responsibilities, in accordance with Vendor's standard employment policies; (ii) provide Customer and its designees full access to such Affected Project Staff Members; and (iii) allow Customer and its designees to meet with, solicit, and hire such Affected Project Staff Members. Vendor shall waive any restrictions that may prevent Affected Project Staff Members from being hired by Customer or its designees pursuant to this Section.

28.04 [TERMINATION ASSISTANCE ON PARTIAL TERMINATION.   Where there is a partial termination of this Agreement, or an insourcing or resourcing of a portion of the Services pursuant to *Section 3.07*, then *Section 28.02* and *Section 28.03* shall apply only in relation to those resources and other items referred to in *Section 28.02* (the *"Affected Resources"*), and those Affected Project Staff Members, which are associated with the Services to be terminated, insourced, or resourced. As soon as practicable after Customer exercises its rights to partially terminate this Agreement, or insource or resource any Services, Vendor shall notify Customer if any such Affected Resources, or any such Affected Project Staff Members, are necessary for the provision of the remaining Services and cannot be duplicated; whereupon Customer and Vendor will agree on, and failing agreement within a reasonable time Customer will specify, an appropriate allocation of such Affected Resources and Affected Project Staff Members.]

ARTICLE 29. INDEMNITIES

29.01 INDEMNITY BY CUSTOMER.   Customer shall indemnify Vendor from, and defend and hold Vendor harmless from and against, any Losses suffered, incurred, or sustained by Vendor or to which Vendor becomes subject, resulting from, arising out of, or relating to any claim:

1. **[That the Customer IP infringes upon the proprietary or other rights of any third-party (except as may have been caused by a modification by Vendor or Vendor Agents).]**

2. Relating to any duties or obligations of Customer or Customer Agents with respect to a third party.

3. Relating to the inaccuracy, untruthfulness, or breach of any representation or warranty made by Customer under this Agreement.

4. Relating to (a) a violation of Law for the protection of persons or members of a protected class or category of persons by Customer or Customer Agents, including unlawful discrimination, (b) work-related injury, except as may be covered by Customer's workers' compensation plan, or death caused by Customer or Customer Agents, (c) accrued employee benefits not expressly assumed by Vendor, (d) any representations, oral or written, made by Customer or Customer Agents to the Affected Employees, and (e) any other aspect of the Affected Employees' employment relationship with Customer or termination of such employment relationship with Customer (including claims for breach of an express or implied contract of employment).

5. Relating to any amounts, including taxes, interest, and penalties, assessed against Vendor, which are the obligation of Customer pursuant to *Article 20.*

6. Relating to personal injury (including death) or property loss or damage resulting from Customer's or Customer Agents' acts or omissions.

7. Relating to a breach of any of the covenants in *Section 24.01.*

[ADD ENVIRONMENTAL INDEMNITY IF APPLICABLE]

Customer shall indemnify Vendor from any costs and expenses incurred in connection with the enforcement of this Section.

29.02 INDEMNITY BY VENDOR.   Vendor shall indemnify Customer from, and defend and hold Customer harmless from and against, any Losses suffered, incurred, or sustained by Customer or to which Customer becomes subject, resulting from, arising out of, or relating to any claim:

1. That the Services, the New IP, the Vendor IP, the Vendor Machines, any enhancements or modifications to the Customer IP performed by Vendor or Vendor Agents, or any other resources or items provided to Customer by Vendor or Vendor Agents infringe upon the proprietary or other rights of any third party (except as may have been caused by a modification by Customer or Customer Agents).

2. Relating to any duties or obligations of Vendor or Vendor Agents in respect of a third party or any subcontractor of Vendor.

3. By a third party arising from services **[or systems]** provided by Vendor or Vendor Agents from a Service Location.

4. Relating to the inaccuracy, untruthfulness, or breach of any representation or warranty made by Vendor under this Agreement.

5. Relating to Vendor's failure to obtain, maintain, or comply with the Consents and Governmental Approvals.

6. Relating to (a) a violation of Law for the protection of persons or members of a protected class or category of persons by Vendor or Vendor Agents, including unlawful discrimination, (b) work-related injury, except as may be covered by Vendor's workers' compensation plan, or death caused by Vendor or Vendor Agents, (c) accrued employee benefits not expressly retained by Customer, (d) any representations, oral or written, made by Vendor or Vendor Agents to Customer's employees, including the Affected Employees, and (e) any other aspect of the Affected Employees' employment relationship with Vendor or the termination of the employment relationship with Vendor (including claims for breach of an express or implied contract of employment).

7. Relating to inadequacies in the facilities and the physical and data security controls at (a) the Customer Service Locations, to the extent the same (i) are controlled or provided by Vendor or Vendor Agents after the Effective Date and (ii) relate to Vendor's or Vendor Agents' provision of the Services and (b) the Vendor Service Locations.

8. Relating to any amounts, including taxes, interest, and penalties, assessed against Customer that are the obligation of Vendor pursuant to *Article 20*.

9. Relating to personal injury (including death) or property loss or damage resulting from Vendor's or Vendor Agents' acts or omissions.

10. Relating to a breach of *Section 15.01* or *Section 15.03*.

11. Relating to a breach of any of the covenants in *Section 24.02*.

[ADD ENVIRONMENTAL INDEMNITY IF APPLICABLE]

Vendor shall indemnify Customer from any costs and expenses incurred in connection with the enforcement of this Section.

29.03 INDEMNIFICATION PROCEDURES.   If any third-party claim is commenced against a Party entitled to indemnification under *Section 29.01* or *Section 29.02* (the *"Indemnified Party"*), notice thereof shall be given to the Party that is obligated to provide indemnification (the *"Indemnifying Party"*) as promptly as practicable. If, after such notice, the Indemnifying Party shall acknowledge that this Agreement applies with respect to such claim, then the

Indemnifying Party shall be entitled, if it so elects, in a notice promptly delivered to the Indemnified Party, but in no event less than 10 days prior to the date on which a response to such claim is due, to immediately take control of the defense and investigation of such claim and to employ and engage attorneys reasonably acceptable to the Indemnified Party to handle and defend the same, at the Indemnifying Party's sole cost and expense. The Indemnified Party shall cooperate, at the cost of the Indemnifying Party, in all reasonable respects with the Indemnifying Party and its attorneys in the investigation, trial, and defense of such claim and any appeal arising therefrom; provided, however, that the Indemnified Party may, at its own cost and expense, participate, through its attorneys or otherwise, in such investigation, trial, and defense of such claim and any appeal arising therefrom. No settlement of a claim that involves a remedy other than the payment of money by the Indemnifying Party shall be entered into without the consent of the Indemnified Party. After notice by the Indemnifying Party to the Indemnified Party of its election to assume full control of the defense of any such claim, the Indemnifying Party shall not be liable to the Indemnified Party for any legal expenses incurred thereafter by such Indemnified Party in connection with the defense of that claim. If the Indemnifying Party does not assume full control over the defense of a claim subject to such defense as provided in this Section, the Indemnifying Party may participate in such defense, at its sole cost and expense, and the Indemnified Party shall have the right to defend the claim in such manner as it may deem appropriate, at the cost and expense of the Indemnifying Party.

ARTICLE 30. INSURANCE

30.01 INSURANCE. During the Term **[and the Termination Assistance Period]**, Vendor shall obtain and maintain at its own expense, and require Vendor Agents to obtain and maintain at their own expense or Vendor's expense, insurance of the type and in the amounts set forth below:

1. statutory workers' compensation in accordance with all Federal, state, and local requirements;

2. employer's liability insurance in an amount not less than $**[SPECIFY DOLLAR AMOUNT]** per occurrence, covering bodily injury by accident or disease, including death;

3. commercial general liability (including contractual liability insurance) in an amount not less than $**[SPECIFY DOLLAR AMOUNT]**; and

4. comprehensive automobile liability covering all vehicles that Vendor owns, hires, or leases in an amount not less than $**[SPECIFY DOLLAR AMOUNT]** (combined single limit for bodily injury and property damage).

[ADD ADDITIONAL INSURANCE COVERAGE IF APPLICABLE]

30.02 INSURANCE DOCUMENTATION.   To the extent third-party insurance is obtained or maintained pursuant to *Section 30.01*, Vendor shall, upon Customer's request, furnish to Customer certificates of insurance or other appropriate documentation (including evidence of renewal of insurance) evidencing all coverages referenced in *Section 30.01* and, if and to the extent applicable, naming Customer as an additional insured. Such certificates or other documentation shall include a provision whereby 30 days' notice must be received by Customer prior to coverage cancellation or material alteration of the coverage by either Vendor or Vendor Agents or the applicable insurer. Such cancellation or material alteration shall not relieve Vendor of its continuing obligation to maintain insurance coverage in accordance with this Article.

30.03 RISK OF LOSS.   Vendor is responsible for the risk of loss of, or damage to, any property of Customer at a Vendor Service Location, unless such loss or damage was caused by the acts or omissions of Customer or a Customer Agent. Customer is responsible for the risk of loss of, or damage to, any property of Vendor at a Customer Service Location, unless such loss or damage was caused by the acts or omissions of Vendor or a Vendor Agent.

ARTICLE 31. MISCELLANEOUS PROVISIONS

31.01 ASSIGNMENT.

1.   Neither Party shall, without the consent of the other Party, assign this Agreement or any amounts payable pursuant to this Agreement, except that Customer may assign this Agreement to an Affiliate or another entity or business unit of Customer or pursuant to a reorganization or Change in Control of Customer without such consent. Upon Customer's assignment of this Agreement to an Affiliate or another Customer entity or business unit or pursuant to a reorganization or Change in Control of Customer, Customer shall be released from any obligation or liability under this Agreement. The consent of a Party to any assignment of this Agreement shall not constitute such Party's consent to further assignment. This Agreement shall be binding on the Parties and their respective successors and permitted assigns. Any assignment in contravention of this subsection shall be void.

2.   **[In the event that Customer divests an entity or business unit of Customer, Vendor shall, for a period of up to two years from the effective date of such divestiture, at Customer's request, continue to provide the Services to such divested Customer entity or business unit at the Fees then in effect.]**

31.02 NOTICES.   Except as otherwise specified in this Agreement, all notices, requests, consents, approvals, agreements, authorizations, acknowledgements, waivers, and other communications required or permitted under this Agreement shall be in writing and shall be deemed given when sent by telecopy to the tele-copy number specified below or delivered by hand to the address specified below. A copy of any such notice shall also be sent by express air mail on the date such notice is transmitted by telecopy to the address specified below:

In the case of Customer:
[ADDRESS]
Attention:
Telecopy No.:

In the case of Vendor:
[ADDRESS]
Attention:
Telecopy No.:

Either Party may change its address or telecopy number for notification pur-poses by giving the other Party **[SPECIFY TIME PERIOD]** notice of the new address or telecopy number and the date upon which it will become effective.

31.03 COUNTERPARTS.   This Agreement may be executed in any number of counterparts, each of which will be deemed an original, but all of which taken together shall constitute one single agreement between the Parties.

31.04 RELATIONSHIP.   The Parties intend to create an independent contractor relationship, and nothing contained in this Agreement shall be construed to make either Customer or Vendor partners, joint venturers, principals, agents (except as expressly set forth in *Article 7*), or employees of the other. No officer, director, employee, agent, affiliate, or contractor retained by Vendor to perform work on Customer's behalf under this Agreement shall be deemed to be an employee, agent, or contractor of Customer. Neither Party shall have any right, power, or authority, express or implied, to bind the other.

31.05 CONSENTS, APPROVALS, AND REQUESTS.   Except as specifically set forth in this Agreement, all consents and approvals to be given by either Party under this Agreement shall not be unreasonably withheld or delayed and each Party shall make only reasonable requests under this Agreement.

31.06 SEVERABILITY.   If any provision of this Agreement is held by a court of competent jurisdiction to be contrary to Law, then the remaining provisions of this Agreement, if capable of substantial performance, shall remain in full force and effect.

31.07 WAIVERS.   No delay or omission by either Party to exercise any right or power it has under this Agreement shall impair or be construed as a waiver of such right or power. A waiver by any Party of any breach or covenant shall not be construed to be a waiver of any succeeding breach or any other covenant. All waivers must be signed by the Party waiving its rights.

31.08 REMEDIES CUMULATIVE. No right or remedy herein conferred upon or reserved to either Party is intended to be exclusive of any other right or remedy, and each and every right and remedy shall be cumulative and in addition to any other right or remedy under this Agreement, or under applicable law, whether now or hereafter existing.

31.09 ENTIRE AGREEMENT. This Agreement and the Exhibits to this Agreement represent the entire agreement between the Parties with respect to its subject matter, and there are no other representations, understandings, or agreements between the Parties relative to such subject matter.

31.10 AMENDMENTS. No amendment to, or change, waiver, or discharge of, any provision of this Agreement shall be valid unless in writing and signed by an authorized representative of each of the Parties.

31.11 SURVIVAL. The terms of **[TO BE FILLED IN]** shall survive the expiration or termination of this Agreement.

31.12 THIRD-PARTY BENEFICIARIES. Each Party intends that this Agreement shall not benefit, or create any right or cause of action in or on behalf of, any person or entity other than the Parties.

31.13 GOVERNING LAW. **[Except as required by Law in any jurisdiction outside of the United States,]** this Agreement and the rights and obligations of the Parties under this Agreement shall be governed by and construed in accordance with the Laws of the State of **[SPECIFY]**.

31.14 SOLE AND EXCLUSIVE VENUE. Each Party irrevocably agrees that any legal action, suit, or proceeding brought by it in any way arising out of this Agreement must be brought solely and exclusively in **[the United States District Court for the [SPECIFY] District of [SPECIFY] or in the state courts of the State of [SPECIFY]]** and irrevocably accepts and submits to the sole and exclusive jurisdiction of each of the aforesaid courts in personam, generally and unconditionally with respect to any action, suit, or proceeding brought by it or against it by the other Party; provided, however, that this Section shall not prevent a Party against whom any legal action, suit, or proceeding is brought by the other Party in the state courts of the State of **[SPECIFY]** from seeking to remove such legal action, suit, or proceeding, pursuant to applicable Federal Law, to the district court of the United States for the district and division embracing the place where the action is pending in the state courts of the State of **[SPECIFY]**, and in the event an action is so removed each Party irrevocably accepts and submits to the jurisdiction of the aforesaid district court. Each Party hereto further irrevocably consents to the service of process from any of the aforesaid courts by mailing copies thereof by registered or certified mail, postage prepaid, to such Party at its address designated pursuant to this Agreement, with such service of process to become effective 30 days after such mailing.

31.15 COVENANT OF FURTHER ASSURANCES.   Customer and Vendor covenant and agree that, subsequent to the execution and delivery of this Agreement and, without any additional consideration, each of Customer and Vendor shall execute and deliver any further legal instruments and perform any acts that are or may become necessary to effectuate the purposes of this Agreement.

31.16 NEGOTIATED TERMS.   The Parties agree that the terms and conditions of this Agreement are the result of negotiations between the Parties and that this Agreement shall not be construed in favor of or against any Party by reason of the extent to which any Party or its professional advisors participated in the preparation of this Agreement.

31.17 EXPORT.   Customer and Vendor shall not knowingly export or re-export any personal computer system, part, technical data, or subelements under this Agreement, directly or indirectly, to any destinations prohibited by the U.S. government. The term "technical data" in this context, means such data as is defined as technical data by applicable United States export regulations.

31.18 NONSOLICITATION.   Except as contemplated by *Article 11*, during the Term, Vendor shall not hire any individual while that individual is an employee of Customer.

31.19 CONFLICT OF INTEREST.   Vendor shall not pay any salaries, commissions, fees, or make any payments or rebates to any employee of Customer, or to any designee of such employee, or favor any employee of Customer, or any designee of such employee, with gifts or entertainment of significant cost or value or with services or goods sold at less than full market value. Vendor agrees that its obligation to Customer under this Section shall also be binding upon Vendor Agents. Vendor further agrees to insert the provisions of this Section in each contract with a Vendor Agent.

31.20 PUBLICITY.   [Each Party shall (1) submit to the other all advertising, written sales promotions, press releases, and other publicity matters relating to this Agreement in which the other Party's name or mark is mentioned or which contains language from which the connection of said name or mark may be inferred or implied and (2) not publish or use such advertising, sales promotions, press releases, or publicity matters without the other Party's consent.]

* * * *

IN WITNESS WHEREOF, each of Customer and Vendor has caused this Agreement to be signed and delivered by its duly authorized representative.

[CUSTOMER]

By: _____
Name:
Title:

[VENDOR]

By: _____
Name:
Title:

INFORMATION TECHNOLOGY OUTSOURCING AGREEMENT (VENDOR FORM)[6]

---

6.   Note: This sample agreement is intended to illustrate the types of legal issues that vendors typically wish to address in connection with information technology outsourcing transactions. The provisions included in this sample agreement, while comprehensive, may not cover all of the issues that may arise in a particular transaction. Legal issues will likely vary depending on the type of information technology process being outsourced and the scope of the outsourcing transaction. This sample agreement or any part thereof should only be used after consultation with your legal counsel. Legal counsel should be consulted prior to entering into or negotiating any outsourcing transaction.

TABLE OF EXHIBITS

Exhibit 1: Definitions
Exhibit 2: Description of Services
Exhibit 3: Fees
Exhibit 4: Customer Assets
Exhibit 5: Customer Service Locations
Exhibit 6: Service Levels
Exhibit 7: Customer Responsibilities and Resources
Exhibit 8: Customer Intellectual Property
[Exhibit 9: Third-Party Contracts]
[Exhibit 10: Transferred Assets and Forms of General Assignment and Bill of Sale]
[Exhibit 11: Human Resources Provisions]
[Exhibit 12: Termination Assistance Services]

SERVICES AGREEMENT

by and between

[VENDOR]
and
[CUSTOMER]

Dated as of **[FILL IN DATE].** This SERVICES AGREEMENT, dated as of [FILL IN DATE], is by and between Vendor and Customer.

NOW, THEREFORE, for and in consideration of the agreements set forth below, Vendor and Customer hereby agree as follows:

ARTICLE 1. DEFINITIONS AND CONSTRUCTION

1.01 DEFINITIONS.   The defined terms used in this Agreement shall have the meanings specified in *Exhibit 1*.

1.02 INTERPRETATION.

1. In this Agreement and the Exhibits to this Agreement, the Exhibits to this Agreement shall be incorporated into and deemed part of this Agreement and all references to this Agreement shall include the Exhibits to this Agreement.

2. The Article and Section headings, Table of Contents, and Table of Exhibits are for reference and convenience only and shall not be considered in the interpretation of this Agreement.

3. In the event of a conflict between the terms of this Agreement and the terms of any of the Exhibits, the terms of [this Agreement] [the Exhibits] shall prevail.

ARTICLE 2. TERM

The initial term of this Agreement shall commence on the Effective Date and continue until 23:59 (**[SPECIFY TIME STANDARD]** Time) on **[SPECIFY DATE],** or such earlier date upon which this Agreement may be terminated pursuant to *Article 17* (the "*Initial Term*"). Upon expiration of the Initial Term, the term of this Agreement shall automatically extend for successive one-year periods (each, a "*Renewal Term*") unless this Agreement is terminated earlier pursuant to *Article 17* or either Party gives the other Party notice at least 12 months prior to the expiration of the Initial Term or the applicable Renewal Term, as the case may be, that it does not desire to extend the term of this Agreement (the Initial Term and the Renewal Term collectively, the "*Term*").

ARTICLE 3. SERVICES

3.01 GENERALLY.   [IF REQUIREMENTS CONTRACT: During the Term, Vendor shall be the exclusive provider of, and Customer shall purchase from Vendor, all of Customer's requirements for the services described in *Exhibit 2* **(the "*Services*"), all upon and subject to the terms and conditions set forth in this Agreement.] [FOR CONTRACTS THAT ARE NOT REQUIREMENTS-BASED: During the Term, Vendor shall provide to Customer, and Customer shall purchase from Vendor, the services described in** *Exhibit 2* **(the "*Services*").]**

3.02 SERVICE LOCATIONS.

1.   Vendor shall provide the Services to the Customer Service Locations.

2.   Each Party, while on the other Party's premises, shall comply with the reasonable requests, standard rules and regulations of such Party regarding safety and health and personal and professional conduct generally applicable to such premises.

3.03 VENDOR MANAGEMENT.   During the Term, Vendor shall maintain an individual (the "*Vendor Account Manager*"), who shall serve as the primary Vendor representative under this Agreement. The Vendor Account Manager shall (a) have overall responsibility for managing and coordinating the performance of Vendor's obligations under this Agreement and (b) be authorized to act for and on behalf of Vendor with respect to all matters relating to this Agreement.

3.04 [MARKET AWARENESS.   Vendor shall periodically meet with Customer in accordance with the procedures agreed upon by the Parties to inform Customer of any new developments or trends of which Vendor becomes aware that could reasonably be expected to have an impact on Customer's business. The acquisition and implementation of any such new assets, methodologies, or technology by Vendor at Customer's request shall be an Out-of-Scope Service.]

3.05 [ASSET TRANSFER.   On [the Effective Date], Vendor shall purchase from Customer, the Transferred Assets for the purchase price set forth in *Exhibit 10.* **[Customer] [Vendor] shall be responsible for and shall pay all sales, use, and other similar taxes arising out of or in connection with the transfer of the Transferred Assets by Customer to Vendor on [the Effective Date]. On [the Effective Date], Customer shall assign, transfer, and convey to Vendor good and valid title in and to the Transferred Assets free and clear of all liens by delivery of one of more general assignments and bills of sale in the form set forth in** *Exhibit 10,* **duly executed by Vendor and Customer.]**

ARTICLE 4. CONTRACT ADMINISTRATION

4.01 THIRD-PARTY CONTRACTS.   Subject to Customer's obtaining and maintaining the Consents, Vendor shall have financial and administrative responsibility during the Term for the Third-Party Contracts. Vendor shall be responsible for the performance of all obligations of Customer under the Third-Party Contracts, including payment of all related expenses attributable to periods on or after the Effective Date, to the extent that such obligations were disclosed to Vendor on or before the Effective Date through receipt by Vendor of a copy of the relevant documents, including the applicable Third-Party Contracts. Customer represents and warrants that all obligations with respect to the Third-Party Contracts accruing prior to or attributable to periods prior to the Effective Date have been satisfied. Customer shall, upon Vendor's request from time to time, terminate any Third-Party Contracts and Vendor shall reimburse Customer for any termination charges arising out of any such terminations.

4.02 CUSTOMER OBLIGATIONS.   Commencing as of the earlier of the date this Agreement is executed by the Parties and the Effective Date, Customer shall not enter into any new or amend any existing agreements or arrangements, written or oral, affecting or impacting the Third-Party Contracts **[or the Transferred Assets],** without Vendor's consent.

ARTICLE 5. SERVICE LEVELS

5.01 SERVICE LEVELS.   [OPTION 1: Within [SPECIFY TIME PERIOD] days after the Effective Date, the Parties shall agree to the (1) service levels that Vendor shall meet in the performance of the Services in the categories set forth in *Exhibit 6* (the "*Service Levels*") and (2) time period during which the Service Levels shall be measured.] [OPTION 2: Vendor shall perform the Services in accordance with the service levels set forth in *Exhibit 6* (the "*Service Levels*").]

5.02 REPORTING.   Vendor shall provide to Customer performance reports according to a schedule and in the format agreed upon by the Parties.

5.03 REMEDIES.   [OPTION 1: BE SILENT] [OPTION 2: Customer agrees that the remedies available to it in the event of a failure of Vendor to provide the Services in accordance with the Service Levels should be addressed to correcting problems that resulted in such failure, rather than to penalizing Vendor. In recognition of this, (1) failures not of a general and consistent nature to meet a Service Level shall not be deemed a material breach by Vendor and (2) Customer's sole and exclusive remedies for such failure shall be as set forth in this Section and *Exhibit 6*. If Vendor fails to meet a Service Level for any Service, then Vendor shall (a) complete performance of the Service as near as reasonably possible to the applicable Service Level

and (b) use commercially reasonable efforts to remedy the problem that caused it to fail to meet such Service Level.] [OPTION 3: In the event Vendor fails to provide the Services in accordance with the Service Levels, Vendor shall incur the performance credits identified in and according to the schedule set forth in *Exhibit 6*. Customer agrees that (1) Vendor shall not be obligated to issue a Performance Credit to Customer if the failure to meet the Service Level was not caused by Vendor or Vendor Agents; (2) any Performance Credit due to Customer shall be applied against amounts otherwise payable to Vendor by Customer pursuant to this Agreement within [90] days after the end of the applicable Contract Year; (3) the Performance Credits shall be Customer's sole and exclusive remedy for Vendor's failure to meet such Service Level; and (4) such failure to meet such Service Level shall not be grounds for termination of this Agreement pursuant to *Section 17.02*.]

ARTICLE 6. CHANGES IN THE SERVICES

1. Vendor reserves the right in its discretion to designate and make changes to the Services and the Service Levels (each, a "*Change*"); provided, however, that any such Change shall not have a material adverse impact on the Service Levels or cause a material increase to the Fees.

2. [OPTION 1: Subject to subsection (3) below, in the event Vendor intends to make a Change that would have a material adverse impact on the Service Levels or cause a material increase to the Fees, Vendor shall (a) notify Customer of the Change and its impact on the Service Levels and the Fees, and (b) if Customer requests within 15 days of receipt of such notice, discuss means to reduce any negative impact and implement such means as are practical and reasonable.]

    [OPTION 2: Except as set forth in subsection (1) above, in the event a Party wishes to make a Change, such Party shall submit a written proposal to the other Party describing such desired Change. The other Party shall reject or accept the proposal in writing within a reasonable period of time, but in no event more than 30 days after receipt of the proposal. In the event the proposal is rejected, the writing shall include the reason for the rejection. In the event the proposal is accepted, the Parties shall determine the additions or modifications to be made to this Agreement (including the Fees). Any such addition or modification shall be set forth in a written Change Order signed by the Parties. Neither Party shall be obligated to accept a proposal submitted by the other Party pursuant to this subsection. Vendor shall have no obligation to provide any service or otherwise act pursuant to any proposal submitted by Customer pursuant to this subsection, except to the extent such proposal is set forth in an executed Change Order.]

3. Customer shall promptly identify and notify Vendor of any changes in Law, including Customer's regulatory requirements, that may relate to Customer's use of the Services. The Parties shall work together to identify the impact of such changes on how Customer uses, and Vendor delivers, the Services. Customer shall be responsible for any fines and penalties arising from any noncompliance by Customer with any Law relating to Customer's use of the Services. Subject to the following sentence, if a change in Law prevents or delays Vendor from performing its obligations under this Agreement, the Parties shall develop and implement a suitable workaround until such time as Vendor can perform its obligations under this Agreement without such workaround. If a change in Law, including the development or implementation of a workaround, results in Vendor's use of additional resources or an increase in Vendor's costs of providing the Services, Customer shall **[OPTION 1: pay for such additional resources and increased costs at rates agreed upon by the Parties] [OPTION 2: reimburse Vendor for such additional resources and increased costs].**

ARTICLE 7.   THIRD-PARTY SERVICES

7.01 VENDOR OPPORTUNITY.   [OPTION 1: Vendor shall have the right to match the material terms of any third-party offer received by Customer with respect to any Out-of-Scope Service. If Vendor offers to provide such Out-of-Scope Service to Customer upon substantially similar terms as those set forth in such third-party offer, Vendor shall provide to Customer, and Customer shall purchase from Vendor, pursuant to a Change Order or separate agreement, as the case may be, such Out-of-Scope Services upon terms set forth in such Change Order or separate agreement, including Vendor's charges for such Out-of-Scope Service.] [OPTION 2: With respect to any Out-of-Scope Service, Customer shall (1) notify Vendor at or about the same time that it notifies other vendors that it is considering acquiring an Out-of-Scope Service and provide Vendor with the same information that it provides such other vendors and (2) allow Vendor the opportunity to compete with such other vendors for the provision of such Out-of-Scope Service. If Vendor is selected by Customer to provide such Out-of-Scope Service, Vendor and Customer shall negotiate a Change Order or separate agreement, as the case may be, including Vendor's charges for such Out-of-Scope Service.]

7.02 COOPERATION WITH THIRD-PARTY SERVICE PROVIDERS.   Upon Customer's request and reasonable notice, Vendor shall, as an Out-of-Scope Service, cooperate with third-party service providers of Customer; provided, however, that (1) such cooperation does not impact the Services or Vendor's ability to meet the Service Levels and (2) Vendor shall not be required to disclose any of Vendor's Confidential Information to such third-party service provider.

ARTICLE 8. HUMAN RESOURCES

[The transition of employees of Customer to Vendor [or Vendor Agents] shall be effected in accordance with the terms and conditions set forth in *Exhibit 11*.]

ARTICLE 9. CUSTOMER RESPONSIBILITIES

9.01 CUSTOMER PROJECT MANAGER. During the Term, Customer shall maintain a senior executive of Customer (the *"Customer Project Manager"*), who shall serve as the primary Customer representative under this Agreement. The Customer Project Manager shall (1) have overall responsibility for managing and coordinating the performance of Customer's obligations under this Agreement and (2) be authorized to act for and on behalf of Customer with respect to all matters relating to this Agreement.

9.02 CUSTOMER RESPONSIBILITIES. During the Term and in connection with Vendor's performance of the Services under this Agreement, Customer shall, at its expense: (1) be responsible for the obligations and responsibilities set forth in *Exhibit 7*; (2) upon Vendor's request, make available to Vendor personnel familiar with Customer's business requirements; (3) provide to Vendor complete and accurate information regarding Customer's business requirements in respect of any work to be performed by Vendor under this Agreement; (4) respond within the time period specified in this Agreement (or if no time period is specified within three business days) to all deliverables presented to Customer by Vendor for Customer's approval, which approval shall not be unreasonably withheld (if Customer fails to respond within such three-day or other specified period, Customer shall be deemed to have accepted such deliverable); (5) cooperate with Vendor; (6) promptly notify Vendor of any (a) third-party claims that may have an impact on this Agreement and (b) invalid or nonexistent licenses or leases; and (7) perform all other obligations of Customer described in this Agreement.

9.03 CUSTOMER RESOURCES. Commencing on the Effective Date and continuing for so long as Vendor requires the same for the performance of the Services, Customer shall provide to Vendor, at no charge to Vendor:

1. the use of the space in Customer's premises that Vendor may from time to time require in connection with the performance of the Services, together with office furnishings, telephone equipment and services, janitorial services, utilities and office-related equipment, supplies, and duplicating services reasonably required in connection with the performance of the Services;

2. full access to, and use of, the Customer Assets; and

3. the resources set forth in *Exhibit 7*.

9.04 CONSENTS. All Consents shall be obtained and maintained by Customer with Vendor's cooperation. Customer shall pay any costs of obtaining and maintaining the Consents.

9.05 USE OF SERVICES. Customer may not remarket or sell all or any portion of the Services provided under this Agreement, or make all or any portion of the Services available to any party other than Customer, without Vendor's consent.

ARTICLE 10. PROPRIETARY RIGHTS

10.01 [CUSTOMER INTELLECTUAL PROPERTY. Customer hereby grants to Vendor at no cost to Vendor a nonexclusive right to access and Use in connection with the provision of the Services (1) the Customer Proprietary Intellectual Property and (2) the Customer Third-Party Intellectual Property. Upon the later of the expiration of this Agreement or termination of this Agreement and the end of the Termination Assistance Period, the rights granted to Vendor in this Section shall immediately revert to Customer and Vendor shall, at Customer's cost and expense, deliver to Customer a current copy of all the Customer Intellectual Property (including any related source code in Vendor's possession) in the form in use as of such date. Customer shall pay all costs and expenses with respect to the Customer Intellectual Property, including the costs associated with maintenance, license payments, insurance, taxes, and the Consents.] [While Vendor shall manage the operation of the Customer Intellectual Property as described in *Exhibit 2*, Customer is responsible for maintaining, upgrading, and replacing the Customer Intellectual Property as necessary for Vendor to provide the Services. In the event that Customer does not comply with such obligations, Vendor shall be excused from its obligation to perform the Services, including Vendor's obligation to meet the Service Levels, to the extent that its inability to meet such obligation is caused by Customer's failure to comply with its obligations under this Section.]**

10.02 VENDOR INTELLECTUAL PROPERTY. All Vendor Intellectual Property shall be and shall remain the exclusive property of Vendor or its licensor and Customer shall have no rights or interests in the Vendor Intellectual Property except as described in *Section 17.04*. Customer hereby irrevocably assigns to Vendor any and all rights or interests in the Vendor Intellectual Property. **[OPTION: Upon expiration or termination of this Agreement, if Customer has fully complied with all of its obligations and is not in default under this Agreement, Vendor hereby grants to Customer, to the extent possible and without additional cost to Vendor, a nonexclusive, nontransferable license to Use "as-is" the then-current, in-use versions of the Vendor Proprietary Intellectual Property set forth in Exhibit ___, in accordance with *Section 10*. Vendor makes no representations or warranties with respect to the Vendor Proprietary Intellectual Property.] [LIMIT RIGHT TO MODIFY/ENHANCE?]**

10.03 DEVELOPMENTS. [SEE OPTIONS IN *APPENDIX 4.6*, "PROPRI-ETARY RIGHTS RIDER"]

10.04 TOOLS. [Notwithstanding anything contrary in this Agreement, Vendor shall retain all right, title, and interest in and to any and all ideas, concepts, know-how, development tools, methodologies, processes, procedures, technologies, or algorithms (*"Tools"*), which are based on trade secrets or proprietary information of Vendor. Nothing contained in this Agreement shall restrict Vendor from the use of any Tools that Vendor develops for Customer or has access to under this Agreement.]

ARTICLE 11. PAYMENTS TO VENDOR

11.01 FEES.   In consideration of Vendor providing the Services, Customer shall pay to Vendor the Fees, as may be adjusted from time to time pursuant to this Agreement.

11.02 COST-OF-LIVING ADJUSTMENT.   Customer shall pay a cost-of-living adjustment in accordance with *Exhibit 3*, beginning in the January following the Effective Date.

11.03 TIME OF PAYMENT.   Vendor shall deliver an invoice on or about the **[first]** day of each month for the Services to be performed during such month and each such invoice shall be due within **[SPECIFY TIME PERIOD]** days of receipt by Customer. Any sum due Vendor pursuant to this Agreement for which a time of payment is not otherwise specified shall be due and payable **[SPECIFY TIME PERIOD]** days after receipt by Customer of an invoice from Vendor. Any amounts not paid by Customer to Vendor when due shall bear interest **[at a rate of [SPECIFY PERCENTAGE] percent per year (or, if lesser, the maximum rate permissible by applicable law),] [at the Default Rate,]** measured from the date such amount was due until the date such amount is paid by Customer to Vendor. Without prejudice to any other rights it has under this Agreement, Vendor shall have the right to suspend the provision of the Services to Customer if Customer is more than **[SPECIFY TIME PERIOD]** days late in paying an invoice.

11.04 DISPUTED AMOUNTS.   If Customer, in good faith, disputes any invoice charges regarding the Services, it may withhold from its payment of the relevant invoice any such disputed amounts (except for applicable taxes), up to a maximum of the lesser of the amount for the Services to which the dispute relates and **[SPECIFY PERCENTAGE]** percent of the average monthly Fees for the previous 12 months. Customer shall pay to Vendor withheld amounts, plus interest **[at a rate of [SPECIFY PERCENTAGE] percent per year (or, if lesser, the maximum rate permissible by applicable law),] [at the Default Rate,]** measured from the date such amount was due until the date such amount is paid by

Customer to Vendor, in accordance with the resolution of the dispute. Notwithstanding any dispute and in accordance with this Section, Customer shall remit to Vendor the invoiced amount, less the disputed amount, in accordance with this Section and *Section 11.03*.

11.05 PERMITS AND APPROVALS.   Customer shall be responsible for and carry the risk of obtaining all consents, permissions, approvals, and assurances of whatever nature, which may be needed to make payments as required under this Agreement.

11.06 EXPENSES.   Unless otherwise agreed, Customer shall reimburse Vendor for all travel expenses, living, hotel, and transportation allowances and other normally reimbursable expenses and allowances for any member of the Project Staff travelling in connection with the Services, all as reasonably incurred and in accordance with Vendor's generally applicable personnel practices and procedures.

11.07 PRORATION.   All periodic charges under this Agreement are to be computed on a calendar month basis and shall be prorated on a per diem basis for any partial month.

11.08 VERIFICATION OF INFORMATION.   [OPTION 1: The obligations of the Parties and the charges set forth in this Agreement are based on information furnished by Customer to Vendor, but such information has not been independently verified by Vendor. Customer believes that such information is accurate and complete. However, if Vendor determines during the first Contract Year that any such information should prove to be inaccurate or incomplete in any adverse material respect, Vendor and Customer shall negotiate appropriate adjustments to the provisions of this Agreement, including the Fees.]

[OPTION 2: The Services, Fees, and Service Levels are based on circumstances, estimates, metrics, principles, financial data, standards, and general information disclosed by Customer or used by Vendor (collectively, "*Assumptions*"). Customer shall be responsible for the accuracy of any representation it made as part of the due diligence and negotiation process and on which the Assumptions are based. In the event of any material deviation from the Assumptions, Vendor and Customer shall negotiate to define and agree upon adjustments that shall be consistent with the intent of each of Vendor and Customer. Any such adjustments shall be set forth in a Change Order.]

11.09 TAXES.   The Fees paid to Vendor are exclusive of any applicable sales, use, gross receipts, excise, value-added, withholding, personal property, or other taxes attributable to periods on or after the Effective Date. In the event that a sales, use, excise, gross receipts, or services tax is assessed on the provision of the Services by Vendor to Customer or on Vendor's charges to Customer under this Agreement, however levied or assessed, Customer shall bear and be responsible for and pay the amount of any such tax, or, if applicable, reimburse Vendor for the amount of any such tax.

11.10 EXTRAORDINARY CHANGES IN WORKLOAD. If, during the Term, Customer experiences significant changes in the scope or nature of its business that have or are reasonably expected to have the effect of causing a sustained substantial decrease of **[SPECIFY PERCENTAGE]** percent or more in the amount of resources Vendor uses in performing the Services, provided such decreases are not due to Customer resuming the provision of such Services by itself or Customer transferring the provision of such Services to another vendor, Customer shall notify Vendor of any event or events that Customer believes may result in such sustained decrease and Vendor shall identify, in a plan that shall be submitted to Customer for review and acceptance, any changes that can be made to accommodate the extraordinary decrease of resource requirements in a cost-effective manner, without disruption to Customer's ongoing operations. Upon Customer's acceptance of Vendor's plan, Vendor shall make any applicable adjustments to the Fees to reflect the foregoing and distribute an amended *Exhibit 3* to Customer.

ARTICLE 12. AUDIT

12.01 VERIFICATION OF FEES.   Upon 30 days' notice from Customer and not more than once during each Contract Year, Vendor shall furnish to Customer a certificate by Vendor's external auditors verifying the Fees. The cost of the verification shall be paid by Customer **[; provided however, that if an overcharge over [SPECIFY AMOUNT] is disclosed, Vendor shall reimburse such costs to Customer].** Such certificate shall be conclusive. Any requests for verification of the Fees shall be made no later than **[SPECIFY TIME PERIOD]** years from the end of the Contract Year in which the Fees were incurred.

12.02 AUDIT EXPENSES.   If Vendor is required to provide services or incur costs, other than of a routine nature, in connection with any audit pursuant to this Article, then Customer shall **[pay for such resources and costs at rates agreed upon by the Parties] [reimburse Vendor for such resources and costs].**

ARTICLE 13. DATA AND REPORTS

13.01 PROVISION OF DATA.   Customer shall supply to Vendor, in connection with the Services, required data in the form and on such time schedules as may be agreed upon by Vendor and Customer ("*Customer Data*") in order to permit Vendor to perform the Services in accordance with the terms of this Agreement, including the Service Levels. All Customer Data is, or shall be, and shall remain the property of Customer.

13.02 INSPECTION OF REPORTS. Customer shall use reasonable efforts to inspect and review reports and provide Vendor with notice of any errors or inaccuracies (1) in daily or weekly reports, within **[SPECIFY TIME PERIOD]** business days of receipt of such reports, and (2) in monthly or other reports, within **[SPECIFY TIME PERIOD]** business days of receipt of such reports. Vendor shall provide Customer with such documentation and information as may be requested by Customer in order to verify the accuracy of the reports. If Customer fails to reject any such report within the applicable period, Customer shall be deemed to have accepted such report.

13.03 CORRECTION OF ERRORS. Upon notice from Customer and at Customer's expense, Vendor shall promptly correct any errors or inaccuracies in Customer Data and reports prepared by Vendor as part of the Services, to the extent not caused by Vendor or Vendor Agents.

13.04 DATA PROTECTION. **[In the event the Services require the access to or use of personal data, each Party shall be responsible for taking all necessary steps required by applicable Law to ensure the protection of the privacy of such personal data to be accessed or used. In the event that applicable Law requires registration with a Governmental Authority, the Parties shall determine which Party shall register, or cause such registration, with such Governmental Authority.]**

ARTICLE 14. CONFIDENTIALITY AND SECURITY

14.01 GENERAL OBLIGATIONS.

1. All Confidential Information relating to or obtained from Customer or Vendor shall be held in confidence by the recipient to the same extent and in at least the same manner as the recipient protects its own confidential or proprietary information.

2. Neither Customer nor Vendor shall disclose, publish, release, transfer, or otherwise make available Confidential Information of, or obtained from, the other in any form to, or for the use or benefit of, any person or entity without the disclosing Party's consent. Each of Customer and Vendor shall, however, be permitted to disclose relevant aspects of the other's Confidential Information to its officers, directors, employees, and Agents, to the extent that such disclosure is not restricted under this Agreement or any governmental approvals and only to the extent that such disclosure is reasonably necessary for the performance of its duties and obligations under this Agreement; provided, however, that the recipient shall be responsible or ensuring that such officers, directors, employees, and Agents abide by the provisions of this Agreement.

14.02 EXCLUSIONS. The obligations in *Section 14.01* shall not restrict any disclosure pursuant to any applicable Law or by order of any court or Governmental Authority (provided that the recipient shall give prompt notice to the disclosing Party of such order) and, except to the extent that local Law provides otherwise, shall not apply with respect to information that (1) is independently developed by the recipient without violating the disclosing Party's proprietary rights as shown by the recipient's written records, (2) is or becomes publicly known (other than through unauthorized disclosure), (3) is disclosed by the owner of such information to a third party free of any obligation of confidentiality, (4) is already known by the recipient at the time of disclosure, as shown by the recipient's written records, and the recipient has no obligation of confidentiality other than pursuant to this Agreement or any confidentiality agreements entered into before the Effective Date between Customer and Vendor, or (5) is rightfully received by a Party free of any obligation of confidentiality.

14.03 UNAUTHORIZED ACTS. Without limiting either Party's rights in respect of a breach of this Article, each Party shall:

1. promptly notify the other Party of any unauthorized possession, use, or knowledge, or attempt thereof, of the other Party's Confidential Information by any person or entity that may become known to such Party, including any incidents involving a breach of security, and any incidents that might indicate or lead to a threat to, or weakness in, security and any attempt to make unauthorized use of the Services or the Customer Data;

2. promptly furnish to the other Party full details of the unauthorized possession, use, or knowledge, or attempt thereof, and assist the other Party in investigating or preventing the recurrence of any unauthorized possession, use, or knowledge, or attempt thereof, of Confidential Information;

3. cooperate with the other Party in any litigation and investigation against third parties deemed necessary by the other Party to protect its proprietary rights; and

4. promptly use its best efforts to prevent a recurrence of any such unauthorized possession, use, or knowledge, or attempt thereof, of Confidential Information.

Each Party shall bear the cost it incurs as a result of compliance with this Section.

14.04 INJUNCTIVE RELIEF. Each Party recognizes that its disclosure of Confidential Information of the other Party may give rise to irreparable injury to such Party and acknowledges that remedies other than injunctive relief may not be adequate. Accordingly, each Party has the right to equitable and injunctive relief to prevent the unauthorized possession, use, disclosure, or knowledge of any Confidential Information, as well as to such damages or other relief as is occasioned by such unauthorized possession, use, disclosure, or knowledge.

14.05 PUBLICITY.   [OPTION 1: Neither Party shall use the other Party's name or refer to it directly or indirectly, without such Party's consent, which consent shall not be unreasonably withheld, in any media release, public announcement, or public disclosure, except for promotional or marketing materials, customer lists or business presentations.] [OPTION 2: BE SILENT]

ARTICLE 15. REPRESENTATIONS AND ADDITIONAL COVENANTS

15.01 BY CUSTOMER.   Customer represents and warrants that:

1. it is either the owner of the Customer Data, each Transferred Asset, each Customer Asset, and the Customer Intellectual Property or is authorized by its owner to include it under this Agreement; and

2. it is authorized to permit Vendor access to and use of the Customer Service Locations used in connection with performing the Services, and Vendor is performing the Services for Customer at the Customer Service Locations at Customer's request.

[ADD ENVIRONMENTAL AND ERISA COMPLIANCE REPS IF APPLICABLE]

15.02 MUTUAL.   Each Party hereby represents and warrants that:

1. it has all requisite corporate power and authority to enter into this Agreement and to carry out the transactions contemplated hereby;

2. the execution, delivery, and performance of this Agreement and the consummation of the transactions contemplated hereby have been duly authorized by all requisite corporate action on the part of such Party;

3. this Agreement has been duly executed and delivered by such Party and (assuming the due authorization, execution, and delivery hereof by the other Party) is a valid and binding obligation of such Party, enforceable against it in accordance with its terms; and

4. its entry into this Agreement does not violate or constitute a breach of any of its contractual obligations with third parties.

15.03 REGULATIONS.   [OPTION 1: Each Party shall obtain all necessary regulatory approvals applicable to its business, obtain any necessary permits, and comply with any regulatory requirements, in each case, applicable to the performance, or receipt, of the Services.]

   [OPTION 2: Customer shall obtain and furnish to Vendor any approvals, consents, licenses, and permits required or recommended by any Law or Governmental Authority in connection with (a) the execution of this Agreement and (b) the performance and receipt of the Services.]

15.04 DISCLAIMERS.

1. [Vendor does not warrant the accuracy of any advice, report, data or other product delivered to Customer that is produced with or from Customer Data, Customer Assets or Intellectual Property provided by Customer. Such products are delivered "AS IS", and Vendor shall not be liable for any inaccuracy thereof.]

2. EXCEPT AS EXPRESSLY SET FORTH IN *SECTION 15.02*, VENDOR DOES NOT MAKE ANY OTHER WARRANTIES OR REPRESENTATIONS AND EXPRESSLY DISCLAIMS ALL OTHER REPRESENTATIONS AND WARRANTIES, EXPRESS OR IMPLIED, INCLUDING ANY IMPLIED WARRANTIES OF MERCHANTABILITY AND FITNESS FOR A SPECIFIC PURPOSE. VENDOR DOES NOT WARRANT THAT THE SERVICES SHALL MEET CUSTOMER'S REQUIREMENTS, THAT THE PERFORMANCE OF THE SERVICES SHALL BE UNINTERRUPTED OR ERROR-FREE, THAT ALL ERRORS IN THE SERVICES SHALL BE CORRECTED [OR THAT THE CUSTOMER ASSETS, CUSTOMER INTELLECTUAL PROPERTY, VENDOR INTELLECTUAL PROPERTY, DEVELOPMENTS OR SERVICES ARE OR SHALL BE YEAR 2000 READY OR COMPLIANT].

ARTICLE 16. DISPUTE RESOLUTION

16.01 CUSTOMER PROJECT MANAGER AND VENDOR ACCOUNT MANAGER.   Any dispute arising under this Agreement shall be considered in person or by telephone by the Customer Project Manager and the Vendor Account Manager within **[seven]** business days of receipt of a notice from either Party specifying the nature of the dispute; provided, however, that a dispute relating to *Article 14* shall not be subject to this Section. **[Unless the Customer Project Manager and the Vendor Account Manager otherwise agree, either Party may pursue its rights and remedies under *Section 16.02* after the occurrence of such meeting or telephone conversation.]**

16.02 [RESOLUTION PROCEDURES.   ADD   MEDIATION/ARBITRATION PROCEDURES IF APPLICABLE]

ARTICLE 17. TERMINATION

17.01 BY VENDOR.   Vendor shall have the right to terminate this Agreement if: (1) Customer fails to pay any amounts payable under this Agreement when due; (2) Customer fails to perform any of its material nonmonetary obligations under this Agreement, and does not cure such default within **[SPECIFY TIME PERIOD]** of receipt of notice of default from Vendor; or (3) Customer becomes or is declared insolvent or bankrupt, is the subject of any proceedings relating to its liquidation, insolvency, or for the appointment of a receiver or similar officer for it, makes an assignment for the benefit of all or substantially all of its creditors or enters into an agreement for the composition, extension, or readjustment of all or substantially all of its obligations.

17.02 BY CUSTOMER.   If Vendor materially fails to perform any of its material obligations under this Agreement, Customer may give Vendor notice of such failure. Vendor shall within **[SPECIFY TIME PERIOD]** days of receipt of such notice remedy the failure specified therein. In the event Vendor fails to remedy the failure within such **[SPECIFY TIME PERIOD]** period, Customer may give a termination notice to Vendor and may terminate this Agreement under which the breach occurred; provided, however, that the time to cure a breach shall be extended if Vendor has promptly commenced to cure the breach and continues to use reasonable efforts to cure such breach.

17.03 TERMINATION ASSISTANCE.   Except in the event this Agreement is terminated by Vendor pursuant to *Section 17.01,* upon the expiration or termination of this Agreement, if (1) all payments due to Vendor under this Agreement have been paid and (2) Customer has requested termination assistance at least **[SPECIFY TIME PERIOD]** prior to the expiration of this Agreement or upon notice of termination of this Agreement, Vendor shall **[OPTION 1: (a) cooperate with Customer in effecting the orderly transfer of the Services to a third party or the resumption of the Services by Customer upon Customer's request and (b) continue to perform such portion of the Services requested by Customer ((a) and (b) collectively, the *"Termination Assistance Services"*).] [OPTION 2: provide the services described in *Exhibit 12* (the *"Termination Assistance Services"*).]** Except in the event this Agreement is terminated by Vendor pursuant to *Section 17.01*, Vendor shall provide the Termination Assistance Services for up to **[SPECIFY TIME PERIOD]** to the expiration of this Agreement or up to 90 days after the effective date of the termination of this Agreement by Customer (the *"Termination Assistance Period"*). To the extent such Termination Assistance Services cause Vendor to use resources beyond those otherwise then being provided by Vendor as part of the Services or incur additional costs, such Termination Assistance Services shall constitute and be performed as Out-of-Scope Services.

17.04 EXIT RIGHTS.   Upon the expiration or termination of this Agreement (except in the event this Agreement is terminated by Vendor pursuant to *Section 17.01*):

1. Vendor shall provide the Termination Assistance Services in accordance with *Section 17.03*;

2. Customer shall allow Vendor to use, at no charge, those Customer facilities, Customer Assets, and Customer Intellectual Property being used to perform the Termination Assistance Services for as long as Vendor is providing the Termination Assistance Services to enable Vendor to effect an orderly transition of Vendor's resources;

3.   each Party shall have the rights specified in *Article 10* to be applicable upon expiration or termination of this Agreement in respect of Intellectual Property;

4.   [upon Customer's request, with respect to generally commercially available Vendor Third-Party Intellectual Property, which Vendor has licensed and is dedicated full-time to providing the Services as of the date of the expiration or termination of this Agreement, Vendor shall transfer, assign, or sublicense such Vendor Third-Party Intellectual Property to Customer; provided, however, that Customer provided Vendor with reasonable notice prior to the acquisition of a license to such Vendor Third-Party Intellectual Property that Customer may desire such assignment or sublicense and Customer pays any costs associated with such assignment or sublicense;] and

5.   upon Customer's request, with respect to any contracts applicable to the Services being provided to Customer on a dedicated, full-time basis for maintenance, disaster recovery services, and other necessary third-party services being used by Vendor to perform the Services as of the date of the expiration or termination of this Agreement, Vendor shall transfer or assign such agreements to Customer or its designee, on terms and conditions acceptable to both parties; provided, however, that Customer provided Vendor with reasonable notice prior to entering into such contracts that Customer may desire such transfer or assignment and Customer pays any costs associated with such transfer or assignment.

ARTICLE 18. INDEMNITIES

18.01 INFRINGEMENT.   Vendor agrees to indemnify, defend, and hold Customer harmless from and against any and all Losses incurred by Customer arising from any **[third party]** claim of **[United States] [SPECIFY COUNTRY/ TERRITORY]** patent, trade secret, or copyright infringement asserted against Customer by virtue of Customer's use of the Vendor Proprietary Intellectual Property or the Developments; provided, however, that (1) Vendor is given prompt notice of any such claim, (2) Vendor has the right to control and direct the defense of such claim, and (3) Customer fully cooperates with Vendor in such defense. Vendor shall have no liability for any claim of infringement that results from or relates to (a) any modification or enhancement to the Vendor Proprietary Intellectual Property or the Developments by Customer, (b) any failure by Customer to implement or install the Vendor Proprietary Intellectual Property or the Developments as directed by Vendor, (c) the combination, operation, or use of the Vendor Proprietary Intellectual Property or the Developments with non-Vendor programs, data, or documentation, and (d) materials, items, resources, or services provided or performed by Customer (whether or not used in connection with or incorporated into the Vendor Proprietary Intellectual Property or the Developments). In the event the Vendor Proprietary Intellectual

Property or the Developments, in Vendor's opinion, are likely to or do become the subject of a claim of infringement, Vendor shall have the right at its sole option and expense to (i) modify the Vendor Proprietary Intellectual Property or the Developments to be noninfringing, (ii) obtain for Customer a license to continue using the Vendor Proprietary Intellectual Property or the Developments, or (iii) terminate this Agreement and the license granted hereunder, accept return of the Vendor Proprietary Intellectual Property or the Developments, and refund to Customer a pro rata portion of the fee paid to Vendor hereunder for that portion of the Vendor Proprietary Intellectual Property or the Developments which is the subject of such infringement, such portion based on a straight-line depreciation over a five-year term beginning on the delivery of such portion of the Vendor Proprietary Intellectual Property or the Developments to Customer.

THE FOREGOING STATES CUSTOMER'S SOLE AND EXCLUSIVE REMEDY AND THE ENTIRE LIABILITY AND OBLIGATION OF VENDOR AND VENDOR AGENTS WITH RESPECT TO ANY INFRINGEMENT OR CLAIMS OF INFRINGEMENT BY THE VENDOR INTELLECTUAL PROPERTY, THE DEVELOPMENTS OR THE SERVICES, OR ANY PART THEREOF, OF ANY PATENT, COPYRIGHT, TRADE SECRET, OR OTHER PROPRIETARY RIGHT.

18.02 PERSONAL AND PROPERTY DAMAGE BY VENDOR.   Vendor agrees to indemnify, defend, and hold Customer harmless, from and against any and all Losses incurred by Customer arising from any **[third party]** claim for (1) bodily injuries to, including fatal injury or disease to, Vendor employees and (2) damage to tangible real or personal property of Vendor and Vendor employees arising from or in connection with this Agreement. **[EXCEPT GROSS NEGLIGENCE/INTENTIONAL ACTS?]**

18.03 PERSONAL AND PROPERTY DAMAGE BY CUSTOMER.   Customer agrees to indemnify, defend, and hold Vendor and Vendor Agents harmless from and against any and all Losses arising from any claim for (1) bodily injuries to, including fatal injuries or disease to, Customer employees and (2) damage to tangible real or personal property of Customer and Customer employees arising from or in connection with this Agreement. **[EXCEPT GROSS NEGLIGENCE/ INTENTIONAL ACTS?]**

18.04 BY CUSTOMER.   Customer agrees to indemnify, defend, and hold Vendor and Vendor Agents harmless from and against any and all Losses arising from any claim relating to: (1) the infringement by or of Customer Data, the Transferred Assets, the Customer Assets, the Customer Intellectual Property, or any other resources or items provided to Vendor or Vendor Agents by Customer or Customer Agents; (2) any amounts, including taxes, interest, and penalties, which are obligations of Customer pursuant to *Section 11.09*; (3) any products or services provided by Customer or Customer Agents to third parties; (4) any breach or default by Customer in the performance of Customer's obligations under agreements with third parties; and (5) **[any environmental claim arising out of this Agreement or as a result of the Services performed at the Customer Service Locations, unless Vendor has caused the environmental damage by actions unrelated to and unauthorized by this Agreement.]**

18.05 INDEMNIFICATION PROCEDURES. If any third-party claim is commenced against a Party entitled to indemnification under *Section 18.02*, *Section 18.03* or *Section 18.04* (the "*Indemnified Party*"), notice thereof shall be given to the Party that is obligated to provide indemnification (the "*Indemnifying Party*") as promptly as practicable. If, after such notice, the Indemnifying Party shall acknowledge that this Agreement applies with respect to such claim, then the Indemnifying Party shall be entitled, if it so elects, in a notice promptly delivered to the Indemnified Party, but in no event less than 10 days prior to the date on which a response to such claim is due, to immediately take control of the defense and investigation of such claim and to employ and engage attorneys reasonably acceptable to the Indemnified Party to handle and defend the same, at the Indemnifying Party's sole cost and expense. The Indemnified Party shall cooperate, at the cost of the Indemnifying Party, in all reasonable respects with the Indemnifying Party and its attorneys in the investigation, trial, and defense of such claim and any appeal arising therefrom; provided, however, that the Indemnified Party may, at its own cost and expense, participate, through its attorneys or otherwise, in such investigation, trial, and defense of such claim and any appeal arising therefrom. No settlement of a claim pursuant to this Section that involves a remedy other than the payment of money by the Indemnifying Party shall be entered into without the consent of the Indemnified Party, which consent shall not be unreasonably withheld. After notice by the Indemnifying Party to the Indemnified Party of its election to assume full control of the defense of any such claim, the Indemnifying Party shall not be liable to the Indemnified Party for any legal expenses incurred thereafter by such Indemnified Party in connection with the defense of that claim. If the Indemnifying Party does not assume full control over the defense of a claim subject to such defense as provided in this Section, the Indemnifying Party may participate in such defense, at its sole cost and expense, and the Indemnified Party shall have the right to defend the claim in such manner as it may deem appropriate, at the cost and expense of the Indemnifying Party.

18.06 SUBROGATION. In the event that a Party is obligated to indemnify the other Party pursuant to *Section 18.01*, *Section 18.02*, *Section 18.03*, or *Section 18.04* the Indemnifying Party shall, upon payment of such indemnity in full, be subrogated to all rights of the indemnified Party with respect to the claims and defenses to which such indemnification relates.

18.07 EXCLUSIVE REMEDY. The indemnification rights of each Indemnified Party pursuant to *Section 18.01*, *Section 18.02*, *Section 18.03*, or *Section 18.04* shall be the sole and exclusive remedy of such Indemnified Party with respect to the claims to which such indemnification relates.

ARTICLE 19. LIABILITY
[ADD LIABILITY/DAMAGE PROVISIONS AS APPLICABLE]

ARTICLE 20. MISCELLANEOUS PROVISIONS

20.01 NOTICES.   Except as otherwise specified in this Agreement, all notices, requests, consents, approvals, agreements, authorizations, acknowledgements, waivers, and other communications required or permitted under this Agreement shall be in writing and shall be deemed given when sent by facsimile to the facsimile number specified below or delivered by hand to the address specified below. A copy of any such notice shall also be sent by express air mail on the date such notice is transmitted by facsimile to the address specified below:

In the case of Customer:
[ADDRESS]
Attention:
Facsimile No.:

In the case of Vendor:
[ADDRESS]
Attention:
Facsimile No.:

Either Party may change its address or facsimile number for notification purposes by giving the other Party [SPECIFY TIME PERIOD] days' notice of the new address or facsimile number and the date upon which it shall become effective.

20.02 ASSIGNMENT AND THIRD-PARTY BENEFICIARIES.   Customer may not, without the consent of Vendor, assign this Agreement or any of its rights under this Agreement, in whole or in part, and may not delegate its obligations under this Agreement. Any such purported assignment or delegation in contravention of this Section shall be null and void. Each Party intends that this Agreement shall not benefit, or create any right or cause of action in or on behalf of, any person, or entity other than the Parties.

20.03 RELATIONSHIP.   The Parties intend to create an independent contractor relationship and nothing contained in this Agreement shall be construed to make either Customer or Vendor partners, joint venturers, principals, Agents, or employees of the other. **[Except as expressly set forth in Article ___,]** no officer, director, employee, or Vendor Agent retained by Vendor to perform work on Customer's behalf under this Agreement shall be deemed to be an employee of Customer or a Customer Agent. Neither Party shall have any right, power, or authority, express or implied, to bind the other. Vendor shall have the sole right to supervise, manage, contract, direct, procure, perform, or cause to be performed, all work to be performed by Vendor under this Agreement.

20.04 SEVERABILITY AND WAIVERS.   If any provision of this Agreement is held by a court of competent jurisdiction to be contrary to Law, then the remaining provisions of this Agreement, if capable of substantial performance, shall remain in full force and effect. No delay or omission by either Party to exercise any right or power it has under this Agreement shall impair or be construed as a waiver of such right or power. A waiver by any Party of any breach or covenant shall not be construed to be a waiver of any succeeding breach or any other covenant. All waivers must be signed by the Party waiving its rights.

20.05 SURVIVAL.   [The terms of **[TO BE FILLED IN] shall survive the expiration or termination of this Agreement.][OPTION: BE SILENT]**

20.06 GOVERNING LAW.   This Agreement and the rights and obligations of the Parties under this Agreement shall be governed by and construed in accordance with the Laws of **[SPECIFY LAW]**.

20.07 SOLE AND EXCLUSIVE VENUE.   Subject to the provisions of *Article 16* **[and except as required by local law]**, each Party irrevocably agrees that any legal action, suit, or proceeding brought by it in any way arising out of this Agreement must be brought solely and exclusively in **[SPECIFY COURT]** and irrevocably accepts and submits to the sole and exclusive jurisdiction of each of the aforesaid courts in personam, generally and unconditionally with respect to any action, suit, or proceeding brought by it or against it by the other Party**[; provided, however, that this Section shall not prevent a Party against whom any legal action, suit, or proceeding is brought by the other Party from seeking to remove such legal action, suit, or proceeding, pursuant to applicable federal law, to the district court of the United States of America for the district and division embracing the place where the action is pending in the state courts of [SPECIFY], and in the event an action is so removed each Party irrevocably accepts and submits to the jurisdiction of the aforesaid district court] [; provided, however, that this Section shall not prevent a Party from enforcing a judgment or court order in another jurisdiction or court].** Each Party hereto further irrevocably consents to the service of process from any of the aforesaid courts by mailing copies thereof by registered or certified mail, postage prepaid, to such Party at its address designated pursuant to this Agreement, with such service of process to become effective 30 days after such mailing.

20.08 EXPORT.   Neither Party shall export, directly or indirectly, any information acquired under this Agreement or any product utilizing such information to any country for which the U.S. government or any agency thereof or any other governmental authority at the time of export requires an export license or other governmental approval without first obtaining such license or approval.

20.09 *FORCE MAJEURE.* [ADD APPLICABLE *FORCE MAJEURE* PRO-VISION]

20.10 NONPERFORMANCE. To the extent any nonperformance by either Party of its nonmonetary obligations under this Agreement results from or is caused by the failure of the other Party or the other Party's Agents to perform its obligations under this Agreement, such nonperformance shall be excused.

20.11 RIGHT TO PROVIDE SERVICES. Each Party recognizes that Vendor personnel providing services to Customer under this Agreement may perform similar services for others and this Agreement shall not prevent Vendor from using the personnel and equipment provided to Customer under this Agreement for such purposes. Nothing in this Agreement shall impair Vendor's right to acquire, license, or develop for itself or others or have others develop for Vendor similar technology performing the same or similar services as contemplated by this Agreement. Vendor may perform its obligations under this Agreement through the use of Vendor Agents; provided, however, that Vendor shall not be relieved of its obligations under this Agreement by such use of such Vendor Agents.

20.12 NONDISPARAGEMENT. [Each Party shall refrain, and shall use commercially reasonable efforts to cause its employees and Agents to refrain, from making negative or disparaging comments about the other Party; provided, however, that Vendor shall not be deemed to be in breach of this Section due to comments made during the first [SPECIFY TIME PERIOD] of the Term by those former employees of Customer who accept Vendor's offer of employment pursuant to *Article 8.*]

20.13 FURTHER ASSURANCES. Each of the Parties acknowledges and agrees that, subsequent to the execution and delivery of this Agreement and without any additional consideration, each of the Parties shall execute and deliver any further legal instruments and perform any actions that are or may become necessary to effectuate the purposes of this Agreement.

20.14 SOLICITATION. During the Term and for **[SPECIFY TIME PERIOD]** after the expiration of this Agreement or termination of this Agreement, Customer shall not solicit **[or hire]** any Vendor employees without Vendor's consent.

20.15 LIMITATION PERIOD. [Neither Party may bring an action, regardless of form, arising out of this Agreement more than [SPECIFY TIME PERIOD] after the cause of action has arisen or the date such cause of action was or should have been discovered.]

20.16 NEGOTIATED TERMS. The Parties agree that the terms and conditions of this Agreement are the result of negotiations between the Parties and that this

Agreement shall not be construed in favor of or against any Party by reason of the extent to which any Party or its professional advisors participated in the preparation of this Agreement.

20.17 ENTIRE AGREEMENT; AMENDMENTS; COUNTERPARTS. This Agreement and the Exhibits to this Agreement represent the entire agreement between the Parties with respect to its subject matter, and there are no other representations, understandings, or agreements between the Parties relative to such subject matter. No amendment to, or change, waiver, or discharge of, any provision of this Agreement shall be valid unless in writing and signed by an authorized representative of each of the Parties. This Agreement may be executed in any number of counterparts, each of which shall be deemed an original, but all of which taken together shall constitute one single agreement between the Parties.

* * * *

IN WITNESS WHEREOF, each of Customer and Vendor has caused this Agreement to be signed and delivered by its duly authorized representative.
[CUSTOMER]

By: _____
Name:
Title:

[VENDOR]

By: _____
Name:
Title:

EXHIBIT 1   DEFINITIONS

1. *"Agents"* shall mean Customer Agents or Vendor Agents, as the case may be.

2. *"Agreement"* shall mean this Services Agreement, dated as of **[SPECIFY DATE]**, by and between Vendor and Customer.

3. **[*"Assumptions"* shall have the meaning set forth in *Section 11.08*.]**

4. *"Change"* shall have the meaning set forth in *Article 6*.

5. *"Change Order"* shall mean a document agreed upon by the Parties (1) implementing a Change or (2) adding an Out-of-Scope Service under this Agreement.

6. *"Confidential Information"* [OPTION 1: of Customer or Vendor shall mean all information and documentation that is (1) marked as confidential by Customer or Vendor or (2) disclosed verbally by Customer or

Vendor and subsequently summarized and designated as confidential in writing by the disclosing Party, in each case, whether disclosed to or accessed by Customer or Vendor in connection with this Agreement, including (a) with respect to Customer and Vendor, the terms of this Agreement and (b) with respect to Vendor, the Vendor Intellectual Property.] [OPTION 2: shall mean (1) with respect to Customer, any information, technical data, or know-how of Customer that is identified by Customer as confidential at the time of disclosure; (2) with respect to Vendor, any information, technical data, or know-how of Vendor disclosed to or relating to Vendor, including the Vendor Intellectual Property; and (3) with respect to Customer and Vendor, the terms of this Agreement.]

7. *"Consents"* shall mean all licenses, consents, authorizations, and approvals that are necessary to allow Vendor and Vendor Agents to use Customer's owned and leased assets, including the Customer Data and the Customer Intellectual Property.

8. *"Contract Year"* shall mean each 12-month period during the Term commencing on the Effective Date and thereafter upon the completion of the immediately preceding Contract Year.

9. *"Control"* shall mean, with respect to any entity, the possession, directly or indirectly, of the power to direct or cause the direction of the management and policies of such entity, whether through the ownership of voting securities (or other ownership interest), by contract or otherwise.

10. *"Customer"* shall mean **[CUSTOMER]**, a **[SPECIFY LOCATION OF INC./FORMATION]** **[corporation/partnership/other]**, having its principal place of business at **[SPECIFY ADDRESS]**.

11. *"Customer Agents"* shall mean contractors and agents of Customer.

12. *"Customer Assets"* shall mean the assets owned or leased by Customer that are listed in *Exhibit 4*, as may be modified by agreement of the Parties from time to time during the Term.

13. *"Customer Data"* shall have the meaning set forth in *Section 13.01*.

14. *"Customer Intellectual Property"* shall mean the Customer Proprietary Intellectual Property and the Customer Third-Party Intellectual Property, collectively.

15. *"Customer Project Manager"* shall have the meaning set forth in *Section 9.01*.

16. *"Customer Proprietary Intellectual Property"* shall mean the Intellectual Property owned by Customer that is listed in *Exhibit 8*, as may be modified by agreement of the Parties from time to time during the Term.

17. *"Customer Service Location(s)"* shall mean any service location of Customer set forth in *Exhibit 5*.

18. *"Customer Third-Party Intellectual Property"* shall mean the Intellectual Property licensed or leased by Customer from a third party that is listed in *Exhibit 8*, as may be modified by agreement of the Parties from time to time during the Term.

19. *"Default Rate"* shall mean **[SPECIFY]**.

20. *"Developments"* shall mean **[SEE OPTIONS IN PROPRIETARY RIGHTS RIDERS ATTACHED AS APPENDIX 4.6]**.

21. *"Effective Date"* shall mean **[INSERT COMMENCEMENT DATE OF SERVICES]**.

22. *"Fees"* shall mean the fees for the Services set forth in *Exhibit 3*.

23. **[*"Force Majeure* Event" shall have the meaning set forth in *Section 20.09*.]**

24. *"Governmental Authority"* shall mean any international, national, provincial, municipal, local, territorial, or other governmental department, regulatory authority, judicial, or administrative body, domestic, international, or foreign.

25. *"Indemnified Party"* shall have the meaning set forth in *Section 18.05*.

26. *"Indemnifying Party"* shall have the meaning set forth in *Section 18.05*.

27. *"Initial Term"* shall have the meaning set forth in *Article 2*.

28. *"Intellectual Property"* shall mean **[Software]**, methodologies, processes, procedures, and algorithms and Related Documentation, in whatever form or media.

29. *"Law"* shall mean any declaration, decree, directive, legislative enactment, order, ordinance, regulation, rule, or other binding requirement of or by any governmental authority.

30. *"Losses"* shall mean any and all damages, fines, penalties, deficiencies, losses, liabilities (including settlements and judgments), and expenses (including interest, court costs, reasonable fees and expenses of attorneys, accountants, and other experts or other reasonable fees and expenses of litigation or other proceedings or of any claim, default, or assessment).

31. *"Out-of-Scope Service(s)"* shall mean any **[SPECIFY SERVICES]** service that is not expressly included within the scope of the Services.

32. *"Parties"* shall mean Customer and Vendor, collectively.

33. *"Party"* shall mean either Customer or Vendor, as the case may be.

34. **[*"Performance Credits"* shall mean the performance credits set forth in *Exhibit 6*.]**

35. *"Project Staff"* shall mean the personnel of Vendor and Vendor Agents who provide the Services.

36. "*Related Documentation*" shall mean, with respect to Intellectual Property, all materials, documentation, specifications, technical manuals, user manuals, flow diagrams, file descriptions, and other written information that describes the function and use of such Intellectual Property, as applicable.

37. "*Renewal Term*" shall have the meaning set forth in *Article 2.*

38. "*Service Levels*" shall have the meaning set forth in *Section 5.01.*

39. "*Services*" shall have the meaning set forth in *Section 3.01.*

40. [**"*Software*" shall mean the object [and source] code versions of any applications programs, operating system software, computer software languages, utilities, other computer programs, and Related Documentation, in whatever form or media, including the tangible media upon which such applications programs, operating system software, computer software languages, utilities, other computer programs, and Related Documentation are recorded or printed.]**

41. "*Term*" shall have the meaning set forth in *Article 2.*

42. "Termination Assistance Period" shall have the meaning set forth in *Section 17.03.*

43. "Termination Assistance Services" shall have the meaning set forth in *Section 17.03.*

44. [**"*Third Party Contracts*" shall mean the third-party contracts listed in *Exhibit 9.*]**

45. [**"*Third-Party Intellectual Property Licenses*"] shall mean the third-party agreements pursuant to which Intellectual Property Used in connection with this Agreement is licensed to Customer or Vendor.]**

46. "*Tools*" shall have the meaning set forth in *Section 10.04.*

47. [**"*Transferred Assets*" shall mean the assets set forth in *Exhibit 10.*]**

48. "*Use*" shall mean the right to load, execute, store, transmit, display, copy, maintain, modify, enhance, create derivative works, make, and have made.

49. "*Vendor*" shall mean **[VENDOR]**, a **[SPECIFY LOCATION OF INC./FORMATION]** **[corporation/partnership/other]** having its principal place of business at **[SPECIFY ADDRESS]**.

50. "*Vendor Account Manager*" shall have the meaning set forth in *Section 3.03(1).*

51. "*Vendor Affiliate*" shall mean any entity that, directly or indirectly, Controls, is Controlled by, or is under common Control with Vendor.

52. "*Vendor Agents*" shall mean Vendor Affiliates and subcontractors, suppliers, and agents of Vendor and Vendor Affiliates.

53.   *"Vendor Intellectual Property"* shall mean the Vendor Proprietary Intellectual Property and the Vendor Third-Party Intellectual Property, collectively.

54.   *"Vendor Proprietary Intellectual Property"* shall mean the Intellectual Property owned or developed by or on behalf of Vendor that is used in connection with the Services.

55.   *"Vendor Third-Party Intellectual Property"* shall mean the Intellectual Property licensed or leased by Vendor from a third party that is used in connection with the Services.

PROPRIETARY RIGHTS RIDER (VENDOR FORM)[7]

PROPRIETARY RIGHTS RIDER

[OPTION 1. VENDOR OWNS NEW DEVELOPMENTS WITH LICENSE
TO CUSTOMER]
[ADD TO DEFINITIONS:]

"*Developments*" shall mean any Intellectual Property, and any modifications or enhancements to Intellectual Property, developed or acquired in connection with this Agreement (but excluding Tools) by or on behalf of (1) Vendor and Vendor Agents, separately or jointly, or (2) Vendor and Vendor Agents, separately or jointly, and Customer and Customer Agents, separately or jointly.

[ADD TO ARTICLE 10:]

__.03 *Developments.*

1. All Developments are and shall be owned by Vendor. Vendor shall have all right, title, and interest, including worldwide ownership of copyright and patent rights, in and to the Developments and all copies made from it. Customer hereby irrevocably assigns, transfers, and conveys, and shall cause Customer Agents to assign, transfer, and convey, to Vendor without further consideration all of its right, title, and interest in and to such Developments, if any, including all rights of patent, copyright, trade secret, and any other proprietary rights in such materials. **[ADD IF VENDOR WILL LICENSE DEVELOPMENTS TO CUSTOMER: Upon expiration or termination of this Agreement (except for a termination pursuant to *Section 17.01*), Vendor hereby grants to Customer a nonexclusive, nontransferable license to use the Developments in accordance with sub-Section (2) below.] [OPTION 1: IF**

---

7. Note: This sample agreement is intended to illustrate the types of legal issues that vendors typically wish to address in connection with information technology outsourcing transactions. The provisions included in this sample agreement, while comprehensive, may not cover all of the issues that may arise in a particular transaction. Legal issues will likely vary depending on the type of information technology process being outsourced and the scope of the outsourcing transaction. This sample agreement or any part thereof should only be used after consultation with your legal counsel. Legal counsel should be consulted prior to entering into or negotiating any outsourcing transaction.

THERE WILL BE A LICENSE FEE: at rates to be agreed upon by the Parties at such expiration or termination] [OPTION 2: IF THERE WILL BE A LICENSE FEE: at Vendor's then-current standard commercial rates].

2. **[ADD IF VENDOR WILL LICENSE DEVELOPMENTS TO CUS-TOMER:** Customer's use of the Developments upon expiration or termination of this Agreement (except for a termination pursuant to Section 17.01) shall be subject to, and Customer shall comply with, the following terms and conditions:

   a. The Developments shall (i) not be Used directly or indirectly by persons other than an employee of Customer **[or an Approved Service Provider], [(ii) only be operated on equipment owned or leased by Customer which is located on Customer's premises] and (iii) only be Used in connection with the internal work of Customer. [LIMIT RIGHT TO MODIFY/ENHANCE?] ["*Approved Service Provider*" shall mean a third party providing services to Customer that has entered into a nondisclosure agreement with Vendor in a form acceptable to Vendor [and that does not compete directly or indirectly with Vendor].]**

   b. Except as set forth in sub-Section (2)(a) above, at no time may the Developments or their components or any modifications thereto be disclosed to third parties or sold, assigned, leased, or otherwise disposed of or commercially exploited or marketed in any way, with or without charge. Except as may be necessary for archival purposes, Customer shall not copy, and shall not permit the copying by a third party of, the Developments in whole or in part.

   c. Upon Vendor's request, Customer shall affix to all copies of the Developments in Customer's possession any form of copyright or other proprietary notice specified by Vendor.

The licenses granted pursuant to this Section in respect of a component of the Developments shall terminate if (i) Customer ceases use of such component of the Developments or (ii) Customer breaches the terms of this license. Upon request after termination of this license, Customer will(a) deliver to Vendor a current copy of such component (including all Related Documentation and source code in Customer's possession) in the form in use as of such date and (b) destroy or erase all other copies of such component in Customer's possession.]

[OPTION 2: JOINTLY OWNED]
[ADD TO DEFINITIONS:]

"*Developments*" shall mean all Intellectual Property developed [for Customer] in connection with the Services (but excluding Tools) by or on behalf of (1) Vendor and Vendor Agents, separately or jointly, or (2) Vendor and Vendor

Agents, separately or jointly, and Customer and Customer Agents, separately or jointly.

[ADD TO ARTICLE 10:]

__.03   *Developments.* **[Subject to the provisions of the Third-Party Intellectual Property, Licenses,] [t] [T]**he Parties shall jointly own the Developments. Neither Party will have a duty of accounting with respect to the Developments, and each Party will take such actions as the other Party reasonably requests to evidence the joint ownership of the Developments. Except as otherwise provided by this Agreement, neither Party will have any obligation to maintain the Developments or to provide the other Party with any modifications or enhancements to the Developments.

[OPTION 3: CUSTOMER OWNS NEWLY CREATED DEVELOPMENTS ONLY]
[ADD TO DEFINITIONS:]

"*Developments*" shall mean any Intellectual Property [and other items] expressly designated as deliverables in Exhibit ___ are developed by Vendor or Vendor Agents.

[ADD TO ARTICLE 10:]

__.03   *Developments.* **[Subject to the provisions of any Third-Party Intellectual Property, Licenses,] [a] [A]**ll Developments shall be owned by Customer. Customer shall have all right, title and interest in and to the Developments. **[Customer hereby grants to Vendor a nonexclusive, irrevocable, worldwide, fully paid-up, royalty-free license to use, and sublicense the use of, the Developments [in connection with the provision of the Services] [for any purpose].]** All other Intellectual Property, materials, data, information, and other items developed by, on behalf of, or in conjunction with Vendor under this Agreement shall be owned by Vendor. Customer hereby irrevocably assigns, transfers, and conveys, and shall cause Customer's subcontractors and agents to assign, transfer, and convey, to Vendor without further consideration all of its right, title, and interest in and to such Intellectual Property, documentation, materials, data, information, and other items, if any, including all rights of patent, copyright, trade secret, and any other proprietary rights.

[OPTION 4: CUSTOMER OWNS DERIVATIVE WORKS OF CUSTOMER SOFTWARE; VENDOR OWNS DERIVATIVE WORKS OF VENDOR SOFTWARE; VENDOR OWNS ALL OTHER DEVELOPMENTS WITH LICENSE BACK TO CUSTOMER]

[ADD TO DEFINITIONS:]

"*Derivative Work*" shall mean Intellectual Property based on one or more preexisting works, including, a condensation, transformation, expansion for adaptation, which, if prepared without authorization of the owner of the copyright of such preexisting work, would constitute a copyright infringement, but excluding Tools.

"*Customer Derivative Work*" shall mean a Derivative Work for which the preexisting copyright is owned by Customer.

"*Developments*" shall mean Intellectual Property developed or acquired by or on behalf of (1) Vendor and Vendor Agents, separately or jointly, or (2) Vendor and Vendor Agents, separately or jointly, and Customer and Customer Agents, separately or jointly, which does not constitute (a) Vendor Intellectual Property, (b) a Customer Derivative Work or a Vendor Derivative Work or (c) Tools.

"*Vendor Derivative Work*" shall mean Intellectual Property which constitutes a Derivative Work for which the preexisting copyright is owned by Vendor or Vendor Agents.

[ADD TO ARTICLE 10:]

__.03   Developments.

1. *Customer Derivative Works.* All Customer Derivative Works are and shall be owned by Customer or its licensors. Customer or its licensor shall own all rights, title, and interests in and to the Customer Derivative Works, and Vendor hereby assigns, transfers, and conveys (and shall cause Vendor Agents to so assign, transfer, and convey) to Customer without further consideration any rights, title, or interests that Vendor may have or acquire in or to the Customer Derivative Works and any copy, translation, modification, adaptation, enhancement, or derivation of the Customer Derivative Works, including any improvement or development thereof. Customer hereby grants to Vendor a nonexclusive, irrevocable, worldwide, fully paid-up, royalty-free license to Use, and sublicense the Use of, the Customer Derivative Works **[in connection with the provision of the Services] [for any purpose]**.

2. *Vendor Derivative Works.* All Vendor Derivative Works are and shall be owned by Vendor or its licensors. Vendor or its licensor shall own all rights, title, and interests in and to the Vendor Derivative Works, and Customer hereby assigns, transfers, and conveys (and shall cause Customer Agents to so assign, transfer, and convey) to Vendor without further consideration any rights, title, or interests that Customer may have or acquire in or to the Vendor Derivative Works and any copy, transla-

tion, modification, adaptation, enhancement, or derivation of the Vendor Derivative Works, including any improvement or development thereof.] **[ADD IF VENDOR WILL LICENSE VENDOR DERIVATIVE WORKS TO CUSTOMER: Upon expiration or termination of this Agreement (except for a termination pursuant to *Section 17.01*),] [Vendor hereby grants to Customer a nonexclusive, nontransferable license to Use the Vendor Derivative Works in accordance with sub-Section (2) below [OPTION 1: IF THERE WILL BE A LICENSE FEE: at rates to be agreed upon by the Parties at such expiration or termination] [OPTION 2: IF THERE WILL BE A LICENSE FEE: at Vendor's then-current standard commercial rates]. [LIMIT RIGHT TO MODIFY/ENHANCE?]**

3. *Developments.* All Developments are and shall be owned by Vendor or its licensors. Customer shall not take any actions that jeopardize Vendor's or its licensor's proprietary rights or acquire any right in the Developments[**, except the limited use rights expressly set forth herein**]. Vendor or its licensor shall own all rights, title, and interests in and to the Developments, and Customer hereby assigns, transfers, and conveys (and shall cause Customer Agents to so assign, transfer, and convey) to Vendor without further consideration any rights, title, or interests that Customer may have or acquire in or to the Developments and any copy, translation, modification, adaptation, enhancement, or derivation of the Developments, including any improvement or development thereof.] **[ADD IF VENDOR WILL LICENSE DEVELOPMENTS TO CUSTOMER: Upon expiration or termination of this Agreement (except for a termination pursuant to *Section 17.01*), Vendor hereby grants to Customer a nonexclusive, nontransferable license to Use the Developments in accordance with sub-Section (2) below.] [OPTION 1: IF THERE WILL BE A LICENSE FEE: at rates to be agreed upon by the Parties at such expiration or termination] [OPTION 2: IF THERE WILL BE A LICENSE FEE: at Vendor's then-current standard commercial rates]. [LIMIT RIGHT TO MODIFY/ENHANCE?]**

4. *License Terms.* **[ADD IF VENDOR WILL LICENSE VENDOR DERIVATIVE WORKS/DEVELOPMENTS TO CUSTOMER:** Customer's use of the Developments upon expiration or termination of this Agreement for any reason (except for a termination pursuant to *Section 17.01)* shall be subject to, and Customer shall comply with, the following terms and conditions:

   a. The Developments shall (i) not be Used directly or indirectly by persons other than an employee of Customer **[or an Approved Service Provider], [(ii) only be operated on equipment owned or leased by Customer which is located on Customer's premises] and (iii) only be used in connection with the internal work of**

Customer. [LIMIT RIGHT TO MODIFY/ENHANCE?] ["*Approved Service Provider*" shall mean a third party providing services to Customer that has entered into a nondisclosure agreement with Vendor in a form acceptable to Vendor and that does not compete directly or indirectly with Vendor.]

b.   Except as set forth in sub-Section (2)(a) above, at no time may the Developments or their components or any modifications thereto be disclosed to third parties or sold, assigned, leased, or otherwise disposed of or commercially exploited or marketed in any way, with or without charge. Except as may be necessary for archival purposes, Customer shall not copy, and shall not permit the copying by a third party of, the Developments in whole or in part.

c.   Upon Vendor's request, Customer shall affix to all copies of the Developments in Customer's possession any form of copyright or other proprietary notice specified by Vendor.

The licenses granted pursuant to this Section in respect of a component of the Developments shall terminate if (i) Customer ceases use of such component of the Developments or (ii) Customer breaches the terms of this license. Upon request after termination of this license, Customer shall (a) deliver to Vendor a current copy of such component (including all Related Documentation and source code in Customer's possession) in the form in use as of such date and (b) destroy or erase all other copies of such component in Customer's possession.]

TEAMING AGREEMENT[8]

---

8. Note: This sample agreement is intended to illustrate the types of legal issues that vendors typically wish to address in connection with information technology outsourcing transactions. The provisions included in this sample agreement, while comprehensive, may not cover all of the issues that may arise in a particular transaction. Legal issues will likely vary depending on the type of information technology process being outsourced and the scope of the outsourcing transaction. This sample agreement or any part thereof should only be used after consultation with your legal counsel. Legal counsel should be consulted prior to entering into or negotiating any outsourcing transaction.

THIS TEAMING AGREEMENT (this *"Agreement"*), dated as of **[DATE]** (the *"Agreement Date"*), by and between **[PRIMARY CONTRACTOR],** with a principal place of business at **[ADDRESS]** (the "Primary Contractor") and **[SUBCONTRACTOR],** with a principal place of business at **[ADDRESS]** (the "the Subcontractor") (the Primary Contractor and the Subcontractor each, a "Party"; collectively, the "Parties").

WITNESSETH:

WHEREAS, **[CUSTOMER]** ("Customer") has requested that the Primary Contractor submit a proposal for certain services and products, described more particularly in Exhibit A (the "Services"); and

WHEREAS, the Parties wish to work together, in accordance with the terms and conditions of this Agreement, to develop a quality approach to the provision of the Services and to prepare a proposal describing such approach to be submitted by the Primary Contractor to the Customer (the "Proposal").

NOW, THEREFORE, for and in consideration of the agreements of the Parties set forth below, the Parties hereby agree as follows:

ARTICLE 1. DEFINITIONS

The following defined terms shall have the meanings specified in the portion of this Agreement indicated below:

TERM	DEFINED IN
AAA	Section 9.2
Agreement	Heading
Agreement Date	Heading
Confidential Information	Section 5.1
Customer	Recitals
Force Majeure	Section 12.16
Indemnitee	Section 10.3
Indemnifying Party	Section 10.3
Party(ies)	Heading
Primary Contractor	Heading
Primary Contractor Representative	Section 9.1
Prime Contract	Section 3.1
Proposal	Recitals
Services	Recitals
Subcontracted Services	Section 3.2
Subcontracting Agreement	Section 3.3
Subcontractor	Heading
Subcontractor Representative	Section 6.1
Term	Article 2
Work Product	Section 5.2

ARTICLE 2. TERM

This Agreement shall commence on the Agreement Date and continue until terminated pursuant to *Article 7* (the "Term").

ARTICLE 3. RESPONSIBILITIES

3.1 PRIMARY CONTRACTOR. The Primary Contractor shall have sole responsibility for (1) developing and directing the format and content of the Proposal, including preparing and revising portions of the Proposal, (2) presenting the Proposal to Customer, and (3) negotiating a prime contract between Customer and the Primary Contractor (the "Prime Contract") as may be requested by Customer after review of the Proposal.

3.2 SUBCONTRACTOR. The Subcontractor shall (1) provide information and data relating to its performance of certain of the Services identified by the Primary Contractor in [***] (the "Subcontracted Services") and (2) assist the Primary Contractor in the Primary Contractor's development and presentation of the Proposal as requested by the Primary Contractor. The Subcontractor shall provide access to qualified personnel and resources as may be requested by the Primary Contractor.

3.3 PRIME CONTRACT. If the Primary Contractor enters into the Prime Contract with Customer, the Primary Contractor shall subcontract to the Subcontractor the Subcontracted Services, as may be amended during negotiations with Customer; provided, that (1) the Primary Contractor and the Subcontractor negotiate and execute an appropriate subcontract (the "Subcontracting Agreement"), (2) Customer approves of the Subcontractor and the scope of the work to be performed by the Subcontractor, and (3) this Agreement has not been terminated pursuant to *Article 7.*

3.4 SUBCONTRACTING AGREEMENT. Within **[NUMBER]** days after the award to the Primary Contractor of the Prime Contract, the Parties shall commence to negotiate the Subcontracting Agreement. The Subcontracting Agreement shall (1) contain those terms and conditions as may be required in the Prime Contract and (2) reflect the scope and requirements set forth in the Prime Contract.

3.5 THIRD PARTIES. In the event that the Parties are not able to negotiate the Subcontracting Agreement within **[NUMBER]** days from award of the Prime Contract to the Primary Contractor, the Primary Contractor may negotiate with and enter into subcontracts with third parties for the performance of the Subcontracted Services or provide such Subcontracted Services itself. The right to subcontract to third parties or provide the Subcontracted Services itself shall be in addition to other rights the Primary Contractor may have. In the event the Primary Contractor subcontracts to a third party or notifies the Subcontractor that it will provide the Subcontracted Services itself, this Agreement shall terminate.

3.6 RIGHT TO COMMUNICATE WITH CUSTOMER. The Subcontractor shall not contact or communicate with Customer or its employees or agents, directly or indirectly, without the Primary Contractor's approval. The Subcontractor shall notify the Primary Contractor immediately if it is approached or contacted by Customer.

ARTICLE 4. RELATIONSHIP

During the Term, the Subcontractor shall not team with any other party or work individually in connection with the preparation of a proposal to be submitted to Customer for the provision of any of the Services. The performance by the Subcontractor of its duties and obligations under this Agreement shall be that of an independent contractor and nothing contained in this Agreement shall create or imply an agency relationship between the Parties, nor shall this agreement be deemed to constitute a joint venture, partnership, or formal business organization between the Parties.

ARTICLE 5. PROPRIETARY RIGHTS

5.1 CONFIDENTIAL INFORMATION. Each Party shall use at least the same standard of care in the protection of confidential or proprietary information ("Confidential Information") of the other Party as it uses to protect its own Confidential Information. Each Party shall use the Confidential Information of the other Party only in connection with the purposes of this Agreement and shall make such Confidential Information available only to its employees, subcontractors, or agents having a "need to know" with respect to such purpose. In the event of the termination of this Agreement for any reason, all Confidential Information of a Party disclosed to and all copies thereof made by the other Party shall be returned to the disclosing Party or, at the disclosing Party's option, erased, or destroyed. The recipient of the Confidential Information shall provide to the disclosing Party certificates evidencing such destruction. The obligations in this *Section 5.1* shall not restrict any disclosure by a Party pursuant to any applicable law, or by order of any court or government agency (provided that the disclosing Party shall give prompt notice to the nondisclosing Party of such order). Confidential Information of a Party shall not be afforded the protection of this Agreement if such data was (1) developed by the other Party independently, (2) rightfully obtained by the other Party without restriction from a third party, (3) publicly available other than through the fault or negligence of the other Party, or (4) released without restriction to anyone.

5.2 PROPRIETARY RIGHTS. All information, documentation, data, and other materials developed, created, or provided solely by a Party in connection with its obligations under this Agreement ("Work Product") **[shall remain the property of the such Party].** Each Party grants the other Party the right to use its Work Product for the limited purpose of preparing and amending the Proposal and negotiating the Prime Contract and the Subcontracting Agreement. **[DISCUSS HOW WORKS CREATED JOINTLY WILL BE TREATED]**

ARTICLE 6. PROJECT TEAM

6.1 SUBCONTRACTOR REPRESENTATIVE.   The Subcontractor shall appoint an individual who from the Agreement Date shall serve as the contact person in respect of, and shall be responsible for, the performance of the Subcontractor's obligations under this Agreement (each such individual, the "Subcontractor Representative"). **[The Subcontractor Representative shall work on the Proposal and the Subcontractor's other responsibilities under this Agreement on a full-time basis.]** The Subcontractor's appointment of any Subcontractor Representative shall be subject to the Primary Contractor's consent. The initial Subcontractor Account Representative shall be **[NAME]. [The Subcontractor shall not reassign or replace the Subcontractor Representative until the earlier of (1) the termination of this Agreement and (2) the date on which the Prime Contract and the Subcontracting Agreement are entered into by the appropriate parties.]**

6.2 PROJECT STAFF.   The Subcontractor shall appoint sufficient staff of suitable training and skills to perform the Subcontractor's responsibilities under this Agreement.

ARTICLE 7. TERMINATION
Except as set forth in *Section 12.16*, this Agreement shall terminate:

1.   if Customer has not awarded a prime contract for the Services within **[NUMBER]** days from the Agreement Date;

2.   if Customer enters into a prime contract for the Services to a party other than the Primary Contractor;

3.   if the Primary Contractor notifies the Subcontractor that the supplies or services to be offered by the Subcontractor are unsatisfactory or do not otherwise meet Customer's requirements;

4.   if the Parties do not enter into the Subcontracting Agreement within **[NUMBER]** days of the date that the Prime Contract is entered into by the Primary Contractor and Customer;

5.   if either Party is ineligible to receive an award or to enter into a contract for the provision of the Services;

6.   if the Primary Contractor enters into the Prime Contract; or

7.   pursuant to *Section 3.5*.

ARTICLE 8. EXPENSES

Each Party shall bear all of its own expenses incurred in connection with the preparation and negotiation of the Proposal, the Prime Contract, and the Subcontracting Agreement.

ARTICLE 9. DISPUTE RESOLUTION

9.1 ACCOUNT REPRESENTATIVES. All disputes shall initially be referred jointly to (1) the Subcontractor Representative and (2) the individual appointed by the Primary Contractor to serve as its primary contact with the Subcontractor (the "Primary Contractor Representative"). If the Subcontractor Representative and the Primary Contractor Representative are unable to resolve the dispute within **[NUMBER]** business days after referral of the matter to them, the parties shall submit the dispute to members of the senior management of both Parties.

9.2 ARBITRATION. If a dispute is not resolved pursuant to *Section 9.1*, then either Party may, within **[NUMBER]** business days after the completion of the procedures set forth in *Section 9.1*, upon notice, submit the dispute to [formal binding] arbitration in accordance with this *Section 9.2*.

1. The arbitration shall be held in [***] before a panel of three arbitrators. Either the Primary Contractor or the Subcontractor may by notice to the other Party demand arbitration, by serving on the other Party a statement of the dispute, controversy, or claim, and the facts relating or giving rise thereto, in reasonable detail, and the name of the arbitrator selected by it.

2. Within **[NUMBER]** days after receipt of such notice, the other Party shall name its arbitrator, and the two arbitrators named by the Parties shall, within **[NUMBER]** days after the date of such notice, select the third arbitrator.

3. The arbitration shall be governed by the Commercial Arbitration Rules of the American Arbitration Association, as may be amended from time to time (the "AAA"), except as expressly provided in this *Section 9.2*; provided, however, that the arbitration shall be administered by any organization agreed upon by the parties. The arbitrators may not amend or disregard any provision of this *Section 9.2*.

4. The arbitrators shall allow such discovery as is appropriate to the purposes of arbitration in accomplishing fair, speedy, and cost-effective resolution of disputes. The arbitrators shall reference the rules of evidence of the Federal Rules of Civil Procedure then in effect in setting the scope and direction of such discovery. **[The arbitrators shall not be required to make findings of fact or render opinions of law.]**

5. **[The decision of and award rendered by the arbitrators shall be final and binding on the Parties.]** Judgment on the award may be entered in and enforced by any court of competent jurisdiction. The arbi-

trators shall have no authority to award damages in excess or in contravention of *Article 11.*

Except (a) for an action to seek injunctive relief to prevent or stay a breach of *Article 5* or (b) any action necessary to enforce the award of the arbitrators, the provisions of this *Section 9.2* are a complete defense to any suit, action, or other proceeding instituted in any court or before any administrative tribunal with respect to any dispute, controversy, or claim arising out of or related to this Agreement or the creation, validity, interpretation, breach, or termination of this Agreement.

ARTICLE 10. INDEMNIFICATION

10.1 BY PRIMARY CONTRACTOR. The Primary Contractor shall indemnify the Subcontractor from, and defend the Subcontractor against, any liability or expenses (including attorneys' fees and expenses as incurred) arising out of or relating to (1) any claim by a third party that the Work Product developed, created, or provided by the Primary Contractor infringes upon the proprietary rights of any third party and (2) **[personal injury, death or damage to tangible personal or real property in any way incident to, or in connection with or arising out of the act or omission of the Primary Contractor, its employees, contractors or agents]**. The Primary Contractor shall be responsible for any costs and expenses incurred by the Subcontractor in connection with the enforcement of this *Section 10.1.*

10.2 BY SUBCONTRACTOR. The Subcontractor shall indemnify the Primary Contractor from, and defend the Primary Contractor against, any liability or expenses (including attorneys' fees and expenses as incurred) arising out of or relating to (1) any claim by a third party that the Work Product developed, created or provided by the Subcontractor infringes upon the proprietary rights of any third party, (2) any claim by a third party in respect of services or systems provided by the Subcontractor to a third party, and (3) personal injury, death, or damage to tangible personal or real property in any way incident to, or in connection with or arising out of the act or omission of the Subcontractor, its employees, contractors, or agents. The Subcontractor shall be responsible for any costs and expenses incurred by the Primary Contractor in connection with the enforcement of this *Section 10.2.*

10.3 INDEMNIFICATION PROCEDURES. If any third party makes a claim covered by *Section 10.1* or *Section 10.2* against any indemnitee (an "Indemnitee") with respect to which such Indemnitee intends to seek indemnification under *Section 10.1* or *Section 10.2,* such Indemnitee shall give notice of such claim to the indemnifying party (under *Section 10.1* or *Section 10.2*) (the "Indemnifying Party") including a brief description of the amount and basis therefore, if known. Upon giving such notice, the Indemnifying Party shall be obligated to defend such Indemnitee against such claim, and shall be entitled to assume control of the defense of the claim with counsel chosen by the Indemnifying Party, reasonably satisfactory to the Indemnitee. Indemnitee shall cooperate fully with, and assist, the Indemnifying Party in its defense against such claim. The Indemnifying Party shall keep the Indemnitee fully apprised at all times as to the status of the defense. Notwithstanding the foregoing, the Indemnitee shall have the right to employ its own separate counsel in any such action, but the fees and expenses of such counsel shall be at the expense of such Indemnitee; provided, however, (1) if the parties agree that it is advantageous to the defense for the Indemnitee to employ its own counsel or (2) in the reasonable judgment of the Indemnitee, based upon an opinion of counsel which shall be provided to the Indemnifying Party, there is a conflict of interest with respect to such claim, then reasonable fees and expenses of the Indemnitee's counsel shall be at the expense of the Indemnifying Party, provided that the Indemnifying Party approves such counsel. Neither the Indemnifying Party nor any Indemnitee shall be liable for any settlement of any action or claim effected without its consent.

Notwithstanding the foregoing, the Indemnitee shall retain, assume, or reassume sole control over, and all expenses relating to, every aspect of the defense that it believes is not the subject of the indemnification provided for in *Section 10.1* or *Section 10.2*. Until both (a) the Indemnitee receives notice from the Indemnifying Party that it will defend and (b) the Indemnifying Party assumes such defense, the Indemnitee may, at any time after **[NUMBER]** days from the date notice of claim is given to the Indemnifying Party by the Indemnitee, resist or otherwise defend the claim or, after consultation with and consent of the Indemnifying Party, settle or otherwise compromise or pay the claim. The Indemnifying Party shall pay all costs of the Indemnitee arising out of or relating to that defense and any such settlement, compromise or payment. The Indemnitee shall keep the Indemnifying Party fully apprised at all times as to the status of the defense.

Following indemnification as provided in *Section 10.1* or *Section 10.2*, the Indemnifying Party shall be subrogated to all rights of the Indemnitee with respect to the matters for which indemnification has been made.

ARTICLE 11. DAMAGES
NEITHER PARTY SHALL BE LIABLE FOR, NOR WILL THE MEASURE OF DAMAGES INCLUDE ANY INDIRECT, SPECIAL OR CONSEQUENTIAL DAMAGES OR AMOUNTS FOR LOST INCOME.

ARTICLE 12. MISCELLANEOUS PROVISIONS

12.1 ASSIGNMENT.   Neither Party may assign this Agreement in whole or in part without the consent of the other Party; provided, however, that a Party may assign this Agreement pursuant to a change of control, including a merger, corporate reorganization, or sale of all or substantially all of its assets. Any purported assignment in contravention of this *Section 12.1* shall be null and void. The consent of either Party to any assignment, or any other assignment permitted hereunder, shall not constitute consent to further assignment. This Agreement shall be binding on the Parties and their respective successors and permitted assigns.

12.2 NOTICES.   Except as otherwise specified in this Agreement, all notices, requests, approvals and consents and other communications required or permitted under this Agreement shall be in writing and shall be sent by telecopy to the telecopy number specified below. A copy of any such notice shall also be personally delivered or sent by (1) first class U.S. Mail, registered or certified, return receipt requested, postage prepaid, or (2) U.S. Express Mail, FedEx, or other, similar overnight bonded mail delivery services to the address specified below:

In the case of the Primary Contractor:
Attention: **[NAME]**
Telecopy Number: **[TELECOPY NUMBER]**

In the case of the Subcontractor:
Attention: **[NAME]**
Telecopy Number: **[TELECOPY NUMBER]**

Either Party may change its address or telecopy number for notification purposes by giving the other Party notice of the new address or telecopy number and the date upon which it will become effective.

12.3 COUNTERPARTS.   This Agreement may be executed in any number of counterparts, all of which taken together shall constitute one single agreement between the Parties.

12.4 HEADINGS.   The article and section headings and the table of contents are for reference and convenience only and shall not be considered in the interpretation of this Agreement.

12.5 CONSENTS, APPROVALS, AND REQUESTS.   Unless otherwise specified in this Agreement, all consents and approvals, acceptance, or similar actions to be given by either Party under this Agreement shall not be unreasonably withheld or delayed and each Party shall make only reasonable requests under this Agreement.

12.6 SEVERABILITY.   If any provision of this Agreement is held by a court of competent jurisdiction to be contrary to law, then the remaining provisions of this Agreement will remain in full force and effect.

12.7 WAIVER.   No delay or omission by either Party to exercise any right or power it has under this Agreement shall impair or be construed as a waiver of such right or power. A waiver by any Party of any breach or covenant shall not be construed to be a waiver of any succeeding breach or any other covenant. All waivers must be in writing and signed by the Party waiving its rights.

12.8 PUBLICITY.   Neither Party shall use the other Party's name or refer to the other Party directly or indirectly in any media release, public announcement, or public disclosure relating to this Agreement or its subject matter, including in any promotional or marketing materials, customer lists, or business presentations without consent from the other Party for each such use or release.

12.9 ENTIRE AGREEMENT.   This Agreement and each of the Attachments, which are hereby incorporated by reference into this Agreement, is the entire agreement between the Parties with respect to its subject matter, and there are no other representations, understandings, or agreements between the Parties relative to such subject matter.

12.10 AMENDMENTS.   No amendment to, or change, waiver, or discharge of, any provision of this Agreement shall be valid unless in writing and signed by an authorized representative of the Party against which such amendment, change, waiver, or discharge is sought to be enforced.

12.11 GOVERNING LAW.   This Agreement shall be interpreted in accordance with and governed by the laws of **[SPECIFY LAW]**.

12.12 SURVIVAL.   The terms of *Article 4, Article 5, Article 8, Article 10, Article 11, Section 9.2, Section 12.8, Section 12.11*, this *Section 12.12* and *Section 12.15* shall survive the termination of this Agreement for any reason.

12.13 THIRD PARTY BENEFICIARIES.   Each Party intends that this Agreement shall not benefit, or create any right or cause of action in or on behalf of, any person or entity other than the Primary Contractor or the Subcontractor.

12.14 COVENANT OF FURTHER ASSURANCES.   The Primary Contractor and the Subcontractor covenant and agree that, subsequent to the execution and delivery of this Agreement and without any additional consideration, each of the Primary Contractor and the Subcontractor will execute and deliver any further legal instruments and perform any acts which are or may become necessary to effectuate the purposes of this Agreement.

12.15 SOLICITATION.   The Subcontractor shall not solicit any Primary Contractor employees during the Term and for **[NUMBER]** days after the termination of this Agreement for any reason.

12.16 *FORCE MAJEURE.* [ADD APPROPRIATE *FORCE MAJEURE* LANGUAGE]

IN WITNESS WHEREOF, each of the Parties have caused this Agreement to be signed and delivered by its duly authorized representative.

[PRIMARY CONTRACTOR]

By: _____
[NAME]
[TITLE]

[SUBCONTRACTOR]

By: _____
[NAME]
[TITLE]

CHAPTER 5

EXHIBITS

5.1 CRITICAL PART OF THE OUTSOURCING CONTRACT

While the outsourcing contract provides the general framework under which services are to be provided by the vendor, and the remedies if obligations are not performed, it is in the exhibits to the outsourcing agreement that the particular services to be provided are described, hardware and software assets and configurations are identified, service levels and security requirements are specified, base and incremental pricing is provided, and the scope and implementation of projects are detailed. Many of the hidden costs in outsourcing transactions can be found in the data and information contained in, or more likely omitted from, the exhibits.

(a) WHAT SHOULD BE INCLUDED IN THE EXHIBITS? There are three general philosophies regarding what should be included in the exhibits: (1) be as detailed as possible with respect to the services to be provided, projects to be implemented, and assets and users covered in order to avoid any future dispute over what is included; (2) be as detailed as possible but leave areas where due diligence is necessary until after contract signing; and (3) be as general as possible (e.g., "the vendor will provide the services provided by the IT department prior to the agreement date") so that there is no room for the vendor to argue that items not listed are not "in scope." Obviously, there are benefits and risks to all three approaches. To the extent that the data is available and time allows, the more detailed the parties can be with respect to each of the exhibits, the more the parties will identify open issues and be able to reach an understanding on these issues before contract signing.

(b) DON'T LEAVE THE EXHIBITS UNTIL THE END! Too often, the parties focus the majority of their attention on the contract and leave the exhibits until the end. In most cases, the vendor will produce its own version of the exhibits and the customer won't read them at all or waits until there is little room left for negotiation. After the customer reviews the exhibits, it almost always discovers that the exhibits (1) do not reflect the business deal as the customer understands it; (2) do not cover the scope of services that the customer believes it is receiving; and (3) are in conflict with what is in the contract. A checklist of general issues to consider with respect to the exhibits is set forth as follows:

- What types of lists/inventories should be attached as exhibits? (Begin a checklist early in the process and delegate preparation to different groups if possible, particularly with respect to inventory lists.)
- Have you read all of the exhibits?
- Have the necessary subgroups reviewed exhibits dealing with their particular areas of expertise?
- Do the exhibits accurately reflect the business deal?
- Are the contents of the exhibits as complete as possible?
- Do the exhibits cover all of the points that the contract says they should? (It is often helpful to do a search for the exhibits in the contract and prepare a cross-reference checklist.)
- What is missing from the exhibits that could mean add-on costs at a later point (e.g., upgrades, replacement equipment, additional equipment, additional capacity, additional users, shadow support services that are provided today)?
- Are the contents of the exhibits negotiable? Have the contents of the exhibits been negotiated?

(c) DELEGATE RESPONSIBILITY.   The outsourcing team should read the exhibits with as much (or more) attention as the contract. In some instances, it may make sense to delegate responsibility for the review of different exhibits to subteams that specialize in the specific area under review. For example, the exhibit describing help desk services could be delegated to a help desk manager, the exhibit describing security services could be delegated to a subteam consisting of data control and audit personnel, the business continuity and disaster recovery exhibit could be delegated to the risk management team, and the human resources exhibits could be delegated to the human resources representative. After the subteams have reviewed and approved the exhibits, each of the exhibits should be reviewed by other members of the outsourcing team to ensure consistency with the other exhibits as well as the contract.

(d) BUSINESS AND LEGAL REVIEWS.   It is a common myth that the contract is for the legal team and the exhibits are for the business team. Both teams need to be involved in the preparation and negotiation of the contract and the exhibits. As much as the parties try to reserve legal issues for the contract and business issues for the exhibits, the two types of issues always overlap.

5.2   EXHIBIT LISTINGS

The types, number, and scope of the exhibits to be attached to the outsourcing contract will vary depending on the scope, location, and value of the services to be outsourced and the time frame in which the contract is to be negotiated. For example, the exhibits for a desktop outsourcing transaction (which would include more detail regarding end users, hardware/software inventory, field support, remote site maintenance) will be different from the exhibits for a data center deal (which would focus more on processing services, file services, capacity, and recovery management) or an application maintenance deal (which would focus more on types of applications, third-party contract, and acceptance procedures).

Although the content of the exhibits are tailored to the requirements of each deal, several general exhibit categories are included in almost all outsourcing deals (e.g., description of services, service levels, pricing, termination assistance). In some deals the parties combine information and data in one exhibit (e.g., the description of services to be provided) that may be broken out into four or five exhibits in other deals (e.g., general processing services, help desk services, security services, maintenance services, training). A list of possible exhibits to the outsourcing contract is listed in Exhibit 5.1 in alphabetical order.

Exhibit Name	Description
1. Application Installation Standards	Description of the standards that vendor must follow when installing existing and new application software.
2. Application Development Measurement Procedures	Procedures used to measure application development (e.g., function point counting manual).
3. Architecture and Product Standards	Description of the technical architecture and product standards used by the customer as of the contract date that vendor must comply with (customer should reserve right to change standards).
4. Base Fees	Detail of fees payable to vendor for the base services; typically annual amounts are provided with provisions that the annual amounts are to be divided over a 12-month period.
5. Benchmarkers	List of preapproved benchmarkers that may conduct the benchmarks permitted by the agreement.
6. Benchmarking Process	Detailed description of benchmarking process and contract ramifications.
7. Change Control Procedures	The form of procedures or the table of contents of the procedures may be attached. This exhibit may be part of the Governance exhibit.

EXHIBIT 5.1   POSSIBLE EXHIBITS TO THE OUTSOURCING CONTRACT

Exhibit Name	Description
8. Communications	Infrastructure.
9. Compliance Requirements	List of regulatory requirements (such as FDA) that are specific to the customer.
10. Confidentiality Agreement	If the outsourcing contract requires vendor employees, vendor subcontractors, customer auditors, or customer third-party vendors to sign a confidentiality agreement, a copy of the agreement to be signed is typically attached.
11. Continuous Improvement Plan	Detailed plan outlining improvements vendor commits to make during the term of the contract.
12. Critical Services	List of services that customer considers critical to its business (if these services are not performed, customer has certain remedies, e.g., liquidated damages, expedited termination).
13. Customer Expense Policy and Procedures	Copy of customer expense policies (if vendor is required to follow these policies under outsourcing contract when providing services for which customer pays expenses).
14. Customer Proprietary Software	Inventory of customer proprietary software that will be transferred to vendor or that vendor will manage, operate, maintain, have financial responsibility for, and/or otherwise need access to.
15. Customer Hardware (Leased and Owned)	Inventory of customer hardware that will be transferred to vendor or that vendor will manage, operate, maintain, have financial responsibility for, and/or otherwise need access to.
16. Customer Employees	List of employees to whom vendor will be making offers of employment; may be prudent to reference employees by social security number rather than name for confidentiality purposes; be mindful of not including any information that may be discriminating (e.g., age, sex, race, health condition).
17. Customer Entities (Service Recipients)	List of customer affiliates, subsidiaries, venture partners, business associates, customer, or supplier that may receive services under the agreement.
18. Customer Third-Party Software	Inventory of customer third-party software that will be transferred to vendor or that vendor will manage, operate, maintain, have financial responsibility for, and/or otherwise need access to.

Exhibit 5.1   (Continued)   Possible Exhibits to the Outsourcing Contract

Exhibit Name	Description
19. Customer Competitors	List of customer competitors that vendor is restricted in providing services to under the agreement or if vendor merges with/purchases/is purchased by any such competitors, customer may terminate the outsourcing contract.
20. Customer Satisfaction Survey	Example of customer satisfaction survey to be distributed within the customer organization.
21. Description of Services	Typically a detailed description of the services to be provided by vendor; typically tracks all of the services provided today by the affected group of employees as well as any supplemental services agreed upon by the parties or additional services to be provided in a "new" environment; in some instances, certain services are broken out and described in other exhibits (e.g., implementation of new systems/projects, help desk, training).
22. Disaster Recovery Services	Description of disaster recovery/business continuation plan and services to be provided by vendor.
23. Employee Release	Form release to be signed by employee when accepting employment with vendor (may not be required for all locations; may vary from location to location).
24. Employee Transition Procedures	Description of how vendor will transition the employees, including employee comunications, offers, acceptance periods, start dates.
25. Employee Plans	Copy of any customer or vendor plans that are relevant for determining financial or administrative responsibility between the parties (e.g., profit sharing, severance, savings, pension); it is useful to attach the plans if there may be a dispute over which plan (or version of the plan) the parties are referring to in the agreement.
26. Governance	Description of governance procedures, escalation points, and change management.
27. Guarantee	Copy of guarantee to be signed by the parent or subsidiary of vendor or customer.
28. Help Desk	Detailed description of help desk services to be provided by vendor, including levels of services, volume of service, escalation procedures.
29. Human Resource Claims	List of any pending or threatened claims against the customer by the affected employees.

Exhibit 5.1 (Continued)   Possible Exhibits to the Outsourcing Contract

Exhibit Name	Description
30. Incremental Fees	Detail of additional fees payable to vendor for services above baselines (hourly, daily, weekly, monthly, with/without notice). Detail of reduction in fees for services below baselines.
31. Invoice Detail	List of information to be included in vendor invoices; example of an invoice.
32. Key Employee Listing	List of employees considered key to the outsourcing transactions and whose appointment/replacement is subject to certain approvals/rights/restrictions under the outsourcing contract.
33. Liquidated Damages for Failing to Meet Service Levels	Description of how liquidated damages for failing to meet service levels areapplied and the amounts payable by vendor.
34. Local Country Agreement	
35. Long-Range Plan	Description of customer long-term IT plan over 5- to 10-year period, including budgeted asset/service/miscellaneous costs.
36. Maintenance Terms	Description of maintenance services to be provided by vendor (typically separated from description of services schedule in desktop deals where end-user maintenance is different than other data center, midrange, network maintenance).
37. Management Procedures Manual	Because the procedures are typically developed within 30 to 180 days after the contract date, an example of the form of procedures or the table of contents of the procedures may be attached.
38. Master Lease Agreement	Copy of master lease agreement to be signed between customer and vendor for equipment to be procured by vendor under the agreement.
39. Migration Plan	Description of how vendor will manage the migration of services from a customer to a vendor site.
40. New Environment	Description of new environment to be implemented by vendor, including ser vices/assets to be provided, implementation schedules, remedies for failing to meet schedule.
41. New Services Schedule	Example of work order to be used when engaging vendor to provide out-of-scope services.
42. New Services Fees	List of fees payable to vendor for out-of-scope services (e.g., time and materials rates).
43. Organizational Structure	Chart of vendor-proposed account organizational structure (typically covers top tiers of structure).
44. Performance Reporting Requirements	Description of performance reports that vendor must provide.

Exhibit 5.1 (Continued) Possible Exhibits to the Outsourcing Contract

Exhibit Name	Description
45. Personal Policies	Typically customer personnel policies are attached or referenced (e.g., code of conduct, acceptable use guidelines).
46. Price List	List (or catalog) of price for different hardware/software that customer may request vendor to procure on customer's behalf.
47. Project Staff Profile	Headcount/description of personnel to be providing services.
48. Projects	Description of projects to be implemented by vendor, including services/assets to be provided, implementation schedules, remedies for failing to meet schedule.
49. Quality Assurance	Description of quality assurances processes and procedures to be followed by vendor.
50. Reports	List of in-scope reports that vendor will create and provide to customer.
51. Retained Operators	List of customer employees who will be retained by customer to run certain software and who will be transferred to vendor when software is no longer being run.
52. Security Procedures	Description of data and/or physical security services to be provided by vendor and procedures to be followed by vendor.
53. Service Levels	List of service levels that must be met by vendor.
54. Service Locations	List of customer sites and vendor service locations.
55. Standardized Environment	Description of standardized environment that customer must comply with (typically included in desktop deals).
56. Subcontractor Agreements	Copies of any agreements directly between customer and vendor subcontractor (e.g., software license agreement for which vendor will be providing customization or maintenance services).
57. Subcontractors	List of subcontractors that customer has approved for use by vendor, together with list of services to be provided.
58. Supplemental Agreements	Copy of any supplemental agreement (e.g., escrow agreement, asset transfer/purchase agreement).
59. Supporting Data	Compilation of background data distributed by customer and vendor (e.g., RFP, proposal, addenda to proposal, other notes and memoranda).
60. System Life Cycle	Description of system life cycle to be followed by vendor when developing new systems.
61. Termination Assistance Services	Description of termination assistance services to be provided by vendor for a period before and after effective date of termination/expiration.

EXHIBIT 5.1   (CONTINUED)   POSSIBLE EXHIBITS TO THE OUTSOURCING CONTRACT

EXHIBIT NAME	DESCRIPTION
62. Termination Fees	List of fees payable by customer upon termination of agreement for certain reasons (typically for convenience); list may include only fixed fees or fixed and variable fees.
63. Third-Party Contracts	List of third-party contracts that will be transferred to vendor. List of third-party contracts for which vendor will assume managerial, administrative, and/or financial responsibility.
64. Training	Description of training to be provided by vendor (e.g., end-user, operational, train the trainer).
65. Transition Plan	Description of how vendor will transition managerial, administrative, and operational responsibility for the IT services from customer to vendor.
66. Vacation Summary	Summary of vacation days available to each of the affected employees for the remainder of the calendar year and/or amount of vacation days to be "bought out" by customer or vendor.
67. Value-Added Services	Description of any value-added services to be provided by vendor (e.g., cross-marketing opportunities, shared benefits).
68. Vendor Proprietary Software	Inventory of vendor proprietary software that will be used by vendor to provide the services.
69. Vendor Employment Agreement	Copy of employment agreement to be signed by employees accepting offers of employment with vendor.
70. Vendor Third-Party Software	Inventory of vendor third-party software that will be used by vendor to provide the services.

EXHIBIT 5.1   (CONTINUED)   POSSIBLE EXHIBITS TO THE OUTSOURCING CONTRACT

5.3   CHECKLISTS

What is included in the exhibits depends largely on the business deal and the customer's philosophy with respect to the exhibits. Set forth as follows are checklists of common service-related exhibits attached to the outsourcing contract:

General Description of Services

- Will the vendor provide different services for the current environment and a future or new environment? If so, should the description of services exhibit be separated into two parts—current and future services?
- Mainframe/Midrange Operations
  Operate System
  Tape Management

Data Entry

File Services

Print and Microfiche

Print Distribution

Backup/Recovery

Test Environments

Documentation of Operations Procedures

Production Control

    Operate/Monitor Systems Console

    Manage Schedules

    Implement Automated Scheduling

    Batch Management

    Report Balancing

    Special Forms Inventory

Hardware Planning, and Installation

    Upgrades

    Replacements

    Additional Equipment

Systems Management

    Capacity Management

    Performance Management

    Change Management

    Problem Management

    Recovery Management

    Configuration Management

    Inventory Management

Facilities

Quality Assurance

- System Software

Requirements

Procurement

Acceptance Testing

Maintenance

Upgrades

New Releases

Enhancements

Replacements

Additional Software

System Monitoring

Performance Tuning (Systems/Applications)

Problem Resolution

Backup/Recovery

Vendor/Subcontractor Performance

Reporting

- Applications Software

Requirements

Procurement

Development/Enhancement of Packages

Acceptance Testing

Maintenance

Upgrades

New Releases

Enhancements

Replacements

Additional Software

Government/Regulatory Changes

Training

Development (see below)

Problem Resolution

Backup/Recovery

Vendor/Subcontractor Performance

Reporting

- Database Administration

Requirements

Modeling

Design

System Maintenance

User Access

Capacity Planning

Performance Management

Backup/Recovery

Problem Resolution

- Telecommunications

Scope

    Voice

    Data

    Facsimile

    Electronic Data Interchange (EDI)

Technical Requirements

Voice/Data Network Management

Network Connectivity and Operations

Bandwidth Management

Hardware Operations

Hardware Maintenance

Vendor Dispatch/Coordination

Problem Resolution

Cabling/Wiring

Project Planning

Hardware/Software Installation (Remote Sites)

Systems/Applications Software Operations

Systems/Applications Software Maintenance

Data Lines Management

Telephone Instruments/Stations

Local/Long Distance

Telephone Directory Publication/Maintenance

Telephone Operators

Voice Mail

Product Evaluation

Product Procurement

Capacity Management

Performance Management

Change Management

Problem Management

Recovery Management

Configuration Management

Inventory Management

Facilities

Quality Assurance

- LAN Network

Technical Requirements

LANs/Servers—Equipment and Software

Management, Operations, and Maintenance

Third-Party Vendor Management

Additional, Replacement, Upgrades

PCs/Workstations

Management, Operations, and Maintenance

Third-Party Vendor Management

Additional, Replacement, Upgrades

Cabling/Wiring

Product Evaluation

Product Procurement

LAN Network

Design

Project Planning

Problem Resolution

Capacity Management

Performance Management

Change Management

Problem Management

Recovery Management

Configuration Management

Inventory Management

Facilities

Quality Assurance

- Data Transmission

Current and Future Methods of Data Transmission

Financial Responsibility for Data Transmission

Management/Financial Responsibility for Contracts with Third Parties (e.g., subscriber agreements)

- Desktop

Scope—Existing and New Devices

Fixed-Function Terminals

PCs—Desktop, Laptop, Mobile

Other Workstations

Servers

Routers

Bridges

Hubs

Associated Modems, Cards, Interface Boards, Printers, Cabling, Supplies, and Accessories

Technology Selection

Technology Standards

Corporate/Site-Specific Guidelines

Catalog for Standard Products and Services

Configuration and Design Assistance

Compatibility Assurance

Design Assistance

Evaluation Lab

Deployment Strategy

Procurement

Acquisition Services/Assistance

Acquisition and Approval Process

Track and Report Order Status

Delivery/Shipping

Installation

Moves, Adds, and Changes

Delivery Process

Installation Hardware/Software

Office

Remote

Field

Network Provisioning

System Setup Requirements

Testing

Removal of Packaging Materials

Systems Management

Technical Support

Capacity Management

Performance Management

Change Management

Problem Management

Recovery Management

Configuration Management

Inventory Management

Quality Assurance

Maintenance

Preventive Maintenance

Problem Management/Resolution/Escalation

Identify, Track, Report, and Initiate Resolution of Problems

Interface with Hardware/Software Vendors

Inventory of Replacement Parts

Repair Service—On-Site/Carry-In

Upgrades

New Releases

Asset Management

Inventory

Tagging Assets

Loading of Databases

Track Move, Adds, and Changes

Ensure License Compliance

Register/Verify/Track Warranties

Technology Disposal

Resale assistance

Reuse procedures

- Help Desk Services

    Location

    Centralized vs. Dispersed

    Levels of Support (Level 1, 2, 3)

    Receive, Log, and Track Calls

    Call Tracking System

    Toll-Free Number

    Languages Spoken at Help Desk

    Support Standard/Nonstandard Systems

    Hours of Operation

    Change Management

    Root Cause Analysis

    Remote Site (Store) Support

    Support Rollout of New Systems

    Coordinate with Third-Party Vendors

    Escalation Procedures

    Administration Support

        Coordinate Equipment/Parts Distribution

            Issue Supplies

            File Transfers

            Control File

            Inventory Control

            Polling

            Asset Management

            Warranty Management

            Services Management

    Reporting

        Number of Calls Received

        Number of Calls Answered

        Response Time

        Priority of Calls Received

- Application Development Services

    Procedures for Requesting/Receiving Proposals

    Baselines

Measurement Metric

    Person Hours

    Person Days

    Function Points

    Other Methodology

Services

    Upgrades

    New Releases

    Enhancements

    Government and Regulatory Changes

    Training

    Reporting

Development Process

    Development Request

    Submit Proposal

    Develop Plan

    Design

    Coding

    Documentation

    Testing

    Acceptance

    Implementation

    Support

Prioritize Projects

Training Quality

Assurance

- Disaster Recovery Services

Customer's Current Disaster Recovery Plan

Will Customer's Current Plan Be Terminated?

Location of Vendor Hotsite

Hotsite Configuration

Customer Priority at Vendor Hotsite?

Response/Recovery Times

Scope of Vendor Services

Notification Procedures

List of Customer/Vendor Contacts

Identify/Prioritize Critical Services

Escalation Procedures

Periodic Testing of Plan

Allow for Growth

- Data Security Services

Data Security

Controls to Detect and Report Intentional or Accidental Invalid Data Access Attempts

Installation, Maintenance, Upgrade of Existing/New Data Access Control Software

Protect Application Resources via the Access Control Software

Protect End User Data via Access Control Software

Security Procedures Manual

Establish, Change, Deactivate, and Remove Logon IDs

Review, Approve, and Grant Request for Privileged User Authorities

Notify Data Owners and Customer of Invalid Data Access Attempts

Emergency Security Requests

Controls for Printed Output from Unauthorized Access while under Vendor Control

Knowledge of Latest Concepts/Techniques Associated with System and Data Security

Storage and Security for Portable Media

EMPLOYEE CONFIDENTIALITY AGREEMENT[1]

My full name is [EMPLOYEE NAME] and I am employed by or acting as a consultant to Vendor ("Vendor").

I understand and agree that I will have access to Confidential Information during my employment [consultancy] with Vendor. In consideration for and as a condition to my employment by Vendor [assignment to the CUSTOMER account], I agree to be bound by the terms set forth herein.

For the purposes of this agreement, "Confidential Information" means materials, data, processes, methodologies, tools, business and technological information, software programs and code, intellectual property, and other information, including individually identifiable medical, dental, or financial information, regardless of form, media, or whether conveyed orally, in writing or electronically, belonging or relating to Vendor and its clients and their direct and indirect subsidiaries and affiliates.

I hereby understand and agree:

That any and all Confidential Information shall be deemed by me to be highly confidential and proprietary in nature having substantial intrinsic and/or monetary value.

That unauthorized use or disclosure of Confidential Information will likely result in substantial monetary and other damages to Vendor and its clients and their direct and indirect subsidiaries and affiliates and will subject me to disciplinary action, including termination of employment, civil and criminal legal proceedings, and recovery of monetary damages as may be determined in a court of law.

Not to deliver to or disclose or otherwise make available to anyone any Confidential Information except as authorized in writing by Vendor and its clients and their direct and indirect subsidiaries and affiliates regardless of the term of this agreement.

---

1. Note: This sample agreement is intended to illustrate the types of legal issues that vendors typically wish to address in connection with information technology outsourcing transactions. The provisions included in this sample agreement, while comprehensive, may not cover all of the issues that may arise in a particular transaction. Legal issues will likely vary depending on the type of information technology process being outsourced and the scope of the outsourcing transaction. This sample agreement or any part thereof should only be used after consultation with your legal counsel. Legal counsel should be consulted prior to entering into or negotiating any outsourcing transaction.

That Confidential Information, and all copyright, patent, and other proprietary rights therein, shall remain property of Vendor or its clients or their direct and indirect subsidiaries and affiliates, as the case may be, at all times and that I shall on demand return it to Vendor within 24 hours of a written or oral demand.

That during the course of my employment, I may work on and be a part of the development of technology, processes, methodologies, and other work product for Vendor. I hereby assign to Vendor any technology, processes, methodologies, and other work product developed by me and such technology, processes, methodologies, and other work product shall become the sole and absolute property of Vendor.

That any and all inventions, improvements, discoveries, technologies, processes, methodologies, and other work product developed or discovered by me as a result of my employment at [or consultancy with] Vendor shall be fully disclosed to Vendor, and I hereby assign the same to Vendor and the same shall become the sole and absolute property of Vendor. Upon the request of Vendor, I shall execute, acknowledge, and deliver such assignments and other documents as Vendor may consider necessary or appropriate to vest all rights, titles, and interests therein to Vendor.

That the disclosure of Confidential Information may give rise to irreparable injury and acknowledge that remedies other than injunctive relief may not be adequate. Accordingly, Vendor and its clients and their direct and indirect subsidiaries and affiliates have the right to equitable and injunctive relief to prevent the unauthorized disclosure of Confidential Information, as well as such damages or other relief as is occasioned by such unauthorized use or disclosure.

That I am bound by the obligations under this agreement until such time as said Confidential Information lawfully becomes part of the public domain.

This agreement shall be governed by and construed in accordance with the laws of the [STATE], excluding its conflicts of laws provisions.

This agreement sets forth the entire agreement between Vendor and me as to the subject matter of this agreement. The terms of this agreement shall not be amended or modified except in writing signed by each of Vendor and me.

_____

SIGNATURE

_____

DATE

CUSTOMER SATISFACTION SURVEY CHECKLIST[2]

1. Define general categories that are to be measured by the satisfaction survey. What are the areas of concern that the survey is targeting? Examples of measurements include:

    o Delivery

    o Performance

    o Support

    o Responsiveness

    o Quality

    o Cost

    o Value

    o Business relationship

2. Develop specific questions to ask in the survey for each category. For example, with respect to cost, identify areas of interest and focus questions on those areas, such as the following:

    o Baseline costs (designated fees)

    o Application development costs

    o Incremental costs

    o Project costs

    o Cost-of-living adjustments

    o Baseline adjustments

    o Add/delete business units

    (See specific topics in (7) below).

---

2. Note: This checklist is intended to illustrate the types of legal issues that customers may wish to consider in connection with contracting for application services. The items included in this checklist may not cover all of the issues that may arise in a particular transaction. Legal issues will likely vary depending on the type of service being provided and the scope of the services. This checklist or any part thereof should only be used after consultation with your legal counsel. Legal counsel should be consulted prior to entering into or negotiating any transaction covering the provision of application services.

3. Determine the frequency with which the survey will be distributed:
   - ○ Monthly
   - ○ Quarterly
   - ○ Semi annually
   - ○ Yearly
     - • Calendar year
     - • Contract year

4. Develop a mechanism to rate or score the vendor's performance. For example:

   5 = Excellent
   4 = Very Good
   3 = Good
   2 = Fair
   1 = Poor
   0 = Unacceptable

   0–10 with:
   10 = Exceptional
    8 = Exceeds Expectations
    5 = Meets Expectations
    3 = Below Expectations
    0 = Unacceptable

5. Decide how index will be computed and reviewed. The results should be reviewed with the account managers and published in the monthly account status report.

6. Determine group to be surveyed (e.g., end users, executives, both).

7. Examples of topics to be surveyed follow.

DELIVERY

- Ability to provide products and services that contribute to business success
- Delivery of products that perform as specified
- Ability to roll out new systems
- Implementation of updates, changes, enhancements, or new releases with minimal disruption

PERFORMANCE/SUPPORT

- Ability to meet service levels

- Uptime
- Continuous improvement
- Dependable and accurate performance of products and services
- Technical ability
- Open/productive communication between customer and vendor personnel
- Degree to which contractual terms and conditions have been met
- Use of proper resources on a timely basis to satisfy customer's business needs (e.g., providing emergency contacts or the assistance in interacting with other organizations to resolve problems)

RESPONSIVENESS

- Willingness to help customers and provide prompt service
- Response to customer questions and requests
- Willingness to take the initiative to identify problems and improvements and new technologies
- Personal attention
- The timeliness of requested program change

QUALITY

- Quality of equipment, software, and services
- Appearance of staff, equipment, documents, and facilities
- Vendor understanding of customer industry
- Vendor experience
- Vendor expertise/know-how
- Demonstration of interest, understanding, timeliness, and accuracy

COST

- Accurate/fair pricing
- Competitive pricing
- Delivery in cost-effective manner
- Ability to keep costs down with minimal impact on quality
- Perception of the quantity and quality of services received for the time, effort, and money invested
- Willingness to share in risk
- Flexibility
- No surprises

VALUE

- Problem identification and resolution
- Ability to identify improvement opportunities
- Application of innovative solutions
- Degree to which vendor demonstrates leadership in customer industry
- Flexibility in approach
- Impact vendor has on customer's businesses
- Information provided regarding new products and services

BUSINESS RELATIONSHIP

- Ability to breed confidence based on professionalism and knowledge of industry and business
- Understanding of and sensitivity to customer's business goals, objectives, and needs
- Ability of vendor and customer to work together in the outsourcing arrangement
- Vendor commitment to customer's success
- Overall rating of vendor's performance

GENERAL ASSIGNMENT AND BILL OF SALE AGREEMENT[3]

THIS GENERAL ASSIGNMENT AND BILL OF SALE is entered into this **[NUMBER VARIATION]** day of **[MONTH] [YEAR],** by and between **[],** a **[]** corporation (*"Purchaser"*) and **[ ],** a **[ ]** corporation (*"Seller"*).

W I T N E S S E T H:

WHEREAS, Purchaser and Seller are entering into an Agreement dated **[DATE]** (the *"Services Agreement"*); (capitalized terms not defined herein shall have the meanings ascribed to them in the Services Agreement);

WHEREAS, pursuant to the Services Agreement, Seller has agreed to sell and Purchaser has agreed to purchase the Assets on the Effective Date; and

WHEREAS, Seller desires to transfer and assign the Assets and Purchaser desires to accept the transfer and assignment thereof.

NOW, THEREFORE, in consideration of the mutual covenants contained herein and for other good and valuable consideration, the receipt and sufficiency of which are hereby acknowledged, Seller hereby irrevocably sells, transfers, conveys, and assigns to Purchaser all of Seller's right, title, and interest in the Assets, TO HAVE AND TO HOLD the same unto Purchaser, its successors, and assigns, forever.

Purchaser hereby accepts the sale, transfer, conveyance, and assignment of the Assets.

At any time or from time to time after the date hereof, at Purchaser's request and without further consideration, Seller shall execute such other instruments of transfer, conveyance, assignment, and confirmation; provide such materials and information and take such other actions as Purchaser may reasonably deem necessary or desirable in order more effectively to transfer, convey, and assign to Purchaser; and confirm Purchaser's title to, all of the Assets, and, to the full extent permitted by law, to put Purchaser in actual possession and operating con-

---

3. Note: This sample agreement is intended to illustrate the types of legal issues that vendors typically wish to address in connection with information technology outsourcing transactions. The provisions included in this sample agreement, while comprehensive, may not cover all of the issues that may arise in a particular transaction. Legal issues will likely vary depending on the type of information technology process being outsourced and the scope of the outsourcing transaction. This sample agreement or any part thereof should only be used after consultation with your legal counsel. Legal counsel should be consulted prior to entering into or negotiating any outsourcing transaction.

trol of the Assets and to assist Purchaser in exercising all rights with respect thereto.

This General Assignment and Bill of Sale may be executed in any number of counterparts, each of which will be deemed an original, but all of which together will constitute one and the same instrument.

This General Assignment and Bill of Sale shall be governed by the laws of the State of **[STATE].** Purchaser and Seller agree that the Federal courts of [***] shall have exclusive jurisdiction over disputes under this General Assignment and Bill of Sale, and the parties agree that jurisdiction and venue in such courts is appropriate.

IN WITNESS WHEREOF, the undersigned have caused their duly authorized officers to execute this General Assignment and Bill of Sale on the date first written above.

[PURCHASER]

By: _____
[NAME]
[Title:]

[NOTARIZE]

[SELLER]

By: _____
[NAME]
[Title:]

[NOTARIZE]

EXAMPLE OF JOINT MANAGEMENT PROCEDURES

I. GENERAL

The Parties acknowledge that Vendor is providing services under this Master Agreement that are critical to the overall operations and business of Customer. In the event of a Critical Failure (as defined below), Customer will not be able to effectively carry out critical business functions. Therefore, the overarching objective of the Parties is for Customer to receive the Services in accordance with the Service Levels, thereby allowing Customer to meet its business and financial obligations. In the event of a Critical Failure, in an effort to minimize harm and disruption to the operations and business of Customer, Customer may request to, and if so requested Vendor shall allow Customer to, participate in the remediation of the Service failures or deficiencies and to implement the joint management procedures described herein (the "*Joint Management Procedures*").

II. JOINT MANAGEMENT PERIOD

The period during which the Joint Management Procedures shall be in effect shall commence as of the time specified in the notice from Customer of its desire to implement the Joint Management Procedures and continue until the date terminated by Customer, which termination date shall not be later than (a) the date that Customer notifies Vendor that the Services are being performed in accordance with the Service Levels for two consecutive reporting periods and provision by Vendor of adequate assurances that the Service shall be provided in accordance with the Service Levels on an ongoing basis or (b) the End Date in the event this Master Agreement is terminated (the "*Joint Management Period*").

III. CUSTOMER PARTICIPATION

Upon the implementation of the Joint Management Procedures, Customer may take such actions as are necessary or recommended to remediate any service failures or deficiencies in accordance with this Exhibit. It is the objective of the Parties to remedy any Critical Failure immediately and provide all Services in accordance with the Service Levels. Customer may participate in its discretion in the remediation of any service failure or deficiencies, including sending resources to the Service Locations to assist in, and where considered appropriate by Customer assume management and/or operational control over, all or a portion of the Services. In connection with such participation, Vendor shall provide to Customer and its representatives access to (and hereby grants Customer and its representatives the right to Use and operate) the Vendor Service Locations and the resources and assets contained therein (including personnel resources, hardware, and software) solely in connection with the provision of the Services. Customer shall have the right to, and Vendor shall assist Customer in, deal directly with (a) members of the Vendor Personnel, including Key Vendor Personnel, and (b) Vendor Agents, as may be necessary or recommended to facilitate the ongoing provision of the Services in accordance with the Service Levels.

Customer's participation during the Joint Management Period may be in an assistance or management role (or increase from an assistance to a management role) depending on the severity of the Critical Failure, as follows:

1. Upon the occurrence of a Level 2 Critical Failure (as defined below), Vendor shall have five Business Days to develop and implement a plan to remedy the failure, during which time Customer may at its discretion assist Vendor in the develop and implementation of the plan and the management and provision of the Services. If Vendor is not providing the Services in accordance with the Service Levels within the next reporting period to Customer's reasonable satisfaction, Customer may at its discretion assume control of the management and operation of the Services for the remainder of the Joint Management Period.

2. Upon the occurrence of a Level 1 Critical Failure (as defined below), Customer may at its discretion assume control of the management and operation of the Services during the Joint Management Period.

3. Customer may at its discretion reduce its role (if applicable) from control of management and operation of the Services to an assistance role.

As used herein, "*Level 2 Critical Failure*" means any failure to meet a Service Level.

As used herein, "*Level 1 Critical Failure*" means _____.

As used herein, "*Critical Failure*" means a Level 1 Critical Failure or a Level 2 Critical Failure.

IV. VENDOR COOPERATION

Vendor shall cooperate fully with Customer's efforts to remedy the critical failures and remediate Service failures and deficiencies in provision of the Services in accordance with the Service Levels as set forth in this Schedule. Such cooperation shall include upon Customer's request:

- Provision of technical information and technical assistance
- Access to and provision of personnel resources

- Access to technology and third party resources
- Access to Service Locations
- Access to benchmark and historical information

V. ROOT CAUSE ANALYSIS AND REMEDIATION PLAN

As part of the Joint Management Procedures, Vendor shall work with Customer to (a) perform a root cause analysis of the service failures and deficiencies in an effort to identify, and develop a plan to remediate, the failures and deficiencies in the provision of the Services in accordance with the Service Levels, and (b) develop and implement a plan to remediate the failures and deficiencies (if such a plan is practicable in Customer's discretion). If Customer so directs, all efforts and prioritization and use of resources during the Joint Management Period shall be directed or otherwise approved by Customer or its representative.

VI. RESPONSIBILITY FOR VENDOR PERSONNEL AND RESOURCES

The employees and consultants of Vendor and Vendor Agents shall remain employees and consultants of Vendor and Vendor Agents during the Joint Management Period. Vendor shall, and shall cause Vendor Agents to, retain and compensate (including salary and benefits) all Vendor Personnel during the Joint Management Period unless otherwise approved or directed by Customer. Customer shall not be deemed an employer of any Vendor Personnel during the Joint Management Period.

Vendor shall maintain and continue to have financial and, unless otherwise directed by Customer, operational, maintenance, and administrative responsibility for all hardware, software, Vendor Service Locations, and other resources used in connection with the Services during the Joint Management Period.

VII.   RIGHTS DURING JOINT MANAGEMENT PERIOD

During the Joint Management Period, Customer shall be responsible for the xxx Fees as set forth in the Master Agreement. Customer shall not be responsible for any other fees or costs incurred by Vendor in connection with Vendor's cooperation and assistance during the Joint Management Procedures.

FINANCIAL CONSIDERATIONS[1]

6.1 INTRODUCTION

Financial considerations tend to dominate all aspects of the outsourcing life cycle. It is critical, therefore, for a company considering an outsourcing transaction to understand its current financial position so as to assess the feasibility of cost savings through outsourcing and to evaluate vendor proposals to determine

---

1. This chapter was originally written by Tim Scudder and has been updated and revised by the authors for this edition.

if, in fact, they would provide cost savings over the length of the agreement. It is just as essential to structure an outsourcing agreement in a way that ensures the customer receives fair and predictable pricing and is able to understand and control the expenditure of IT dollars.

6.2   BASE CASE

An essential starting point in the outsourcing life cycle is the creation of a base case, or comparison baseline. The base case is a detailed determination of the operating costs of the IT services being considered for outsourcing (typically referred to as the in-scope services). This analysis should summarize annual costs, starting with the current fiscal year and extending throughout the expected term of the agreement. Estimates of future costs should take into account reasonable assumptions regarding future changes to the scope of the series (increases or decreases, in use) as well as price performance trends of the resources required to provide the in-scope services. The result of this analysis should be an accurate representation of the expected costs for the in-house organization to provide in-scope services over the target term.

There are two reasons for conducting a base case financial analysis. The first is to establish a basis for performing an outsourcing assessment. A key element of the outsourcing assessment is comparing actual and projected in-house costs to the marketplace and expected marketplace cost trends. The purpose is to establish the magnitude of expected IT expenditure and any anticipated savings that may be realized through outsourcing. This is essential to both setting management expectations and deciding whether to proceed further with vendor solicitation. The second reason for creating a base case is to provide the point of comparison for vendor proposals. This information will be essential to establishing the business case for entering into an outsourcing arrangement. Senior management generally needs to be convinced that outsourcing will provide high-quality services for less than expected internal costs. The only exceptions to this trend occur when significant quality problems need to be corrected.

(a) ARCHITECTURE.   The first step in building the base case is to create a model (architecture) of how costs will be categorized. A top-down approach is recommended to streamline the process. The first tier of this architecture, shown in Exhibit 6.1, categorizes major IT services from the IT customer's perspective. There are several advantages to starting with this approach. The first, and perhaps most obvious, is that it should correspond to the way in which IT customers view the services they consume, making it easy to communicate. Second, all IT services can be grouped into a small number of overall categories, which facilitates understandability. Finally, a subtle advantage is that it helps the project team, which is typically dominated by IT professionals, start to change its perspective from that of service provider to customer. This is a critical element in structuring the request for proposal (RFP) as well as the overall outsourcing agreement.

IT SERVICE	DESCRIPTION
Application Delivery	The computing, communications, and human resources needed to allow users to access and utilize existing computer applications.
Application Development	The human and system resources needed to create and test new computer applications.
Customer Service	The human and system resources needed to facilitate the use of IT resources.
Professional Services	The human and system resources that provide specialized services, such as training and consulting.

EXHIBIT 6.1 FIRST TIER OF ARCHITECTURE FOR BUILDING A BASE CASE

The simplicity of the model depicted in Exhibit 6.1 belies the complexity involved in the IT industry. The Application Delivery category, for example, is composed of a myriad of processing platforms and network protocols. The high-level approach shown in Exhibit 6.1 must be further refined to the technology categories shown in Exhibit 6.2. It will be necessary to build separate base cases

IT SERVICE	TECHNOLOGY CATEGORY
Application Delivery	Mainframe computing
	Midrange computing
	Distributed computing
	Super computing
	Output services
	Wide-area data communications
	Local-area data communications
	Voice communications
	Video communications
	Premises systems support
Application Development	Design
	Coding and testing
	Quality assurance
	Database administration
	Implementation services
Customer Service	Help desk
	Information center
	Business liaison
Professional Services	Training
	Consulting
	Data entry

EXHIBIT 6.2 TECHNOLOGY CATEGORIES FOR BASE CASES

RESOURCE CATEGORY	DESCRIPTION
Hardware	The physical devices that comprise processing, data storage, output, and communications systems. Also includes the cabling used to connect the devices.
Software	The electronically coded instructions that control the activities of the hardware devices.
Personnel	The technical, operational, and administrative staff responsible for IT services.
Facilities	The physical sites in which IT hardware, software, and personnel reside.
Outside Services	Services acquired from outside firms in lieu of creating them through in-house resources. This includes transmission facilities from third-party carriers and disaster recovery agreements.

EXHIBIT 6.3   RESOURCE CATEGORIES WITHIN TECHNOLOGY CATEGORIES

for each of the technology categories that are within the scope of your outsourcing investigation for two important reasons. The first is purely pragmatic: the magnitude of effort involved in creating a base case is substantial. It needs to be broken down into manageable components to create a practical project plan. Second, it becomes difficult to compare vendor proposals that are not differentiated along the same lines.

Within each of the technology categories described in Exhibit 6.2, there are similar Resource Categories, as described in Exhibit 6.3. The exact nature and relative importance of each category will vary from one technology category to the next. A large percentage of costs in the mainframe computing category, for example, are devoted to hardware, as shown in Exhibit 6.4. It would be a mistake, however, to assume that even closely related technology categories have similar cost distributions. This is illustrated dramatically in Exhibit 6.5, which

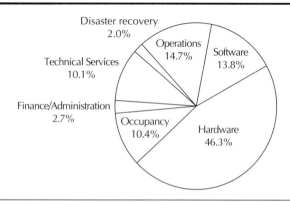

EXHIBIT 6.4   MAINFRAME COMPUTING COST DISTRIBUTION

Source: Gartner

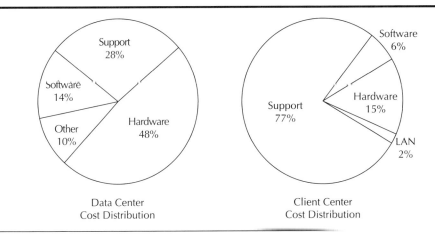

Data Center
Cost Distribution

Client Center
Cost Distribution

EXHIBIT 6.5 COMPARISON OF COST DISTRIBUTION OF MAINFRAME AND CLIENT/SERVER COMPUTING

Source: Gartner

compares the cost distributions of the mainframe (data center) computing and client/server computing categories.

Budgetary myopia is a common mistake made in creating the base case. Each IT organization deals with an operating budget that conforms to the accounting norms of the company as a whole. Corporate practices and, in some cases, business industry conventions may dictate whether a variety of cost elements are included in the IT budget. Common examples of cost elements that vary from one company to the next in budgetary treatment are capital expenditures, occupancy costs, and personnel benefits. If these kinds of cost elements are excluded from your base case, it will be impossible to compare your true costs to those proposed by vendors.

Therefore, it is critical to develop a business model base case rather than a budget model base case. The business model approach identifies all functional resource category elements required to create and deliver a given IT service if the IT organization were an independent business unit. Identification of the cost elements can be straightforward, but finding the costs may be a daunting task. For example, all capital expenditures may be grouped into large financial pools for the purpose of calculating corporate depreciation. It may require manual calculations based on purchase orders to determine the equivalent depreciation for various telecommunications devices (e.g., multiplexors and modems). Exhibits 6.6 through 6.13 provide examples of business model base cases for major IT services. Please note that it is critical to differentiate budget expenses from corporate expenses in order to reconcile total IT expenditures to management perceptions.

(b) FINANCIAL CONCEPTS. Each of the resource categories in the base case models consists of several different kinds of cost elements. It is essential to understand the characteristics of each element to ensure the creation of an

PERSONNEL

FINANCE AND ADMINISTRATION
Vendor Management, System Procurement
Financial Accounting, Chargeback Administration
Quality Management
Administrative Management and Support

OPERATIONS
System Operations, Operations Support
Tape Operations
Print Operations, Fiche Operations
Production Control
Operations Management

TECHNICAL SERVICES
Operating System Support, Subsystem Support, Internal Systems Support
Performance Analysis, Capacity Planning
Storage Management
System Security, Contingency Planning
Technical Management

NONPERSONNEL

MAINFRAME HARDWARE
Processors (CPU, channels, modems)
Disk Storage (disk drives, control units)
Tape Storage (tape drives, silos, control units)
Optical Storage
Printers (locally attached, high-speed printers)

MAINFRAME SUPPLIES
Print (paper, forms, ribbons, toner)
Tape (cartridges, reels)
Microfilm/Microfiche

MAINFRAME SOFTWARE
System (e.g., MVS, VM, CICS, IMS, FOCUS, SAS, COBOL, utilities)
Applications (e.g., accounts payable, payroll, order entry)

FACILITIES
Office Space (floor space, furniture, office *equipment and* supplies, phones)
Other Space (raised floor, tape library, storage)
Power (electricity, gas, UPS, batteries)
Site Management (security, janitorial, maintenance)

OUTSIDE SERVICES
Disaster Recovery Site

EXHIBIT 6.6   MAINFRAME COMPUTER PROCESSING BASE CASE

PERSONNEL

FINANCE AND ADMINISTRATION
Vendor Management, System Procurement
Financial Accounting, Chargeback Administration
Quality Management
Administrative Management and Support

OPERATIONS
System Operations, Operations Support
Tape Operations
Print Operations, Fiche Operations
Production Control
Operations Management

TECHNICAL SERVICES
Operating System Support, Subsystem Support, Internal Systems Support
Performance Analysis, Capacity Planning
Storage Management
System Security, Contingency Planning
Technical Management

NONPERSONNEL

MIDRANGE HARDWARE
Processors (CPU, channels, modems)
Disk Storage (disk drives, control units)
Tape Storage (tape drives, silos, control units)
Optical Storage
Printers (locally attached, high-speed printers)

MIDRANGE SUPPLIES
Print (paper, forms, ribbons, toner)
Tape (cartridges, reels)
Microfilm/Microfiche

MIDRANGE SOFTWARE
Operating System (e.g., VMS, Unix, Oracle, utilities)
Applications (e.g., accounts payable, payroll, order entry)

FACILITIES
Office Space (floor space, furniture, office equipment and supplies, phones)
Other Space (raised floor, tape library, storage)
Power (electricity, gas, UPS, batteries)
Site Management (security, janitorial, maintenance)

OUTSIDE SERVICES
Disaster Recovery Site

EXHIBIT 6.7 MIDRANGE COMPUTER PROCESSING BASE CASE

PERSONNEL

FINANCE AND ADMINISTRATION
Financial Accounting, Billing
Requisitions, Inventory Maintenance
Administrative Management and Support

OPERATIONS
PBX Installation and Maintenance
Process Centralized Receipt of Inbound Calls

TECHNICAL SERVICES
Planning, Design
Product Management
Vendor Liaison

NONPERSONNEL

LOCAL VOICE HARDWARE
PBX
Handsets
Service Modules

LOCAL VOICE SOFTWARE
Accounting, Engineering
Least Cost Routing
Automatic Call Distribution
Voice Mail
Local Directory

FACILITIES
Wiring (cable, twisted pair, fiber optics)
Floorspace, Furniture

OUTSIDE SERVICES
Central Office, Exchange Lines, Customer Access Calcs
Local Usage, Message Units

EXHIBIT 6.8   LOCAL VOICE BASE CASE

accurate base case. The first kind of cost element is ordinary expenses, which are incurred for items that are considered to be consumed as they are used. Expenses are recognized in the time period in which they are used. However, the acquisition cost of items that will be used over a long time (more than one year) are recognized over a greater period. Depreciation "is a process of allocating the acquisition cost to the particular periods or products that are related to the use of the assets."[2] Depreciation applies to asset purchases and involves the notion of a

2.   Horngren, Charles T. *Introduction to Financial Accounting* (Englewood Cliffs, NJ: Prentice Hall, 1981), p. 355.

PERSONNEL

FINANCE AND ADMINISTRATION
Accounting and Billing
Order Processing and Inventory Maintenance
Administrative Management and Support

OPERATIONS
Circuit Monitoring
Analyze Call Detail Records
System Installation and Maintenance

TECHNICAL SERVICES
Planning, Design, Engineering
Vendor Liaison

NONPERSONNEL

LONG-DISTANCE VOICE HARDWARE
Multiplexors (include CSUs/DSUs)
Backbone Switches (NTU/NTRs)
Routers
Call Detail Recorders, SMDRs
Microwave, Satellite

LONG-DISTANCE VOICE SOFTWARE
Accounting, Engineering
Least Cost Routing
Engineering
Accounting and Management
Long Distance Directory

FACILITIES
Floorspace, Furniture

OUTSIDE SERVICES
Virtual Network Services (Dedicated, Outbound, Inbound)
Tie, FX lines, DDD, Out-WATS

EXHIBIT 6.9   LONG-DISTANCE VOICE BASE CASE

useful life. In theory, the useful life is an accurate measure of the duration of an asset's life span. In practice, "useful lives are almost always more heavily affected by economic and technological factors than by when equipment may disintegrate."[3] Most assets have some residual value (also called salvage value, scrap value, or terminal value).[4] at the end of their useful life. In other words, another party would be willing to acquire the asset from the original owner for

---

3.   Ibid, p. 355.
4.   Ibid.

PERSONNEL

FINANCE AND ADMINISTRATION
Accounting, Billing, Chargeback
Circuit Inventory
Administrative Management and Support

OPERATIONS
System Monitoring and Problem Resolution
System Installation and Maintenance
Change Management

TECHNICAL SERVICES
Planning, Design, Engineering
Network Management Software Support
Computer Telephone Interface (CTI) Applications Development
Vendor Liaison

NONPERSONNEL

WIDE-AREA DATA HARDWARE
Network CPU/DASD, FEPs, Matrix Switches
Multiplexors: T1/E1, Other
Protocol Converters, Packet Switches, PADS
Modems, Test Equipment, CSUs/DSUs
Routers, Bridges, Gateways, FRADs
Network Management Hardware

WIDE-AREA DATA SOFTWARE
Access (e.g., ACF/VTAM, NPSI, TCP/IP)
Switching/Routing (e.g., ACF/NCP, T/R Bridge)
Network Management (e.g., NetView, HP OpenView, CAUnicenter)

FACILITIES
Floorspace, Furniture

OUTSIDE SERVICES
Access Lines, Bypass MAN
Backbone Circuits, Microwave, Satellite
Value Added Network Usage
Inward Dial (800 Service)
Outward Dial
Network Disaster Recovery, Dial Backup

EXHIBIT 6.10   WIDE-AREA DATA BASE CASE

some amount less than the purchase price, because the useful life is as much a function of the asset user as it is of the asset.

Several depreciation methods exist. In general terms, depreciation may be straight-line or accelerated. In straight-line depreciation, costs are recognized in

PERSONNEL

FINANCE AND ADMINISTRATION

Services Management (e.g., asset management, administration/accounting, service level reporting)

OPERATIONS

Hardware Services (premises maintenance, distribution, moves, adds, and changes)

Software Services (premises maintenance, distribution)

User Support (premises support of user community)

Application Support (premises development and maintenance of business applications, integration of purchased application software)

Facilities Management (management of shared facilities: operations, capacity planning, backup and recovery, security, disaster recovery, quality control)

TECHNICAL SERVICES

Connectivity Services (design and maintenance of local networks and their connection to other networks)

Data Support (maintenance and administration of shared databases and files)

Technology and Process Management (standards development, evaluation of new technologies)

NONPERSONNEL

DISTRIBUTED COMPUTER PROCESSING HARDWARE

Premises

Desktop (general-purpose networked or stand-alone computers intended for individual use)

Portables (general-purpose computers designed to be transported, docking stations)

Workstations (networked or stand-alone computers with a special orientation toward calculation- or graphics-intensive applications, e.g., statistical analysis, 3-D imaging and modeling, CAD)

Terminals (devices used to interact with a host computer but incapable of independent processing)

Communications Controllers (cluster controllers, concentrators, PADS, 3x74s)

Personal Peripherals (peripheral devices attached to individual PCs or workstations, e.g., printers, plotters, scanners, modems, faxes, CD-ROMs)

Shared Peripherals (peripheral devices attached to the network, e.g., printers, plotters, scanners, modems, faxes, CD-ROMs)

Connectivity

Interface Cards

Internetwork Equipment (bridges, routers, brouters, gateways, hubs, power supplies, and conditioners)

Network Management/Servers

Data Storage (disk, CD-ROM, optical storage)

EXHIBIT 6.11 DISTRIBUTED COMPUTER PROCESSING BASE CASE

DISTRIBUTED COMPUTER PROCESSING SOFTWARE

Premises

    Operating System (e.g., DOS, Windows, OS/2, System 7, Unix)

    Utilities (e.g., disk management, backup/recovery, file compression, memory manager, security, virus protection)

    Applications (e.g., e-mail, groupware, spreadsheet, desktop publishing, word processing, compilers, CASE tools)

Connectivity

    Network Operating System (e.g., Novell, Banyan VINES, OS/2 LAN server, LAN Manager, Decnet, Appletalk)

    Network Management (metering, software distribution, audit, inventory, performance monitors)

FACILITIES

    Floorspace, Furniture

OUTSIDE SERVICES

    Vendor Maintenance Agreements

EXHIBIT 6.11   (CONTINUED)   DISTRIBUTED COMPUTER PROCESSING BASE CASE

---

equal amounts over the course of the useful life. For example, if an asset was acquired for $100, had a useful life of five years, and had no salvage value at the end of the five years, then $20 would be recognized as a depreciation expense each year. This is the most common method of depreciation.[5] Straight-line depreciation is simple to calculate, easy to understand and justify, and easy to use to predict the cost stream over time. In addition to the straight-line method, there are several accelerated depreciation methods, for example, sum of the years' digits (SYD) and double-declining balance (DDB).[6] Each method attempts to match the value received from an asset with the appropriate time period. The reader should consult accounting texts for further information on the formulae and rationales for each method. For the purpose of preparing for an outsourcing evaluation, it is sufficient to understand that when using accelerated depreciation, more costs are recognized early in the useful life, with lesser amounts in each successive period.

    Leasing is an alternative to acquiring assets through a purchase. A lease "is a contract whereby an owner (lessor) grants the use of property to a second party (lessee) for rental payments."[7] There are two types of leases: operating leases and capital leases. As Horngren explains:

> In 1976, the Financial Accounting Standards Board (FASB) reduced the chaos in accounting for leases with its Statement No. 13. Leases are divided into two major kinds: capital leases and operating leases. Capital leases are

---

5.   Ibid, p. 356.
6.   Ibid, p. 357.
7.   Ibid, p. 426.

PERSONNEL

FINANCE AND ADMINISTRATION
Accounting, Billing, Chargeback
Administrative Management and Support

OPERATIONS
Tier 1 Customer Service (Call Response, Incident Logging)
Tier 2/3 Customer Service (Special Diagnostics and Problem Resolution)

NONPERSONNEL

CALL CENTER HARDWARE
Call Center Management (e.g., workstations, predictive dialers, call prompters, alert message systems)
Agent Telephone Expenses (e.g., ACD, VRU, PBX, handsets, voice mail, automated attendant)

CALL CENTER SOFTWARE
Call Center Management (e.g., problem tracking, desktop software)
Agent Telephone Expenses (e.g., VRU software)

FACILITIES
Floorspace, Furniture

OUTSIDE SERVICES
Network Services (e.g., local telco (dedicated CO, DID, Centrex), tie lines (dedicated to IT Help Desk support only), toll free ("800" service), inbound lines, ANI (Automatic Number Identification))

EXHIBIT 6.12   IT HELP DESK BASE CASE

those that transfer substantially all the risks and benefits of ownership. They are equivalent to installment sale and purchase transactions. The asset must be recorded essentially as having been sold by the lessor and having been purchased by the lessee. All other leases are operating leases. Examples of the latter are telephones rented by the month and cottages rented by the day, week, or month. Operating leases are accounted for as ordinary rent revenues and expenses; no changes in rented property owned by the landlord or related liabilities of the renter should be reflected in the body of the balance sheet.[8]

For accounting purposes, operating leases are treated like ordinary expenses and capital leases are treated like depreciation.

Although expenses, depreciation, and leases account for the majority of IT costs, two other cost elements also need to be considered in an outsourcing evaluation: maintenance and cost of capital. Maintenance fees are common for hardware and software. In the case of hardware, maintenance is typically a fee paid

---

8.   Ibid.

PERSONNEL

FINANCE AND ADMINISTRATION
Accounting, Billing, Chargeback
Administrative Management and Support

TECHNICAL SERVICES
Design
Application Development
Testing/Quality Assurance
Database Administration
Implementation
Application Maintenance and Support

NONPERSONNEL

APPLICATION DEVELOPMENT HARDWARE
Development Workstations

APPLICATION DEVELOPMENT SOFTWARE
CASE Tools

FACILITIES
Floorspace, Furniture

OUTSIDE SERVICES
Contract programmers

EXHIBIT 6.13   APPLICATIONS DEVELOPMENT
AND SUPPORT BASE CASE

to the hardware vendor to periodically check the hardware and respond to problems. In the case of software, maintenance fees generally cover the cost of upgrades in addition to customer support. In either case, the cost associated with maintenance must be included in the base case.

Calculating the cost of capital can be considerably more difficult. The first obstacle to this is that the term *cost of capital* may have different meanings. Some companies look at the cost of capital simply as interest rates. Others include debt financing as well. Still others include investment opportunity costs. As used in this text, the cost of capital refers to the cost of financing the acquisition of IT assets. This financing may include an interest-financing component (such as obtaining a loan from a bank) as well as a debt-financing component (such as issuing a bond to raise capital). Interest is "the rental charge for the use of principal."[9] Typically, IT assets are pooled with other corporate assets, ranging from buildings to generators to aircraft for the purposes of raising capital. This creates the second major obstacle in calculating the actual cost.

---

9.   Ibid, p. 399.

RESOURCE CATEGORY	COST ELEMENTS
Hardware	Expenses
	Operating Leases
	Depreciation
	Capital Leases
	Maintenance
Personnel	Salary/Overtime Expenses
	Incentive/Bonus Expenses
	Personnel Development Expenses
	Fringe Benefit Expenses
Facilities	Expenses
	Operating Leases
	Depreciation
	Capital Leases
Outside Services	Expenses
	Operating Leases
	Depreciation
	Capital Leases

EXHIBIT 6.14   PERSONNEL AND NONPERSONNEL COST ELEMENTS

Most corporations use a blended cost for a given time period, which may be used to approximate the cost of capital. A representative cost of capital should be added to the base case for an accurate comparison to vendor proposals.

Special attention must be given to personnel expenses. The base case must be based on total compensation, which includes much more than salary information. Typically, salary and overtime expenses are grouped together in the base case. Incentive and bonus plans form another. Personnel development expenses, which primarily consist of training, but also include tuition assistance, form a third category. The final area is fringe benefits. In many corporations some or all of these costs are held at the corporate level, not at the budget-center level. There may be an overall allocation that approximates the total cost. It is essential to understand the exact benefit areas that are and are not included in such an allocation to adequately build the base case. The delineation of personnel and nonpersonnel cost elements is summarized in Exhibit 6.14.

(c) TIME FRAME.   The concepts and definitions developed in the prior sections provide the tools needed to start building the base case. The final issue is over what time period the base case should be built. It is best to begin with the current year, which typically includes a combination of actual and projected costs. The costs should be summarized for the entire year. Under certain circumstances (e.g., a significant midyear restructuring of the firm or the IT organization), it may be preferable to annualize the costs following the restructuring. This will provide a more useful foundation for future comparisons. Exercise caution, however, in trying to continually adjust for budget to actual variances or unique financial events. Many IT organizations experience sufficient fluctuation that trying to pin down actuals will be an elusive goal and detract energies from the other activities required in an outsourcing evaluation.

In addition to looking at costs for the current year, it is essential to estimate what the IT organization's costs will be during the expected duration of an outsourcing arrangement. This requires understanding several factors: historic trends in IT workload volumes, business forecasts and their relationship to IT usage, expected staffing needs, and future price-performance assumptions for systems and outside services. Each of these elements needs to be reflected in the RFP, so that vendors can use realistic assumptions in pricing the arrangement. Similarly, the prospective outsourcing client needs to understand its costs in order to determine if vendors can reasonably be expected to provide the same services for less money. One might be tempted to seek a shortcut to this activity by assuming that if the vendor's price in the first year of the agreement is less than in-house costs, then the vendor will remain more cost effective over the course of the contract. As the next section shows, this is a dangerous and incorrect assumption.

6.3   RETAINED COSTS

Clients of outsourcing arrangements will retain some costs related to the outsourced function. Exhibit 6.15 illustrates some of the functions typically retained by clients. As shown in Exhibit 6.16, the nature and extent of retained functions

---

MANAGEMENT

> IT Management
> IT Strategic Planning and Architecture
> Contract Management
> Agreement Audit

QUALITY ASSURANCE

> Quality Control
> System Design Validation and Authorization
> Performance Analysis
> Production Control
> Storage Management Analysis and Tuning
> Data Dictionary and Administration

BUSINESS INTERFACE

> Business Requirements Definition
> Business Unit Liaison
> Chargeback Management
> Job Scheduling

EXHIBIT 6.15   TYPICAL CLIENT-RETAINED IT FUNCTIONS

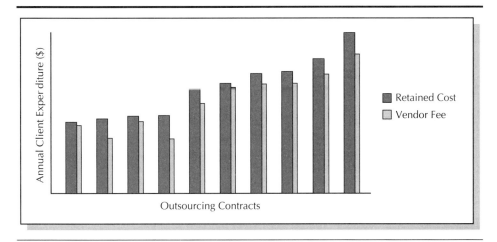

EXHIBIT 6.16 RETAINED COST EXAMPLES

Source: Gartner

varies from one outsourcing arrangement to the next and depends on many factors. Elements that affect the nature and quantity of retained costs are the client's IT vision, need for contract management and audit, requirement for confidentiality, demand for quality assurance, desire to retain control, and comfort level with the vendor.

(a) IN PROPOSAL COMPARISON. The issue of retained costs must first be dealt with when modeling vendor proposals for the purposes of comparison. Those cost elements that the customer will continue to bear after the outsourcing agreement has been completed need to be added to vendor fees to perform an accurate comparison. Before the receipt of vendor proposals, an initial calculation of retained costs can be undertaken, but the exact determination of retained costs will need to be reconsidered with each proposal. Each vendor will propose solutions that may affect the determination of retained costs. There may be slight variances in the base proposal, assuming the customer put together a well-written RFP.

In addition, the vendor may come back with alternative proposals that have significant ramifications. A good example of the latter situation might occur as part of a data center outsourcing situation. The requirement for the original proposal is to include the standard mainframe computer processing functions, including processing, data storage, and output services. One vendor might propose an additional alternative solution where the client performs the output services (e.g., printing, microfiche, plotting). The client, in this second scenario, would retain hardware, facilities, personnel, and possibly, software costs. This second scenario, even with the retained costs, may be the lowest overall cost solution. An accurate modeling of all the vendor charges, coupled with the client-retained costs, is the only way to arrive at this conclusion.

(b) IN FINANCIAL PLANNING.   A successful venture into outsourcing is predicated on realistic expectations by the potential customer management. The experiences of too many parties to outsourcing deals is that originally anticipated cost savings did not materialize.[10] Part of the reason for this is that the requirement for retained functionality and the associated costs was underestimated. The retained costs must be added to projected vendor fees to forecast the customer's future IT expenditures. This process helps avoid some of the hidden costs in an outsourcing deal.

6.4   UNIT VS. TOTAL COST

A chief motivating factor in the decision to consider outsourcing is the desire to reduce expenditures for IT services. This perspective may be fueled by the fact that senior management does not understand what is driving increasing total IT costs. For example, data center costs may have increased by 2 percent over the prior year, but 30 percent more computing product is being delivered. It becomes difficult to manage IT expenditures by only looking at the totals. It is much more productive to manage unit costs. Companies that have rate-based chargeback systems are familiar with this concept. Using the base case models described in Exhibits 6.6 through 6.13 provides half of the equation needed to establish unit costs (also known as unit rates). The second half of the equation is determining the units to divide into each IT area's costs. These units will be described later in this chapter.

There are added benefits to going through this exercise. The first is that it starts the process of "productizing" IT services. *Productizing* is the process of packaging and delivering IT services in a manner that is understandable and controllable by the end user. The second benefit is that it reinforces the practice of viewing IT from the perspective of services, not the underlying manufacturing processes. This is an essential transition for the outsourcing relationship. Finally, it establishes the starting point from which future price-performance changes can be gauged.

(a) IDENTIFYING THE UNITS IN UNIT COST.   The goal of defining a unit of IT work is to determine a measure or indicator of usage that the customer understands and can control. The desire to establish a usage indicator tends to lead to finer levels of granularity in the measurement process. The requirement of ease of understanding indicates simpler, less detailed measures. In practice, a compromise between the two must be reached. Exhibit 6.17 presents an outline of the units that might apply to each of the major technology categories. Data for most of the units can be obtained relatively easily through standard IT automated tools. Although each unit is a technology measure, it can be presented in terms that are understandable and relevant to nontechnical users. Each unit can also be

---

10.   Lacity, Willcocks, and Feeny. "IT Outsourcing: Maximize Flexibility and Control," *Harvard Business Review*, May-June 1995, pp. 84–93.

Technology Category	Representative Units
Mainframe computing	Processing Hour
	Storage Space (GB)
	Printed Page
Distributed computing	Desktop Count
	User Count
Wide Area Data communications	Data Transmitted
	Business Locations Supported
	Desktop Count
Voice Communications	Call Minute
	Extension Count
Application Development	Function Point
Customer Service	Support Call Count

Exhibit 6.17   Outline of Representative Units per Technology Category

directly related to each user's interaction with an IT area. The calculation of each unit can also be defined in sufficient detail so there is no confusion about what the measure actually represents. Precise definition of calculations is a practical consideration, both while soliciting bids from a variety of different vendors and while establishing the pricing basis for the contract, to ensure auditability.

(b) COST TRENDS.   Total IT costs for many companies continue to rise. The rate of change is a function of industry and individual company performance and goals. Different stakeholders in the IT organization may have different perspectives. The CEO, for example, will tend to focus on the bottom line and see a gradual increase in overall IT spending. The CIO, however, may view a declining baseline cost (e.g., as a result of increased efficiencies in computer processing), with a concomitant increase in total spending driven by substantial increased workload volumes. From yet another vantage point, the outsourcing vendor is looking at the same cost trends and identifying opportunities to drive down the cost of providing the same service.

As you might expect, trends vary by IT area. In general, unit costs (remember, not total costs) are decreasing over time in system-intensive IT areas, such as mainframe computer processing. Exhibit 6.18 illustrates the dramatic changes that are continuing to occur in the mainframe computer processing area. Trends are expected to continue into the foreseeable future, primarily because of continuing improvements in hardware price-performance and increased data center automation.

The cost trends for distributed computer processing (including desktop computer processing and client/server processing) have been quite different. Exhibit 6.19 shows that unit costs in this IT area are, in fact, increasing. The hardware and software component of this IT area is decreasing slightly. The support requirements, because of the rapidly increasing complexity of the operating environment and the applications being supported, are the primary contributors

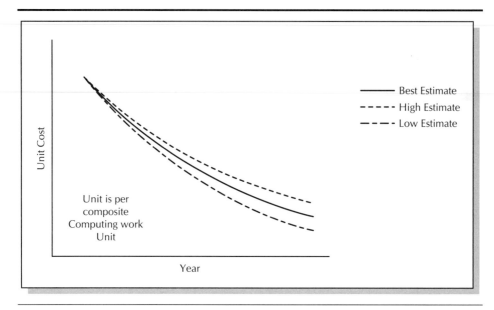

EXHIBIT 6.18 MAINFRAME COMPUTING UNIT COST TRENDS

Source: Gartner

to this cost trend. As this area continues to mature, unit costs are expected to flatten out and eventually decrease. Because of the relatively high percentage of support costs (see Exhibit 6.5), unit cost decreases in the distributed computing environment are not expected to match those in the mainframe computing arena.

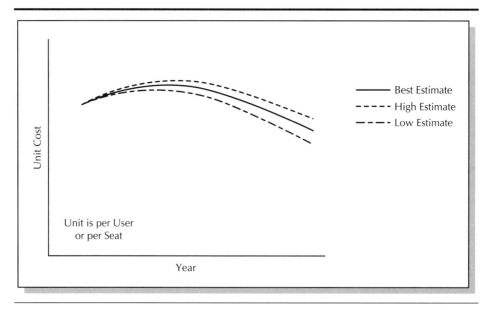

EXHIBIT 6.19 DISTRIBUTED COMPUTING UNIT COST TRENDS

Source: Gartner

(c) USING COST TRENDS. The previous section demonstrated the difference in costs trends in two related IT areas: mainframe and distributed computer processing. Trends in areas such as application development, voice telecommunications, and wide-area data communications also vary considerably. It is essential first to understand and account for these patterns to determine if outsourcing will be feasible from an expense perspective. It is just as important to use this information to validate vendor offers. It should be expected that professionals in the IT industry recognize these trends and are prepared to provide a solution that uses this information to the customer's advantage. Finally, it provides another tool to use in negotiation to ensure that you are entering the arrangement from a position of mutual knowledge and respect. It also provides insights into where the vendor expects to gain financial advantage.

6.5 PRICING OPTIONS

A key issue during negotiations is not only the amount that the customer will pay for the services to be provided by the vendor, but also how (or according to what schedule) such payments will be made. Set forth in the following sections are some of the possible pricing options to consider when structuring your outsourcing transaction. This list is by no means exhaustive. Many customers and vendors are creative in the ways that the fee schedules are engineered to address the needs and concerns of the parties.

(a) PRICING STRUCTURE.

(i) Fixed Fee. In fixed-fee deals, the customer pays a fixed (typically monthly) fee agreed on during contract negotiation for the base services. The fixed fee may include "all services" within a particular function (i.e., all application maintenance) or services up to a "baseline" (i.e., a specified number of help-desk calls or maintenance hours). It is of particular importance in fixed-fee deals to have a clear understanding of the scope and amount of services that are included in the fixed fee. In most cases, the customer wishes to attach a detailed description of the base services. Any service not included in the description of base services or above a baseline will be considered an additional service and subject to an additional charge. A common problem in fixed-fee deals is that no matter how detailed the description of services, it does not (and likely cannot) account for all of the possible business changes that may occur.

(ii) Rate-Based Pricing. In deals with rate-based pricing, the customer and the vendor negotiate a set rate for a particular resource (e.g., application development hours, number of reports). The customer then pays for the amount of that resource that it uses. Depending on the amount of ramp-up resources needed to service the customer or the resources required to be held in reserve for the customer, the outsourcing deal may include a requirement that the customer purchase a minimum amount of services from the vendor. In addition, if the

transaction involves more than one geographic location, the parties should consider whether there should be global rates or country-specific rates.

(iii) Fixed-Fee and Rate-Based Pricing.   A combination of fixed-fee and rate-based pricing is the most common type of pricing structure. Those services that can be described in detail and quantified are subject to a fixed fee (e.g., application maintenance), and those services that will likely increase and decrease over the term (e.g., application development) are subject to rate-based pricing.

(iv) Resource Pool.   In cases in which the customer has not defined a project or its application development needs, the pricing may include a resource pool (e.g., a certain number of development hours). The customer may then draw on the resource pool during the term of the outsourcing agreement, subject in some instances to certain restrictions (e.g., notice periods, limits on use of resources within a specified period).

(v) Cost-Plus Pricing.   In cost-plus pricing deals, the customer pays the vendor's cost plus overhead plus a specified profit. The parties negotiate which costs are allowable costs (e.g., person-hours devoted to application development are allowable, but person-hours devoted to administration and training are not). Overhead is calculated according to a fixed formula, typically including such items as benefits, office space, and supplies. The profit varies from deal to deal but typically ranges from 3 to 10 percent. Vendors typically resist cost-plus pricing on the grounds that they do not wish to disclose their costs. If the parties agree to cost-plus pricing, the customer should keep in mind that broad audit rights of all vendor costs are essential to monitoring whether the fees charged to the customer are accurate.

(vi) Time and Materials.   Time and materials pricing is typically used when the scope or potential duration of a project is not known or the specifications of a project cannot be defined. This type of pricing gives the customer the flexibility to start a project without knowing all of the variables. In some instances, the customer may elect to change from a time and materials contract to a fixed-fee contract after the project specifications are defined. The customer should ensure that the vendor is required to provide detailed backup for all time logged in as well as materials purchased.

(vii) Pass-Through Expenses.   The customer may wish to negotiate the pass-through of certain expenses. The most typical examples are out-of-pocket expenses and travel. The vendor should be required to provide detailed backup for pass-through expenses. The customer may even wish to consider having the vendor abide by the customer's internal expense policy (particularly with respect to travel expenses).

(viii) Lump-Sum Payment for Assets. In outsourcing transactions where assets are being transferred from the customer to the vendor, the parties may negotiate a lump-sum payment to the customer due at contract signing. Such a lump-sum payment may provide the customer with a needed capital infusion or offset other transition costs.

(ix) Spending Commitments. The customer may try to negotiate a lower price or a particular pricing structure (e.g., rate-based or cost-plus pricing) in exchange for a commitment that it will purchase all of its requirements from the vendor or that it will purchase a minimum amount of services from the vendor. This is a potentially dangerous approach from a customer's point of view and should only be undertaken carefully and with proper exit rights.

(x) Other Cost Considerations.

- Travel
- Out-of-pocket expenses
- Cost-of-living adjustments
- Taxes
- Severance
- Transition costs

(b) PAYMENT TERMS. Most vendors propose that payments be made in advance of the services being provided. Because the customer will lose the cost of money if payments are made in advance, the customer typically wishes to pay net 15 to 45 days. The customer's position may depend on its current payment practices with other vendors.

(c) NO CUSTOMER'S BUSINESS REMAINS STATIC OVER THE TERM OF THE OUTSOURCING AGREEMENT. Therefore, it is important that the parties consider during contract negotiations possible changes in the customer's (and the vendor's) business over the term of the outsourcing agreement and include provisions in the outsourcing agreement that allow for business variability. Examples of provisions that deal with business variability are:

- *Additional and Reduced Resource Charges*. The outsourcing agreement typically includes rates at which the customer may receive additional resources/services, as well as rates by which the baseline fee will be reduced if lesser resources/services are used. The rates may vary depending on the amount of resources needed and the amount of notice given.
- *Renegotiation Trigger*. The outsourcing agreement may include a renegotiation right if the customer's demand for services increases or decreases above or below a certain level. An example of such a provision is set forth as follows:

In the event that Customer's use of the Services increases or decreases more than ____ percent the aggregate] [per Service], Customer and Vendor shall negotiate and implement an appropriate adjustment to the Fees. In the event Customer and Vendor cannot agree on the adjustment to the Fees required by this Section, such disagreement shall be submitted to dispute resolution.

- *Termination Right.* The outsourcing agreement may include a partial/full termination right if the customer's demand for services decreases below a certain level. Such a termination right may be tied to a termination fee.

(d) ONGOING PRICE REDUCTIONS. A common question for customers to ask is how they can ensure that the vendor will deliver continuing price reductions over the term of the outsourcing agreement. The desire to obtain continuing price reductions is based on the customer's perception (which is often accurate) that over the term of the outsourcing agreement: (a) the vendor should be able to become more efficient; (b) the vendor should be able to better leverage its economies of scale; and (c) the overall cost of technology should decrease. Although the vendor's ability to deliver ongoing price reductions may depend on how the fee schedule is structured (e.g., are any large capital expenses deferred to the later years?), it is possible to build some provision for ongoing price reductions into the outsourcing deal.

(i) May Depend on Pricing Structure.   The payment stream in fixed-fee deals will likely be subject to financial engineering (e.g., a flat payment stream over the term of the outsourcing agreement, lower costs in the early years), and, therefore, the customer may not see constantly reducing prices over the term.

(ii) Productivity Improvements.   The pricing structure may include a requirement that the vendor demonstrate specific productivity improvements annually (e.g., constantly improving service levels, increased output, more efficient software developers).

(iii) Market Comparisons.   Other mechanisms often found in an outsourcing agreement that may result in pricing reductions include the following:

- Technology indexing
- Price indexing
- Benchmarking

Other Pricing Considerations That May Impact Price Reductions

- Cost-of-living adjustments
- Taxes
- Scope changes
- New projects

(e) COST-OF-LIVING ADJUSTMENTS.   The outsourcing arrangement must also take into account economic changes that impact the outsourcing relationship. The most common area is changes in the cost of living, also termed *inflation*. Cost-of-living adjustment (COLA) clauses are common in outsourcing agreements. They recognize the changing value of money over time. The following must be considered in determining how COLA should be treated in an outsourcing arrangement. First, there is generally no COLA guarantee for in-house IT organizations (COLA guarantees may exist if some of the IT staff is unionized). Second, COLA should apply to personnel only. Hardware/software systems generally experience price-performance improvements that offset inflationary trends. Third, make sure that you understand the index that is being used to establish the cost of living (there are several) and determine that it is the best indicator for your company.

6.6 OTHER FINANCIAL CHARGES

A variety of other financial charges associated with an outsourcing arrangement should be considered when determining the overall financial impact of the outsourcing transaction. These charges should be factored into the analysis of vendor proposals in order to be truly comparable to in-house costs. The vendor generally adds these charges to the base fee, so that the customer pays for them directly. In some limited cases, the vendor may be able to include some of these charges in the base fee.

(a) TAXES.   Taxes are an important consideration in structuring an outsourcing arrangement. There may be options to reduce the customer's tax liabilities through outsourcing. Internal organizations pay income and property taxes. These tax burdens typically remain as retained costs. The outsourcer generally assumes the income and property tax liability for these areas for the personnel and assets that are transferred. If the outsourcer is given flexibility in where these personnel and assets will be located, there may be opportunities to relocate these resources to remote locations with a lower tax rate, with potential savings to the customer.

A relocation such as the one suggested may have the opposite effect in terms of sales taxes. Sales taxes may be levied from local and state jurisdictions. In international outsourcing arrangements, taxes may be levied from provincial and national jurisdictions; for example, the Provincial Sales Tax (PST) and General Sales Tax (GST) in Canada, Value Added Tax (VAT) in the United Kingdom and Europe. There may be use taxes in addition to, or in lieu of, sales taxes. From an analysis perspective, use and sales taxes may be treated in the same fashion.

A key consideration is identifying and documenting which party to the outsourcing relationship is responsible for which tax liabilities.

(b) INSURANCE.   Insurance costs should be taken into account in structuring any outsourcing arrangement. The vendor typically assumes all obligations for the insurance related to the resources transferred to the vendor. This includes property and casualty insurance for physical assets (e.g., hardware, buildings, furniture, power generation equipment, security systems). It also includes life and disability insurance for transferred employees. The vendor may be able to achieve cost savings through a lower-cost provider or participating in lower-risk insurance pools. As in the case of taxes, it is key to identify and document the insurance responsibilities of both parties. If any type of special or additional insurance or bond is required, the cost of such insurance or bond will need to be built into the fees or (if a retained cost) the customer's overall business case.

(c) EXPENSES.   Travel is typically required as a part of delivering an IT service. The nature and amount of travel varies considerably by technology category, as Exhibit 6.20 illustrates. Wide-area data communications may involve the least amount of travel, whereas application development often requires the most. Most companies can estimate the amount of travel required by their current in-house staff and may be able to make reasonable approximations of the change in travel needed, if the service were to be transferred to an external provider. The physical location(s) of prospective vendors may impact travel costs significantly. It is

TECHNOLOGY CATEGORY	SAMPLE TRAVEL REQUIREMENTS
Mainframe Computing	Requirements Definition
	Client Operational Reviews
	Client Training Sessions
	Disaster Recovery Testing
Distributed Computing	Requirements Definition
	Client Operational Reviews
	Client Training Sessions
	Disaster Recovery Testing
	Moves/Adds/Changes
Wide-Area Data Communications	Requirements Definition
	Client Operational Reviews
Voice Communications	Requirements Definition
	PBX Upgrade/Installation
	Moves/Adds/Changes
Application Development	Requirements Definition
	On-Site Development
	Client Status/Acceptance Reviews
	System Testing
	System Implementation
Customer Service	Requirements Definition
	Client Focus Sessions

EXHIBIT 6.20   TRAVEL REQUIREMENTS BASED ON TECHNOLOGY CATEGORIES

essential to define which party will bear travel cost responsibility and under what circumstances. For example, the vendor may be expected to include the cost of monthly operational reviews in the base fee to the customer. However, the vendor is typically allowed to charge travel expenses for special requests made on behalf of the customer. Even in the latter case, there may be exceptions if it appears there is marketing or sales potential for the vendor through this activity.

Outsourcing arrangements may involve several pass-through charges in addition to the vendor's fees. One of the attractions of outsourcing in certain circumstances is the transfer of administrative responsibility for managing payments to multiple vendors. Pass-through charges are common in telecommunications outsourcing contracts. The primary vendor typically acts as an agent of the client and collects, for example, circuit charges from a variety of carriers and presents the outsourcing client with a consolidated bill. Another example of pass-through arrangements occurs for certain software licenses. This arrangement occurs most frequently because (1) the software supplier will not transfer license to the outsourcing vendor; (2) the license transfer would result in increased costs; or (3) the client wishes to retain direct control of critical applications.

Most pass-through arrangements prohibit a markup on the initial invoiced amount, but it should be kept in mind that, even though there is no explicit bill, this service does not come free. The vendor must recover the administrative costs of performing this service through the base charge (or management additive).

(d) EXCHANGE RATE. With the ever-increasing number of international outsourcing arrangements, the handling of exchange rates becomes more critical. Most international, or multinational, deals require that the vendor bills in one currency. The currency selected is typically that of the country in which the parent company is headquartered. The basis for the exchange rate must be established as part of the agreement. While it is possible that a separate method may be selected for each affected country, in practice it makes the most sense to select a method that is common to all.

There are several bases for calculating the exchange rate, and the impact of each method varies primarily as a result of the rate of inflation in each affected country. One method is to use the closing exchange rate at the time of billing. This has the advantages of being easy to validate and calculate. It has the disadvantage of being subject to unpredictability in countries with volatile economies. A second method is to use an average exchange rate for the billing period. If the billing period is monthly, then the exchange rate would be calculated by adding all of the daily exchange rates for the billing period and dividing by the number of days involved. This smoothes out fluctuations in currency valuation, but is more difficult to calculate and validate. In either case, it is essential to identify and document the basis for the exchange rate and audit the vendor invoices to ensure compliance with the agreement.

(e) AUDIT RIGHTS AND REQUIREMENTS. Audit rights and requirements are receiving heightened attention with the implementation of Sarbanes-Oxley and increased regulation in the pharmaceutical, energy, and financial services industry. The cost of conducting the necessary audits, maintaining the requisite supporting documentation, and creating the audit reports (e.g., SAS 70 reports) should be considered when assessing overall transaction costs.

6.7   FINANCIAL IMPACT OF CHANGE

Outsourcing means change. Several terms have been used interchangeably to describe this period of change, including *transition, migration,* and *transformation.* There are two primary motivations for this change. The first is to have a more efficient and/or effective service provider take over operation of an existing IT function. The second goal is to establish a mechanism for fundamentally changing the process or vehicles by which an IT service is created and/or delivered. The following terms will be used for the purposes of this chapter to eliminate misunderstanding: *Transfer* is the period during which the vendor assumes operational and, possibly, financial responsibility for IT functions, and *transformation* is the period during which the vendor moves IT operation from one platform to another. Both may include one-time or unique charges that should be considered.

(a) TRANSFER FINANCES.   Substantial short-term costs are typically incurred as part of the transfer of financial and operational responsibilities in an outsourcing relationship. These costs result from the extra effort required to plan the transfer, the test procedures to ensure that the transfer occurs without a problem, the termination penalties associated with discontinuing leases, the relocation expenses to transport assets and personnel, and severance fees to compensate personnel whose positions are eliminated as part of the outsourcing agreement. Many of the extra costs are the responsibility of the vendor, but the customer may incur some of the costs as well. The impact of these cost elements must be factored into the financial assessment of the outsourcing deal.

Additional costs may be incurred before the transfer period. The first one usually encountered relates to planning and testing. The vendor may need to bring in specialists who will be involved in the transaction only for the transfer period. In addition to supporting day-to-day operations, the vendor may need to perform the detail planning required to maximize the success of a transfer that goes without interruption to the user community. Integral to this planning process is a learning curve that also adds to the vendor's costs. One of the key elements of the planning process is developing and implementing tests to ensure that the vendor is capable of performing the transfer without a hitch. The customer may also incur some additional costs as a part of the testing process (e.g., test travel to the vendor site), but this is typically a small expense.

The vendor typically assumes responsibility for the costs associated with the transfer and/or relocation of assets and personnel. The transfer of purchased assets involves acquisition costs, either at book or market value. The transfer of leased assets may involve a conveyance fee. The transfer of personnel does not involve a payment to the customer, but may involve sign-up incentives. The relocation of assets involves freight and installation/deinstallation charges. The relocation of personnel involves house-hunting assistance, moving fees, and other living considerations.

The customer typically assumes responsibility for the costs associated with the termination of assets and personnel. Purchased assets do not have termination charges, but there may be termination charges with the associated maintenance. There may be costs associated with discarding or selling the asset. Leased assets that will not be assumed by the vendor will typically have some kind of termination penalty associated with terminating the lease before the end of the lease period. The impact of termination charges can be minimized by timing the transfer period to coincide with the expiration of major leases. In preparation for this transfer, leases can also be renegotiated or renewed to align termination periods or make them short term.

(b) TRANSFORMATION FINANCES. Transformational outsourcing arrangements involve moving IT functions from one technology platform to another. In recent years, transformational outsourcing has most often been associated with moving applications from mainframe computers to client-based systems. Development expenses are a major component of the transformation. These costs are associated with creating replacement systems on the new technology platform. It may also be necessary to develop temporary conversion tools to facilitate migration from the old to the new platforms. At the same time, it may be necessary to invest in the infrastructure for the new platform.

As the transformation becomes more of a reality, it will be necessary to maintain parallel systems until the transformation is complete. This results in an overlap of expenses for the parallel testing period. After the transformation is complete, there may be termination expenses related to the old system. At the same time, it will be necessary to begin training end users in the new system.

(c) TRANSFER AND TRANSFORMATION FUNDING. The cost streams for transfer and transformation activities are similar. One-time or limited costs that are above and beyond normal operating expenses occur at the beginning of the outsourcing relationship. If the transfer or transformation costs are recognized in the period during which they occur, it may create a significant financial deterrent to entering into the deal.

This is illustrated in Exhibit 6.21. Many vendors, recognizing the obstacle this represents, are able to structure deals to amortize these initial costs over a longer term. An example of this is shown in Exhibit 6.22. It is important to recognize that if this second option is selected, the customer is committed to a long-term financing option. This may adversely affect the competitiveness of future pricing. In the best case, the additional transfer or transformation costs are offset by the vendor's reduced operational costs.

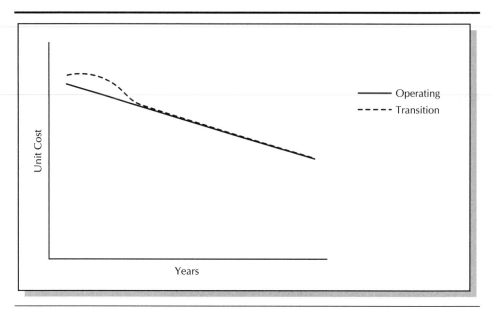

EXHIBIT 6.21   FRONT-LOADED TRANSFORMATION COST RECOVERY

Source: Gartner

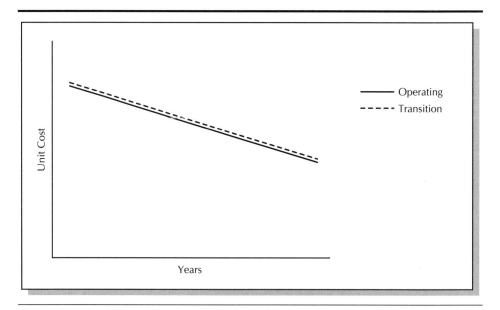

EXHIBIT 6.22   LIFE CYCLE TRANSFORMATION COST RECOVERY

Source: Gartner

6.8 PAYMENTS

The method and timing of payments can also have real financial impact on the effectiveness of an outsourcing deal. All of the details of payments should be negotiated and documented before the commencement of actual service by the vendor. The customer must ensure that the protocol established is consistent with internal practices in other areas of the corporation.

Increasingly, the method of payment is becoming an automated electronic transfer to the vendor's account. Ensuring that the amount is correct and providing reasonable avenues for problem resolution is more critical.

(a) TIMING. There are two aspects to the timing of payments. The first is the timing relative to the delivery of service. There are two general approaches. The most typical is that billing is done in arrears. This means the service has been rendered by the vendor and the customer has the opportunity to review the supporting documentation to ensure the service was delivered according to specifications. Another option is billing in advance, with subsequent adjustments as needed. This approach may be more common in fixed-price arrangements. Even flat-fee arrangements may require adjustments after the fact because of exceedance and underage clauses or service-level penalty provisions.

The second aspect of timing is the frequency of the billing. In most cases, billing is performed monthly. Few vendors can afford to do otherwise. Other options include quarterly and annual billings, but if a vendor offers these options, make sure you are not incurring a financing charge for the unpaid balances.

(b) LATE CHARGES. A typical clause in any purchasing agreement deals with late charge penalties. Most outsourcing arrangements establish Net 30 or Net 45 payment terms. This means that payment in full is expected within 30 or 45 days, respectively, of the invoice date. Although late charges are often waived in practice, it is not recommended that this contractual area be overlooked in the negotiation of the contract. It is critical, first, to understand the vendor's invoicing practices. It is incumbent upon the potential customer to investigate the average time between creation of an invoice and its delivery to the customer. What are the vendor's standard terms for late charges? Will there be any hidden financial charges for changing the terms to ones that are more favorable to the customer? It is also essential that the vendor be willing to accept, at a minimum, the customer's standard terms and conditions in this area.

(c) DISPUTES. As in any working relationship, most outsourcing arrangements experience periodic disagreements regarding portions of bills. These disputes may arise out of misunderstandings, miscommunications, or disagreements regarding the responsibility for incurring a specific charge, and, in the worst case, suspicion regarding the validity or accuracy of a charge. Many outsourcing agreements have a contractual provision that permits withholding, as well as the suspension of late charges, on amounts that are being disputed in good faith. A common part of that kind of clause is the statement that, despite some of the amounts being in dispute, the payment of amounts not in dispute will not be hindered. It is also important to have a resolution mechanism for payment disputes so they can be settled within a reasonable time frame in a manner agreed to by both parties. The resolution mechanism typically involves some internal resolution within both parties with the option to escalate the matter to some external binding arbitration as a last resort.

6.9   CHARGEBACK

One of the often overlooked aspects of an outsourcing relationship is in the area of chargeback. Chargeback, as used in this context, is the need to allocate or assign IT expenditures to the end users who consume the services. The need for chargeback does not disappear with outsourcing, but in fact may be heightened because of the recognition that IT expenditures amount to significant funds. The need to conserve and justify these dollars becomes very real. An outsourcing agreement may, in fact, be of benefit to companies that have not established internal chargeback methods. Vendors are typically required to provide detailed, itemized invoices, so they have established the methodologies to create cost pools, identify unit costs, and charge based on those units. Companies that do not have chargeback systems also benefit from the fact that the vendor can be enlisted to do much of the dirty work (e.g., establishing naming conventions and assigning charge codes). This added administrative and technical effort typically comes at a cost. The customer should to understand and agree with the bases for any additional fees associated with chargeback systems.

(a) PAYING FOR CHARGEBACK SERVICES.   One of the thorniest issues in the use of chargeback in an outsourcing relationship is that of which party bears the cost responsibility. This arises most often when the issue of chargeback is not addressed in the customer's RFP or through negotiations. Chargeback can be treated as part of baseline service or in the same fashion as any user computing activity. Remember, the customer ultimately pays for everything that an outsourcer does. However, it should be established as part of the initial agreement which elements of chargeback fall within the vendor's base fee and what the customer's responsibilities are.

Exhibit 6.23 illustrates the wide range of functions associated with IT chargeback. Some might be assumed to clearly fall within the vendor's purview (e.g., implementing and modifying data collection tools, maintaining chargeback databases, and auditing and correcting data collection), whereas others might be assumed to be clearly the customer's responsibility, such as determining charging levels (e.g., individual, department, cost center, or business unit). In reality, most of the functions have a shared element of responsibility. For example, the data collection auditing function may rely, in part, on a table of authorized account codes. The coding and execution of the chargeback auditing routine may be the respon-

DATA COLLECTION

Identifying Data Requirements
Selecting Data Collection Software
Implementing and Modifying Data Collection Tools
Maintaining Chargeback Databases
Auditing and Correcting Data Collection

CUSTOMER INTERFACE

Determining Charging Level
Authorizing Charge Codes
Educating End Users on System Usage
Assisting Users and Management on Information Interpretation
Receiving and Resolving Credit Requests

CHARGEBACK REPORTING

Creating Standard Invoices
Generating Supporting Detail
Creating Special Reports
Running Special Reports

EXHIBIT 6.23   IT CHARGEBACK FUNCTIONS

sibility of the vendor, but the customer will probably want to retain control over
the creation and validation of the table that authorizes outside expenditures. If the
auditing routine identifies an invalid account code, the vendor will need to work
with the customer to identify the discrepancy and help the customer determine
where the code was used. The customer, in turn, must work with the vendor to
quickly resolve the problem and determine how the vendor will be compensated
for the services that were delivered. In many cases, this may simply be the result of
an expired account code that needs to be replaced with a current one. This can be
reconciled through a rerun of the system with the corrected information. In other
cases, some mutually satisfactory solution must be reached to resolve the problem.
The roles and responsibilities must be spelled out in the same level of detail as all
other working relationships within the contract.

(b) OUTSOURCING AN EXISTING CHARGEBACK PROCESS.   The same considerations hold true with an existing chargeback process. The roles and responsibilities of each party must be defined in great detail. Entering into an
outsourcing relationship with an existing chargeback system provides an opportunity to reexamine the merits of that system. In most cases, customers simply
continue using their existing processes and tools.

   Vendors may, however, be in a position to lend their expertise in the area of
charging and substantially improve the process in terms of user acceptance and/
or the efficiency and reliability of providing chargeback information.

(c) CHARGEBACK VS. CHARGING.   Keep in mind that there may be a difference between chargeback and charging. The vendor may have a standard method of charging clients (e.g., based on capacity or total utilization). Some of this utilization would be for the benefit of the vendor management group; some may be system overhead. The basis that the vendor is using to charge real dollars to a company may not be applicable as chargeback to end users. The vendor management group may even desire to use chargeback to effect behavioral changes that are not similar to those resulting from the vendor's methodology. The key is that the customer must first decide what is necessary for internal chargeback purposes and segregate that need, if necessary, from vendor charges.

APPENDIX **6.1**

COST-OF-LIVING ADJUSTMENT (COLA) PROVISIONS CHECKLIST[11]

1. What is a COLA provision? (A provision that calls for an adjustment to the fees to reflect inflation)

2. At what point during the term of the Agreement will COLA apply?
   - Is any inflation built into the fees?
   - To what extent should the vendor be managing inflation?

3. To what fees does COLA apply? (Typically labor portions only; even for fees that are labor based, there is typically some portion attributable to overhead/ administration)

4. To what extent should a COLA increase be offset by a pricing decrease (e.g., productivity gains)?

5. Will there be any risk-sharing mechanisms (e.g., if COLA exceeds 4 percent, then the parties will share amounts over 4 percent on a 50/50 basis)?

6. Different indices for the Unites States and other countries

7. Choosing an index
   - Consumer Price Index
   - Employment Cost Index
   - General indices vs. specific goods/services
   - No IT services index
   - U.S. vs. Regional/City indices

8. Sample Indices (see attached):
   - Percentage increases vs. percentage point increases
   - Mechanisms for changes to the indices

9. New developments

---

11. Note: This checklist is intended to illustrate the types of legal issues that customers may wish to consider in connection with contracting for application services. The items included in this checklist may not cover all of the issues that may arise in a particular transaction. Legal issues will likely vary depending on the type of service being provided and the scope of the services. This checklist or any part thereof should only be used after consultation with your legal counsel. Legal counsel should be consulted prior to entering into or negotiating any transaction covering the provision of application services.

CHAPTER 7

HUMAN RESOURCES[1]

7.1 TRANSITIONING EMPLOYEES TO THE VENDOR

As part of the outsourcing arrangement, the outsourcing vendor is often required to make offers of employment to all or a substantial number of the outsourcing customer's employees who currently provide the services to be outsourced. The customer and the vendor will need to discuss and negotiate the number of employees to be offered employment with the vendor, the terms of the employment offers, the timing of the employee transition, the schedule for employee communications, and, in some cases, procedures for dealing with precontract staffing problems (e.g., stay incentives, provision of temporary vendor personnel). The outcome of

---

1. The authors wish to thank Jane Hansen of Milbank Tweed for her ongoing assistance on HR-related issues.

these discussions and negotiations will depend on several factors, including the following:

- The customer's outsourcing objectives (e.g., cost savings)
- The existing services to be outsourced (e.g., data center, application development, business processes)
- The services to be provided by the vendor (e.g., migration from legacy system to client/server system)
- The service levels desired by the customer
- The ability of the vendor to be more efficient than the customer
- The need for the vendor to acquire business or systems knowledge of the customer
- Employee morale and expectations
- Customer precedent
- Comparability of customer and vendor benefits (e.g., bonuses, health insurance, severance)
- Customer–vendor negotiations

The reduction in personnel costs caused by the transfer of employees to the vendor often accounts for a large percentage of the total cost savings anticipated by the outsourcing customer. Although these cost savings may be significant, the customer considering outsourcing should be mindful of the associated business and legal issues. The costs and inconvenience associated with the administration and resolution (e.g., litigation, arbitration, settlement, government proceedings) of a mismanaged employee transition may prevent the customer from realizing many of the anticipated benefits of the outsourcing transaction.

Personnel issues warrant particular consideration throughout the negotiation process. A representative or representatives from human resources should be included on the outsourcing team as early as possible. The number of representatives will depend on the scope of the transaction, whether the legal and personnel/human resources departments assign representatives to handle the human resources issues, and the number of sites or locations of transitioning employees (particularly if there are sites outside of the United States). For the purposes of this chapter, human resources issues have been divided into five categories. The applicability and importance of each of these categories will vary from transaction to transaction. The categories are as follows:

1. Due diligence (i.e., preliminary information gathering and analysis)
2. The employment offer
3. The employee transition
4. Contract-related issues (e.g., warranties, indemnities, rights upon termination)
5. Stay incentives

7.2 DUE DILIGENCE

(a) EMPLOYEES AFFECTED BY TRANSITION. Before sending out the request for proposal (RFP) (or, if the customer does not intend to send out an RFP, at the early stages of the negotiation process with the outsourcing vendor), the customer's outsourcing team should determine how it wishes to structure the human resources part of the outsourcing transaction. Which employees are in-scope? Does the customer want to transfer all of the in-scope employees? Does the customer want the vendor to make the most cost-effective bid, with the option to hire all or a portion of the in-scope employees? Which employees does the customer want to retain?

A useful exercise to get the process started is for the customer to prepare a list of all employees who currently provide the services to be outsourced (including those employees who may be transitioned to the vendor, laid off, or retained by the customer) (see Exhibit 7.1). When preparing this list, the customer typically looks at those employees who are included in the budget of the department or function to be outsourced. The customer should also be mindful of employees who are not in the budget, but who provide shadow support.

Once the in-scope employees have been identified, the customer should make a preliminary assessment as to which employees it wishes to retain (usually management-level employees and in some cases key employees with critical knowledge or expertise), which employees it wishes to transition to the vendor, and among those employees whether some are critical to the services and should be given extra job protections and incentives to remain with the customer, and which employees, if any, should be laid off. The assessment of

EMPLOYEE NAME OR ID NUMBER	SITE/LOCATION	JOB DESCRIPTION	COMMENTS

EXHIBIT 7.1 IDENTIFYING IN-SCOPE EMPLOYEES[a]

---

[a]NOTE WITH RESPECT TO PERSONNEL DATA AND INFORMATION:
This template, the template set forth in Exhibit 7.2, and most other HR-related data and information compiled in connection with the outsourcing transaction contain sensitive information. In order to limit the disclosure of this information, the customer should consider the following protective measures:
- Designate one individual who will be responsible for preparing and revising the list
- Maintain a limited number of copies of the list, preferably one master
- Mark the document "Strictly Confidential"
- Shred any drafts and copies of the list
- Notify the vendor(s) of these measures and require vendor compliance.

In addition, the customer and the vendor should be mindful of the type of information contained in these exhibits. The customer should not identify the employees by any protected class (e.g., sex, race, religion, age, health status) or give the appearance of such identification.

whether employees will be retained, transitioned, or laid off is often made in conjunction with the information contained in the vendor proposals or even with direct vendor input.

The following are some of the options that should be considered when deciding which employees to transfer to the vendor and some of the benefits of these options:

- *Transitioning all employees to the vendor*, with staggered protections (e.g., no termination for a period of time, retention bonuses) for:

  - Critical employees (identified by customer) who are needed long term

  - Rank-and-file employees who may be needed only for a transition or shorter period

  One of the biggest advantages outsourcing offers to the in-scope population is the opportunity for advancement with the vendor. For example, a senior IT professional with a manufacturer is likely to have greater chances for expanded responsibilities with a vendor/IT service provider than with the customer/employer.

  A fundamental goal of most outsourcing transactions is cost savings; thus, invariably some measure of downsizing of the in-scope population will be necessary. If the customer requires the vendor to hire all of the affected employees, even if the customer knows that downsizings will be necessary, it may put the downsized employees in a better position for finding employment with the vendor than they would have had if they had been downsized by the customer.

- *Downsizing some employees before transitioning others to the vendor*, with the customer identifying and downsizing certain noncritical or non-essential employees before the Effective Date.

  Eliminating positions can be difficult for any employer, particularly from a morale standpoint. However, if the customer knows ahead of time that the business plan will call for reduced headcounts, it may decide to avoid transition costs by making the first cut among the affected employees before transition.

  In addition, in some instances, a customer may have some in-scope employees who are amenable to downsizing. For example, some in-scope employees who have accrued substantial years of service may be amenable to a voluntary downsizing that can be accomplished through a voluntary early retirement program (VERP). Implementing a downsizing of this nature before the Effective Date can result in a savings of transition costs and a reduction in the administrative burdens associated with transition.

- *Transitioning some employees to the vendor and retaining others*, in circumstances in which there are reasons not to transfer certain employees, for example:
  - Critical or essential employees who will provide oversight of the process
  - Unionized employees whom many vendors are reluctant to take

Many customers are reluctant to lose key personnel who will provide the link between the customer and the vendor in ensuring that the services are provided in the most efficient and beneficial manner to the customer. The customer may decide to retain these employees.

In addition, many vendors do not have unionized employees in their workforces and are reluctant to take on that obligation. At the same time, a customer may have unionized employees who are in-scope and are essential to the services to be provided. These employees may be retained by the customer and "seconded" or leased to the vendor.

- *Transitioning no employees*, but:
  - Seconding or leasing the in-scope employees to work with the vendor
  - Developing a collaborative relationship with the vendor

As a variation on the preceding theme, occasionally a customer will decide that transferring employees as a part of the outsourcing of a function is not appropriate for its operations. The customer may nevertheless find that a vendor can offer long-term solutions, including in-depth skills overhauling. A customer in this position may decide to establish a long-term collaboration with a vendor in which the vendor supplies project staff at all levels to work with the customer's employees with the goal that as the skills are acquired by the customer's employees, the vendor's employees will be phased out of the project.

A discussion of additional factors to consider when deciding which employees to retain is provided in Appendix 7.2. An example of a template used to compile the employee information is set forth in Exhibit 7.2. This information should be updated throughout the course of the negotiations.

EMPLOYEE NAME OR I.D. #	SITE/ LOCATION	JOB DESC.	TRANSFERRED (Y/N)	RETAINED (Y/N)	COMMENTS

NOTE: If employees are to be laid off, add a column to reflect this additional category.

EXHIBIT 7.2 DETERMINING EMPLOYEE STATUS

The general information included in Exhibit 7.2 can be elaborated on and separated into more specific charts relating to employees being transferred, retained, and, if applicable, laid off (see Exhibits 7.3, 7.4, and 7.5). As with Exhibit 7.2, these exhibits should be updated throughout the course of the negotiations because the information contained in them is often used by the customer's financial analysts or controllers in assessing the cost benefits of the vendor's proposal and by the vendor's financial analysts in preparing pricing.

Employee Name or I.D. #	Site/ Location	Job Desc.	Salary	Bonus	Overhead Costs (e.g., office, admin., benefits)	Vacation	Separation Costs Assumed by Vendor (e.g., severance, stay bonuses)*	Separation Costs Assumed by Customer (e.g., severance, stay bonuses)*	Comments

*Because it is often difficult to definitively assess separation costs, it may be useful to include a high and low number for evaluation purposes.

EXHIBIT 7.3 TRANSFERRED EMPLOYEES

Employee Name or I.D. #	Site/ Location	Job Desc.	Salary	Bonus	Overhead Costs (e.g., office, admin., benefits)	Vacation	Comments

EXHIBIT 7.4 RETAINED EMPLOYEES

Employee Name or I.D. #	Site/ Location	Job Desc.	Salary	Bonus	Overhead Costs (e.g., office, admin., benefits)	Vacation	Separation Costs Assumed by Vendor (e.g., severance, stay bonuses)*	Separation Costs Assumed by Customer (e.g., severance, stay bonuses)*	Comments

*Because it is often difficult to definitively assess separation costs, it may be useful to include a high and low number for evaluation purposes.

EXHIBIT 7.5 LAID-OFF EMPLOYEES

(b) COMPENSATION AND BENEFITS ANALYSIS. A standard requirement or offering in most RFPs and vendor proposals is that the vendor provide the customer's employees with equivalent or better compensation and benefits (in the aggregate) than those being provided by the customer. Comparable compensation and benefits may also be necessary to avoid triggering rights under the customer's severance plan. (Severance plans often provide that the employer will not be responsible for severance if the employee is offered employment with another employer upon comparable—in some cases, substantially comparable—terms and conditions of employment.) For transactions involving countries outside of the United States, employers may be required by statute to offer comparable terms and conditions of employment in order to avoid having to pay redundancy payments.

Both the customer and the vendor will need to perform an analysis of the compensation and benefits provided by the customer and to be provided by the vendor to assess comparability. In order to perform this assessment, the customer and the vendor will need to have access to each other's compensation and benefits plans and programs. The timing for this exchange of information varies from transaction to transaction. In some cases, the customer will include compensation and benefit information in the RFP with a request that the vendor provide a comparison of customer–vendor compensation and benefits together with a proposal for dealing with differences between the two. In other cases where the customer is less inclined to disseminate personnel-related data in the RFP, the customer may request a description of the vendor's proposed compensation and benefit plans and then disseminate its own information at a later date for a formal comparison.

The customer and the vendor should be careful to include all benefits in the comparability analysis. Seemingly minor benefits that are often forgotten but that are hot points for employees include fitness facilities, transportation discounts, store discounts, cafeteria access, and parking. Although often contentious, an issue that should also be taken into account when determining comparability is whether the vendor will count the transitioned employees' years of service with the customer when determining vesting, eligibility, and accrual rights with respect to certain benefits (particularly vacation, savings, stock options, and retirement benefits).

(c) REVIEW OF SEVERANCE/REDUNDANCY POLICIES. A task that the customer should undertake early in the due diligence process is the review of its severance/redundancy policies. In such a review, the customer should identify the events that trigger severance/redundancy obligations. The customer's potential severance/redundancy liability is important in assessing the total cost of the deal. Although severance/redundancy plans typically contemplate mergers, acquisitions, and sales, they do not always contemplate outsourcing. There is a risk that, unless the customer's plan is worded correctly, even those employees transferred to the vendor may be eligible for severance/redundancy payments.

In addition to reviewing its own policy, the customer will need to review the vendor's severance/redundancy policies. Often the vendor's policies are not as generous as those of the customer. In addition, many vendors do not offer credit for years of service with the customer for severance/redundancy calculations. Many customers choose to negotiate enhanced severance/redundancy for transitioned employees, so that if an employee is terminated by the vendor within a certain number of years from contract signing, the employee will receive supplemented severance/redundancy payments either comparable to, or a percentage of, what the employee would have received if he or she had remained employed by the customer. The customer and the vendor will need to negotiate the administration of and financial responsibility for enhanced severance. Will the cost be built into the base fees or will the customer reimburse the vendor on a pass-through basis? The customer should also consider restricting enhanced severance/redundancy to those employees who are still on the customer's account at the time of termination, which will depend largely on the vendor's staffing plans.

Another part of due diligence will be to determine whether there are any legal or regulatory requirements affecting severance/redundancy. Are the employees entitled to any severance/redundancy pay by law or regulation? Is there any way to reduce or eliminate this liability? This due diligence is particularly relevant to employee transitions outside of the United States.

(d) OUTPLACEMENT BENEFITS.   Many customers offer employees who are to be laid off a variety of outplacement benefits. Such benefits may include the following:

- Job posting for alternative positions with the customer
- Resume preparation assistance
- Job search assistance
- Counseling
- Access to offices, telephones, and computers for a certain period of time
- Extension of loan repayment terms

The customer should consider whether the vendor should assist in outplacement (e.g., by allowing the employees to post for vendor jobs).

(e) LAWS AND REGULATIONS.   The customer and the vendor will need to determine whether notice requirements must be complied with or special authorizations or consents must be obtained in connection with the employee transition. Relevant U.S. statutes that may require specific types of notice are as follows:

- Worker Adjustment and Retraining Notification Act (WARN)
- Federal and state banking regulations
- Employee Retirement Income Security Act (ERISA)
- Health Insurance Portability and Accountability Act (HIPAA)

In Europe, the Acquired Rights Directive and Work Council regulations typically include specific notice, authorization, consultation, and consent requirements.

(f) DUE DILIGENCE CHECKLIST. A list of issues for the customer's human resources team to consider is set forth as follows. Many customers find it useful to involve the vendor in this due diligence.

- Will any customer employees be needed by the vendor for only a short transition period?
- Are any customer employees on an approved leave from active employment with the customer for reasons other than layoff (e.g., leave of absence, family and medical leave, or disability leave)? When will the vendor be required to extend offers of employment to them (e.g., at the time other offers are extended or on the first day they return from their absence)?
- Are any union employees or other employees subject to collective bargaining agreements?
- Should there be a hiring freeze in the months leading up to the effective date?
- How long will the customer employees have to consider an offer of employment from the vendor (this period may be very short, e.g., 5 to 10 days)?
- Who will be making the offer of employment, the vendor or a subcontractor? What will the customer's relationship be with the subcontractor (particularly for liability purposes)?
- When will the affected employees commence employment with the vendor? Will all employees start on the same day? When will employees on an approved leave of absence start their employment (e.g., on the first day they return from the leave or at a later date if the employment offer is delayed until the return date)?
- Will there be any hiring requirements (e.g., background checks, credit checks, drug testing)?
- Will the vendor require the customer employees hired by the vendor to sign an employment/confidentiality agreement? If so, a copy of such agreement(s) should be obtained.
- Will the customer want any type of release from the transitioned employees (e.g., as a condition of receiving an offer of employment from the vendor)?
- How will starting salaries be set? How will differences in the timing of merit increases be handled?
- How will bonuses be handled? Will there be any salary adjustments to reflect bonuses or matching programs not provided by the vendor? Will

other adjustments be necessary to account for differences in the timing of payment of bonuses between the customer's and the vendor's bonus plans?

- When will the affected employees be put on the vendor's payroll? (There may be some timing issues with respect to payroll administration.)

- When will the first performance reviews be given?

- What are the opportunities for promotion within the vendor?

- Will the vendor be required to extend offers of employment with comparable positions?

- Does the customer reimburse for tuition? If so, who will pay the tuition for courses commencing before the date the employees are transitioned but continuing after such date?

- How will vehicles and personal computers be handled? Are there any housing subsidies or loans? Are there any meal allowances?

- How will savings plans be handled? Will the vendor accept the rollover of account balances and/or outstanding loans?

- Have any former customer employees retired from the customer who may be hired by the vendor? Does the customer wish to limit the vendor's hiring such persons?

- How will claims for health care benefits that arose before the effective date of the agreement be handled?

- How will payments toward medical deductibles be handled? How will co-payments be handled?

- How will credit for service be handled for eligibility, vesting, and benefit accrual (e.g., voluntary pension, deferred vested pension, surviving spouse's benefit)?

- How will the vendor deal with preexisting conditions and waiting periods?

- How will pension plans be handled?

- Does the vendor treat its retirement plans differently from its other benefits plans with respect to the manner in which years of service are credited?

- How will retiree medical benefits be handled?

- Are there any stock purchase or stock option issues?

- What is the vendor's vacation policy? How will time off that is accrued but unused before transition to the vendor be handled?

- How will vacation and designated holidays be prorated during the first year of the agreement?

- What holidays do the vendors observe?

- What is the vendor's working day? Is it the same length as the customer's working day?

- What is the vendor's dress code? How will it be implemented for employees working at a customer location?

- Do any miscellaneous benefits (e.g., health facility, employee discounts, access to cafeteria, parking) need to be addressed?

- Will the customer require information regarding employees after the transfer to the vendor for benefits administration or other purposes?

- How will severance/redundancy be handled? What are the customer's severance/redundancy obligations?

- Will the vendor provide any redeployment assistance or outplacement services to terminated employees?

- Review relevant customer–vendor policies, which may include:
  - Human resources procedures manuals
  - Employee handbooks
  - Equal employment opportunity (EEO) policies
  - Disciplinary/grievance procedures
  - Safety policies
  - Performance appraisal process
  - Union/collective bargaining agreements
  - Recruiting and offer letters

7.3 THE EMPLOYMENT OFFER

The employment offer is often one of the most negotiated provisions of the outsourcing contract. A useful negotiation tactic is to take a position on certain important terms in the RFP and, for other terms, ask the vendor what its position is. This tactic is helpful when the customer is not certain what its position will be on an issue or does not necessarily want to take a position early in the process. It also forces the customer to perform substantial, necessary due diligence at the RFP stage and allows the customer to use the vendors' responses to the human resources section of the RFP as part of the selection process.

The parties will need to draw on information contained in the RFP, the vendor's proposal, and further due diligence performed as part of the negotiation process when drafting the human resources section of the outsourcing agreement. The following sections show issues that the parties should consider when drafting the human resources terms.

(a) **EMPLOYEES TO BE TRANSITIONED.** The employees who will have offers made to them are typically listed in an exhibit to the agreement. This exhibit often lists each affected employee by identification number, together with his or her salary (adjusted for bonuses and matching contributions), the date that the employee started work with the customer, and the number of accrued vacation days. The employment start date should be specified with extensions of the start date for employees on leaves of absence or disability leave. Special provisions will need to be negotiated and included if affected employees are covered by collective bargaining agreements.

(b) VENDOR VS. SUBCONTRACTOR HIRING.   In some cases, a subcontractor rather than the vendor will make offers of employment to certain employees. This is more likely to occur in international transactions in countries where the vendor does not have a presence or in transactions where a significant part of the services are being subcontracted (e.g., network services). The customer should require the vendor to reveal any planned use of subcontractors in its proposal. The customer will need to consider what relationship, if any, it wishes to have with the subcontractor. The customer also may wish to obtain an indemnity from the vendor for any claims resulting from the subcontractor's actions.

(c) START DATE.   In most cases, the customer will prefer that the employees being transferred to the vendor become vendor employees as of the date the vendor commences providing services. The vendor will in most cases resist a start date on or close to the date the agreement is signed on the grounds that the vendor needs time to prepare for the transition (e.g., preemployment screening, transfer of benefits). The transition period proposed by the vendor typically ranges from 30 to 90 days after the date the agreement is signed. In special circumstances, the parties may agree to allow the vendor to commence the transition process before signing the agreement. The customer, therefore, will need to begin to notify the employees to be transitioned of the proposed outsourcing transaction before the vendor takes any action. Any communications with the customer's employees before the signing of the agreement should be prefaced with a notice that all activity is contingent upon signing an agreement with the vendor.

(d) HIRING REQUIREMENTS.   Often vendors will make offers of employment contingent upon the employee meeting certain preemployment screening requirements. Examples of such requirements include the following:

- Credit check
- Background check
- Drug screening
- Reference check

Many customers are able to successfully negotiate the vendor's acceptance of employees as is, without any preemployment screening. The ability of the customer to get the vendor to waive preemployment screening may depend on the strength of the customer's own policies. (If the customer administers drug tests as a condition of employment, the vendor is more likely to be willing to waive its own drug testing.)

> *Sample Clause.* Vendor shall hire the Customer Employees who:
>
> 1. Are employed by Customer and have not been reassigned to an out-of-scope position within Customer as of the date the offer is made,
>
> 2. Accept the offer of employment from Vendor within __ business days from the date the offer is made; and
>
> 3. If requested by Customer, sign a release substantially in the form set forth in Schedule __
>
> (clauses (1) through (3) collectively, the "Hiring Requirements") (the Customer Employees hired by Vendor collectively, the "Transitioned Employees"; each, a "Transitioned Employee"').
>
> Vendor shall make hiring decisions regarding the Customer Employees based on the Hiring Requirements. Vendor shall be solely responsible for making such hiring decisions, subject to the provisions of this Section.

(e) VENDOR EMPLOYMENT AGREEMENT. The customer should inquire as to whether the vendor will require the transitioned employees to sign an employment or confidentiality agreement as a condition of employment. If the vendor does require any such agreements, the customer should request a copy of the proposed agreements for its review and comment. Provisions that warrant particular consideration include noncompetition, ownership, and training provisions.

(f) BASE SALARY. The agreement should specify the base salary to be offered to each of the transitioned employees and when the employees will be eligible for increases and should include adjustments for bonuses and other amounts agreed upon by the parties to account for disparities in employee benefits.

> *Sample Clause.* Each offer of employment to a Customer Employee shall include an initial base salary of not less than the base salary that each such Customer Employee received from Customer as of the Agreement Date, with any adjustments thereto made by Customer in accordance with Customer's normal salary adjustment policies. The Customer Employees' base salaries as of the Agreement Date, **[plus the applicable adjustments],** are set forth in **Schedule *****.

(g) POSITIONS. A concern of many employees is whether they will be offered employment for comparable positions. A manager may not wish to accept an offer of employment for a nonmanagement job even if the compensation is comparable. In addition to being an issue of employee morale, the customer's severance plan may provide that severance payment will not be due if the employee is offered employment in a comparable position with comparable compensation.

> *Sample Clause.* **[TRACK LANGUAGE IN SEVERANCE PLAN IF APPLICABLE]** Vendor shall offer the Customer Employees employment in positions that are comparable to the positions in which such Customer Employees are employed as of the Agreement Date.

(h) MINIMUM EMPLOYMENT PERIOD.   When structuring the human resources portion of the deal, the customer should consider whether it wishes the vendor to commit to employing certain employees transitioned to the vendor for a certain period. Obtaining such a commitment from the vendor typically improves employee morale. The customer may wish to require the vendor to keep certain transitioned employees assigned to its account for a period (e.g., for a minimum of one to two years, through the migration to the vendor, through the migration to a new platform/system to be implemented by the vendor). In some instances, the vendor may suggest separating the employees into two classes: (1) temporary employees, who will only be employed for a set number of months, and (2) regular employees, for whom the customer may wish to obtain a longer employment commitment from the vendor.

(i) HEALTH CARE BENEFITS.   The agreement should specify which health benefits the transitioned employees will be eligible for, when the employees are eligible, and whether preexisting conditions and waiting provisions have been waived.

> *Sample Clause.* Each Customer Employee shall be eligible as of his or her Start Date for enrollment in Vendor's healthcare plans, including *[major medical, hospitalization, dental, vision, long-term disability, prescription, life insurance, and personal accident coverage]*. Vendor shall provide each Customer Employee with health care coverage so that on the Start Date for the Customer Employee, he or she (and any qualified dependents) is covered by Vendor's healthcare plans, and all pre-existing condition exceptions, exclusionary provisions, and waiting periods are waived with respect to the Customer Employee (and any qualified dependents). Vendor shall be responsible for any medical or health expenses incurred by the Transitioned Employees on or after the Start Date.

(j) DEDUCTIBLE/CO-PAYMENT REIMBURSEMENT.   Unless the employee start date coincides with the beginning of a new plan year, the customer should consider including a provision in the agreement that gives the transitioned employees credit under the vendor's plan for deductibles and co-payments made during the existing plan year.

(k) VACATION.   Because vacation is often calculated based on the employee's years of service, this is an area where the customer may wish to negotiate that transitioned employees will receive credit for years of service with the customer for the purpose of calculating vacation with the vendor. The parties will also need to consider how accrued (but not taken) vacation will be dealt with. Will the vendor pick up the accrued vacation at least for the remainder of the calendar year? Will the customer buy the employee out of accrued vacation?

> *Sample Clause.* Vendor shall calculate paid time off for vacation [and sick leave] purposes for each Customer Employee using each Customer Employee's length of service with Customer and Vendor.

(l) SAVINGS PLANS. The customer will need to negotiate with the vendor how, if at all, the vendor will deal with the savings plan benefits of the transitioned employees. In some instances, the vendor will agree to roll over the benefits of all or some employees into the vendor's plan. The ability and willingness of the vendor to roll over the transitioned employee's benefits will depend largely on the terms of the vendor's plan. If rollover is agreed to, the customer will need to assess whether the administrative costs for the rollover are included in the base fee. Additional issues to consider include the following:

- If the customer has a matching contribution policy, does the vendor have a similar policy or, if not, is the transitioned employee receiving other benefits of comparable value?
- How will unvested matching contributions with the customer be handled?
- How will employee loans be handled?

(m) PENSION PLANS. Questions to ask with respect to pension benefits include the following:

- How will the existing pension benefits of the transitioned employees be handled?
- Can they be transferred to the vendor's plan?
- What are the vendor's pension benefits?
- Are the transitioned employees immediately eligible to participate?
- Will the transitioned employees immediately vest, will vesting be determined by recognizing service with the customer, or will vesting be based only on service with the vendor?
- Without immediate vesting and recognition of customer service, which employees are disadvantaged?

Typically, the vendor will grant credit for years of service for vesting and eligibility purposes under the vendor's plan but not for accrual purposes.

> *Sample Clause.* Vesting and eligibility under *[Vendor-Defined Benefits Plan]* shall be determined by the Customer Employee's length of service with Customer and Vendor.

(n) RETIREE MEDICAL BENEFITS. Does the customer provide retiree medical benefits? How will retiree medical benefits be handled by the vendor? Does the customer expect the vendor to assume responsibility for retiree medical benefits?

(o) SEVERANCE/REDUNDANCY. The customer will need to perform due diligence (see Section 7.2) to determine what its severance/redundancy obligations are in an outsourcing context under its plans as well as pursuant to any legal or regulatory requirements. Provided that the customer does not owe severance/

redundancy payments to the transitioned employees, the customer will need to consider how severance/redundancy payments will be handled after transition. Many customers choose to negotiate enhanced severance/redundancy for transitioned employees, so that if an employee is terminated by the vendor within a certain number of years from contract signing, the employee will receive supplemented severance/redundancy payments either comparable to, or a percentage of, what the employee would have received if he or she was still with the customer. The customer and the vendor will need to negotiate the administration of and financial responsibility for "enhanced" severance. Will the cost be built into the base fees or will the customer reimburse the vendor on a pass-through basis? The customer should also consider restricting enhanced severance/redundancy to those employees who are still on the customer's account at the time of termination, which will depend largely on the vendor's staffing plans.

(p) SERVICE CREDIT.   Of particular importance to customer employees with a number of years of service is the extent to which the vendor will give them credit for their years of service with the customer for eligibility, participation, vesting, and accrual purposes for certain benefits (e.g., vacation, savings plans, pension plans, severance).

> *Sample Clause.* Except with respect to those plans for which the Customer Employee shall immediately vest pursuant to this Article, the Customer Employee shall be eligible for Vendor's vacation and holiday program, disability plan and retiree health plan and other welfare plans based on the Customer Employee's "service date" with Customer.

(q) TUITION AID.   If the customer currently provides tuition aid to the transitioned employees, the parties may wish to clarify each of their responsibilities with respect to classes in progress and classes that have been approved but have not commenced.

(r) LOCATION.   The customer's severance plan may provide that severance payment is due if the employee is not offered employment within a certain geographic distance from his or her current position. In order to avoid unanticipated severance liability, the customer should review its plan and, if appropriate, include language in the agreement regarding location. If the location of the job will not be in or near the employee's current position, the parties may also need to discuss how relocation expenses will be handled.

> *Sample Clause.* **[TRACK LANGUAGE IN SEVERANCE PLAN IF APPLICABLE]** The Customer Employee shall be offered a position as of the Start Date that is at the same location to which the Customer Employee was assigned by Customer prior to that time or at a location within a reasonable commuting distance [definition to be negotiated] from the Customer Employee's home.

(s) MISCELLANEOUS BENEFITS.   The customer should be sure that it has considered all of the benefits it offers to employees. This is particularly important in international transactions, where a large portion of compensation is often provided in in-kind benefits.

(t) WORK HOURS.   What are the vendor's work days and work hours? If they conflict with the customer's work days or hours, the customer may wish to consider including a provision requiring the vendor to allow the transitioned employees to follow the customer's work days and hours while on the customer's premises. Does the vendor permit flex time and job sharing arrangements?

> *Sample Clause.* The work days, including daily work hours and holidays, of the Customer Employees located at any Customer location shall be the same as the work days and work hours in effect at that Customer location.

(u) DRESS CODE.   What is the vendor's dress code? If it conflicts with or is stricter than the customer's dress code, the customer may wish to consider including a provision requiring the vendor to allow the transitioned employees to follow the customer's dress code while on the customer's premises.

(v) PERFORMANCE APPRAISALS.   An issue that may be a concern of the employees is when performance appraisals will be administered. This is of interest particularly if the employees were scheduled to receive a performance review within a few months after contract signing and the reviews are tied to merit increases.

(w) REPLACEMENTS.   The parties will need to consider how jobs for employees not accepting offers from the vendors will be filled. Typically, the vendor will be responsible for filling these positions at its expense.

> *Sample Clause.* Vendor shall be responsible for filling the positions of any Customer Employees not hired by Vendor pursuant to this Article at comparable skill levels. Vendor shall be responsible for the salary and benefits for such replacements.

(x) HUMAN RESOURCES REPRESENTATIVE.   The customer should consider requiring the vendor to appoint one (or more depending on the size of the transaction) representative who will be responsible for the transition. The representative should be located at the customer's site and not replaced or reassigned until the transition is complete.

> *Sample Clause.* The Vendor representative responsible for the transition of the Customer Employees from Customer to Vendor shall be _____ (the "HR Representative"). The HR Representative shall be located at _____. Vendor shall not replace or reassign the HR Representative without Customer's consent (except due to voluntary resignation, death or disability) until _____ months days after the Start Date. There shall be no additional charge for the services of Vendor's human resources team.

(y) ADMINISTRATIVE AND FINANCIAL RESPONSIBILITY. The agreement should set forth each of the parties' administrative and financial responsibilities with respect to the transitioned employees. This includes payroll responsibilities (often there is a lag between the start dates and when the employees are transferred over to the vendor's payroll system), severance administration and financial responsibilities, and responsibility for stay incentives.

> *Sample Clause.* Customer shall continue to pay wages, provide benefits and make employer contributions on behalf of the Customer Employees until the Start Date, and Vendor shall promptly reimburse Customer for all such wages, benefits and employer contributions paid by Customer from the [Agreement Date] until the Start Date. Customer's obligation to continue to pay wages, provide benefits and make employer's contributions shall terminate on the Start Date.

7.4   COMMUNICATION AND TRANSITION PLAN

The customer and the vendor will need to prepare a rollout schedule for implementing the transition (or, if applicable, termination) of the employees. General guidelines for communicating and transitioning are set forth as follows:

- General Tips for Communicating with Employees

  - Keep records of all information communicated to the employees by the customer and the vendor. A representative from the customer should attend and keep a record of all meetings the vendor has with the customer's employees. (The customer may want to consider taping such meetings.)

  - All communications sent to customer employees should be reviewed and approved by the customer in advance.

- Communication/Transition Plan

  - Identify and orient customer–vendor transition teams

  - Develop a communication/transition plan that deals with the concerns of senior management, IT management, and employees to be retained, transitioned, and laid off at each site

  - Define a timetable for communications and transition

  - Develop communication materials (in the appropriate languages), including employee handouts, employee bulletins, e-mail announcements, vendor materials, and questionnaires

  - Conduct initial employee meetings (determine at which meetings the vendor should be present)

  - Address union/collective bargaining issues

- Once the agreement is signed, the customer and vendor should conduct meetings with senior management, IT management, and employees to be retained, transitioned, and laid off at each site
- Vendor to make employment offer
- Vendor to send out offer letters or, in certain countries outside of the United States, transfer letters confirming the transfer of employment
- Employees to accept employment offer within a specified number of days
- Customer to transition administrative responsibility to the vendor (e.g., payroll)
- Customer and vendor to ensure that all notification, authorization, and consent requirements have been complied with

7.5 CONTRACT-RELATED ISSUES

In addition to the section or exhibit of the outsourcing contract that outlines the terms upon which the employees will transition to the vendor, human resources–related issues typically are addressed in several of the general sections of the outsourcing contract. As discussed as follows, these general sections may include the representations and warranties, the indemnities, and rights upon termination.

(a) REPRESENTATIONS AND WARRANTIES. The customer is often asked to represent that there are no pending claims by the employees being transitioned. If there are claims, these claims are typically identified in an exhibit to the outsourcing agreement.

(b) INDEMNITIES. Each party should indemnify the other party against (1) representations made by the party to the employees, (2) violations of federal, state, or other laws or regulations for the protection of persons or members of a protected class or category of persons by the indemnifying party's employees and the employees of the party's agents and subcontractors, (3) work-related injury, illness, or death caused by the indemnifying party (except as may be covered by the indemnifying party's workers' compensation insurance), and (4) any claim by the transitioned employees arising out of the employment relationship [for the customer, add: "before the start date"] [for the vendor, add: "on or after the start date"].

(c) RIGHTS UPON TERMINATION OF THE OUTSOURCING CONTRACT. The customer should consider whether, upon the termination or expiration of the agreement with the vendor, the customer wants the right to solicit employees of the vendor. In addition, the customer may wish to restrict the vendor's ability to solicit certain employees of the customer.

7.6   STAY INCENTIVES

Often the customer and the vendor wish to provide incentives to certain employees to stay through a critical period. Examples of the types of employees to whom stay incentives are typically offered include the following:

- Employees who are to be laid off because the data center (or other location) that they service will be closed but whose services are necessary until the closing
- Key employees either retained by the customer or transitioned to the vendor who are critical to the transition process or to a particular project
- Employees to be hired by the vendor on a short-term basis whose services are necessary for that term
- All employees who stay with the vendor through the transition to the vendor or migration to new systems

A discussion of the different types of stay incentives that may be used is provided in Appendix 7.1.

APPENDIX **7.1**

STAY INCENTIVES

I. EXAMPLES OF STAY INCENTIVES

This appendix includes examples of various types of stay incentives to consider when seeking to increase the likelihood that employees being transferred to the vendor ("Affected Employees") will accept employment with the vendor and remain in the vendor's employ through migration.

STAY INCENTIVE	SAMPLE CONTRACT LANGUAGE
1. Lump-sum payment to all Affected Employees; same percentage/amount offered to all Affected Employees; payable upon transfer to the vendor	Each Affected Employee will be hired by the vendor at a base salary rate equal to 105 percent of the base salary rate he or she was receiving as of his or her last date of employment with the customer. The vendor will pay each Affected Employee an additional amount equal to 15 percent of his or her base salary with customer within 30 days of his or her effective date of employment. Affected Employees designated as part-time will be paid a prorated payment based on the ratio of hours worked per week at customer.
2. Lump-sum payment to all Affected Employees; same percentage/amount offered to all Affected Employees; **payable if the Affected Employee has not quit or been terminated for cause prior to the completion of the migration of the Affected Employee's location**	The vendor will pay each Affected Employee an amount equal to 10 percent of his or her base salary as of his or her last date of employment with the customer if the Affected Employee has not voluntarily resigned or been terminated for cause prior to the migration completion date for the Affected Employee's location.
3. Lump-sum payment to all Affected Employees; **varied percentage/ amount offered to Affected Employees; payable upon transfer to the vendor**	
4. Lump-sum payment to all Affected Employees; varied percentage/amount offered to Affected Employees; **payable if the Affected Employee has not quit or been terminated for cause prior to the completion of the migration of the Affected Employee's location**	

STAY INCENTIVE	SAMPLE CONTRACT LANGUAGE
5. Lump-sum payment to **selected** Affected Employees; varied percentage/amount offered to selected Affected Employees; payable if the Affected Employee has not quit or been terminated for cause prior to the completion of the migration of the Affected Employee's location	Customer will pay stay bonuses in an amount not to exceed $____ to selected Affected Employees on the migration completion date.
6. Enhanced severance (customer's severance plus a supplemental payment) for all Affected Employees, payable if the Affected Employee does not, prior to completion of the migration, (a) receive an offer to continue in the vendor's employment or (b) is terminated by the vendor (other than for cause)	If an Affected Employee **[does not accept an offer from or]** is terminated by the vendor without cause (a) after completion of the minimum employment period and (b) prior to or on the migration completion date for such Affected Employee's location, such Affected Employee shall receive: • A completion allowance equal to _____ weeks of the Affected Employee's base salary for each full year and partial six-month period of employment with customer, provided that the maximum allowance may not exceed _____ weeks of such Affected Employee's base salary, and • A health benefit allowance equal to the amount of the employer's contribution for the Affected Employee's health insurance during his or her employment, which shall be payable as a part of said employee's COBRA payment to continue such coverage for a period of time equal to the number of weeks calculated above.
7. Severance "comparable to customer's severance" for all Affected Employees, payable if the Affected Employee does not, prior to completion of the migration, (a) receive an offer to continue in the vendor's employment or (b) is terminated by the vendor (other than for cause)	If an Affected Employee is terminated by the vendor (a) after completion of the minimum employment period and (b) prior to or on the migration completion date for such Affected Employee's location, such Affected Employee shall receive: • A separation allowance equal to ____ weeks of the Affected Employee's base salary for each full year and partial six-month period of employment with customer, provided that the maximum allowance may not exceed ____ weeks of such Affected Employee's base salary.
8. Same as (7), which is only payable if the Affected Employee is not offered another job or is terminated—and a lump-sum payment, **payable if the Affected Employee has not quit or been terminated for cause prior to the completion of the migration of the Affected Employee's location**	

STAY INCENTIVE	SAMPLE CONTRACT LANGUAGE
9. Good-faith efforts to encourage employees to stay	Customer will encourage Affected Employees to accept employment with the vendor and provide representatives of the vendor with access to such Affected Employees for the purposes of discussing potential employment.
10. No stay incentive	

II. ALTERNATIVE METHODS

Following are examples of other incentives that may be used by outsourcing customers to increase the likelihood that Affected Employees are available during the migration of systems operations to the vendor:

- Retention of certain key or critical support Affected Employees by customer
- Minimum guarantee period of employment with the vendor (subject only to termination for cause)
- Mandatory notice period of ___ months prior to termination
- Attractive employment/advancement opportunities
- Training
- Continuation of educational tuition advances and reimbursements for Affected Employees
- Payment of relocation expenses

III. CHECKLIST

Following are additional issues to consider prior to implementing a stay incentive program:

- Remember that the structure of incentives being offered to Affected Employees will vary from country to country. Local counsel from each of the locations should review and approve any incentive plan prior to it being announced to Affected Employees.
- Beware of misrepresentation claims: carefully communicate in writing terms of employment to Affected Employees who will receive stay incentives. Do not make oral representations.
- Be careful not to create special classes of employees based on protected classifications (e.g., age, race, sex).
- Prepare an agreement for Affected Employees to sign who are to receive stay incentives.
- Include a release of claims against customer in the agreement.
- Identify customer representative responsible for administering stay incentives.

- Beware of noncompetition provisions in vendor employment agreements.

- Beware of other restrictions in vendor employment agreements (e.g., requirement that certain training expenses be reimbursed if employee leaves the vendor).

- Identify all perks that Affected Employees currently receive and determine whether they will be offered once the Affected Employees are outsourced.

  - Recreational programs
  - Fitness centers
  - Travel programs
  - Banking benefits
  - Discounts
  - Automobiles
  - Transportation
  - Housing
  - Medical benefits
  - Medical deductible
  - Dental benefits
  - Stock options
  - Vacation
  - Holidays
  - Day care
  - Special care
  - Performance reviews
  - Bonuses

- Discuss incentive plans with the vendor.

ISSUES TO CONSIDER WHEN SELECTING RETAINED EMPLOYEES

Listed as follows are issues and questions that organizations contemplating outsourcing should consider when determining which employees to retain and which employees to transfer to the vendor. This list is intended to illustrate the types of issues and questions that customers typically raise when making this decision and is by no means exhaustive. The issues and questions will likely vary depending on the size, skill group, and internal environment of the customer.

1. The vast number of retained employees are typically managers and key technical employees.

   ○ The vendor will request the company to identify a project executive who will represent and make final decisions on behalf of the company with respect to the outsourcing contract.

   ○ In addition, the company is typically asked to identify two or three additional employees from the company who will serve with the project executive on a management committee.

   ○ Many companies also find it helpful to retain managers or key technical employees who understand and are able to manage the day-to-day operations (e.g., review of reports, batch scheduling, end-user contacts) of the company being outsourced.

2. The number of employees retained varies from company to company depending on the size, geographic diversity, and complexity of the IT department. The numbers range from 6 to 60 employees for IT staffs ranging from 200 to 400 employees.

3. In order to ensure that the company is able to continue to review and manage all areas of IT operations, companies typically chose to retain at least one person from each IT division (e.g., data center, application development, telecommunications).

4. Perhaps the most important factor to consider when determining which employees to retain is which employees have the greatest overall understanding of the company's operations. Identifying these individuals is important in order to allow the company to make informed decisions. It

is also important in the event the agreement terminates, so that the company has the ability to oversee the transfer of operations to another vendor or back in-house.

5. If the customer's operations are dispersed throughout the world, the customer may wish to consider identifying individuals who are familiar (or can be easily familiarized) with the operations at each of the locations. One individual can typically be identified to oversee the locations in a particular region (e.g., European operations).

6. For many companies, determining which and how many employees to retain is largely a cost issue. Although not willing to jeopardize the quality of the retained staff, companies generally wish to minimize retained costs to the extent possible. Questions typically raised when considering the cost of retaining employees are:

    o How much would it cost to retain this employee (salary, bonus, other compensation)?

    o How much would it cost to terminate this employee (consider stock options, severance)?

    o Is this employee able to fill more than one role (eliminating the need to retain two or more employees)?

7. Finally, it is important that the retained employees are willing to communicate and work with the chosen vendor. If an employee is hostile to the outsourcing transaction, the employee may not be supportive at the beginning of the transaction (the migration to the vendor), which is when the retained employees typically play a critical role.

CHAPTER 8

INFORMATION PRIVACY AND SECURITY ISSUES

FRANÇOISE GILBERT[1]

---

1. © 2004–2005 Françoise Gilbert, IT Law Group, Palo Alto, CA. All rights reserved. Françoise Gilbert is the founder and President of IT Law Group PC, *www.itlawgroup.com*, a law firm based in Palo Alto, California. Ms. Gilbert focuses on the information technology and ecommerce markets. For more than 24 years, she has assisted global companies as well as start-up developers of innovative software products or services on leading-edge technology legal issues, including data governance issues—information privacy, information security, and other data management issues. Ms. Gilbert holds a graduate degree in Mathematics from Paris University (France) and law degrees from Paris University (France) and Loyola University in Chicago (Illinois). She is admitted to practice in California, Illinois, and France.

8.1   INTRODUCTION

For most companies, databases have become a critical asset, essential for record keeping, customer relations, product support, and other core functions. Typically, companies' databases might include nonpublic personal information about employees, clients, or prospects such as home addresses, unlisted phone numbers, family status, children's or dependents' names, race, ethnicity or national origin, employment history, salary, tax withholdings, financial statements, medical information, sexual orientation, hobbies, personal interests, travels, political opinion, philosophical beliefs, or membership in community or business organizations. In some cases, this information might be highly sensitive.

Given the strategic and monetary value of these compilations, databases have been copied, stolen, misused, or even altered. Disputes and litigation have ensued. Numerous federal and state laws were passed, and government and private actions have taken place, out of concern for the protection of individuals, to combat identity theft and for other purposes. In the United States, the Federal Trade Commission (FTC) and state Attorney General offices have conducted investigations of companies' data management practices, which have resulted in fines and other penalties when deficiencies were identified. Abroad, foreign data protection agencies have investigated local companies, including subsidiaries of U.S. companies within their jurisdiction, as well.

News of these disputes, investigations, and suits, widely reported in the press, have caused public relations disasters, disruption of the company's activities, and unexpected financial losses. Companies that were scrutinized and were found to have deficient data protection practices incurred substantial expenses and were required by court order to implement costly changes. In other instances, government action precluded or hampered contemplated transactions and delayed the transfer of assets.

Most outsourcing arrangements require the transfer or sharing of databases. Whether the services pertain to accounting, billing, payroll, call center, document management, or other operation, the vendor is likely to need access to some of the customer's employee, client, or prospect information.

Given the increasing importance of data privacy and security laws and litigation, companies contemplating outsourcing must carefully examine the potential legal barriers to such transaction, as well as the risks and exposure to liability and litigation. They also must understand and appreciate the obligations resulting from having the custody of third parties' personally identifiable information. To be able to receive the needed outsourced services, the customer must ensure that it can transfer its databases to the vendor. It must also ensure that, in addition to providing the specific services, the vendor will have the capacity and ability to perform in a manner consistent with the customer's unique privacy and security obligations and needs. The vendor, concurrently, must understand the nature of the responsibilities that are associated with handling the customer's personal data compilations. It must adequately estimate the costs that might result from addressing the customer's privacy or security requirements. When granted access to or custody of these databases, the vendor must comply with the numerous obligations that might be attached to handling personal information, and impose the same stringent obligations on its own subcontractors.

This chapter analyzes selected information privacy and security issues that affect the negotiation and performance of an outsourcing agreement. Privacy and security requirements in selected U.S. and foreign laws are explained. Practical suggestions are provided for due diligence and contract drafting.

8.2 SELECTED INFORMATION PRIVACY LAWS

(a) BACKGROUND.   Privacy law regulates the use and disclosure of and access to nonpublic personally identifiable information that pertains to an individual—frequently designated as a "data subject." Like confidentiality principles that apply to trade secrets, privacy requires the holder of the protected information to keep it confidential, use it for specific purposes only, and share it only with individuals who have a need to know.

In addition, privacy law encompasses individual rights. For example, the data subjects may be entitled to know which information is collected and how it is used. They may also have the right to review the personal information collected about them or to receive an accounting of the disclosures of this information that were made to third parties.

Privacy or data protection laws worldwide follow most or some of the principles that were developed in the studies, recommendation, and directives of the Organization for Economic Cooperation and Development (OECD),[2] the United Nations (UN),[3] and the European Union (EU).[4] In the United States, the federal government, the states, and other agencies and associations have enacted privacy laws or adopted privacy principles inspired from similar concepts.

Information security laws have many facets, most of which are beyond the scope of this book. However, because security is essential to the protection of personal data, certain aspects of information security laws are relevant to privacy protection. In this case, the goal is to ensure the confidentiality, integrity, and availability of the personal information. As for privacy, information security principles are generally commonly understood in the same manner in most countries. The OECD, for example, has established Guidelines for the Security of Information Systems and Networks[5] and has recommended that these guidelines be used by governments, business, other organizations, and individual users who develop, own, provide, manage, service, and use information systems and networks.

---

2.   *www.oecd.org.* The Council of the Organization for Economic Cooperation and Development (OECD) adopted Guidelines Governing the Protection of Privacy and Transborder Flows of Personal Data on September 23, 1980.

3.   *www.un.org.* The General Assembly of the United Nations adopted the United Nations Guidelines Concerning Computerized Personal Data Files on December 14, 1990.

4.   *http://europa.eu.int/comm/internal_market/privacy/index_en.htm.*

5.   *www.oecd.org/document/42/0,2340,en_2649_37409_15582250_1_1_1_37409,00.html.*

The U.S. legal framework for information privacy and information security is complex; it is impossible to provide a simple overview. The diversity and inconsistency stem from several factors. State courts, using torts principles, addressed the first privacy claims on a common law basis, and in many circumstances, still do rely on common law precedents. When privacy laws were first adopted in the 1970s and 1980s, the American legislators used a sectoral approach. As a result, there are scores of privacy laws. State legislature passed a myriad of privacy laws targeting specific concerns; some states incorporated privacy protection in their constitution and adopted subject matter privacy laws as well. The federal government also passed privacy laws and regulations, to address interstate business and communications. In many instances, such as for the health care or financial markets, state and federal laws may complement or overlap each other. As a result, there are wide discrepancies, depending on history, lobbying, and circumstances.

Numerous laws address or affect the security of information. These include, for example, computer crime laws, such as the Computer Fraud and Abuse Act of 1986 (as amended), the Electronic Communications Privacy Act of 1986, the Computer Security Act of 1987, the Economic Espionage Act of 1996, and the USA Patriot Act of 2001. Recently, information security concepts were introduced in regulations drafted by government agencies, such as the Department of Health and Human Services, in the case of the HIPAA Security Rule. States also have laws that address information security issues. For example, California requires companies to notify customers about security breaches that have caused the loss of certain personal data under its Identity Theft Act, also known as "SB 1386."[6] Since January 1, 2005, it also requires businesses to use safeguards to ensure the security of the personal information (name plus Social Security Number, driver's license or state ID number, or financial account number) of California residents and to contractually require third parties to do the same.[7]

(b) SERVICES TO THE FINANCIAL INDUSTRY. Numerous federal and state laws regulate the handling of financial information. These include, for example, the Right to Financial Privacy Act,[8] the Financial Modernization Act[9] (Gramm-Leach-Bliley), the Fair Credit Reporting Act,[10] and the recent Fair and Accurate Credit Transactions Act of 2003 (FACTA).[11] These laws limit the ability of businesses to collect and disseminate financial information such as credit information and credit worthiness information. There are also many state laws and regulations.

---

6.   California Bill SB 1386 has been incorporated into California's Civil as Sections 1798.82 and 1798.29, and became effective on July 1, 2004.
7.   California Bill AB 1950 has been incorporated into California's Civil Code at Section 1798.81.5, effective January 1, 2005.
8.   29 U.S.C. 3401 *et seq.*
9.   15 U.S.C. §§ 6801-6827.
10. 15 U.S.C. § 1681 *et seq.*
11. Pub. L. No. 108-159 (2003).

The Gramm-Leach-Bliley Act (GLBA) contains several privacy-related provisions that apply to all "financial institutions." The GLBA reaches a broad range of entities offering financial advice, credit counseling, credit cards, data processing, investments, lending, check cashing, wire transfers, tax preparation, debt collection, or providing credit, insurance, lay-a-way, financing, brokerage, financial aid, lease, or account services. Many companies, such as equipment manufacturers, value-added resellers, and hosted exchanges, or even some travel agencies, may be surprised to find that they too may be subject to GLBA's privacy and security requirements. In addition, the provisions also apply to third parties that do not meet the definition of a financial institution, but receive nonpublic personal data from financial institutions with which they are not affiliated or to which they are providing services. Numerous agencies have published separate sets of privacy and security regulations implementing GLBA's requirements: the Securities and Exchange Commission (SEC),[12] Treasury,[13] Treasury Office of Thrift Supervision,[14] Federal Deposit Insurance Corporation (FDIC),[15] FTC,[16] Federal Reserve Board,[17] the Office of the Comptroller of the Currency (OCC),[18] National Credit Union Administration (NCUA),[19] and Commodity Futures Trading Commission (CFTC).[20]

An entity that is subject to GLBA must provide an initial notice about the availability of the privacy policy and state whether it intends to share information outside the permitted exceptions. The organization must also provide an opt-out notice, with the initial notice or separately, before sharing nonpublic personal information with nonaffiliated third parties. Consumers must have a "reasonable opportunity" to opt out before the financial institution may disclose nonpublic personal information about them to nonaffiliated third parties. If a consumer elects to opt out of all or certain disclosures, the financial institution must honor this opt-out direction as soon as reasonably practicable after the opt-out is received. If the organization changes practices and the most recent notice provided to a consumer is no longer accurate or not adequately described in the prior notice, the organization must provide a revised notice. In addition, *annual notices*, restating or updating the policy, must be sent annually to customers for the duration of the relationship. Before attempting to outsource certain functions to third parties, a financial institution should first review the notices that it distributed to its clients to ensure that the representations and commitments made allow for the transfer of consumer personal data to an outsourcing company.

In addition, GLBA and its related regulations contain important provisions that require ongoing safeguards and protection of the personal information.

12. 17 CFR Ch. II, Part 248, et *seq.*
13. 12 CFR Ch. III, Part 40, et *seq.*
14. 12 CFR Ch. V, Part 573, et *seq.*
15. 12 CFR Ch. III, Part 332, et *seq.*
16. 16 CFR Part 313, et *seq.*
17. 12 CFR Part 216.
18. 12 CFR Par. 40.
19. 12 CFR Par. 716.
20. 17 CFR Par. 160.

These requirements would affect the cost of providing outsourcing services to a financial institution.

The law contains many restrictions on the use and disclosure of personal information, as well as a substantial number of exceptions to these restrictions. A vendor should be familiar with these restrictions and understand their scope and consequence on its ability to process the information or subcontract services to third parties.

In addition, GLBA requires the entities subject to the Act to implement substantial security measures. The agencies that implement GLBA (i.e., SEC, Treasury, Treasury Office of Thrift Supervision, FDIC, FTC, Federal Reserve Board, OCC, NCUA, CFTC) have published security standards. Under these rules, entities subject to GLBA must require their service providers, by contract, to implement and maintain such safeguards.[21] For example, Section 314.4(d) of the FTC Security Rule—which applies to the entities subject to GLBA and the FTC—states that in order to develop, implement, and maintain an information security program under GLBA, an entity must, among other things:

> *(d) Oversee service providers, by:*
>
> *(1) Taking reasonable steps to select and retain service providers that are capable of maintaining appropriate safeguards for the customer information at issue; and*
>
> *(2) Requiring [its] service providers by contract to implement and maintain the specific security safeguards listed in the FTC rule.*

The security standards contain other specific requirements for the implementation of security procedures. For example, Section 314.4 of the GLBA Security Rule published by the FTC requires that the entity:

- Designate an employee to coordinate the information security program;
- Identify reasonably foreseeable internal and external risks to the security, confidentiality and integrity of customer information that could result in the unauthorized disclosure, misuse, alteration, distribution or other compromise of such information, and assess the sufficiency of any safeguards in place to control these risks;
- Design and implement information safeguards to control the risks identified through the risk assessment phase, and regularly test or monitor the effectiveness of the safeguards' key control, systems and procedures; and
- Evaluate and adjust the information security program in light of the results of the testing and monitoring.

While these rules and requirements may be consistent with the safeguards that a reasonably prudent and cautious vendor would generally have in place, the specificity of GLBA and related agency rules that are unique to companies in the financial industry may place a substantial burden on both the vendor and the cus-

---

21. GLBA Security rules issued by the Federal Trade Commission. *www.ftc.gov/os/2002/05/67fr36585.pdf.*

tomer. They must comply with clear, specific guidelines, which provide a floor and define a standard.

Responding to an RFP for outsourcing services from an entity that is subject to GLBA will require a vendor to incorporate in the cost of operating the service, the costs, and other additional burdens of complying with the requirements of GLBA. The vendor should also ensure that it will receive specific guidance and instructions from the customer, which arguably should be more knowledgeable about the specific confidentiality, privacy, or security requirements that apply to the financial industry. The customer, however, should ensure that the outsourcing agreement contains specific clauses that ensure continued protection and safeguards of the personal financial information. For example, the outsourcing agreement may contain clauses that would:

- Place on the customer an obligation to keep the vendor informed of all laws, statutes, regulations, or jurisprudence that may affect the handling of personal information

- Define the scope of the services required, such as preparing and mailing annual or other notices, responding to inquiries or opt-out decisions, and ensuring security of operations consistent with the standards defined in the applicable agency rules

- Outline detailed confidentiality and security provisions to ensure the protection the financial information

- Identify how the parties would cooperate in the event of an investigation by a law enforcement agency or a customer inquiry

- Define the vendor's warranty on the services provided

- Define the scope of indemnification

- Identify services to be provided upon the termination of the contract to ensure proper transfer of the personal information to a new vendor and destruction of the data after the transfer

(c) SERVICES TO THE HEALTH CARE INDUSTRY. Although the provision of outsourcing services to the financial industry may require special precautions and result in additional costs, the performance of these activities in the health care field are more complex, more costly, and represent more risk. It is generally admitted that the laws and regulations that govern the privacy and security of health care information are, to date, the most detailed and comprehensive.

With some exceptions, such as Medicaid or Medicare systems, state laws have traditionally governed most matters surrounding health care. However, the growing inconsistencies amongst state health care laws, the evolution of the insurance industry, workforce mobility, the increased use of interstate communications, and other national priorities have forced the federal government to increase its involvement in the regulation of health care matters.

Passed in 1996, the comprehensive Health Insurance Portability and Accountability Act[22] (HIPAA) attempted, among other things, to create uniformity among the states and respond to the growing public concern over the privacy and security of medical records. HIPAA required the creation of statutes or regulations that would address the privacy and security of patient medical records. In addition, to preserve the delicate balance between federal and state laws, HIPAA provided a framework for the concurrent existence of state and federal laws. HIPAA preempts state laws that address the same issues, only to the extent that they provide less protection. If state law would provide more protection, then it would control.

(i) HIPAA Privacy Rule.   After years of consultations and numerous redrafts, the HIPAA Privacy Rule[23] was published in December 2000 and took effect as of April 2001. Completed in the last days of the Clinton Administration, the initial Privacy Rule was adopted, as is, by the Bush Administration on April 14, 2001, but was later modified, with the final text published on August 14, 2002, while keeping the initial compliance dates of April 14, 2003 (and April 14, 2004 for small plans). The Privacy Rule restricts the use and disclosure of patient health information, outlines patient rights, and defines administrative obligations for covered entities.

The HIPAA Privacy Rule applies to specific "covered entities," which are health plans, health care providers, and health care clearinghouses such as billing services, and repricing companies. Health plans include any company-sponsored health plans. The Rule imposes restrictions on the use and disclosure of patient individually identifiable information and defines when and whether an authorization is required, whether disclosure to third parties is permitted, or even mandatory. In addition, any person or company that provides services to the covered entities and that may be handling or getting access to patients' protected information might be subject to the HIPAA Privacy Rule as "business associate" of these covered entities. For example, a company that provides security, legal, or accounting services might be a business associate. The Business Associates provisions in the HIPAA Privacy Rule are especially relevant to companies that intend to purchase or provide outsourcing services. These provisions define the relative obligations and duties of the vendor and the customer.

To help understand the effect of the HIPAA Privacy Rule on outsourcing relationships, it is useful to have a general understanding of the entire regulation:

- *Consent.* Covered entities may communicate freely with patients about treatment options and other health-related information, including disease-management programs. However, their other uses or disclosures of patient health care information is limited, and require the patient's prior permission.

---

22.   42 U.S.C. §§ 1320 et *seq.*
23.   45 CFR §§ 160.103 et *seq.* and 45 CFR §§ 164.102 et *seq.*

- *Authorization*. Patients must give specific authorization before a covered entity may use or disclose protected information in most nonroutine circumstances—such as releasing information to an employer—or use the information in marketing activities.

- *Policies and procedures*. Covered entities must establish policies and procedures for protecting the confidentiality of patients' information and informing patients about their privacy rights. They must also appoint privacy officers to coordinate privacy-related activities and respond to individuals' inquiries.

- *Notice*. Covered entities must provide patients with written notice of their privacy practices and the patients' privacy rights. The patients are asked to sign or acknowledge receipt of the privacy notice from direct treatment providers.

- *Marketing*. Covered entities must obtain the patient's written authorization before using protected health information for marketing purposes except for a face-to-face encounter or a communication involving a promotional gift of nominal value. Communications by the covered entities about a patient's treatment options or the covered entity's own health-related products and services are not considered marketing.

- *Incidental use and disclosure*. Uses or disclosures that are incidental to an otherwise permitted use or disclosure are not considered a violation of the Rule if the covered entity has met the reasonable safeguards and minimum necessary requirements.

- *Minimum necessary*. Only the minimum amount of information necessary may be disclosed.

- *Patients' rights*. Patients have the right to have access to their records, to seek an amendment to those records, to receive an accounting of the disclosures made, to limit the use and disclosure of the records, and to receive responses to their requests pertaining to their right of access, notice, and amendment.

Most relevant to an outsourcing relationship is the requirement that a covered entity enter into a written contract with its business associates, in which the business associate will give adequate assurances that it will protect the patients' protected health information and assist the covered entity in handling its duties and obligations with respect to such information. If the vendor fails to comply with these requirements, the covered entity must terminate its contract with the vendor.

The Privacy Rule outlines with great specificity the required terms of the contract between the covered entity and a business associate. For example, this contract must establish the permitted and required uses and disclosures of the protected health information by the business associate. It must provide that the business associate will (1) not use or further disclose the information other than as permitted or required by the contract or by law; (2) use appropriate safeguards to prevent misuse or disclosure of the information; and (3) report to the covered entity any unauthorized use or disclosure of the information of which it becomes aware.

The business associate must commit to impose the same restrictions and conditions on any agent or subcontractor to which it discloses protected health information. It must also agree to cooperate with the covered entity to ensure compliance with the Privacy Rule. For example, the business associate must agree to make available protected health information for review by the patient. It must also assist the covered entity when required to provide the patient with an accounting of disclosures.

In addition, the business associate must agree to make its internal practices, books, and records relating to the use and disclosure of protected health information available for purposes of determining the covered entity's compliance with the Privacy Rule. It must also agree to return or destroy all protected health information on termination of the relationship.

These mandatory provisions would have to be included in any outsourcing contract between a covered entity and a vendor that qualifies as a "business associate" under the Privacy Rule.

(ii) HIPAA Security Rule.   After gathering dust for almost five years, and being substantially modified, the HIPAA Security Rule was finally published on February 20, 2003 (Security Rule).[24] These standards are separate from and in addition to those set in the Privacy Rule.

The Security Rule lists the measures that the covered entities must take to protect the confidentiality, integrity, and availability of the protected health information in electronic form in their custody or while transmitting it to third parties. These measures include administrative, physical, and technical safeguards (see Exhibit 8.1). Security policies and procedures, and organizational and documentation requirements are also mandated.

The nine *Administrative Safeguards* include requirements for the implementation of security management process, assigning security management responsibility, and establishing workforce security. Covered entities must implement information access management, as well as security awareness and training. Security incident procedures with documented report and response procedures must be in place to ensure that security violations are reported and handled promptly. A contingency plan must be in effect for responding to system emergencies, with a data backup plan, disaster recovery plan, and emergency mode operation plan. In addition, like for the Privacy Rule, the covered entity must obtain satisfactory assurances from its business associates that they will appropriately safeguard the information in accordance with these standards.

The five *Physical Safeguards* include facility access controls, and control of workstation use, workstation security, and other device and media. For example,

---

24. Federal Register, Volume 68, pp. 8334-8381 (February 20, 2003).

CATEGORY	STANDARDS
Administrative Safeguards	Security management process
	Assigned security management responsibility
	Workforce security
	Information access management
	Security awareness, and training
	Security incident procedures
	Contingency plan
	Evaluation
	Business associates contracts
Physical Safeguards	Facility access controls
	Workstation use
	Workstation security
	Device and media controls
Technical Safeguards	Access control
	Audit controls
	Integrity
	Person or entity authentication
	Transmission security

EXHIBIT 8.1 SECURITY STANDARDS

a covered entity must implement policies and procedures to document modifications to the physical components of a facility that are related to security, such as hardware, walls, doors, and locks. Each organization must also put in place physical safeguards to secure workstations and control the use of other equipment. This would involve, for example, policies and procedures that govern the receipt and removal of hardware and/or software (e.g., diskettes and tapes) into and out of a facility.

Five *Technical Safeguards* require policies and procedures for access control, which would involve, among other requirements, unique user authentication and emergency access procedures. Audit controls and mechanisms to authenticate the persons or entities sending the data are also required. Mechanisms to authenticate electronic data and ensure data integrity must be implemented, as well as methods for ensuring transmission security.

For each standard, the Security Rule defines implementation specifications. In all cases, the covered entity must meet the standards. Each standard is associated with implementation specifications, which are either required or "addressable." Covered entities must implement all required implementation specifications. For addressable implementation specifications, the organization must decide whether the security measure fits within the entity's particular security framework. Based on its evaluation, each covered entity can implement the specification if reasonable and appropriate; implement an alternate measure to accomplish the purposes of the standard; or not implement anything if the specification is not reasonable and appropriate and the standard can still be met.

The final responsibility for a covered entity's security must be assigned to one official, who will manage and supervise the personnel and the use of security measures to protect data. The covered entities must implement written policies and procedures, review these policies and procedures periodically, and update them as needed. They must also document in writing their actions, activities, or assessments taken or conducted. All documentation must be retained for six years from date of creation or from the date when last in effect.

The parties to an outsourcing relationship should incorporate the requirements of the Privacy and Security Rules in their agreement and address as well the respective duties and obligations of the parties, and the allocation of responsibilities in the event of a breach of contract. The HIPAA Privacy and Security Rules are much more comprehensive than the equivalent set of standards published for financial institutions. As a result, companies providing outsourcing services to the health care industry should exercise even greater caution.

(iii) HIPAA Penalties.   HIPAA provides for civil and criminal penalties.[25] Any person who violates a provision of the statute can be penalized up to $100 for each such violation; the total amount imposed for all violations of an identical requirement or prohibition during a calendar year may not exceed $25,000. The statute establishes defenses based on the reasonableness of the defendant's conduct.

There are criminal penalties for knowingly obtaining or disclosing health information relating to an individual. In most cases, a person who violates the criminal provision faces a fine of up to $50,000 and up to one year imprisonment or both. If the offense is committed under false pretenses, the fine can reach $100,000 and five-year imprisonment or both, cumulatively. If the offense is committed with the intent to sell, transfer, or use the information for commercial advantage, personal gain, or malicious harm, there may be fines up to $250,000 and up to 10 years' jail sentence. This provision punishes violations that are made knowingly. The act must be done purposefully or be the product of a conscious design.

Although there is little published information about enforcement or clarification of the HIPAA requirements, a recent mishap at Eli Lilly might serve as an example of the type of scrutiny that may result from a failure to implement adequate data security. This event, however, was not addressed under the HIPAA Privacy or Security Rules, which were not in effect at the time, but rather under Section 5 of the FTC Act, which prohibits unfair and deceptive practices.

An Eli Lilly employee's mistake resulted in the disclosure of individual e-mail addresses of the subscribers of a service that distributed information to Prozac patients. An e-mail that was meant to be sent confidentially to more than 600 patients instead prominently displayed the entire mail list in the "to" portion of the header.

---

25.   42 U.S.C. §§ 1320 —5 and 6.

Eli Lilly was sued for privacy violation both by the FTC and by several state Attorney Generals. In January 2002, the company settled with the FTC, agreeing to take steps to ensure the security of data, follow a specific four-stage information security program, and submit to an annual review "by qualified persons" of its information security program. The FTC did not assess any fine. In July 2002, Eli Lilly settled with eight states for the same event. In this case, the settlement provided for a payment of $160,000 to the states and required the company to strengthen its internal standards relating to privacy protection, training, and monitoring. Class actions are pending as well, which will substantially raise the legal costs incurred by the company, while continuing to draw the public's attention to the unfortunate mishap.

(iv) HIPAA Business Associates Agreements and Outsourcing Issues. HIPAA's requirements with respect to business associates are directly relevant to companies and vendors who enter into an outsourcing relationship. HIPAA mandates numerous precautions, restrictions, and obligations of which the vendor as a business associate must be aware. The vendors must agree to comply with the same stringent confidentiality or security requirements and transfer restrictions as those that the HIPAA Rules impose on their clients that are covered entities. For example, being able to respond, within the regulatory time frames, to a patient's request for an accounting of the disclosures of the patient's information in the vendor's custody would require having in place the technology, structure, and personnel necessary to handle the request.

A vendor that offers services to HIPAA-covered entities should take into account the requirements, restrictions, and obligations set forth in the HIPAA Privacy Rule and Security Rule before preparing a proposal for outsourcing services. However, the customer should ensure that the vendor will be able to assist in the compliance, respond to the requests, and ensure the required confidentiality and the like. During the relationship, the customer should continue monitoring the activities of the vendor to ensure continued compliance with the requirements. If the vendor defaults in its obligations, the customer should ensure prompt correction or terminate the contract as required under the HIPAA regulations.

(d) WEB SITES COLLECTING INFORMATION ABOUT CHILDREN. The Children's Online Privacy Protection Act[26] (COPPA), which governs what information online businesses may collect information about children younger than age 13 and the extent to which they can use that information, presents a different set of issues. COPPA imposes certain requirements on Web site operators and online service providers that collect "personal information" (such as name, address, e-mail address, or other identifying information).

COPPA applies to the collection of children's information online and the subsequent uses of that information. Its primary goal is to give parents control over

---

26.   15 U.S.C. sections 6501, *et seq.*

what information is collected online from their children and how such information may be used.

COPPA, however, applies not just to Web sites specifically directed toward children. It also applies to Web sites with a general audience where the Web site operator has actual knowledge that the site collects information from individuals younger than 13 and operators of general audience sites that have a separate children's area and that collect personal information from children younger than 13. Among other things, COPPA requires operators to:

- Post a privacy policy on the homepage of the Web site and link to the privacy policy on every page where personal information is collected

- Provide notice to parents about the site's information collection practices and obtain verifiable parental consent before collecting personal information from children

- Allow parents to choose whether their child's personal information will be disclosed to third parties

- Provide parents with access to their child's personal information, the opportunity to delete the information, and opt-out of future collection or use of the information

- Not condition a child's participation in a game, contest, or other activity on the child's disclosing more personal information than is reasonably necessary to participate in that activity

- Maintain the confidentiality, security, and integrity of personal information collected from children

A company that would subcontract or outsource the operation of its Web site, mailing list, or newsletter would have to ensure that the practices of the vendor are consistent with COPPA's requirements. For example, COPPA requires verifiable parental consent before a Web site operator may collect, use, or disclose children's personal information. If the vendor fails to implement a reliable process to obtain verifiable parent permission, the company would face the scrutiny of the FTC and state Attorney Generals for COPPA violations. Even though the penalties ultimately assessed might seem relatively small, the public relations disaster associated with a failure to comply with the law might cause the demise of a Web site.

The FTC and state Attorney General offices have actively monitored compliance with COPPA. Several companies were prosecuted for improperly gathering and using children's information. For example, in February 2003, Mrs. Fields Cookies and Hershey Foods Corporation each settled FTC charges that they violated COPPA by collecting personal information from children without first obtaining the proper parental consent. Mrs. Fields agreed to pay civil penalties of $100,000 and Hershey $85,000. The settlements bar future COPPA violations and require that the companies delete any information collected in violation of

COPPA. In addition, the companies must implement record-keeping requirements to allow the FTC to monitor compliance.

According to the FTC complaints, the Mrs. Fields and Hershey's Web sites failed to post adequate privacy policies to provide direct notice to parents about the information they were collecting and how it would be used, and to provide a reasonable means for parents to review the personal information collected from their children and to refuse to permit its further use. While the information collected on the *Mrs. Fields'* Web sites—*mrsfields.com, pretzeltime.com,* and *pretzelmaker.com*—was not disclosed to third parties, the company allegedly collected personal information—including full name, home address, e-mail address, and birth date—from more than 84,000 children, without first obtaining parental consent. *Hershey Foods Corporation,* on its 30 Web sites, many of which are directed at children, employed a method of obtaining parental consent that did not meet the standard delineated under the COPPA Rule.

Compliance with COPPA requires strict and meticulous processes. Before outsourcing and delegating its obligations, an entity covered by COPPA must ensure that the vendor will understand the procedures required by the law and follow them scrupulously. A service provider taking on the operation of a Web site for children should be cognizant of the COPPA requirements and anticipate the need for additional staffing to handle the specific registration needs. Consistency in the collection and use of the data gathered from the children, discipline in the operations, and adequate record keeping are essential. Children's names and personally identifiable information and their parents' involvement in the registration process and their consent should be kept together and up-to-date, and saved in an easily accessible format, for audit purposes. Using and applying a strict record-creation and management policy is crucial as well.

Given the increased scrutiny on compliance with COPPA, a company that outsources any portion of a Web site that collects information about children younger than 13 should take strict precautions to ensure compliance with the law, including detailed specific contractual provisions and regular audits of compliance by the vendor.

(e) OUTSOURCING HUMAN RESOURCE FUNCTIONS.   The concern for the protection of personal data does not apply solely to information of clients, patients, or other third parties outside a company. There are also circumstances where privacy and security concerns may affect the relationship of a company with its personnel, full-time, part-time, hourly or temporary employees, with respect to which the company may hold a substantial amount of information.

Numerous aspects of the employer–employee relationship involve the handling of sensitive personal data. Although many aspects of the employment relationship are governed by common law or are regulated by company policies, companies should also be cognizant that numerous state or federal privacy laws govern or apply to activities conducted in the employment context. For example, some laws regulate employers before they have hired potential employees. The

Fair Credit Reporting Act[27] (FCRA) and the Fair and Accurate Credit Reporting Act (FACTA)[28] contain a myriad of rules pertaining to background checks of prospective employees. There are laws about permissible and nonpermissible interview inquiries. Employee drug or psychological testing is regulated both before and during the employment relationship.

In addition, federal and state laws govern personnel records and communications, such as confidentiality, privacy, or employee access. Very serious privacy concerns come into play when issuing or responding to subpoenas for the employment records of current or former employees.

Many companies electronically monitor their employees' Internet and e-mail usage, as a necessity for complying with discrimination and sexual harassment laws or for other compelling business reasons. Employees—naively, perhaps—act as if their desks, drawers, e-mails, or other communications are private and are not accessed by third parties. Employers, however, frequently monitor their personnel (e.g., to prevent theft of company assets and reduce the risk of sexual harassment complaints). Such monitoring raises legal issues under state and federal statutes as well as the employees' right to privacy. Some states, such as Connecticut[29] and Delaware,[30] expressly require employers to notify employees if the employer will monitor Internet usage and e-mail.

Companies that outsource human resources functions should keep in mind the privacy requirements in the employment context and ensure that their service providers will abide by the laws. If the outsourced services are performed on-site, the vendor's employees may receive access to the client's premises, intranet, and e-mail and voice-mail system. In this case, issues of employee monitoring may become even more complex. For example, the company may, while monitoring its own employees, access communication from the vendor's employees. In this case, conversely, the privacy of the outsourcer's employees might be in jeopardy.

The outsourcing agreement should include specific instructions, directions, and procedures on the handling of employee information before, during, and after termination of employment. For example, consider the following:

- Document the e-mail and Internet access policy

- Document the policies with respect to company access, if any, to employee files, desks, offices, or correspondence

- Define the scope of the services required from the vendor, such as compiling employee records, responding to employee inquiries, or handling the processing of health insurance claims and the limitations to the use of the information

---

27.   15 U.S.C. § 1681 *et seq.*
28.   Pub. L. No. 108-159 (2003).
29.   Conn. Gen. Stat. § 31-48d (2001).
30.   141 Del. Laws HB 75 (2001).

- Incorporate into the outsourcing agreement detailed confidentiality and information security provisions to ensure the protection of employee information that is collected or processed by the vendor

- Address the vendor's obligations when performing services on the company's premises

- Identify how the parties would cooperate with each other if there was a need to access employee confidential information or to respond to a court subpoena

- Negotiate appropriate warranty and indemnification provisions

- Identify services to be provided upon the termination of the outsourcing contract to ensure proper transfer of the employee personal information to a new service provider

(f) MARKETING AND CUSTOMER RELATIONS. Companies that intend to outsource marketing and customer relationship activities should remain aware of the requirements in the new Controlling the Assault of Non-Solicited Pornography and Marketing Act (CAN-SPAM Act) and instruct their service providers to perform accordingly. The CAN-SPAM Act of 2003 establishes requirements for those who send e-mails whose primary purpose is advertising or promoting a commercial product or service, including content on a Web site, and identifies specific requirements for commercial e-mails. A commercial e-mail must include the following:

- *NO false or misleading header information.* The e-mail's "From," "To," and routing information—including the originating domain name and e-mail address—must be accurate and identify the person who initiated the e-mail.

- *NO deceptive subject lines.* The subject line cannot mislead the recipient about the contents or subject matter of the message.

- *An opt-out method.* The email must provide a return e-mail address or another Internet-based response mechanism that allows a recipient to ask not to send future e-mail messages to that e-mail address, and the sender must honor the requests. Any opt-out mechanism must be able to process opt-out requests for at least 30 days after the commercial e-mail is sent. The sender has 10 days after receiving an opt-out request to stop sending e-mail to the requestor's e-mail address.

- *An identification that it is an advertisement.*

- *The sender's valid physical postal address.*

Finally, it is illegal to sell or transfer the e-mail addresses of people who choose not to receive e-mail, even in the form of a mailing list, unless the addresses are transferred so another entity can comply with the law.

The Act also provides rules for sending "transactional or relationship messages"—e-mail that facilitates an agreed-upon transaction or updates a customer in an existing business relationship. These emails may not contain false or misleading routing information, but otherwise are exempt from most provisions of the CAN-SPAM Act.

Because the CAN-SPAM Act is recent, most companies have not yet implemented procedures that ensure compliance with the law. An outsourcing contract with a company that may have access to personal data should include adequate provisions that ensure that the outsourcer will comply with the specific requirements of the CAN-SPAM Act. Consider, for example, specific representations and warranties about the vendor's ability to handle opt-out requests, audit provisions that allow monitoring e-mails sent by the outsourcer on behalf of the company, or specific processes to ensure that databases are scrubbed from both opt-out notices received by the outsourcer as well as those received directly by the company.

(g) MONITORING ELECTRONIC COMMUNICATIONS.   Several laws govern access to electronic communications and telephone communications. The Electronic Communications Privacy Act (ECPA)[31] governs the interception of electronic and wire communications. It imposes duties on those involved in providing telecommunications services and restricts third parties' abilities to access or disclose telephone or other electronic communications. It also provides for criminal penalties and civil liability for those who intercept wire or electronic communications, or have access to stored communications, in violation of the Act.

The Federal Stored Wire and Electronic Communications Act[32] (Stored Communications Act) prohibits unauthorized access to electronic communications while in electronic storage. The Wiretap Act[33] provides, with some exceptions, for criminal punishment and a private right of action for the intentional interception of wire, oral, or electronic communications. In addition, many state laws limit access to electronic communications.

The Computer Fraud and Abuse Act[34] (CFAA) establishes criminal penalties for unauthorized access to computers or networks, and may give rise to civil claims for damage or destruction of information. In applying the CFAA, the courts have determined that companies can bring a civil claim for money damages and injunctions against a person who gained unauthorized access to the companies' computers in violation of the Act.

While most of these laws might come into play in connection with employee monitoring, as described previously, they have been used as well in privacy litigation to prevent access to electronic communications of Web site users. For example, DoubleClick[35] was accused of improperly obtaining information

---

31.   18 U.S.C. §§ 2510-2521, 2701-2711, 3121-3127.
32.   18 U.S.C. § 2701.
33.   18 U.S.C. 2511.
34.   18 U.S.C. § 1030.
35.   See, for example, *In re* Double-Click Privacy Litigation, 154 F. Supp 2d 497 (S.D.N.Y. 2001).

regarding Internet users through the use of Web-based technology, including cookies, and using the information to identify and track users and obtain users' confidential information without their consent. These suits were based on violation of ECPA and CFAA. After months of investigations by the FTC and state Attorney General offices, and class action suits, DoubleClick settled the pending cases, agreeing to pay substantial fines and damages, including more than $1.8 million in the plaintiff's attorneys' fees and court costs related to class action suits.

The recent Pharmatrak[36] privacy litigation is also of great interest. In this case, several pharmaceutical companies (Pfizer Inc., Pharmacia Corp., Smith-Kline Beecham PLC, Glaxo Welcome PLC, Novartis Corp., and American Home Products Corp) had outsourced to Pharmatrak the monitoring of certain Web site traffic. Pharmatrak sold a service that permitted users to compare the Web traffic on a company's Web site with that of its competitors' sites with similar content. The pharmaceutical companies installed code on their Web sites that caused a user's computer to contact Pharmatrak's servers when the user visited these sites. These servers, in turn, embedded a persistent cookie on the user's computer. These cookies permitted Pharmatrak to track the use of a client's sites and to determine which Web site the user visited just before and just after visiting the client's site. The pharmaceutical companies had specifically instructed Pharmatrak not to collect any personal information. Pharmatrak presented the data it obtained in monthly reports, which contained no personally identifiable information.

The complaint alleged that Pharmatrak violated the Wiretap Act by using cookies to monitor Web usage because Pharmatrak had intercepted electronic communications and acquired user information simultaneously with the communication. The pharmaceutical companies were named as defendants as well. Ultimately, after lengthy litigation, it was determined that there was no intentional interception of the communications.

The case is an example of the vulnerabilities and risks in outsourcing relationships. It also shows that how user data is collected, who is gathering the information, and what personal information is gathered is very important. If cookies or similar technologies are to be used, or if any personal information may be aggregated or disclosed to third parties, then the customer and vendor should ensure that such activities are clearly disclosed in the applicable privacy policies. Users should be given a meaningful opportunity to refuse or consent to cookie placement, data aggregation, or data disclosure, and the terms of the company's privacy policies and consumer consents should be meticulously followed. If the privacy policies do not contain sufficient disclosure, vendors should have to provide written assurances that personal information will not be intercepted, collected, or disseminated without the prior written consent of the client. Periodic audit of the vendor's practices would be prudent as well.

---

36. Copy of the appellate court decision at *http://caselaw.lp.findlaw.com/scripts/getcase.pl?court=1st&navby=case&no=022138&exact=1.*

8.3   SELECTED INFORMATION SECURITY LAWS

(a) SARBANES-OXLEY ACT.   Although it is not an information security law *per se*, the Sarbanes-Oxley Act has had a substantial influence in bringing companies' attention to the need for information security measures. In effect, Sections 302, 404, and 409 of the Sarbanes-Oxley Act require public companies to ensure that they have implemented appropriate information security control for their financial information.[37] By providing that CEOs and CFOs must attest to the quality of the financial data provided to the SEC and shareholders, the Sarbanes-Oxley Act has caused company management to focus on data collection, reporting, monitoring, and supervision, provoking in turn a massive revamping and updating of many public companies' information security procedures.

Section 302 requires that company management certifies the disclosures of financial information made in the company's quarterly and annual reports; section 404 requires that companies establish and maintain an internal control structure and procedures for financial reporting, and provide an assessment of the effectiveness of these controls. Section 409, in addition, provides for real-time disclosures of material changes in the financial condition and operations of the issuers.

The Sarbanes-Oxley Act has had a tremendous ripple effect on service providers who have access to or generate information needed for financial reporting of public companies. As a result, entities that use outsourcing are imposing on their service providers security and quality standards consistent with their own obligation to establish and maintain an internal control structure and procedures for financial reporting. Outsourcing agreements in turn must include adequate provisions to address these concerns, tighten the methods and procedures related to the creation, processing, and use of information needed in financial reports, and ensure the needed security for the related data. The following issues, for example, may have to be addressed with specificity to ensure quality of the data provided to, or used by, the public company client in its own reporting:

- Representations and warranties with respect to the accounting processes and other procedures used in financial reporting
- Policies to restrict, control, or monitor systems accessed by personnel
- Security awareness training for personnel
- Physical access policies to protect computer systems and data
- Due diligence and auditing
- Security incident reporting and remediation of these incidents

(b) REQUIRED SECURITY PRACTICES: CALIFORNIA INFORMATION SECURITY LAW.   In addition to the information security requirements specifically imposed by federal laws such as the Gramm-Leach-Bliley Act or HIPAA discussed previ-

---

37.   Sarbanes-Oxley Act, Pub. Law. 107-204 (2002).

ously, state laws are also beginning to require the implementation of security measures. For example, since January 1, 2005, California requires, with a few exceptions, all entities that own or license personal information about a California resident to implement and maintain reasonable security procedures and practices to protect the personal information from unauthorized access, destruction, use, modification, or disclosure. The protected information includes an individual's first name or first initial and his or her last name in combination with any one or more of the following data elements, when either the name or the data elements are not encrypted or redacted: (a) Social Security number; (b) driver's license number or California identification card number; (c) account number, credit or debit card number, in combination with any required security code, access code, or password that would permit access to an individual's financial account; or (d) individually identifiable information, in electronic or physical form, regarding the individual's medical history or medical treatment or diagnosis by a health care professional. Information that is lawfully made available to the public from federal, state, or local government records is not protected by this law.

Although the law does not indicate what constitutes adequate security measures, it is clear that any company that retains the services of an outsourcing vendor should require that vendor to provide at least the level of security that the company has adopted for its own operations. There are currently no legal standards broadly adopted to define what constitutes "reasonable security measures." There are many "technical standards" for information security, but none of them has yet become generally accepted in all industries. One that is commonly cited is ISO 17799 Code of Practices for Information Technology Management, which was adopted by the International Organization for Standardization (ISO) in 2000.[38]

The law specifically addresses the retention of third-party service providers. If an entity discloses personal information about a California resident to a nonaffiliated third party, it must contractually require the third party to implement and maintain reasonable security procedures and practices appropriate to the nature of the information, to protect the personal information from unauthorized access, destruction, use, modification, or disclosure. Consequently, companies that hold data about a California resident that is protected under this law must ensure that their outsourcing agreement contain the necessary provisions to impose on the provider the adequate security measures. Concurrently, outsourcing vendors who are working with, or contemplating transactions with, companies subject to this law should be aware of this requirement and plan adequately to ensure that they will be able to satisfy the need of their clients or prospects.

(c) BREACH OF SECURITY: CALIFORNIA'S IDENTITY THEFT LAW.   Since July 1, 2003, California's Identity Theft Act (also known as SB 1386)[39]

---

38. The text of the ISO 17799 standard is available for purchase from the ISO website: *www.iso.org.*
39. California's SB 1386 has been incorporated into the California Civil Code as Sections 1798.29 (for government agencies) and 1798.82 (for companies and businesses).

requires most entities that hold personal data pertaining to California residents to notify these individuals of computer security breaches that expose their personal data. This law requires a business or a state agency that maintains computerized data that includes specified personal information to disclose any breach of the security of that data to any California resident whose unencrypted personal information was, or is reasonably believed to have been, acquired by an unauthorized person. By giving consumers such notice, the law intends to give them the opportunity to take proactive steps to ensure that they do not become victims of identity theft. This law has important consequences for outsourcing relationships and will require the addition of appropriate provisions in outsourcing contracts.

The law affects any person or business that conducts business in California and owns or licenses computerized data that includes California residents' personal information or maintains computerized data that includes California residents' personal information that the person or business does not own. It requires the affected entities to notify their California customers if a breach of security occurred (or is suspected to have occurred) that resulted in the unauthorized access to the customers' data.

The law defines a "breach of security of the system" as the unauthorized acquisition of computerized data that compromises the security, confidentiality, or integrity of personal information. The affected entity must disclose any breach of security following discovery or notification of the breach to any California resident whose unencrypted personal information was, or is reasonably believed to have been, acquired by an unauthorized person. The disclosures to the affected customers must be made in the most expedient time possible and without unreasonable delay, consistent with the legitimate needs of law enforcement, or any measure necessary to determine the scope of the breach and restore the reasonable integrity of the data system.

In the case of an entity that maintains information on behalf of another, this entity must notify the owner or licensee of the information of any breach of security immediately following discovery, if the personal information was, or is reasonably believed to have been, acquired by an unauthorized person. This provision would be applicable to an outsourcer that processes or maintains data on behalf of a company that does business with California residents.

Two requirements must be satisfied for a notice to be given to an individual. First, the security breach must expose an individual's first name or first initial and last name in combination with any one or more of the following data elements: Social Security number; driver's license number or California identification card number; or account number, credit or debit card number, in combination with any required security code, access code, or password that would permit access to an individual's financial account. Publicly available information that is lawfully made available to the public from federal, state, or local government records is not protected by the law.

The second requirement for triggering a notice is that either the name data or the other data elements must not be encrypted at the time of the security incident. The law, however, does not provide guidance as to the nature of the encryption (i.e., where or how encryption is to be applied).

The law requires notice to be provided in writing. Electronic notices are appropriate only to the extent that the notice provided is consistent with the provisions regarding electronic records and electronic signature. The law also provides for substitute notice, if the affected entity can demonstrate that the cost of providing notice would be too onerous (more than $250,000 expense or affecting more than 500,000 persons). In this case, substitute notice is acceptable. The substitute notice may be given by e-mail, conspicuously posted on the Web site, or made through major statewide media.

The law creates a safe harbor for companies that have their own notification procedures in place as part of their information security policy. However, the notice must be given within the time frames required by the law. Companies face some challenging questions in determining what types of security incidents may trigger the notice requirements and what kinds of security control they must implement to provide appropriate protection to the relevant personal information.

Although the law involves only the processing of personal information of California residents, it is clear that it affects, indirectly, companies doing business with nationwide operations as well. It may be difficult to segregate California residents from the others clients or users. As a result, businesses may find it more prudent to notify all individuals affected by the breach of security, rather than just the mandatory California residents.

In the context of outsourcing, it is clear that this new law affects both the customer and the vendor. Outsourcing contracts should provide for taking reasonable steps to secure customer records and implementing procedures to promptly notify the affected customer if a breach of security occurs. In addition, the outsourcing contract should detail the respective parties' obligations in the event of a security breach, how the parties would proceed in the event of a security breach, how they would comply with the notice requirements, and how they would allocate the responsibility and liabilities for damages resulting from the incident.

8.4 COMPANY PRIVACY POLICIES

Because U.S. information privacy and security laws use a sectoral approach that relies on a mix of legislation, regulations, and common law, numerous fields are not yet regulated. The U.S. government has encouraged companies to self-regulate and to adopt policies tailored to their own business purposes and business ethics. Thus, even if a company does not operate in a market that has been regulated through information privacy or security laws, it may have voluntarily elected to address privacy and security concerns.

(a) COMPLYING WITH PUBLISHED POLICIES. Companies that are not subject to specific laws such as HIPAA or GLBA described previously, or similar laws, are free to adopt privacy or security policies and procedures adapted to their operations. There are no floor or minimum obligations, only many recommended best practices. Frequently, these policies are posted on company Web sites. They may apply to any types of data or only to the data collected from the Web site.

These policies and procedures are likely to differ drastically because there are no requirements, although most policies generally follow a similar structure. The company's published policy may contain representations about the nature of the data collected, the use of the data, or the security measures taken to protect the collected data. The company should remain aware of these restrictions when conducting its own activities and ensure that its practices conform to the representations made. It should also ensure compliance by third parties as well, such as outsourcing vendors. If the policy contains representations or commitments, adequate measures are required to ensure compliance with the statements made.

Companies intending to outsource certain operations should carefully examine their own privacy and security policies and procedures before entering into an outsourcing contract. They should, in addition, review and understand those of their proposed service provider to ensure that there are no discrepancies. The customer should ensure that its proposed vendor will be able to provide at least the same level of privacy and security protection for the personal data in its custody as those described in the company's privacy or security policy. For example, a company's policy might be not to use customer data for anything other than the services requested by the customer. The outsourcing vendor, however, may want to use the data for marketing or market research purposes. During performance of the contract, the company should frequently audit the vendor's practices to ensure that the vendor continues to collect, use, or process the data as agreed in the outsourcing contract. The vendor should evaluate whether it has adequate procedures and policies, sufficient technology, and staff to provide the required privacy and security in a manner consistent with the customer's published and other privacy or security policies.

(b) RESTRICTIONS TO TRANSFER OF DATABASES.   In many cases, company privacy policies contain statements about the use of the data collected. Some policies state that the company will not share any private data with anyone. For example, the privacy policy on the Web site of SRI International, a not-for-profit research and development organization, states: "SRI will not sell or rent your personally identifiable information to anyone."[40] Other companies carve out exceptions. For example, Amazon.com's privacy notice states:

> We employ other companies and individuals to perform functions on our behalf. Examples include fulfilling orders, delivering packages, sending postal mail and email, removing repetitive information from customer lists, analyzing data, providing marketing assistance, providing search results and links (including paid listings and links), processing credit card payments, and providing customer service. They have access to personal information

---

40.   *www.sri.com/privacy.html* (last visited February 15, 2004).

needed to perform their functions, but may not use it for other purposes. . . . Other than as set out above, you will receive notice when information about you might go to third parties, and you will have an opportunity to choose not to share the information.[41]

Before outsourcing its databases to a vendor, a company should verify that its policies permit such transfer. In the United States, several courts have prohibited, substantially hampered, or limited the transfer of databases, when the original owner of these databases had previously made public commitments, promises, or representations that it would not transfer any personal data to third parties.

These cases focused on the attempted transfer of personal data compilations by companies that has previously represented to their customers that their information would "not be transferred to any third party." Although these cases occurred in the context of bankruptcy, they might as well apply in connection with an outsourcing transaction where there is a *de facto* transfer of data or information to a third party—whether the transfer is physically performed through loading data onto the third party's computer or the transfer is virtually completed through giving access to the data located on the client's computer. Examples of transactions where there is a transfer of data include, for example, business process outsourcing such as customer service or customer hotlines. Unless the policy is carefully drafted, a provider of outsourced services might be deemed a *third party* to which the transfer would be restricted, if the company's preexisting policy included a commitment not to transfer the personally identifiable information to *any third party*.

This issue first arose in connection with the Toysmart bankruptcy.[42] Toysmart, an online seller of children's toys, collected information from adults and children visiting the Toysmart Web site, including their names, addresses, e-mail addresses, and shopping preferences. Toysmart's online privacy policy, posted on its Web site, proclaimed it would "never share" this information with a third party. When Toysmart sought bankruptcy protection, in the course of the proceedings, its trustee offered for sale the company's database of customer information. The FTC intervened to block the sale, arguing that the proposed sale of the customer list contradicted Toysmart's statements in its privacy policy. The FTC alleged that this transfer violated Section 5 of the FTC Act, which prohibits "unfair or deceptive acts or practices in or affecting commerce." After months of negotiations between Toysmart, the FTC, and the judge, Toysmart agreed that any buyer of Toysmart's customer information would have to be in the same business as Toysmart and would have to agree to follow all of the requirements of Toysmart's privacy policy. The FTC commissioners who participated in the case stated that they felt the privacy of Toysmart customers would be better protected if the customers were given prior notice of the transfer and a choice to not

---

41. *www.amazon.com/exec/obidos/tg/browse/-/468496/103-2268312-0947041.*
42. *In re Toysmart.com, LLC,* No. 00-13995-CJK (US Bankr. Ct. Mass.) filed in May, 2000 and *FTC v. Toysmart.com, LLC,* No. 00-11341-RGS (U.S.D.C., D.Mass) filed July 10, 2000).

have their information transferred (an opt-out opportunity) before their personal information was shared with another corporate entity. The third commissioner felt the sale should not have been allowed at all, but was satisfied with the protections that were put in place. Ultimately, Disney, who was a minority shareholder of the company, agreed to purchase the database and destroy it immediately.

After the Toysmart case, the FTC and state Attorneys Generals (who enforce so-called little FTC Acts, the state equivalent of the FTC Act) intervened in the sale of customer information in connection with other bankruptcies. The opt-out remedy suggested by the FTC commissioners in Toysmart proved to be acceptable to the FTC and state Attorney General offices. For example, the sale of customer information databases as part of the Egghead.com[43] and Living.com[44] bankruptcies were allowed to proceed after these companies gave an opt-out opportunity to their customers before sale of the information to a third party.

Before entering into an outsourcing transaction where personal information databases will be disclosed or transferred to a vendor, the customer should ensure that its privacy policies or other representations made to data subjects do not prevent the transfer or disclosure of the databases to third parties. Otherwise, the customer risks actions by clients, customers, or state or federal agencies, which would attempt to block the transfer.

(c) FEDERAL TRADE COMMISSION AND STATE ATTORNEY GENERAL OFFICES.   The FTC and states Attorney General offices have taken an active role in addressing online privacy and security as a consumer issue. Although companies expect that failure to comply with data protection law would expose them to liability, they may be surprised by an FTC or Attorney General's investigation of their security practices. Even if a company is not subject to any specific data protection law, it risks prosecution, fines, and other obligations it if fails to abide by the commitments it has made to the public, such as in statements displayed on its Web site privacy policy. These violations may come under Section 5 of the FTC Act, which prohibits unfair deceptive business practices, or the similar provision of the state's law.

In recent years, numerous well-known companies were prosecuted for privacy or security violations by the FTC, such as Guess.com Inc., Microsoft, Eli Lilly and Company, Tower Records, and Petco. Lesser-known companies were also investigated and fined (e.g., Educational Research Center of America Inc., Student Marketing Group Inc., International Outsourcing Group Inc., Focus Medical Group Inc., Trimline Inc., and Affordable Accents Inc.). State Attorneys General have also prosecuted companies for privacy or security violations, either in conjunction with similar FTC actions or independently. For example, the New York State Attorney General has prosecuted Ziff Davis Media, the American

---

43.   *In re Egghead.com, Inc.*, Case No. 01-32125-SFC-11 (Bankr. N.D. Cal.).
44.   *In re Living.com, Inc.*, Case No. 00-12522-FRM (Bankr. W.D. Tex.).

Civil Liberties Union, and most recently Victoria's Secret for false claims about data security.

Given the substantial risks of suits and related damages and other disruption, even when a company is not directly regulated by specific information privacy or security laws, its outsourcing contracts should address in sufficient detail the need for privacy and information security protection, the methods and tools required, and the policies and procedures needed to protect customer information. Requiring the vendor to have adequate privacy and security measures might help reduce the risk of data spills or other embarrassment.

When a privacy violation or a breach of security occurs, the client is likely to be responsible for the vendor's actions. Because it failed to keep adequate control of its customers' personal data, the company might face substantial trouble. Negative press reports, public relations disaster, fines, and stringent consent decrees are likely to result from the prosecution. Any company that contemplates outsourcing must ensure that its vendor will have adequate privacy and security practices, sufficient to comply with the company's own representations as to the privacy or security of customer data. A vendor that contemplates providing outsourcing services to another entity shouldalso ensure that it has in place the process and procedures required to avoid inadvertently violating the client's policies.

8.5   OUTSOURCING AND GLOBAL COMPANIES

If the contemplated outsource services require sending or receiving personal data protected by foreign laws, the company should anticipate the need for compliance with those laws and budget for adequate financial, human, and other resources to comply with these requirements. Thirty years after the first data protection law was enacted,[45] more than 45 countries now have substantial data protection laws. These laws are relevant to U.S.-based companies with global operations, in connection with outsourcing projects. Foreign subsidiaries, suppliers, agents, or other subcontractors of U.S. corporations are subject to the jurisdiction of the countries in which they are located. Any use of their databases is controlled by the local laws. Attempting to transfer the databases to a third party outside of the country may be problematic if there are restrictions in the local data protection law.

Many of the foreign data protection laws require companies within their jurisdiction to register their databases of personally identifiable information with the local Data Protection Agency and/or to respond to requests for information and records within specific time frames imposed by the local law. These laws may also restrict transborder transfers of personal information.

To ensure a free flow of data or information in a global outsourcing project, U.S. corporations intending to outsource the custody or processing of data collected by foreign companies must ensure that they conform to the requirements

---

45. The first data protection law was enacted in the Land of Hessen, Germany, in 1970.

of the laws of the countries in which these foreign entities are located. Failure to do so may jeopardize the activities of their suppliers, agents, subcontractors, or subsidiaries. A vendor bidding on an outsourcing project must also be aware of these requirements. Performing services under such laws undoubtedly would require additional technical, human, and other resources to ensure compliance with the local laws after the vendor has received access to the databases.

(a) EUROPEAN UNION AND EUROPEAN ECONOMIC AREA. All countries in the European Union (EU) and the European Economic Area (EEA)[46] have enacted laws that restrict the collection, use, and dissemination of personal information. Although there might be discrepancies, each country's data protection law follows the guidelines set forth in the *EU Directive 95/46/EC on the Protection of Individuals with Regard to the Processing of Personal Data.*[47] These include the following:

- *Purpose limitation.* Data should be processed only for specific purpose(s) and only used or further communicated to the extent compatible with the specific purpose(s) disclosed to the data subject.

- *Data quality and proportionality.* Data should be accurate and, where necessary, kept up to date. The data should be adequate, relevant, and not excessive in relation to the specific purpose(s).

- *Transparency.* Individuals should be notified of the purpose(s) of the processing and the identity of the data controller, and other information as is necessary to ensure fairness.

- *Security.* The data controller/data processor should take technical and organizational security measures that are appropriate to the risks presented by the processing.

- *Rights of access, rectification, and opposition.* The data subject should have the right to obtain a copy of all information relating to him or her, and to rectify these data where they are shown to be inaccurate.

- *Restrictions on onward transfers.* Further transfers of data should be permitted only where the recipient is also subject to rules affording an "adequate level of protection." There are exceptions to this restriction, including informed consent given by the data subject.

Special attention and additional restrictions must be placed on the collection and processing of "sensitive" data (i.e., data with respect to race/ethnic origin, political opinions, religion/philosophy, trade union membership, health information, sexual preference information, and criminal conviction information), on direct marketing, and on automated individual decision making.

---

46. The European Economic Area (EEA) comprises Norway, Iceland, Lichtenstein, and the countries that are members of the European Union.
47. *http://europa.eu.int/comm/internal_market/privacy/index_en.htm.*

Data controllers must show a high degree of awareness of their obligations, and data subjects must be made aware of their rights and the means of exercising them. Effective and dissuasive sanctions must exist, as well as systems of direct verification of compliance by authorities, auditors, or independent data protection officials.

Individuals must be able to enforce their rights rapidly and effectively, and without prohibitive cost. An institutional mechanism must allow independent investigation of complaints. An injured party must have a way to recover from violations. This should involve a system of independent adjudication or arbitration that allows compensation to be paid and sanctions to be imposed where appropriate.

EU member states are also modifying their law to comply with *EU Directive 2002/58/EC for the Protection of Personal Data and Privacy in the E-communications Sector* and its predecessor *EU Directive 97/66/EC Concerning the Processing of Personal Data and the Protection of Privacy in the Telecommunications Sector.*[48] This directive mandates that EU member countries enact legislation placing restrictions on telecommunication companies and Internet service providers with respect to spam, telemarketing, interception of communications, traffic data, and customers' personal data. Among other things, the Directive addresses the use of invisible tracking devices, such as cookies. Cookies may collect information on Internet users only if the users are provided with adequate information about the purposes of such devices and have the possibility to reject these tracking devices.

(b) RESTRICTIONS TO THE TRANSFER OF DATABASES. Countries that are members of the EU and the EEA prohibit transfers of personal information outside the EEA unless the entity transferring the data has obtained "adequate" assurances that the personal information and the data subjects will receive at least the same level of protection in that foreign country as they do in the EU or EEA country where the database was created.[49]

Outside the EU and EEA, most countries that have enacted data protection laws have followed data protection principles substantially similar to those in the guidelines drafted by the OECD,[50] the United Nations (UN),[51] or the EU.[52] As a result, many foreign privacy laws also impose restrictions on the transfer of data to third parties. For example, the Australian Federal Data Privacy Law restricts the transfer of personally identifiable information to any third party if the data subject has not been informed in advance that such transfer might occur.[53]

---

48. *http://europa.eu.int/comm/internal_market/privacy/index_en.htm.*
49. The Data Protection Laws of each of the country members of the EU and the EEA contain provisions that incorporate the mandate of Article 25 and 26 of the 1995 EU Data Protection Directive.
50. *www.oecd.org.*
51. *www.un.org.*
52. *http://europa.eu.int/comm/internal_market/privacy/index_en.htm.* The European Union has 24 members: Austria, Belgium, Cyprus, the Czech Republic, Denmark, Estonia, Finland, France, Germany, Greece, Hungary, Ireland, Italy, Latvia, Lithuania, Luxembourg, Malta, Poland, Portugal, Slovakia, Slovenia, Spain, Sweden, the Netherlands, and the United Kingdom.
53. Australian Federal Data Privacy Law: *www.privacy.gov.au/publications/ipps.html.*

Frequently, in addition, data subjects can sue a data collector for misuse of data and receive monetary damages. A state Data Protection Authority can take action against the collector as well, including imposing administrative fines or sanctions and prison terms. For example, Data Protection Agencies in EU member states have dragged subsidiaries of U.S. corporations into court over the misuse of data. The Spanish Data Protection Agency, for example, has found Microsoft liable for violation of the Spanish Data Protection Laws and assessed a $57,000 fine for unauthorized transfer of personally identifiable information outside of Spain.

Given the increased spread of data protection laws, it is highly likely that a company established abroad may be subject to a local data privacy protection law that restricts the exportation or transfer of private data. Companies intending to send or receive personal data about individuals protected by foreign data protection laws should carefully identify the requirements and restrictions before attempting to frame an outsourcing arrangement. The company may need to obtain specific permission from the data subjects before transferring its databases. The parties exchanging protected data may have to enter into specific contracts for the transfer of personal data. The recipient of the personal data may have to commit to privacy and security procedures that are consistent with the local law. The proposed transaction may face the scrutiny of the local data protection agency.

(c) MODEL CONTRACTS: U.S. SAFE HARBOR.   Although the United States and the EU share the goal of enhancing privacy protection for their citizens, the United States takes a different approach from that of the EU. The United States uses a sectoral approach that relies on a mix of legislation, regulation, and self-regulation. EU members rely on legislation that, among other things, requires creation of government data protection agencies, registration of databases with those agencies, and in some instances prior approval before personal data processing may begin. Because of these different privacy approaches, the European Commission has determined that the United States does not offer the "adequate" protection required under the data protection laws of the EU member states. Few countries have successfully passed the review of the European Commission. To date, only Switzerland, Canada, Argentina, and the U.K. territories of Guernsey and the Isle of Man have data protection regimes that are recognized by the Commission as offering adequate data protection.

Data pertaining to EU residents may not be exported to the United States or most countries outside of the EU community if there is not a specific commitment from the entity receiving the data that it will provide the data subjects with the rights and protections consistent with those that are offered in the EU. Several methods are available to provide these "adequate assurances": (1) using model contracts that have been approved by the European Commission, (2) self-certification under the Safe Harbor program, or (3) use of a code of conduct.

(i) Model Contracts.   The European Commission has published two sets of model contracts that must be used verbatim, without modifications. These contracts are between the data exporter (located in the EU) and the data importer (located in the United States or other non-EU country). These contracts define the responsibilities of the parties, make the European individual a third-party beneficiary, and require the data importer to commit to provide the individual with substantially the same rights and protections as those enjoyed in the country of residence.

The first set of model contracts was published in 2001 and the second set in February 2005. Set two takes into account concerns expressed by many that set one imposed terms that were too stringent. Companies believe that some of the new clauses, such as those on litigation, allocation of responsibilities, or auditing requirements, are more business-friendly. Yet they provide for a similar level of data protection as those of 2001 and to prevent abuses, the data protection authorities are given more powers to intervene and impose sanctions where necessary. The implementation of this new set of clauses will be reviewed in 2008.

If a global company elects to use the model contracts in order to comply with the EU data protection law requirements that govern its subsidiaries, and if it elects to outsource to a third party the processing of data pertaining to EU residents, it will have to ensure that its outsourcing contract takes into account the numerous constraints created in these model clauses and adequately consider the allocation of responsibilities among the participants.

(ii) Safe Harbor as an Alternative to Use of Model Clauses.   The U.S. Department of Commerce in consultation with the European Commission developed a "safe harbor" privacy program.[54] Self-certifying to the safe harbor assures that the U.S. company provides "adequate" privacy protection, as defined by the Directive. To qualify for safe harbor, a U.S. company must provide individuals with the following:

- Notice of the company's data-related procedures
- Choice to opt-out or opt-in to the transfer (depending on the nature of the data and its subsequent use)
- Assurance that any third party that receives the data will adequately protect it
- Access to the data
- Reasonable security to protect the data
- Reasonable measures to ensure that the data is accurate and complete
- A suitable recourse mechanism and remedy for breach of the company's privacy promises

---

54. *www.export.gov/safeharbor/index.html.*

To receive the benefit of the safe harbor program, a U.S. company must self-certify with the U.S. Department of Commerce that it complies with these principles. In its self-certification application, among other things, it must describe its privacy policy program, identify the persons designated to receive complaints, and describe its process for verifying compliance with its policies. Only entities that are subject to the regulation of the FTC and the Department of Transportation may benefit from the safe harbor program. This restriction excludes banking and credit institutions and others.

Once the U.S. company has joined the safe harbor program, it receives a presumption from all EU member states that it offers the required "adequate protection" of personal information in a manner consistent with the protection that is granted in the EU member states. Of course, the U.S. company must act in accordance with the representations made as part of the certification process, or it risks prosecution under U.S. laws. In addition, the foreign company that would be transferring information to the U.S. company still needs to comply with its own data protection law as well, and both EU and U.S. companies must enter into the proper written agreements.

The safe harbor program only applies to data transfers between the EU and the United States. Use of personal data from other countries with data transfer restrictions must comply with the requirements in those countries, and would not benefit from the safe harbor program.

Before entering into an outsourcing relationship with a company that has self-certified under the safe harbor program, a co-contractant should review all applicable documentation, the representations and commitments made, and verify that the company has in place policies and procedures that are consistent with the statements and promises made in the self-certification application.

An outsourcing contract that involves a company that has self-certified under the U.S. safe harbor program should contain clauses that require continued validity of the representations made in the self-certification statements, adequate attention to the yearly renewal of the self-certification, and compliance with the procedures dictated by the safe harbor program. In addition, there should be adequate communications with the EU co-contractants, which rely on the representations made.

(iii) **Binding Corporate Rules.**   The third alternative is the use of binding corporate rules (i.e., the use of codes of conduct instead of model contracts for the transfer of personal data to third countries). This process is not yet widespread because it is cumbersome and requires review and approval by the data protection agencies, which makes it a cumbersome and lengthy process.

(d) INFORMATION PRIVACY AND SECURITY OUTSIDE THE EU AND THE EEA.   Whereas the first data privacy laws enacted anywhere in the world were passed in the mid-1970s in Eastern Europe, and worldwide organizations such as the OECD and the UN followed with privacy-focused guidelines and proclamation, the adoption of the *EU Directive 95/46/EC on the Protection of Individuals* *with Regard to the Processing of Personal Data* was the major triggering event that caused the enactment of numerous data protection laws worldwide.

The tremendous influence of the 1995 EU Directive is clear. Many countries outside of the EU have opted to follow the model created by the European Commission so that their own country's law is consistent with the EU Data Protection Directive, and their constituents do not face substantial hurdles when attempting to exchange personal data with EU companies. As a result, in more than 40 countries, the collection of personally identifiable information from individuals, as well as the manipulation, correlation, disclosure, transmittal, and other data processing, are heavily regulated. The countries include, for example, Argentina, Australia, Canada, the Czech Republic, Hong Kong, Hungary, Lithuania, Poland, and Switzerland. Still, many countries offer no or very limited data protection. This deficiency should be of concern to companies contemplating offshore outsourcing because there may be limited recourse in case of loss or misuse of data.[55]

8.6 OFFSHORE OUTSOURCING

About 75 percent of the countries in the world lack privacy protection. Only about 40 to 50 countries have data protection laws. Examples include, in addition to the 25 EU members and EEA countries, Argentina, Australia, Brazil, Bulgaria, Canada, Chile, Hong Kong, Israel, Japan, New Zealand, Paraguay, Russia, Switzerland, and Tunisia. Although these countries may not offer data protection and rights as substantial and comprehensive as those defined in the EU Data Protection Directive, their laws generally follow most of the principles set forth in the OECD Guidelines.

In other countries, data protection laws might be so new that there is little or no information about the efficacy of the law and its enforcement. Japan, for example, only recently added a Data Protection Act that established general restrictions on the use and sharing of personal data, and gave individuals the right to obtain information collected by some private-sector bodies. The law prohibits companies from sharing personal information without an individual's approval and limits the use of the information to specific purposes. It also requires private-sector companies to notify individuals when they acquire information about them.

In other cases, bills might be pending, and there is still uncertainty as to when a law will be enacted, what it will cover, or how it will be enforced. For example, the Philippines currently has no general data protection law, although a draft has been proposed. According to press reports, the bill would adhere to the EU data protection standards.

India, which is a substantial participant in the outsourcing market, does not yet have a data protection law, despite several announcements that it was considering a new Data Privacy Act. India's Ministry of Information Technology is

55. See Chapter 11, Global Transactions.

said to be preparing a draft in cooperation with the National Association of Software and Services Company. According to press reports, India's proposed law would take into account the floor set by the EU Directive, so that the law satisfies the concern of the EU Commission and ensures that EU companies can outsource services and operations to India.

In most countries, though, despite the general interest for information privacy and security elsewhere, there is no protection of personal data. This is the case, for example, in Mexico and Central America, most of the Middle East (except Israel), Africa, China, Malaysia, Singapore, and most of Asia (except Russia).

The Republic of Korea (South Korea) has adopted the OECD Guidelines, and its constitution provides explicit protection of privacy and freedom from instruction into correspondence and place of residence. In practice, however, government agencies and private-sector entities are said to pay little respect to privacy rights.

There is no general data protection or privacy law in Singapore. The government is frequently criticized for surveillance of political opposition groups and ordinary citizens. Singapore has no governmental authority affiliated with privacy or data protection.

Similarly, Malaysia does not specifically recognize a right to privacy, and there has been little progress in the development of a regime for the protection of personal data. The constitution of Malaysia does not specifically recognize the right to privacy. A controversial law, the Internal Security Act, allows police to search without a warrant the homes of persons suspected of threatening national security. They may also seize evidence.

Even though Hong Kong and Taiwan have data protection laws, the People's Republic of China does not have general data protection legislation. The Chinese constitution provides for limited rights to privacy. Freedom and privacy of correspondence are protected by law. No organization or individual may infringe on citizens' freedom or privacy of correspondence, except for state security or criminal investigations. Hong Kong, however, has legislation based on the EU Directive, with a personal data ordinance, covering public and private data users. Similarly, the Taiwanese constitution articulates a restricted right of privacy, and the 1995 law on Computer Processed Personal Data Protection governs the collection and use of personal information by government agencies and many areas of the private sector.

A company contemplating offshore outsourcing should understand the scope of privacy protection—or lack thereof—in the country where the outsourced services would be performed. Although the outsourcing contract may require specific privacy or security policies, the companies may need more tools to prosecute the theft or misuse of data entrusted to the outsourcer. There may be a breach of the contractual provisions. The data may be stolen and misused by third parties. In these cases, the customer may need protection or assistance from the local police and law enforcement agencies. In some cases, it may be possible to sue for breach of contract. However, it the data is misused by a third party with which there is no privity of contract, or if the data is stolen, the action might be based on copyright infringement, negligence, or data protection violation. If there is limited local intellectual property or data protection, or if laws are not existent or not enforced, the U.S. company will find it very difficult, or perhaps impossible, to find recourse and protect the data of its clients or personnel. Even in countries where there are data protection laws, these countries may not use the high standards expected from certain U.S. laws or may not adequately enforce the laws in existence.

8.7 PRACTICE TIPS

When preparing to outsource certain operations, and when planning other relationship with third parties such as distributors, suppliers, joint venturers, or acquirers, where personal data will be transferred to third parties, companies should be very attentive to privacy and information security issues. These issues are complex. They require specific detailed knowledge and understanding of the applicable laws, regulations, and other constraints. A cookie-cutter approach can only lead to a disaster. Even though the customer must relinquish most controls over critical or confidential information, it remains ultimately responsible for the activities of the vendor. However, the vendor must perform and deliver results while executing directions over which it may have had little say, or performing under a strategic plan about which it may have no knowledge. Failure from either party to fully understand the privacy and security constraints may lead to disruptive litigation and/or unanticipated cost and expenses.

(a) EVALUATE THE NEEDS AND POTENTIAL LEGAL LIABILITIES. Given the complex legal, regulatory, and judicial background, the potential privacy and information security issues should be addressed before entering into or negotiating an outsourcing agreement. As part of its precontract due diligence, a company should identify and understand the privacy and information security issues involved. Addressing these issues early on may prevent unnecessary disruption and waste of time and resources. The proposed arrangement should be evaluated in light of the respective players' privacy and security policies and other restrictions before signing a contract.

Essential to a successful transaction is the customer's understanding of its data collection and data protection practices, how its databases are created and used, and the policies, contracts, and laws that apply to the use or disclosure of data necessary for its business. If it is contemplated that subsidiaries, affiliates, distributors, or other third parties will use the outsourced services, the inquiry should include these companies as well.

In preparation for the transaction, the parties should analyze whether the proposed outsourcing structure may lead to, or require the collection, use, maintenance, or access to private data. If due diligence has identified databases of private information, the parties should determine whether collection, use, sharing, or transfer of personal data is permitted and/or regulated under the applicable laws, each participant's data policy, and other contracts that the parties might have executed.

The parties must also evaluate the privacy and security needs associated with the specific transaction and whether the vendor has the economic, technical, and human resources necessary to handle privacy and security obligations. The customer must also determine whether the vendor will be able to perform according to the customer's needs. For example, the vendor might be subject to restrictions in other contracts or in the local law of the country where it operates. In addition, the customer may want to know whether the laws, judicial systems, and the political climate in the vendor's country will provide sufficient protection consistent with the customer's needs.

The customer must be assured that in the course of performance of the contemplated agreement, the required privacy and information security protections and procedures will be in place and respected, consistent with the subject matter of the contract.

(b) DRAFT APPROPRIATE AGREEMENT.   The parties should remain sensitive to data privacy and security issues in the negotiation of the contract terms and in all phases of the relationship. The written agreement should define, as appropriate, how data privacy and security issues will be addressed during the term of the contract and upon termination.

Appropriate clauses might include detailed requirements with respect to the use or handling of the data, such as segregating the protected data from other customers' data or implementing specific security measures. Allocation of responsibilities, liability obligations, and risk management provisions should be incorporated into the definitive agreement as well. The parties may wish to negotiate covenants or representations and warranties with respect to the data and the scope of use of the data. Indemnification provisions and limitation of liability provisions might be appropriate, to address liability that may result from loss or misuse of data or breach of contract. The customer should plan to conduct periodic audits of data protection practices, to ensure that they comply with the contract.

The contract should also anticipate that new laws will be enacted. Companies should be concerned about the many restrictions and the need to be informed of the new developments, to ensure that the outsourcing contract is updated as needed.

(c) MONITOR LEGAL DEVELOPMENTS.   Information privacy and information security is a fertile field for the creation of new laws and regulations at the federal and state levels. In addition, the FTC and State Attorneys General have actively pursued companies that were breaching the FTC Act and equivalent state unfair trade practices acts. As a result, this area is evolving drastically. Consequently, the outsourcing agreement should address these changes and allow for amendments of the contract in case of change in the legal landscape. In addition, companies should constantly monitor legal and legislative developments because they may affect the outsourcing structure under which they operate, and in particular drastically modify the financial conditions or the respective liabilities and obligations of the parties.

MEASURING PERFORMANCE

9.1 OVERVIEW

This chapter covers some of the mechanisms that customers and vendors may wish to consider including in the IT outsourcing contract to measure vendor performance. Measuring performance is an important part of the outsourcing arrangement because it allows the parties to assess the quality of service being delivered. In some instances, such mechanisms may be tied to a monetary charge for failure to perform in accordance with a certain level or a monetary incentive if performance meets or exceeds a certain level. The mechanisms focused on in this chapter are the establishment and monitoring of service levels, benchmarking, customer satisfaction, and gainsharing.

9.2 SERVICE LEVELS

Service levels are now included in most outsourcing contracts. During the early phases of outsourcing, the inclusion of service-level commitments in the outsourcing contract was typically resisted by the vendor and, accordingly, the subject of much negotiation between the parties. At that point, if the vendor did agree to service levels, it was often based on some commitment to establish the service levels at some date in the future (which in many instances never happened). As customers have become more sophisticated and the marketplace has matured, service-level commitments have now become the norm rather than the exception. Vendors—who once considered service levels as mechanisms used to hold their "feet to the fire"—are taking a different approach to service levels. In the outsourcing market, end users always want better, more efficient services (at lower costs), regardless of the terms of the outsourcing contract. End-user perception, therefore, about the level of service they should be receiving is not always in line with what the outsourcing contract requires the vendor to provide. Vendors are now viewing service levels as helpful tools for monitoring and demonstrating performance and compliance with the terms of the outsourcing contract.

(a) OBJECTIVES FOR USING SERVICE LEVELS.   As discussed earlier, in many instances, both the customer and the vendor wish to include service-level commitments in the outsourcing contract. Set forth as follows are some common objectives for using service-level commitments:

- *Setting end-user expectations.* It is important in any outsourcing transaction for the customer to not oversell the outsourcing deal. End users may view the proposed outsourcing as a means for obtaining better and more efficient services. Although this is often the case, end-user expectations may exceed the services (and prices) agreed to under the contract. The customer may use the service-level agreements as tools for communicating with end users about what to expect. Many customers survey the end users (or a core group of end users) and ask them to buy in to the service-level agreements before the service-level agreements are negotiated with the vendor.

- *Setting management expectations.* Just as important as setting end-user expectations is setting management expectations for the level of service to be provided by the outsourcing vendor. Setting management expectations is a key task for the customer and the vendor. The vendor's first encounter with customer management is typically during the sales phase of the outsourcing transaction. In an effort to sell the deal, the vendor often uses general language, such as "best of breed" and "state of the art" when presenting the proposed deal to customer management. Customer management often hears these terms and envisions better, more efficient services—and thinks that is what gets documented in the outsourcing contract. The outsourcing contract is much more specific and typically outlines the vendor's service-level commitment in detail. It is important for both the customer and the vendor to set management's expectations vis-à-vis the actual terms of the outsourcing contract.

- *Meeting end-user requirements.* As well as setting end-user and management expectations, service-level agreements are often used to ensure that the outsourcing contract meets the end users' requirements. It is often good practice to survey the end users to determine their requirements and sort out what is required as opposed to what is a wish list item. Requirements may change once the end user understands the price associated with the better or enhanced service level. End-user accountability for service-level requirements and associated costs leads to fewer perception problems.

- *Monitoring performance.* Both customers and vendors use service level agreements to monitor the vendor's performance. In most instances, the vendor is responsible under the outsourcing contract for providing to the customer performance reports that document whether the service-level commitments are being met.

- *Demonstrating contract compliance or noncompliance.* By monitoring service levels, the vendor is able to demonstrate its compliance (or noncompliance) with the terms of the outsourcing contract.

- *Targeting areas of needed improvement or overachievement.* In addition to demonstrating vendor compliance or noncompliance with the contract terms, monitoring service levels enables the customer and the vendor to see whether there are any areas that require improvement and, perhaps, the use of additional or enhanced resources. Similarly, the performance reports may reveal areas where the vendor is consistently exceeding the agreed-upon service level. In these instances, the customer may wish to eliminate or reallocate resources.

(b) ESTABLISHING SERVICE LEVELS. Although the parties may agree that the outsourcing contract should include service-level commitments, discussions around the actual service-level commitments to be used are often lengthy. The customer obviously wants the best service-level commitments it can negotiate. However, the customer may not have service-level agreements in place before the outsourcing begins or historical data necessary to validate the desired service levels. The vendor—who is often providing the services using equipment, software, and personnel inherited from the customer—only wants to commit to service levels that it knows it can meet (often with some buffer) using the resources at hand. Some common techniques used for establishing service levels are as follows:

- *Existing service-level agreements.* More and more customers (but by no means all customers) have service-level agreements in place before outsourcing. This enables the customer to include the service-level agreements in the RFP, if there is one, or at least show the vendor the expected service-level commitments so that the vendor can make certain assumptions as it prices and allocates resources to the deal. Even if there are service-level agreements in place, the vendor may wish to see performance reports documenting whether the customer actually met the service-level commitments consistently. If the customer was not able to meet the service-level commitments, the vendor may need to upgrade or enhance the resources (such as equipment, software, and personnel) being used in order to be able to meet the service-level commitments consistently going forward.

- *Historical data.* If the customer has historical data that documents performance before the outsourcing begins, the customer and the vendor may be able to use such data to assess and establish service levels using the resources being transferred to the vendor. Again, the vendor may be willing to commit to better service levels by upgrading or enhancing the resources being used.

- *Benchmarking future performance.* Often, the customer does not have historical data to document past performance. In these cases, the customer and vendor may agree to collect data and monitor performance during some representative period (e.g., the 180-day period after the commencement date). Such data will then be used to establish the service-level commitments. Note: This method would not apply to time-sensitive service levels (e.g., tax filings or reporting) where the service level is tied to a specified date.

- *Customer requirements.* Another approach is to establish the service levels based on end-user requirements. Although historical data and benchmarking may reveal that actual uptime is 92 percent, end users may require uptime of 98 percent. The service level to be met by the vendor is 98 percent, with the agreement that the vendor will upgrade or enhance resources as part of the base fees in order to be able to meet the 98 percent requirement.

- *Business/regulatory requirements.* Service levels may also be driven by business or regulatory requirements. For example, the vendor may be responsible for generating reports that need to be filed with the tax authorities by a certain time or date. This deadline is likely to be met on a quarterly or annual basis. Arguably, the service level for this service should be 100 percent because, if the vendor misses the deadline, the customer may be penalized or fined.

- *Service levels during initial transition.* As part of contract negotiations, the customer and the vendor should discuss the level of service to be delivered to the customer during the transition of services from the customer to the vendor. For example, the customer may wish to include in the outsourcing contract a commitment from the vendor that the service levels will not be degraded during such transition. The vendor, however, may wish to include a commitment to use "reasonable efforts" to meet service levels during such transition without an outright commitment to do so.

(c) SERVICE-LEVEL AGREEMENTS.   The customer will need to decide the level of detail that it wishes to include in the service-level agreements. For example, will there be a general service level for response time for help desk calls, or will there be more specific service levels for types of calls (e.g., priority 1, 2, and 3)? In most instances, customers have found the more specificity, the better. Vendors, in turn, may commit to specific service levels with the understanding that they will only incur "performance credits" (see Section 9.2(h)) with respect to certain critical service levels.

(d) EXCUSED PERFORMANCE. Although most vendors are agreeing to include service levels in the outsourcing contract, they also seek to limit their commitment in certain events. For example, in most instances, at least with respect to certain processing and response-based service levels, the parties agree to some scheduled or anticipated period during which services are unavailable. In addition, the vendor typically wishes to exculpate itself from liability to the extent that failure to meet a service level is caused by the customer's failure to perform its obligations or the failure of third-party equipment or resources that are not the vendor's responsibility. The customer and the vendor should carefully review the instances for which the vendor is excused from meeting the service levels to ensure that they are not overly broad or too narrow in light of the services being provided.

(e) INNOVATIVE SERVICE LEVELS. As the concept of service levels is becoming more commonplace, customers and vendors are becoming more innovative with regard to the types of service-level commitments being included in the outsourcing contract. Examples of innovative service levels include the following:

- *Customer satisfaction.* The vendor guarantees a certain percentage of positive customer satisfaction, or the vendor guarantees a certain percentage of increase in customer satisfaction.
- *Productivity.* The vendor guarantees certain productivity improvements over a specified period.
- *Cost savings.* The vendor guarantees certain cost savings over a specified period. These cost savings may be tied to the vendor's ability to identify areas where services can be reduced, eliminated, or consolidated.

(f) REPORTING. In order to monitor the vendor's performance in accordance with the service levels, the vendor typically undertakes to implement performance-monitoring tools that generate performance reports documenting vendor performance on a weekly, monthly, quarterly, and/or annual basis, depending on the service. The customer and the vendor typically discuss the content and breakdown of these reports during contract negotiations. It is important for the customer to review these reports regularly to ensure that they are accurate and to document any service-level failures on a consistent and ongoing basis.

(g) ADJUSTMENT OF SERVICE LEVELS. Service levels, like the underlying services, typically do not remain static over the term of the contract. Therefore, the outsourcing contract should include a mechanism for reviewing and adjusting service levels. Examples of such mechanisms include the following:

- An agreement for the management or advisory committee to meet once every calendar quarter to review the service levels in light of changes to services and technology as well as the customer's changing business needs and to adjust them (and the fees if applicable) as necessary

- The adjustment of service levels based on the results of a benchmark study conducted that shows the service levels are below industry standards

- A requirement that the vendor automatically adjust service levels to comply with certain business and regulatory requirements that are driven by external forces

(h) REMEDIES.   Once the service levels have been agreed on by the customer and the vendor, the next step (at least from the customer's perspective) is to discuss what happens if the vendor fails to meet the service levels. What is the customer's remedy? There are a variety of approaches for dealing with service-level failures. The selected approach will depend on several factors, including the types of services being provided (e.g., Are they critical to the customer's business? Are certain services more critical than others?), the amount of responsibility of the vendor for missed service levels (e.g., Is the outsourcing vendor only one of multiple vendors responsible for a particular service?), and the value of the deal (e.g., How much revenue is the vendor willing to put at risk?). Some approaches to service-level failures include the following:

- *Root cause analysis.* The outsourcing customer may wish to include a mechanism in the outsourcing contract that requires the vendor, upon the occurrence of a service-level failure, to investigate the cause of the failure, remedy the failure, and provide assurances to the customer that the failure will not occur again. The vendor, although often willing to include some type of root cause obligation in the outsourcing contract, may wish to limit its obligation to perform root cause analyses to repeated failures (at least for noncritical failures). In addition, the vendor may wish to be absolved of responsibility (as well as the imposition of any performance credits) and compensated for the root cause analysis if the failure turns out to be the result of third-party services or resources that are not the vendor's responsibility.

- *Performance credits.* Most customers now wish to include a scheme by which the customer in effect receives a credit for reduced or failed performance. The performance credit scheme varies from transaction to transaction. In many instances, the customers and vendors do not tie performance credits to every service level but rather focus on certain critical service levels that would cause particular problems if they were missed. In addition, for service levels based on percentages (e.g., 98 percent uptime rather than a specified delivery date), the vendor's performance is often measured over a specified period (typically monthly) so that credits would only apply if the vendor failed to meet the service levels on the average during such measurement period. The amount of revenue at risk as performance credits is the subject of much negotiation. Examples include performance credits calculated as a percentage of the monthly fees, a fixed dollar amount, or the amount of fines that the customer would incur for missed deadlines.

- *Performance bonuses.* The vendor may argue that if the customer insists on performance credits, then it is only fair that the vendor be entitled to performance bonuses if it exceeds the service levels. Many customers welcome the opportunity for the vendor to "overachieve" and agree to put some amount into a bonus pool (which would be netted out against the credit pool). Other customers reject such an argument on the basis that they are comfortable with the service levels that they have agreed to and there is no additional value to the customer if the vendor overachieves (e.g., production is not enhanced or revenue increased).

- *Termination.* A remedy in addition to or in lieu of performance credits is termination. If the vendor fails to meet the service levels (at least critical service levels or other service levels on a repeated basis), the customer often wants the ability to terminate the vendor for breach of contract. Although this may be an implied right under the termination provisions in the outsourcing contract, many customers wish to add an explicit right to terminate upon the failure to meet certain service levels or if the performance credits exceed a certain amount over a specified period.

9.3 BENCHMARKING

It has become increasingly common for customers to negotiate some type of benchmarking provision into the outsourcing contract. The general objective of a benchmarking provision is to provide a mechanism by which the parties periodically compare the services being provided and/or prices being charged against similar services being provided and/or prices being charged to a specified customer or industry group. Although the effectiveness of benchmarking provisions is debatable, most customers feel that the inclusion of such a provision will at a minimum give the customer some leverage if the pricing, technology, or service levels are significantly different from market standards. Vendors typically resist the inclusion of benchmarking provisions on the grounds that the comparative data is easily manipulated and the results are difficult to interpret.

(a) SCOPE OF BENCHMARK. An overriding question that arises when considering the scope of a benchmarking provision is what will be benchmarked. Areas that may be benchmarked include the following:

- Total/aggregate cost
- Unit or element cost
- Types of technology

- Manner of providing services
- Service levels

A related issue is the geographic scope of the benchmark. For example, will the benchmark assess whether the customer is receiving pricing as good as or better than other organizations in a particular country or region (e.g., organizations in the customer's industry in the United States), or will the benchmark assess whether the customer is receiving the best pricing offered to other organizations anywhere in the world? With respect to international transactions, the pricing structure may affect the scope of the benchmark. For example, if the customer pays one global rate for all data center processing resources, the benchmark will likely assess whether the customer is receiving the best global pricing. However, if the customer pays different rates on a country-by-country basis, the benchmark may assess whether the customer is receiving favorable rates on a country-by-country basis (rather than globally). An example of contract language dealing with the scope of the benchmark is as follows:

> Customer and Vendor shall jointly implement the objective benchmarking measurement and comparison process described in Exhibit ___ in order to ensure that Vendor provides Customer with [unit pricing] [technology] [service levels] equal to or greater than other organizations receiving similar services.

(b) ORGANIZATIONS USED FOR COMPARISON. The parties will need to select the peer group against which the costs, technology, and/or service levels will be benchmarked. The group of organizations may include the following (and variations thereof):

- Organizations in the customer's industry generally
- Agreed-upon competitors of the customer
- Organizations in the customer's industry that outsource similar services
- Other customers of the vendor generally
- Other customers of the vendor that are in the customer's industry
- Outsourcing customers generally
- Other outsourcing customers in the customer's industry in a particular geographic location (e.g., all retailers in the Southeastern United States; all manufacturing companies in the United Kingdom)
- All outsourcing customers in the customer's industry worldwide

The customer and the vendor typically wish to identify peer group members with as many characteristics similar to the customer's characteristics as possible, including the following:

- Similar types of services
- Similar volumes

- Similar services provided by an outsourcing vendor (rather than internally)
- Similar geographic location(s) (this is applicable if the scope of the benchmark is limited to a geographic or regional pool of organizations, rather than a worldwide pool of organizations)

The customer and the vendor may wish to agree on a method for level-setting organizations included in the benchmark that are not an exact match. For example, if the benchmark will assess whether the customer is receiving pricing as good as or better than prices received by other outsourcing customers in the customer's industry anywhere in the world, the benchmark may need to take into account market rates for personnel, inflation, and currency exchange rates. An example of a clause attempting to define the peer group to be included in the benchmark is set forth as follows:

> As part of the benchmarking process, the parties will identify the group of organizations against which the services and pricing provided to Customer will be measured (the "Peer Group"). The parties will consider the following guidelines when identifying the Peer Group: [LIST; E.G., SIMILAR BUSINESS; SIMILAR SERVICES; SIMILAR VOLUMES]. The parties shall review in a timely manner the Peer Group prior to each implementation of the benchmarking process and, upon agreement of the parties, add and delete organizations from the Peer Group. If there is any disagreement between the parties as to the inclusion or exclusion of an organization in the Peer Group, [Customer] [the benchmarker] [the Management Committee] shall make the final decision.

(c) **BENCHMARKER.** The next question to be addressed when structuring a benchmarking process is who will perform the benchmark. There are several options to consider when deciding on the benchmarker, including the following:

- An independent third party
- The customer's consultants (affiliated or nonaffiliated)
- The vendor's employees assigned to the outsourcing project
- The vendor's employees not assigned to the outsourcing project (to ensure that the resources that should be dedicated to providing services and achieving service levels are not diverted to perform the benchmark)
- The vendor's consultants (affiliated or nonaffiliated)
- The vendor's employees/consultants initially, with disputes handled by an independent third party

The choice of who will conduct the benchmark typically depends on cost (it is expensive to have a third party conduct the benchmark) and the intended use of the benchmarking results (if the results are for informational purposes only, then having the customer's or the vendor's in-house personnel perform the benchmark may be acceptable, but if the results will require the vendor to adjust the fees to be more in line with other outsourcing customers or require the vendor to refresh certain technology so that it is more up to date, then an independent third party may be more appropriate). The customer may wish to reserve the right to have different organizations or resources conduct the benchmark for different types of services (e.g., one benchmarking organization may be better at benchmarking data center services, whereas another is better at benchmarking application development services). Many customers insist on including the identity of the initial benchmarker, or a list of acceptable benchmarkers, in the outsourcing agreement, thereby limiting the vendor's ability to delay the benchmarking process by disqualifying the customer-proposed benchmarkers. Some potential issues to consider when evaluating third-party benchmarkers include the following:

- Is the organization an independent entity (e.g., not affiliated with the customer or the vendor)?
- Is the organization a competitor of the customer?
- Does the organization have experience in conducting this type of benchmark for these particular services in this geographic area?
- What type of methodology does the organization use?
- Does the organization have any potential conflict of interest?

As mentioned previously, the potential costs of performing the benchmark may be expensive. The parties will need to discuss how the costs of the internal or third-party resources used to perform the benchmarking are to be allocated. Cost allocation schemes may include the following:

- The vendor builds the cost of third-party or internal resources into its price.
- The vendor charges the customer on a pass-through basis for the cost of the third-party benchmarker.
- The vendor and the customer share the cost of the third-party benchmarker.
- The vendor absorbs the cost of the benchmark if it reveals that the vendor's fees and technology are not in-line with industry standards.

An example of a clause appointing the benchmarker is as follows:

> The benchmark shall be conducted by _____, or his or her replacement as provided in this Section (each, a "Benchmarker"). In the event (1) a Benchmarker is no longer providing the services necessary to conduct the benchmarking, (2) another individual or organization has a more appropriate benchmarking system or methodology as agreed by Customer and Vendor, or (3) Customer and Vendor otherwise agree that the Benchmarker should be replaced, Customer and Vendor shall promptly replace such Benchmarker. The fees and expenses charged by the Benchmarker shall be paid by [Customer] [Vendor].

(d) THE PROCESS.

(i) Timing. Benchmarking may be conducted regularly (e.g., annually, biannually, quarterly) or on an as-requested basis, often with a cap on the number of requests made during a year (e.g., on request but not more than four times a year). Because benchmarking can be time consuming and expensive (particularly if a third party is engaged to perform the benchmarking), most customers and vendors wish to limit the amount of benchmarking that is required.

(ii) Underlying Data. The benchmark will be based on data compiled by the parties or by an independent organization. The parties may wish to agree, either during negotiations or before the initial benchmark, on the types and scope of underlying data to be used in the benchmarking process (e.g., data obtained from a company in a comparable position, from a group of companies, from an index, from a group of indices). The benchmarker will analyze the data and determine whether any assumptions need to be built into the analysis as well as whether the data should be leveled in any way (e.g., discounted).

(iii) The Results. The benchmarker will then take the data and assess whether the vendor's prices, technology, and services meet the benchmark requirements (e.g., are in-line with industry standards, best of breed). If the benchmarking results reveal that the vendor is not performing in accordance with the benchmark requirements, the vendor may then be required to:

- Adjust the prices, technology, and services at the vendor's cost.
- Notify the customer of any necessary adjustment to the prices, technology, and services and allow the customer to assess whether it wishes to implement changes at the customer's cost.

The vendor may try to contest the results on the grounds that the underlying data is flawed. The vendor may argue that the services being provided to the organizations studied are not the same as the services being provided to the customer or that the fees being charged to the customer are not in-line with other organizations because they have been streamlined to allow for steady payments or have been engineered, for example, to reflect greater savings in the early years.

(iv) Reports. The customer should ensure that it receives copies of any benchmarking reports, as well as copies of the underlying data if such data is made available to the vendor.

(v) Dispute Resolution. A major problem with benchmarking provisions is that it is difficult to construct a satisfactory dispute resolution mechanism. A common scenario is that the benchmarking results reveal that pricing is too high, the vendor disputes the results, and then the parties are at an impasse, with the only alternative being arbitration or litigation, which is typically undesirable for both parties. Some outsourcing agreements have tried to deal with this problem by

making the interim findings of the benchmarker subject to review and discussion but making the final findings binding, or by building a mini-arbitration into the benchmarking provision with the arbitrator being an independent benchmarking company other than the company that performed the original benchmarking. Again, the decision of the arbitrator would be final and binding on the parties.

(e) ALTERNATIVES TO BENCHMARKING.

(i) Technology/Price Indexing.   Similar to benchmarking but less common, technology/price indexing is a mechanism that ties technology/pricing to a published industry index. If the index reveals that the technology/pricing used by the vendor is not in-line with the industry index or indices, the vendor must implement new technology, at the customer's request and at the vendor's cost, to bring the technology in-line with industry trends. An example of a simple price-indexing provision is as follows:

> On an annual basis, Vendor will compare its prices for each element against a composite of industry indices selected by Customer Vendor will reduce its prices to reflect the results of this comparison, subject to Customer's approval.

Vendors typically object to the inclusion of technology/price-indexing provisions. The vendor may argue that its overall pricing assumes a certain amount of profit in the later years and therefore cannot be tied to an industry index in a particular year. The customer, however, may argue that there may be instances where technology costs are reduced significantly because of new technological developments that the vendor did not account for when establishing its pricing. Such cost reductions should not be a windfall to the vendor but rather should be shared by the parties.

(ii) Most-Favored-Customer Provision.   In lieu of or in addition to a benchmarking provision, the customer may wish to include a most-favored-customer provision that requires the vendor to provide technology/pricing similar to or better than other similarly situated customers. The parties will need to negotiate what is intended by the term "similarly situated" (e.g., similar volumes, similar types of services in the aggregate/service categories).

(iii) Notification of New Technologies.   One of the purposes of the benchmarking clause is to ensure that the customer is kept abreast of industry standards and trends. The customer may wish to include in the outsourcing agreement a requirement that the vendor periodically update the customer about new technologies and developments.

(iv) Right to Competitively Bid.   Some customers have taken the position that the only effective way to benchmark technology, pricing, and services is to reserve the right to competitively bid (and source) all or a portion of the services periodically. Most vendors resist such a provision because it may be difficult to

segregate parts of the outsourcing contract (particularly if there has been some financial engineering) and because they may lose all or a portion of the outsourcing contract.

9.4 CUSTOMER SATISFACTION

A common way for in-house operations to assess end-user and management perception and, accordingly, performance is through the use of end user and management satisfaction surveys. Many outsourcing contracts require the vendor to perform similar surveys during the term of the outsourcing contract. The type, content, and scope of these surveys are negotiated on a deal-by-deal basis. In some instances, as discussed earlier, the results of customer satisfaction surveys are included as actual service levels against which the vendor must monitor performance and for which the vendor may be subject to service-level credits if certain levels of satisfaction are not achieved.

GAINSHARING IN OUTSOURCING TRANSACTIONS: OVERVIEW

A favorite buzzword during negotiations of outsourcing transactions is *gainsharing*. Customers and vendors alike are intrigued by the concept of gainsharing. What is meant by gainsharing, however, is nebulous at best. On its face, the term means that the parties will share in the gain (interpreted as savings or revenue) realized by a party. Gainsharing has come to mean anything from simple cost-saving mechanisms included in the outsourcing contract (e.g., the vendor agrees to work with the customer to identify areas that can be eliminated or handled using fewer resources, without having a material impact on front-end services, and the parties will share in the savings to the customer) to options or warrants granted to the vendor in the customer (or granted to the customer in the vendor) and actual joint venture relationships (e.g., the parties will form a joint venture that will initially provide services to the customer and will ultimately provide similar services to other companies in the customer's industry).

The success of the implementation of gainsharing arrangements has been questionable. Often, at least early in the deal, the gainsharing provisions are overshadowed by transition and performance issues (e.g., if the customer is dissatisfied with the level of service that it is receiving, the implementation of a gainsharing arrangement such as co-marketing of a new product or application becomes a secondary concern). Other common problems include (1) incentive payments or obligations becoming due at the same time a balloon payment is due under a financially engineered outsourcing deal, (2) a change in customer management, with the new management not able to understand why it is paying incentives to the vendor when services are not perceived as being satisfactory, and (3) the gainsharing incentive is tied to customer or vendor revenue/profit that skyrockets in a particular year for reasons not related to the business process and, therefore, results in an unforeseen windfall to a party.

The attached chart provides examples of several generic gainsharing arrangements. These arrangements are intended to be illustrative only. Gainsharing arrangements tend to be the subject of much negotiation and are, therefore, specifically tailored to the deal at hand. As with any business arrangement, gainsharing arrangements should be reviewed carefully by the parties from a business, legal, and tax perspective.

GAINSHARING AGREEMENT	HOW IT WORKS	ISSUES TO CONSIDER
1. The vendor receives an incentive based on the actual savings against *budget* realized by the customer. The vendor receives an incentive based on the actual savings against *previous year's spending* realized by the customer.	The customer submits base budget or the previous year's spending to the vendor; the vendor commits to a certain percentage of savings over the portion of the budget/spend outsourced.	The vendor should require that budget/spend numbers reflect inflation. The parties will need to discuss which inflation indices apply.
	Savings commitment needs to be adjusted to reflect scope changes, volume changes, capacity changes, additional/ fewer units, partial termination of services. Savings commitment does not pertain to retained portion of the budget/spend.	The customer may wish to require that budget is adjusted to reflect unanticipated changes resulting in windfall savings.
2. The vendor commits to provide the services at prices that are comparable to the customer's peer organizations; the vendor receives an incentive for any savings below peer index.	The parties agree to benchmark services provided to comparable organizations. If the vendor can show savings against market rates, then the vendor receives an incentive.	The parties will need to negotiate who will perform the benchmarking (e.g., independent third party), what organizations will be surveyed, and whether benchmark will apply to aggregate or unit services. Although vendors typically resist benchmarking provisions, this is an instance where benchmarking may be acceptable to the vendor.
3. The vendor receives an incentive based on the amount of areas or projects that the vendor eliminates or reduces without cutting front-end services.	The incentive compensation is typically based only on the vendor's ideas that are actually implemented.	The vendor must have access to the customer's organization. The process should be clear and agreed to during contract negotiations (e.g., what services will be targeted; ideas are submitted to a committee then added to a database). The customer may argue that the idea to eliminate certain services was not completely initiated by the vendor.

GAINSHARING AGREEMENT	HOW IT WORKS	ISSUES TO CONSIDER
4. The customer provides incentive compensation to the vendor for any business improvements delivered over the term through business process reengineering.	(Similar to item 3)	
5. The customer commits to "respond" certain dollar amounts in services with the vendor to the extent vendor effectively eliminates/ reduces services.	If the customer saves $_____, then the customer must respend a certain percentage of such savings within a specified time period.	
6. The vendor enters into a requirements contact with the customer.	If cost savings are realized, then the customer must obtain certain types of services from the vendor only.	
7. The vendor commits to performance or productivity levels; if the vendor does not meet the specified levels, the vendor must give the customer a credit; if the vendor exceeds the levels, the vendor receives an incentive payment.	The parties need to agree to and set performance levels.	Most contracts include some type of performance charge if performance levels are not met; few include a bonus for overachievement on the basis that after a certain level, the customer is not benefited from the overachievement (e.g., 98% vs. 99% uptime).
8. The vendor and the customer agree to share the risk or benefit of the implementation of new methodologies or technology.	The parties may share in implementation costs or the vendor may agree to spread the up-front costs over the term of the contract in return for the sharing in realized cost savings. The vendor agrees to liquidated damages in the event the rollout is delayed due to the vendor's fault; the customer will compensate the vendor if the rollout is delayed due to the customer's fault.	

GAINSHARING AGREEMENT	HOW IT WORKS	ISSUES TO CONSIDER
	If certain milestones are achieved (e.g., rollout, achievement of requirements), the vendor receives an incentive payment.	
9. The vendor receives a bonus if the customers [gross] [net] profits exceed a certain amount.	Partnership approach Alternative to taking an equity interest and sharing in profits Arguably more relevant when the vendor is investing up-front resources in the customer	The customer is often dissatisfied because there is no clear indication that the increased profits are directly linked to the business process services or improvements (as opposed to market or other business process improvements).
	The vendor is given an incentive to make the customer more efficient/more marketable. Provision typically applicable on an annual basis	The vendor may become frustrated if the customer has unanticipated write-offs for the year that are not related to the business process.
		If profits are tied to annual report, financials may be subject to certain engineering. The parties will need to discuss appropriate caps or thresholds.
10. The vendor receives a bonus if the customer's [gross] [net] revenues exceed a certain amount.	(Similar to item 9)	
11. The vendor receives options/warrants in the customer in return for reduced fees.	Typically implemented when the customer is in financial trouble	
12. The customer receives options/warrants in the vendor as an incentive for entering into the outsourcing deal.	Typically implemented in large transactions or when the customer has significant negotiating leverage	
13. A party receives a seat on the board of directors of the other party.		

GAINSHARING AGREEMENT	HOW IT WORKS	ISSUES TO CONSIDER
14. The vendor has the right to use or market any newly developed methodology or technology with its other customers.	The vendor either owns the methodology or technology with a nonexclusive, limited license granted to the customer or the customer owns the methodology or technology with a license granted back to the vendor.	The vendor may provide a reduced development rate to the customer or commit additional resources/know-how to the development effort.
15. The parties agree to market methodology or technology to third parties and share in the revenues.	Parties may enter into a co-marketing agreement, where both parties market new products and share in any generated revenues or may form a joint venture or new entity to market the methodology or technology (see items 16 and 17 below).	
16. The parties form a joint venture or new entity to market methodologies, technology, or services to other companies in the customer's industry.	Formation of a joint venture or net entity	Will the joint venture or new entity provide services back to the customer or will its sole purpose be to act as a vehicle to market methodologies, technology, or services to third parties? What resources or capital will each party contribute? How will equity or profits be allocated?
17. The parties form a joint venture/new entity to develop, implement, and market new methodologies/technology/services.	Formation of joint venture or new entity	What resources or capital will each party contribute? How will equity or profits be allocated?

CHECKLIST OF ISSUES TO CONSIDER WHEN ESTABLISHING SERVICE LEVEL METHODOLOGIES[1]

1. Defining Service Levels
   a. Define what service levels should be included in the Agreement.
   b. Include fixed service levels for those service levels which have historical data supporting the metrics or for those service levels to which the customer requires the vendor to commit as part of the vendor's solution (there may be a ramp up period if the service level is significantly better than what the customer does today).
   c. Include a benchmarking provision for those services that do not have historical data.
   d. Determine which service levels are critical vs. noncritical—this determination may drive whether a service level failure triggers:
      - Service level credits
      - Expedited termination
      - Joint management rights
      - Step in rights
      - Rights to use alternate providers
   e. Use the right terminology—most customers want "commitments" not "targets" (though there may be instances where targets are appropriate).
2. Measuring Service Levels
   a. Define and document points of measurement (e.g., response time is measured from the time of receipt of a request to time that vendor actually speaks with a customer designee).
   b. Ensure that the tools/systems can capture the data that is necessary to measure the service level.

---

1. Note: This checklist is intended to illustrate the types of legal issues that customers may wish to consider in connection with contracting for application services. The items included in this checklist may not cover all of the issues that may arise in a particular transaction. Legal issues will likely vary depending on the type of service being provided and the scope of the services. This checklist or any part thereof should only be used after consultation with your legal counsel. Legal counsel should be consulted prior to entering into or negotiating any transaction covering the provision of application services.

3. Reporting on Service Levels

    a. Tools.

- How will the service levels be measured—using customer or vendor tools? Are these tools in use today or will the tools need to be developed, purchased, or customized?
- If customer tools will be used (e.g., to ensure that a standard problem management tool is used), will it be necessary to purchase additional seats or use licenses? How will the costs for such licenses be allocated?
- Are there any third party consents issues with respect to the use of any third party tools?
- How will reports be generated?

    b. Measurement periods.

- Daily
- Weekly
- Monthly
- Quarterly
- Annually

    c. Access to reports.

- Real time
- Electronic access

4. Adjusting Service Levels

    a. Include a mechanism for periodic reviews in the agreement?

    b. Will adjustments be unilateral or subject to mutual agreement?

    c. Are there any automatic adjustments to reflect guaranteed continuous improvement?

5. What Happens When There Is a Service Level Failure?

    a. Service level credits.

- Consider whether a certain percentage of the fees should be put at risk each month for service level failures. How are the amounts at risk measured (e.g., for international deals, will the amounts be calculated locally, by region or globally)? How are the amounts at risk calculated (e.g., fees projected, fees invoiced or fees paid)
- Will the service level methodology include weighting factors for the service levels (e.g., the customer has 300 percentage points to allocate amongst all service levels)?
- Specify whether the credits are actually credits, fee reductions, or liquidated damages?

- Will service level credits be provided automatically or must the customer elect to take the credit?
- Will the vendor have any opportunity to "earn back" the service level credit?
- Will there be any grace periods prior to service levels applying?
- Will service level credits apply during transition?

b. Damages: The contract should specify whether the service level credits are an exclusive or nonexclusive remedy. If they are a nonexclusive remedy (which obviously is a more favorable position to the outsourcing customer), what other monetary remedies are available?

c. Termination: The contract may allow for termination rights specific to service level failures that are in addition to the customary termination for breach rights. Such additional termination rights may include:

- Expedited termination (e.g., if there is a failure to provide certain critical services, then the customer does not have to wait for the full cure period afforded other breaches).
- Predefined termination rights, e.g.:
  - Termination for the failure to met xxx number of service levels in a specified period
  - Termination if the service level credit maximum is hit for one or more months

d. Other remedies that may be available to the customer include:

- Joint management rights
- Customer step in rights
- Right to go to an alternate provider

e. Business continuity: The contract should specify what the vendor's business continuity obligations are (e.g., disaster recovery—hot site/cold site) and when certain services should be triggered (e.g., at what point is a service failure a disaster?).

6. Examples of Excuses from Service Level Failures

a. *Force majeure* (consider whether *force majeure* events should excuse service level failures, especially if the vendor has business continuity/back up/disaster recovery responsibilities).

b. Problems with third party software (not managed by the vendor).

c. Problems with third party hardware (not managed by the vendor).

d. Problems with third party networks (not managed by the vendor).

e. Customer actions (consider limiting to specific types of actions; e.g., failure to perform certain defined obligations).

7.   Examples of Services Levels in IT Outsourcing Transactions
  a.   System Availability
  b.   Database Availability
  c.   Network Availability
  d.   System Response Time
  e.   Application Response Time
      • Critical Applications
      • NonCritical Applications
  f.   Call Center—Time to Answer
  g.   Call Center—Number of Calls Put on Hold
  h.   Call Center—Length of Automated Message
  i.   Call Center—Number of Hang Ups
  j.   Call Center—Average Time of Call
  k.   Call Center—First Call Resolution
  l.   Time to Respond
      • Severity Level 1
      • Severity Level 2
      • Severity Level 3
      • Severity Level 4
  m. Time to Resolve
      • Severity Level 1
      • Severity Level 2
      • Severity Level 3
      • Severity Level 4
  n.   Percentage of Projects Completed On Time
  o.   Customer Satisfaction
  p.   Time to Implement/Integrate/Test Software
  q.   Time to Implement/Integrate/Test Hardware
  r.   Time to Install/Implement/Test Patch
  s.   Asset Inventory Accuracy
  t.   Fault Monitoring—Time to Detect and Respond
  u.   Time to Move/Add/Change/Delete
  v.   Time to Add/Change/Disable Passwords
  w.   Batch Turnaround Time
  x.   Batch Monitoring—Time to Respond to Job Failures
  y.   Batch Scheduling—Time to Make Add/Change/Deletion
  z.   Tape Storage—Time to Deliver
  aa. Data Restoration Time
  ab. Security—Time to Report Problem
  ac. Security—Time to Detect Virus
  ad. Security—Time to Install Virus Patch

CHAPTER 10

TRANSFORMATIONAL OUTSOURCING

10.1   MOVING FROM A TO C

Many customers view outsourcing as a means for implementing new technologies or processes or standardizing existing technologies or processes of a type and at a rate that they would not be able to implement using their current IT resources without incurring significant up-front equipment, software, personnel, change management, and training costs. In most cases, if the customer transformed its IT environment on its own, the transformation typically would be implemented in three or more phases:

A = Identify new systems or processes, continue to operate existing systems or processes

B = Interim phase during which legacy systems or processes are operated in some locations and new systems or processes in other locations (may include refresh or upgrade of legacy technology before new technology is implemented; typically staff is trained in new technology at Step B and ramp up of staff and subcontractors is necessary)

C = Full rollout of new technologies or processes

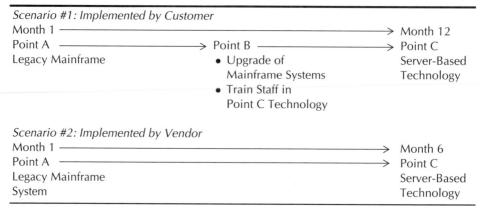

Scenario #1: Implemented by Customer
Month 1 ⟶ Month 12
Point A ⟶ Point B ⟶ Point C
Legacy Mainframe   • Upgrade of   Server-Based
                            Mainframe Systems   Technology
                          • Train Staff in
                            Point C Technology

Scenario #2: Implemented by Vendor
Month 1 ⟶ Month 6
Point A ⟶ Point C
Legacy Mainframe   Server-Based
System   Technology

EXHIBIT 10.1   COMPARISON OF TIME FRAME SHOWING NEW TECHNOLOGY IMPLEMENTED BY CUSTOMER (SCENARIO 1) AND VENDOR (SCENARIO 2)

The customer is looking to the vendor to move from Step A to Step C at a more rapid, more cost-effective rate by leveraging the vendor's experience and personnel. As demonstrated by the scenarios set forth in Exhibit 10.1, the vendor is often able to substantially reduce the duration of Step B because of its ability to provide additional, temporary resources trained in the new technologie or processes and experienced in implementing comparable systems or processes, thereby allowing for a quicker implementation of the target technology or processes and reducing ramp-up and training costs.

Common scenarios in which customers look to the outsourcing vendor to provide transformational services include (1) the implementation of new, state-of-the-art front-end technologies or processes, (2) the replacement of legacy back-office systems with server-based technology, and (3) the rollout of standardized systems to sites in several locations. Each of these scenarios is described in more detail in the following examples.

Example 1

A retail chain wishes to upgraqde its point-of-sale (POS) computing. The new POS technology will help modernize existing stores and help put the customer at the forefront of its market. Without such technology, the customer may lose much of its competitive edge. The customer is looking to the vendor to provide actual handheld equipment pieces and new registers as well as installation, implementation, field support and maintenance.

Example 2

An outsourcing customer wishes to replace outdated mainframe systems with server-based technology. The customer wants the vendor to maintain the existing technology and implement the new technology with minimal disruption to the customer's business. In some cases, customers look to the vendor to operate the existing technologies so that the customer can focus its resources on the implementation of a new system.

Example 3

An international outsourcing customer wishes to implement new, global applications at all sites worldwide. The vendor will develop the new applications and implement them at each site. The customer's objective is to have all locations on the same systems so that information can be easily interchanged, standard reports can be generated, and input data and customer service communications will be uniform at all locations.

10.2 INTERNAL CONSIDERATIONS

Before implementing a major new project, the customer will need to consider several internal issues, ranging from defining business objectives and direction to assessing the need to realign the customer's organization to absorb change. A list of general issues for consideration by the outsourcing customer that plans to introduce significant change to its organization are set forth as follows. The level of the outsourcing vendor's involvement in addressing and resolving the internal business issues described previously varies from customer to customer. In many cases, the customer chooses to engage a third-party consultant to provide objective assistance and direction.

Business Direction

- *Business direction/strategy.* What strategic direction is the customer moving toward? Is the proposed technology or processes consistent with this direction? Will the implementation of the proposed technology or processes assist the customer in moving toward this direction? Is the proposed implementation schedule too rapid or too slow? What are other organizations in the customer's industry doing?

- *Business priorities.* What are the customer's business priorities? How should these priorities be considered when planning the project? Should the rollout schedule focus on a particular site or type of technology or process first? What sites/technology/process is critical to the customer?

Project Definition

- *Process design.* What will the new technologies or processes do? What will they not do? What is the impact on the customer (at all levels)? How will the customer implement the new technologies or processes? How will the project be managed? What is the responsibility structure? How will the different users be educated in the objectives/operation of the new technologies or processes?

- *Identify objectives.* What are the customer's goals in implementing the new technologies or processes? What does the customer wish to achieve? How will the customer be able to assess whether its objectives are achieved?

- *Prototype of future environment.* What will the new environment look like? How will it work?

- *Implementation schedule.* Identify priorities for rollout. Are all sites ready for rollout? Are the new technologies/processes more critical at certain sites? Should one or two noncritical sites be used as pilot sites?

Risk Assessments

- *Risk/benefit assessment.* Identify the risks of implementing the new technologies/processes. How can the risks be reduced (e.g., parallel environments testing labs, pilot phases)? Identify the benefits of implementing the new technologies/processes. Are the benefits consistent with the customer's business direction/strategy? Are the benefits consistent with the project objectives?

- *Cost analysis.* What is the overall cost of implementing the new technologies/processes? Will ongoing IT costs be reduced as a result of implementing the new technologies/processes. Will any non-IT costs be reduced? Is the cost of the new technology/process, warranted by the business benefit achieved?

- *Worst-case scenario.* What is the worst thing that can happen during implementation? What is the most the project could cost? How can the worst case/costs be minimized? How can the contract be drafted to protect the customer (e.g., liquidated damages for delays/failures, deferral of payment)?

Management/Organizational Issues

- *Project management.* How will the project be managed internally? Who will be on the customer's project team? Does the customer have the resources and expertise to manage the project? Have all of the affected areas of the organization been consulted to provide input? Are outside consultants necessary?

- *Management commitment.* Has senior management been made aware of the project? Has senior management given its support?

- *Assessment of organization's ability to absorb change.* What aspects of the customer's business will change? What aspects of the customer's business will be affected? What parts of the customer's business will benefit? What parts will be disadvantaged? Are all users ready to absorb the change that will take place as a result of the new technology? What type of training and communication is necessary? How will the change be handled?

- *Staffing/management reorganization.* Will the new technology/process create different or new staffing needs? Will any functions be reduced or eliminated? Will personnel need to be reorganized? Will tasks need to be reprioritized or restructured? Will the existing management structure work in the new environment? Does this reorganization work with broader enterprisewide reorganizations that are occurring simultaneously as part of a larger reorganization?

- *Organizational awareness.* Who will be affected by the IT changes? By the larger enterprisewide changes? Are all of the areas that will be affected by the change aware of the change? What types of plans should be put into place? How will organizational awareness be managed?

- *Communications—internal and external.* The communication plan should provide for the following:
  - Building sponsor and change agent commitment
  - Communicating customer's vision
  - Developing high-level transition strategy
  - Developing communications plan
  - Training change implementation personnel
  - Implementing educational and development programs

10.3 PROJECT DEFINITION

With any new project, one of the most difficult tasks is defining the project requirements. The first step is to determine who will be responsible for preparing the project requirements. Will the customer, the vendor, or an outside consultant be responsible for project definition? In the event that the customer turns over the task of defining the project to another party, it should always retain approval rights over all aspects of the requirements.

The next step is to determine the scope of the project requirements. How detailed should the project requirements be? The customer will need to weigh the benefits of being as detailed and specific as possible against the benefits of allowing room for flexibility and changing business needs. Detail and specificity will enable the customer to hold the vendor to fixed pricing and timetables, whereas general requirements will allow both parties room to reprioritize. Often the parties will agree to developing two project plans—the initial project plan reflecting the customer's general business requirements (usually done at an early stage in the project development) and a later or final project plan developed after vendor due diligence in which the vendor will commit to specific deliverables and deadlines. Depending on the level of understanding of the customer's business requirements at the time of contract signing, the parties may include a detailed project plan as an appendix to the agreement or include an initial project plan, with an agreement to develop a more detailed project plan within a specified number of days after contract signing. It is preferable from a contractual perspective to have detailed commitments in the contract; however, this is not always practical from a business perspective.

A checklist of topics typically included in the project plan is set forth as follows:

- Detailed project specifications
- Project management
- Site surveys
- Site requirements
- Inspections
- Hardware requirements (including third-party vendors)
- Software requirements
- Configuration requirements
- Pilot/test labs
- Installation and implementation requirements (cabling, wiring, electrical outlets)
- Methodologies
- Cutover requirements
- Testing requirements
- Acceptance requirements
- Milestones
- Deliverables
- Implementation schedules
- Incentives
- Training
- Documentation
- Conversion requirements (data and software)
- Environmental requirements
- Operating requirements
- Disposal/relocation requirements
- Reports (including risk assessment)
- Meetings
- Permits/authorizations
- Clearances (e.g., building clearances for VSAT installation)
- Resource commitments
- Quality plans
- Customer responsibilities

10.4 MAINTAINING MULTIPLE ENVIRONMENTS

A key resource that the customer hopes to gain from the outsourcing vendor is the ability to ramp up with additional personnel, equipment, and software as necessary to implement new projects and use proven, tested processes to handle and implement the associated changes. Often customers will want the vendor to maintain existing environments at each site, maintain parallel environments during transition, and then implement and/or maintain the new environment while disconnecting the old environment. Customers look to the vendor to perform all or some of these tasks. For example, a customer engaging in a short-term outsourcing transaction may expect the vendor to maintain its legacy systems/processes while the customer redirects resources to the implementation of its new systems/processes. This allows the customer to retain the knowledge base for the operation of future systems while not requiring additional hiring. Other customers agree to maintain existing environments while engaging the vendor to develop, implement, and maintain new systems/processes. The knowledge necessary to keep the old environments going is not lost in the transformation, and the vendor is able to start anew with the implementation of new technology/processes.

Key issues to keep in mind during the transformation, on are as follows:

- *Service levels.* A key issue for the customer to keep in mind is that service levels should be maintained during all phases of the implementation.

- *Resource commitments.* What resources is the vendor committing to the implementation? Are there unlimited resources until project completion or are resources capped, so that additional resources will be at an additional expense? Are the resources experienced with the appropriate expertise?

- *Parallel environments.* To what extent will the vendor operate parallel environments and for how long?

- *Recovery mechanisms.* What mechanisms (in addition to parallel environments) will be in place to ensure limited disruption to the customer's business (e.g., data backup, availability of comparable systems)? Is the implementation schedule realistic? How long before a disaster recovery plan is in place?

10.5 USING SUBCONTRACTORS

Frequently, if the vendor does not have the requisite resources or expertise to implement the proposed project or the customer or the vendor targets a third-party vendor with particular expertise or a specific product, the vendor will engage the third party to provide all or part of the services. The third party may provide all or part of the resources necessary to implement the new technologies, such as equipment, software (often in the form of a mature applications system), customization services, installation services, cabling, connectivity, and ongoing support. Third-party resources may be required in specific locations (e.g., the outsourcing vendor may need to subcontract resources in South America to handle the customer's South American locations if it does not have a presence there).

Depending on the role of the subcontractor and how the pricing will be handled, the customer may want to be involved in the selection of (or at least have approval rights with respect to) the third party, as well as be involved in negotiations with the subcontractor. In any event, the customer should enter into an understanding with the vendor regarding the vendor's responsibility for the subcontractor. The degree to which the vendor will assume responsibility for the subcontractor often depends on which party recommended the subcontractor or whether the vendor supports the selection of the subcontractor. The customer will want the vendor to accept responsibility for the subcontractor on the basis that the vendor can contract directly with the subcontractor to protect itself in the event the subcontractor does not perform. The liability provisions in the subcontracting agreement should mirror the liability provisions in the outsourcing agreement, with the subcontractor liable to the vendor for any damages that the vendor is liable to the customer for as a result of the subcontractor's performance.

Other key issues to consider when agreeing to allow the vendor to subcontract to a third party include the following:

- *Software licenses.* The customer should consider whether it should be the licensee of record to the license agreement for the new technologies. This is often a prudent step for several reasons: (1) in the event the relationship between the customer and the outsourcing vendor goes sour, the customer has a direct relationship with the licensor and can presumably continue to use the software if it takes IT operations back in-house; and (2) if the licensor goes bankrupt, the customer will be able to exercise its rights under the Bankruptcy Code as licensee of the software (otherwise the customer would have to rely on the vendor to exercise these rights). If the customer is the licensee of the software, the customer should ensure that the license allows the outsourcing vendor (and any other agent who requires access in connection with the operation of the customer's business) to have access to the software (including rights of modification and enhancement if appropriate) and allow the customer to assign such rights to another third-party service provider in the event the relationship with the outsourcing vendor terminates.

- *Ownership issues.* The customer will need to consider who will own modifications and enhancements to any software used in connection with the project. This should include modifications and enhancements made by the customer, the vendor, and the subcontractor.

- *Ongoing support.* Is the vendor contracting with the subcontractor for ongoing support or maintenance? If so, does the vendor and/or the customer have the right and ability (e.g., access to source code) to provide support if the subcontractor goes out of business or otherwise fails to provide support?

- *Assignability.* The customer should consider whether it should, as part of the outsourcing agreement, require the subcontracting agreement to be assignable to the customer and/or its alternative service provider

- *Pass-through warranties and indemnities.* The customer will also wish to ensure that all warranties and indemnities that are provided by the subcontractor are passed through to the customer, particularly warranties for free support.

10.6 CONTRACT TERMS

(a) **PROJECT DEFINITION.**   As noted in Section 10.3, one of the most difficult tasks in any project is defining and creating the project requirements. What does the customer want the vendor to deliver? In Exhibit 10.1, what is phase C? What are the customer's objectives? What are the design requirements? What are the specifications? What equipment/software is necessary? What equipment/software is included? What are the compatibility requirements? What are the site and installation requirements? What are the deliverables? What documentation is required? What training is required? What are the uptime/response time requirements? What are the runtime requirements? Often the customer will engage the vendor to identify and understand the customer's existing environment, business objectives, and desired environment and produce recommendations or a preliminary report before creating the project plan.

(b) **PROJECT PLAN.**   Once the project requirements are prepared, or often at the same time, the parties should prepare the project plan which typically includes project management, definition of specific vendor tasks with milestone and deliverable dates, implementation schedules, the creation of a test environment, rollout, identification of necessary hardware and software, documentation, and training. (See Section 10.3 for a checklist of topics typically included in a project plan.) The final project plan should be as detailed as possible with input or, at a minimum, sign-off from the customer. The more definition the parties can give to the project early in the process, the better off the customer will be.

(c) **CUSTOMER RESPONSIBILITIES.**   The vendor likely will want to include customer responsibilities in the project plan, which typically include project representatives, that is, a description of customer tasks that must be performed in connection with the project. The vendor will look to these responsibilities as releases from responsibility if the implementation schedule is delayed or interrupted as a result of the customer's failure to perform its responsibilities. From the customer's perspective, it is useful to clarify those functions or responsibilities that will be retained and not included in the fees, those areas that it has approval rights over, and its acceptance testing responsibilities.

(d) IMPLEMENTATION SCHEDULE.   It is in the customer's interest to include a detailed implementation schedule in the project plan that commits the vendor to certain dates while allowing the customer the flexibility to reprioritize or delay rollout schedules in the event a customer location is not ready. Dates should be included for the implementation of a pilot site or sites, delivery, installation, cutover, dates by which the systems must be accepted, and milestones or key dates. If the project is priced separately (i.e., not included in the base fees), the customer may wish to tie payments to certain key dates or deliverables. For critical projects, most customers wish to impose some type of monetary incentive or damage on the vendor if such dates are not met. (A discussion of incentives, together with examples of contract provisions, is provided in section 10.6(l), "Incentives.")

(e) RIGHT TO REPRIORITIZE OR DELAY.   The customer will need to weigh its need to have the vendor commit to a tight implementation schedule with its desire to be able to reprioritize or delay resources during the course of the project. It is not uncommon for the customer to determine *after* the implementation schedule has been prepared that certain locations should be rolled out before others or that certain locations are not ready for, or cannot absorb, the proposed change within the specified timetable. What if management has decided to change the business strategy in a way that would make the proposed technology impractical? What if the company is not ready to absorb change? What if management wants more definition with respect to the project before rollout? Depending on the potential for changes from within the customer's organization, it is useful to build the ability to shift or reprioritize resources into the outsourcing contract. Typically, the contract will include detailed change control procedures, or a mechanism for developing them, to be followed in the event of a change to equipment, software, or schedules. In addition to, or in lieu of, these procedures, the customer may wish to include guidelines pursuant to which schedule changes will be handled. (A discussion of changes to equipment and software appears in section, 10.6(f) "Change Orders.")

The vendor may resist allowing the customer to shift resources if the vendor will be ramping up staff at different levels for part of the rollout. In addition, the vendor may expect the customer to compensate it for additional costs incurred as a result of the reprioritization or delay. Such costs may be negotiated, for example, actual, outof-pocket costs, costs plus markup, a base rate. The customer may argue that there should not be any additional cost for reprioritization or delay because the vendor was aware of the possibility of such reprioritization or delay early on in the process and because the vendor (as an experienced, multicustomer vendor) should be able to shift its own resources to minimize costs. Often a key negotiating point for both parties is the amount of notice the customer has to give the vendor of a change or delay in order to avoid incremental costs. If the customer provides the vendor a reasonable period of notice, the vendor should be able to reorganize its staffing to minimize or eliminate additional costs. The vendor's willingness to implement a change at no cost may depend on the impact of the reprioritization on the overall rollout schedule. For example, if the reprioritization causes the entire schedule to be extended (causing the vendor to have to retain resources longer than anticipated), the vendor may argue that additional costs should apply. While the customer wants the flexibility to delay, it typically does not want the vendor to have the same flexibility. What happens if the vendor delays? At a minimum, the customer would look to the vendor to absorb any additional costs associated with the delay. In addition. many customers include incentives for the vendors to stay on schedule. (See Section 10.6(l) "Incentives."). An example of a contract clause that sets out the parties' responsibilities in the event of a delay in the implementation schedule by the customer, by the vendor, and by agreement of the parties is set forth as follows:

(1) Upon at least [***] days' notice from the customer that the customer desires the vendor to extend or reprioritize an Implementation Schedule by more than [***] days, or an Implementation Schedule is extended for more than [***] days as a result of delays materially caused by the customer, the vendor shall extend or reprioritize an Implementation Schedule as requested or required by the customer. The customer shall not be responsible for any incremental or additional costs to the vendor as a result of such extension or reprioritization.

(2) Upon less than [***] days' notice from the customer that the customer desires the vendor to extend or reprioritize an Implementation Schedule by more than [***] days, or an Implementation Schedule is extended for more than [***] days as a result of delays materially caused by the customer, the vendor shall extend or reprioritize an Implementation Schedule as requested or required by the customer. The customer shall not be responsible for any incremental or additional costs to the vendor as a result of such extension or reprioritization other than the costs of the incremental resources necessary at the rates set forth in the exhibits.

(3) In the event an Implementation Schedule is extended as a result of delays materially caused by the vendor or subcontractors or agents of the vendor, (i) the customer shall pay the Base Fees subject to the customer's deferral rights and (ii) the vendor shall be responsible for the customer's direct costs that would have otherwise been reduced or eliminated if the migration had occurred as scheduled.

(4) In the event customer and the vendor agree to extend the Implementation Schedule, customer and the vendor shall negotiate and implement an appropriate adjustment to the Base Fees.

(5) Prior to commencing a project, the customer and the vendor shall agree upon the effect of an extension or reprioritization of or delay in the applicable Implementation Schedules as a result of requests from or delays by customer, the vendor, and their subcontractors and agents.

(6) In the event an Implementation Schedule is extended, customer and the vendor shall each use commercially reasonable efforts to minimize incremental or additional costs to the other Parry.

(f) CHANGE ORDERS.   As noted in the previous section, the outsourcing contract typically includes detailed change control procedures or a mechanism for developing them. Once a project is started, it is typical for one or both parties to identify more compatible equipment, software or processes or for changing business needs to arise that necessitate changing the equipment, software or processes originally set out in the project plan. While the customer wishes to retain the ability to make changes, the vendor will look to extend the implementation schedule or adjust the pricing to account for the change. The vendor may wish to freeze the date on which the customer can change the requirements. Any changes made after that date will result in significant additional fees, including equipment return charges and contract termination charges. Similarly the customer will want to limit the vendor's ability to come back and make changes resulting from design or compatibility miscalculations and, therefore, run up additional time and materials or attempt to impose additional fees.

(g) INSTALLATION.   As part of the project, the vendor may be required to install equipment and software or implement processes at a customer site or sites or; in cases where operations are being migrated to or consolidated at vendor locations, at a vendor site. For installations at a customer site, the customer may be required to prepare the site. If possible, it is prudent for the customer to have the vendor inspect and approve such preparations before installation. An example of a standard installation provision is set forth as follows:

> The vendor shall install the equipment and the software described in the Project Plan and make such equipment and software operational. Installation of equipment consists of uncrating and unpacking, connection to peripherals, the power source, communication and other utilities, and performing the vendor's standard diagnostic tests. Installation of software consists of loading the software onto the applicable equipment and performing the vendor's standard diagnostic tests. The vendor shall provide the customer with a written installation report on the date such installation is completed.

(h) RISK OF LOSS.   The vendor may wish to pass the risk of loss of equipment purchased by the customer and to be used at a customer site to the customer upon delivery of the equipment to a carrier. The customer, however, would favor risk of loss for such equipment to pass to it upon installation at the customer's site or acceptance by the customer. Responsibility for risk of loss of leased equipment used at a customer site may depend on the leasing arrangements, particularly whether the cost of insurance is included in the lease fees. Risk of loss of customer and vendor equipment used at a vendor site typically rests with the vendor. An example of a risk of loss provision is set forth as follows:

> **Purchased Equipment**
>
> The customer shall be responsible for all risks of loss or damage to equipment being purchased [upon acceptance by the customer of the equipment] [after delivery to the carrier at the vendor's point of origin], except as may be caused by the vendor, its agents, or subcontractors. [If second alternative is

chosen add: The vendor shall provide the customer, _____ days prior to the shipment of the equipment, with a notice describing the date and time of shipment of the equipment and the carrier that will be used by the vendor for the shipment Upon the customer's request, the vendor shall arrange for the equipment to be insured at the amounts and in accordance with the requirements described by the customer in its request. The customer shall be billed directly by the third party carrier for any such insurance or reimburse the vendor on a pass-through for the costs of such insurance.] The customer's responsibility for risk of loss or damage to purchased equipment shall terminate upon the customer's return of the equipment to the vendor.

Leased Equipment

While leased equipment is in transit and in the possession of the customer, the vendor shall relieve the customer of responsibility for loss or damage to leased equipment from theft, fire, and other casualty insured by customary forms of insurance. The vendor shall be responsible for risk of loss or damage to leased equipment while in the vendor's possession or control.

(i) CUTOVER/PARALLEL ENVIRONMENTS. The customer and the vendor will need to negotiate when an environment is ready to cut over from the legacy environment to the new environment. When will the cutover occur? During business hours? On a weekend? Will there be overtime charges? Which sites will cut over first? Last? For critical systems or processes, most customers require the vendor to operate parallel environments for a period of time before and after cutover to ensure limited disruption to the customer services in the event of problems with the new systems. For standardized environments, the customer may wish to have the vendor support nonstandardized software/hardware/processes for a period after standardization with cutoff date, thereby allowing time for transition and training.

(j) ACCEPTANCE TESTING. The project plan should specify the criteria for acceptance of project deliverables, as well as the scope and type of acceptance testing to be performed by the customer and by the vendor. An example of a provision for acceptance testing is set forth as follows:

Upon completion of the installation of each System (as defined in the Project Plan), the vendor shall notify the customer that the System has been properly installed and is fully operational. After receipt of such notification, the customer and, if required, the vendor shall perform the acceptance tests described in the Project Plan (the "Acceptance Tests"). If the customer determines that the Product fails to meet the acceptance criteria set forth in the Project Plan (the "Acceptance Criteria"), the customer shall (a) promptly notify the vendor of such failure and (b) specify the nature of the failure. Upon receipt of such notice, the vendor shall promptly make such repairs, adjustments, modifications or replacements as are necessary to cause the System to meet the Acceptance Criteria Upon completion of such repairs, adjustments, modifications, or replacements, the vendor shall demonstrate that the System meets the Acceptance Criteria. At such time as the System meets the Acceptance Criteria and operates in accordance with the applicable specifications for the period specified in the Project Plan, but in any event a minimum of *** consecutive days, the customer shall issue a certificate of conformance and accept the System (the "Acceptance Date"). The Acceptance Tests shall not extend for more than the number of days specified in the Project Plan (the "Acceptance Test Period") unless otherwise extended by the customer.

(k) FAILURE TO PASS ACCEPTANCE TESTS. The customer should consider including in the outsourcing contract a provision specifying the remedies available to the customer in the event the system fails to pass the acceptance tests described in the project plan. Typically, the vendor is first subject to specified monetary damages in the event the system fails to pass the applicable acceptance tests. (See following section.) If the system fails to perform for a certain number of days, the customer should have the right to one or all of the following: (1) the right to terminate the project and, depending on the project, the outsourcing contract, (2) a refund of all, or prorated amount of, monies paid with respect to the project, and (3) the right to engage an alternate provider to complete the project at the vendor's cost or an amount equal to the difference between what the customer would have paid the vendor and the alternate provider's costs. An example of a provision relating to the failure to pass acceptance tests is set forth as follows:

> In the event the Acceptance Date (as defined in the clause under "Acceptance Testing") has not occurred prior to the expiration of the Acceptance Test Period (as defined in the clause under "Acceptance Testing"), the customer may, upon notice to the vendor, reject the System and terminate the applicable Project [and this Agreement). Upon termination of a Project Plan, (a) the vendor shall, upon the customer's request, promptly (i) remove the System from the customer's premises in such a manner as to minimize the disruption of the services being performed by the vendor and the customer's business and (ii) refund to the customer all payments it has received under the applicable Project Plan, plus interest at the rate of one percent per month from the date each such payment was made, and the customer shall not be obligated to make any further payments pursuant to such Project Plan and (b) the customer may procure an alternate source to implement the Project In addition to any payment owed pursuant to this Section and Section ____ (dealing with liquidated damages for delays), the vendor shall be liable to the customer for the difference between (x) any commercially reasonable amount of the customer's payments to such alternate source associated with such implementation and (y) the payments that would have been owed to the vendor pursuant to this Agreement to complete the Project.

(l) INCENTIVES. A common contract provision is a clause whereby the customer provides an incentive to the vendor to implement the project on time. As a general matter, there are three basic types of incentives: (1) liquidated damages, (2) deferrals, and (3) retainages. Examples of each of these incentives are provided as follows:

Liquidated Damages

The vendor acknowledges that the customer will suffer damages, the amounts of which are difficult to specify at this time, should the vendor fail to implement the Project in accordance with schedule set forth in the Project Plan. Accordingly, the vendor shall pay to the customer the following amounts as liquidated damages and not as a penalty if the vendor fails to meet the milestone dates set forth in the Project Plan:

(a) within _____ days of the milestone date (or such other date as may be agreed upon by the parties), $_____:

(b) within _____ days of the milestone date (or such other date as may be agreed upon by the parties), an additional $_____;

(c) within _____ days of the milestone date (or such other date as may be agreed upon by the parties), an amount equal to the difference, if any between $_____ and _____ percent of the total price of the applicable Project Plan.

If the vendor's payments to the customer equal or exceed $_____, the customer may (i) terminate this Agreement upon notice to the vendor and (ii) procure an alternate source to implement the Project. In addition to any payment owed pursuant to this Section, the vendor shall be liable to the customer for the difference between (x) any commercially reasonable amount of the customer's payments to such alternate source associated with such implementation and (y) the payments that would have been owed to the vendor pursuant to this Agreement to complete the Projects. The customer's right to terminate this Agreement shall be without the right to cure.

Deferrals

For each _____-day period that the vendor fails to achieve any of the milestones specified in the Project Plan, the customer shall defer, upon the customer's election, an amount for each such milestone equal to the amounts specified in the Project Plan for the preceding month. The customer shall pay to the vendor (a) _____ percent of the deferred amount for a milestone if the milestone is achieved in _____ days from the scheduled milestone date, (b) _____ percent of the deferred amount if the milestone is achieved in _____ days from the scheduled milestone date, (c) _____ percent of the deferred amount if the milestone is achieved in _____ days from the scheduled milestone date and (d) _____ percent of the deferred amount if the milestone is achieved in _____ days from the scheduled milestone data. If the vendor fails to meet a milestone by more than _____ days, the customer tray terminate this Agreement without a right to cure. The customer's deferral rights shall not limit the customer's right to recover other damages as incurred by the customer as a result of such failure.

Retainage

Within _____ days of the Acceptance Date for a deliverable required to be delivered for a specific milestone tinder the Project Plan, the customer shall pay to the vendor the amount specified in the Project Plan for such milestone, less a retainage of _____ percent.

The accumulated retainage shall be paid to the vendor within _____ days of the Acceptance Date.

The customer may withhold payment for deliverables until the Acceptance Date or, where a defect in a Deliverable arises, the defect is corrected and the vendor provides written notice of such correction to the customer. The vendor shall not be entitled to interest on retainage or payments due to the vendor's failure to meet the Acceptance Date.

(m) STAFFING.   The project plan should describe the vendor's staffing commitment, which may vary depending on the type of payment scheme agreed upon. For example, the business deal may be that the vendor will supply a certain number of person-hours in connection with the project. If it takes longer, then the parties will need to adjust the price. This is typically the arrangement when there is not much definition to the project and there is a likelihood of redefinition. Alternatively, the customer may negotiate a fixed-fee deal where the vendor must implement the new environment at an agreed-upon price, in which case the staffing commitment to the vendor. There are also modified versions of the straight time and materials and fixed-fee deal. For example, the vendor may estimate a resource commitment. If after further project definition, incremental resources are necessary, the parties will share in the incremental cost or the customer will pay a reduced resource fee up to a cap. In addition to specifying the amount of resources the vendor will provide, the outsourcing contract should also require the vendor to commit qualified, trained staff. Similarly, if the vendor is required to provide specific expertise, this should be committed to in advance.

(n) PROJECT MANAGEMENT.   As part of the staffing commitment made by the vendor, the vendor should propose and implement a management structure for the project, with an overall project manager, site managers, and key personnel approved by the customer. The vendor's management structure should complement the customer's management structure in order to facilitate communication and cooperation between managers. In addition, many customers wish to impose restrictions on the vendor's ability to reassign and replace project managers and key personnel.

(o) PROGRESS MEETINGS AND REPORTS.   As part of the project plan, the vendor's project team should be required to meet with the customer's project team regularly to discuss the progress of the project. Many customers appoint a member of their own project team to take minutes of the meeting. In addition to meetings, the customer may wish to consider requiring the vendor to submit written reports documenting the progress of the project. An example of a provision regarding project reports is set forth as follows:

Upon the customer's request, the vendor shall submit to the customer written progress reports describing the status of the vendor's performance under the Project Plan, including the service performed, the products shipped and installed, and the progress expected to be made during the period specified by the customer. The progress reports shall describe the vendor's activities by reference to the Delivery/Implementation Schedules and the manner in which the vendor intends to overcome past delays.

(p) HARDWARE AND SOFTWARE. In many projects, the vendor will be procuring equipment for the customer. Depending on the extent to which the project requirements are defined, the customer may wish to (1) specify the particular type and quality of equipment in the project plan (reserving the right to substitute the specified equipment), (2) include an amount in the base fee to be applied toward the purchase of equipment, or (3) require the vendor to estimate the cost of the equipment and have this cost passed through to the customer (in some cases, up to a cap). In addition, the customer may wish the vendor to warrant that the equipment described in the project plan (or a functional equivalent) is all of the equipment necessary to implement the project and that the equipment is compatible with other aspects of the customer's environment.

In addition to the procurement of equipment, the customer may require the vendor to procure third-party software, customize third-party software or the customer's own software, or develop new software as part of the project.

(q) SOFTWARE AND DATA CONVERSION. An often hidden cost not accounted for by the parties as either a cost assumed by the vendor or retained by the customer is the cost of converting existing software for use in the new environment. Does any software need to be converted? Who will be responsible for the conversion? Who will be responsible for the cost? Similar to software conversion is the responsibility for ensuring that the customer's existing data can be used on the new systems. This may require data conversion via electronic means or in some instances even direct data input.

(r) DOCUMENTATION. The customer will want to ensure that as part of the project deliverables it will receive operating and user manuals, as well as detailed specifications. The documentation should follow agreed-upon methodologies and formats, and the parties should agree upon the software used to develop the documentation. It is helpful to have the documentation delivered in paper, as well as a designated electronic format. Some vendors distinguish between deliverable and nondeliverable documentation. Deliverable documentation includes manuals and reports. Nondeliverable documentation includes such items as notes, design specifications, and drawings. Although nondeliverable documentation may not be tied to a milestone or delivery date, the customer should still request copies of such because they may prove important in the provision of future maintenance and support.

(s) TRAINING. An important part of the implementation of new systems is the training provided to customer operations staff, as well as end users. The parties will need to negotiate whether training is in scope and, if so, the type of training to be provided. Issues to consider with respect to training include: Will training be on or off site? How many classes will be offered? Who will attend classes? What will the syllabus cover? What documentation will be provided? Will the training be direct to the end user or will the vendor "train the trainer"? What expenses are not included (e.g., travel, accommodation)? Will a test environment/lab be provided? What equipment/software will be provided?

(t) PAYMENT.   The parties will need to negotiate the pricing structure of the project. Although the customer may pay the project fees as part of the overall base fees, the payment structure for the project generally falls within one of four types:

1.   Fixed fee

2.   Time and materials with certain amount of resources built into fee

3.   Certain amount of resources built into the base fees with a cap on incremental exposure

4.   Fees based on an estimate and if required resources exceed estimate a sharing above the estimate

(u) WARRANTIES.   The customer may wish the vendor to make several warranties with respect to the project and the project deliverable, such as the following:

- A warranty that the system will perform in accordance with specifications
- A warranty that the new system will be compatible with the customer's existing systems
- A warranty that valid title is being transferred free and clear of all liens or encumbrances (for purchased equipment and software)
- A warranty that the equipment and software being provided does not and will not infringe on the rights of any third party
- A requirement that the vendor pass through any warranties made to a third party with respect to the equipment or software

(v) INDEMNITIES.   The parties typically negotiate certain indemnities relating to the project, including responsibility for the following:

- Subcontractor claims
- Actions of subcontractors
- Use by or sale to third parties or other vendor customers
- Infringement claims
- Time bombs/viruses

(w) PROPRIETARY RIGHTS.   The customer and the vendor need to consider several ownership issues, including the following:

- Will the equipment be leased to or owned by the customer?
- Will the software/processes be licensed or owned by the customer?
- Will the documentation be licensed or owned by the customer?
- Will improvements, modifications, enhancements be licensed or owned by the customer?

Ownership and right-to-use issues relating to software, processes, and documentation are often contentious. The customer ideally would want to own or have unlimited rights to use the software, processes, and documentation. The vendor, however, may try to limit the customer's use (and re-use) or obtain a license back to certain software, processes, and documentation. The parties will need to determine whether the software license is for object code only or object code and source code. If source code is not provided, the customer may want the source code escrowed so that it will have access upon the occurrence of certain events. The vendor may also attempt to impose restrictions on third-party use and access. The customer should determine the extent to which third parties (contractors, suppliers, customers) may require access to the software and ensure that a license is broad enough to permit such use. Finally, the customer should consider the extent of the customer's rights to use equipment, software, processes, and documentation upon termination or expiration of the outsourcing contract. Will the license be perpetual? Will the customer or another third-party service provider have the ability to maintain/enhance the software or processes upon expiration/termination? Are the software/process documentation licenses and equipment leases assignable?

(x) THIRD-PARTY LICENSES. The project plan should specify whether any third-party software will be provided as project deliverables. If so, the parties will need to consider how the third-party software is acquired and in whose name the software will be purchased or licensed. The answers to these issues may depend on whether the software is packaged or customized software. For packaged software, the vendor may be required to procure the software, but the ownership or license typically lies with the customer. Alternatively, the customer may choose to let the vendor license the software in its name with the right to assign the license upon termination or expiration of the agreement. In light of certain rights of licensees under the bankruptcy code, the customer may wish to license the software in its name in order to have direct privity with the software vendor. If the software is customized, the parties will need to negotiate with the third party whether the software will be licensed or owned by the customer. In many instances, the third party will be customizing existing packages for the customer. Who owns the modifications or enhancements? Furthermore, who owns modifications or enhancements made by the customer, vendor, third party after implementation?

(y) RIGHT TO COMPETE. The systems and processes developed as part of the project may play a critical role in business reengineering efforts. The systems themselves may give the customer a competitive edge. If the customer owns the systems and processes, the customer may wish to include a provision in the outsourcing agreement prohibiting the vendor from providing similar services to certain competitors or from assigning the project staff to the account of a competitor. If the vendor owns the system and processes and licenses them to the customer, the customer may wish to ensure that the systems and processes are not licensed to customer's competitors, that similar services are not provided to competitors, or that project staff is not assigned to the account of a competitor. The extent of the noncompetition provision will depend on the uniqueness of the system/processes, the impact of the system/processes on the customer's business, and the cost of the new environment.

(z) MARKETING ARRANGEMENTS. The customer may wish to consider some type of marketing arrangement with the vendor under which the vendor markets the systems/processes developed for the customer to other customers and third parties with a royalty payable to the customer.

(aa) ADDITIONAL UNITS. The project plan typically identifies the specific locations to which the new systems/processes will be rolled out. The customer may wish to consider reserving the right to roll out additional locations at agreed-upon rates during or after the planned project implementation.

GLOBAL TRANSACTIONS

11.1 OVERVIEW

Many of the largest and most complex IT outsourcing transactions have been international deals involving customers and vendors with global operation. As the term suggests, international outsourcing involves the outsourcing of the IT operations of a company or organization (often including subsidiaries and affiliates) at sites in multiple countries. The international aspects of these transactions significantly increase the scale and complexity of the transactions, due to the need to understand, coordinate, conduct due diligence with respect to, and negotiate the contractual terms relating to current and future local technical, business, and legal requirements. Coordinating managers, staff, human resources, and legal counsel in different geographical locations is often an exercise in understanding different corporate organizations, different corporate and local cultures and customs, and different work ethics, work techniques, and languages. (Exhibit 11.1 lists several of the largest international outsourcing transactions

Vendor	Customer	Estimated Value (US Millions)	Term
1. AT&T	Merrill Lynch		
2. Atos Origin/HP/CSC	Renault	$1,000	5
3. BT	Volkswagen		
4. CSC	DuPont	$1,900	5
5. CSC	General Dynamics	$1,630	7.25
6. CSC	Motorola	$1,600	10
7. EDS	General Motors		
8. EDS	Kooperativa		
9. EDS	Lumenis		8
10. Equant	STMicroelectronics	$100	Multiyear
11. HP	Ericsson		5
12. IBM	American Express	$4,000	5
13. IBM	Astrazeneca	$1,700	7
14. IBM	Deutsche Bank	$2,500	10
15. IBM	Ericsson	$250	5
16. IBM	Michelin IBM	$1,000	5
17. IBM	Nokia IBM	$255	5
18. NIIT	ING		
19. Perot	Global Motorsport Group	$22	10
20. SAIC	Marathon		7

Exhibit 11.1   International Outsourcing Transactions

involving vendors with base operations in the United States. This list is by no means exhaustive.)

Often the international outsourcing transaction is part of the customer's global initiative to consolidate geographically dispersed and distinct IT organizations and resources throughout its company or organization, to standardize systems and processes and information output across the company or organization and, in most instances, to provide enterprisewide connectivity.

While the focus of this chapter is on international outsourcing (outsourcing in multiple countries), it is also worth pointing out the large amount of outsourcing that is happening outside of the United States that may not be referred to as international. A sampling of some of the larger transactions outside of the United States is provided in Exhibit 11.2. Again, this list is by no means exhaustive. It is also worth noting that there is an overlap between international outsourcing transactions and offshore outsourcing transactions in that both involve multi-country legal and business requirements. The distinction is that offshoring involves a country that is not the primary location of the customer. A more detailed discussion of offshoring is in Chapter 4.

Customer	Vendor
1. Abbey (Grupo Santander)	BT
2. Allianz Life Korea	IBM
3. Allied Irish Bank	BT
4. Anglian Water (UK)	CSC
5. Aon UK	LogicaCMG
6. Australian Taxation Office	EDS
7. Bank of India	HP
8. Bank of Queensland (Australia)	EDS
9. Banque Hervet (France)	EDS
10. Barclays	Accenture
11. Blanco Santander Totta	IBM
12. CAT Group (Europe)	Cognizant
13. Central Bank of India	Tata
14. China Pacific Property Insurance	CSC
15. Confederation of Business Industry (UK)	Getronics
16. Delta Lloyd (Danish)	IBM
17. Federal Institute of Labour (Germany)	EDS
18. First International Bank of Israel	EDS
19. Fonterra	EDS
20. Geogis (France)	IBM
21. Hydro One (Canada)	Cap Gemini
22. ING (Japan0	CSC
23. Inland Revenue (UK)	Cap Gemini
24. Manulife Financial (Canada)	CGI
25. Maybank	CSC
26. NTL (UK)	IBM
27. Renault	CSC
28. Royal Australian Navy	CSC
29. Royal Mail Group (UK)	CSC (Alliance)
30. Schroders	CSC
31. State Gov't of Victoria (Australia)	Keane
32. TAM (Brazil)	Unisys
33. TD Bank Financial Group	HP
34. TDC (Danish)	CSC
35. Techspace Aero (Belgium)	CSC
36. UK Ministry of Defense	EDS (Consortium)
37. Vesta (Norway)	CSC
38. Western Australia Dept. of Health	Fujitsu Australia
39. WHSmith	Fujitsu
40. Zurich Financial	CSC

Exhibit 11.2 Outsourcing Deals Outside the United States[a]

[a.] The data contained in this exhibit has been gathered from annual reports, press releases, and other public information. This list is not exhaustive by any means. It is intended to provide a sampling of the types of deals that customers have been entering into in the last couple of years.

The actual and potential growth statistics of international outsourcing are-astounding.

Gartner Group has predicted in a recent Gartner Group survey that the world-wide IT outsourcing market will grow from $180.5 billion in revenue in 2003 to $253.1 billion in 2008 at a compound annual growth rate (CAGR) of 7.2 percent.[1]

11.2   CONTRACT AND LEGAL ISSUES

This section will examine many of the contractual, legal, and regulatory issues that a company or organization wishing to outsource international IT operations will need to consider.

The applicability of each of the topics addressed in this section to a particular deal will differ depending on the countries that are being dealt with and the type of transaction. For example, relocating a data center from a customer to a vendor site in Germany may require the permission of the German authorities, while the relocation of a data center from a customer to a vendor site in the United States would not require permission. Similarly, a variety of governmental approvals will likely have to be obtained in an international data center deal, whereas different, and likely fewer, approvals are necessary for desktop transactions.

(a)   PREPARING THE CONTRACT.

(i) Contract Structure.   An issue of particular interest to the legal team will be how to structure the contractual framework. Companies with multinational offices will need to determine whether to structure the agreement as a single service contract or as a master contract (containing terms applicable to all sites receiving services) with schedules of work or local country agreements for each of the sites receiving services. For the most part, the contract structure will be driven by tax and permanent establishment considerations, as well as the service and/or invoicing model is local/on-site or centralized.

(ii) Defining the Scope of Services.   The first step in structuring any out-sourcing transaction is to understand and define the scope of services to be provided to each of the in-scope sites. This task is, in many cases, more difficult than it seems, particularly if the customer does not have a centralized IT department with an existing definition of its tasks or the customer is moving to a new environment and therefore does not know what the scope of services will be. To the extent that the customer is able to define the scope of services at an early

---

1.   Gartner Group Report (B. Caldwell, A. Young, E. Goodness, R. DeSouza, R. Sillman): "Continued Growth Forecast for IT Outsourcing Segments" (October 5, 2004).

stage (ideally while preparing its request for proposal), the more comprehensive the vendors' proposals will be and the easier the drafting of the outsourcing agreement will be. Defining the scope of services will also be helpful in selecting the vendor or vendors from whom the customer wishes to receive proposals. For example, if the services being outsourced involve data center and application development, the customer may consider one group of vendors, whereas if the transaction involves only telecommunication services, the customer will likely consider a different group of vendors.

(iii) Identifying Service Locations. An issue to resolve early in discussions with vendors is to which customer locations services will be provided and from which customer and vendor locations services will be provided. This issue is of importance for several reasons: (1) identifying the customer locations to receive services will help in defining the scope of services; (2) the customer may wish to have its IT locations based in a certain city or country and the vendor may not have the requisite resources or facilities in such location; and (3) the customer may need to obtain special local approvals or authorizations to allow the vendor to provide or relocate services at that location.

(iv) The Effective Date. An issue that is often overlooked but is very important for determining financial and employee management responsibility is identifying effective dates. The effective date typically refers to the date on which the vendor will assume control of the customer's operations. Such a date may vary on a site-by-site basis. External or internal events may control when the effective date will be (e.g., government or third party-vendor consents that must be obtained before vendor assumption of responsibility, site readiness for vendor management, terms of third-party vendor contracts, employee communications, other corporate initiatives).

(v) Liability. Probably the most contentious issue in any global deal is the allocation of liability. Will the vendor agree to a global or regional liability cap? If so, now will the vendor allocate such liability internally?

(b) CONTRACT GOVERNANCE AND APPROVAL PROCEDURES.

(i) Customer Governance. How will the customer manage each of the sites receiving services on a local level? How will the customer centrally manage each of the individual sites? In order to have a successful outsourcing contract, it is necessary to put into place an effective management team on a local and global level. Frequently, as part of the outsourcing transaction, the customer is looking to reorganize its existing management structure (often distinct local organizations with limited central management) into a strong, centralized management structure with local management forming part of, and reporting directly

to, central global management. In conjunction with the outsourcing transaction, it will be necessary to develop:

- The customer's internal organizational structure after IT operations are outsourced

- The vendor's organizational structure, which should mirror the customer's organization

- A mechanism pursuant to which the two structures will interact, typically a management committee or committees

(ii) Vendor Governance.   An important part of the management process is the vendor's managers. The success of an outsourcing relationship is often dependent on the vendor's global and site project managers The customer should insist that the vendor provide it with nominees for these positions before contract signing so that the managers can be appointed (and familiar with the transaction) as of contract signing. Qualification requirements and reassignment provisions pertaining to project managers and other key personnel should also be provided for in the outsourcing contract. A common solution in international transactions in which the selected vendor does not have required expertise or resources in a certain location is for the vendor to subcontract part of its service obligations. The customer should require the vendor to identify the names of any proposed subcontractors and the services that each subcontractor will be responsible for, while retaining the right to approve subcontractors for all or, at a minimum, certain critical or core services.

(iii) Approvals.   In order to avoid confusion regarding who may grant approvals for particular tasks, many customers have found it useful to develop and implement an approval system (e.g., termination for failure to provide the critical services requires approval from senior executives, changes to software may be approved by the site project manager). This system can be incorporated into the outsourcing contract or implemented through a separate procedures manual.

(iv) Uniform Policies and Procedures.   An issue that is tied in many ways to management is the implementation and use of uniform policies and procedures at all sites. Examples of procedures that should be standardized include procedures relating to management, operations, change control, training, reports, invoicing, and dispute resolution. To the extent possible and practical, the vendor should be required, as part of the outsourcing arrangement, to develop procedures manuals for use by the customer and the vendor.

(c) **TRANSFER OF EMPLOYEES.**   Typically one of the most complicated areas in international outsourcing transactions is the transfer of employees to the vendor. Local law requirements are often rigid and may vary significantly from country to country. It typically takes several months to compile the necessary employee information, conduct a comprehensive comparison of benefits, and implement the transition (including allowing time for termination/transfer notices, offers, and a period for acceptance). The first step in determining employee-related issues is to identify those employees who will be transitioned and the countries in which these employees are employed. This is often not as easy a task as it may seem because when you are identifying the employees to be transitioned you are in effect defining the scope of the services to be outsourced. Once the outsourcing customer's list of affected employees is compiled, the customer may determine that, for certain countries where there are only a few employees to be transitioned and where the employee laws are stringent, it is easier to retain or lay off these employees than transfer them to the vendor.

Other areas to consider in connection with the transfer of employees are the following:

- Will the IT employees be transferred to the vendor or a subcontractor? It is not uncommon for an outsourcing vendor to propose that a subcontractor will hire the customer's employees in those countries where the vendor does not have a presence. In addition, some outsourcers do not have an international contracting entity, so instead of having one company perform the services, they have a corporate affiliate in each of the countries act as the subcontractor to provide the services. This may result in the less-than-seamless provision of services.

- A task that will require significant involvement from the human resources department is the evaluation of whether the customer's and the vendor's benefits are comparable in each of the affected countries. This comparison is necessary to ensure that severance/redundancy obligations are not triggered. As a result, benefits packages may have to be developed on a country-by-country basis.

In deals involving the transfer of employees in Europe, a significant amount of time is typically devoted to understanding and complying with the European Commission's Acquired Rights Directive. The Acquired Rights Directive provides for the protection of employees in the event of a change in employer by ensuring that the employee's rights under the previous employment contract are safeguarded. The Directive allows employees to work for the transferee on the same employment terms as those existing with the transferor as of the date of transfer. Although there is some debate as to whether an outsourcing transaction constitutes a transfer for the purposes of the Acquired Rights Directive, the European Court of Justice (ECJ) tends to interpret the Directive's concept of legal transfer liberally. For example, the ECJ has held that a transfer of an entire operating business unit or department falls under the authority of the Directive. Some key aspects of the Directive include the following:

- Article 3(1) provides for the transfer from the transferor to the transferee of the rights and obligations arising under the employment contract between the transferor and the employee.

- Article 4(1) protects the employee against dismissal merely by reason of the transfer. Article 6 includes obligations of notice and consultation to the employees or representatives of the employees.

- Article 7 permits member states to implement legislation that affords greater, but not less, protection to the employees. The United Kingdom, for example, has implemented the Transfer of Undertaking (Protection of Employment) Regulations of 1981 and the Trade Union Reform and Employment Rights Act of 1993, in addition to the U.K. implementation of the Acquired Rights Directive.

If the customer provides cars or meal allowances, which are common in European countries, the customer and the vendor must ensure that the vendor will provide the same or comparable benefits after the transfer is effective in order to avoid triggering redundancy payments. The outsourcing customer must flesh out all of its benefits (from medical benefits and health clubs to housing subsidies). In many countries where taxes are high, companies compensate the employees with in-kind benefits, such as child care, health care, cars, and housing. The customer will need to determine the extent to which these benefits will be provided to the employees once they are transitioned to the vendor. Negotiations typically focus on who bears the costs of providing the benefits. The parties will also need to discuss how long the benefits will be available because there is an argument that, if the benefits are materially reduced soon after the transfer is effected, then the employees were not transferred on comparable terms. Finally, an important issue to discuss with the human resources team is the employee communication plan—how and when information will be communicated to the affected employees—keeping in mind the possibility that the migration of duties to the vendor may be contingent on obtaining regulatory approvals.

(d) LAWS AND REGULATIONS.

(i) Industry-Specific Regulations.   This category is particularly relevant to financial institutions and other heavily regulated industries. Four preliminary questions to ask when performing due diligence are as follows:

- What regulatory authorities are called into question? For example, if the customer is a bank, it will need to look at federal, state, and local banking authorities.

- If the customer is regulated, are there regulations specific to computer operations?

- Do the regulations apply in this case?

- What actions, usually in the form of notice requirements or approvals, are necessary precontract and postcontract signing? The issues addressed in this last point are typically divided into conditions precedent and conditions subsequent. Making this distinction allows the customer to prioritize action items.

It is important to identify and understand the regulations that apply to the transaction early on. The requirements that are most daunting, and that could potentially change the time frame and scope of the deal, are those that require the customer or the vendor to obtain the permission of governmental or regulatory authorities (particularly with respect to financial institutions). For larger transactions dealing with several countries, it is helpful, as part of due diligence, to divide the countries into four categories:

1. Countries where approval from a regulatory agency is necessary before the vendor takes over data processing operations

2. Countries where approval from a regulatory agency is necessary before migrating data processing operations to a vendor site

3. Countries where notice, either formal or informal, is necessary. This category can be further divided into two subcategories in order to reflect whether notice is required before the vendor takes over data processing operations or whether notice can be given afterward

4. Countries where no action is necessary

This due diligence is important to do at an early stage of the transaction because getting input from the numerous local counsels about the applicable laws and regulations, then getting approval from, for example, the Bank of England, can take a significant period. And if approval is not to be received, it is better for everyone to learn this as early as possible. The transfer of customer employees to the vendor and assumption of operational and financial responsibility may have to be delayed until necessary approvals are obtained. If authorities are not cooperative, the timing of the entire transaction can be thrown off. Most important, the pricing may change if the customer has to retain certain assets and responsibilities for a longer period than contemplated while the vendor is ramping up for transitioning employees, migrating data centers, and rolling out new systems. Particular concern typically revolves around communications to the employees. It would not look good from a human resources perspective if the customer is not able to convey to the employees a definite date for transition or, worse yet, has to change the date it had communicated. In some cases, it could be more than a communications problem. Legal notice requirements may need to be complied with, which are contingent on the date the vendor takes over operations.

In addition to industry regulators, the outsourcing customer who acts as a government contractor should investigate whether any government regulations affect the outsourcing of data processing services. The government may wish to approve the outsourcer or, in some cases, ensure that there has been an arm's-length transaction.

Once the outsourcing customer has determined the impact of industry-specific regulations on the transaction, the parties should consider what will happen if certain conditions precedent do not occur. This is typically done by requiring the outsourcing vendor to implement necessary workarounds, with as little impact on the outsourcing customer's business as possible. For example, common workarounds include: (1) continuing to run the customer's data processing operations out of the customer's facility and (2) running the data center out of a location acceptable to the regulatory authority. Perhaps just as important as identifying a suitable workaround is for the parties to negotiate which party will be responsible for the costs associated with the workaround.

(ii) Transborder Data Flow.   Most countries impose some restriction on transborder data flow. This issue may not be so significant if the customer already processes its data in another country because the customer likely will already have obtained permission for such data flow. If, however, the outsourcing transaction contemplates a different flow of data—through a new country or with a data center at a different location—the customer may have to reapply for permission.

(iii) Data Privacy Regulations.   The customer's obligations with respect to protection of client's data will vary from country to country. For example, some countries require the customer to obtain government consent before giving third parties access to client data. Some countries require certain minimal security measures (e.g., the use of access code, security software). Other countries require or prohibit encryption. Many countries require a testing environment that does not use production data. Data protection requirements may be industry-specific. For example, a financial institution may have to obtain the consent of each of its customers before allowing a third party to process customer data. This requirement may be met by simply putting a notice on the customer's next statement (negative consent) or by requiring a reply from the customer (affirmative consent), depending on the country. Some countries prohibit all third-party access to certain types of data.

(iv) Import/Export Controls.   Many countries restrict, and impose duties on, the import/export of data and technology. The United States, for example, has restrictions on which type of technology can be imported/exported from the country. Many countries including the United States find it difficult to value data and technology, particularly software. Often duties are imposed on the media on which the data and technology is carried. Because of the potentially high value of certain data and technology, countries are searching for a way to tax the import and export of technology. The applicability and scope of such restrictions should be assessed on a country-by-country basis.

(v) Relocation of Data Centers. Many countries may require the customer to obtain government consent or notify the government before relocating a data center outside that country's borders. Other countries may expressly require the customer to maintain a data center in that country. Similar to transborder data flow, if the customer is currently processing its data outside a country's border, additional permission may not be necessary.

(vi) Third-Party Processing. In addition to permission or notice requirements relating to the relocation of a data center, some countries require the customer to obtain consent before allowing a third party to process data. This may be a general requirement or a requirement based on specific industries.

(vii) Changes in Laws and Regulations. The final issue relating to legal and regulatory concerns is how to go forward into the future with the outsourcing vendor. Laws and regulations will undoubtedly change over the term of the contract, and the contract should be drafted to deal with these changes in laws and regulations, as well as who will bear the costs of implementing such changes. In addition, the parties will need to determine responsibility for making changes required by external/internal auditors. If certain services or activities are prohibited or impeded because of a change in law, the contract should provide for suitable workarounds.

(viii) Ownership Issues. Issues relating to the ownership of software, both developed and newly acquired, may be complex depending on the applicable local law. For example, the definition of a work made for hire will likely differ in the United Kingdom and India. In addition, customers that perform a good deal of government contracting work, or that are government entities, will need to identify and understand the regulations applicable to software and technical data ownership in order to ensure that the ownership provisions of the contract are effective.

(e) AUDIT REQUIREMENTS. The internal and external audit requirements of each affected site will need to be assessed and addressed in the contract. Financial Institutions, in particular, have a wide range of external and internal auditors, all of whose requirements must be met. The regulations applicable to the particular industry may require the customer to incorporate some minimum audit rights into the outsourcing agreement.

With the implementation of Sarbanes-Oxley, many customers and vendors are strugglines to assess how to comply with its obligations on an international basis. In the United States, SAS-70 reporting is becoming more accepted for most services. However, it is not clear how this requirement will or can be enforced globally.

(f) NEW ENVIRONMENTS. Many outsourcing transactions serve as the platform from which the customer will move from one environment to another, or in many instances, from several different environments to a standardized environment. The customer will need to consider how the rollout to each of the individual sites should be handled. What are the local requirements for the rollout? Are the acceptance criteria the same for each site? What is the rollout schedule? Act what if the schedule is changed or delayed? What are the penalties for failing to meet the schedules on a site-by-site and global basis?

(g) MONITORING PERFORMANCE.

(i) Performance Standards.   Global and site-specific performance standards should be specified in the contract. The mechanism for measuring performance on a global and site-by-site basis, as well as the penalties applicable if performance standards are not met, should also be addressed in the contract.

(ii) Benchmarking.   It has become more and more typical for companies to require as part of the outsourcing contract that the vendor benchmark technology and services against technology and services provided to other vendor customers, as well as other companies in the customer's industry. Other topics to consider are whether benchmarking should be performed on a global/per-site basis, the allocation of the costs of the benchmarker, and the procedures for implementing improvements.

(iii) Customer Satisfaction.   Not all performance-related issues are quantifiable and may only be measured by monitoring end-user or management satisfaction. Many outsourcing contracts contain robust customer satisfaction survey provisions. Such provisions include the surveying process, the scope of individuals to be surveyed, the content of the surveys and the cost of implementing and reviewing the surveys.

(h) PRICING-RELATED ISSUES.

(i) Pricing.   Some issues to consider with respect to pricing include the following:

- In some cases, the structure of the contract may affect the pricing. For example, pricing should be more favorable if the customer commits in the outsourcing contract to include a certain number of sites in scope rather than having a master agreement with an option for the customer to add sites.

- The customer should evaluate the budget for each of the affected locations when assessing whether the vendor's base fee is acceptable.

- When negotiating price, the parties should discuss appropriate mechanisms for adjusting the price in the event of increases and decreases in services. This mechanism will likely vary on a site-by-site basis because the cost of providing services in the United Kingdom is more than the cost in India.

- The base fees typically include a baseline of service, with the customer paying incremental fees for services above and below the baselines. In order to reflect substantial changes in the customer's use of the services over the term (e.g., +/– 20 percent), many customers wish to include in the outsourcing agreements a mechanism pursuant to which baselines can be adjusted periodically. The customer will need to determine whether baselines will be set on a global or a site-by-site basis and, similarly, whether adjustments will be made globally or on a site-by-site basis.

- The vendor should be required to segregate its fees for each site receiving services (this is particularly important when assessing tax liability).

(ii) Currency Risks.   The contract should provide for when, where, and in what currency payments will be made. The currency or currencies in which payments are to be made is typically the subject of much discussion because one of the parties will always be bearing the risk of fluctuating exchange rates.

(iii) Cost-of-Living Adjustments (COLA).   The applicability of COLA, if any, will likely vary from country to country. The parties will need to determine how inflation-sensitive countries are to be handled.

(iv) Taxes.   The potential tax liability imposed in connection with outsourcing transactions may be substantial. The customer should work with the vendor to determine the potential tax exposure. The customer may wish to consider allocating responsibility for taxes (sales, use, service, VAT) on a country-by-country basis.

(v) Asset Sales.   Many outsourcing transactions involve the sale of all or some of the customer's IT assets to the vendor in exchange for a lump-sum payment or a reduction in annual fees. If assets are being sold or transferred by the customer to the vendor, the customer typically inventories those assets being transferred on a site-by-site basis. In addition, the customer will need to assess the most favorable means (from a tax and regulatory perspective) of transferring such assets on a site-by-site basis.

(i) RETAINED RESPONSIBILITIES.   The parties will need to determine for which assets the customer will retain managerial, administrative, operational, and/or financial responsibility on a global/per-site basis. If the vendor assumes financial responsibility for assets retained by the customer, the parties will need to determine how, by whom, and in which currency invoices will be paid.

(j) TERMINATION. Just as important as planning a smooth transition of IT operations to the vendor is safeguarding oneself in the event the relationship does not work out. There are several different types of possible terminations: termination for convenience, for change of control of vendor/customer, for cause, for failing to provide critical services, for failing to meet service levels, and for failing to restore services in the event of a disaster or a *force majeure* event. The customer will need to focus particular attention on how global/site terminations will be handled, including termination for the following:

- Convenience
- Change of control of customer/vendor
- Breach
- Failure to provide critical services

With respect to multisite transactions, cross-termination rights (e.g., what is the effect on the master contract as individual sites are terminated?) will need to be spelled out. In addition to negotiating the rights of the parties to terminate, the parties will need to negotiate the applicable fees (if any) for global/site terminations and the manner and currency in which such fees are payable.

(k) CONTINUATION OF SERVICES. An issue that is critical to any outsourcing transaction is how and when critical functions will be restored at each site in the event of a disaster or force majeure event. What is the minimum amount of service that the customer can live with on a site-by-site or global basis? With respect to disasters, the customer will need to determine whether disaster recovery is in scope. The parties will need to put plans into place for each of the sites, and possibly a global escalation plan if more than one site is affected. With respect to *force majeure*, the parties should examine closely the definition of a *force majeure* event. Are all of the possibilities for a particular country included? Should anything be excluded? Is a disaster at one site a force majeure event at another site?

INTERNATIONAL TRANSACTIONS KEY ISSUES CHECKLIST[2]

1. **Structure of Agreement**

    o Define scope of services for each of the entities receiving services to determine whether to structure the agreement as a single service contract or as a master contract. (A master contract or MSA typically contains general terms and conditions applicable to all entities receiving services with schedules of work detailing the specific services to be provided to each of the entities.)

2. **Contract Management**

    o Determine how Customer will manage the contract in each of the locations receiving services and how Customer will centrally manage each of the locations

    o Construct:

    • Customer's internal organizational structure

    • Vendor's organizational structure

    • Mechanism pursuant to which the two structures will interact

    o Define change control procedures:

    • Services

    • Assets

3. **Approvals**

    o Specify the levels of approval necessary, for example:

    • Level 1—Senior Executives (Parent/Contracting Party)

    • Level 2—Management Committee

    • Level 3—Global Project Manager

---

2. Note: This checklist is intended to illustrate the types of legal issues that customers may wish to consider in connection with contracting for application services. The items included in this checklist may not cover all of the issues that may arise in a particular transaction. Legal issues will likely vary depending on the type of service being provided and the scope of the services. This checklist or any part thereof should only be used after consultation with your legal counsel. Legal counsel should be consulted prior to entering into or negotiating any transaction covering the provision of application services.

- Level 4—Location/Site Project Manager
- Level 5—(Other)
  - ○ Determine whether a specific level of approval is necessary for a particular task (e.g., termination for failure to provide the critical services = Level 1 approval)

4. **Effective Date**
   - ○ When will Vendor assume responsibility for providing services to Customer?
   - ○ Determine whether there should be different effective dates for different locations (the term typically runs from the first/last effective date—so that there is a single expiration date)

5. **Entities Receiving Services from the Vendor**
   - ○ Determine which entities (intercompany and third party) will be receiving services

6. **Services Being Provided**
   - ○ Determine scope of services being provided to each entity and locations from which services will be provided

7. **Vendor/Subcontractors**
   - ○ Will Vendor personnel be responsible for providing services to all locations or will a subcontractor be responsible?
   - ○ Determine scope of subcontracting
   - ○ Create mechanisms to restrict subcontracting

8. **Conditions Precedent**
   - ○ Identify (with local counsel) country-specific approvals, consents, and authorizations that are a condition to the provision of services, for example:
     - Migration
     - Provision of services by a third party
     - Personnel transfer
     - Industry-specific approvals (e.g., banking, insurance, EC)
   - ○ Determine consequences if condition precedent does not occur (workaround, associated costs)

9. **Service Locations**
   - ○ Determine from, through, and to which countries services will be provided

10. **Local Laws/Regulations**
    - ○ Identify (with local counsel) country-specific laws/regulations affecting transaction

  ○ Determine consequences of changes in laws/regulations during term of Agreement (work around, associated costs)

11. Transborder Data Flow

  ○ Determine compliance requirements relating to TDF laws/regulations

12. Assets

  ○ Identify asset requirements for each entity

  ○ Will Customer/Vendor be providing assets?

  ○ Determine ownership/license rights during term and upon expiration/termination of Agreement

13. Agreements to Be Reviewed

  ○ Assess which third-party contracts will need to be reviewed for each of the affected entities, for example:

   • Contracts covering assets that will be transferred to Vendor

   • Contracts covering assets for which Vendor will have administrative, operational, and/or financial responsibility

   • Issues to consider in Customer review:

    ○ What are access/transfer rights?

    ○ Will third-party vendor consent be necessary?

    ○ Will additional charges/fees be applicable?

    ○ When does agreement terminate/renew?

    ○ Will renewal/termination/cancellation fees be applicable?

14. Performance Standards

  ○ Determine performance standard for each of the affected entities and/or global performance standards

  ○ Determine local/global penalties

  ○ Determine local/global termination rights if penalties reach certain amounts

15. Retained Assets/Responsibilities

  ○ Determine which assets Customer will retain management, administrative, operational, and/or financial responsibility on a global/local level

  ○ If Vendor will assume financial responsibility for assets retained by Customer, determine how, by whom, and in which currency invoices will be paid (*see also* item 13)

16. Employee Transfer

  ○ Identify number of employees to be transferred and the countries in which employees will be transferred

- o Summarize employee benefits in each affected country
- o Compare Vendor's benefits
- o Review local laws/regulations (i.e., transfers, benefits, severance, vacation)
- o Develop benefit package on a country-by-country basis

17. **Project Staff**
- o Identify global/location project managers for Customer/Vendor
- o Identify any other key personnel
- o Specify qualification/reassignment provisions pertaining to project manager/key personnel

18. **Reports**
- o Identify reports that Customer currently prepares on a country-by-country basis
- o Identify any additional reports that may be required/desired on a country-by-country basis
- o Determine who will receive which reports on a global/local level

19. **Audits (Processing/Charges)**
- o Determine local audit requirements
- o Determine responsibility for making changes required by internal/external auditors
- o Pricing
- o Determine global/location pricing mechanisms
- o Which services will incremental charges apply to?
- o When will credits apply?
- o How will charges/credits be paid (e.g., net out global charges/credits)?

20. **Cost-of-Living Adjustment**
- o Will COLA apply on a global/location level?
- o How will inflation-sensitive countries be handled?
- o Will Vendor share in the risk?

21. **Method of Payment**
- o Determine when, where, and in what currency payment will be made
- o Assess currency risks

22. **Benchmarking**
- o Determine whether benchmarking procedures are appropriate
- o If so, implement on a global/location basis
- o Create mechanism for implementing improvements

23. Baselines/Baseline Adjustments
    ○ Determine whether baselines apply on a global/location level
    ○ Discuss baseline adjustment mechanisms, for example:
      • Quarterly/annual adjustments
      • Adjustments upon significant change in volume

24. Improvements
    ○ How will significant changes in methodologies/technology be handled?
    ○ What are Vendor's notice obligations regarding improvements in methodologies/technology?

25. Taxes
    ○ Determine potential tax liability
    ○ Allocate responsibility for taxes (sales, use, service, VAT) on a location-by-location basis

26. Additional Services
    ○ How will additional assets be handled on a location-by-location basis
    ○ Does Customer want the ability to contract with third parties
    ○ Does Customer want the ability to add or take away entities or locations

27. Early Termination
    ○ How will global/location terminations be handled, including:
      • Termination for convenience (in whole or in part)
      • Termination upon change of control of Customer
      • Termination for change of control of Vendor
      • Termination for breach
      • Termination for nonpayment
      • Termination for failure to provide the critical services
      • Termination due to force majeure event
      • Termination due to a disaster
      • Termination upon the occurrence of a regulatory event
      • Discuss cross-termination rights (e.g., if more than one location terminated, agreement terminates)

28. Termination Fees
    ○ Determine applicable fees for global/local termination for convenience (in whole or in part)
    ○ Determine manner and in which currency payment is made

29. Rights upon Termination[3]

  o Determine rights to purchase or use Vendor or third-party assets upon termination

  o Have assets been amortized?

  o Determine rights to assign third-party service contracts upon termination

  o Allocate responsibility for transfer/ongoing fees

  o Specify Vendor's obligations to provide assistance upon termination

30. Business Recovery

  o Specify disaster recovery/business continuation requirements for each Customer/Vendor location

  o Identify Customer responsibilities

  o Identify Vendor responsibilities

  o Determine consequences if Vendor is not able to restore services within specified period

31. Security Procedures

  o Specify data security requirements for each Customer/Vendor location

  o Specify physical security requirements for each Customer/Vendor location

  o Identify who will be responsible for maintaining security

  o Determine how changes in security requirements will be handled

---

3. See also "Due Diligence Checklist for Customers Considering Termination" set forth in Appendix 15.2.

GLOBAL MASTER SERVICES AGREEMENT (VENDOR FORM)[4]

ATTACHMENT 2

WORKING DRAFT — *************

GLOBAL MASTER SERVICES AGREEMENT

by and between

[VENDOR]
and
[CUSTOMER]

Dated as _____

This **GLOBAL MASTER SERVICES AGREEMENT**, dated as of _____,
is by and between **[VENDOR]**, a _____ corporation with a principal place
of business at _____ and **[CUSTOMER]** a _____ corpora-
tion with a principal place of business at _____.

   NOW, THEREFORE, for and in consideration of the agreements set forth
below, Vendor and Customer hereby agree as follows:

ARTICLE 1. AGREEMENT FRAMEWORK

1.01 PURPOSE. The purpose of this Master Agreement is to establish the general terms and conditions applicable to Vendor's provision of _____
and related services to Customer for which Vendor and Customer shall have
entered into one or more service contracts to this Master Agreement describing
the responsibilities and obligations specific to the applicable services, in a form
substantially similar to the form attached as <u>Exhibit 2</u> (each, a "<u>Local Service</u>

---

4. Note: This sample agreement is intended to illustrate the types of legal issues that vendors typically
   wish to address in connection with information technology outsourcing transactions. The provisions
   included in this sample agreement, while comprehensive, may not cover all of the issues that may
   arise in a particular transaction. Legal issues will likely vary depending on the type of information
   technology process being outsourced and the scope of the outsourcing transaction. This sample
   agreement or any part thereof should only be used after consultation with your legal counsel. Legal
   counsel should be consulted prior to entering into or negotiating any outsourcing transaction.

Contract; collectively, the "Local Service Contracts"; when referring to the specific Local Service Contract that references and incorporates this Master Agreement, the "Local Service Contract").

1.02 MASTER AGREEMENT. This Master Agreement is intended to serve as a framework for the provision of services under one or more Local Service Contracts. Vendor shall only be obligated to provide those services agreed to under an executed Local Service Contract.

1.03 LOCAL SERVICE CONTRACTS. Customer intends to invite Vendor to bid on providing [SPECIFY TYPE OF SERVICES] various call center and related services. If Vendor is selected as the vendor to provide any such services to Customer, Customer and Vendor shall enter into a Local Service Contract. The Local Service Contracts shall reference and incorporate this Master Agreement, and the terms and conditions set forth in this Master Agreement shall govern Vendor's provision of services under the Local Service Contracts, except as may be amended by a Local Service Contract in respect of the specific services being provided under such Local Service Contract.

1.04 NATURE OF RELATIONSHIP. Neither this Master Agreement nor any Local Service Contract gives Customer sole and exclusive access or rights to the services provided by Vendor. Subject to the execution of a Local Service Contract or Change Order covering the services, Vendor will endeavor to make resources and services available to Customer.

ARTICLE 2. DEFINITIONS AND CONSTRUCTION

2.01 DEFINITIONS. Unless otherwise defined in the Local Service Contract, the defined terms used in this Master Agreement and the Local Service Contract shall have the meanings specified in Exhibit 1.

2.02 INTERPRETATION.

1. The Article and Section headings, Table of Contents, Table of Exhibits, and Table of Schedules are for reference and convenience only and shall not be considered in the interpretation of this Master Agreement or the Local Service Contract.

2. In the event of a conflict between the terms of this Master Agreement and the terms of a Local Service Contract, the terms of the Local Service Contract shall prevail. In the event of a conflict between the terms of a Local Service Contract and the terms of the Schedules to such Local Service Contract, the terms of the Schedules to such Local Service Contract shall prevail. In the event of a conflict between the terms of one or more Local Service Contracts, the terms of the latest dated Local Service Contract shall prevail. **[OPTION: BE SILENT]**

ARTICLE 3. TERM

3.01 MASTER AGREEMENT. The term of this Master Agreement shall commence on the Master Effective Date and continue until terminated pursuant to Article 16 (the "Master Term")

3.02 LOCAL SERVICE CONTRACT. The initial term of the Local Service Contract shall commence on the Local Service Contract Effective Date and continue until 23:59 **[SPECIFY TIME STANDARD]** on the anniversary of the Local Service Contract Effective Date, or such earlier data upon which the Local Service Contract may be terminated pursuant to Article 16 (the "Initial Local Service Contract Term"). Upon expiration of the Initial Local Service Contract Term, the term of the Local Service Contract shall automatically extend for successive one-year periods (each, a "Renewal Local Service Contract Term") unless the Local Service Contract is terminated earlier pursuant to Article 16 or a Party gives the other Parties notice at least 180 days prior to the expiration of the Initial Local Service Contract Term or the applicable Renewal Local Service Contract Term, as the case may be, that it does not desire to extend the term of the Local Service Contract.

ARTICLE 4. SERVICES

4.01 GENERALLY. During the Local Service Contract Term, Vendor shall provide to Customer, and Customer shall purchase from Vendor, the Services.

4.02 VENDOR PERSONNEL.

1. During the Master Term, Vendor shall maintain an individual (the "Vendor Account Manager"), who shall serve as the primary Vendor representative under this Master Agreement and the Local Service Contracts. The Vendor Account Manager shall (a) have overall responsibility for managing and coordinating the performance of Vendor's obligations under this Master Agreement and the Local Service Contracts and (b) be authorized to act for and on behalf of Vendor with respect to all matters relating to this Master Agreement and the Local Service Contracts.

2. During the Local Service Contract Term, Vendor shall maintain an individual (the "Vendor Project Manager"), who shall serve as the primary Vendor representative under the Local Service Contract. The Vendor Project Manager shall (a) have overall responsibility for managing and coordinating the performance of Vendor's obligations under the Local Service Contract and (b) be authorized to act for and on behalf of Vendor with respect to all matters relating to the Local Service Contract.

3. **[Vendor shall appoint individuals to the Project Staff with suitable training and skills to perform the Services.]**

[WILL SERVICES BE CUSTOMER LOCATION SPECIFIC? IF SO, THIS NEEDS TO BE ADDED]

ARTICLE 5. SERVICE LEVELS

5.01 SERVICE LEVELS.   Vendor shall provide the Services in accordance with the Service Levels. If Vendor fails to meet the Service Levels, the procedures and remedies described in the Local Service Contract shall apply and shall be the sole and exclusive remedy of the other Parties for such failure.

5.02 REPORTING.   Vendor shall provide to Customer performance reports according to a schedule and in the format agreed upon by the Parties.

ARTICLE 6. CHANGES IN THE SERVICES

1.   Vendor reserves the right in its discretion to designate and make changes to the Services, the Service Levels, standards, operation procedures, access periods, Customer identification procedures, allocation and quantity of system resources utilized, and administrative and operational algorithms (each, a "Change"); provided, however, that any such Change shall not have a material adverse impact on the Service Levels or cause a material increase to the Fees.

2.   Except as set forth in subsection (1) above, in the event a Party wishes to make a Change, such Party shall submit a written proposal to the other Parties describing such desired Change. The other Parties shall reject or accept the proposal in writing within a reasonable period of time, but in no event more than 30 days after receipt of the proposal. In the event the proposal is rejected, the writing shall include the reason for the rejection. In the event the proposal is accepted, the Parties shall determine the additions or modifications to be made to the Local Service Contract (including the Fees). Any such addition or modification shall be set forth in a written Change Order signed by the Parties. None of the Parties shall be obligated to accept a proposal submitted by another Party pursuant to this subsection. Vendor shall have no obligation to provide any service or otherwise act pursuant to any proposal submitted by Customer pursuant to this subsection, except to the extent such proposal is set forth in an executed Change Order.

3.   Customer shall promptly identify and notify Vendor of any changes in Law, including Customer's regulatory requirements, that may relate to Customer's use of the Services. The Parties shall work together to identify the impact of such changes on how Customer uses, and Vendor delivers, the Services. Customer shall be responsible for any fines and penalties arising from any noncompliance by Customer with any Law relating to Customer's use of the Services. Subject to the following sen-

tence, if a change in Law prevents or delays Vendor from performing its obligations under this Master Agreement or the Local Service Contract, the Parties shall develop and implement a suitable workaround until such time as Vendor can perform its obligations under this Master Agreement or the Local Service Contract, as the case may be, without such workaround. If a change in Law, including the development or implementation of a workaround, results in Vendor's use of additional resources or an increase in Vendor's costs of providing the Services, Customer shall pay for such additional resources and increased costs at rates agreed upon by the Parties.

ARTICLE 7. THIRD-PARTY SERVICES

7.01 VENDOR OPPORTUNITY. [OPTION 1: Vendor shall have the right to match the material terms of any third party offer received by Customer with respect to any Out-of-Scope Service. If Vendor offers to provide such Out-of-Scope Service to Customer upon substantially similar terms as those set forth in such third party offer, Vendor shall provide to Customer, and Customer shall purchase from Vendor, pursuant to a Change Order or separate agreement, as the case may be, such Out-of-Scope Services upon the terms set forth in such Change Order or separate agreement, including Vendor's charges for such Out-of-Scope Service.] [OPTION 2: With respect to any Out-of-Scope Service, Customer shall (1) notify Vendor at or about the same time that it notifies other vendors that it is considering acquiring an Out-of-Scope Service and provide Vendor with the same information that it provides such other vendors and (2) allow Vendor the opportunity to compete with such other vendors for the provision of such Out-of-Scope Service. If Vendor is selected by Customer to provide such Out-of-Scope Service, Vendor and Customer shall negotiate a Change Order or separate agreement, as the case may be, including Vendor's charges for such Out-of-Scope Service.]

7.02 COOPERATION WITH THIRD-PARTY SERVICE PROVIDERS. Upon Customer's request and reasonable notice, Vendor shall, as an Out-of-Scope Service, cooperate with third-party service providers of Customer; provided, however, that (1) such cooperation does not impact the Services or Vendor's ability to meet the Service Levels and (2) Vendor shall not be required to disclose any of Vendor's Confidential Information to such third party service provider.

ARTICLE 8. CUSTOMER RESPONSIBILITIES

8.01 CUSTOMER MANAGERS.

1. During the Master Term, Customer shall maintain an individual (the "Customer Account Manager"), who shall serve as the primary Customer

representative under this Master Agreement and the Local Service Contracts. The Customer Account Manager shall (a) have overall responsibility for managing and coordinating the performance of Customer's obligations under this Master Agreement and the Local Service Contracts and (b) be authorized to act for and on behalf of Customer with respect to all matters relating to this Master Agreement and the Local Service Contracts.

2. During the Local Service Contract Term, Customer shall maintain a senior executive of Customer (the "<u>Customer Project Manager</u>"), who shall serve as the primary Customer representative under the Local Service Contract. The Customer Project Manager shall (a) have overall responsibility for managing and coordinating the performance of Customer's obligations under the Local Service Contract and (b) be authorized to act for and on behalf of Customer with respect to all matters relating to the Local Service Contract.

8.02 CUSTOMER RESPONSIBILITIES.   During the Local Service Contract Term and in connection with Vendor's performance of the Services under the Local Service Contract, Customer shall, at its expense: (1) be responsible for the obligations and responsibilities set forth in <u>Schedule C to the Local Service Contract</u>; (2) upon Vendor's request, make available to Vendor Customer technical personnel familiar with Customer's business requirements; (3) provide to Vendor complete and accurate information regarding Customer's business requirements in respect of any work to be performed by Vendor under the Local Service Contract; (4) respond within the time period specified in this Master Agreement or the Local Service Contract (or if no time period is specified within three business days) to all deliverables presented to Customer by Vendor for Customer's approval, which approval shall not be unreasonably withheld (if Customer fails to respond within such three-day or other specified period, Customer shall be deemed to have accepted such deliverable); (5) cooperate with Vendor; (6) promptly notify Vendor of any third-party claims that may have an impact on this Master Agreement or the Local Service Contract; and (7) perform all other obligations of Customer described in this Master Agreement and the Local Service Contract.

8.03 CUSTOMER RESOURCES.   Commencing on the Local Service Contract Effective Date and continuing for so long as Vendor requires the same for the performance of the Services, Customer shall provide to Vendor, at no charge to Vendor access to and use of (1) the Customer Technology and (2) the resources set forth in <u>Schedule C to the Local Service Contract</u>.

8.04 CONSENTS.   All Consents shall be obtained and maintained by Customer with Vendor's cooperation. Customer shall pay any costs of obtaining and maintaining the Consents.

8.05 RELIANCE ON INSTRUCTIONS.   In performing its obligations under this Master Agreement or a Local Service Contract, Vendor shall be entitled to rely on instructions, authorizations, approvals, or other information provided to Vendor by Customer. Vendor shall incur no liability or responsibility of any kind in relying or complying with any such instructions or information.

8.06 USE OF SERVICES.

1.   Customer shall not permit any third party to access or use the Services without the consent of Vendor. In the event that Customer authorizes any third party to access or use the Services, the authorizing Party agrees to indemnify, defend and hold Vendor harmless in accordance with the procedures set forth in Section 17.02 from and against any and all Losses arising from or in connection with the access to or use of such Services by such third parties.

2.   Customer may not remarket or sell all or any portion of the Services provided under this Master Agreement or any Local Service Contract, or make all or any portion of the Services available to any party other than Customer, without Vendor's consent.

ARTICLE 9. PROPRIETARY RIGHTS

9.01 [CUSTOMER TECHNOLOGY.   Customer hereby grants to Vendor at no cost to Vendor a nonexclusive right to access and Use in connection with the provision of the Services the Customer Technology. Upon the expiration or termination of the Local Service Contract, the rights granted to Vendor in this Section shall immediately revert to Customer and Vendor shall, at Customer's cost and expense, deliver to Customer a current copy of all the Customer Technology (including any related source code in Vendor's possession) in the form in use as of such date. Customer shall pay all costs and expenses with respect to the Customer Technology, including the costs associated with maintenance, license payments, insurance, taxes, and the Consents. Customer is responsible for maintaining, upgrading, and replacing the Customer Technology as necessary for Vendor to provide the Services. In the event that Customer does not comply with such obligations, Vendor shall be excused from its obligation to perform the Services, including Vendor's obligation to meet the Services Levels, to the extent that its inability to meet such obligation is caused by Customer's failure to comply with its obligations under this Section.]

9.02 VENDOR TECHNOLOGY.   All Vendor Technology (including any modifications, enhancements or changes thereto and derivative works thereof) shall be and shall remain the exclusive property of Vendor or its licensor and Customer shall not have any rights or interests in the Vendor Technology. Customer hereby irrevocably assigns to Vendor any and all rights or interests in the

Vendor Technology (including any modifications, enhancements or changes thereto and derivative works thereof).

9.03 GENERAL SKILLS.   Notwithstanding anything to the contrary in this Master Agreement, the Local Service Contracts or otherwise, Vendor shall retain all right, title, and interest in and to any and all ideas, concepts, know-how, development tools, methodologies, processes, procedures, technologies, and algorithms ("Tools") used, accessed, or developed when providing the Services. Nothing in this Master Agreement or the Local Service Contracts shall restrict Vendor from the use of the Tools. Vendor shall not be prohibited or enjoined at any time from using skills or knowledge of a general nature acquired during the course of providing the Services, including information publicly known or available that could reasonably be acquired in similar work performed for another client of Vendor.

ARTICLE 10.   PAYMENTS TO VENDOR

10.01 FEES.   In consideration of Vendor providing the Services, Customer shall pay to Vendor the Fees, **[subject to the minimum fee requirements set forth in Schedule D to the Local Service Contract]**, as may be adjusted from time to time pursuant to the terms of this Master Agreement and the Local Service Contract.

10.02 TIME OF PAYMENT.   Vendor shall deliver an invoice on or about the **[first]** day of each month for the Services **[to be performed during such month] [performed during the preceding month],** and each such invoice shall be due within ___ days of receipt by Customer. **[CONSIDER INVOICING ON AN ESTIMATED BASIS IN ADVANCE WITH RECONCILIATION AT THE END OF THE MONTH.]** Any sum due Vendor pursuant to this Master Agreement or the Local Service Contract for which a time of payment is not otherwise specified shall be due and payable ___ days after receipt by Customer of an invoice from Vendor. Any amounts not paid by Customer to Vendor when due shall bear interest at a rate of ___ percent per month (or, if lesser, the maximum rate permissible by applicable law), measured from the date such amount was due until the date such amount is paid by Customer to Vendor. Without prejudice to any other rights it has under this Master Agreement or the Local Service Contract, Vendor shall have the right to suspend the provision of the Services to Customer, modify the payment terms to require full payment before providing additional Services, or terminate this Master Agreement or the applicable Local Service Contract(s) for breach without the opportunity for cure, if Vendor has not received payment of an invoice within ___ days after the invoice date. Customer shall pay to Vendor all expenses incurred by Vendor in exercising any of its rights under this Master Agreement, the Local Service Contracts or applicable Law with respect to the collection of a payment, including reasonable attorneys' fees and collection agency fees.

10.03 DISPUTED AMOUNTS.   If Customer, in good faith, disputes any invoice charges regarding the Services, it may withhold from its payment of the relevant invoice any such disputed amounts (except for applicable taxes), up to a maximum of the lesser of the amount for the Services to which the dispute relates and ___ percent of the average monthly Fees for the previous   months. Customer shall pay to Vendor withheld amounts, plus interest at a rate of ___ percent per month (or, if lesser, the maximum rate permissible by applicable law), measured from the date such amount was due until the date such amount is paid by Customer to Vendor, in accordance with the resolution of the dispute. Notwithstanding any dispute and in accordance with this Section, Customer shall remit to Vendor the invoiced amount, less the disputed amount, in accordance with this Section and Section 10.02.

10.04 PERMITS AND APPROVALS.   Customer shall (1) be responsible for and carry the risk of obtaining all consents, permissible, approvals, and assurances of whatever nature, which may be needed to make payments as required under this Master Agreement and the Local Service Contract and (2) use all reasonable efforts to obtain all such consents, permissible, approvals, and assurances required by any law or governmental authority.

10.05 EXPENSES.

1.   Unless otherwise agreed, Customer shall reimburse Vendor for all travel expenses, living, hotel, and transportation allowances and other normally reimbursable expenses and allowances for any member of the Project Staff traveling in connection with the Services, all as reasonably incurred and in accordance with Vendor's generally applicable personnel practices and procedures.

2.   The Fees and the Service Levels each relate to normal expected operation. Customer recognizes that in the event of an emergency, Vendor may incur additional costs and expenses to ensure continuation of the Services, including by providing the Services from the premises of a third party. If such resources or costs are reasonable in the light of the emergency, then Customer shall pay for such additional resources and increased costs at rates agreed upon by the Parties.

10.06 PRORATION.   All periodic charges under this Master Agreement and the Local Service Contract are to be computed on a calendar month basis and shall be prorated on a per diem basis for any partial month.

10.07 VERIFICATION OF INFORMATION.   The obligations of the Parties and the charges set forth in the Local Service Contract are based on information furnished by Customer to Vendor, but such information has not been independently verified by Vendor. Customer believes that such information is accurate and complete. However, if Vendor determines that any such information should prove to be inaccurate or incomplete in any adverse material respect, Vendor and Customer shall negotiate appropriate adjustments to the provisions of this Master Agreement and the Local Service Contract, including the Fees.

10.08 TAXES.   The Fees paid to Vendor are exclusive of any applicable sales, use, gross receipts, excise, value-added, withholding, personal property, or other taxes attributable to periods on or after the Local Service Contract Effective Date. In the event that a sales, use, excise, gross receipts, or services tax is assessed on the provision of the Services by Vendor to Customer or on Vendor's charges to Customer under this Master Agreement or the Local Service Contract, however levied or assessed, Customer shall bear and be responsible for and pay the amount of any such tax or, if applicable, reimburse Vendor for the amount of any such tax.

10.09 EXTRAORDINARY CHANGES IN WORKLOAD.   **[If, during the Local Service Contract Term, Customer experiences significant changes in the scope or nature of its business that have or are reasonably expected to have the effect of causing a sustained substantial decrease of [___] percent or more in the amount of resources Vendor uses in performing the Services, provided such decreases are not due to Customer resuming the provision of such Services by itself or Customer transferring the provision of such Services to another vendor, Customer shall notify Vendor of any event or events which Customer believes may result in such sustained decrease and Vendor shall identify, in a plan that shall be submitted to Customer for review and acceptance, any changes that can be made to accommodate the extraordinary decrease of resource requirements in a cost-effective manner, without disruption to Customer's ongoing operations. Upon Customer's acceptance of Vendor's plan, Vendor shall make any applicable adjustments to the Fees to reflect the foregoing and distribute an amended <u>Schedule D to the Local Service Contract</u> to the Parties.]**

ARTICLE 11.   AUDIT

11.01 VERIFICATION OF FEES.   Upon __ days' notice from Customer and not more than __ during each Local Service Contract Year, Vendor shall furnish to Customer a certificate verifying the Fees. The cost of the verification shall be paid by Customer. Such certificate shall be conclusive. Any requests for verification of the Fees shall be made no later than two years from the end of the Local Service Contract Year in which the Fees were incurred.

11.02 AUDIT EXPENSES.   If Vendor is required to provide services or incur costs, other than of a routine nature, in connection with any audit pursuant to this Article, then Customer shall pay for such resources and costs at rates agreed upon by the Parties.

ARTICLE 12. DATA AND REPORTS

12.01 PROVISION OF DATA. Customer shall supply to Vendor, in connection with the Services, required data in the form and on such time schedules as may be agreed upon by Vendor and Customer ("Customer Data") in order to permit Vendor to perform the Services in accordance with the terms of the Local Service Contract, including the Service Levels. All Customer Data is, or shall be, and shall remain the property of Customer.

12.02 INSPECTION OF REPORTS. Customer shall use reasonable efforts to inspect and review reports and provide Vendor with notice of any errors or inaccuracies (1) in daily or weekly reports, within two business days of receipt of such reports, and (2) in monthly or other reports, within five business days of receipt of such reports. Vendor shall provide Customer with such documentation and information as may be requested by Customer in order to verify the accuracy of the reports. If Customer fails to reject any such report within the applicable period, Customer shall be deemed to have accepted such report.

12.03 CORRECTION OF ERRORS. Upon notice from Customer and at Customer's expense, Vendor shall promptly correct any errors or inaccuracies in Customer Data and reports prepared by Vendor as part of the Services, to the extent not caused by Vendor or Vendor Representatives.

12.04 DATA PROTECTION. **[In the event the Services require the access to or use of personal data, each Party shall be responsible for taking all necessary steps required by applicable Law to ensure the protection of the privacy of such personal data to be accessed or used. In the event that applicable law requires registration with a governmental authority, the Parties shall determine which Party shall register, or cause such registration, with such governmental authority.] [ADD RELEVANT DATA PRIVACY LANGUAGE.]**

ARTICLE 13. CONFIDENTIALITY AND SECURITY

13.01 GENERAL OBLIGATIONS.

1. All Confidential Information relating to or obtained from Customer or Vendor shall be held in confidence by the recipient to the same extent and in at least the same manner as the recipient protects its own confidential or proprietary information.

2. Neither Customer nor Vendor shall disclose, publish, release, transfer, or otherwise make available Confidential Information of, or obtained from, the other in any form to, or for the use or benefit of, any person or entity without the disclosing Party's consent. Each of Customer and Vendor shall, however, be permitted to disclose relevant aspects of the

other's Confidential Information to its officers, directors, employees, representatives, and professional and legal advisors to the extent that such disclosure is not restricted by law or by order of any court or governmental authority and only to the extent that such disclosure is related to the performance of its duties and obligations under this Master Agreement and the Local Service Contract; provided, however, that the recipient shall be responsible for ensuring that such officers, directors, employees, representatives, and professional and legal advisors abide by the provisions of this Master Agreement and the Local Service Contract.

13.02 EXCLUSIONS. The obligations in Section 13.01 shall not restrict any disclosure pursuant to any applicable law or by order of any court or governmental authority (provided that the recipient shall give prompt notice to the disclosing Party of such order) and, except to the extent that applicable law provides otherwise, shall not apply with respect to information that (1) is independently developed by the recipient without violating the disclosing Party's proprietary rights as shown by the recipient's written records, (2) is or becomes publicly known (other than through unauthorized disclosure), (3) is disclosed by the owner of such information to a third party free of any obligation of confidentiality, (4) is already known by the recipient at the time of disclosure, as shown by the recipient's written records, and the recipient has no obligation of confidentiality other than pursuant to this Master Agreement, any Local Service Contract, or any confidentiality agreements entered into before the Master Effective Date between Customer and Vendor, or (5) is rightfully received by a Party free of any obligation of confidentiality.

13.03 UNAUTHORIZED ACTS. Without limiting the other Parties' rights in respect of a breach of this Article, each Party shall:

1. promptly notify the other Parties of any unauthorized possession, use, or knowledge, or attempt thereof, of the other Parties' Confidential Information by any person or entity that may become known to such Party, including any incidents involving a breach of security and any incidents that might indicate or lead to a threat to, or weakness in, security and any attempt to make unauthorized use of the Services or the Technology used in connection with the provision of the Services;

2. promptly furnish to the other Parties full details of the unauthorized possession, use, or knowledge, or attempt thereof, and assist the other Parties in investigating or preventing the recurrence of any unauthorized possession, use, or knowledge, or attempt thereof, of Confidential Information;

3. cooperate with the other Parties in any litigation and investigation against third parties deemed necessary by the other Parties to protect their proprietary rights; and

4. promptly use its best efforts to prevent a recurrence of any such unauthorized possession, use, or knowledge, or attempt thereof, of Confidential Information.

Each Party shall bear the cost it incurs as a result of compliance with this Section.

13.04 INJUNCTIVE RELIEF. Each Party recognizes that its disclosure of Confidential Information of the other Parties may give rise to irreparable injury to such Party(ies) and acknowledges that remedies other than injunctive relief may not be adequate. Accordingly, each Party has the right to equitable and injunctive relief to prevent the unauthorized possession, use, disclosure, or knowledge of any Confidential Information, as well as to such damages or other relief as is occasioned by such unauthorized possession, use, disclosure, or knowledge.

13.05 SECURITY POLICIES. **[Upon Customer's request and agreement of the Parties as to scope and implementation, Vendor shall makes change necessary to comply with security requirements and specifications of Customer at rates to be agreed upon by the Parties.]**

ARTICLE 14. REPRESENTATIONS AND ADDITIONAL COVENANTS

14.01 MUTUAL. Each Party hereby represents and warrants that:

1. it has all requisite corporate power and authority to enter into this Master Agreement and the Local Service Contract and to carry out the transactions contemplated hereby;

2. the execution, delivery, and performance of this Master Agreement and the Local Service Contract and the consummation of the transactions contemplated hereby have been duly authorized by all requisite corporate action on the part of such Party;

3. this Master Agreement and the Local Service Contract has been duly executed and delivered by such Party and (assuming the due authorization, execution and delivery hereof by the other Party) is a valid and binding obligation of such Party, enforceable against it in accordance with its terms; and

4. its entry into this Master Agreement or the Local Service Contract does not violate or constitute a breach of any of its contractual obligations with third parties.

14.02 REGULATIONS. Customer shall obtain and furnish to Vendor any approvals, consents, licenses, and permits required or recommended by any law or governmental authority in connection with (a) the execution of this Master Agreement and the Local Service Contract and (b) the performance and receipt of the Services.

14.03 DISCLAIMERS.

1. Vendor does not warrant the accuracy of any advice, report, data, or other product delivered to Customer that is produced with or from Customer Data or Technology provided by Customer. Such products are delivered "AS IS," and Vendor shall not be liable for any inaccuracy thereof.

2. **EXCEPT AS EXPRESSLY SET FORTH IN <u>SECTION 14.01</u>, VENDOR DOES NOT MAKE ANY OTHER WARRANTIES OR REPRESENTATIONS WITH RESPECT TO THE SERVICES AND EXPRESSLY DISCLAIMS ALL OTHER REPRESENTATIONS AND WARRANTIES, EXPRESS OR IMPLIED, INCLUDING ANY IMPLIED WARRANTIES OF MERCHANTABILITY AND FITNESS FOR A SPECIFIC PURPOSE. VENDOR DOES NOT WARRANT THAT THE SERVICES SHALL MEET CUSTOMER'S REQUIREMENTS, THAT THE PERFORMANCE OF THE SERVICES SHALL BE UNINTERRUPTED OR ERROR-FREE, THAT ALL ERRORS IN THE SERVICES SHALL BE CORRECTED.**

3. **VENDOR DOES NOT AND CANNOT CONTROL THE FLOW OF DATA TO AND FROM CUSTOMER'S NETWORK AND SYSTEMS AND THE INTERNET. SUCH FLOW DEPENDS ON THE PERFORMANCE OF NETWORK, SYSTEMS AND INTERNET COMPONENTS AND SERVICES CONTROLLED BY CUSTOMER OR THIRD PARTIES. VENDOR CANNOT GUARANTEE THAT DISRUPTIONS AND PROBLEMS WILL NOT OCCUR, AND EXPRESSLY DISCLAIMS ANY AND ALL LIABILITY ARISING THEREFROM.**

ARTICLE 15. DISPUTE RESOLUTION

15.01 LOCAL SERVICE CONTRACT.   Any dispute arising under the Local Service Contract shall be considered in person or by telephone by the Customer Project Manager and the Vendor Project Manager within seven business days of receipt of a notice from a Party specifying the nature of the dispute; provided, however, that a dispute relating to <u>Article 13</u> shall not be subject to this Section. In the event the Customer Project Manager and the Vendor Project Manager are unable to resolve, or do not anticipate resolving, the dispute within such seven-day period, the Customer Project Manager and the Vendor Project Manager shall submit the dispute to the Vendor Account Manager and the Customer Account Manager for their consideration in accordance with <u>Section 15.02</u>.

15.02 MASTER AGREEMENT.   Any dispute arising under this Master Agreement or, subject to <u>Section 15.01</u>, the Local Service Contract shall be considered in person or by telephone by the Customer Account Manager and the Vendor

Account Manager within seven business days of receipt of a notice from a Party specifying the nature of the dispute; provided, however, that a dispute relating to Article 13 shall not be subject to this Section. Unless the Customer Account Manager and the Vendor Account Manager otherwise agree, a Party may pursue its rights and remedies under Section 15.03 after the occurrence of such meeting or telephone conversation.

15.03 ARBITRATION.   [IF U.S. TRANSACTION: Failing the settlement of a dispute pursuant to Section 15.01 or Section 15.02, as applicable, such dispute shall be finally and exclusively settled by binding arbitration in accordance with the then-current C.P.R. Institute for Dispute Resolution Rules for Non-Administered Arbitration of Business Disputes, and this Section. The arbitration shall be governed by the United States Arbitration Act, 9 U.S.C. §~ 1-16, to the exclusion of any provision of state law inconsistent therewith or which would produce a different result, and judgment upon the award rendered by the arbitrator may be entered by any court of competent jurisdiction. The arbitration shall be held in _____. There shall be one arbitrator. The arbitrator shall set forth the reasons for the award in writing.]

ARTICLE 16. TERMINATION

16.01 BY VENDOR.   Vendor shall have the right to terminate this Master Agreement or the Local Service Contract if: (1) Customer fails to pay any amounts payable under this Master Agreement or the Local Service Contract when due; (2) Customer fails to perform any of its material nonmonetary obligations under this Master Agreement or the Local Service Contract, and does not cure such default within 15 days of receipt of notice of default from Vendor; or (3) Customer becomes or is declared insolvent or bankrupt, is the subject of any proceedings relating to its liquidation, insolvency, or for the appointment of a receiver or similar officer for it, makes an assignment for the benefit of all or substantially all of its creditors, or enters into an agreement for the composition, extension, or readjustment of all or substantially all of its obligations.

16.02 BY CUSTOMER.   If Vendor materially fails to perform any of its material obligations under the Local Service Contract, Customer may give Vendor notice of such failure. Vendor shall within 45 days of receipt of such notice remedy the failure specified therein. In the event Vendor fails to remedy the failure within such 45-day period, Customer may give a termination notice to Vendor and may terminate the Local Service Contract under which the breach occurred; provided, however, that the time to cure a breach shall extend for up to 30 days from the date on which the notice of breach is received by Vendor if Vendor has promptly commenced to cure the breach and continues to use reasonable efforts to cure such breach during the 30-day period.

16.03 FOR CONVENIENCE. [Either Vendor or Customer may terminate a Local Service Contract upon no less than 90 days' notice to all of the other Parties. Customer shall pay for all services performed by Vendor through the effective date of termination (including works-in-progress), plus any wind-down fees set forth in the Local Service Contract.]

16.04 TERMINATION OF MASTER AGREEMENT. [Upon the termination of this Master Agreement, all Local Service Contracts then in effect shall simultaneously terminate.]

ARTICLE 17. INDEMNITIES

17.01 BY CUSTOMER. Customer agrees to indemnify, defend, and hold Vendor and Vendor Representatives harmless from and against any and all Losses arising from any claim relating to (1) the infringement by or of the Customer Technology and any other resources or items provided to Vendor or Vendor Representatives by Customer or Customer Representatives; (2) any amounts, including taxes, interest, and penalties, which are obligations of Customer; (3) any products or services provided by Customer or Customer Representatives to third parties; and (4) any claim by or relating to an end user of the Services.

17.02 INDEMNIFICATION PROCEDURES. If any third-party claim is commenced against a Party entitled to indemnification under Section 8.05 and Section 17.01 (the "Indemnified Party"), notice thereof shall be given to the Party that is obligated to provide indemnification (the "Indemnifying Party") as promptly as practicable. If, after such notice, the Indemnifying Party shall acknowledge that this Section applies with respect to such claim, then the Indemnifying Party shall be entitled, if it so elects, in a notice promptly delivered to the Indemnified Party, but in no event less than 10 days prior to the date on which a response to such claim is due, to immediately take control of the defense and investigation of such claim and to employ and engage attorneys reasonably acceptable to the Indemnified Party to handle and defend the same, at the Indemnifying Party's sole cost and expense. The Indemnified Party shall cooperate, at the cost of the Indemnifying Party, in all reasonable respects with the Indemnifying Party and its attorneys in the investigation, trial, and defense of such claim and any appeal arising therefrom; provided, however, that the Indemnified Party may, at its own cost and expense, participate, through its attorneys or otherwise, in such investigation, trial, and defense of such claim and any appeal arising therefrom. No settlement of a claim pursuant to this Section that involves a remedy other than the payment of money by the Indemnifying Party shall be entered into without the consent of the Indemnified Party. After notice by the Indemnifying Party to the Indemnified Party of its election to assume full control of the defense of any such claim, the Indemnifying Party shall not be liable to the Indemnified Party for any legal expenses incurred thereafter by such Indemnified Party in connection with the defense of that claim. If the Indemnifying Party does not assume full control over the defense of a claim subject to such defense as provided in this Section, the Indemnifying Party may participate in such defense, at its sole cost and expense, and the Indemnified Party shall have the right to defend the claim in such manner as it may deem appropriate, at the cost and expense of the Indemnifying Party.

ARTICLE 18. DAMAGES

18.01 DIRECT DAMAGES.

1. **ANY AND ALL CLAIMS ASSERTING LIABILITY OF VENDOR OR VENDOR REPRESENTATIVES TO CUSTOMER OR ANY THIRD PARTY ARISING FROM OR IN CONNECTION WITH THE SERVICE CONTRACT OR THE PROVISION OF SER VICES, HOWEVER CAUSED, REGARDLESS OF THE FORM OF ACTION AND ON ANY THEORY OF LIABILITY, INCLUDING CONTRACT, STRICT LIABILITY, NEGLIGENCE, OR OTHER TORT, SHALL BE BROUGHT UNDER THE APPLICABLE SERVICE CONTRACT.**

2. **THE ENTIRE LIABILITY OF VENDOR AND VENDOR REPRESENTATIVES TO CUSTOMER OR ANY THIRD PARTY ARISING FROM OR IN CONNECTION WITH THE SERVICE CONTRACT OR THE PROVISION OF SERVICES, HOWEVER CAUSED, REGARDLESS OF THE FORM OF ACTION AND ON ANY THEORY OF LIABILITY, INCLUDING CONTRACT, STRICT LIABILITY, NEGLIGENCE, OR OTHER TORT, SHALL BE LIMITED TO DIRECT DAMAGES NOT TO EXCEED IN THE AGGREGATE THE AMOUNT ACTUALLY PAID BY CUSTOMER TO VENDOR UNDER THE APPLICABLE SERVICE CONTRACT FOR THE AFFECTED SERVICES DURING THE [FILL IN NUMBER OF MONTHS] PRIOR TO THE OCCURRENCE OF THE FIRST EVENT WHICH IS THE SUBJECT OF THE FIRST CLAIM.**

18.02 CONSEQUENTIAL DAMAGES.   In no event shall a Party have any liability, regardless of the form of action and on any theory of liability, including contract, strict liability, negligence, or other tort, for any loss of interest, profit or revenue, replacement goods, loss of technology, rights or services, loss of data or interruption, or loss of use of service or equipment by another Party or for any consequential, indirect, incidental, special, punitive, or exemplary damages suffered by another Party, arising from or related to this Master Agreement or the Local Service Contract, even if such Party has been advised of the possibility of such losses or damages; provided, however, that this Section shall not prevent Vendor from recovering amounts payable under this Master Agreement or any Local Service Contract for the provision of the Services.

18.03 EXCLUSIONS AND LIMITATIONS.

1. The limitations or exclusions of liability set forth in this Article are not applicable to the obligation or failure of Customer to make payments due or past due under this Master Agreement or the Local Service Contract. In addition, in no event shall Vendor or Vendor Representatives be liable for any damages if, and to the extent, caused by Customer's failure to perform its responsibilities, as set forth in this Master Agreement or the Local Service Contract. The limitations and exclusions set forth in this Master Agreement and the Local Service Contract apply to Vendor and Vendor Representatives and represent the maximum aggregate amount for which Vendor and Vendor Representatives are collectively responsible.

2. In no event shall Vendor or Vendor Representatives be responsible or liable for (a) any corruption, damage, loss, or mistransmission of data or (b) the security of data during transmission via public telecommunications facilities.

18.04 ACKNOWLEDGMENT.   Vendor and Customer each acknowledge that the limitations and exclusions set forth in this Master Agreement and the Local Service Contract have been the subject of active and complete negotiations between the Parties and represent the Parties' agreement based on the level of risk to Vendor and Customer associated with their respective obligations under this Master Agreement and the Local Service Contract and the payments made to Vendor pursuant to this Master Agreement and the Local Service Contract.

[ADD INSURANCE OBLIGATIONS]

ARTICLE 19. MISCELLANEOUS PROVISIONS

19.01 NOTICES.   Except as otherwise specified in this Master Agreement or the Local Service Contract, all notices, requests, consents, approvals, agreements, authorizations, acknowledgements, waivers, and other communications required or permitted under this Master Agreement and the Local Service Contract shall be in writing and shall be deemed given when sent by facsimile to the facsimile number specified below or delivered by hand to the address specified below. A copy of any such notice shall also be sent by express air mail on the date such notice is transmitted by facsimile to the address specified below:

In the case of Vendor:
[ADDRESS]
Attention:
Fax No.:

In the case of Customer:
[ADDRESS]
Attention:
Fax No.:

A Party may change its address or facsimile number for notification purposes by giving the other Parties 10 days' notice of the new address or facsimile number and the date upon which it shall become effective.

19.02 ASSIGNMENT AND THIRD PARTY BENEFICIARIES.   Customer may not, without the consent of Vendor, assign this Master Agreement or any Local Service Contract or any of its rights under this Master Agreement or any Local Service Contract, in whole or in part, and may not delegate its obligations under this Master Agreement or any Local Service Contract. Any such purported assignment or delegation in contravention of this Section shall be null and void. Each Party intends that this Master Agreement and the Local Service Contract shall not benefit, or create any right or cause of action in or on behalf of, any person or entity other than the Parties.

19.03 RELATIONSHIP.   The Parties intend to create an independent contractor relationship, and nothing contained in this Master Agreement or the Local Service Contract shall be construed to make either Vendor or Vendor partners, joint venturers, agents, principals, representatives, or employees of the other. Except as expressly set forth in the Service Agreement, no officer, director, employee, or Vendor Representative retained by Vendor to perform work on Customer's behalf under this Master Agreement or the Local Service Contract shall be deemed to be an employee of Customer or Customer Representative. None of the Parties shall have any right, power, or authority, express or implied, to bind the other. Vendor shall have the sole right to supervise, manage, contract, direct, procure, perform, or cause to be performed all work to be performed by Vendor under this Master Agreement and the Local Service Contract.

19.04 SEVERABILITY AND WAIVERS.   If any provision of this Master Agreement or the Local Service Contract is held by a court of competent jurisdiction to be contrary to Law, then the remaining provisions of this Master Agreement or the Local Service Contract, if capable of substantial performance, shall remain in full force and effect. No delay or omission by a Party to exercise any right or power it has under this Master Agreement or the Local Service Contract shall impair or be construed as a waiver of such right or power. A waiver by any Party of any breach or covenant shall not be construed to be a waiver of any succeeding breach or any other covenant. All waivers must be signed by the Party waiving its rights.

19.05 [SURVIVAL.   The terms of [TO BE FILLED IN] shall survive the expiration or termination of this Master Agreement and the Local Service Contract.] [OPTION: BE SILENT]

19.06 GOVERNING LAW.   This Master Agreement and the Local Service Contract and the rights and obligations of the Parties under this Master Agreement and the Local Service Contract shall be governed by and construed in accordance with the Laws of _____, without giving effect to the principles thereof relating to the conflicts of Laws.

19.07 SOLE AND EXCLUSIVE VENUE.   Subject to the provisions of <u>Article 15</u>, each Party irrevocably agrees that any legal action, suit, or proceeding brought by it in any way arising out of this Master Agreement or the Local Service Contract must be brought solely and exclusively in _____and irrevocably accepts and submits to the sole and exclusive jurisdiction of each of the aforesaid courts in personam, generally and unconditionally with respect to any action, suit, or proceeding brought by it or against it by another Party[; **provided, however, that this Section shall not prevent a Party against whom any legal action, suit, or proceeding is brought by another Party from seeking to remove such legal action, suit, or proceeding, pursuant to applicable federal law, to the U.S. district court for the district and division embracing the place where the action is pending in the state courts of _____, and in the event an action is so removed the Parties irrevocably accept and submit to the jurisdiction of the aforesaid district court.**] Each of the Parties hereto further irrevocably consents to the service of process from any of the aforesaid courts by mailing copies thereof by registered or certified mail, postage prepaid, to such Party at its address designated pursuant to this Master Agreement or the Local Service Contract, with such service of process to become effective 30 days after such mailing.

19.08 [EXPORT.   None of the Parties shall export, directly or indirectly, any information acquired under this Master Agreement or any Local Service Contract or any product utilizing such information to any country for which the U.S. government or any agency thereof or any other governmental authority at the time of export requires an export license or other governmental approval without first obtaining such license or approval.] [Nothing in this Section shall be construed as a submission by the Parties to the Laws or the jurisdiction of any court, state or federal, of the United States of America.]

19.09 *FORCE MAJEURE.*   If and to the extent that a Party's performance of any of its nonmonetary obligations pursuant to this Master Agreement or the Local Service Contract is prevented, hindered, or delayed by fire, flood, earthquake, elements of nature or acts of God, acts of war, terrorism, riots, civil disorders, rebellions, revolutions, strikes, labor disputes, compliance with laws, any acts by a third party, any third-party products or services, or any other cause beyond the reasonable control of such Party, including failures or fluctuations in electrical power, heat, light, air conditioning or telecommunications equipment (each, a "*Force Majeure* Event"), then the nonperforming, hindered, or delayed Party shall be excused for such nonperformance, hindrance, or delay, as applicable, of those obligations (except for monetary payment obligations) affected by the *Force Majeure* Event for as long as such *Force Majeure* Event continues and such Party continues to use commercially reasonable efforts to recommence performance whenever and to whatever extent possible without delay, including through the use of alternate sources, workaround plans, or other means. The Party whose performance is prevented, hindered, or delayed by a *Force Majeure* Event shall immediately notify the other Parties of the occurrence of the *Force Majeure* Event and describe in reasonable detail the nature of the *Force Majeure* Event.

19.10 NONPERFORMANCE. In the event that Vendor's performance of the Services requires or is contingent on the performance by Customer of an obligation under this Master Agreement or the Local Service Contract, and Customer delays or withholds such performance beyond the agreed-upon time period (or beyond five days, if a time period is not specified), the time for the performance of Vendor's obligations shall be extended for the period of such delay in, or withholding of, performance.

19.11 RIGHT TO PROVIDE SERVICES. Each Party recognizes that Vendor personnel providing services to Customer under this Master Agreement and the Local Service Contract may perform similar services for others, and neither this Master Agreement nor the Local Service Contract shall prevent Vendor from using the personnel and equipment provided to Customer under this Master Agreement or the Local Service Contract for such purposes. Nothing in this Master Agreement nor any Local Service Contract shall impair Vendor's right to acquire, license, or develop for itself or others or have others develop for Vendor similar technology performing the same or similar services as contemplated by this Master Agreement or any Local Service Contract. Vendor may perform its obligations under this Master Agreement and the Local Service Contract through the use of Vendor Representatives; provided, however, that Vendor shall not be relieved of its obligations under this Master Agreement or the Local Service Contract by such use of such Vendor Representatives.

19.12 NONDISPARAGEMENT. Each Party shall refrain, and shall use commercially reasonable efforts to cause its employees and Representatives to refrain, from making negative or disparaging comments about the other Parties.

19.13 FURTHER ASSURANCES. Each of the Parties acknowledges and agrees that, subsequent to the execution and delivery of this Master Agreement and the Local Service Contract and without any additional consideration, each of the Parties shall execute and deliver any further legal instruments and perform any actions which are or may become necessary to effectuate the purposes of this Master Agreement or the Local Service Contract.

19.14 SOLICITATION. During the Local Service Contract Term and for __ months after the expiration or termination of the Local Service Contract, neither Customer may not solicit or hire directly or directly, on its own behalf or on behalf of others, any Vendor employees or contractors without Vendor's consent.

19.15 LIMITATION PERIOD. None of the Parties may bring an action, regardless of form, arising out of this Master Agreement or the Local Service Contract more than __ years after the cause of action has arisen or the date such cause of action was or should have been discovered.

19.16 NEGOTIATED TERMS. The Parties agree that the terms and conditions of this Master Agreement and the Local Service Contract are the result of negotiations between the Parties and that neither this Master Agreement nor the Local Service Contract shall be construed in favor of or against any Party by reason of the extent to which any Party or its professional advisors participated in the preparation of this Master Agreement or the Local Service Contract.

19.17 ENTIRE AGREEMENT; AMENDMENTS; COUNTERPARTS. This Master Agreement and the Local Service Contract represent the entire agreement between the Parties with respect to its subject matter, and there are no other representations, understandings, or agreements between the Parties relative to such subject matter. No amendment to, or change, waiver, or discharge of, any provision of this Master Agreement or the Local Service Contract shall be valid unless in writing and signed by an authorized representative of each of the Parties. This Master Agreement and the Local Service Contract may be executed in any number of counterparts, each of which shall be deemed an original, but all of which taken together shall constitute one single agreement between the Parties.

IN WITNESS WHEREOF, each of Vendor and Customer has caused this Master Agreement to be signed and delivered by its duly authorized representative.

Vendor
By: _____
Name:
Title:

Customer
By: _____
Name:
Title:

EXHIBIT 1. DEFINITIONS

1. "Change" shall have the meaning set forth in Article 6.

2. "Change Order" shall mean a document agreed upon by Vendor and Customer (1) implementing a Change or (2) adding an Out-of-Scope Service under the Service Agreement.

3. "Confidential Information" shall mean (1) with respect to Customer, any information, technical data or know-how of Customer, which is identified by Customer as confidential at the time of disclosure; (2) with respect to Vendor, any information, technical data, or know-how of Vendor disclosed by or relating to Vendor, including the Vendor; and (3) with respect to Customer and Vendor, the terms of this Master Agreement and the Local Service Contract.]

4. "Consents" shall mean all licenses, consents, authorizations, and approvals that are necessary to allow Vendor and Vendor Representatives to provide the Services to Customer, including the use and access of the Customer Technology.

5. "Control" shall mean, with respect to any entity, the possession, directly or indirectly, of the power to direct or cause the direction of the management and policies of such entity, whether through the ownership of voting securities (or other ownership interest), by contract or otherwise.

6. "Customer Account Manager" shall have the meaning set forth in Section 8.01(1).

7. "Customer" shall mean [CUSTOMER] a [SPECIFY LOCATION OF INC. OR FORMATION] [corporation/partnership/other], having its principal place of business at [_____].

8. "Customer Data" shall have the meaning set forth in Section 12.01.

9. "Customer Project Manager" shall have the meaning set forth in Section 8.01(2).

10. "Customer Representatives" shall mean contractors and agents of Customer.

11. "Customer Technology" shall mean the Technology owned by Customer or licensed by Customer from a third party (excluding any Vendor Technology) that Vendor uses or accesses in connection with the provision of the Services.

12. "Fees" shall have the meaning set forth in Section *** of the Local Service Contract.

13. "*Force Majeure* Event" shall have the meaning set forth in Section 19.09.

14. "Governmental Authority" shall mean any international, national, provincial, municipal, local, territorial, or other governmental department, regulatory authority, judicial, or administrative body, domestic, international or foreign.

15.   "Indemnified Party" shall have the meaning set forth in Section 17.02.

16.   "Indemnifying Party" shall have the meaning set forth in Section 17.02.

17.   "Initial Local Service Contract Term" shall have the meaning set forth in Section 3.02.

18.   "Law" shall mean any declaration, decree, directive, legislative enactment, order, ordinance, regulation, rule or other binding requirement of or by any Governmental Authority.

19.   "Local Service Contract(s)" shall have the meaning set forth in Section 1.01.

20.   "Local Service Contract Year" shall mean each 12-month period during the Local Service Contract Term commencing on the Local Service Contract Effective Date and thereafter upon the completion of the immediately preceding Local Service Contract Year.

21.   "Local Service Contract Effective Date" shall have the meaning set forth in Section *** of the Local Service Contract.

22.   "Local Service Contract Term" shall mean the Initial Local Service Contract Term and the Renewal Local Service Contract Terms, collectively.

23.   "Losses" shall mean any and all damages, fines, penalties, deficiencies, losses, liabilities (including settlements and judgments), and expenses (including interest, court costs, reasonable fees, and expenses of attorneys, accountants, and other experts or other reasonable fees and expenses of litigation or other proceedings or of any claim, default, or assessment).

24.   **["Machines" shall mean computers and related equipment, including central processing units and other processors, controllers, modems, communications and telecommunications equipment (voice, data and video), cables, storage devices, printers, terminals, other peripherals and input and output devices, and other tangible mechanical and electronic equipment intended for the processing, input, output, storage, manipulation, communication, transmission, and retrieval of information and data.]**

25.   "Master Agreement" shall mean this Master Services Agreement, dated as of _____, by and between Vendor and Customer.

26.   "Master Effective Date" shall mean _____.

27.   "Master Term" shall have the meaning set forth in Section 3.01.

28.   "Out-of-Scope Service(s)" shall mean any service that is not expressly included within the scope of the Services.

29.   "Parties" shall mean Vendor and Customer, collectively.

30.   "Party" shall mean either Vendor or Customer, as the case may be.

31.   "Project Staff" shall mean the personnel of Vendor and Vendor Representatives who provide the Services.

32. "Related Documentation" shall mean, with respect to Technology, all materials, documentation, specifications, technical manuals, user manuals, flow diagrams, file descriptions, and other written information that describes the function and use of such Technology, as applicable.

33. "Renewal Local Service Contract Term" shall have the meaning set forth in Section 3.02.

34. "Representatives" shall mean Customer Representatives or Vendor Representatives, as the case may be.

35. "Service Levels" shall have the meaning set forth in Section *** of the Local Service Contract.

36. "Services" shall have the meaning set forth in Section *** of the Local Service Contract.

37. "Technology" shall mean (1) applications programs, operating system software, computer software languages, utilities, other computer programs, (2) processes, methodologies, procedures, and trade secrets, (3) literary works and other works of authorship, including reports, drawings, charts, graphics, and other documentation, (4) Related Documentation, in whatever form or media, and (5) the tangible media upon which the foregoing are recorded or printed.

38. **["Threshold Limits" shall mean, with respect to a Service, the maximum increase or decrease in resource requirements for performing such Service that Vendor shall undertake, as set forth in Schedule D to the Local Service Contract.]**

39. "Tools" shall have the meaning set forth in Section 9.03.

40. "Use" shall mean the right to load, execute, store, transmit, display, copy, maintain, modify, enhance, create derivative works, make, and have made.

41. "Vendor" shall mean _____

42. "Vendor Account Manager" shall have the meaning set forth in Section 4.02(1).

43. "Vendor Project Manager" shall have the meaning set forth in Section 4.02(2).

44. "Vendor Representatives" shall mean Vendor Affiliates and subcontractors, suppliers, and agents of Vendor and Vendor Affiliates.

45. "Vendor Technology" shall mean the Technology owned or developed by or on behalf of Vendor or licensed by Vendor from a third party, that Vendor uses in connection with the Services.

EXAMPLE OF LOCAL COUNSEL QUESTIONNAIRE FOR INTERNATIONAL OUTSOURCING TRANSACTIONS

[To be provided to local counsel in each of the countries to/from which services will be provided by Vendor. Please note that this questionnaire is intended to cover as many issues as possible. Depending on the scope of the transaction, Customer's internal resources, and Customer's experience with the topics set forth below, it may not be necessary to submit all of the issues set forth below to local counsel.]

CONFIDENTIAL

[DATE]

[NAME OF LOCAL COUNSEL]:

Customer intends to enter into **[DESCRIBE PROPOSED TRANSACTION]**. All information relating to the proposed transaction is strictly confidential and should not be disclosed to or discussed with any third parties. Information relating to this transaction should be disclosed to personnel of your firm only on a need-to-know basis. Please provide answers to each of the questions set forth below. You should respond as comprehensively as possible based on the facts as you know them at this time.

1. **Response Date**. All responses should be sent to the individual set forth below by **[DATE].**

   [NAME]

   [TITLE]

   [ADDRESS]

   [TELEPHONE NUMBER]

   [FAX NUMBER]

   If you are unable to meet this deadline, please advise the above individual as soon as possible.

2. **General**. Please identify and summarize any local laws and regulations (including laws of international commissions and treaties, e.g., EU regulations) that would govern or regulate the provision/performance of

506

information technology services by a third-party service provider to Customer or its affiliate or subsidiaries.

3. **Contract Structure**. We are intending to structure the contract as **[a single agreement] [a master agreement with country agreements]**. Please advise as to whether there is a problem with the intended contract structure (for tax, regulatory, or other reasons) and whether there is a preferred approach. To the extent possible at this time, please advise as to if and under what circumstances the contract will need to be filed. Also, indicate whether English-language versions are sufficient or whether the contract will also need to be translated into the local language.

4. **Notice Requirements**. Please specify whether notice would be required to be given to any governmental or regulatory authority in connection with Customer's entering into new service contracts with Vendor. If notice is required, please specify:

   a. the entity that must provide notice;

   b. the form of notice; and

   c. the timing of such notice (e.g., how many days; must it be before or after contract execution/effectiveness?).

5. **Governmental/Regulatory Consents**. Please specify whether any governmental or regulatory permission, consent, or authorization would be required to be obtained in connection with Customer's entering into new service contracts with Vendor. If so, please specify:

   a. the entity that must obtain the permission, consent, or authorization;

   b. the process for obtaining such permission, consent, or authorization; and

   c. the timing of such permission, consent, or authorization (e.g., how many days; must it be before or after contract execution/effectiveness?).

6. **Transborder Data Flow**. Please specify any local laws or regulations relating to transborder data flow that may impact the proposed transaction. If you are aware of Customer's current compliance with such laws/regulations, please specify the details of such compliance and indicate whether any further steps need to be taken in light of the new transactions.

7. **Data Privacy**. Please specify any local laws or regulations relating to data privacy that may impact the proposed transaction. If you are aware of Customer's current compliance with such laws/regulations, please specify the details of such compliance and indicate whether any further steps need to be taken in light of the new transactions.

8. **Insurance Levels**. Please indicate any minimum insurance levels and types that would be required under local law.

9. **Ownership of Software**. Please specify whether there are any local requirements regarding ownership of newly developed software or the allocation of proprietary rights with respect to such software.

10. **Ownership of Equipment**. Please specify whether there are any local requirements regarding ownership of information technology equipment used by a third-party service provider.

11. **Noncompetition Provisions**. Please specify whether there are any prohibitions/limitations regarding provisions in a services agreement that:

    a.   prohibit Vendor from providing services to competitors of Customer,

    b.   restrict Vendor from using certain of Vendor's software/technology with competitors of Customer,

    c.   prohibit Vendor from reassigning personnel assigned to Customer's account to the account of a competitor of Customer for a certain time period,

    d.   prohibit either Customer or Vendor from prohibiting the hiring of employees of the other party during the term and for a period of time after the expiration/termination of the agreement, and

    e.   restrict Vendor from reassigning the project executive and certain key employees from Customer's account for a number of years.

12. **Facilities**. Please specify any local laws or regulations relating to the use of leased or owned facilities by a third-party service provider.

13. **Taxes**. Please discuss generally the potential tax exposure that Customer may incur as a result of receiving information technology services from a third-party service provider. Please specify any recommendations for limiting Customer's tax exposure.

14. **Currency**. Please specify any restrictions relating to the payment for services in a currency other than the local currency.

15. **Provision of Services**. Please discuss any restrictions relating to the provision of services by a vendor outside the country that the recipient of services is in (e.g., providing development services from a different country).

16. **Liability**. Please discuss any restrictions or exclusions relating to limiting a party's liability under a service contract.

17. **Disaster Recovery**. Please discuss any business recovery or disaster recovery requirements that a third-party service provider would be required to comply with under local law or regulation.

18. **Security**. Please discuss any data/facility security requirements that a third-party service provider would be required to comply with under local law or regulation.

19. **Audit Requirements**. Please discuss any audit requirements that a third-party service provider would be required to comply with under local law or regulation.

20. **Termination Rights**. Please discuss any termination rights that a customer or vendor would be required to include in a service contract of this type or termination right that a party would have by operation of law.

21. **Dispute Resolution**. Please discuss any local laws or regulations limiting a party's ability to contract to be bound by:

   a.   arbitration,

   b.   mediation, or

   c.   court decision.

22. **Jurisdiction**. Please discuss any local laws or regulations limiting a party's ability to contract to be bound by:

   a.   a governing law other than local law,

   b.   jurisdiction other than local jurisdiction, and

   c.   venue other than local venue.

23. **Disasters**. Please advise as to whether any events (natural or otherwise) are likely to occur in your country that may cause a party not to be able to perform (e.g., floods, electrical shortages, labor strikes). This is important in allocating risk for such events in the contract and determining the appropriate amount of backup/disaster recovery procedures.

24. **Precedent**. Please describe any precedent you are aware of in your country of transactions of this nature. If you are aware of any problems that have arisen in connection with these agreements, please describe.

25. **Additional Information**. Please provide any additional information or raise any additional issues that you think would be relevant at this time.

CHAPTER 12

BUSINESS PROCESS OUTSOURCING

12.1 THE EMERGING MARKET

Business process outsourcing (BPO)—the management of one or more specific business *processes or functions* (e.g., procurement, accounting, human resources, asset or property management) by a third party, together with the IT that supports the process or function—is being heralded in the marketplace as the next generation of outsourcing. As IT outsourcing services become more commoditized, customers and vendors alike are looking to BPO as a means to revitalize their organizations, reduce costs, or both. For the customer, the outsourcing of business processes would allow the customer to focus on its core competencies, while having a qualified third party focus on and add value to noncore processes. For the typical vendor, BPO, a natural extension of IT outsourcing, offers a possible means to expand its primary service offering, with the opportunity to introduce innovative service and pricing structures (and realize higher pricing margins) in a relatively untapped market.

The potential revenue that can be generated from outsourcing business processes is significantly greater than that generated by more traditional forms of outsourcing. Analysts are looking at the potential revenue to be generated from BPO transactions and are making astounding growth predictions for the BPO market in the next few years. If the predictions prove to be correct, the BPO market will dwarf the IT outsourcing market in the United States and abroad.

Although BPO is emerging as a market in and of itself, it has also become more common for IT outsourcing vendors to market business process services, such as business process management and business process reengineering, as part of a comprehensive IT outsourcing deal. It is likely, therefore, that many IT outsourcing deals will include some level of business process management in the next few years. As a result, the conventional IT vendor is being forced to realign its organizational structure, marketing strategies, and resource capabilities to account for the market's interest in business process and IT outsourcing services.

Although the BPO market is expected to experience significant growth in the next three to five years, the concept of outsourcing some business processes is not new to most companies. A large percentage of companies have already out-sourced one or more business processes to external service providers. BPO, in many ways, dovetails with the growing idea of the virtual company, where the company offers limited core services and receives all noncore services from a third party, thereby reducing headcount and overhead. Although the concept of BPO is not new, the expected increase in the scope of the processes outsourced (e.g., a company may outsource only part of its benefits management today, leaving open the possibility of broadening the scope of its human resource out-sourcing) and the various types of processes outsourced is new.

12.2   WHAT IS BPO?

As discussed earlier, BPO is becoming, if it has not already become, the hot topic in the outsourcing industry, receiving a good deal of attention in the press as well as outsourcing and industry-specific seminars. But what is covered by the term BPO?

The typical IT outsourcing deal focuses mainly on the IT component of business operations, such as data center and desktop operations. The outsourcing of a customer's data center, for example, provides back-office support to several business functions, thereby providing a service that is shared by several, often unrelated, business functions. Rather than providing IT support to multiple functions, BPO refers to the outsourcing of one or more *specific business processes or functions* to a third-party vendor, together with the IT that supports it. BPO focuses on how an overall process or function is run—from manager to end user—rather than on the technology that supports such process or function. IT is only a component of the overall business process. A formal definition of BPO is set out in *The End-User Executive's Guide to BPO,* which defines BPO as "the delegation of one or more IT-intensive business processes to an external provider who, in turn, administrates and manages the selected processes based upon defined and measurable performance metrics."[1]

One of the challenges of discussing BPO is that it refers to the outsourcing of any business process, which covers a wide spectrum of possibilities, from procurement to accounting to human resources to asset and property management. In the next section, we will try to place some parameters around the general cat-

---

1.   G2R, TPI, and Milbank, Tweed, Hadley & McCloy LLP, *The End-User Executive's Guide to Business Process Outsourcing* (1998) (hereinafter the "End-User's Executive Guide to BPO") at p. 9.

egories of business processes that companies have focused on as potential targets for outsourcing.

12.3 AREAS TARGETED FOR BPO

(a) **GENERAL CATEGORIES.** Business processes that have come under close examination as potential candidates for outsourcing typically fall within one of the following nine categories:

1. Administration (audit, tax)
2. Asset and property management
3. Finance (accounting, billing, accounts payable, accounts receivable)
4. Human resources (benefits administration, payroll, personnel administration, recruitment, training)
5. Miscellaneous (energy services, customer service, clinical data management)
6. Procurement/logistics
7. Call center
8. Claims processing
9. Data management

These categories have been established to facilitate the discussion of the general types of business processes that are the subject of consideration for outsourcing. Because a business process often touches different areas within an organization, customers and vendors may categorize certain business processes under different headings depending on the organization's internal structure. For example, in some companies, payroll is considered a human resource function, whereas in others it is considered a finance function. Similarly, tax compliance may be considered an administrative function in some companies and a finance function in others.

As the BPO market evolves, customers and vendors will undoubtedly identify more business processes that can—and will—be outsourced. The potential reach of BPO is evidenced by the scope of what is even now being considered for outsourcing. Business processes targeted for outsourcing are expanding beyond the traditional corporate support functions into the supply chain. For example, an increasing number of companies are considering outsourcing their customer service functions. The voice behind that toll-free customer service number may not be an employee of the manufacturer but an employee of a third-party outsourcing vendor.

(b) **ADMINISTRATION.** Because business processes that fall within the administration category are generally not considered core to a company's operations, more companies are examining processes such as tax compliance and internal auditing to assess whether they should be outsourced. Tax compliance has been the subject of outsourcing for longer than most other business processes. Companies have historically outsourced some or all of their tax compliance function to outside accounting firms. Because tax compliance, in many ways like the practice of law, requires being constantly apprised of the laws, regulations, and rules in multiple jurisdictions, many companies have found it more efficient to rely on outside firms to effectively manage this process.

However, companies are just beginning to consider some administrative functions for outsourcing. One example is internal auditing. Many companies have considered this function as one that should remain internal because it often involves looking closely at many of the company's sensitive operations. A potential problem is a possible conflict with the external audit function. However, with the negotiation of strict confidentiality provisions, companies are beginning to allow outside firms to manage this process.

(c) ASSET AND PROPERTY MANAGEMENT.   An area that financial institutions, particularly investment companies, are considering for outsourcing is asset management. If, for example, an investment company manages a small amount of certain assets as part of a larger service offering or to be able to market itself as a full-service company, it may consider outsourcing the underlying business process to a more experienced company with larger portfolios of these types of assets and greater infrastructure and resources to manage such assets. An issue that arises with asset management outsourcing is the extent, if any, to which permission from or notice to the outsourcing customer's clients is necessary. Such an approval or notice requirement may dissuade certain financial institutions and investment companies from outsourcing for fear that clients may find it more cost effective to do business directly with the outsourcing vendor.

Although asset management outsourcing has just begun to gain attention, property or real estate management operations have been the subject of outsourcing for some time. The management of property or real estate typically involves responsibility for such noncore functions as physical security, maintenance, customer service, cafeteria, parking, leasing, rent collection, and disaster recovery. Because the owner of real estate often purchases property for investment purposes, the owner is often eager to turn over management responsibility to a third party.

(d) FINANCE.   Many of the traditional vendors and a growing number of niche providers offer outsourcing services that provide support for a company's financial functions. These functions may include the following:

- General accounting
- Payroll (note: may alternatively be included under the HR function)
- Treasury/cash management
- Accounts payable

- Accounts receivable
- Credit
- Fixed assets
- Contract maintenance
- Collections
- Financial systems
- Tax compliance
- Budgeting
- SEC reporting

Companies that do outsource all or part of their finance function often want to turn over managerial and operational responsibility of a finance function in conjunction with the reengineering of their financial methodologies and systems. Such reengineering may involve the development and implementation of new methodologies and/or systems or customization of off-the-shelf or standard third-party methodologies and/or systems (e.g., an SAP implementation). Outsourcing transactions that include business process reengineering and BPO are more complex, often involving multiple documents and requiring the parties to address issues such as cross-termination and cross-default.

(e) HUMAN RESOURCES. What is covered by human resources varies from company to company. For example, some companies consider payroll to be a human resource function, whereas others consider it to be a finance function. For the purposes of this discussion, the human resources category covers all employee-related functions, from recruitment to benefits management, claims administration, and payroll.

Some companies opt to outsource the entire human resource process to one vendor, but it is more common to identify particular functions within the human resource process for outsourcing to different vendors, largely because different vendors have different expertise within this area. For example, if a company wanted to outsource payroll, it might consider a vendor with accounting expertise, whereas if it wanted to outsource benefits management, it might consider a vendor with more ERISA and insurance expertise. This outsourcing to multiple vendors may change as vendors develop—or more likely obtain through merger, acquisition, or strategic alliance/partnership—the expertise to become full-service human resource outsourcers.

Customers (and vendors) considering an arrangement that involves the outsourcing of one or more human resources functions will need to consult representatives from a variety of disciplines. Such disciplines typically include, at a minimum, the following:

- Legal
- Audit

- Personnel
- ERISA
- Tax

(f) MISCELLANEOUS.   In addition to the general business process categories discussed in this section, companies are beginning to consider for outsourcing several other, less easily categorized, processes. Such business processes include clinical data management, energy services, customer service, mail and copying services, and food services (which, in some cases, may fall under the category of property management). The spectrum of business processes that are the subject of outsourcing will likely grow as companies identify noncore areas that may be effectively managed by a third party or, if outsourced, will lead to a reduction in costs.

Examples of transactions that involve the outsourcing of business processes that fall under the miscellaneous category include the following:

- A transaction between Accenture and Wyeth for clinical data management (CDM)
- Transactions between Aramark and Salvation Army and Better Care for laundry and housekeeping services
- A transaction between Merrill Lynch and Pitney Bowes Management Services for the outsourcing of interoffice mail
- A transaction between Covansys and SIRVA for the outsourcing of employee relocation services

(g) PROCUREMENT/LOGISTICS.   An area that is receiving significant attention, particularly in the vendor community, is procurement outsourcing. Procurement outsourcing covers some or all aspects of noncore purchasing and supplies management, including the following:

- Product selection
- Acquisition
- Delivery
- Inventory
- Packing
- Warehouse management
- Installation
- Moves, adds, and changes
- Refreshes
- Maintenance
- Help desk services

The types of goods and services that may be included in the procurement out-sourcing arrangement depend largely on which goods and services the customer considers nonproduction goods and services. In some instances, the customer focuses the outsourcing on specific goods and services, such as office supplies or office equipment. In the typical procurement outsourcing transaction, the cus-tomer is typically looking to the vendor to standardize supply options and offer cost savings based on efficiency and economics of scale.

A business process that often overlaps with procurement is logistics. In addi-tion to several midsize and smaller companies that focus primarily on logistics outsourcing, several of the large transportation and shipping companies, such as Ryder, FedEx, and UPS, are offering logistics outsourcing services.

- An arrangement between WaWa and McLane for logistics services
- An arrangement between Philips Consumer Electrics of North America and Ryder for outbound logistics
- An arrangement between Honeywell and UPS Supply Chain Solutions

Because procurement and logistics outsourcing typically involves the acquisi-tion, handling, and/or transportation of goods, many legal and regulatory issues specific to such services may arise, such as warehouse liens, security interests, insurance, and allocation of risk during transportation. As with any BPO transac-tion, the customer and the vendor should consult legal and other counsel, as appropriate, to flesh out all of the applicable legal and regulatory issues and assist in identifying the risks and benefits of the transaction.

(h) CALL CENTER. Many companies have long histories of outsourcing call centers, which include internal call centers (or help desks) for such areas as help desk support as well as call centers that deal directly with external cus-tomers and third parties. Call center outsourcing is one of the first processes to move offshore, with many companies looking to low-cost providers in countries with similar language capabilities to provide level-one (or first con-tact) support. Call center outsourcing has also enabled global companies to provide 24/7 support by utilizing different centers around the world in multi-ple time zones.

The scope of call center outsourcing can range from simply answering the phone (e.g., serving as an answering service) to providing low-level support (e.g., tracking orders, taking inquiries) to more sophisticated support (e.g., appli-cation support). The ability of the outsourcing customer to share know-how and company knowledge, thereby enabling the outsourcing vendor to institute an effective training program, is critical to a successful call center outsourcing transaction.

(i) CLAIMS PROCESSING. Because claims processing often involves some fairly administrative steps that can be segregated (such as data input, document scanning, data audit), it is one of the back-office functions that companies that process claims are targeting as ripe for outsourcing. Many companies use the line between the administration functions of claims processing and the actual review and settlement of claims as the demarcation of what services get outsourced and what services are retained, although some more sophisticated vendors provide review and settlement services as well.

Similar to call center outsourcing, because of the administrative nature of some of the work, it is an area that companies are starting to move offshore to centers with leverage resources and low overhead and infrastructure costs. The ability to transfer data over data lines enables companies to easily move data between onshore and offshore centers.

(j) DATA MANAGEMENT. Data management outsourcing comes in many variations, including data entry, document entry, exception processing, data storage, data audit, and data compilation. Data management services are typically industry specific and require the vendor to have knowledge of the relevant privacy and validation issues that may arise depending on the type of business the customer is in as well as the type of data that is being handled.

In the pharmaceutical industry, for example, companies are looking at clinical data management as an area with outsourcing potential. Clinical data management requires knowledge of patient data privacy issues (including HIPAA) as well as FDA regulations regarding system validation and processes around good supporting documentation.

12.4 REASONS FOR OUTSOURCING BUSINESS PROCESSES

Vendors are marketing BPO as an alternative to the typical IT outsourcing deal, encouraging customers to identify noncore processes that are inefficient, too costly, or difficult to manage. The entire process (except, in most cases, a high-level management position or positions) is then turned over to the vendor, which, in turn, agrees to productivity, customer satisfaction, and cost savings commitments.

As the IT outsourcing marketplace becomes more commodity based (e.g., number of CPUs provided, help desk calls answered), BPO customers are looking for innovative ways to increase the efficiency and quality of an entire business process through value-added services, customer satisfaction, and, ideally, a direct, quantifiable impact on share price and profit. Because BPO focuses on an entire process rather than part of the process, as with IT outsourcing, it is often easier to identify the benefits derived from the BPO relationship. Some of the key business drivers for customers considering BPO include the following:

- Transferring the entire function (not just the IT component) out-of-house
- Enhancing and improving methodologies
- Benefiting from industry knowledge or experience
- Streamlining or standardizing processes across its organization

- Sharing resources or technologies
- Committing less up-front investment to new methodologies or technologies
- Obtaining flexibility with respect to the rollout of methodologies or technologies
- Increasing productivity
- Quantifying savings or benefits more easily
- Tracking customer satisfaction
- Enhancing shareholder value

Obviously, a customer's objectives for outsourcing one or more business processes will vary on a deal-to-deal basis. The objectives are typically shaped by management's overarching goal in outsourcing (e.g., transition to new methodology or technology, reduction in costs or expenses).

12.5 INTEGRATION: MAKING BPO FIT

As customers are beginning to outsource one or more business processes, several issues are emerging with respect to the integration of the services and systems being provided by the BPO vendor with the services and systems used in connection with other business processes being provided internally or by a third party. Some of these integration issues are as follows:

- *Systems integration.* As part of the BPO transaction, the BPO vendor often introduces new, state-of-the-art systems that are specific to the business process being outsourced. The customer will need to consider how these systems will interrelate with the systems being used in connection with other business processes. How will BPO impact the customer's move toward standardization?

- *Existing IT outsourcing arrangements.* What impact will the BPO transaction have on existing outsourcing, particularly IT outsourcing, arrangements? Will there be a reduction or termination of services under existing outsourcing contracts? How do the customer's other outsourcing contracts deal with such reduction or termination?

- *Vendor management.* How will responsibility be allocated among the outsourcing vendors if there is a service failure? How will the various outsourcing vendors be managed?

12.6 BPO VENDORS

When identifying vendors to provide BPO services, the customer's spectrum of possible vendors will depend on the particular process under consideration as well as the scope of the outsourcing. The vendor pool for payroll administration will usually be different from the vendor pool for procurement outsourcing. Similarly, the customer will probably consider different vendors if it wishes to simply have the vendor continue the operation of existing process service rather than a more complex outsourcing that requires the development, implementation, and management of new methodologies and/or technologies. Another factor to consider when selecting possible vendors is the geographic scope of the outsourcing. For multinational transactions or transactions in foreign countries, the customer should identify vendors with resources in the particular locations that are under consideration for outsourcing.

Many of the leading vendors in the BPO industry have capabilities and experience in process-related services (e.g., business process reengineering, management consulting, change management, consulting), as well as technology services. Often, the BPO transaction is preceded by or entered into in conjunction with a reengineering project. In addition to the conventional IT outsourcers, several of the top accounting firms—those with both process and technology capabilities—are leading the BPO market. To be able to provide the full-scale services that the BPO customer desires, many vendors are looking outside their own organizations to other companies with established service experience. The vendor who seeks to be a full-service BPO outsourcer may acquire the resources and experience offered by such an outside company through an outright acquisition or some type of teaming or strategic alliance relationship. For example, EDS entered into a joint venture with Towers Parson to market HR outsourcing; and Hewitt Associates acquired Exult to provide human resource outsourcing services.

Another growing trend among BPO vendors is to team or form an alliance with a software provider with a product designed to serve particular business processes. A relatively new but growing market is being forged by Web-based outsourcers that offer specialized services via the Internet. Such outsourcers are offering a wide range of low-cost services primarily to smaller and start-up organizations. Such services include document storage, payroll administration, data backup, and benefits management.

CHAPTER **13**

INTERNET-ENABLED OUTSOURCING: THE VIRTUAL FRONTIER

13.1 INTRODUCTION

The first frontier was traditional IT outsourcing. This model began with service providers taking over and managing a company's mainframes, but grew into a multibillion-dollar industry with service providers managing all aspects of a company's IT operations, including application development, desktop deployment and maintenance, client/server implementation, telecommunications, and customer support centers. Then came business process outsourcing (BPO), in which entire business functions (e.g., procurement, accounting, and real estate) were outsourced to functional experts such as logistics companies, accounting firms, and facility management companies. The next frontier, Internet-enabled outsourcing, promises to dwarf and possibly encompass (at least in part) all previous means of outsourcing.

Use of the Internet has unleashed many new and dynamic outsourcing models that are being shaped not only by the existing (and formidable) outsourcing heavyweights but also outsourcing newcomers, because of minimal infrastructure costs. These companies are using the Internet to provide traditional IT and business process services to all sizes and types of customers; the most noteworthy "e-sourcers" are application service providers (ASPS). In addition to e-sourcers, the existence of the Internet has spawned other types of outsourcers. For example, a multitude of companies are emerging whose primary mission is to manage Web/sites or provide infrastructure for the provision of e-centric services (such as co-location providers and Internet incubators).

13.2 POTENTIAL PROBLEMS AND ISSUES

The Internet-enabled outsourcing market is still in its infancy, so the potential risks and pitfalls are still largely unknown. As with most emerging markets, Internet-enabled outsourcers are looking to more established, analogous markets for guidance in identifying and minimizing these risks and pitfalls. Although the lion's share of the issues dealt with in traditional outsourcing models arise again in Internet-enabled outsourcing transactions, some of these issues are taking on different, often heightened, levels of importance (such as access to customer data), and new, unprecedented issues are emerging (such as liability for hacking). With the law and the corresponding legal issues being crafted and shaped as the Internet-enabled outsourcing industry is crafting and shaping itself, legal and business advisors have a daunting (albeit exciting) task keeping pace with the rapidly growing and changing outsourcing industry.

Appendices 13.1 through 13.5 contain checklists and sample vendor agreements. These checklists and sample agreements focus primarily on the provision of application services, but many of the issues facing ASPs and ASP customers are similar to the issues facing other Internet-enabled service providers and customers. These checklists and sample agreements are intended to illustrate the types of issues that arise in connection with transactions involving application (and other Internet-enabled) services. They are by no means exhaustive. The scope and complexity of the agreement for a particular transaction will vary depending on the actual deal at hand. The relevant legal issues and pitfalls are changing rapidly with the rapidly changing market. Legal counsel should be consulted by outsourcers and customers alike before entering into any transaction for Internet-enabled outsourcing services.

KEY LEGAL ISSUES TO CONSIDER WHEN NEGOTIATING CONTRACTS FOR THE PROVISION OF APPLICATION SERVICES[1]

1. Structure of the Application Services Agreement
  - Determine how the application services agreement will be structured:
    - A single services agreement
    - A master agreement with product/service orders
    - Numerous agreements for license, customization, support, hosting, and escrow (to the extent applicable)
    - Standard vendor form
    - Standard customer form
    - Negotiated agreement
    - Click-wrap agreement
  - Determine the inter-relationship between these agreements if separate (e.g., cross-termination, payment)
  - Factors that may affect the agreement structure include:
    - *Manner in which services will be delivered.* Will Customer sign up for services online? To what extent (if any) will there be face-to-face marketing/negotiation efforts?
    - *Scope of services.* Will Vendor be providing any customization or development services or will all services be standardized?

---

1. Note: This checklist is intended to illustrate the types of legal issues that customers may wish to consider in connection with contracting for application services. The items included in this checklist may not cover all of the issues that may arise in a particular transaction. Legal issues will likely vary depending on the type of service being provided and the scope of the services. This checklist or any part thereof should only be used after consultation with your legal counsel. Legal counsel should be consulted prior to entering into or negotiating any transaction covering the provision of application services.

- *Services to be provided at different sites.* Will all Customer sites receive the same services or will each Customer site receive different services?
- *Geographic scope.* Single country vs. international agreement
- *Types of entities receiving/delivering the services.* Is the contracting entity for each of the parties able to bind the entities that will receive/deliver the services or must each of the recipient/delivering entities agree to be bound by the master agreement?
- *Cost allocation.* Are there any cost allocation requirements internal to Customer that would drive separate site/entity agreements?
- *Taxes.* Are there any tax requirements that would drive separate service agreements?

2. Contracting Party

- Who will sign the agreement on behalf of Customer? On behalf of Vendor?
- Does the signing entity have the capacity to obligate the other entities receiving/providing the services?
- What is the relationship among the parties receiving the services (e.g., corporate relationship, alliance)? Should there be multiple signatures?
- What is the relationship among the parties providing the services? Does Customer want direct contractual privity with any affiliated parties or subcontractors? Should there be multiple signatures?
- If there is a master agreement with separate product/service orders, will the same party that signs the master agreement sign the product/service orders?

3. Entities Receiving Services from Vendor

- Determine which entity or entities will directly or indirectly receive services from Vendor.
- Will one entity retain overall responsibility for acts/obligations of other related entities (e.g., will parent receive (and guarantee) services/payments on behalf of its subsidiaries)?
- Entities may include:
  - Customer affiliates
  - Joint ventures/alliances
  - Contractors
  - Suppliers
  - Clients of Customer

- ○ Will Customer have the option of adding/deleting entities over the term?

- ○ How will mergers/acquisitions/divestitures be handled? What will Customer's and Vendor's ongoing obligations be in the event of a change in control/divestiture?

- ○ Which entity(ies) will have payment obligations? Are recipients of services third-party beneficiaries?

4. Entities Providing Services to Customer

- ○ Determine which entity (or entities) will provide the products/services to Customer.

- ○ Will there be any subcontracting/teaming relationships?

- ○ For international deals, how will Vendor provide resources/services in each country? Will Vendor use affiliated entities or subcontractors?

- ○ What are Customer's rights to approve/remove subcontractors?

- ○ Which entity(ies) will have performance/indemnification obligations?

5. Term

- ○ What is the commencement date of services? Will there be one commencement date for all sites? Will there be one commencement date for all products/services?

- ○ How long is the term of the agreement? If the transaction includes multiple agreements, are all of the agreements co-terminus? If there is a master agreement with separate product/service orders, are all of the documents co-terminus?

- ○ Will there be a pilot period?

- ○ What are each party's renewal rights? What type of notice is required for renewal?

6. Scope of Services

- ○ Determine the general scope of services to be provided by Vendor:

  - License/access to application
  - Development/customization
  - Processing
  - Data backup
  - Hosting
  - Co-location
  - Security
  - Maintenance/support
  - Training

- Installation
- Business continuity/disaster recovery

  ○ Determine those services that will be provided in-house by Customer or to Customer by a third party.

  ○ Describe in detail the services (typically by service category) to be provided by Vendor.

  ○ Define Customer's responsibilities with respect to the services to be provided by Vendor (i.e., definition of requirements, strategic direction, approvals).

  ○ Define existing and future requirements (e.g., capacity requirements, volume changes, business changes). Allocate managerial and financial responsibility.

7. Transition Plan

   ○ How will the transition of services to Vendor be handled?

   ○ Will there be any redundant/parallel environments?

   ○ Determine the performance standards during transition.

   ○ How long will the transition period be?

   ○ Will there be a similar plan for the transition away from Vendor in the event of expiration/termination? (See discussion point on "Termination Assistance.")

8. Methodologies

   ○ What methodologies will be used by Vendor? Are the methodologies proprietary to Vendor or licensed from a third party? If licensed from a third party, are there any use restrictions? What are Customer's rights to use during the term and after expiration/termination?

   ○ Will any of Customer's methodologies continue to be used during the term of the transaction? What are Vendor's use rights (e.g., use in connection with services to Customer only; use in connection with other customers)?

   ○ How will Vendor transition Customer to Vendor's methodologies (if applicable)?

   ○ How will the methodologies introduced by Vendor be integrated with Customer's existing and future methodologies (with respect to the applicable application as well as other applications)?

   ○ Will Vendor be developing/providing any new methodologies? If so, how will ownership/use rights be allocated? How will new methodologies be rolled out (e.g., define time period, consequences for failure to meet deadlines, each party's responsibilities)?

9. Technology

   o What technology will be used by Vendor? Is the technology propri-
     etary to Vendor or licensed from a third party? If licensed from a
     third party, are there any use restrictions? What are Customer's
     rights to use/access during the term and after expiration/termination?

   o Will any of Customer's technology continue to be used during the
     term of the transaction? What are Vendor's use rights (e.g., use in
     connection with services to Customer only; use in connection with
     other customers)?

   o Will part or all of the environment be dedicated/shared?

   o How will Vendor transition Customer to Vendor's technology (if
     applicable)?

   o How will the technology introduced by Vendor be integrated with
     Customer's existing or future technology (e.g., is Vendor technol-
     ogy compatible with technology used by Customer's information
     system group)?

   o Will Vendor be developing/providing any new technology? If so,
     how will ownership/use rights be allocated? How will new technol-
     ogy be rolled out (e.g., define time period, consequences for failure
     to meet deadlines, each party's responsibilities)?

10. Documentation

   o What are Vendor's responsibilities to create/provide documentation
     (e.g., procedures, manuals, training materials)?

   o Which party will own documentation?

   o What are the parties' rights to copy and use the documentation?

11. Projects

   o Identify any projects that Vendor will be responsible for imple-
     menting/managing as part of the transaction.

   o Will Vendor be responsible for any development/customization? If
     so, what are each party's responsibilities? What are the conse-
     quences if the development/customization is not completed by the
     deadlines specified?

   o What is the inter-relationship of Vendor's development/customiza-
     tion responsibilities and Vendor's ongoing service responsibilities
     (e.g., are they cross-terminable)?

   o Which party will be responsible for purchase/license of third-party
     methodologies/technologies (if applicable)?

12. Integration

   o How will the methodologies/technologies introduced by Vendor be
     integrated with other methodologies/technologies used by Customer?

       ○ Have other Customer business areas been contacted for input (e.g., information systems, human resources)?

13. Project Staff

    ○ Identify management structure of Vendor as well as Customer in connection with the provision/receipt of services.

    ○ Are there any limitations/restrictions with respect to reassignment/ replacement of key Vendor personnel?

    ○ Are there any limitations/restrictions with respect to "churning" of employees?

    ○ How will Customer complaints regarding Vendor personnel be handled?

    ○ Are any special clearances of Vendor personnel necessary?

    ○ Are there any limitations/restrictions with respect to subcontractors?

14. Management

    ○ How is Vendor's senior management structured? Are there any retention incentives for senior management?

    ○ To whom does Vendor account representative report?

    ○ (For start-up ASPs) Who controls Vendor's strategic direction? Who is on the Vendor's board (any competitors, conflicting interests)?

15. Retained Assets

    ○ Identify which assets Customer will continue to manage and, of those assets, whether Vendor will have any financial responsibility.

    ○ How will the parties act in the event it is not clear where a problem originates from (e.g., root cause analysis)?

16. Agreements to Be Reviewed

    ○ Identify any third-party agreements/relationships that may be impacted by the outsourcing, including:

        • Development/outsourcing agreements

        • Hosting/co-location agreements

        • Maintenance agreements

        • Subcontracting relationships

        • Other service agreements

        • Methodology/technology licenses

        • Equipment/asset leases

        • Real estate leases/subleases

    ○ Are there any restrictions with respect to third-party management/ access or assignment to a third party?

    ○ What are the terms relating to termination/renewal?

- ○ What are the pricing terms and will they be impacted by the transaction?
- ○ Develop a strategy for notifying third parties, if applicable.

17. Third-Party Consents
- ○ Are any third-party consents necessary in connection with the commencement of the transaction? If so, which party is responsible for obtaining such consents and how will financial responsibility be allocated?
- ○ How will third-party consents be obtained upon the expiration/termination of the transaction (in order to transition agreements/assets back to Customer or Customer's designee)? How will financial responsibility be allocated?

18. Performance Standards
- ○ Identify those services that will be tied to performance standards.
- ○ Identify the performance standards (e.g., availability, response time, reporting).
- ○ Will existing performance standards be used or will performance standards be established on a going-forward basis?
- ○ Identify any permitted downtime and testing.
- ○ Will any events excuse Vendor from performance (e.g., *force majeure* event, acts/omissions of Customer)?
- ○ How will failures to meet performance standards be handled (e.g., liquidated damages or termination)?
- ○ Will there be any procedures for assessing/determining causes of failures to meet performance standards (e.g., root cause analysis)?
- ○ What performance standards will apply during transition/implementation?

19. Customer Satisfaction
- ○ Will Vendor be responsible for any type of Customer satisfaction reporting?
- ○ Determine pool of employees surveyed (e.g., management, end users).
- ○ How will the results of such surveys be used (e.g., as basis for performance standard)?

20. Benchmarking
- ○ Determine whether the agreement will include any benchmarking procedures (e.g., benchmarking of services or prices).
- ○ Develop benchmarking procedures (e.g., scope of benchmark, group against which services/prices will be benchmarked).

o   Identify benchmarker (e.g., third party, Vendor group).

o   How will benchmarking results be reviewed and how will changes, if applicable, be implemented?

21.   Gainsharing

o   Determine whether any gainsharing provisions will be included in the agreement (e.g., bonuses tied to stock price).

o   Develop procedures for implementing gainsharing agreement.

o   How will disputes be handled?

22.   Compliance Issues

o   Identify any regulatory/governmental requirements (e.g., timing, notice, consent). (Note: These requirements are typically driven by the type of transaction, e.g., rules governing accounting services, and the type of organization receiving services, e.g., rules governing financial institutions. In addition, compliance issues may vary from country to country or if the transaction involves more than one country.)

o   Are there any Euro compliance issues?

o   Determine which party is responsible for ensuring compliance. Allocate costs of compliance due to changes in laws, rules or regulations after commencement.

o   Identify any license/permits required to be obtained by Customer and/or Vendor.

o   Consult with legal, regulatory, tax, and audit departments.

23.   Transaction-Specific Issues

o   Identify any transaction-specific requirements.

o   Consult with legal, regulatory, tax, and audit departments.

24.   Customer Responsibilities

o   Identify Customer's responsibilities (e.g., provision of supplies, computers).

o   Will Customer be providing any space/facilities to house Vendor's employees/equipment? What are the terms of Vendor's use (e.g., sublease)?

o   Is Customer retaining staff necessary to perform the retained responsibilities (e.g., management, definition of requirements, approvals)?

25.   Service Locations

o   Where will Vendor be providing the services from? If such locations are not Customer locations, are there any restrictions on where Vendor may provide services from? Will any company location facilities be used?

o   Will the service locations be dedicated to Customer or shared facilities?

o   Describe physical security requirements. Are uniforms or other identification required? Does Customer or Vendor have specific codes of conduct?

o   How will breaches of security be handled?

o   Are there any environmental concerns?

26.   Management Procedures

o   Will the parties develop management procedures to be used in connection with the provision of the services?

o   How will change control be handled?

27.   Reports

o   Identify the performance and other reports that Customer currently generates or receives with respect to the services being outsourced.

o   Identify those reports that Customer wishes to receive from Vendor.

o   Establish deadlines for each report.

o   Will Customer be required to review the reports within a specific time period?

o   How will errors in reports be handled?

28.   Data

o   Discuss procedures for handling Customer data. What are Vendor's use rights?

o   How will errors in Customer data be handled?

o   Describe data security requirements at service locations. Are passwords required?

o   How will breaches of security be handled?

29.   Proprietary Rights

o   Establish Vendor's right to use Customer proprietary methodologies and technology during the term and after expiration/termination of the agreement.

o   Establish Vendor's right to use during the term and after expiration/termination of the agreement methodologies and technology licensed by Customer from third parties and used in connection with the provision of the services.

o   Establish Customer's right to use Vendor's proprietary methodologies and technology during the term and after expiration/termination of the agreement.

- o   Establish Customer's right to use during the term and after expiration/termination of the agreement methodologies and technology licensed by Vendor from third parties and used in connection with the provision of the services.

- o   Establish each party's ownership/use rights with respect to methodologies and technology developed or acquired as part of or in connection with the provision of the services.

- o   Establish any restrictions governing the use of confidential information.

- o   Establish any restrictions governing the use of mentally retained information.

- o   Discuss whether noncompetition provisions are appropriate.

30.   Audit

- o   What are Customer's rights to audit the services and the service locations? How often may Customer exercise any such audit rights?

- o   How will the results of any such audit be dealt with? What are Customer's rights to audit the fees?

- o   How will overpayments/underpayments be handled?

- o   Will interest be charged?

31.   Fees

- o   Determine the applicable fee structure:
  - Initial set-up fees
  - Subscription fees
  - Usage-based fees
  - Support/maintenance fees
  - Training fees
  - Installation fees
  - Ancillary fees

- o   Customer should assess actual cost savings, if any. Such analysis should include any new taxes, employee transfer costs, and other expenses resulting from the outsourcing.

- o   Vendor should assess actual profit margin.

- o   Other Fee Provisions:
  - If a base fee structure is used, determine structure for increasing and decreasing fees/resources.
  - Determine the rights of the parties to set off monies owed.
  - To what extent, if any, will Customer be responsible for Vendor expenses (e.g., travel)? Will Vendor use Customer or Vendor expense guidelines?

- Will there be any cost-of-living adjustments?
- For international deals, is there any currency risk?
- Consider a most-favored-customer provision.
- How will fees be paid (e.g., in what currency, in what manner, and according to what schedule)?
- How, when, and to what Customer entity(ies) will invoices be issued? Determine the degree of detail to be included on invoices.
- How will disputed fees/credits be handled (e.g., escrow)? What are the parties' obligations to perform in the event of a dispute?
- How will changes in business volumes be handled?

32. Taxes
   - Determine liability for sales, use, and other taxes.
   - Determine liability for additional taxes resulting from Vendor's relocation of service locations or rerouting of services.

33. Additional Services
   - How will the provision of additional services be handled? Will Vendor be required to submit a bid? Will there be any rights of first refusal granted to Vendor?
   - What type of detail must be included in a Vendor proposal?
   - To what extent does Customer wish to reserve the right to contract with third parties?

34. Insurance
   - Assess Vendor's insurance coverage, for example:
      - Errors and omissions
      - Liability
      - Workers' compensation
      - Automobile
      - Environmental
   - Specify any specific bonding requirements.
   - Determine whether any parental or other type of guarantee is appropriate.

35. Termination
   - Consider early termination rights, for example:
      - Termination for convenience in whole
      - Partial termination for convenience
      - Termination upon change of control of Vendor

- Termination upon change of control of Customer
- Termination for breach
- Termination for nonpayment
- Termination for failure to provide critical services
- Termination for failure to meet the performance standards
- Termination for substantial changes in business
- Termination upon the occurrence of a regulatory event
- Cross-termination with other agreements

  o Determine whether and in what instances termination fees are applicable. If so, establish formula for determining applicable termination fees.

36. Exit Rights

  o Determine each party's ongoing rights after expiration/termination with respect to proprietary and third-party methodologies, technology, equipment, facilities, subcontracting arrangements, and third-party service agreements.

  o Determine which party will be responsible for transfer/assignment fees imposed by third parties.

  o If Customer has right to purchase certain Vendor assets used to provide the services, how will the purchase price be determined?

37. Termination Assistance

  o Determine the types of assistance Vendor and/or its subcontractors will provide Customer upon expiration/termination.

  o Determine duration of Vendor's termination assistance obligations.

  o How will termination assistance be paid for (e.g., fee schedule, time schedule for payment)?

38. Liability Provisions

  o Assess liability exposure.

  o Determine any liquidated damages to be imposed upon Vendor (e.g., for failure to meet performance standards, for failure to meet implementation schedules).

  o What are each party's indemnification obligations (e.g., for claims of infringement, employee claims).

  o Determine the representations and warranties to be made by each party.

39. Dispute Resolution

  o How will disputes be handled? Will the agreement include an escalation procedure?

  o Will unresolved disputes be handled through arbitration or litigation?

40.   Disaster Recovery and Business Continuation Procedures

- o   What are Vendor's responsibilities in the event of a disaster or *force majeure* event? How are disaster and *force majeure* event defined?
- o   Does Vendor maintain, or contract with a third party to provide, a hotsite or backup facilities?
- o   What are Vendor's system and data backup procedures?
- o   Determine Vendor response times for delivery of business recovery services. Describe escalation procedures.
- o   How does Vendor allocate priority among customers in the event of service interruption?
- o   Does Customer have an existing business recovery plan? Will Customer's existing plans be terminated?
- o   (For start-up ASPs) Does Vendor have a plan that allows Customer to experience minimal disruption to services in the event Vendor goes out of business?
  - •   Access to source code
  - •   Right to receive services directly from subcontractors?
  - •   Standby service provider
- o   (For start-up ASPs) Does Customer have a plan that allows Customer to experience minimal disruption to services in the event Vendor goes out of business?

41.   Assignment

- o   Specify each party's right to assign its rights/obligations under the agreement in whole or in part.
- o   Will there be any special assignment rights in the event of a merger, acquisition, or divestiture?
- o   May either party assign to an affiliate/related entity?

42.   Solicitation of Employees

- o   Will there be any limitations/restrictions on Customer's or Vendor's right to solicit and/or hire the other party's employees?
- o   When will such limitations/restrictions apply (e.g., during the term, after expiration/termination)?
- o   Will there be any exceptions for blind solicitations (e.g., newspaper advertisements)?

43.   Miscellaneous Provisions

- o   *Notices.* How will notices be given (e.g., by hand, by facsimile)? To whom (e.g., to business manager and/or counsel)?

○ *Publicity.* Are there any limitations/restrictions on each party's ability to make public statements regarding the other party and/or the transaction?

○ *Governing law.* Determine which state/country law will govern the transaction (or if international transaction with multiple documents, determine which law will govern each part of the transaction).

○ *Venue.* Will there be a requirement that any action be brought in a particular venue?

○ *Import/export.* Provide any limitations/restrictions on the export/import of data and/or technology.

○ *Interpretation of documents.* How will the transaction documents be interpreted in the event of a dispute (e.g., the main agreement will take precedence over the exhibits/schedules, change orders will take precedence over earlier dated documents)?

○ *Counterparts.* Specify whether the various transaction documents may be executed in counterparts.

○ *Relationship of the parties.* Specify that Vendor is an independent contractor to Customer and that the provision of services does not constitute any type of partnership or joint venture (unless that is expressly the intent).

○ *Severability.* Specify that if any provision is held to be invalid that the remaining provisions shall remain in full force and effect.

○ *Waivers.* Specify that any delay or omission does not constitute a waiver of rights and that any waiver should not be construed to be a waiver of a subsequent breach/covenant.

○ *Entire agreement.* Specify that the transaction documents constitute the entire agreement between the parties.

○ *Amendments.* Specify how the transaction documents may be amended (e.g., by writing signed by both parties).

○ *Survival.* Specify which provisions of the agreement will survive termination and/or expiration of the agreement.

○ *Third-party beneficiaries.* Expressly state that there will not be any third-party beneficiaries under the transaction documents or, if there will be third-party beneficiaries, identify such beneficiaries.

○ *Covenant of further assurances.* Expressly state that each party will execute any documents or perform any actions necessary to effectuate the purposes of the agreement.

LEGAL CHECKLIST FOR ASPs[2]

1. Incorporation/Partnership Documents
2. Financial Documents
3. Financing Documents
4. Process for Handling Customer Contracts
5. Process for Handling Vendor/Supplies Contracts
6. Legal Terms and Condition
   - Standard Forms
   - Service Levels
   - Third-Party Performance/Warranties
7. IP Protection
   - Trademark
   - Copyright
   - Patent
   - Trade Secret
   - Confidential Information
8. Web Site Protection
   - Copyright Notice
   - Disclaimers
   - Privacy
   - Acceptance User Guidelines
   - Affiliations/Non-Affiliations

---

2. Note: This checklist is intended to illustrate the types of legal issues that customers may wish to consider in connection with contracting for application services. The items included in this checklist may not cover all of the issues that may arise in a particular transaction. Legal issues will likely vary depending on the type of service being provided and the scope of the services. This checklist or any part thereof should only be used after consultation with your legal counsel. Legal counsel should be consulted prior to entering into or negotiating any transaction covering the provision of application services.

9. Systems Security
    o   Disclaimers
    o   Passwords
    o   Electronic Signatures
    o   Encryption
10. Data Security
11. Insurance
12. Employee Issues
    o   Nondisclosure
    o   Employment Contracts
13. Public Communications
14. Alliances/Joint Ventures
15. Nondisclosures
16. Contractor Agreements
17. Business Continuity

LEGAL DUE DILIGENCE CHECKLIST FOR COMPANIES TRANSACTING WITH ASPs[3]

1. Corporate Documents
   - If privately held, request or obtain through a search agency articles of incorporation, by-laws and certificates of good standing
   - If publicly held, check filings with SEC
2. Financial Documents
   - Request or obtain through a search agency most recent quarterly and annual financial statements
   - Perform search of financial databases (D&B) if applicable/accessible
   - Consider preliminary issues:
     - Funding
     - Working capital
     - Debt
     - Expenditures
     - Profitability
     - Existing and prospective client base
     - Expansion plans
3. Media Search
   - Review recent press releases
   - Review articles/references in press

---

3. Note: This checklist is intended to illustrate the types of legal issues that customers may wish to consider in connection with contracting for application services. The items included in this checklist may not cover all of the issues that may arise in a particular transaction. Legal issues will likely vary depending on the type of service being provided and the scope of the services. This checklist or any part thereof should only be used after consultation with your legal counsel. Legal counsel should be consulted prior to entering into or negotiating any transaction covering the provision of application services.

4. Litigation Search

- Search legal databases for litigation involving Vendor
- Ask for representation regarding potential and actual claims and lawsuits
- Search for UCC filings, liens, and judgments

5. Vendor Management Structure

- Request or obtain names/information regarding board members and officers
- Review structure of senior management
- Determine whether there are any retention incentives for key management members

6. Personnel Relationships

- Access use of nondisclosure agreements
- Access use of employment contracts
- Review consulting agreement

7. Vendor Account Structure

- Determine point person responsible for Customer account
- Determine to whom the Customer's account manager reports
- Review replacement/reassignment procedures
- Determine incentive/bonus structure

8. Legal Terms and Conditions

- Prior to discussions regarding the relationship, agree upon and sign nondisclosure agreements (if click-wrap agreement, review confidentiality and privacy policies)
- Determine whether the parties will first negotiate a letter of intent or memorandum of understanding
- Determine whether a Vendor standard form, a Vendor click-wrap agreement, or "Customer-prepared" form will be the basis for negotiations
- Review and negotiate:
  - Letter of Intent/Memorandum of Understanding (if applicable)
  - Contract
  - Scope of services
  - Performance standards (and liquidated damages/bonuses)
  - Fee structure
- Review pass-through of third-party performance/warranties

9. Protection of Intellectual Property
   - Review extent to which Vendor has protected/maintains its:
     - Trademark and service marks (registered and unregistered)
     - Copyright
     - Inventions (registered and unregistered)
     - Patents
     - Trade secrets
     - Confidential information
   - Review policies and procedures to be followed by Vendor to protect Customer's intellectual property

10. Web Site Protection
    - Review extent to which Vendor has protected its Web site:
      - Domain name registration
      - Service mark/trademark registration
      - Copyright notices
      - Disclaimers
      - Privacy policies
      - Acceptance use guidelines
      - Statement of affiliation/nonaffiliation
    - Review data and system security measures

11. Security
    - Review physical security measures
      - Restricted access
      - Access policies and procedures
    - Review data security measures
      - Passwords
      - Electronic signatures
      - Encryption
      - Segregation of data
    - Review systems security measures
      - Keys
      - Passwords

12. Review Insurance Coverage
    - Review Vendor's insurance coverage:
      - E-risk

- Errors and omissions
- General liability
- Worker's compensation
  - Review performance/fidelity bond coverage (if applicable)
  - Review Customer insurance coverage to ensure that it adequately covers damages that may be suffered/caused by Customer

13. Public Communications
  - Negotiate extent to which Vendor may use Customer's name in press releases/public communications
  - Negotiate extent to which Customer may use Vendor's name in press releases/public communications

14. Alliances/Joint Ventures
  - Review any publicly disclosed alliances/joint ventures (and status thereof)
  - Determine extent of any such relationships

15. Change in Control/Reorganization
  - Consider possibility of Vendor merger, acquisition, IPO, divestiture, or reorganization
  - If such an event is possible, consider impact on the provision of the services and instances where Customer would not want to continue to do business with Vendor (e.g., purchase by Customer competitor)

16. Business Continuity Plan (BCP)
  - Determine plan to continue business operations:
    - In the event of a disaster/force majeure event
    - In the event Vendor ceases operations or fails to perform
  - BCP may include:
    - Right to use infrastructure components
    - Right to use intellectual property
      - Object code
      - Source code
      - Access to personnel
      - Ability to replace Vendor
    - Review proposed/actual recovery times

APPLICATION SERVICES (VENDOR SAMPLE FORM) AGREEMENT[4]

This Agreement for Application Services (this "Agreement") is between [User] ("User") and [Vendor] ("Vendor") and is effective as of _____ (the "Effective Date").

The following capitalized terms shall have the meanings set forth below:

"Applications" means the applications set forth on the User Information Page, and any modifications, enhancements or changes thereto provided or made available by Vendor hereunder.

"Authorized User Representative(s)" means the employee(s) of User authorized to access the Applications in the manner and in accordance with the terms and conditions set forth herein, each of whom are specified on the User Information Page.

"Authorized Site(s)" means the specific location(s) set forth on the User Information Page of the User organizations set forth on the User Information Page.

"Service(s)" means, collectively, the Consulting Services, the Hosting and Reporting Services and the Support Services, if applicable.

"User Information" means the data and information inputted by the Authorized User Representatives and processed using the Applications.

"Third Party Provider(s)" means a third party or third parties engaged by Vendor to provide data center, infrastructure or other services or equipment in connection with the performance of the Services under this Agreement.

Reference to this Agreement includes the Schedules to this Agreement. The Schedules to this Agreement are hereby incorporated into, and made part of, this Agreement.

---

4. Note: This sample agreement is intended to illustrate the types of legal issues that vendors typically wish to address in connection with information technology outsourcing transactions. The provisions included in this sample agreement, while comprehensive, may not cover all of the issues that may arise in a particular transaction. Legal issues will likely vary depending on the type of information technology process being outsourced and the scope of the outsourcing transaction. This sample agreement or any part thereof should only be used after consultation with your legal counsel. Legal counsel should be consulted prior to entering into or negotiating any outsourcing transaction.

1. APPLICATIONS

1.1 ACCESS. Upon (a) acceptance by Vendor and User of this Agreement, including User's agreement to be bound by the terms of the fee arrangement set forth in Schedule A, and (b) User's payment in full of the Subscription Fees for the first year [and any one-time set-up fees], Vendor shall issue passwords for the number of Authorized User Representatives set forth on the User Information Page to allow the Authorized User Representatives access to the Applications using a User-provided internet connection and User Systems (as defined in Section 1.4). Vendor may provide access to the Applications through its own website or through a link in the website of Vendor's parent or an Vendor affiliate.

1.2 RIGHT TO USE. Vendor hereby grants to User, and User hereby accepts from Vendor, a non exclusive, non-transferable right to access [and use] the Applications for the limited purposes, and pursuant to the terms and conditions, set forth herein. The Applications shall be accessed and used only by the Authorized User Representatives and only for [DESCRIBE PURPOSES]. [Authorized Users must be full-time employees of Users.] User shall not use the Applications to act as a service bureau or to process or report any third party information. User shall not delete any identifying marks, copyrights or proprietary right notices from any web pages of, or reports or documentation generated by, the Applications. User shall not modify, translate, decompile, create or attempt to create, by reverse engineering or otherwise, the object or source code of the Applications or adapt the Applications or any reports or documentation generated thereby in any way or use them to create derivative works.

1.3 CHANGES. Vendor reserves the right in its sole discretion, and from time to time, to change the format or content of the Applications or update, modify or enhance the Applications, whether or not such changes, updates, modifications or enhancements would require changes to the User Systems (as defined in Section 1.4) or User's modes of operation. Vendor shall not be responsible for providing any updates, replacements, revisions, enhancements, additions or conversions or otherwise maintaining the User Systems.

1.4 USER SYSTEMS. User is solely responsible for acquiring and installing all of the equipment, software (including web browser software), telecommunications lines, Internet access connections and other items necessary to access the Applications (the "User Systems"). User acknowledges that Vendor makes no representations or warranties as to the User Systems.

1.5 RIGHT OF INSPECTION/AUDIT. Vendor shall have the right to access the premises and systems of User to ensure compliance with the provisions of this Agreement. User agrees to furnish User on request with such information concerning its use of the Applications as Vendor shall reasonably request for the purposes of monitoring compliance with this Agreement.

1.6 ON-LINE CONDUCT. User shall ensure that the information it transmits and receives complies with all applicable laws, rules and regulations and the rules and regulations of Vendor and Third Party Providers, if applicable. User must at all times conform its use of the Applications to Vendor's acceptable use guidelines, as Vendor may issue and update from time to time. If Vendor is informed by government authorities or other parties of inappropriate or illegal use of the Applications or other networks accessed through the Applications, or Vendor otherwise learns of such use or has reason to believe such use may be occurring, then User shall cooperate in any resulting investigation by Vendor or government authorities. Any government determinations shall be binding on User. If User fails to cooperate with any such investigation or determination, or fails to immediately rectify any illegal use, Vendor may immediately suspend User's service or access to the Applications. Further, upon notice to User, Vendor may modify or suspend User's service or access to the Applications (a) as necessary to comply with any law or regulation as reasonably determined by Vendor or (b) if deemed reasonably necessary by Vendor to prevent any harm to Vendor and its businesses.

2. SERVICES

2.1 CUSTOMIZATION, IMPLEMENTATION, AND TRAINING. User may from time to time request Vendor to provide consulting services in connection with the customization, implementation and use of the Applications and training of users in respect of the Applications ("Consulting Services"). Upon Vendor's agreement to perform Consulting Services and the execution of a work order detailing the Consulting Services to be provided, Vendor shall perform such services subject to staff availability. User shall pay for the Consulting Services at Vendor's then-current standard consulting rates and the cost of materials and expenses plus [***] percent.

2.2 HOSTING AND REPORTING SERVICES. Vendor shall provide to User the hosting and reporting services described in Schedule C (the "Hosting and Reporting Services") as part of the Subscription Fees. [User hereby acknowledges and agrees that Vendor will use a Third Party Provider to host the Applications and the data inputted into and generated by the Applications.]

2.3 MAINTENANCE AND SUPPORT. During the Term, Vendor agrees to:

A. Maintain the Applications by correcting system defects (where a "defect" is a reproducible, substantial failure of the system to conform to the system features); and

B. Provide telephone and online support as described on Vendor's website [ADDRESS], which is subject to change from time to time during the Term ((a) and (b) collectively, the "Support Services").

2.4 ACCURACY AND QUALITY OF INFORMATION.   User shall be responsible for the accuracy, completeness and quality of any and all User Information. User shall provide User Information in the format and manner requested by Vendor and in accordance with the standards set by Vendor from time to time. Vendor reserves the right to reject or refuse to use, distribute or display any User Information that it considers offensive, defective, libelous, inaccurate, incomplete or of a quality that does not meet Vendor's standards (which standards Vendor may change at any time). Any changes or amendments to User Information shall be performed at User's own cost and expense. If an error or defect in User Information occurs that was caused solely by Vendor, User's sole remedy shall be the correction of such error after notice to Vendor.

2.5 VENDOR USE OF INFORMATION.   During the Term and subject to the terms of this Agreement, User hereby grants to Vendor the right to use, distribute, reformat, recompile and display the User Information in connection with providing the Services. User shall be responsible for obtaining all consents and approvals necessary for Vendor to use the User Information as contemplated hereunder.

3. PROPRIETARY RIGHTS

3.1 APPLICATIONS.   Vendor represents that it is the owner or licensee of the Applications and that it has the right to grant the access to User to the Applications as set forth in this Agreement. User acknowledges that all rights, title and interest in and to the Applications, including all modifications, changes and enhancements thereto, are and shall be the sole and exclusive property of Vendor or its licensor. User hereby assigns, and shall cause its employees, agents and contractors to assign to Vendor, all rights, title and interest in and to the Applications, including all modifications, changes and enhancements thereto.

3.2 CONFIDENTIALITY.   User may have access to information that is proprietary or confidential to Vendor and other Users (the "Vendor Confidential Information"). Vendor may have access to information that is proprietary or confidential to User ("User Confidential Information"). [User Confidential Information shall be limited to information that is marked "Confidential" by User.] User shall: (a) hold the Vendor Confidential Information in confidence by taking reasonable measures to prevent unauthorized disclosure of such Vendor Confidential Information, in any form, to any third party; and (b) use Vendor Confidential Information only for the purposes specified in Agreement. Vendor shall: (i) hold the User Confidential Information in confidence by taking reasonable measures to prevent unauthorized disclosure of such User Confidential Information, in any form, to any third party (other than as permitted in accordance with this Agreement); and (ii) use User Confidential Information only for the purposes specified in this Agreement. User may not use, disclose, exploit or sell to third parties, or allow third parties to access, any information or data regarding the performance of the Applications, the Services or Vendor for benchmarking or other purposes.

3.3 EXCLUSIONS FROM CONFIDENTIALITY.   Vendor Confidential Information and User Confidential Information shall not include information which: (a) is or becomes publicly known through no act or omission of the recipient; (b) the recipient can demonstrate with competent written proof was in the recipient's possession prior to such access or disclosure (other than through an unauthorized disclosure); (c) is disclosed to the recipient by a third party having legitimate possession thereof without restriction on such disclosure; or (d) is independently developed by the recipient without violating the proprietary rights of the disclosing party and is so documented by the recipient.

3.4 GENERAL SKILLS.   Notwithstanding anything to the contrary in this Agreement or otherwise, Vendor shall retain all right, title and interest in and to any and all ideas, concepts, know-how, development tools, methodologies, processes, procedures, technologies or algorithms ("Vendor Know-How") developed when providing the Services. Nothing contained in this Agreement shall restrict Vendor from the use of any Vendor Know-How. Vendor shall not be prohibited or enjoined at any time by User from utilizing any skills or knowledge of a general nature acquired during the course of providing the Services including information publicly known or available or that could reasonably be acquired in similar work performed for another client of Vendor.

3.5 USE OF NAME.   User hereby grants to Vendor and Vendor's parent and affiliates the right to use User's names, characters, artwork, designs, trade names, copyrighted materials, trademarks or service marks or any of its related or subsidiary companies, parent, employees, directors, shareholders, assigns, successors or licensees ("User Marks") in its publicity, press releases, and/or promotions of Vendor. In addition, User hereby grants to Vendor and Vendor's parent and affiliates to promote User as a participating user of the Applications and the Services.

4. TERM

4.1 TERM.   The term of this Agreement shall commence on the Effective Date and continue until the [***] anniversary of the Effective Date, unless otherwise renewed or terminated pursuant to this Agreement (the "Initial Term"). Upon expiration of the Initial Term, this Agreement shall be automatically renewed for additional successive [***] month periods (each, a "Renewal Period"; Initial Term and Renewal Period collectively, the "Term"), unless this Agreement is terminated in accordance with the provisions contained herein or a party provides [***] days' notice before the expiration of the Initial Term or a Renewal Period, as the case may be, that User does not with to enter into a Renewal Period and desires to terminate this Agreement.

4.2 FOR NONPAYMENT.   After [***] days of non-payment of amounts from the due date, or such longer period as Vendor may provide, Vendor may disable access to the Applications or cease provision of any service upon prior notice to User. To re-enable access or service, Vendor will require a re-access fee. After [***] days of nonpayment from the invoice due date, or such longer period as the Applications may provide, Vendor may terminate this Agreement permanently. Termination does not relieve User of its obligations under this Agreement, including the obligation to pay all fees for the committed term.

4.3 UNACCEPTABLE USE; BANKRUPTCY.   Vendor may terminate this Agreement immediately if User becomes the subject of a voluntary petition in bankruptcy or any voluntary proceeding relating to insolvency, receivership, liquidation, or composition for the benefit of creditors or becomes the subject of an involuntary petition in bankruptcy or any involuntary proceeding relating to insolvency, receivership, liquidation, or composition for the benefit of creditors, if such petition or proceeding is not dismissed within 60 days of filing.

4.4 FOR CAUSE.   Either party may terminate this Agreement if the other party breaches any material term or condition of this Agreement and fails to cure such breach within 30 days after receipt of written notice of the same, except in the case of failure to pay fees which is subject to Section 4.2 or for failure to comply with Vendor's acceptable use guidelines pursuant to Section 1.6.

4.5 EFFECT OF TERMINATION.   Upon the effective date of expiration or termination of this Agreement: (a) Vendor shall immediately cease providing access to the Applications and cease provision of the services under this Agreement; (b) any and all payment obligations of User under this Agreement shall become due immediately, [including fees through the end of the term indicated in Schedule A adjusted for the net present value of the prospective payments;] and (c) within 30 days after such expiration or termination, User shall return all Vendor Confidential Information in its possession at the time of expiration or termination and shall not make or retain any copies of such.

5. FEES

5.1 SUBSCRIPTION FEES.   In consideration of the access rights described in Section 1.1, the Hosting and Reporting Services and the Support Services, User shall pay to Vendor the subscription fees set forth in Schedule A (the "Subscription Fees") [in addition to the one-time set-up fees set forth in Schedule A]. [***] Authorized User Representatives are included in the base Subscription Fees. Additional Authorized User Representatives may be added at an additional charge upon Vendor's approval.] User agrees to pay the Subscription Fees on an annual basis in advance. The Subscription Fees for the first year shall be due upon execution of this Agreement. Vendor reserves the right to increase the Subscription Fees effective at the beginning of each calendar year, provided, that it has notified User of such increase.

5.2 CONSULTING FEES. Unless otherwise agreed by Vendor pursuant to a work order executed by the parties, User shall pay to Vendor its then current consulting rates and materials and expenses plus [***] percent for all Consulting Services.

5.3 EXPENSES. Except as otherwise provided herein, User shall reimburse Vendor for any out-of-pocket expenses incurred by Vendor in connection with Vendor's performance of its obligations hereunder.

5.4 PAYMENT SCHEDULE. User shall pay all invoices within 30 days after the invoice date. All payments shall be made in United States Dollars. If User fails to pay any amount due within 30 days after the invoice date, User shall pay late charges of 1.5% per month on such balance (unless such amount exceeds the highest rate of interest permitted by law, in which case such late charge shall automatically be reduced to an amount equal to the highest rate so permitted by law), together with all of Vendor's collection costs, including reasonable attorneys' fees, incurred in enforcing this Agreement.

5.5 TAXES. User shall, in addition to the payments required hereunder, pay all applicable sales, use, or transfer taxes and all duties, whether international, national, state or local, however designated, which are levied or imposed by reason of the transaction(s) contemplated hereby, excluding, however, income taxes on profits which may be levied against Vendor. User shall reimburse Vendor for the amount of any such taxes or duties paid or accrued directly by Vendor as a result of this transaction.

6. WARRANTIES

User represents and warrants that (a) the User Information and the User Marks do not infringe the intellectual property rights of any third party and (b) the User Information is timely, complete and accurate.

THE APPLICATIONS AND THE SERVICES PROVIDED HEREUNDER ARE MADE AVAILABLE TO USER "AS IS," WITH NO ADDITIONAL WARRANTIES OF ANY KIND, EXPRESS OR IMPLIED, INCLUDING ANY IMPLIED WARRANTIES OF MERCHANTABILITY, FITNESS FOR A PARTICULAR PURPOSE, ARISING OR IMPLIED FROM USAGE OF TRADE OR COURSE OF DEALINGS AND NON-INFRINGEMENT OF THIRD PARTY RIGHTS. VENDOR DOES NOT WARRANT THE ACCURACY, TIMELINESS, AVAILABILITY, COMPLETENESS, ADEQUACY, MER-CHANTABILITY OR FITNESS FOR A PARTICULAR PURPOSE OF THE APPLICATIONS OR THE SERVICES PROVIDED HEREUNDER AND VENDOR SHALL NOT BE LIABLE TO USER OR TO ANY THIRD PARTY WITH RESPECT TO ANY ACTUAL OR ALLEGED INACCURACY, UNTIMELINESS, UNAVAILABILITY, INCOMPLETENESS, INADE-QUACY, UNMERCHANTABILITY OR UNFITNESS.

[Vendor agrees that it will pass through to User any right it obtains under warranties and indemnities given by Third Party Providers in connection with any
services, software, equipment or other products provided by Vendor pursuant
this Agreement to the extent permitted by the Third Party Providers at no additional cost to Vendor.]

7. LIABILITY

7.1 USER INDEMNITY.   User shall indemnify Vendor and its directors, officers,
employees, parent, subsidiaries and affiliates (collectively, the "Covered Entities") from, and defend and hold the Covered Entities from and against any and
all Losses (as defined below) suffered, incurred or sustained by any of the Covered Entities or to which any of the Covered Entities become subject, resulting
from, arising out of or relating to any claim, action or demand: (1) with respect
to the User's business, resources or services or the User Information for: (a)
infringement or misappropriation of any intellectual property rights; (b) defama-
tion, libel, slander, obscenity, pornography, or violation of the rights of privacy
or publicity; or (c) spamming, or any other offensive, harassing or illegal conduct or violation of Vendor's acceptable use guidelines; (2) any personal injury
or property damage to any User employee, contractor or representative or other
User designee; (3) claims by Third Party Providers; or (4) any other damages
arising from User's business, resources or services or the User Information.
"Losses" means any and all damages, fines, penalties, deficiencies, losses, liabilities (including settlements and judgments) and expenses (including interest,
court costs, reasonable fees and expenses of attorneys, accountants and other
experts and professionals and other reasonable fees and expenses of litigation or
other proceedings or of any claim, default or assessment).

7.2 DAMAGES.   IN NO EVENT SHALL VENDOR OR ANY OTHER COV-
ERED ENTITY BE LIABLE TO USER OR ANY THIRD PARTY FOR ANY
DIRECT, INDIRECT, INCIDENTAL, CONSEQUENTIAL, SPECIAL, OR
PUNITIVE DAMAGES ARISING OUT OF THIS AGREEMENT OR ITS
EXPIRATION OR TERMINATION, SERVICES PROVIDED BY VENDOR
OR USE OF THE APPLICATIONS OR THE PROVISION OF INFORMA-
TION, RESOURCES OR SERVICES WHETHER LIABILITY IS ASSERTED
IN CONTRACT OR TORT (INCLUDING NEGLIGENCE AND STRICT
PRODUCT LIABILITY) AND IRRESPECTIVE OF WHETHER VENDOR
HAS BEEN ADVISED OF THE POSSIBILITY OF ANY SUCH LOSS OR
DAMAGE.
   In the event that Vendor or any other Covered Entity is liable to User for any
damages arising out of this Agreement or its expiration or termination, services
provided by Vendor or the use of the Applications, the aggregate liability of
Vendor and the other Covered Entities shall not exceed in the aggregate the
amounts actually paid to Vendor by User under this Agreement for the [***]
month period preceding the events that gave rise to the claims.

7.3 SECURITY AND AVAILABILITY.   User is required to comply with all Vendor security procedures, as modified by Vendor from time to time, in order to maximize the security of the Applications. Only individuals identified as "Authorized User Representatives" shall be permitted to access the Applications or request service, either by telephone or email. For good cause, Vendor may suspend the right of any Authorized User Representative or other person to access the Applications. Vendor does not warrant or guarantee the security of the Applications. Vendor may assist in site and network security breach detection and identification, but shall not be liable for any failure or error in providing such assistance.

7.4 AVAILABILITY AND DISCLAIMER OF THIRD PARTY ACTIONS AND CONTROL.   Vendor does not and cannot control the flow of data to or from the Applications and (a) the User Systems and (b) other portions of the Internet Such flow may depend on the performance of User, User Systems and services provided or controlled by third parties. Actions or omissions of User or third parties may result in connections to the User Systems or Internet (or portions thereof) being impaired or disrupted. Although Vendor will use commercially reasonable efforts to take actions it deems appropriate to remedy and avoid such events, Vendor cannot guarantee that they will not occur. Accordingly, Vendor disclaims any and all liability resulting from or related to such events.

8. GENERAL

8.1 NO PARTNERSHIP OR JOINT VENTURE.   The parties are independent contractors and neither party is the legal representative, agent, joint venturer, partner or employee of the other party for any purpose whatsoever. Neither party has any right or authority to assume or create any obligations of any kind or to make any representation or warranty, whether express or implied, on behalf of or to bind the other party in any respect.

8.2 ASSIGNMENT AND RESALE OF SERVICES.   User may not directly or indirectly sell, transfer, assign, convey, pledge, encumber or otherwise dispose of its rights or obligations under this Agreement without the prior written consent Vendor. Any assignment in contravention of this Section shall be void. User may not resell any services provided by Vendor or via Applications without Vendor's consent.

8.3 SURVIVAL.   Upon any expiration or termination of this Agreement, Section 1.5, Article 3, Section 4.5, Article 6, Article 7, this Section 8.3, Section 8.5, Section 8.6, Section 8.8 and Section 8.10 shall remain in full force and effect.

8.4 *FORCE MAJEURE*.   Vendor shall not be liable for any failure or delay in its performance under this Agreement due to any cause beyond its reasonable control, including act or war, acts of God, earthquake, flood, embargo, riot, sabotage, labor shortage or dispute, governmental act, [acts of third parties,] [failures of third party software or equipment,] [power or electrical failures] and [internet and connectivity failures].

8.5 GOVERNING LAW AND JURISDICTION.   This Agreement shall be governed by and construed under the laws of the State of [***], excluding the conflicts of law provisions.

8.6 LIMITATION OF ACTIONS.   No action, regardless of form, arising out of this Agreement may be brought by either party more than [***] year after the cause of action has arisen, with the exception of User's breach of its confidentiality or non-disclosure obligations or violation of Vendor's proprietary rights.

8.7 GOVERNING REGULATIONS.   User shall not export, re-export, transfer, or make available, whether directly or indirectly, any regulated item or information to anyone outside the U.S. in connection with this Agreement without first complying with all export control laws and regulations which may be imposed by the U.S. Government and any country or organization of nations within whose jurisdiction User operates or does business.

8.8 NO SOLICITATION.   User agrees not to solicit for employment or enter into consultant relationships with employees or consultants of Vendor during the Term and for a period of [***] from the expiration or termination of this Agreement.

8.9 NONPERFORMANCE.   In the event that Vendor's performance under this Agreement requires or is contingent upon User's performance of an obligation under this Agreement, and User delays or withholds such performance beyond the agreed-upon time period (or beyond five days, if a time period is not specified), the time for the performance of Vendor's obligations shall be extended for the period of such delay in, or withholding of, performance.

8.10 RIGHT TO PROVIDE SERVICES.   Each party recognizes that Vendor personnel providing services to User under this Agreement may perform similar services for others and this Agreement shall not prevent Vendor from using the personnel provided to User under this Agreement for such purposes. Nothing in this Agreement shall impair Vendor's right to acquire, license or develop for itself or others or have others develop for Vendor similar services as contemplated by this Agreement. Vendor may perform its obligations under this Agreement through the use of subcontractors and other third parties.

8.11 ENTIRE AGREEMENT.   This Agreement and any attachments, schedules or appendices hereto, constitute the entire agreement and understanding between the parties hereto with respect to the subject matter hereof and supersedes any and all other agreements, written or oral, that the parties heretofore may have had with respect to the subject matter herein.

IN WITNESS WHEREOF, each of Vendor and User acknowledge that they have read and agree to this Agreement and any attachments, schedules or appendices hereto, and have each caused this Agreement to be signed and delivered by its duly authorized representative.

VENDOR

By:

Date:

USER

By:

Date:

SCHEDULE A

USER INFORMATION PAGE

Contract No.: _____

Effective Date: _____

VENDOR CONTACT INFORMATION

Contact: _____

Address: _____

Phone Number: _____

Fax Number: _____

E-Mail Address: _____

USER CONTACT INFORMATION

Contact: _____

Address: _____

Phone Number: _____

Fax Number: _____

E-Mail Address: _____

AUTHORIZED USER REPRESENTATIVES   TOTAL NUMBER:

_____

_____

_____

_____

_____

AUTHORIZED SITES

_____

_____

_____

_____

_____

APPLICATIONS

_____

_____

_____

_____

_____

_____

_____

_____

_____

SCHEDULE B

FEE SCHEDULE

SCHEDULE C

HOSTING AND REPORTING SERVICES

BUSINESS CONTINUITY ISSUES FOR CUSTOMERS TO CONSIDER WHEN EVALUATING AN APPLICATION SERVICE PROVIDER[5]

1. Service Levels

   o Review service levels to which the ASP has committed:

      • Availability

      • Response time

      • Processing Time

      • Delivery of Reports

   o Review actual levels of services that the ASP has been able to meet (are they consistent with the proposed service levels?)

   o When will the ASP be excused from meeting the service levels (e.g., customer acts/omissions, third party fault and scheduled downtime)? What procedures are in place to minimize business interruption even if not caused by the ASP (Customer may need to look to the ASP for procedures as well as in-house resources)?

   o To what extent are the service levels under the control of a third party? Is the ASP stepping up to the service levels of third party providers or is it "passing through" the service levels thereby allowing Customer direct priority with the third party?

   o Has due diligence been performed on any "key" or "critical" third parties (e.g., co-location facilities, maintenance providers to access their ability to meet the service levels?

---

5. Note: This checklist is intended to illustrate the types of legal issues that customers may wish to consider in connection with contracting for application services. The items included in this checklist may not cover all of the issues that may arise in a particular transaction. Legal issues will likely vary depending on the type of service being provided and the scope of the services. This checklist or any part thereof should only be used after consultation with your legal counsel. Legal counsel should be consulted prior to entering into or negotiating any transaction covering the provision of application services.

2. Support and Maintenance
   - What procedures does the ASP have in place to support and maintain:
     - ASP-owned software and equipment
     - ASP-licensed/leased software and equipment
     - Customer software and equipment (if applicable)
   - What are the hours of support (e.g., 24/7 or 9-5)? Does the ASP exclude any holidays (if so, the ASP's holidays or Customer's holidays)?

3. Back-Up
   - Review the ASP's data back-up policies (twice a day, daily, every two days)
   - Where are data back-ups stored, on what media, in what format, and for how long?
   - Review the ASP's system back-up policies
   - Does the ASP have redundant environments in place? Are the production and back-up systems synchronized on a regular basis?

4. Business Continuity Plans
   - Does the ASP have a business continuity plan in place in the event of:
     - Service failure
     - Financial/credit problems
     - Cessation of services
     - Cessation of support
   - Review continuity plan for:
     - Access to data
     - Access to personnel
     - Access to software:
       - Right to use object code
       - Right to use source code
       - Assignment of third party licenses or right to license software directly
     - Access to escrowed materials (source code, key files, documentation)
     - Access to equipment:
       - Sale/transfer of dedicated equipment
       - Ability to continue to use for a period of time
     - Access to Vendor procedures/methodologies
     - Access to Vendor-owned and leases facilities

- Access to third party providers:
  - Subcontractors
  - Maintenance providers
- Ability to take over management of operations specific to Customer
- Stand-by service providers
  - Does Customer have a business continuity plan in place?
    - Back-up/redundant infrastructure
    - In-house or accessible third party capabilities
    - What is maximum amount of downtime that is permitted prior to termination? What is potential exposure if business is interrupted for longer than permitted period?

5. **Insurance/Bonding**
   - Review Vendor's insurance coverage:
     - E-risk
     - Errors and omissions
     - General liability
     - Worker's compensation
   - Review performance/fidelity bond coverage (if applicable)

6. **Due Diligence of Financial and Legal Documents**
   - Are there any legal disputes that could potentially impact the ASP's financial position and ultimately its ability to perform? Search for:
     - UCCs
     - Litigation
     - Judgments
     - Liens
   - Conduct an analysis of the ASP's financials to determine financial strength, including:
     - Request or obtain through a search agency most recent quarterly and annual financial statements
     - Perform search of financial databases (D&B) if applicable/accessible
     - Consider preliminary issues:
       - Funding
       - Working capital
       - Debt
       - Expenditures
       - Profitability
       - Existing and prospective client base
       - Expansion plans

CHAPTER 14

POST-NEGOTIATION ACTIVITIES

14.1   CONTRACT SIGNING

Having agreed upon the terms and conditions under which the services will be provided, the parties are ready to move into contract execution mode. Typically, the parties have undergone tough, time-consuming negotiations, often away from home or off-site and are eager to firm the deal up. A few final due diligence and internal tasks may need to be completed in order to prepare for the signing. Following is a quick list to check off before moving on to contract signing:

- In accordance with policy, notify or obtain approvals from senior management and board of directors. (If board notification or approval is necessary, coordinate signing with board meeting.)

- Determine who will sign the outsourcing agreement for the customer and the vendor. Make sure the signing party is authorized to sign on behalf of the company.

- Identify date for signing and make sure all necessary parties are available. Some considerations must be coordinated:

  - Determine whether any other internal events must be coordinated with signing (public offering, announcement of business reorganization).

  - Determine whether announcement will have an effect on stock prices and assess best time for announcement.

  - If signing requires all parties to be in one location, make sure that all necessary parties can be in that location. Confirm travel plans and itineraries.

  - Coordinate with internal, employee, and press communications.

- Identify location for signing. Confirm the signing particulars (e.g., lunch, number of people).

- Determine how many copies of the documentation will be signed and make sure that number is ready and available at signing.

- If the parties have a formal signing with all parties present, confirm who should be invited to signing and ensure invitations are made.

- Prepare, gain approval of, and implement internal notification/announcement plan. This should include general announcement, management announcements, and affected employee announcements. The affected employee announcements may be phased (general and individual) to ensure that timing is coordinated.

- Determine whether a press release will be issued. Prepare content and obtain approval. Determine when and how press release will be made. Determine whether press will be invited to signing.

- Determine how communications will be made to the customer's third-party vendors affected by the outsourcing transaction. Determine a schedule for distributing consent letters to third parties from whom consent is necessary to allow the outsourcing vendor access to third-party assets or to manage third-party contracts (if applicable).

14.2   THE PRESS RELEASE

In many instances, particularly with respect to large outsourcing transactions, the parties agree to issue a press release outlining the major objectives and highlights of the transaction. In other transactions, the parties choose not to alert the press. This typically applies with respect to smaller transactions or in situations where the customer does not wish to draw attention to the transaction or is concerned that the outsourcing, coupled with other corporate events, will be viewed negatively by the press.

If the parties agree to issue a press release, one of the parties will need to take control of the drafting. Bigger companies or organizations will rum the task over to their public relations departments. Both parties will need to review and approve the content and form of the release, as well as to whom the release will be issued and the mechanics of the release. The framework for a brief press release is set forth in Exhibit 14.1.

In addition to issuing a press release, the parties will need to consider how inquiries from the press and outside parties will be handled. Typically, each party prepares procedures that should be followed by all employees and subcontractors receiving inquiries from the press. These procedures should be disseminated in an employee newsletter or bulletin so that employees and subcontractors are put on notice. In most cases, inquiries must be directed to a particular manager or to the public relations department who will then have (to the extent possible) prepared preapproved responses to inquiries.

Contact:

FOR IMMEDIATE RELEASE.

CUSTOMER CHOOSES VENDOR TO MANAGE
COMPUTER OPERATIONS

[ADDRESS; DATE] – Customer chose Vendor, a [   ] company, to provide [   ] services in a $_____ outsourcing agreement. The outsourcing agreement will cover Customer's operations in [   ].

[DESCRIBE CUSTOMER'S BUSINESS AND BUSINESS OBJECTIVES IN OUTSOURCING]

[QUOTE FROM CUSTOMERIVENDORI _____ of [Customer] [Vendor] who is [   ] noted that [   ].

The Vendor agreement covers [   ] technologies. [DESCRIBE HIGHLIGHTS OF DEAL].

EXHIBIT 14.1 FRAMEWORK FOR PRESS RELEASE

14.3 THE AUTOPSY

Depending on the availability of the outsourcing team, a useful exercise is to perform an autopsy of the RFP, proposal, and negotiation process to determine whether the team achieved its objectives and to identify the strengths and weaknesses of the team's positions and tactics. If the team elects to do an autopsy, it should prepare an outline of the objectives of the autopsy and what areas will be reviewed. (This process also allows the team to vent its frustrations and share its positive experiences—often a healthy idea for a bunch of people who have been working around the clock in a closed area for many months.)

The first step in performing the autopsy is to retrieve the initial objectives prepared by management and the outsourcing team. The team should review the objectives one by one and analyze whether each objective was achieved. For example, in the area of cost reduction, what are the overall projected savings? The analysis should take into account the customer's retained responsibilities (financial and administrative) as well as value-added services that the customer would not have been able to perform with its own resources. Other areas that the team may wish to consider in the autopsy include the following:

- Dissect each part of the process—the RFP, the proposal, proposal evaluation, vendor selection, employee communications, and negotiations. What were the high points? What was done well? What could have been done better? How?

- Look at the different components of the deal—the legal provisions, the description of services, transformational services, service levels, project management, staffing, pricing.

- Look at the organization of the outsourcing team. Was it the right group of people? Should other areas have been involved?
- Look at the performance of the different parts of the outsourcing team— management, team leaders, technical, financial, human resources, risk assessment, audit, public relations, consultants, legal.

14.4   RISK ANALYSIS

Another useful task that can be done immediately before or after contract sign-ing is to analyze the potential risks of the transaction and how the contract han-dles such risks. Often the general counsel's office, senior management, or the board will ask for such an analysis usually followed by a recommendation as to whether the benefits outweigh the risks. An example of a risk analysis is pro-vided in Exhibit 14.2. The terms in the risk analysis are for illustrative purposes only and would need to be modified to reflect the particular transaction.

INFORMATION TECHNOLOGY SERVICES AGREEMENT BETWEEN _____ AND _____

A. RISK ASSESSMENT

1. **RISK: SERVICE FAILURES.**
    CONTRACT PROVISIONS FOR REDUCING RISK:
    a.   Service level requirements (with associated liquidated damages in the event of a failure to meet such service level requirements and the right to terminate if the liquidated damages exceed certain amounts)
    b.   Critical milestone requirements for the data center migrations/project imple-mentations
    c.   Root cause analysis in the event of a failure to meet service levels
2. **RISK: LOSS OF CONTROL OVER IT OPERATIONS.**
    CONTRACT PROVISIONS FOR REDUCING RISK:
    a.   Flexibility to use third party package software rather than developed software
    b.   Approval rights over:
        ○ any material changes to the services and the systems
        ○ new service locations
        ○ project executive and certain key employees
    c.   Benchmarking
    d.   Customer satisfaction survey
    e.   Audit rights of services and charges
3. **RISK: ABILITY TO INSOURCE OR CONTRACT WITH A THIRD PARTY FOR SERVICES**
    CONTRACT PROVISIONS FOR REDUCING RISK:
    a.   Right to contract with third parties
    b.   Termination assistance
    c.   Rights to use software and hardware upon termination

EXHIBIT 14.2   RISK ASSESSMENT

4. **RISK: CHANGES IN CUSTOMER BUSINESS/REGULATORY REQUIREMENTS**
   CONTRACT PROVISIONS FOR REDUCING RISK:
   a. Right to increase/decrease services
   b. Right to add/delete business units
   c. Renegotiation rights if change in usage above/below certain percentages
   d. Parties' responsibilities for changes in laws/regulations

5. **RISK: INFLEXIBLE PRICING**
   CONTRACT PROVISIONS FOR REDUCING RISK:
   a. Right to use discretionary resources for additional work/new projects
   b. Adjustments of baselines/fees to reflect increases/decreases in services
   c. Sharing in savings resulting from new technology
   d. Technology indexing

6. **RISK: ABILITY TO TERMINATE CONTRACT**
   CONTRACT PROVISIONS FOR REDUCING RISK:
   a. Convenience in whole or in part
   b. Change in control
   c. Cause
   d. Failure to provide critical services
   e. Insolvency

7. **RISK: POTENTIAL LIABILITY**
   CONTRACT PROVISIONS FOR REDUCING RISK:
   a. Indemnities
   b. Deferral rights/Liquidated damages for failures to meet critical milestones/ service levels
   c. Direct damages up to _____ (except for_____)
   d. Consequential damages for _____
   e. Insurance

B. AREAS OF SIGNIFICANT EXPOSURE

1. Conditions Precedent/Changes in Circumstances
   a. Provision of the services
   b. Effect on rollout of new systems
   c. Effect on human resources
   d. Additional costs
2. Customer Readiness for Rollout of New Systems
3. Vendor as exclusive provider of _____ services
4. Consents
5. Human Resource Issues
   a. Transition
   b. Severance
   c. Litigation exposure
6. Cost of Living Adjustments
7. Taxes
8. Limitation of Liability

EXHIBIT 14.2 (CONTINUED) RISK ASSESSMENT

14.5   CONTRACT ADMINISTRATION

Once the contract is executed and the vendor is commencing work, the customer's most important task (in addition to managing the impact of the change) is administering the contract. A great contract is of little help to the customer if it is not administered effectively. Depending on the size and scope of the transaction, the customer may want to appoint an individual or team responsible for contract administration, including following up on any to-be-determined items in the schedules to the contract, tracking customer and vendor tasks that are to be performed taking deliverables, managing customer use of vendor resources, and auditing invoices. The contract administrator(s) may be part of the customer's team responsible for strategic IT decisions and issuing approvals or a separate administrative team. A thorough understanding of the contract is the key to successful contract administration. If possible, the contract administrators) should be involved in contract negotiations.

As a starting point, the contract administrator(s) may wish to prepare several documents that have proven to be helpful in the understanding and management of the contract:

- *The executive summary.* A summary of the key contract provisions. This document can serve as a big picture checklist for the contract administrators and as a useful tool when briefing senior management on the terms of the contract as well as the status of key items.

- *Tracking the to-be-determined (TBD) list.* A list of items in the contract that were not agreed upon at contract signing because of insufficient information. Examples of such items include service levels for which there was no historical data, project definition, deliverables, and milestones for projects that were only in the conceptual stage as of contract signing. This list will need to be revised and updated regularly.

- *Tracking the deliverables.* A list of items to be provided by the vendor during the term of the contract. Examples include project deliverables, new equipment (including pursuant to refreshes) inventory lists and reports. This list will need to be revised and updated regularly.

14.6   IMPLEMENTING THE TRANSITION PLAN

The first of the vendor's tasks will be to manage the transition of responsibility for the systems and facilities being outsourced from the customer to the vendor, as well as to manage the transfer of employees from the customer to the vendor. In some instances, particularly in data center transactions, the transition plan will include the migration of systems from a customer to vendor site. If the vendor will continue to operate the customer's systems at a customer site for a period before migration to a vendor site, the migration plan may be provided in a separate document with separate completion dates. The time frame for implementing the transition plan is typically from 30 to 180 days, with the employee transition portion taking from 0 to 60 days depending on the transaction.

14.7 NOTIFYING THIRD PARTIES

An action item that is often part of the transition plan is the notification of third parties of the transaction. The third parties to be notified should have been identified during due diligence and contract negotiations. Relevant third parties typically include the following:

- *Third-party vendors.* If the vendor requires access to certain customer software/equipment or certain software/equipment contracts are being transferred to the vendor, are consent letters to the relevant third-party vendors being sent out? If not, should certain vendors at a minimum be notified of the transaction (particularly those whose invoices will now be paid by the vendor)? Have any addresses for the purposes of invoicing and sending notices changed? Have contact names changed? Are any third-party vendors being terminated? Are any third-party vendors' duties changing? If so, the customer should consider which vendors should be notified and how the notifications should be sent out.

- *Government/regulatory authorities.* Should any government, regulatory, or taxing authorities be notified? For example, it is typical in an outsourcing transaction involving a financial institution that the financial institution notify (and possibly obtain the consent of) certain regulatory authorities. (The financial institution should assess the timing of this notice, which in some instances must be made before the vendor begins providing outsourcing services.)

- *Stockholders.* The customer (and the vendor) should consider whether it needs to notify its stockholders of the transaction (or at least include it in securities reports). The customer (and the vendor) should also consider whether any special securities filings are necessary as a result of the transaction. This is particularly applicable in large transactions and transactions with large asset pieces.

RENEGOTIATION AND TERMINATION

15.1 OVERVIEW

The contract is signed, operations are being or have been transferred to the out-sourcing vendor, and, in many cases, employees have been transitioned and/or assets have been sold or disposed of—the customer essentially has handed over to the outsourcing vendor ownership of the infrastructure used to manage the in-scope IT on a day-to-day basis. Then something unanticipated happens. There is an organizational change or a real or perceived performance problem. The customer feels vulnerable and the vendor feels overburdened, causing both parties to become at least a little defensive. Although this is an unpleasant and dreaded scenario (and one that neither party wants to think about during the precontract court-ship phase), it is a common one. A surprisingly high percentage of outsourcing contracts are renegotiated during the first few years of the term. Although fewer contracts are actually terminated (at least in their entirety), it is not unheard of for outsourcing contracts to be terminated for convenience or for breach.

Although there are no prescribed reasons that drive a party's desire to renego-tiate, we have attempted to highlight in Exhibit 15.1 some of the more common

CUSTOMER REASONS FOR RENEGOTIATING

- Unrealized cost savings
- Unanticipated charges
- Excessive pricing (real or perceived)
- Change in management (with new management having different objectives)
- Unsatisfactory performance (real or perceived)
- Inadequate service levels
- Change in organizational structure
- Acquisition, merger, or divestiture
- Increased or reduced volumes
- New projects (not reflected in contract)
- Implementation of new environment (not reflected in contract)
- Delay or cancellation of rollout of new environment
- Desire to bring certain services in-house
- Change in scope or project definition
- Change in strategic or infrastructure direction
- Desire to restructure relationship
- Contract expiration

VENDOR REASONS FOR RENEGOTIATING

- Unanticipated costs
- Unrealized profit
- Need for additional resources
- Unsatisfactory input from the customer
- Acquisition, merger~or divestiture
- Increased or reduced volumes
- Desire to increase or decrease scope
- New projects (not reflected in contract)
- Implementation of new environment (not reflected in contract)
- Delay or cancellation of rollt~ut of new environment
- Change in scope or project cr'efinition
- Desire to restructure relationship
- Means to avoid termination
- Desire to increase length of term

EXHIBIT 15.1   REASONS FOR RENEGOTIATING

reasons for renegotiating the IT outsourcing arrangement from both the customer's *and* the vendor's perspective.

Termination is a more draconian consequence than renegotiation in the event of an organizational change or dissatisfaction with the IT outsourcing arrangement, but many of the reasons underlying a party's desire to terminate the IT outsourcing contract are the same as the reasons for renegotiating highlighted in Exhibit 15.1. In fact, termination is often viewed as the next step if

CUSTOMER REASONS FOR SEEKING TERMINATION

- Excessive pricing (real or perceived)
- Unsatisfactory performance (real or perceived)
- Change in organization structure
- Acquisition, merger, or divestiture
- Implementation of new environment
- Failure to roll out new environment
- Poor customer or vendor relations
- Change in scope or project definition
- Change in strategic or infrastructure direction
- Means to initiate renegotiation

VENDOR REASONS FOR SEEKING TERMINATION

- Unanticipated costs
- Acquisition, merger, or divestiture
- Nonpayment by the customer

EXHIBIT 15.2 REASONS FOR SEEKING TERMINATION

renegotiation is not a successful or viable option. A common, often effective strategy is for the customer or the vendor to head down the path to termination, when the party's real objective is to bring the other party to the table to renegotiate. (This strategy, however, is typically effective only if there are substantive reasons for termination.)

Some of the more common reasons that both the customer and the vendor seek to terminate the IT outsourcing contract are set forth in Exhibit 15.2.

15.2 RENEGOTIATION/TERMINATION PROCESS

Once a party has decided to consider renegotiating or terminating the outsourcing contract, the next step is to outline the renegotiation or termination process. As was the case when negotiating the contract that is now the subject of renegotiation or termination, the party's objectives underlying renegotiation or termination largely drive the process. For example, if a customer's primary objective in renegotiating is to obtain better pricing, the process will be different than if it is renegotiating to adjust the contract to reflect a change in scope. Some of the action items that each of the parties should consider as part of any renegotiation or termination are provided in Exhibit 15.3.

15.3 WHAT DOES THE CONTRACT SAY?

When renegotiating or terminating a IT outsourcing contract, the precise language of the contract, which was once considered the dalliance of lawyers, is now extremely important. Seemingly innocuous provisions are being closely

- Define objectives
- Obtain management support
- Obtain support from IT department
- Obtain empowerment from management
- Identify point people for renegotiations or termination discussions
  - Management
  - Financial
  - Technical
- Involve legal counsel
- Involve human resources (if there are personnel issues)
- Review the contract (all provisions!) (see Section 14.3)
- Review all ancillary agreements with vendor
- Review the file
  - Correspondence
  - Memoranda
  - Amendments
  - Change orders
  - New service orders
  - Invoices
- Know the history of the deal
  - Original goals in outsourcing
  - The vendor's primary commitments
  - Concessions by the customer
  - Concessions by the vendor
  - Financial engineering
  - Customer promises or representations
  - Vendor promises or representations
- Document problems
  - Nonperformance
  - Failure to meet service levels
  - Failure to provide deliverables
  - Customer-vendor relations
  - Churning of employees
- Anticipate other party's objectives
- Develop strategy
  - Assess current and future business needs
  - Assess strength of any nonperformance or breach claims
  - Calculate any credits or fees owing for nonperformance or delayed performance
  - Identify and access alternatives
    - Insource
    - Resource
  - Determine the customer's willingness or ability to use a third party
  - Determine impact of termination on other IT functions and business processes of the customer
  - Initiate contact or dialogue with the other party

EXHIBIT 15.3   ACTION ITEMS

reviewed and dissected. Each party is looking for contractual support, however thin, to bolster its position. The document that was intended to forge the outsourcing relationship is now being used to dissolve or at least restructure it. The use of the contract to dissolve or restructure the outsourcing relationship is an important point to keep in mind during renegotiation or termination, as well as during the initial negotiation and structuring of the IT outsourcing contract.

The following sections provide an overview of some of the key provisions typically included in the IT outsourcing contract that each of the parties should review when renegotiation or termination is being considered.

(a) TERM OF AGREEMENT. The parties should review the contract provision setting out the term of the contract. How long is the relationship supposed to go for under the terms of the contract? Is there an expiration date? Is there a pilot period with an early out right? What are the renewal options, and have they been exercised? An additional issue to consider is how the length of the term came to be agreed upon. For example, did the parties agree to a shorter or longer term with the understanding that the customer would receive some financial relief in the early years or that the vendor would recoup up-front costs over the term of the contract? What other commitments were made as part of the negotiations around term? Were there any incentives to agreeing to a longer term?

(b) RIGHT TO RENEGOTIATE/TERMINATE.

(i) Renegotiation. Is there any contractual basis for requesting a renegotiation (e.g., a provision that calls for renegotiation if volumes exceed or go below a certain amount)? Has there been any event of termination (discussed next) that could be used as a lever to request renegotiation?

(ii) Termination. What events may trigger a termination right (e.g., convenience, change of control, regulatory event, breach)? Has any termination event occurred? If the basis for a termination for breach exists, what are the procedural requirements (e.g., has the cure period passed, has proper notice been given)?

(c) TERMINATION FEES. The IT outsourcing contract typically includes a specific termination fee or formula that is applicable upon termination for certain events (e.g., termination for convenience). What types of termination trigger the termination fee? The applicability of a termination fee may drive the strategy pursued by each of the parties. For example, if a termination fee applies for termination without cause and does not apply for termination for cause, the customer will likely argue that there has been a breach and the vendor will argue that the customer is terminating for convenience.

(d) DATA. The contractual provisions relating to ownership and return of data are important when renegotiating or terminating an outsourcing contract. The customer may have a weakened negotiating position if it does not own its data (in any modified form) or does not have the right to obtain copies of its data on demand (whether at any time during the term or upon termination). It is undesirable, from the customer's perspective, to be in a position where it is threatening to go to another service provider when it does not have copies of its data necessary to maintain business operations. A related issue is the cost of recovering data (e.g., delivery charges, storage, media costs).

(e) INTELLECTUAL PROPERTY.   As part of renegotiation and termination discussions, both parties will want to review the intellectual property provisions in the IT outsourcing contract to determine their ownership and use rights of certain key intellectual property (e.g., software, methodologies, tools, documentation) upon termination. Some of the issues that should be considered include the following:

- Who owns new developments?
- Who owns modifications or enhancements to the customer's intellectual property (including methodologies, technology, and documentation)?
- Who owns modifications or enhancements to the vendor's intellectual property (including methodologies, technology, and documentation)?
- Does the customer have the right to use the vendor's proprietary intellectual property during the term? Upon termination?
- Does the customer's right to use the vendor's proprietary intellectual property include software object and source code (if applicable)? Does it include the right to maintain the software?
- What are the customer's rights to use intellectual property licensed by the vendor from a third party during the term? Upon termination? Is there any associated cost (e.g., transfer or consent fee)?
- What are the customer's rights to use tools used to provide the services? During the term? Upon termination?
- Who owns work product?
- What are the customer's rights to require the vendor to transfer knowledge (e.g., training, configuration designs) to the customer or its designee during the term? Upon termination?
- What are the customer's rights to request copies of all work product? To request an inventory?
- What are the vendor's rights to use residual knowledge?

(f) EQUIPMENT/FACILITIES.   Similar to intellectual property, each of the parties should review the provisions in the IT outsourcing contract to determine its rights with respect to key equipment and facilities. If the agreement were to terminate, what are the party's ongoing rights? Several issues to consider are as follows:

- Who owns equipment acquired in connection with the provision of the services?

- Who owns upgrades, enhancements, and add-ons to the customer's equipment or facilities?

- Who owns upgrades, enhancements, and add-ons to the vendor's equipment or facilities?

- Does the customer have the right to access or use vendor-owned equipment or facilities during the term? Does the customer have a purchase right upon expiration or termination? At what cost?

- What are the customer's rights to access or use equipment or facilities leased by the vendor from a third party during the term? Upon termination?

- Does the vendor occupy any customer space? Has the vendor leased any facilities in connection with the provision of services?

(g) THIRD-PARTY SERVICE CONTRACTS. The parties will need to assess their respective rights under third-party service contracts in the event of a termination of the IT outsourcing contract. For example, are there any limitations on the customer's rights to use the vendor's subcontractors upon the termination of the IT outsourcing contract? What are the customer's rights to assume the vendor's third-party service contracts upon termination? Are there any associated costs (e.g., transfer or consent fee)?

(h) SERVICE LEVELS. For a customer seeking to assert a claim that the vendor has failed to perform, key provisions to focus on are the provisions relating to service levels. What are the vendor's obligations with respect to service levels? Has the vendor met all of its service-level obligations? Under what circumstances is the vendor excused from performance? Is the vendor obligated to perform a root cause analysis of the service failure upon the customer's request? Is there a termination right associated with the failure to meet service levels (in addition to the right to terminate for material breaches)? Does the customer have the right to request liquidated damages?

(i) CUSTOMER SATISFACTION. More and more IT outsourcing contracts include a provision regarding customer satisfaction. Both parties should review the IT outsourcing contract (and the exhibits) to determine if the vendor is obligated to conduct a customer satisfaction survey. Has the vendor complied with this obligation? What do the results of the survey reveal? Is the vendor obligated to improve customer satisfaction? If so, have such improvements been achieved?

(j) DELIVERABLES OR MILESTONES. Often at the center of renegotiation or termination discussions is a project that was not successfully implemented, not implemented on time, delayed, or cancelled. The parties will need to review the IT outsourcing contract to determine each party's obligations with respect to the project and the impact on the IT outsourcing contract if the project was not implemented as designed or on schedule or was delayed or cancelled. As is frequently the case with projects, the parties will find that some to-be-determineds (TBDs) were never completed. Issues for the parties to consider include the following:

- Has the vendor provided all deliverables in a timely manner? Has the vendor met all required milestones?

- Is there a termination right associated with the failure to provide deliverables or meet milestones (in addition to the right to terminate for material breaches)?

- Does the customer have the right to request liquidated damages?

- Did any third parties not perform that have impacted project implementation? If so, which party bore the risk of third-party nonperformance?

- If a party delayed or cancelled a project, how was the contract impacted? Is there an adjustment or renegotiation mechanism?

- Have the fees associated with the project been segregated or bundled into one base fee?

(k) FEES. Many renegotiations or terminations are driven by a dispute over the fees. The customer may believe that it is being overcharged, the vendor may feel that it is not making the profits that it anticipated, or either or both parties may think that the deal has changed so that the pricing structure in the contract is no longer appropriate. Issues to consider when reviewing the contract provisions relating to fees include the following:

- How is the customer charged?

- Are there fixed rates for additional or reduced resource usage?

- Can baselines be adjusted?

- Are there any minimum revenue commitments?

- Are there any cost-of-living adjustments?

- Who is responsible for what taxes?

- How is termination assistance charged?

- Does the customer have any right to offset, withhold, or escrow payments?

- What are the customer's rights to audit? Have such rights been exercised?

(l) BENCHMARKING. In instances where the customer feels that it is being overcharged compared to other organizations receiving similar services, the parties will need to review the contract to determine whether there is a benchmarking provision. If so, has a benchmark been performed? Do the results reveal inconsistencies with industry standards? Do the benchmarking results allow either party to request a readjustment of pricing or services or implementation of new methodologies or technology?

(m) GAINSHARING. Were any gainsharing provisions negotiated as part of the business deal? For example:

- Does the contract contain any guaranteed savings?
- Are there any shared benefits or shared risks?
- Are there any cross-marketing opportunities that have been exercised? That should have been exercised?

If there are gainsharing provisions, have they been implemented? Are they still appropriate in light of the overall business deal?

(n) DAMAGES. If a party is claiming that the other party has not performed as a basis for renegotiation or termination, each of the parties should assess its liability in the event of nonperformance. Accordingly, an in-depth review of the damages provisions in the contract should be reviewed. What is each party's liability for failure to perform? Are there any types of damages that cannot be recovered?

(o) CONFIDENTIAL INFORMATION. Often during renegotiation and termination discussions, several outside parties will need access to confidential information. What does the contract say regarding disclosing information to consultants, lawyers, and so on? In addition, if there is a termination, the parties should determine their obligations regarding proprietary data and confidential information upon termination.

(p) DISPUTE RESOLUTION. Most renegotiations and terminations are preceded by a dispute that is not resolved and escalates. What are the dispute procedures in the contract? Must dispute claims be made in writing and referred to certain individuals? Is there an escalation track? Can action be taken without going to the management committee or senior management? Has proper notice been given? Must disputes be arbitrated or litigated?

(q) CONTINUED PERFORMANCE. The parties will need to review the IT outsourcing contract to assess each party's obligations to continue to perform. Does the vendor have any right to cease performance (e.g., nonpayment)? Do any protections prohibit the vendor from ceasing to perform (particularly during a dispute)? Often, parties are excused from performance upon the occurrence of certain events beyond their control (e.g., force majeure events). What constitutes a force majeure event? Has one occurred? What constitutes a disaster? What are the parties' obligations upon the occurrence of a disaster? Has a disaster taken place?

(r) TERMINATION OR TRANSITION ASSISTANCE. Each of the parties should determine what, in the event renegotiation or termination discussions go sour, the vendor's obligations are to provide assistance to the customer in connection with the termination of the IT outsourcing arrangement and the transition back in-house or to another service provider. Issues to consider include the following:

- What in-scope services is the vendor obligated to perform?
- What out-of-scope services is the vendor obligated to perform?
- What is the extent of the vendor's assistance obligations? Does it include cooperation with third parties? Do third-party vendors need to sign a confidentiality agreement?
- What are the costs of termination or transition assistance?
- Can the customer hire the vendor personnel?

(s) RIGHTS TO RESOURCE/INSOURCE. Does the customer have any contractual right to source services to a third party? Does the customer have any contractual right to bring any of the services back in-house? If so, the customer may be able to use these rights to prompt renegotiation or implement a partial termination.

(t) ASSIGNMENT. Renegotiation and termination are often driven by an organizational change (e.g., merger, acquisition). What are each of the party's rights to assign the agreement, in whole or in part, to a new entity or organization?

(u) EMPLOYEE ISSUES. As part of the IT outsourcing transaction, the customer's employees responsible for the day-to-day operations of the IT function have been transferred to the vendor. The vendor in effect has employed most, if not all, of the persons with residual knowledge of the customer's operations and has trained its own employees in any new operational requirements.

The customer at best has retained some high-level understanding about how things are run. Issues to consider relating to employees and personnel include the following:

- What are the customer's rights to hire the vendor's employees?
  - Right to rehire employees transferred to the vendor by the customer
  - Right to hire the vendor's employees assigned to the customer's account (Is there a restriction on vendor employees primarily assigned to the customer's account? Determine time contribution of employees that the customer is interested in hiring.)
  - Right to hire other vendor employees
- Are there any exceptions from the restrictions on hiring for blind solicitations (e.g., through newspapers)?

- If there is a partial termination, customer should ascertain whether hiring restrictions or allowances only apply upon full termination.

- May third-party service providers assuming responsibility for part or all of the services hire any vendor employees previously assigned to the customer's account?

- Are there any restrictions on the use by the customer or its third-party service provider of the vendor's subcontractors?

- What are the vendor's rights to hire the customer's employees?

- Are there any noncompete provisions in the contract?

(v) STRATEGIC ALLIANCE OR JOINT VENTURE. The parties should determine if any strategic alliance or joint venture was formed as part of the transactions and, if so, review any documents relating to the formation and operations of the strategic alliance or joint venture. What are the cross-negotiation or termination rights (if any)? Would any other rights in the strategic alliance or joint venture documents affect the agreement or have to be amended in connection with renegotiation or termination?

(w) ANCILLARY AGREEMENTS. In addition to the IT outsourcing contract and any strategic alliance or joint venture documents discussed earlier, the parties should be sure to review other agreements entered into in conjunction with the transaction (e.g., reengineering, specific projects, consulting, training). Would any of these agreements be affected by a renegotiation or termination? What are the termination rights in these agreements?

15.4 ADDITIONAL ISSUES TO CONSIDER

In addition to the issues raised in the IT outsourcing contract documents, the parties should take into account other external factors when considering renegotiation or termination. Some of these issues are summarized in the following sections. The applicability and importance of these issues will vary from deal to deal and depend largely on the type and scope of transaction at issue.

(a) INTERNAL POLITICS. Who or what is driving renegotiation or termination? Is this a senior management directive? Is there senior management support? Is a general corporate reorganization taking place? What are the reasons underlying renegotiation or termination? Is there a corporate initiative to cut cost? The "who" and "what" driving renegotiation or termination will shape how discussions proceed and how serious each party addresses the other party's concerns. Another political issue to consider is the status of other relationships the party has with the other party. For example, if this IT outsourcing contract is small compared to a larger, unrelated relationship between the two parties, the parties may be more cautious about how discussions proceed.

(b) PUBLICITY. What is the potential impact to the parties if news of renegotiation or termination leaks internally or to the press? How would negative publicity affect the customer's and the vendor's ability to do or obtain additional business? Would there be any impact on stock price?

(c) TERMINATION/TRANSITION COSTS. Implementing the termination of an IT outsourcing contract will undoubtedly cause each of the parties to incur additional costs. The questions then are as follows:

- Does the additional cost outweigh the risk or cost of not terminating?
- How much are the costs and can they be mitigated?

Examples of such costs may include additional fees to the vendor for providing termination services, such as maintaining parallel environments and training of customer employees.

(d) TRANSITION TIME FRAME. In the event of a termination, both parties will need to consider the tasks necessary to complete transition back to the customer or to another service provider. How long will transition take? How will service levels be affected? Will users be affected? How much transition can the customer's organization absorb?

(e) ASSESSING IN-HOUSE CAPABILITIES. As part of renegotiation, the customer should assess whether the in-house capabilities that it maintains are in fact sufficient to manage the IT outsourcing contract and whatever other IT functions it retained. Too often the customer transfers all of its IT personnel to the vendor and does not maintain enough staff to effectively manage and administer the outsourcing contract. Renegotiation may give the customer an opportunity to assess whether additional resources are necessary. If the customer is terminating the IT outsourcing contract, the customer should assess whether it has the capabilities to bring the IT function back in-house (which it typically does not) and, when transitioning to another vendor, what additional resources are necessary.

(f) OTHER SERVICE PROVIDERS. If the customer is considering terminating and does not wish to or does not have the capabilities to bring the IT function back in-house, it will need to determine whether any other service providers can provide the services. In assessing the strengths and weaknesses of other service providers, the customer should investigate whether the service provider has successfully transitioned services from another service provider (as opposed to from a customer's in-house operations). For example, how would the service provider handle staffing issues?

15.5 TERMINATION PLAN

If the parties are moving toward termination, it is in both parties' interest to develop a termination plan (a plan outlining each party's rights and obligations upon termination, including the obligation to provide termination assistance, transition assistance, and ongoing services). Just as important as the content of such plans is how any services provided under them will be paid for.

The vendor is typically contractually obligated to provide reasonable assistance for a period after the termination date. Termination assistance services may include the following:

- Continued provision of certain services for a period
- Parallel environments
- Testing
- User acceptance
- Provision of backup tapes
- Provision of operating documentation
- Freezing of all methodology or technology changes
- List of procedures to be followed during transition
- Review of all systems libraries
- Analysis of space required for databases and systems libraries
- Unloading of production and test databases
- Return of customer equipment
- Return of customer software or tools
- Return of customer data
- Copies of all methodologies or technology used to provide the services
- Generation of reports during transition
- Maintenance of service levels during transition

The IT outsourcing contract may also require the vendor to provide assistance to the customer and its third-party service provider in transitioning services to the third-party service provider. Transition assistance may be in addition to termination assistance. Examples of transition assistance services include the following:

- Making vendor employees available for consultation
- Making vendor subcontractors available for consultation
- Providing copies of all customer-owned and -licensed methodologies or technology (for software: object and source code)
- Providing access to vendor methodologies or technology and copies of all vendor methodologies or technology to be licensed to the customer or the customer's designee
- Providing access to vendor tools and copies of all vendor tools to be licensed to the customer or the customer's designee
- Providing documentation of customer configurations

- Providing manuals
- Providing procedures
- Providing passwords or security codes
- Providing access to vendor hardware
- Providing access to facilities
- Allowing third-party service provider to hire vendor employees assigned to customer account
- Providing an inventory
  - Equipment
  - Methodologies
  - Software
  - Networks
  - Tools
  - Cabling or lines
  - Documentation
  - Manuals
  - Configurations
  - Procedures
  - Work product
  - Third-party agreements (e.g., licenses, leases, service contracts, tariff agreements)
- Identifying which party owns which assets and how ownership was determined (i.e., under which contract provision)
- Identifying whether assets are used in a dedicated or shared environment
- Identifying where assets are being used
- Identifying which customer entity the asset is being used for
- Listing vendor employees or subcontractors used to provide services
- Identifying key personnel
- Listing works in progress, including a status report and report about the work necessary to complete the project
- Listing any contract negotiations in progress, including a status report and name and contact person for other negotiating parties
- Listing all facilities
- Listing all reports generated

CHECKLIST FOR RENEGOTIATING/ TERMINATING INFORMATION TECHNOLOGY OUTSOURCING TRANSACTIONS[1]

1. Overview
   - Why Customers Seek to Renegotiate/Terminate
   - Common Customer Objectives
   - The Renegotiation Process
   - Key Success Factors
   - Key Business Issues
   - Key Contract Issues
   - Assessing Customer's Rights under the Contract
   - Being Prepared to Terminate

2. Why Customers Seek to Renegotiate/Terminate
   a. Publicly Announced Reasons:
      - Expiration:
         - Of outsourcing contract
         - Of initial pilot period
      - Change in Customer's business:
         - Reorganization
         - Acquisition of Customer by third party
         - Acquisition by Customer of other businesses
         - Downsizing of Customer's business

---

1. Note: This checklist is intended to illustrate the types of legal issues that customers may wish to consider in connection with contracting for application services. The items included in this checklist may not cover all of the issues that may arise in a particular transaction. Legal issues will likely vary depending on the type of service being provided and the scope of the services. This checklist or any part thereof should only be used after consultation with your legal counsel. Legal counsel should be consulted prior to entering into or negotiating any transaction covering the provision of application services.

- o Expansion of Customer's business
- o Insolvency
- o Redirection of Customer's product/market
- Material deviations from original scope of services:
  - o Decision to delay/not to implement certain projects
  - o Customer's desire to implement new projects/technology that materially impact overall delivery of services (e.g., change from data center to client server)
  - o Need to implement new technology to maintain service levels/stay competitive
- Changes in technology:
  - o More efficient hardware/software
  - o New developments in industry-specific applications
- Need for significantly more/fewer resources than contemplated by outsourcing contract:
  - o Need to adjust baselines
  - o Additional/reduced resource charges not in-line with market

b. Not Publicly Announced
- Poor performance by Vendor (real or perceived):
  - o Service outages
  - o Failure to meet service levels
  - o Failure to provide deliverables/roll out new systems on time
  - o Failure to provide quality deliverables
  - o Failure to meet cost reduction goals
  - o Failure to increase productivity
  - o Failure to standardize
- Overcharging (real or perceived):
  - o Fees for base services are in excess of market
  - o Fees for new/additional services are in excess of market
- Poor Customer satisfaction
- Poor Customer/Vendor relations:
  - o Cultural disconnect
  - o Mismatched project manager
  - o Poor Vendor responsiveness
- Change in Customer management

- Desire to bring core services back in-house
- Disagreement on interpretation of contract:
  - Dispute regarding which services are in-scope vs. out-of-scope
  - Dispute regarding Vendor responsibility for software upgrades/maintenance
  - Dispute regarding Vendor responsibility for equipment upgrades/refresh and additional equipment
- Three- to five-year itch
- Unrealized expectations:
  - Inadequate access to personnel
  - Inadequate access to cutting edge technology
  - Failure to achieve cost savings
  - Failure to roll out cutting edge systems

3. **Common Customer Objectives**
   - Reduction of fees
   - Addition of new entities (increase volumes)
   - Taking away of entities (decrease volumes)
   - Obtaining more flexibility/control
   - Obtaining certain services from third parties
   - Providing certain core services in-house
   - Restructuring of contract to reflect actual services/technologies being provided
   - Obtaining more control over project staff
   - Termination of contract without fees/liability
   - Recovering past expenses

4. **Renegotiation Process**
   - Define Customer's objectives:
     - Be as specific as possible
     - Process often dictated by Customer's objectives (e.g., reduction of fees vs. restructuring contract to reflect new services being provided)
   - Obtain management support
   - Obtain IT organization support
   - Obtain empowerment from management
   - Identify point people for renegotiations

- Management
- Technical
- Financial
○ Involve legal counsel
○ Involve human resources (if there are personnel issues)
○ Review the contract (all provisions!):
  - Identify any contractual rights to seek renegotiation/termination
  - Identify contractual provisions that Customer must follow in connection with renegotiation/termination (e.g., management meetings, notice provisions, dispute resolution)
  - Identify contractual provisions that allow Customer to audit/monitor Vendor (e.g., audit rights, benchmarking, customer satisfaction)
  - Identify any contractual rights to withhold payments (e.g., offset, withholding, escrow)
  - Identify any contractual provisions that would allow/prohibit Vendor from ceasing to perform the services in the event of a dispute/withholding of payments
  - Identify any contractual rights to insource/resource
  - Identify Vendor pre-transition obligations to provide information/assistance necessary to facilitate transition (e.g., provide inventories, provide key employee lists)
  - Identify Vendor obligations to cooperate with transition of services inhouse or to a third party
○ Review the file:
  - Correspondence
  - Memoranda
  - Amendments
  - Change orders
  - New service orders
  - Invoices
○ Know the history of the deal:
  - Customer's original goals in outsourcing
  - Vendor's primary commitments
  - Concessions by Customer
  - Concessions by Vendor
  - Financial engineering

- Vendor promises/representations
  - Document any problems with Vendor:
    - Nonperformance
    - Failure to meet service levels
    - Failure to provide deliverables
    - Vendor relations
    - Churning of employees
  - Anticipate Vendor's objectives:
    - Increase profit
    - Increase scope
    - Increase length of term
    - Increase efficiencies/consolidation
    - Decrease cost
    - Increase presence/expertise in Customer's industry
    - Decrease scope (i.e., take troubled/unprofitable services out-of-scope)
  - Develop strategy
    - Assess Customer's current and future IT needs
    - Assess strength of any nonperformance/breach claims
    - Calculate any credits/fees owing to Customer for nonperformance/delayed performance
    - Identify and access alternatives
    - Insource
    - Resource
    - Determine Customer's willingness/ability to use a third party
  - Initiate contact/dialogue with Vendor
5. Key Success Factors
  - Practicality of objectives
  - Commitment of management
  - Commitment of organization (time; support)
  - Underlying Customer/Vendor relationship
  - Profitability of original deal
  - External economic factors
  - Customer leverage:
    - Ability to go to another vendor

- Ability to provide services in-house
- Publicity
- Ability to document Vendor's breach

6. Key Business Issues
    ○ What rights does Customer have to compel renegotiation?
    ○ What are the reasons for Customer's dissatisfaction?
    ○ What are the noncontractual leverage points?
    ○ What is the worst-case scenario?
    ○ Who gains by a public disclosure?

7. Key Contract Issues
    c. At Signing
        - What is it?
            ○ Scope of services
            ○ Entities receiving services
        - Who does it?
            ○ Vendor's responsibilities
            ○ Right to use subcontractors
            ○ Customer's responsibilities
        - Who owns it?
            ○ Software
            ○ Documentation
            ○ Data
            ○ Equipment
        - How much will it cost?
            ○ Base fees
            ○ Additional/reduced resource charges
            ○ Cost-of-living adjustments
            ○ Taxes
        - What happens if it isn't done?
            ○ Liquidated damages
            ○ Right to insource
            ○ Right to resource/use third parties
            ○ Right to terminate
            ○ Right to obtain damages

   d. At Renegotiation

- Has there been a default?
- Are there exercisable termination rights?
- Are there exercisable renegotiation rights?
  - Due to change in Customer's business
  - Due to benchmarking results
- Does Customer have the right to access/use
  - Software (proprietary and third party)
  - Tools
  - Equipment (owned and leased)
  - Data
  - Documentation
  - Configurations
  - Passwords
  - Third-party services
  - Facilities
- Can Customer transfer to another vendor without substantial degradation in services?
- What are Vendor's assistance/training obligations?
- What rights does Customer have to hire project staff?

8. Assessing Customer's Rights under the Contract

   a. Term of Agreement

- A typical contract runs for 5 to 10 years
- Is there a pilot period?
- Renewal options

   b. Data

- Does the contract specify that Customer owns data it submits to Vendor?
- Does Customer have the right to recover a copy of its data and software at any time during the term?
- Does Customer have the right to recover a copy of its data and software upon expiration or termination of the contract for any reason?
- What is the cost of recovering data (e.g., delivery charges, storage, media costs)?

   c. Intellectual Property

- Who owns newly developed software?

- Who owns modifications/enhancements to Customer's software?
- Who owns modifications/enhancements to Vendor's software?
- Does Customer have the right to use Vendor's proprietary software during the term? Upon expiration or termination?
- Does Customer's right to use Vendor's proprietary software include object and source code? Does it include the right to maintain the software?
- What are Customer's rights to use software licensed by Vendor from a third party during the term? Upon expiration or termination? Is there any associated cost (e.g., transfer/consent fee)?
- What are Customer's rights to use tools used to provide the services?
- During the term? Upon expiration or termination?
- Who owns work product?
- What are Customer's rights to require Vendor to transfer knowledge (e.g., training on systems, configuration designs) to Customer or its designee during the term? Upon expiration or termination?
- What are Customer's rights to request copies of all work product and source code? To request an inventory?

d.   Equipment/Facilities

- Who owns equipment acquired in connection with the provision of the services?
- Who owns upgrades/enhancements/add-ons to Customer's equipment?
- Who owns upgrades/enhancements/add-ons to Vendor's equipment?
- Does Customer have the right to access/use Vendor-owned equipment during the term? Does Customer have a purchase right upon expiration or termination? At what cost?
- What are Customer's rights to use equipment leased by Vendor from a third party during the term? Upon expiration or termination?
- Does Vendor occupy any Customer space? Has Vendor leased any facilities in connection with the provision of services?

e.   Third-Party Service Contracts

- What are Customer's rights to use Vendor's subcontractors upon expiration or termination?
- What are Customer's rights to assume Vendor's third-party service contracts upon expiration or termination? Is there any associated cost (e.g., transfer or consent fee)?

f.   Service Levels/Customer Satisfaction

- Has Vendor met all of its service-level obligations?

- Can Customer request Vendor to perform root cause analysis of the service failure?
- Is there a termination right associated with the failure to meet service levels (in addition to the right to terminate for material breaches)?
- Does Customer have the right to request liquidated damages?
- Are there any obligations for Vendor to conduct customer satisfaction surveys? Has Vendor complied? What are the results?

g. Deliverables/Milestones

- Has Vendor provided all deliverables in a timely manner? Has Vendor met all required milestones?
- Is there a termination right associated with the failure to provide deliverables/meet milestones (in addition to the right to terminate for material breaches)?
- Does Customer have the right to request liquidated damages?

h. Fees

- How is Customer charged?
- Are there fixed rates for additional/reduced resource usage?
- Can baselines be adjusted?
- Are there any minimum revenue commitments?
- Are there any cost-of-living adjustments?
- Who is responsible for what taxes?
- How is termination assistance charged?
- Does Customer have any right to offset/withhold/escrow payments?
- What are Customer's rights to audit? Have such rights been exercised?

i. Benchmarking

- Is there a benchmarking provision?
- Has a benchmark been performed? Do the results reveal pricing/services/technology consistent with industry standards?
- Do the benchmarking results allow Customer to request a readjustment of pricing/services or implementation of new technology?

j. Gainsharing

- Does the contract contain any guaranteed savings?
- Are there any shared benefits/shared risks?
- Are there any cross-marketing opportunities that have been exercised?
- That should have been exercised?

k.   Limitation of Liability

- What is each party's ultimate liability for failure to perform?
- What types of damages *cannot* be recovered?
- What fees are owed in a termination for convenience?

l.   Confidential Information

- What are each party's obligations regarding proprietary data and confidential information?
- What does the contract say regarding disclosing information to consultants, lawyers, etc.?

m.   Dispute Resolution

- Does the contract establish an informal dispute resolution mechanism?
- Can action be taken without going to a management committee?
- Has notice been given?

n.   Continued Performance

- Is this a *force majeure* event?
- What constitutes a disaster? Are there adequate disaster recovery plans in place?
- Does Vendor have any right to cease performance (e.g., nonpayment)?
- Are there any protections that would prohibit Vendor from ceasing to perform?

o.   Right to Renegotiate/Terminate

- Renegotiate:
  - Is there any contractual basis for requesting a renegotiation (e.g., a provision that calls for renegotiations if volumes exceed/go below a certain amount)?
  - Has there been any breach?
- Termination:
  - What are termination rights (e.g., convenience, change of control, breach)?
  - Is there any basis for termination for breach? What is the cure period?
  - Has proper notice been given?

p.   Termination/Transition Assistance

- What in-scope services is Vendor obligated to perform?
- What out-of-scope services is Vendor obligated to perform?

- What is the extent of Vendor's assistance obligations? Does it include cooperation with third parties? Do third-party vendors need to sign a confidentiality agreement?
- What are the costs of termination/transition assistance?
- Can Customer hire Vendor personnel?

q. Rights to Resource/Insource

- Does Customer have any contractual right to source services to a third party?
- Does Customer have any contractual right to bring any of the services back in-house?

r. Assignment

- Does Vendor have the unfettered right to assign?
- Does Customer have the right to assign under certain circumstances (e.g., merger or other corporate reorganization)?

s. Solicitation of Employees

- Can Customer hire Vendor employees during the term? Upon expiration or termination?
- Can Vendor hire Customer employees?
- Is there a noncompetition clause? What is its scope?

t. Partnership/Joint Venture

- Has a partnership/joint venture been formed?
- What are the cross-negotiation/termination rights (if any)?
- Are there any other rights in the partnership/joint venture documents that would impact/affect or have to be amended in connection with renegotiation/termination?

9. Be Prepared to Terminate

- Know the contract!
- Read the exhibits
- Establish rights to terminate
- Fulfill any notice/dispute resolution requirements
- Prepare for disaster recovery
- Identify key Vendor personnel
- Identify key software/tools
- Identify key documentation/manuals
- Identify key equipment
- Prepare to insource/resource

DUE DILIGENCE CHECKLIST FOR CUSTOMERS CONSIDERING TERMINATION[2]

1. Prepare a summary of all termination provisions
   - Include prerequisites and procedures, such as:
     - Acts that may trigger termination right (expiration of pilot period; change of control; default)
     - Required notice periods
     - Any dispute resolution obligations
     - Cure periods
     - For example, *Prerequisite for Termination for Cause.* The customer may terminate for cause if vendor defaults in the performance of any of its material duties or obligations under the contract. The dispute resolution process [is] [is not] a condition precedent to termination for cause. *Procedures for Termination for Cause.* The customer must provide written notice to Vendor of the alleged default. Vendor has ___ days to cure the default. Customer may terminate upon further notice to Vendor if Vendor is unable to cure within the ___-day cure period.
   - Read all contract provisions to determine whether there are any termination rights not listed in termination section of the contract.
   - Examples of possible termination rights:
     - Termination for convenience in the entirety
     - Termination at the end of a pilot phase
     - Partial termination

---

2. Note: This checklist is intended to illustrate the types of legal issues that customers may wish to consider in connection with contracting for application services. The items included in this checklist may not cover all of the issues that may arise in a particular transaction. Legal issues will likely vary depending on the type of service being provided and the scope of the services. This checklist or any part thereof should only be used after consultation with your legal counsel. Legal counsel should be consulted prior to entering into or negotiating any transaction covering the provision of application services.

- Termination for change of control of customer
- Termination for change of control of vendor
- Termination for cause
- Termination for failing to provide certain critical services
- Termination for failing to meet service levels on a repeated basis
- Termination for failing to reinstitute services within the specified time frame in the event of a disaster or *force majeure* event
- Termination if vendor's liability exceeds damages caps
- Termination upon the occurrence of a regulatory event
- Termination upon the termination/expiration of a lease
- Termination upon the sale of asset
- Termination upon an event of bankruptcy

2. Analyze whether customer may exercise any of its termination rights

   ○ After which date may customer exercise its termination for convenience right?

   ○ When and under what circumstances may customer exercise its partial termination rights (e.g., only if services will be resourced to a third party; if services are resourced or brought back in-house?)

   ○ Can services be substantially reduced through partial termination? At what stage are services reduced enough to constitute termination in the entirety (e.g., is there a floor of services that must be retained?)

   ○ Has there been any change of control (including corporate reorganization)?

   ○ Does customer have any claims of breach (e.g., have all the service levels been met)?

   ○ Has there been a disaster/*force majeure* event? Has vendor successfully reinstituted critical services?

   ○ Has there been a regulatory event that could trigger termination?

   ○ Has a "key" lease expired/terminated or has a "key" asset been sold?

3. Assess termination fee payable by customer under each termination provision

   ○ May depend on the type of termination right being exercised (e.g., termination for convenience is typically tied to a termination fee; termination for cause is not typically tied to a termination fee)

   ○ Calculation of the termination fee may be according to:

     - A fixed amount (agreed upon during contract negotiations)
     - A fixed formula (agreed upon during contract negotiations)

- General statement basing the termination fee on expenditures incurred by vendor and amortized over the contract term (e.g., upfront costs for equipment/technology)

- Fixed amount plus wind down costs (e.g., costs of relocating employees resale/relocation costs of equipment; third party contract termination fees)

- If wind down costs are part of formula/calculation, termination fee may be reduced if customer purchases all or a portion of the assets used to provide the services or if customer hires some or all of the employees that would be relocated

- Some contracts also allow vendor to recover some percentage of lost profits

4. Analyze the parties' rights and obligations upon termination

   a. *Termination Assistance.* Vendor is typically contractually obligated to provide reasonable assistance for a minimum period of time after the termination date. Termination assistance services may include:

   - Continued provision of certain services for a period of time
   - Continued processing
   - Parallel processing
   - Testing
   - User acceptance
   - Provision of back-up tapes
   - Provision of operating documentation
   - Freezing of all methodology/technology changes
   - List of procedures to be followed during transition
   - Review of all systems libraries
   - Analysis of space required for databases and systems libraries
   - Unload production and test databases
   - Return of customer equipment
   - Return of customer software/tools
   - Return of customer data
   - Copies of all methodologies/technology used to provide the services
   - Generation of reports during transition
   - Maintenance of service levels during transition

   b. *Transition Assistance.* The contract may require vendor to provide assistance to Customer and its other third party service provider in transitioning services to the third party service provider. Transition assistance may be in addition to termination assistance. Examples of transition assistance services include:

- Making vendor employees available for consultation
- Making vendor subcontractors available for consultation
- Providing copies of all customer owned and licensed methodologies/technology (for software: object and source code)
- Providing access to vendor technology and copies of all vendor methodologies/technology to be licensed to customer or customer's designee
- Providing access to vendor tools and copies of all vendor tools to be licensed to customer or customer's designee
- Providing documentation of customer configurations
- Providing manuals
- Providing procedures
- Providing passwords/security codes
- Providing access to vendor hardware
- Providing access to facilities
- Allowing third-party service provider to hire vendor employees assigned to customer account
- Providing an inventory:
  - Equipment
  - Methodologies
  - Software
  - Networks
  - Tools
  - Cabling/lines
  - Documentation
  - Manuals
  - Configurations
  - Procedures
  - Work product
  - Third-party agreements (licenses, leases, service contracts, tariff agreements)
- Identifying which party owns which assets and how ownership was determined (i.e., under which contract provision)
- Identifying whether assets are used in dedicated/shared environment

- Identifying where assets are being used
- Identifying which customer entity the asset is being used for
- List of vendor employees/subcontractors used to provide services
- Identification of key personnel
- List of works in progress, including a status report and report as to the work necessary to complete the project
- List of any contract negotiations in progress, including status report and name and contact person for other negotiating parties
- List of all facilities
- List of all reports generated

c. Rights with respect to methodologies, technology, equipment, and third-party contracts

- Does customer have a license to use vendor methodologies/technology upon termination? Are these rights assignable (e.g., to a third-party service provider)?
- Who owns newly developed methodologies/technology? If vendor owns, does customer have a license to use newly developed methodologies/technology upon termination? Are these rights assignable (e.g., to a third-party service provider)?
- Will third-party methodology/technology contracts and third-party maintenance contracts be transferred to customer or customer's designee? Is this at customer's option? Which party is responsible for transfer fees?
- Does customer have the option/obligation to purchase equipment used to provide the services? How will the purchase price be calculated (e.g., fair market value; book value; the lesser/greater of fair market value and book value)?

d. Employee issues

- What are customer's rights to hire vendor employees?
  - ○ Right to rehire employees transferred to vendor by customer
  - ○ Right to hire vendor employees assigned to customer account (is there a restriction on vendor employees primarily assigned to customer's account? Determine time contribution of employees that customer is interested in hiring)
  - ○ Right to hire other vendor employees
- Are there any exceptions from the restrictions on hiring for blind solicitations (e.g., through newspapers)?

- If there is a partial termination, customer should ascertain whether hiring restrictions/allowances only apply upon full termination
- May third-party service providers assuming responsibility for part/all of the services hire any vendor employees previously assigned to customer's account?
- Are there any restrictions on the use by customer or its third-party service provider of vendor's subcontractors?
- What are vendor's rights to hire customer's employees?

TERMINATION ASSISTANCE SERVICES AGREEMENT OUTLINE[3]

1. **Condition Precedent**. Concurrently with, and as a condition of, the Termination Assistance Services Agreement (the "*TASA*"), Customer and Vendor shall execute and deliver the Termination Agreement **[and the Personnel Transition Agreement]**.

2. **Term**. The initial term of the TASA shall commence on **[DATE]** and continue until **[DATE]**. The initial term may renew upon notice from Customer for a period of **[NUMBER]** months.

3. **Transition Services**. Commencing on the effective date of the TASA, Vendor shall perform all functions and services necessary to accomplish the transition of Customer's information technology operations and capabilities back to Customer on or before **[DATE]** (the "*Transition Services*"). The Transition Services shall include those services listed in Exhibit ___.

4. **Transition Manager**. As part of its obligations under the TASA, Vendor shall designate an individual for each of Customer's facilities, functions, and services being transitioned. Each such designee shall be responsible for managing and implementing the Transition Services with respect to such facilities, functions, or services. Until completion of the Transition Services, Vendor's designees shall review the status of the Transition Services on a weekly basis with designated personnel from Customer's management.

5. **Transition Schedule**. Vendor shall perform the Transition Services in accordance with the schedule set forth in Exhibit ___ (the "*Transition Schedule*"). If, however:

    a. Customer desires Vendor to extend the Transition Schedule by more than **[NUMBER]** days, or if the Transition Schedule is

---

3. Note: This sample agreement is intended to illustrate the types of legal issues that vendors typically wish to address in connection with information technology outsourcing transactions. The provisions included in this sample agreement, while comprehensive, may not cover all of the issues that may arise in a particular transaction. Legal issues will likely vary depending on the type of information technology process being outsourced and the scope of the outsourcing transaction. This sample agreement or any part thereof should only be used after consultation with your legal counsel. Legal counsel should be consulted prior to entering into or negotiating any outsourcing transaction.

extended for more than **[NUMBER]** days as a result of delays caused by Customer, (a) Vendor shall extend the Transition Schedule for the applicable period of time and (b) Customer shall pay to Vendor an amount equal to Vendor's direct and actual costs associated with any such extension of the Transition Schedule; or

b.   the Transition Schedule is extended for more than **[NUMBER]** days as the result of delays caused by Vendor, (a) Customer shall continue to pay the fees under the TASA and (b) Vendor shall pay to Customer an amount equal to Customer's direct and actual costs associated with any such extension of the Transition Schedule.

In the event Customer and Vendor agree to extend the Transition Schedule, or if the Transition Schedule is extended for more than **[NUMBER]** days as a result of delays caused by Customer and Vendor, Customer and Vendor shall negotiate an appropriate adjustment to the fees.

6.   **Projects**. Vendor shall perform all tasks requested by Customer that are included in the Transition Services and any projects requested by Customer for information technology and information technology-related services. Vendor is not entitled to decline to perform such Transition Services or projects. Vendor shall receive the designated fees for providing such services or, for services not covered by the designated fees, Vendor shall be entitled to reasonable compensation agreed upon by Customer and Vendor. **[CUSTOMER MAY CONSIDER SETTING FORTH IN AN EXHIBIT LABOR RATES FOR SERVICES AND PROJECTS NOT COVERED BY THE DESIGNATED FEES.]**

7.   **Other Services**. Vendor shall provide the following services/assistance to Customer: **[CUSTOMER LIST OTHER SERVICES, SUCH AS:]**

a.   Documentation

b.   Configuration

c.   ID Numbers/Passwords

d.   Access to Software/Tools

e.   Access to Hardware

f.   Access to Facilities

g.   Training

h.   Assistance to/Cooperation with Third Parties

i.   Transfer of Knowledge

8.   **Required Consents**. All consents to transfer any Vendor or third-party software or services to Customer shall be obtained by Vendor with Customer's cooperation. Vendor shall pay any costs of obtaining the consents.

9.   **Fees**. In consideration of Vendor providing the Transition Services and projects, Customer shall pay to Vendor the designated fees as set forth in

Exhibit ___. Except as expressly set forth in the TASA, there shall be no charges or fees payable by Customer in respect of Vendor's performance of its obligations under the TASA.

10. **Expenses**. Customer shall not be responsible for any of Vendor's expenses incurred in connection with the provision of the Transition Services or projects.

11. **Payment Schedule**. Invoices shall be provided to Customer within **[NUMBER]** days of the provision of service. The fees shall be payable within **[NUMBER]** days of receipt of invoice.

12. **Milestones**. In connection with the Transition Services, Customer and Vendor shall develop a list of milestones relating to Vendor's obligations pursuant to the TASA that are critical to Customer and, for each milestone, (1) a description of the applicable triggering event from which achievement of that milestone shall be measured, (2) the duration of time from the triggering event for completion of that milestone, and (3) an amount of the designated fees that Customer may defer with respect to that milestone if, as a result of Vendor's failure to perform its obligations pursuant to the TASA, Vendor fails by more than **[NUMBER]** days to achieve such milestone by the specified completion date. Exhibit ___ contains a list of milestones agreed upon by Customer and Vendor.

13. **Data**. Customer data is the property of Customer and shall be deemed confidential information of Customer. Customer data shall not, without Customer's approval, be (1) used by Vendor other than in connection with providing the Transition Services, (2) disclosed, sold, assigned, leased, or otherwise provided to third parties by Vendor, or (3) commercially exploited by or on behalf of Vendor. Vendor hereby irrevocably assigns, transfers, and conveys to Customer without further consideration all of its right, title, and interest in and to Customer data.

14. **Confidentiality**. All confidential information or proprietary information relating to either party shall be held in confidence by the other party to the same extent and in at least the same manner as such party protects its own confidential or proprietary information. The terms of the TASA are confidential and shall not be disclosed to any third party except as provided in the TASA.

15. **Customer's Representations and Warranties.** Customer represents and warrants that (1) it has the requisite power and authority to execute the TASA, (2) the execution of the TASA has been duly authorized by Customer, (3) there is no outstanding litigation, arbitration, or other dispute to which Customer is a party that, if decided unfavorably to Customer, would have a material adverse effect on Customer's ability to fulfill its obligation under the TASA, and (4) it shall comply with all

applicable Federal, state, and local laws and regulations in connection with its obligations under the TASA.

16. **Vendor's Representations and Warranties**. Vendor represents and warrants that (1) it has the requisite power and authority to execute the TASA, (2) the execution of the TASA has been duly authorized by Vendor, (3) there is no outstanding litigation, arbitration, or other dispute to which Vendor is a party that, if decided unfavorably to Vendor, would have a material adverse effect on Vendor's ability to fulfill its obligation under the TASA, and (4) it shall comply with all applicable Federal, state, and local laws and regulations in connection with its obligations under the TASA.

17. **Termination**. Customer may terminate the TASA (without any termination fee) effective as of any time upon **[NUMBER]** days' notice to Vendor.

18. **Damages**. Each party shall be liable to the other party for any direct damages arising out of or relating to such party's performance of, or failure to perform, its obligations under the TASA; provided, however, that the liability of either party shall not exceed an amount equal to $**[DOLLAR AMOUNT]**. Neither Customer nor Vendor shall be liable for, nor will the measure of damages include, any consequential or special damages arising out of or relating to its performance or failure to perform under the TASA. The foregoing limitations of liability shall not apply to damages arising in connection with a party's gross negligence or willful misconduct.

19. **Customer's Indemnities**. Customer indemnifies Vendor from, and will defend Vendor against, any losses, liabilities, and damages, and all related costs and expense arising out of or relating to any claim by a third party based on any breach of the TASA by Customer.

20. **Vendor's Indemnities**. Vendor indemnifies Customer from, and will defend Customer against, any losses, liabilities, and damages, and all related costs and expense arising out of or relating to any claim (1) by a third party based on any breach of the TASA by Vendor or (2) that the Transition Services or any software, documentation, or work product provided by Vendor in connection with the TASA infringes another party's proprietary rights.

21. **Insurance**. Vendor shall maintain the following insurance during the term of the TASA: **[LIST INSURANCE REQUIREMENTS]**

22. **Miscellaneous Provisions**

   a. *Assignments:* Neither party may assign the TASA without the consent of the other party.

   b. *Successors and Assigns:* The TASA is binding on and inures to the benefit of successors and permitted assigns.

c. *Notices:* All notices under the TASA shall be in writing and by tele-copy to addresses specified in this provision.

d. *Survival:* The indemnity, confidentiality, representations and war-ranties, and survival provisions shall all survive termination of the TASA.

e. *Counterparts:* The TASA may be executed in counterparts.

f. *Relationship of the Parties:* The TASA does not create an agency, partnership, or joint venture relationship between the parties.

g. *Severability:* If any provision of the TASA is held by a court to be contrary to law, the remaining provisions shall be valid and enforceable to the extent granted by law.

h. *Waiver:* No delay or omission by either party to exercise any right or power it has under the TASA shall be construed as a waiver of such right or power.

i. *Publicity:* Each party shall submit to the other all publicity relating to the Services Agreement or its termination or the TASA and shall not publish such publicity without the written approval of the other party.

j. *Entire Agreement:* The TASA and the appendices constitute the entire agreement between the parties with respect to its subject matter.

k. *Amendments:* No amendment to the TASA will be valid unless properly signed by the party against whom enforcement is sought.

l. *Governing Law:* The TASA shall be governed by **[STATE]** law.

m. *Covenants of Further Assurances:* The parties agree to execute any further agreement between the parties with respect to its subject matter.

EXHIBITS

Exhibit ____ sets forth a detailed list and description of the Transition Services.

Exhibit ____ sets forth the Transition Schedule.

Exhibit ____ sets forth the designated fees payable by Customer in consider-ation of Vendor's performance of the Transition Services.

Exhibit ____ sets forth a list of milestones relating to the Transition Services to be met by Vendor pursuant to the TASA and includes target completion dates for such Transition Services and amounts of the designated fees that may be deferred by Customer if such milestones are not met by Vendor.

TERMINATION AGREEMENT BETWEEN CUSTOMER AND VENDOR[4]

EXHIBIT LISTING

Exhibit 1. Termination Assistance Agreement

Exhibit 2: Personnel Transition Agreement

Exhibit 3: Termination Payments

Exhibit 4: Assets

Exhibit 5: General Assignment and Bill of Sale

Exhibit 6: Transferred Contracts

Exhibit 7: Consent Letter

THIS TERMINATION AGREEMENT, dated as of **[DATE]** (the "*Termination Date*"), by and between **[NAME OF CUSTOMER]** ("*Customer*") and **[NAME OF VENDOR]** ("*Vendor*") (this "*Termination Agreement*"):

WITNESSETH:

WHEREAS, Customer and Vendor entered into an Information Technology Outsourcing Agreement dated as of **[DATE]** (the "*Outsourcing Agreement*");

WHEREAS, pursuant to the Outsourcing Agreement, Customer transferred certain assets **[and made payments to Vendor]** and Vendor performed the services described in the *Outsourcing Agreement*;

WHEREAS, for good and valuable consideration, Customer and Vendor wish to enter into this Termination Agreement in order to terminate the Outsourcing Agreement and to settle and release the other from agreed-upon claims and causes of action;

NOW, THEREFORE, in consideration of the foregoing and the mutual promises, covenants, and undertakings set forth herein, the parties agree as follows:

---

4.   Note: This sample agreement is intended to illustrate the types of legal issues that vendors typically wish to address in connection with information technology outsourcing transactions. The provisions included in this sample agreement, while comprehensive, may not cover all of the issues that may arise in a particular transaction. Legal issues will likely vary depending on the type of information technology process being outsourced and the scope of the outsourcing transaction. This sample agreement or any part thereof should only be used after consultation with your legal counsel. Legal counsel should be consulted prior to entering into or negotiating any outsourcing transaction.

ARTICLE 1. TERMINATION OBLIGATIONS

1.01 CONDITIONS PRECEDENT.   Concurrently with, and as a condition of this Termination Agreement, Customer and Vendor shall execute and deliver a Termination Assistance Agreement in a form substantially similar to *Exhibit 1* **[and a Personnel Transition Agreement in a form substantially similar to *Exhibit 2*].**

1.02 PAYMENTS BY [SPECIFY PARTY].   In consideration of the termination of the Outsourcing Agreement and the release of certain claims and causes of actions pursuant to *Article 3,* **[SPECIFY PARTY]** shall pay to **[SPECIFY PARTY]** the payments set forth on *Exhibit 3* (the "*Termination Payments*").

1.03 SETTLEMENT OF PAYMENTS.   The Termination Payments shall be made to **[SPECIFY PARTY]** by no later than 5:00 P.M. (EST) on the Termination Date.

1.04 ASSETS TRANSFERRED.   On the Termination Date, Customer shall pay to Vendor **[SPECIFY DOLLAR AMOUNT]** for the assets described in *Exhibit 4* (the "*Assets*"). **[NOTE: DISCUSS ALLOCATION OF TAXES, IF ANY, RELATED TO TRANSFER OF ASSETS.]** On the Termination Date, Vendor shall assign and transfer to Customer good and valid title in and to the Assets free and clear of all liens by delivery of (1) a General Assignment and Bill of Sale, in a form substantially similar to *Exhibit 5* (the "*General Assignment and Bill of Sale*"), duly executed by each of Customer and Vendor and (2) such other good and sufficient instruments of conveyance, assignment, and transfer to be prepared by Customer, in form and substance reasonably acceptable to Vendor, as shall be effective to vest in Customer good title to the Assets.

1.05 TRANSFERRED CONTRACTS.   On the Termination Date, Vendor shall transfer or assign to Customer **[in accordance with Section ___ of the Outsourcing Agreement], [to the extent permitted under the applicable third-party agreement]** and except as otherwise provided in *Exhibit 6,* the agreements, including all rights and responsibilities thereunder, for the assets and facilities leased or licensed by Vendor and third-party services and software identified in *Exhibit 6.* To the extent that an applicable third-party agreement is held in Vendor's name, Vendor shall obtain any necessary consents to assignment pursuant to a letter, in a form substantially similar to *Exhibit 7.*

1.06 SOFTWARE AND TOOLS.   On the Termination Date, Vendor shall **[provide access to] [deliver copies of (including object and source code) in the form and on the media designated by Customer]** the software and tools used by Vendor to provide the services under the Outsourcing Agreement prior to the Termination Date **[in accordance with Section ___ of the Outsourcing Agreement] [and the license granted to Customer pursuant to Section ___ of the Outsourcing Agreement shall commence].**

1.07 DOCUMENTATION. On the Termination Date, Vendor shall provide copies of all documentation, configurations, manuals, and other information and work product used by Vendor to provide the services under the Outsourcing Agreement **[in accordance with Section ___ of the Outsourcing Agreement].** Vendor represents and warrants that it has provided to Customer all documentation, configurations, manuals, and other information and work product necessary to operate and maintain Customer's systems.

1.08 KNOWLEDGE TRANSFER. Upon Customer's request, Vendor shall meet with those individuals designated by Customer in order to provide training and direction with respect to the operation and maintenance of Customer's systems **[in accordance with Section ___ of the Outsourcing Agreement].**

1.09 RETURN OF CUSTOMER DATA AND OTHER PROPERTY. On the Termination Date, Vendor shall return to Customer all copies (in the form and on the media designated by Customer) of (1) Customer-owned or -licensed software and tools, (2) data of Customer and Customer's clients, and (3) Customer-owned or -licensed documentation, configurations, manuals, and other information and work product **[in accordance with Section ___ of the Outsourcing Agreement].** Vendor shall promptly erase all files from its computers containing the foregoing information and, upon Customer's request, provide written certification that all such files have been erased.

1.10 VERIFICATION OF PAYMENTS. During the 90-day period following the Termination Date, each of Customer and Vendor reserves the right to confirm, validate, and update any information set forth in *Exhibit 4* and *Exhibit 5*. Vendor shall provide any data, information, and access to software reasonably requested by Customer in connection with the validation of information described in this *Section 1.10* consistent with that provided to Customer prior to the Termination Date. If any such information should prove to be inaccurate or incomplete, unless the parties otherwise agree, there shall be an equitable adjustment to the amounts paid or to be paid by Customer to Vendor under this Termination Agreement. Any amounts to be so paid or reimbursed pursuant to an equitable adjustment as aforesaid shall be paid or reimbursed within 30 days of the determination of such amount.

ARTICLE 2. TERMINATION OF OUTSOURCING AGREEMENT

Effective as of the Termination Date, the Outsourcing Agreement is terminated.

ARTICLE 3. RELEASES

RELEASE OF CLAIMS BY CUSTOMER. Customer hereby releases Vendor and its parent, affiliates, and subsidiaries, and their respective directors, officers, employees, agents, assignees, transferees, and successors from any and all claims, causes of action, suits, damages, losses, liabilities, demands, judgments, and orders of any kind whatsoever, in law or in equity ("*Claims*"), arising out of or relating to (1) the termination of the Outsourcing Agreement and (2) the following payment obligations **[SPECIFY AMOUNTS OWED BY VENDOR]** incurred prior to the Termination Date. The release set forth in this *Section 3.01* shall not apply to Claims that may arise as a result of (a) Vendor's failure to comply with the terms of this Termination Agreement and (b) obligations of Vendor that pursuant to the Outsourcing Agreement survive the termination thereof **[NOTE: CONSIDER EXCEPTIONS TO SURVIVAL CLAUSE]**. Customer shall bear its own costs and attorneys' fees arising out of or relating to the negotiation and preparation of this Termination Agreement.

3.02 RELEASE OF CLAIMS BY VENDOR. Vendor hereby releases Customer and its parent, affiliates, and subsidiaries and their directors, officers, employees, agents, assignees, transferees, and successors from any and all Claims, arising out of or relating to (1) the termination of the Outsourcing Agreement and (2) the following payment obligations **[SPECIFY AMOUNTS OWED BY CUSTOMER]** incurred prior to the Termination Date. The release set forth in this *Section 3.02* shall not apply to Claims that may arise as a result of (a) Customer's failure to comply with the terms of this Termination Agreement and (b) obligations of Customer that pursuant to the Outsourcing Agreement survive the termination thereof **[NOTE: CONSIDER EXCEPTIONS TO SURVIVAL CLAUSE]**. Vendor shall bear its own costs and attorneys' fees arising out of or relating to the negotiation and preparation of this Termination Agreement.

ARTICLE 4. INDEMNITIES

4.01 INDEMNITY BY CUSTOMER. Customer shall indemnify Vendor from, and defend against, any losses, liabilities, and damages (including taxes and related penalties) and all related costs and expenses, including reasonable attorneys' fees and expenses and costs of investigation, litigation, settlement, judgment, appeal, and penalties as relate to either party ("*Losses*"), arising out of or relating to any claim by a third party based on any breach of this Termination Agreement by Customer.

4.02 INDEMNITY BY VENDOR. Vendor shall indemnify Customer from, and defend against, any Losses arising out of or relating to any claim by a third party based on any breach of this Termination Agreement by Vendor. **[NOTE: CONSIDER INDEMNITY PROCEDURES.]**

ARTICLE 5. CONFIDENTIALITY

All confidential or proprietary information, trade secrets, information relating to customers, prospective customers, business plans, practices, procedures, and documentation ("*Confidential Information*") relating to either party or its parent, affiliates, or subsidiaries shall be held in confidence by the other party to the same extent and in at least the same manner as such party protects its own confidential or proprietary information. Neither party shall disclose, publish, release, transfer, or otherwise make available Confidential Information of the other party in any form to, or for the use or benefit of, any person or entity, except as provided in this *Article 5,* without the other party's approval. Each party shall, however, be permitted to disclose relevant aspects of the other party's Confidential Information to its officers, agents, employees, and sub-contractors and to the officers, agents, employees, and subcontractors of its corporate parent, affiliates, or subsidiaries to the extent that such disclosure is reasonably necessary for the performance of its duties and obligations under this Termination Agreement; provided, however, that such party shall take all reasonable measures to ensure that Confidential Information of the other party is not disclosed or duplicated in contravention of the provisions of this Termination Agreement by such officers, agents, employees, and subcontractors. The obligations in this *Article 5* shall not restrict any disclosure by either party pursuant to any applicable law, or by order of any court of competent jurisdiction or governmental agency or to banking regulators in connection with their investigative and audit functions (provided that the disclosing party shall endeavor to give such notice to the nondisclosing party as may be reasonable under the circumstances) and shall not apply with respect to information that is independently developed by the other party, becomes part of the public domain(other than through unauthorized disclosure), or is disclosed by the owner of such information to a third party free of any obligation of confidentiality, or that either party gained knowledge or possession of free of any obligation of confidentiality. The terms of this Termination Agreement are confidential and shall not be disclosed by either party to any third party except as provided in this *Article 5.*

ARTICLE 6. REPRESENTATIONS AND WARRANTIES

6.01 BY CUSTOMER.   Customer represents and warrants that (1) it has all the requisite power and authority to execute, deliver, and perform its obligations under this Termination Agreement; (2) the execution, delivery, and performance of this Termination Agreement have been duly authorized by Customer; and (3) it is not a party to any agreements that would prevent Customer from performing its obligations under this Termination Agreement.

6.02 BY VENDOR.   Vendor represents and warrants that (1) it has all the requisite power and authority to execute, deliver, and perform its obligations under this Termination Agreement; (2) the execution, delivery, and performance of this Termination Agreement have been duly authorized by Vendor, and (3) it is not a party to any agreements that would prevent Vendor from performing its obligations under this Termination Agreement.

ARTICLE 7. MISCELLANEOUS

7.01 ASSIGNMENT. Neither party may assign this Termination Agreement without the consent of the other party. Any assignment in contravention of this *Section 7.01* shall be void.

7.02 SUCCESSORS AND ASSIGNS. This Termination Agreement shall be binding upon, and shall inure to the benefit of, the successors and permitted assigns of each of the parties.

7.03 NOTICES. All notices, requests, approvals, consents, and other communications required or permitted under this Termination Agreement shall be in writing and shall be sent by telecopy to the telecopy number specified below, and the party sending such notice shall telephone to confirm receipt. A copy of any such notice shall also be sent by registered express mail or courier with the capacity to verify receipt of delivery on the date such notice is transmitted by telecopy to the address specified below:

[SPECIFY]

Either party may change its address or telecopy number for notification purposes by giving the other party notice of the new address or telecopy number and the date upon which it shall become effective.

7.04 SURVIVAL. The terms of **[SPECIFY]** shall survive the termination of this Termination Agreement for any reason.

7.05 COUNTERPARTS. This Termination Agreement may be executed in any number of counterparts, all of which taken together shall constitute one single agreement between the parties.

7.06 RELATIONSHIP. Nothing contained in this Termination Agreement shall create or imply an agency relationship between Customer and Vendor, nor shall this Termination Agreement be deemed to constitute a joint venture or partnership between the parties. Except as expressly set forth in *Article 3,* each party intends that this Termination Agreement shall not benefit or create any right or cause of action in or on behalf of any person other than Customer or Vendor and their respective parents, affiliates, and subsidiaries.

7.07 SEVERABILITY. If any provision of this Termination Agreement is held by a court of competent jurisdiction or any arbitral tribunal to be contrary to law, then the remaining provisions of this Termination Agreement or the application of such provisions to persons or circumstances other than those to which it is invalid or unenforceable shall not be affected thereby, and each such provision of this Termination Agreement shall be valid and enforceable to the extent granted by law.

7.08 WAIVER.   No delay or omission by either party to exercise any right or power it has under this Termination Agreement shall impair or be construed as a waiver of such right or power. A waiver by any party of any breach or covenant shall not be construed to be a waiver of any succeeding breach or any other covenant. All waivers must be in writing and signed by the party waiving its rights.

7.09 PUBLICITY.   Each party shall submit to the other all advertising, written sales promotion, press releases, and other publicity matters relating to the Outsourcing Agreement or its termination and this Termination Agreement and shall not publish or use such advertising, written sales promotion, press releases, or publicity matters without approval of the other party. Whenever required by reason of legal, accounting, or regulatory requirements, a party may disclose all or any part of this Termination Agreement following reasonable notice to the other party, and after satisfying all reasonable means for masking, deleting, or otherwise protecting all or portions of this Termination Agreement.

7.10 ENTIRE AGREEMENT.   This Termination Agreement and the Exhibits, which are hereby incorporated by reference into this Termination Agreement, represent the entire agreement between the parties with respect to its subject matter, and there are no other representations, understandings, or agreements between the parties, whether written or oral, relative to such subject matter.

7.11 AMENDMENTS.   No amendment to, or change, waiver, or discharge of, any provision of this Termination Agreement shall be valid unless in writing and signed by an authorized representative of the party against which such amendment, change, waiver, or discharge is sought to be enforced.

7.12 GOVERNING LAW.   This Termination Agreement shall be governed, interpreted, and enforced under the laws of the State of **[SPECIFY]** without regard to its conflict of laws rules. In connection with any judicial proceeding, Customer and Vendor agree that the Federal and State courts of competent jurisdiction in **[SPECIFY]** shall have exclusive jurisdiction over disputes under this Termination Agreement. The parties agree that jurisdiction and venue in such courts is appropriate.

7.13 COVENANT OF FURTHER ASSURANCES.   Each of Customer and Vendor agrees that, subsequent to the execution and delivery of this Termination Agreement and without any additional consideration, each of Customer and Vendor shall execute and deliver any further legal instruments and perform any acts that are or may become necessary to effectuate the purposes of this Termination Agreement.

7.14 INTERPRETATION.   "Including" and all usage of the word "including," or the phrase "e.g.," in this Termination Agreement shall mean "including, without limitation." The article and section headings are for reference and convenience only and shall not be considered in the interpretation of this Termination Agreement.

   IN WITNESS WHEREOF, the parties have caused this Termination Agreement to be executed by their duly authorized representatives.

Sworn to before me **[CUSTOMER]** this _____ day of _____.

_____
By: _____
Notary Public Name:

Title:

Sworn to before me **[VENDOR]** this _____ day of _____.

_____
By: _____
Notary Public Name:

Title:

INDEX